Huebner School Series

McGill's Life Insurance

Tenth Edition

C.W. Copeland

HS323-10

This publication is designed to provide accurate and authoritative information about the subject covered. While every precaution has been taken in the preparation of this material, the authors, and The American College assume no liability for damages resulting from the use of the information contained in this publication. The American College is not engaged in rendering legal, accounting, or other professional advice. If legal or other expert advice is required, the services of an appropriate professional should be sought.

© 2015 The American College Press
270 S. Bryn Mawr Avenue
Bryn Mawr, PA 19010
(888) AMERCOL (263-7265)
theamericancollege.edu
ISBN 10: 1-58293-218-2
ISBN 13: 978-1-58293-218-7
ISSN: 1945-2462
Printed in the United States of America

The American College

The American College® is an independent, nonprofit, accredited institution founded in 1927 that offers professional certification and graduate-degree distance education to men and women seeking career growth in financial services.

The Solomon S. Huebner School® of The American College administers the Chartered Life Underwriter (CLU®); the Chartered Financial Consultant (ChFC®); the Chartered Advisor for Senior Living (CASL®); the Registered Health Underwriter (RHU®); the Registered Employee Benefits Consultant (REBC®); the Chartered Healthcare Consultant™, the Chartered Leadership Fellow® (CLF®); the Retirement Income Certified Professional (RICP®); and the Financial Services Certified Professional (FSCP®); professional designation programs. In addition, The College offers prep programs for the CFP® and CFA® certifications.

The Richard D. Irwin Graduate School® of The American College offers a Master of Science in Financial Services (MSFS) degree, a Master of Science in Management (MSM), a one-year program with an emphasis in leadership, and a PhD in Financial and Retirement Planning. Additionally, it offers the Chartered Advisor in Philanthropy® (CAP®) and several graduate-level certificates that concentrate on specific subject areas.

The American College is accredited by **The Middle States Commission on Higher Education**, 3624 Market Street, Philadelphia, PA 19104 at telephone number 267.284.5000.

The Middle States Commission on Higher Education is a regional accrediting agency recognized by the U.S. of Education and the Commission on Recognition of Postsecondary Accreditation. Middle States accreditation is an expression of confidence in an institution's mission and goals, performance, and resources. It attests that in the judgment of the Commission on Higher Education, based on the results of an internal institutional self-study and an evaluation by a team of outside peer observers assigned by the Commission, an institution is guided by well-defined and appropriate goals; that it has established conditions and procedures under which its goals can be realized; that it is accomplishing them substantially; that it is so organized, staffed, and supported that it can be expected to continue to do so; and that it meets the standards of the Middle States Association. The American College has been accredited since 1978.

The American College does not discriminate on the basis of race, religion, sex, handicap, or national and ethnic origin in its admissions policies, educational programs and activities, or employment policies.

The American College is located at 270 S. Bryn Mawr Avenue, Bryn Mawr, PA 19010. The toll-free number of the Office of Professional Education is (888) 263-7265; the fax number is (610) 526-1465; and the home page address is theamericancollege.edu.

Dedication

To Dr. Dan McGill, who has kept Dr. Solomon S. Huebner's dream alive.

Dr. Dan M. McGill, PhD, CLU, whom, in memoriam, we honor by including his name in the title of this book, is professor emeritus at The Wharton School of the University of Pennsylvania. His ideas continue to make him one of the most influential educators and scholars in the field of insurance for more than 60 years. Considered by many to be the nation's leading life insurance scholar, Dr. McGill taught at The Wharton School for four decades and served as chairman of The Wharton School's prestigious insurance department for 25 years. He also served as executive director of the Solomon S. Huebner Foundation for Insurance Education.

Table of Contents

Acknowledgments

This is intended to be the definitive book on life insurance concepts and therefore not focused on life insurance sales practices. It presupposes no prior knowledge of the subject, and it covers all the topics that constitute the foundation for the study of more specialized aspects of life insurance. Although emphasis is placed on the primary principles, the underlying reasons for contract provisions, actuarial computations, and underwriting practices are also stressed. Technical terms are carefully defined and employed, and visual demonstrations of complex concepts are interspersed throughout the more technical sections of the book.

This book is a major revision of Life Insurance by Dan M. McGill, PhD, CLU. It was first published in 1959. The copyright was originally held by Richard D. Irwin, Inc., Homewood, Illinois, but was subsequently transferred to Dr. McGill, who graciously donated the copyright to The American College so his book could be revised for use in the CLU/ChFC curriculum.

This edition would not be possible without the tireless work of Edward E. Graves, over many prior editions. Edward E. Graves, CLU, ChFC, is a retired associate professor of insurance and former Chairholder of the Charles J. Zimmerman Chair in Life Insurance Education at The American College, serving on the College's faculty from 1976 to 2013. He was responsible for the courses in the Chartered Life Underwriter (CLU) and Chartered Financial Consultant (ChFC) designation programs that deal with individual life insurance products and life insurance law.

Special thanks are also in order to Samuel H. Weese, PhD, CLU, CPCU, former President and CEO of The American College, and Gary K. Stone, PhD, CLU, former Vice President of Academics at The American College, for their tireless efforts in bringing this project to fruition. Both Dr. Weese and Dr. Stone were instrumental in convincing Dr. McGill that his classic text should be the foundation upon which all CLU/ChFC students build. Without their leadership, this revision would never have been started, much less completed.

Many individuals supplied information and other support that permitted this manuscript to culminate in the second edition of McGill's Life Insurance. Especially noteworthy are John Angle, FSA; Ben Baldwin, CLU, ChFC; Joseph Belth, PhD, CLU, CPCU; Kenneth Black, Jr., PhD, CLU; Richard Breen, JD, LLM, CLU, ChFC; William Broundie, CLU, ChFC; Patrick Collins, CLU; James Douds, JD; Joseph Higgins, FSA; Walter Miller, FSA; Alan Press, CLU; James Reiskytl, FSA; George Rejda, PhD, CLU; Gordon K. Rose, CLU; Harold D. Skipper, Jr., PhD, CLU; Fred Stitt, CLU; Edward Stoeber, JD, CLU; and Richard Weber, CLU.

The third edition of McGill's Life Insurance contained several completely new chapters that were not based on the original McGill text. Ram Gopalan, Robert M. Baranoff, and Denise C. Marvel, all from the Life Insurance Marketing Research Association (LIMRA), wrote chapter 23, "Life Insurance Marketing." Harry Garber, FSA, wrote chapters 24 and 25, "Financial Statements" and "Ratings." Jon Hanson, JD, authored chapter 22, "Types of Life Insurance Carriers." Joseph Huver, CLU, ChFC, MSFS, wrote the material on structured settlements in chapter 6 on annuities. Norma Nielson, PhD and Donald Jones, FSA, wrote chapter 16, "Surplus—An Insurance Company's Capital." Ronald F. Duska, PhD, wrote the material on the ethical issues of classifying risk in chapter 18. Francis H. Schott, PhD, wrote chapter 26, "Life Insurance Company Investments."

This revision is the collective effort of experts from insurance companies, colleges and universities, professional insurance associations and societies, actuarial societies, and insurance marketing agencies. Chapter revisions required extensive research and significant rewriting in many cases. All the authors revising chapters contributed significantly to this book and should be recognized for their accomplishments. Norma Nielson and Donald Jones, the authors of chapter 16, revised the chapters dealing with life insurance mathematics, asset shares, and nonforfeiture values (9–11 and 13–15). James Winberg, CLU, ChFC, FLMI, FALU, worked with Jeremy Holmes on behalf of the Home Office Life Underwriters Association to revise the chapters on home office underwriting and on reinsurance (17–20).

The manuscript benefited from the constructive criticism and helpful suggestions of many reviewers. Special acknowledgment is appropriate for the assistance of David Moon, Larry Brown, LLB; Dr. Robert M. Crowe, PhD, CLU, ChFC, CFP; Dr. Gary Stone PhD, CLU; and C. Bruce Worsham, JD, LLM, CLU, each of whom read several chapters, except Dr. Stone, who read the entire manuscript. Helpful suggestions were provided by my former colleagues on the faculty at The American College, especially Stephan R. Leimberg, JD, CLU, and William J. Ruckstuhl, CLU, ChFC, and Robert J. Doyle, Jr., CLU, ChFC., and Edward E. Graves, CLU, ChFC.

Without the pioneering work of Dr. Solomon Stephen Huebner, none of this would have been possible.

Every attempt has been made to ensure that this current volume is accurate and up-to-date. Because I have full confidence in Murphy's law and expect you will find some errors or shortcomings, I would appreciate your critical reactions and suggestions for improvement. With your help we can make future editions of this classic text even better.

C.W. Copeland

About the Authors

C. W. Copeland, PhD is an Assistant Professor of Insurance at The American College of Financial Services. Dr. Copeland conducts scholarly research in Behavioral Economics and teaches graduate-level business courses. He has been a regular guest on radio and television shows across the country where he addresses audiences on financial planning strategies on a regular basis.

Prior to joining The American College, Dr. Copeland served for 13 years as an adjunct professor in the School of Business at Clark-Atlanta University and 15 years as an instructor with R.S. Thomas Training Associates providing pre-licensing training, continuing education, and business development advice for financial services professionals. Dr. Copeland has more than 16 years of industry experience as a financial planner where he coordinates the efforts of attorneys, tax advisors, employee benefits coordinators, estate and business planners, and pension managers for the benefit of his clients. He holds numerous licenses and registrations (Georgia, Missouri, New Jersey, North Carolina, South Carolina, and Tennessee) in the areas of investments and insurance.

Chapter 1
Economic Bases
of Life Insurance

Written by Dan M. McGill

Revised by C.W. Copeland

Special Note to Readers Enrolled in American College Courses

Many readers of this book are using it as part of their work for courses in designation programs of The American College. If you are one of these students, you need to be aware that the book is used in conjunction with materials that are found on The American College Online. It is important that you use this site for additional study materials and instructions on how to prepare for your course. If you have not received instructions on how to access The American College Online, contact the Office of Professional Education at 1-888-263-7265.

Learning Objectives

An understanding of the material in this chapter should enable you to

1. **Describe the role of insurance in preserving a family's economic security.**

2. **Apply the five-step procedure to estimate a person's economic value to the family.**

3. **Explain the role that present-value calculations play in determining the required amount of insurance.**

4. **Compare the human life value approach with the needs approach to determine the appropriate amount of life insurance.**

5. **Describe the business uses of life insurance.**

6. **Identify and explain the expenses commonly associated with death and settling the deceased's estate.**

7. **Identify and explain the ongoing income needs of family survivors.**

8. **Identify and explain the potential sources of retirement income.**

9. **Understand how life insurance can be used to fund charitable donations and bequests.**

10. **Understand the general categories of needs and the kinds of information necessary to evaluate those needs in determining the appropriate amount of life insurance.**

11. Describe the strengths and weaknesses of both liquidating and non-liquidating approaches to funding lifetime income needs.

A human life possesses many values, most of them irreplaceable and not conducive to measurement. These values are founded on religious, moral, and social relationships. From a religious standpoint, for example, human life is regarded as immortal and endowed with a value beyond the comprehension of mortal man. In a person's relationship with other human beings, a set of emotional and sentimental attachments is created that cannot be measured in monetary terms or supplanted by material things. A human life may be capable of artistic achievements that contribute in a unique way to the culture of a society.

Such values, however, are not the foundation of life insurance. Although not oblivious to these values—in fact, the life insurance transaction has strong moral and social over-tones—life insurance is concerned with the economic value of a human life, which is derived from its earning capacity and the financial dependence of other lives on that earning capacity. Because the economic value may arise out of either a family or a business relationship, it seems advisable to discuss the functions of life insurance under two head-ings: family purposes and business purposes.

FAMILY PURPOSES

Source of the Economic Value of the Human Life

In terms of its physical composition, the human body is worth only a few dollars. In terms of earning capacity, however, it may be worth millions of dollars. Yet earning power alone does not create an economic value that can logically serve as the basis of life insurance. A human life has an economic value only if some other person or organization can expect to derive a pecuniary advantage through its existence. If an individual is without dependents and no other person or organization stands to profit through his or her living either now or in the future, then that life, for all practical purposes, has no monetary value that needs to be perpetuated. Such an individual is rare. Most income producers either have dependents or can expect to acquire them in the normal course of events. Even those income earners with no family dependents often provide financial support to charitable organizations. In either case, a basis exists for insurance.

Preservation of Family's Economic Security

In many cases an income producer's family is completely dependent on his or her personal earnings for subsistence and the amenities of life. In other words, the "potential" estate is far more substantial than the existing estate—the savings that the family has been able to accumulate. The family's economic security lies in the earning capacity of each income earner, which is represented by his or her "character and health, training and experience, personality and power of industry, judgment and power of initiative, and driving force to put across in tangible form the economic images of his mind."[1] Over a period of time, these economic forces are gradually converted into income, a portion of which is devoted to self-maintenance, a portion to support of dependents, and if the income is large enough, a portion to savings to meet future needs and contingencies. If the individual lives and stays in good health, the total income potential will eventually be realized, all to the benefit of the family and others who derive financial gain from his or her efforts. If an income earner dies or becomes permanently and totally disabled, the unrealized portion of his or her total earnings potential will be lost, and in the absence of other measures, the family will soon find itself destitute or reduced to a lower income than it previously enjoyed.

This need not happen, however, since there are contracts that can create a fund at death at least to partially, and possibly to fully, offset the lost income of the insured. Those contracts, of course, are life insurance. By means of life insurance, an individual can assure that the family will receive the monetary value of those income-producing qualities that lie within his or her physical being, regardless of when death occurs. By capitalizing this life value, an income earner can leave the family in the same economic position that they would have enjoyed had he or she lived.[2]

The Moral Obligation to Provide Protection

Most people assume major responsibility for the support and maintenance of their dependent children during their lifetime. In fact, they consider it one of the rewarding experiences of life. In any case, the law attaches a legal obligation to the support of a spouse and children. Thus if there is a divorce or a legal separation, the court will normally decree support payments for dependent children and possibly alimony for the dependent spouse. In some cases (if the children are still dependent or if the alimony recipient has

---

1.   S. S. Huebner, *Life Insurance,* 4th ed. (New York: Appleton-Century-Crofts, Inc., 1950), p. 14.
2.   Capitalization is the creation of a fund large enough to generate ongoing investment income approximating the salary or wages of the individual.

not remarried[3]) such payments, including alimony, are to continue beyond the provider's death. Nevertheless, it takes a high order of responsibility for a parent to voluntarily provide for continuation of income to dependents after his or her own death. It virtually always involves a reduction in the individual's own standard of living. Yet few would deny that any person with a dependent spouse, children, or parents has a moral obligation to provide them with the protection afforded by life insurance, as far as his or her financial means permit.

Dr. S. S. Huebner had the following to say concerning the obligation to insure:

> From the family standpoint, life insurance is a necessary business proposition which may be expected of every person with dependents as a matter of course, just like any other necessary business transaction which ordinary decency requires him to meet. The care of his family is man's first and most important business. The family should be established and run on a sound business basis. It should be protected against needless bankruptcy. The death or disability of the head of this business should not involve its impairment or dissolution any more than the death of the head of a bank, railroad, or store. Every corporation and firm represents capitalized earning capacity and goodwill. Why then, when men and women are about to organize the business called a family should there not be a capitalization in the form of a life insurance policy of the only real value and goodwill behind that business? Why is it not fully as reasonable to have a life insurance policy accompany a marriage certificate as it is to have a marine insurance certificate invariably attached to a foreign bill of exchange? The voyage in the first instance is, on the average, much longer, subject to much greater risk, and in case of wreck, the loss is of infinitely greater consequence.

> The growth of life insurance implies an increasing development of the sense of responsibility. The idea of providing only for the present must give way to recognition of the fact that a person's responsibility to his family is not limited to the years of survival. Emphasis should be laid on the "crime of not insuring," and the finger of scorn should be pointed at any man who, although he has provided well while he was alive, has not seen fit to discount the uncertain future for the benefit of a dependent household . . . Life insurance is a sure means of changing uncertainty into certainty and is the opposite of gambling. He who does not insure gambles with the greatest of all chances and, if he loses, makes those dearest to him pay the forfeit.[4]

---

3. In such event, the parent and ex-spouse are required to provide life insurance or to set funds aside in trust.
4. Huebner, *Life Insurance*, p. 23.

Measurement of Monetary Value

It seems agreed that an individual should protect his or her earning capacity for the benefit of dependents by carrying life insurance in an appropriate amount. The question logically arises at this point as to how much is an "appropriate" amount.

Some have suggested that a person should capitalize this economic value at an amount large enough to yield, at a reasonable rate of interest, an income equal to the family's share of those earnings. In an attempt to obtain the same general result, others have recommended that a person capitalize this value at a figure large enough to yield an annual income equal to a specified percentage, such as 50 percent, of those personal earnings at the time of the provider's death. In response to the significant inflation in recent decades, some suggest capitalizing the worker's full income (or more) so that the income portion that would otherwise have gone to income taxes and the insured's self-maintenance can be used to offset general price inflation. All of these approaches are based on the assumption that the income from personal efforts is a perpetuity. All would preserve the capitalized value of a portion of those earnings into perpetuity. Such an assumption is theoretically invalid. Personal earnings are subject to termination at any time by the producer's death or disability and, in any case, will generally not continue beyond the date of retirement. Therefore, in capitalizing the earnings of an individual, their terminable nature can be taken into account.

The technically accurate method of computing the monetary value of a person is too complex for general use.[5] It involves an estimate of the individual's personal earnings for each year from his or her present age to the date of retirement, taking into account the normal trend of earnings and inflation. From each year's income the cost of self-maintenance, life insurance premiums, and personal income taxes is deducted. The residual income for each year is then discounted at an assumed rate of interest and against the possibility of its not being earned. In the latter calculation, the three contingencies of death, disability, and unemployment have to be considered. The sum of the discounted values for each year of potential income is the present value of future earnings or the monetary value of the life in question.[6] When determining the economic value of a human life for purposes of insuring that value against loss by death, one should consider the projected flow of income to the family rather than the probability of the provider's death. The objective is to determine the present value of the income flow to the family if the family provider survives to the end of

---

5.   See Louis J. Dublin and Alfred J. Lotka, *The Money Value of a Man,* rev. ed. (New York: Ronald Press Co., 1946), for a comprehensive discussion of the subject.

6.   Ibid., p. 195.

his or her income-producing period since ideally insurance will be sufficient to permit the family to enjoy the same standard of living that it would have enjoyed had the provider(s) not died.

Elements of Economic Value Estimates:
• Average annual earnings estimate
• Taxes, self-maintenance costs, life insurance premiums
• Remaining years in workforce before retirement
• Estimated interest rate applicable to future working years

Five-step Procedure for Estimating Economic Value

A reasonably accurate estimate of a person's economic value for purposes of life insurance can be derived by a simple-to-understand method that can be used by anyone with access to a computer, a financial calculator, or compound-interest discount tables. There are five steps in this procedure:

1. Estimate the individual's average annual earnings from personal efforts over the remaining years of his or her income-producing lifetime.
2. Deduct federal and state income taxes, life insurance premiums, and the cost of self-maintenance.
3. Determine the number of years between the individual's present age and the contemplated age of retirement.
4. Select a reasonable rate of interest at which future earnings will be discounted.
5. Multiply (1) minus (2) by the present value of $1 per annum for the period determined in (3), discounted at the rate of interest selected in (4).

In the first step an effort should be made to anticipate the pattern of future earnings. In the majority of cases, particularly among semiskilled and clerical workers, earnings will reach their maximum at a fairly early age, perhaps around 40, and will remain at that level (except for inflation adjustments) until retirement. The earnings of professional people continue to increase until about age 55, after which they level off or decline somewhat unless they are adjusted for inflation. The earnings of still other groups may continue to rise until shortly before retirement. It is difficult to estimate accurately the average annual income that can be expected. Inflation, technological change, and increased global competition are accelerating the rate of change and our society's economic volatility.

The costs in the second step are also difficult to estimate, but income taxes and the cost of self-maintenance can be approximated within a reasonably close margin of error unless Congress makes a drastic change in the future tax rates. The purpose of step (2), of course, is to arrive at the family's share of personal earnings. The determination of the income tax liability, life insurance premiums, and the cost of self-maintenance can be dispensed with if the individual can directly estimate what portion of personal earnings goes to the support of the family. In the typical case it is probably relatively accurate to assume that less than half of the provider's gross personal earnings is devoted to the support of the family. In the low-income brackets, the percentage is undoubtedly a little higher but in no event more than two-thirds; in the higher-income brackets, the percentage might be lower than one-half.

The purpose of step (3) is to determine how long the family can expect to receive the income projected in step (2), ignoring, for reasons indicated above, the probability that the individual may die before reaching normal retirement age.

The rate of interest selected in step (4) should be in line with the rate generally payable on proceeds left with the insurance company since it is usually a conservative estimate of conditions over the relevant future period. Another acceptable interest rate estimate is the rate used by the Pension Benefit Guaranty Corporation (PBGC is a federal agency located in Washington, DC) for valuing defined-benefit pension liabilities.

Calculating Present Value

present value of $1 per annum

The **present value of $1 per annum**, the only new element involved in step (5), is obtained directly from a financial calculator or a computer using financial software. Alternatively it can be derived from a compound-discount table that shows the present value of a series of future income payments—specifically, $1 per annum—for various periods of time and at various rates of interest.

Example

Examples of present values of $1 per annum

- Forty annual payments of $1 at the end of each year with an interest rate of 0.0 percent are equal to $40.

- Forty annual payments of $1 at the end of each year with an interest rate of 5.0 percent are equal to $17.16.

- Forty annual payments of $1 at the end of each year with an interest rate of 4.5 percent interest are equal to $18.40.

The entire process of computing the monetary value of a human life can be illustrated with the following example:

Example

Angus McDonald is a married male, aged 35, with gross annual earnings of $40,000 (expected level to retirement) and with an assumed $20,000 available annually to support his family. Angus plans to retire at age 65. The assumed interest rate is 5.0 percent. Thirty years of $1 payments has a present value of $15.37.

The value of future earnings to the family is

$20,000 × $15.37 = $307,400 (rounded from $307,449)

A person aged 35 who can be expected to devote an average of $45,000 per year to his or her family over the next 30 years is worth $691,650 (when $15.37 is the rounded-off version of $15.37245103; $691,760 without rounding) to the family today if the income is discounted at 5 percent. If possible, that income should be capitalized in the form of a life insurance policy on the producer of the income.

Diminishing Nature of the Economic Value

economic value of a producer

It must be apparent that, from any given point, the **economic value of a producer** tends to diminish with the passage of time. His or her earning level may continue to increase for a certain period or indefinitely, but with each passing year, the remaining period of productivity becomes shorter. Each year of income that is realized means that there is less that remains to be earned. Because an individual's economic value is nothing more than the unrealized earning capacity represented by native ability and acquired skills, his or her

value must diminish as potential income is converted into actual income. This principle is illustrated by the diagram in Figure 1-1.

The chord AB represents the lifetime of an individual born at point A and dying at point B. The chord AB represents the cost of maintenance and, during his or her productive years, the individual's income tax liability. The arc CD represents earning capacity. During the period A to C, there are no earnings, but there are costs of maintenance represented by the triangle AEC. Earnings commence at C and may represent part-time work or sums earned for running errands. The area of arc CD that extends above arc AB represents earnings in excess of taxes and the cost of self-maintenance. Point D marks the age of retirement, and the area DFB symbolizes the second major period in the individual's life, during which the cost of self-maintenance exceeds his or her income.

Figure 1-1
Hypothetical Illustration of Economic Value of a Human Life

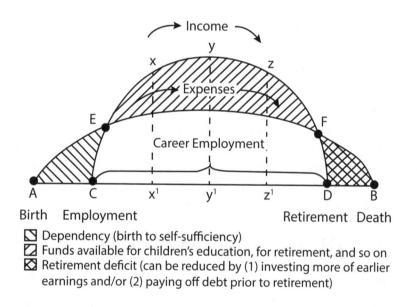

Figure 1-1 is diagrammatic and obviously unrealistic. Neither earnings nor maintenance expenses follow a symmetrical curve. For example, the childhood period starts with a highly unsymmetrical outlay for maternity costs. Income is also likely to commence earlier than at point C, particularly among lower-income groups, and under no circumstances is

it likely to decline so gradually to the age of retirement. In most occupations people reach their maximum earnings in their 40s, and earnings decline only slightly to retirement, when they terminate abruptly. Figure 1-2 shows a fairly typical pattern of earnings among clerical and professional groups.

Figure 1-2
Typical Pattern of Earnings

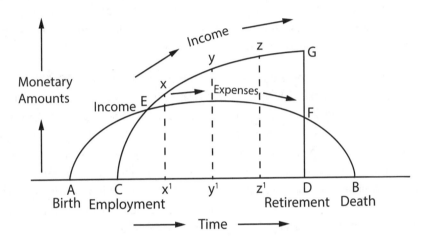

In Figure 1-2 the monetary value of the individual is at its peak at point E since net earnings are just commencing. At the point where xx^1 intersects the arcs, the earnings rate has increased, but potential future earnings have declined. The earnings potential shows further decreases at yy^1 and zz^1; at point F, it has shrunk to zero.

Bases for Insurance

These diagrams roughly illustrate the economic foundation of three broad categories of life insurance. The first is represented by the area AEC. During this period the individual's needs are met by the parents or other persons responsible for the child's welfare. If the child dies before becoming a producer, the investment in nurturing, maintenance, and education is sacrificed. This can be a sizable sum, especially if the child has been educated at private schools. Various studies have shown that the cost of rearing a child to age 18 ranges from 1.5 times to 3.25 times the parents' annual income. At today's prices the cost may be even higher. While most parents regard these expenditures as one of the duties and privileges of parenthood and justifiably shrink from labeling them as an investment to be recovered in

the event of the child's death, such costs do create a substantial insurable value. This value can logically serve as one of the bases for juvenile insurance—a strong segment of the life insurance business.

The second category of insurance is portrayed by the area EGF. The surplus earnings represented by this area are the source of support for the individual's dependents and a broad measure of the economic loss to the family if the producer(s) should die. A portion of these earnings will go toward insurance premiums, and another portion should be set aside for both spouses' old-age needs, but the share that is destined for the care and maintenance of the family should be capitalized and preserved for the family through the medium of life insurance. This is family insurance in the purest sense.

Finally, the individual's retirement needs are represented by the area DFB. Although the income vacuum may be partially filled by federal OASDI (Old Age, Survivors, and Disability Income)—Social Security—benefits, pension plans and other tax-qualified plans (such as profit sharing, income deferral, and thrift or savings), and individual investments, the most realistic source of funds to cover any income shortage is through investment income life insurance and annuities. This remaining need can be satisfied with group life insurance through employment and/or a personal insurance program. For long-term planning purposes, however, individuals should not rely on group life insurance for any more than the funds that can—and will—be kept in force after an unforeseen job loss. Individuals should check their employer's plan to find out how much of the group life insurance they can convert to individual insurance after termination.

Elements of Retirement Income

- Social Security

- Pension plan, if any (401k, 403b, IRA, SEP, and so on)

- Investments, if any

Analysis of Needs

human life value approach

The foregoing approach to the problem of determining how much life insurance a person should carry has been termed the **human life value approach**. It is based on the proposition that a person should carry life insurance in an amount equal to the capitalized value of his or her net earnings. Another approach is to analyze the various needs that the family would experience if the income producer dies. The presumption is that these needs will

have to be met through life insurance, although other resources, particularly federal OASDI benefits, are taken into account in the ultimate determination of the amount of insurance needed. This technique is identified as the needs approach and, purely from a sales stand-point, is regarded as more realistic than the human life value approach. In most cases, the approach to the amount of life insurance is based on some assessment of needs analysis, and the human life value approach would lead to the highest estimate of needs.

It would be difficult, if not impossible, to prepare a list of all needs that might possibly arise after the death of the income producer. Family circumstances differ, and a list of needs that would be appropriate for one family might be quite unsuitable for another. Moreover, within any particular family, the needs picture changes from time to time. The most that can be attempted in this section is to outline the general categories of needs that are likely to be found in any family situation. These categories are discussed in the order in which they arise, which in most cases is also the order of importance. All of the needs approaches assume the life insurance proceeds will be liquidated by the end of the dependents' lifetimes.

needs approach

There is another approach to determine the amount of life insurance which is based on providing a perpetual income adequate to support surviving dependents. It is called the financial **needs approach** and requires even higher amounts of coverage than the human life value approach. It appeals to wealthy clients who are interested in leaving a legacy fund for dependents.

After future income needs have been estimated and combined into a total, there is another important step that must be completed to translate this need into a stated funding objective. Future income payments can be comprised solely of investment earnings on a capital sum, or they can be a combination of investment earnings and liquidation of part of the capital sum. The advantage of using investment earnings only to supply such income streams is that the capital sum is not being depleted, and consequently a termina-tion date on the income stream is not necessary. This means that individuals relying upon the income will not outlive their income stream. The disadvantage of this strategy is that it takes more money in the capital fund to fully fund this approach than it takes to fund a program that relies on liquidation of part of the principal.

Liquidating Approach

- All investment income is distributed

- Part of the investment capital is being distributed with each payment

- Intent is to nearly exhaust the investment fund at the end of recipient's life

- Requires estimation of the remaining lifetime

A serious shortcoming of the liquidating approach is that the fund will eventually be totally dissipated. The strategy requires estimating the insured's likely maximum age at death and planning liquidation for that date or later. Any liquidation planning predicated on the beneficiary's death at an early age runs a high risk of liquidating the proceeds while the beneficiary is still dependent on them. As one famous agent likes to put it, they run out of money before they run out of time. Financial advisers are well advised to plan for a liquidation in such a way that the beneficiary is likely to run out of time before he or she runs out of money.

Nonliquidating Approach (Capital Needs)

- Benefit payments are completely derived from investment income

- Investment fund is not diminished

- Benefits can be paid as long as needed

- Requires larger investment fund than that for a liquidating approach

- Much simpler to calculate

There are essentially two ways of eliminating this potential problem associated with liquidating the principal sum over the beneficiary's lifetime. One approach is to use policy proceeds at death to provide a life income through policy settlement options or separate annuity contracts. These arrangements guarantee lifelong income payments regardless of how long the recipient lives. The other approach (nonliquidating) is the previously mentioned capitalization at a high enough level that all the income benefits can be provided from the investment income only.

financial needs analysis

capital needs analysis

Within the life insurance industry the liquidating approach is often referred to as the **financial needs analysis**, and a nonliquidating approach is often referred to as the **capital needs analysis**.

Another advantage of the nonliquidating approach is the simplicity of calculating the needed capital fund. The desired income level is easily capitalized by dividing that income amount by the applicable interest rate representing the after-tax investment return anticipated on the capital sum. For example, if $100,000 per year is desired, and the capital sum generating those income payments can realistically expect to generate a 5 percent return after taxes, a $2 million fund is sufficient. This is determined by taking the desired income amount and dividing into that the realistic estimate of the after-tax investment return rate. In our example it was .05, or 5 percent. That division yields the $2 million capital fund amount needed. Obviously, the lower the after-tax investment return rate, the higher the capital fund needed to throw off the same amount of income. Similarly, higher marginal tax rates will lower the after-tax return rate and increase the size of the fund needed to generate the income.

SOURCES OF IMMEDIATE FUNDS

The death of an insured family member usually terminates an income stream that the family has relied upon. The costs of daily living for survivors, final expenses for the deceased insured, and emergencies, repairs and replacements associated with events surrounding the family member's death create an immediate need for funds. Families having an adequate source of emergency funds in liquid holdings, such as money market funds, mutual funds, bank balances, cash management accounts, life insurance cash values, and so forth, may easily meet any need for immediate cash following the death. However, the need for additional funds becomes urgent if the family does not have an emergency fund or has depleted it immediately prior to the death.

One of the goals of proper planning is to make sure the emergency fund is adequate to meet the survivors' needs until life insurance proceeds and other potential sources of funds become available. Life insurance proceeds often provide a significant portion of the emergency fund itself. (This reliance on the immediate availability of death benefits should not be associated with policies that are still contestable—in force less than 2 years. There could be some delay in settling claims of contestable life insurance polices. After a policy

becomes incontestable, however, it is reasonable to count on quick availability of death benefits.)

Cleanup Fund

cleanup fund

The first need is a fund to meet the expenses resulting from the insured's death and to liquidate all current outstanding obligations. There are many types of obligations to be met, and ready cash should be available for that purpose. Such a fund is usually referred to as a **cleanup fund**, although some planners prefer to substitute the terms probate fund or estate clearance fund.

The principal items of expense to consider include the following:

- hospital, doctors', and nurses' bills incident to the insured's last illness that are not covered by insurance
- burial expenses, including funeral costs, cemetery lot, and marker
- personal obligations, including unpaid notes, household bills, installment payments, personal loans, and unsatisfied judgments, if any
- unpaid pledges, whether or not they are legally binding obligations
- the cost of estate administration, including executor's or administrator's fee, appraisers' fees, legal fees, and court costs
- estate, inheritance, income, and property taxes

Mortgages might well be included in the list, but in view of their size and the special problems frequently encountered in their connection, they are usually treated as a separate need.

It is difficult to estimate precisely the size of the fund that will be needed since an individual's obligations vary from year to year. Moreover, last-illness expenses can be estimated only within a broad range since the person may die suddenly or may linger for months or years. The needs will also vary with the size of the estate. In the typical estate, for example, estate and inheritance taxes will be insignificant items, if present at all; in a sizable estate, they may constitute the largest item of expense, running into hundreds of thousands or even millions of dollars. Executors' or administrators' fees and legal expenses are based on the size of the estate, the former normally being a fixed percentage of the probate estate. In the typical estate, however, a cleanup fund equal to half the annual family income should suffice, although individual circumstances may justify a larger cleanup fund.

Readjustment Income

readjustment income

Few individuals are able to leave an estate, including life insurance, substantial enough to provide their dependents with an income as large as they enjoyed while the income earner was alive. This means that an adjustment will generally have to be made in the family's standard of living. To cushion the economic and emotional shock, however, it is desirable to postpone that adjustment for a period following the income producer's death. The length of the period depends largely on the magnitude of the change that the family will have to make in living standards. If the adjustment is slight, a year should suffice. If the adjustment is drastic, 2 years or more should be allowed. If the surviving spouse must refresh or acquire skills to gain employment, an even longer period may be needed. Whatever the duration, the **readjustment income** during this period should be approximately equivalent to the family's share of the producer's earnings at the time of his or her death.

Income during Dependency Period

critical period income

After the expiration of the readjustment period, income should be provided in a reduced amount until the children, if any, are able to support themselves. This is sometimes called the **critical period income**. Two concepts are involved: how much income should be provided and for how long.

Obviously, as much income as is consistent with the family's other needs should be provided. As a minimum, there should be enough income that the family can remain intact and the surviving spouse can devote adequate time to the care and guidance of the children during their formative years. Although the children may have to engage in part-time employment, it should not be so extensive that it impairs their health or interferes with their education. The needs of this period constitute a large portion of the total demand for individual life insurance policies.

The most important determinants of the income's duration are the present ages of the insured's children and the type of education they will receive. In any case, income should continue until the youngest child is 18. If there are several children, the income can be reduced somewhat as each reaches the age of self-sufficiency. If the children are to receive a college education, income will have to continue for a longer period. In that event, the income during the period the children are in college may be provided by special educational insurance policies. For planning purposes, the immediate death of the income

producer is assumed. The projected income is then presumed to be needed for a period equal to the difference between the present age of the youngest child and the age at which the child is expected to become self-supporting.

Life Income for Surviving Dependent Spouse

The needs that exist during the readjustment and dependency periods are primarily family needs. It is presumed that the family unit will be preserved under the guidance of the surviving parent and that the resources of the various members of the family will be pooled to meet the needs of the group. After the children have become self-supporting, however, the widow(er) will still have needs as an individual and will require an income from some source.

If the surviving spouse is a full-time homemaker until the children finish at least part of their education, he or she may subsequently be able to obtain employment, but the earning power for people entering the workforce at that age will have declined substantially. After the birth of children, for example, a wife sometimes gives up her job or the opportunity to become self-supporting. As the years pass, whatever occupational skills she may have possessed are either obsolete or have atrophied and she will most likely have to return to the labor market as a middle-aged woman with deficient skills. Under such circumstances, employment opportunities are limited. Many individuals feel a moral obligation, therefore, to provide their spouses with incomes that will continue throughout the remaining years of their lives. The income may be modest, but it can be the difference between complete dependency on welfare services and reasonable self-sufficiency.

Special Needs

special needs of surviving spouse and family

There are certain **special needs of surviving spouse and family** that are not found in every family situation and, even when they are found, are not likely to enjoy as high a priority as those previously discussed. Three of the most prominent of these are mortgage redemption, educational, and emergency needs.

Mortgage Redemption Needs. Home ownership is very prevalent among American families today, but most of the homes are burdened with a mortgage, frequently financed by a life insurance company. These mortgages are usually amortized over a period of 15 or 30 years, but it is highly probable that an unliquidated balance will still be outstanding upon the death of a person with dependent children.

In some cases, of course, the widow(er) may want to sell the house and move into a smaller one or into an apartment, and it would not be essential to provide funds for the liquidation of the mortgage. In fact, it may actually be easier to dispose of a home if it has an assumable mortgage (becoming rare) with favorable terms than if it is clear of debt. In many—if not most—cases, however, it is contemplated that the survivors will continue to occupy the family residence, and funds to pay off the mortgage may be needed. If the family can occupy the home rent free, it will greatly reduce the amount of income that they would otherwise require.

Educational Needs. The income provided for a surviving spouse during the period when the children are dependent should normally be adequate for secondary school expenses, as well as for general maintenance. If a college education for one or more of the children is envisioned, however, additional income will be needed. Under present conditions, college expenses range from about $10,000 to $50,000 per year. The cost might be less if the family happens to live in the vicinity of a college or university and the college student resides at home; it might be considerably higher if the institution has a high tuition schedule. In any event, there is no question that a college or professional education is beyond the means of many dependent children who lose an income-earning parent. Life insurance companies have a variety of policies that will meet this need in a very convenient manner. In many cases, however, the limited funds available for life insurance premiums must be devoted to higher-priority needs.

Emergency Needs. From time to time in the life of a family, unforeseen needs for money arise because of illness, surgery, major dental work, home repairs, or many other reasons. It is unrealistic for the family income providers to leave enough income for the family to subsist on only if everything goes well and no unusual expenditures are incurred. Therefore, a liquid fund should be set up from which additional income can be provided if and when it is needed. Some financial planners suggest that the emergency fund often warrants a higher priority than income for dependents. The actual setting of priorities is properly the responsibility of the income earner(s).

retirement needs

Retirement Needs. Retirement needs do not fall within the categories previously described. On the contrary, the need arises only if the others do not. Yet retirement planning is a contingency that the financial planner and estate planner must anticipate and one that must be considered in arriving at the amount of insurance a family head should carry. To be more precise, this contingency determines the type of insurance the family provider(s) should purchase since if the family needs are met with the right kind of insurance (assuming adequate funds for premiums), the cash values under this insurance

will usually be sufficient to take care of the postretirement needs of the insured and the spouse, if still living.

Elements of Needs Analysis

- Cleanup fund

- Readjustment income

- Income during dependency period

- Life income for surviving dependent spouse

- Special needs

- Mortgage redemption needs

- Educational needs

- Emergency needs

- Retirement needs

Funding Trusts at Death. Trusts are contractual arrangements for the ownership and management of assets by a trustee according to the trust agreement. The trustee manages trust assets on behalf of and for the benefit of the trust beneficiaries. There are many different motivations for the establishment of a trust. One is to get professional management from a corporate entity, such as a trust company or a bank trust department, so that the trustee will not predecease any of the trust beneficiaries. Tax considerations sometimes justify the creation of a trust.

Life insurance is often an integral part of the trust funding. The trust itself often owns life insurance on the grantor, who names the trust as beneficiary of that insurance. Trusts can also be beneficiaries of insurance policies not owned by the trust. Those insurance proceeds provide the funds necessary for the trust to carry out its objectives. Some trusts are set up specifically for the purpose of funding life insurance premiums and receiving proceeds. If estate tax minimization is the objective of the trust, the trust is subject to more stringent requirements that can change many times during the existence of the trust.

Trusts have always been an important means of extending family financial management by the parents beyond the parents' lifetime. In these arrangements the trust is often used to distribute funds periodically rather than in a lump sum. The objective is usually to protect a child from a propensity to spend funds frivolously. By spreading out the distribution, the

child is unable to get access to and squander the entire sum immediately after the parents' death. Final distribution from such trusts is often predicated on the beneficiary's attainment of a specified age and is usually the parents' best guess as to when the child will be mature enough to handle the funds responsibly.

Trusts can also be set up for the benefit of children with mental impairments or other problems that would preclude them from ever becoming capable of managing their own finances. The nature of the trust depends very heavily on the type of care being provided to such children, especially on whether the care is private or public.

Trusts can also be an important tool for sequestering assets from a spouse to prevent the assets from being directed to a stepchild or to an unforeseen family member if the surviving spouse were to remarry after the insured's death.

Trusts

- Contractual agreement created by trustor

- Managed by trustee

- For benefit of trust beneficiaries, such as child or spouse

- Can own and manage assets

- Can be funded with life insurance

- Can own life insurance policies

Life insurance and trusts are often combined in creative ways to fund charitable gifts. Sometimes the entire arrangement is for the exclusive benefit of the charity. In other arrangements the trust is set up for a combination of family objectives and gifts to charitable institutions. Such arrangements usually involve a stream of income payments and subsequent distribution of the trust corpus. The charity or the family member can be the recipient of either the income payments, the corpus, or both.

Charitable Donations. Life insurance policies are often used to increase the value of gifts to charities. This can be accomplished either by giving the policy itself to the charitable organization or by naming the charity as the beneficiary on the existing life insurance policies. Where federal estate tax considerations are important, a new life insurance policy may be purchased by the charity itself at the request of the donor, who would give the necessary permission and information to complete the policy application and would provide the funds for premium payments.

Most states have enacted specific statutes expressly stating that charitable organizations have an insurable interest in the life of the donor. The statutes were prompted by an IRS decision claiming that a charity lacked an insurable interest in the donor. In part that decision was based on a New York statute that has since been modified to recognize such insurable interest.

Life insurance can also be used for charitable giving even if the charity is not a beneficiary of the insurance policy. The donor can use adequate amounts of life insurance to fund all of the needs of surviving family members and thereby free up personal property and other assets for lifetime gifts to the charities. Gift tax and estate tax considerations are often strong motives for making charitable gifts. Because tax laws can—and probably will—change, tax planning should be carefully coordinated by a knowledgeable tax adviser.

Funding for Gifts to Individuals. The use of life insurance is not limited to benefiting family members and related trusts and charities. Life insurance can easily be used to benefit anyone the donor specifies. The motivation could be friendship, long-term loyalty, respect for another's accomplishments, support of a common endeavor, or any other commitment about which the individual feels strongly. The intended recipient can be made beneficiary of a life insurance policy or a beneficiary of a trust funded by life insurance proceeds.

One of the strong factors favoring life insurance policies is that the proceeds do not generally go through probate and are not a matter of public record. The proceeds are payable quickly and directly to the beneficiary. Complications of settling or managing the estate have no bearing on nor do they delay the payment of proceeds under a life insurance policy unless the proceeds are payable directly to the insured's estate. In estates large enough to have a federal estate tax liability, therefore, it is generally not a good idea to have life insurance proceeds payable to the insured's estate.

Funding Home Health Care or Nursing Home Care. The prematurity values of life insurance policies can be used for home health care or nursing home care if that is deemed desirable or necessary. Access to the cash value is available through policy loans, partial withdrawals of the cash value, or outright surrender of the policy.

Long-term-care riders are available with some life insurance policies to provide for home health care or nursing home care needs. In some cases the rider is available without any additional charge; in other cases there is a nominal charge. In essence these riders make a portion of the death benefit, usually one or 2 percent of the face value of the policy, available each month that the insured qualifies for the benefit. The subsequent death benefit payable is reduced dollar-for-dollar for each accelerated benefit payment made under these riders. Their pre-death-benefit payments are usually subject to an aggregate

limitation of 50 percent of the face value of the policy, although a few insurance companies have increased the aggregate limitation to 70 or 80 percent of the policy face value.

Long-term-care riders allow life insurance policies to do double duty. They make benefits available for both the insured's lifetime objectives and the survivors' objectives. This can create a complication, however, in that lifetime uses directly reduce the residual benefit payable upon death. It is important to recognize and evaluate the potential conflicts when planning for these needs.

Transferring Assets to Younger Generations. Life insurance is often used as a way of leveraging assets when transferring property to younger generations. Children, grandchildren, and great-grandchildren can all be recipients of life insurance proceeds. They can also be recipients of life insurance policies. Members of the younger generations may own life insurance policies and also be beneficiaries of the same policies. Parents or grandparents often pay the premiums on policies owned by their children or grandchildren with gifts that are small enough to qualify for the annual gift tax exclusion.

Intergenerational transfers, however, may be subject to generation-skipping taxes as well as to gift and estate taxes. Such asset transfers therefore often involve very sophisticated arrangements to deal with the many complex constraints of both federal and state laws. Improper planning can increase the potential tax liabilities significantly. In many cases the costs of poor planning could be many times the cost of expert tax advice.

Discreetly Providing for Confidential Needs. Because life insurance is a contract and can be situated so that it is not property of the estate, it can escape public disclosure. This makes it a very desirable vehicle for accomplishing discreet postdeath funding, such as private business agreements in which life insurance proceeds are used to retire an outstanding personal debt. Life insurance and disability insurance are sometimes utilized to guarantee future payments under secret liability settlements. The insurance will continue the periodic payments if the liable person dies or is disabled.

Through proper arrangements life insurance proceeds can even be arranged to provide anonymous gifts to the intended recipients. This requires a third party who knows of the arrangement and can file the claim for death benefits. Life insurance has long been used as a funding device for partners in nontraditional living arrangements or those in amorous involvements outside of wedlock. Insurance companies are not eager to issue policies for some of these purposes and may decline the application if the purpose is openly set forth. However, the insurance company is unable to stop a policyowner from changing beneficiary designations on an existing policy. This contractual flexibility allows policyowners to

accomplish their objectives indirectly if they cannot do so directly at the time they apply for the policy.

Monetary Evaluation of the Foregoing Needs

It is interesting to compare the monetary value of the above needs with the economic value of the human life computed earlier. For purposes of comparison, assume—as in the earlier illustration—that the family head is a male aged 35, has gross annual earnings of $40,000, and devotes $20,000 per year to his family. Assume further that he has a wife aged 30 and two children, ages 2 and 5, and that an income of $1,700 per month is to be provided during the first 2 years, $1,460 per month during the next 14 years, and $971 per month thereafter for the life of the surviving spouse.

In computing the present value of the foregoing series of income payments, it is advisable to treat them as a life income of $971 per month payable from the surviving spouse's age 30 with an additional income of $489 per month for 16 years and another $240 per month for 2 years. On the basis of the 1983 Individual Annuity Table and 4 percent interest, a life income of $971 per month for a female aged 30, with payments guaranteed for 20 years, has a present value of approximately $220,000. Provision must be made for guaranteed payments during the children's dependency, since in the event of the widow's early death, the income to the children will be reduced from $971 perx month to $489 ($729 per month during the first 2 years). Guaranteed installments are available only in multiples of 5 years (up to 20 years), and at age 30, a 20-year guarantee can be obtained at a sacrifice of only 1 cent per $1,000 of principal sum, compared to the cost of a 15-year guarantee that would be one year short of the 16-year dependency period. The present value on a 4 percent interest basis of $489 per month for 16 years is $69,263, and the present value of $240 per month for 2 years is $5,526. The present value of the family's income needs when the figures are rounded to the nearest hundred dollars is $294,800.

The total increases when the lump-sum needs (cleanup fund and mortgage redemption fund), educational needs, and emergency needs are added. Even if no provision is made for the children's college education, a cleanup fund of $20,000, a mortgage redemption fund of $80,000, and an emergency fund of $30,000 will increase the total to $424,800. If $80,000 is provided to each of the children for a college education, the total income requirements reach $584,800.

Example

Married male aged 35, spouse aged 30, children ages 2 and 5

Income needed first 2 years	$ 1,700 / month
Income needed next 14 years	$ 1,460 / month
Income thereafter for surviving spouse	$ 971 / month
Assumed interest rate	4.0 percent
Cleanup fund	$ 20,000
Mortgage redemption fund	$ 80,000
Emergency fund	$ 30,000
Education fund for children	$160,000
Combined needs	$584,800

It is not likely that these needs will have to be met entirely through personal life insurance. If the individual in the example is covered under the federal OASDI program with benefits approaching the maximum—which, in view of his earnings, is very probable—nearly two-thirds of the income needed until the youngest child is 18 will be provided by the federal government.[7] This would reduce the personal insurance requirements by approximately $170,000. If the husband had attained "fully" insured status for Social Security at the time of his death—also a reasonable assumption—the widow at age 60 would become entitled to a life income of $800 per month, which would reduce the personal insurance requirements by another $29,600. The individual may also be covered by group life insurance, with benefits of possibly $150,000 or more. Therefore, it is not beyond the realm of possibility that all the needs, including those requiring lump-sum payments, may be met in full with the purchase of $235,000 of additional life insurance.

The retirement needs of the husband do not impose additional quantitative requirements. If the husband purchases $300,000 of life insurance (roughly the equivalent of the income needs computed earlier) on the ordinary life plan (the lowest premium type of permanent insurance) before age 35, it will have accumulated at least $125,000 in cash values by age 65. This will provide him with a life income, with payments guaranteed for 10 years, of more than $1,012 per month. If his wife is also alive and in need of old-age protection, the accumulated sum could be converted into a joint-and-last-survivor annuity,[8] which would provide a lower (a 7.5 percent to 14 percent reduction) income per month as long as either the husband or the wife survives. Such an income, supplemented by federal OASDI benefits and possibly retirement benefits from an employer pension plan, should meet their old-age

---

7. This assumes that the widow will not remarry during the period and that both children survive the period.
8. See chapter 24 for a description of the joint-and-last-survivor annuity.

needs with ample margins. (If the insured keeps premium outlays down through a liberal use of term insurance, the cash values available at age 65 will be reduced accordingly.)

Amount of Insurance Needed

Ideally, the life of each productive member of society should be insured for an amount equal to his or her full economic value, as measured by contributions to those who depend on that income. Upon the death of the income producer, the insured sum should then be liquidated in a manner consistent with the purposes for which it was created, meeting the various needs in the order of their importance. If the insured lives to retirement, the sums accumulated through premium payments should, with the exception of amounts required for cleanup and other necessary purposes, be used to satisfy the postretirement needs of the insured and his or her spouse.

As a practical matter, attaining this ideal is difficult, even when death benefits available under the federal OASDI program and employer benefit plans are taken into account. The basic obstacle is that when both the economic value and the needs are at their maximum—at younger ages—the funds available for premium payments are at their minimum. In the lower income groups, the bulk of the family income is spent on the necessities of life; very little is saved. As the family income rises, aggregate expenditures for consumer goods increase, but they constitute a smaller percentage of total income. Thus, more money is available for insurance premiums and other forms of savings. By that time, however, the need for insurance may have declined somewhat.

Amount of Insurance Needed

- Estimated economic value or amount needed to fund desires
- Less amounts already available (Social Security, investments, existing benefits and so on)
- Equals unfunded amount that can be made up with life insurance

Various formulas have been developed in an attempt to establish the proper relationship between family income and the amount of insurance to carry. A rule of thumb that has gained some acceptance is that 10 percent of gross family income should be devoted to life insurance premiums. Although this ratio is probably unrealistic at lower income levels, it becomes attainable as the income level increases. Another rule states that the typical wage earner should carry insurance equal to some specified multiple of annual gross income, while persons in the higher income brackets should capitalize a higher multiple

of annual earnings. Such rules of thumb are too simplistic because they do not take into consideration either (1) accumulated assets or (2) family composition and objectives.

Shortcomings of Rules of Thumb

- They do not recognize accumulated assets.

- They do not recognize individual family circumstances or family objectives.

Note that in the early 1990s approximately 1.88 percent of American families' disposable personal income[9] went into life insurance premiums.[10] This reflects a long slow decline from the high of 5.5 percent back in 1935 and is approximately the same percentage that prevailed during the last decade.

The average American family in the early 1990s owned enough life insurance of all types to replace approximately 27 months of its disposable income after federal income taxes. This reflects a slight increase from the characteristic 21 months of disposable income coverage prior to 1985.

Many family situations give rise to a need for funds that life insurance can supply. Some of the situations apply to almost all families, while others may be relatively complicated and apply only to special circumstances. Nevertheless there are many planned and unplanned needs for funds that can be satisfied with life insurance policies. Policies with cash values can provide funds during the insured's lifetime and benefits after the insured's death. Death benefits can be paid within a few days of the claim filing and are, therefore, an excellent source of immediate cash to the surviving family members. Life insurance makes the funds available upon death to meet any of the beneficiary's subsequent needs unless the contract intentionally directs the funds to a restricted use or availability.

Example 1

Carol had to start working after her husband died. Her daughter is attending a private school, and her son is attending a private university. By sending them to public institutions, she can reduce tuition costs by $25,000 a year.

---

9. Disposable personal income is gross income minus federal income taxes.
10. *Life Insurance Fact Book 1992,* American Council of Life Insurance, p. 73.

Example 2

The death of a nonincome-earning spouse can greatly increase the costs of the surviving household.

A single parent has to pay for essential services such as child care, transportation, and domestic chores that were previously performed by the deceased spouse and cannot be done by the survivor.

Example 3

Elderly parents can instantly loose their independence and self-sufficiency by means of an accident or sudden change in health. They may be hospitalized after a fall or a stroke and never be able to live by themselves again. Adult children are often overwhelmed by the demands of seeking care for a parent awaiting discharge from a hospital.

Nondependents

Many people make a regular discretionary payment to their adult children to enhance their standard of living although there is clearly no parental obligation to make these gifts, and the children are not dependent on the payments for necessities. Nevertheless, many parents in these circumstances have a strong desire to continue such enhancement payments at least until the grandchildren become self-supporting, even if the period of payments extends beyond the grandparent's life.

Payments to enhance someone's lifestyle, however, are not necessarily restricted to children or other family members. Payments are sometimes extended to lifelong domestic helpers and care givers as an informal pension, perhaps for the recipient's remaining lifetime. Life insurance can fund these payments if the benefactor dies first.

Level of Support

Any sort of plan to provide ongoing income payments to dependents or others after death requires the provider to make decisions about the amount of the payments and their duration. A starting point is to decide whether the income payments constitute partial support, full support, or full support plus an enhancement element. Another factor to consider is whether the payments are intended to be level or to change over time. In some cases there may be an intent to phase out these income payments by decreasing them over a given interval in the expectation that the recipient will achieve financial independence. Conversely, when the intent is to provide full support, income payments may have to be increased to compensate for the effects of inflation.

qualified terminal interest property trust (QTIP)

The duration of support payments can vary widely, depending on the provider's objectives. Payments may go to a very specific and predictable date, such as age 21 of the grandchild, age 35 of a child, age 90 of a spouse or other dependent, or to a specified calendar year. Alternatively, payments may be designed to continue for an unknown length of time, such as the remaining lifetime of the recipient, until the recipient remarries, or until the birth of a child. Income payments can even be designed to be perpetual so that the capital sum supporting the income payments is not reduced or depleted. By using a perpetual-funding approach for lifetime incomes, the capital sum is a transferable asset after the income objectives are satisfied. A common application is the **qualified terminal interest property trust (QTIP)** used for estate planning purposes. In such a trust a lifetime income is paid to the surviving spouse, and the trust corpus is then distributed to children (or others) after the spouse dies.

BUSINESS PURPOSES

Life insurance serves a wide variety of purposes in the business world, but most of the services can be grouped under these four headings:

- key person indemnification
- credit enhancement
- business continuation
- employee benefit plans

Key Person Indemnification

Perhaps the most direct application of the principles of family insurance to the business world is key person insurance. Its purpose is to indemnify a business concern for the loss of earnings caused by the death of a key officer or employee. In many business concerns, there is one person whose capital, technical knowledge, experience, or business connections make him or her the most valuable asset of the organization and a necessity to its successful operation. This is more likely to be true of a small organization, but innumerable examples can also be found in large organizations. A manufacturing or mining enterprise may depend on one or a few individuals whose engineering talents are vital to the concern. An employee with unusual administrative ability or the ability to develop and motivate a superior sales organization may also be a key person. An educational institution or

other organization that depends partly on charitable giving may regard a highly successful fund-raiser as a key person.

It is difficult to estimate the economic loss that the organization would suffer in the event of the key person's death. In most cases the loss is measured in terms of earnings, but occasionally it is based on the additional compensation that would have to be paid to replace the key employee. In some cases, the reduction in earnings is assumed to be temporary (5 years, for example), while in other cases, a permanent impairment of earning power is envisioned. The basis for indemnity can usually be established rather accurately when the key person protection is required in connection with a specific research project or other undertaking of temporary duration.

Insurance is purchased on the life of the key employee by the business and is made payable to the business as beneficiary. In most cases, some form of permanent insurance, usually ordinary life, is purchased, and the accumulating cash values are reflected as an asset on the business's books. If key person protection is needed for only a temporary period, term insurance is normally used. Premiums paid for key person insurance are not deductible as a business expense, but in the event of death, the proceeds are received free of federal income tax.

Elements of Key Person Valuation

- Profits directly attributable to person's efforts

- Additional compensation necessary to replace

- Recruiting and training costs to find or create a replacement

- Lost revenue anticipated

Credit Enhancement

Life insurance can enhance a business concern's credit in two general ways: by improving its general credit rating and by making collateral available.

The first credit function of life insurance is closely allied to (if not identical with) key person insurance. Anything that stabilizes a business concern's financial position improves its credit rating. Insuring the lives of key personnel not only assures banks and other prospective lenders that the business will have a financial cushion if a key person dies, it also improves the firm's liquidity through the accumulation of cash values that are available at all times. As a result, the firm is able to command more credit and obtain it on better terms.

A more specific use of life insurance for credit purposes is pledging it for collateral. It is important to note, however, that the collateral can serve two different purposes. It can protect the lender only against loss arising out of the death of a key person or the borrower, or it can provide protection against the borrower's unwillingness or inability to repay the loan.

An example of the first situation is a firm that has borrowed as much as is justified on the basis of conventional operating ratios but would like to borrow additional sums to take advantage of an unusual business opportunity. If the bank has confidence in the business and feels that the only contingency to fear is the death of the business head or other key person, it can safely extend the additional credit upon assigning to the bank a life insurance policy in an appropriate amount on the life of the proper official. The policy need not have cash values; therefore, term insurance is frequently used. The basic security behind the loan is the earning capacity of the business and the integrity of its officials. The policy provides protection only against the death of the person whose business acumen assures the loan's repayment. Such loans, secured only by the assignment of a term insurance policy on the borrower's life, are common in personal or nonbusiness transactions—for example, an aspiring doctor who borrows money from a benefactor for medical school, repaying the funds after establishing a practice. In the interim, the benefactor is protected by a term insurance policy on the budding physician's life. This is a character loan, pure and simple; the only hazard to repayment is premature death.

A loan based on cash values is in a different category. The basic security lies in the policy values; the amount of the loan, therefore, is always less than the cash value under the policy assigned to the lender. If the borrower dies before the loan is repaid, the lender recovers funds from the death proceeds, with the difference paid to the insured's designated beneficiary. If the borrower lives but the loan is not paid at maturity, the lender can recover the funds by surrendering the policy for cash or by exercising the policy loan privilege. If the loan is repaid at maturity, the policy is reassigned to the borrower. Life insurance policies are widely used for this purpose in both business and personal situations. Policyowners frequently borrow from an insurance company through the policy loan privilege, rather than through assignment to a bank or other lender.

Business Continuation

One of the important forms of business organization in this country is the general partnership, which is subject to the rule of law that any change in the membership of the partnership causes its dissolution. In accordance with this rule, the death of a general partner dissolves the partnership, and the surviving partners become liquidating trustees, charged

with the responsibility of paying over the deceased's fair share of the business's liquidated value to his or her estate. Liquidation of a business, however, almost invariably results in severe shrinkages among the assets. Accounts receivable yield only a fraction of their book value, inventory is disposed of at sacrifice prices, furniture and fixtures are sold as second-hand merchandise, and goodwill is lost completely. Moreover, liquidation deprives the surviving partners of their means of livelihood.

In the absence of a prior agreement among the partners, any attempt to avoid liquidation is beset with legal and practical complications. Even if the surviving partners can raise the cash to purchase the deceased's interest—an unrealistic assumption in most cases—they have to prove, as liquidating trustees, that the price paid for the interest is fair. In some states, their fiduciary status prevents their purchasing the deceased's interest at any price since it is virtually tantamount to trustees purchasing trust property. Furthermore, it is seldom practical for the widow(er) or other heir to become a member of the reorganized partnership or to purchase the surviving partner's interests.

In order to avoid this impasse, it is becoming increasingly common for the members of a partnership to enter into a buy-sell agreement. Such an agreement binds the surviving partners to purchase the partnership interest of the first partner to die at a price set forth in the agreement and obligates the deceased partner's estate to sell his or her interest to the surviving partners. The various interests are valued at the time the agreement is drawn up and revised from time to time thereafter. Each partner is insured for the amount of his or her interest, and either the partnership or the other partners own the insurance. Upon the first death among the partners, the life insurance proceeds are used by the partnership or the partners, as the case may be, to purchase the deceased's interest. Thus, the business continues in operation for the benefit of the surviving partners, and the deceased's heirs receive the going value of his or her business interest in cash.

All parties benefit by the arrangement. After the first death, the surviving partners can enter into a new buy-sell agreement, or they can continue under the original agreement with the necessary valuation and insurance adjustments. Life insurance is uniquely suited to financing such agreements since the very event that creates the need for cash also provides the cash. The same sort of agreement is desirable for the stockholders in a closely held corporation. Closely held corporations are so similar in basic characteristics to partnerships that they have been described as "incorporated partnerships." Although the death of a stockholder does not legally dissolve the corporation, the same practical difficulties may be encountered in any attempt to continue the business. These difficulties arise because stockholders of a closely held corporation are also its officers, earnings are distributed primarily in the form of salaries, and no ready market exists for the stock.

Objectives of Buy-Sell Agreements

- Provide for transfer of deceased person's ownership interest

- Establish an agreed-upon method of valuing the interest

- Facilitate the continuation of the business despite the termination of the deceased person's participation and ownership

- Establish the desired method of financing the ownership interest transfer(s)

- Provide an equitable method for terminating the interest of nonparticipating heirs

Upon the death of a principal stockholder in a closely held corporation, the surviving stockholders are faced with three choices (apart from liquidation), all of which may prove undesirable: (1) to accept the widow(er) or other adult heir of the deceased into the active management of the corporation, (2) to pay dividends, approximately equivalent to the salary of the deceased stockholder, to the widow(er) or other heir without any participation in management on the heir's part, or (3) to admit outside interests to whom the deceased's stock may have been sold into active management of the company. The surviving spouse faces the possibility of having to dispose of the deceased's stock at a sacrifice price, either to the surviving stockholders or to outsiders, neither of whom would normally be inclined to offer a fair price, or of retaining the stock and receiving no dividends. These difficulties can be avoided through a binding buy-sell agreement financed by life insurance. Under such an agreement, the surviving stockholders will get the corporation's stock, and the widow(er) will receive cash for a speculative business interest.

Similar agreements can be arranged between a sole proprietor and one or more key employees. Life insurance can provide at least a portion of the purchase price, and the remainder can be financed by interest-bearing notes to be paid off from the business's earnings after the proprietor's death.

Employee Benefit Plans

Employee benefit plans provide three broad types of benefits that can be financed through insurance:

- disability benefits, including income replacement and indemni-fication of medical, surgical, and hospital costs
- death benefits
- old-age benefits

The plans that provide such benefits are usually referred to, respectively, as group health insurance, group life insurance, and pensions, including group annuity plans. While accidental death benefits may be—and usually are—provided under a group health plan, life insurance contracts, per se, are used only in connection with group life insurance and certain forms of pensions. Suffice it to say that death benefits under a group life insurance contract may be provided in the form of yearly renewable term insurance, permanent types of contracts, or a combination of the two. The employer always bears a portion of the cost, and some may pay it all. The benefits payable on behalf of any particular employee are determined by a formula that minimizes selection against the insurer. In other words, the employees are not permitted to choose the amount of coverage since those in poor health could be expected to apply for the largest amounts of insurance.

CHAPTER REVIEW

Key Terms and Concepts

present value of $1 per annum
economic value of a producer
human life value approach
needs approach
financial needs analysis
capital needs analysis
cleanup fund

readjustment income
critical period income
special needs of surviving spouse and
    family
retirement needs
qualified terminal interest property
    trust (QTIP)

Chapter 1 Review Questions

1. What is meant by the economic value of a human life? [2]

2. Explain why earning power alone does not create an economic value that can logically serve as the basis of life insurance. [2]

3. Describe Dr. S. S. Huebner's views concerning the obligation to insure. [2]

4. List the five steps in the recommended procedure to compute a person's monetary value for purposes of life insurance. [2]

5. Explain why it takes substantially less than $1.2 million of life insurance to provide $40,000 per year for 30 years to a provider's dependents. [3]

6. Describe the three broad categories of life insurance. [6]

7. Describe the six categories of needs to consider in determining the amount of insurance a person should carry. [1]

8. Describe in general terms how a typical family with dependent children can determine the amount of insurance needed on an income provider's life. [4]

9. What is the advantage of purchasing ordinary life insurance instead of term insurance to provide the insurance required in the preceding question? [4]

10. Describe the use of life insurance for the following business purposes: (a) key person indemnification; (b) credit enhancement; (c) business continuation; (d) employee benefit plans. [5]

11. Identify the expenses commonly associated with a family breadwinner's death. [6]

12. Identify the most common ongoing needs for funds to support surviving family members. [7]

13. Explain why trusts are often used in providing for the support of surviving dependents. [8]

14. Identify the potential sources of retirement income and supplements to it. [8]

15. Explain how life insurance can be used to make charitable donations or specific bequests. [9]

16. Explain why using simple rules of thumb to determine the amount of life insurance an individual needs may result in the wrong amount for that person's actual needs. [10]

17. How can simplistic rules of thumb about the amount of life insurance that is needed be used positively? [10]

18. Indicate the types of information to assemble and analyze before recommending the appropriate amount of life insurance for a person. [10]

19. Describe the types of expenses to anticipate when estimating the lump-sum funds needed at death. [10]

20. Why is it important to evaluate each prospective life insurance purchaser's needs individually? [10]

21. Explain how existing liquid assets and near-liquid assets affect the emergency fund portion of estimating life insurance needs. [10]

22. What information is necessary to make an accurate estimate of educational expenses for dependent children as a component of life insurance needs? [10]

23. What special life insurance planning problems are presented by dependent children who are unable to ever become self-sufficient? [10]

24. List four common categories of income needs for surviving spouses. [10]

25. Describe the categories of survivors entitled to income benefits from Social Security after a covered worker dies. [10]

26. Describe the contracts available from life insurers that can provide income on a liquidating basis and still guarantee a life income. [11]

27. Why do some financial advisers suggest using simplifying assumptions and working with rounded-off amounts to estimate income needs, rather than calculating every item to the last penny? [11]

28. Explain the pros and cons of planning to fund survivors' income needs on a liquidating basis. [11]

29. Calculate the capital sum required to provide $80,000 of income per year if: (a) the funds earn a 4 percent return after taxes; (b) the funds earn an 8 percent return after taxes. [11]

Chapter 1 Review Answers

1. *A human life has an economic value if it has both (1) earning power and (2) some other person or organization can expect to derive financial advantage through its existence.*

2. *Life insurance is concerned with the economic value of a human life, which is derived from (1) its earning capacity and (2) the financial dependence of others on that earning capacity. If an individual has earning capacity but is without dependents and no other person or organization stands to benefit financially through his or her living either now or in the future, then that life, for all practical purposes, has no monetary value that needs to be protected with life insurance.*

3. *Concerning the obligation to insure, Dr. S.S. Huebner viewed the family as a parent's most important business venture that, like other business ventures run on a sound basis, should be protected against "needless bankruptcy" due to death or disability by the purchase of insurance by the parent as a matter of responsibility to his or her dependents.*

4. *An estimate of a person's monetary value for purposes of life insurance can be derived by the following 5 steps:*
    a. *Estimate the individual's average annual earnings from personal efforts over the remaining years of his or her income-producing lifetime.*
    b. *Deduct federal and state income taxes, life insurance premiums, and the cost of self-maintenance.*
    c. *Determine the number of years between the individual's present age and the contemplated age of retirement.*
    d. *Select a reasonable rate of interest at which future earnings will be discounted.*
    e. *Multiply (1) minus (2) by the present value of $1 per annum for the period determined in (3), discounted at the rate of interest selected in (4).*

5. *The insured's goal is to provide dependents with $40,000 a year for 30 years. In total $1.2 million will be distributed over the 30-year period. The question is, how much is required*

today to provide the desired income stream? Because not all the funds are distributed immediately, the lump sum can be conservatively invested. Each annual $40,000 payment will be part principal from the lump sum and part interest earnings. The earnings on the funds reduce the initial required principal sum to less than $1.2 million.

A compound discount table shows the present value of a series of $1 income payments for various time periods. The present value of a series of $1 income payments received at the end of each year for 30 years at an assumed 5 percent interest rate is $15.37. This means that if $15.37 is invested today earning 5 percent annual interest, an income stream of $1 per year payable at the end of each year can be provided to the insured's family for 30 years. At the end of the 30-year period, the account balance will be zero—all funds, principal, and interest will have been paid out to the dependents.

Because the goal is to provide income of $40,000 per year, simply take the present value of $1 invested at 5 percent for 30 years—$15.37—and multiply it by the required annual payment—$40,000—to arrive at the principal sum needed today—$614,800.

The amount of insurance ($614,800) needed today to provide $40,000 of annual income over 30 years is substantially less than $1.2 million because the funds will be invested and the annual distributions will come from both the insurance principal amount and the interest earnings.

6. *The three broad categories of life insurance are:*

   a. *Juvenile insurance. This is life insurance purchased on a child's life to enable the parents' to recover the financial investment made in raising the child if the child dies between birth and self-sufficiency.*

   b. *Family insurance. This is life insurance purchased on a parent's life to provide for care and maintenance of the family in the event of the parent's death.*

   c. *Income shortage in retirement. This is life insurance and annuities purchased to fill income gaps in retirement years.*

7. The six categories of needs to consider in determining the amount of insurance a person should carry are:

    a. Cleanup fund—a fund to meet the expenses resulting from the insured's death and to liquidate all current outstanding obligations. The principal items of expense to consider include the following:

        •   hospital, doctors', and nurses' bills incident to the insured's last illness that are not covered by insurance

        •   burial expenses, including funeral costs, cemetery lot, and marker

        •   personal obligations, including unpaid notes, household bills, installment payments, personal loans, and unsatisfied judgments, if any

        •   unpaid pledges, whether or not they are legally binding obligations

        •   the cost of estate administration, including executor's or administrator's fee, appraisers' fees, legal fees, and court costs

        •   estate, inheritance, income, and property taxes

    b. Readjustment income—the need for income approximately equivalent to the family's share of the income producer's earnings at the time of his or her death that will be continued for a period following the income producer's death in order to cushion the adjustment that generally will have to be made in the family's standard of living.

    c. Income during the dependency period—After the expiration of the readjustment period, income should be provided in a reduced amount until the children, if any, are able to support themselves.

    d. Life income for surviving dependent spouse-Many individuals feel a moral obligation to provide their spouses with incomes that will continue throughout the remaining years of their lives.

    e. Special needs—There are certain needs that are not found in every family situation. Three of the most prominent of these are mortgage redemption, educational, and emergency needs.

        •   Mortgage redemption—In many—if not most—cases, it is contemplated that the survivors will continue to occupy the family residence, and funds to pay off

the mortgage may be needed. If the family can occupy the home rent free, it will greatly reduce the amount of income that they would otherwise require.

- Educational needs—If a college education for one or more of the children is envisioned, additional income will be needed.

- Emergency needs—A liquid fund should be set up from which additional income can be provided if and when it is needed for unforeseen needs such as illness, surgery, major dental work, home repairs, or many other reasons.

f. Retirement needs—These needs do not fall within the categories previously described. On the contrary, the need arises only if the other do not. This contingency determines the type of insurance the family provider(s) should purchase because if the family needs are met with the right kind of insurance (assuming adequate funds for premiums), the cash values under this insurance will usually be sufficient to take care of the postretirement needs of the insured and the spouse, if still living.

8. First, for each of the income needs (readjustment income, income during the dependency period, life income for surviving dependent spouse and income for education) compute the present value today of the needed income streams. Second, add the amounts of the lump-sum needs (cleanup fund, mortgage redemption fund, and emergency fund) to the total present value of the income needs to get the amount of the family's total needs if the income producer were to die today.

Next, identify the sources of income that would be available to help meet the family's income needs if the income producer were to die (for example, Social Security benefits streams and add them together. Then add any lump sums that would be available to help meet the family's lump-sum needs if the income producer were to die (for example, savings and investments, death benefits under the income producer's retirement plan, and so on) to get the total funds that would be available to meet the family's needs if the income producer were to die.

Subtract the total funds currently available from the total family needs to determine the amount of life insurance needed.

9. While both term insurance and ordinary life insurance would meet the gap between family needs and currently available resources if the income producer were to die, ordinary life insurance would also accumulate cash values that could be used to help meet retirement needs if the income producer were to survive.

10. *The following are some uses of life insurance for business purposes:*

   a. *Key person indemnification—Life insurance is used to indemnify a business concern for the loss of earnings (and extra expenses) caused by the death of a key officer or employee. Insurance is purchased on the life of the key employee by the business and is made payable to the business as beneficiary. In most cases, some form of permanent insurance, usually ordinary life, is purchased, and the accumulating cash values are reflected as an asset on the business's books. If key person protection is needed for only a temporary period, term insurance is normally used.*

   b. *Credit enhancement—Life insurance can enhance a business concern's credit in two general ways: by improving its general credit rating and by making collateral available. The first credit function of life insurance is closely allied to (if not identical with) key person insurance. Anything that stabilizes a business concern's financial position improves its credit rating. Insuring the lives of key personnel not only assures banks and other prospective lenders that the business will have a financial cushion if a key person dies, it also improves the firm's liquidity through the accumulation of cash values that are available at all times. The second use of life insurance for credit purposes is pledging it for collateral. It is important to note, however, that the collateral can serve two different purposes. It can protect the lender only against loss arising out of the death of a key person or the borrower, or it can provide protection against the borrower's unwillingness or inability to repay the loan.*

   c. *Business continuation—Life insurance can be used (1) to fund a buy-sell agreement that will prevent a partnership from having to be dissolved upon the death of a general partner and (2) to fund a buy-sell agreement that will prevent a closely held corporation from passing into the hands of an heir or outside party upon the death of a principal stockholder.*

   d. *Employee benefit plans—Death benefits are provided under a group life insurance contract that may be in the form of yearly renewable term insurance, permanent types of contracts, or a combination of the two.*

11. *Expenses commonly associated with a breadwinner's death include bills for uninsured medical bills, as well as deductibles and copay portions; convalescent case, funeral, burial or other disposition of the body, transportation, managing and settling the estate and, in large estates, taxes; and emergencies that cause death sometimes create the need for immediate repairs or replacement of property.*

12. *Common ongoing needs include food, clothing, shelter, education, transportation, utilities, taxes, lifetime support for disabled dependents, support until self-dependency of young children, dependent parents, debt repayment (mortgages, loans, and so on).*

13. *Sometimes a trust is used to provide professional management of the finances. Trusts can be used to control assets after the death of a parent and, in some cases, disabled dependents, and prevent the squandering of funds by beneficiaries who cannot manage money.*

14. *Social Security, corporate pensions, IRAs, qualified plans, investments, life insurance proceeds, life insurance surrenders, life insurance cash withdrawals, life insurance policy loans are all sources of retirement/supplemental income.*

15. *Life insurance policy proceeds may be directed to a charity or person by making them the beneficiary. The policy itself may be given to the intended party. Cash can be obtained from permanent life insurance policies either as withdrawals or policy loans. Policies can also be surrendered (terminating coverage) for their cash value. Life insurance can be used to fund a trust that has the desired recipient named as trust beneficiary.*

16. *The rule-of-thumb approach ignores information about the specific needs of the client's dependents, how much the client has already accumulated, and any existing external sources of finance such as trusts and inheritances. The simplistic rule-of-thumb approach can err in either direction, that is, it can either overinsure or underinsure the client.*

17. *Simplistic rules of thumb may perform a positive function if they are the only approach or logic that motivates the client to purchase needed insurance. Sometimes clients do resist providing the information necessary for an appropriate and thorough analysis of their needs.*

18. *Before recommending the appropriate amount of life insurance for a person, the financial services professional must gather and analyze complete and accurate information about current income, potential future income, accumulated assets, investments, pensions, and other qualified plan holdings. In addition, it is important to develop a profile of the client's priorities and goals or objectives.*

19. *The cash (lump-sum) needs at death include such items as final costs not covered by insurance; repayment of outstanding debt that becomes due and payable upon death; estate taxes, if applicable; the expenses of the funeral, burial, and cremation, if applicable;*

the costs of probate court to prove the validity of the will; attorneys' fees; and operational expenses to cover the ongoing costs of the survivors' household. Because future interest would be saved, funds to pay off the outstanding balance of the mortgage are also often handled as lump sum needs.

20. *Because the amounts associated with each category of needs vary widely from one individual to another and from one family to another, each case must be evaluated individually.*

21. *An important factor in setting the level of the emergency fund is whether the family has other liquid or near-liquid assets that could easily be used to cover such emergencies. Money market accounts and listed security holdings may be acceptable sources of funds to cover all or part of any potential emergency, thus reducing or eliminating the amount of funds from life insurance death proceeds needed to cover emergencies.*

22. *The amount needed to prefund children's education with life insurance is a function of the current ages of those children, the costs associated with the intended educational institutions, the number of years for which educational support is intended to be provided, and the proportion of financing for education the parents intend to prefund.*

23. *In most families, there is both a desire and the financial ability to prefund the survivors' income needs at least until the youngest child becomes self-sufficient, often when he or she completes formal education. This type of evaluation becomes more difficult when there are children with special needs that will keep them from ever becoming self-sufficient. Such special children may actually have ongoing income needs many years beyond the death of the surviving parent.*

24. *It is common to classify the survivors' (spouse and/or dependents) ongoing income needs in four categories:*

    • *income for a readjustment period immediately after death*

    • *adjusted income starting after the initial transition period and continuing until the youngest child becomes self-sufficient*

- income, if any, for the surviving spouse after the children have become self-sufficient (the blackout period)

- the surviving spouse's income after eligibility for Social Security benefits and private pension benefits

25. The most commonly available source of income is Social Security benefits. The surviving spouse and each child will be eligible for benefits as long as the children are under age 16 and living with the surviving spouse. The children's benefits will actually continue until they are aged 18, but the surviving spouse's benefit will stop when the youngest child reaches age 16. The surviving spouse then becomes eligible for widow's/widower's benefits at age 60. There are also benefits for dependent parents at age 62.

26. Life insurance policy proceeds at death can provide a guaranteed life income through policy settlement options or separate annuity contracts. Annuity contracts can also be used to provide a guaranteed life income from other sources, such as funds accumulated in the deceased's retirement plan.

27. Because this is an estimation process, numbers can be rounded off. Also, because no one knows the future with precision, simplifying assumptions must be made.

28. A serious problem associated with the liquidating approach is that the fund will eventually be totally dissipated. However, the liquidating approach requires less capital at death than the nonliquidating approach.

29. a.　It takes $2 million to provide $80,000 per year from a 4 percent after-tax return ($80,000 divided by 0.04).

　　b.　It takes $1 million to provide $80,000 per year from an 8 percent after-tax return ($80,000 divided by 0.08).

Chapter 2
Basic Principles

By Dan M. McGill

Revised by C.W. Copeland & Edward E. Graves

Learning Objectives

An understanding of the material in this chapter should enable you to

1. **Explain the concept of risk pooling and how it applies to life insurance.**

2. **Describe how the premium for yearly renewable term insurance is determined.**

3. **Explain the operation of the level premium plan and its application to term insurance and ordinary life policies.**

4. **Explain the tax treatment of life insurance.**

Insurance has been defined in many different ways. Willett, for example, has defined it as "that social device for making accumulations to meet uncertain losses of capital which is carried out through the transfer of the risks of many individuals to one person or to a group of persons."[1] Kulp states that "insurance is a formal social device for the substitution of certainty for uncertainty through the pooling of hazards."[2] In the same vein, Riegel and Miller say that from a functional standpoint, "insurance is a social device whereby the uncertain risks of individuals may be combined in a group and thus made more certain, small periodic contributions by the individuals providing a fund out of which those who suffer loss may be reimbursed."[3] Finally, Pfeffer, in his search for a generic definition, concludes that "insurance is a device for the reduction of the uncertainty of one party, called the insured, through the transfer of particular risks to another party, called the insurer, who offers a restoration, at least in part, of economic losses suffered by the insured."[4]

1. Allan H. Willett, *The Economic Theory of Risk and Insurance* (Philadelphia: University of Pennsylvania Press, 1951), p. 72.
2. C. A. Kulp, *Casualty Insurance,* 3d ed. (New York: Ronald Press Co., 1956), p. 9.53.
3. Robert Riegel and Jerome S. Miller, *Insurance Principles and Practices* (New York: Prentice-Hall, Inc., 1947), p. 19.
4. Irving Pfeffer, *Insurance and Economic Theory* (Homewood, Ill.: Richard D. Irwin, Inc., 1956), p. 53.

CONCEPT OF RISK POOLING

risk pooling

Underlying all of these definitions is the concept of **risk pooling**, or group sharing, of losses. That is, persons exposed to loss from a particular source combine their risks and agree to share losses on some equitable basis. The risks may be combined under an arrangement whereby the participants mutually insure each other, a plan that is appropriately designated "mutual insurance," or they may be transferred to an organization that, for a consideration called the "premium," is willing to assume the risks and pay the resulting losses. In life insurance, such an organization is a stock life insurance company. While several elements must be present in any sound insurance plan, the essence of the arrangement is the pooling of risks and losses.

Illustration of the Insurance Principle

The basic principle involved in insurance can best be illustrated in terms of a simple form, such as fire insurance. Suppose that in a certain community there are 1,000 houses, each worth $100,000 and each exposed to approximately the same probability of destruction by fire. The probability that any one of these houses will be destroyed by fire in any particular year is extremely remote, possibly no more than one out of 1,000. Yet if that contingency should occur, the loss to the owner would be staggering—$100,000. If it could be assumed, however, that only one of the 1,000 houses would be destroyed by fire in a particular year, a contribution of only $100 by each home owner would provide a fund large enough to reimburse in full the unfortunate person whose home was lost. If each homeowner were willing to assume a certain loss of $100, he could rid himself of the risk of a $100,000 loss. Over the years, only a relatively small percentage of the homes would be destroyed; and through their willingness to contribute a series of small annual sums to a mutual indemnity fund, the property owners would eliminate the possibility of a catastrophic loss to any of their group. The aggregate premium payments over 60 years of home ownership for any one person would still be very small, relative to the protection against the potential loss.

Application to Life Insurance

The principle of loss sharing can be applied in identical fashion to the peril of death. The simplest illustration involves insurance for one year, with all members of the group the same age and possessing roughly similar prospects for longevity. The members of this

group might mutually agree that a specified sum, such as $100,000, will be paid to the designated beneficiaries of those members who die during the year, the cost of the payments being borne equally by the members of the group. In its simplest form, this arrangement might envision an assessment upon each member in the appropriate amount as each death occurs. In a group of 1,000 persons, each death would produce an assessment of $100 per member. Among a group of 10,000 males aged 35, 21 of them could be expected to die within a year, according to the Commissioners 2001 Standard Ordinary Mortality Table (2001 CSO Table); if expenses of operation are ignored, cumulative assessments of $120 per person would provide the funds for payment of $100,000 to the beneficiary of each of the 12 deceased persons. Larger death payments would produce proportionately larger assessments based on the rate of $1.24 per $1,000 of benefit.

Example

Ten thousand males aged 35 contribute to a life insurance pool. Twelve of the 10,000 are expected to die while aged 35 (based on 2001 CSO mortality table). If each of the 10,000 contributes $120 to fund death benefits (ignoring costs of operation), a death benefit of $100,000 could be paid for each of the 12 expected deaths.

The 1980 CSO mortality table is sex distinct and therefore has different rates at each age for men and women. The rate per $1,000 of benefit for women aged 35 is $1.65, according to the 1980 CSO table. However, it is $1.00 for the same group of 35 year old women according to the 2001 CSO table. It is very important to note that most large insurance companies base their rates on their own statistics rather than 1980 or 2001 CSO tables. The companies that issue policies only to the healthiest applicants will have rates significantly lower than those of the CSO tables used for reserving purposes by the regulators. Even insurance companies issuing policies to applicants in just average health usually experience a rate lower than either the 1980 or 2001 CSO rates.

Assessment Insurance

assessment insurance

Over a century ago, plans based on the **assessment insurance** technique were widely used in the United States, although confined to fraternal societies and so-called "business assessment associations."[5] Assessments were levied to cover future claims rather than to pay claims that had already been incurred.

---

5. Business assessment associations were local societies organized for the sole purpose of offering insurance at rates much lower than those charged by regular or old-line life insurance companies. They were neither fraternal in

Example

The Ancient Order of United Workmen, organized in 1868 and the first society to provide death benefits—$2,000 each—levied an assessment of $1 against each member after the payment of each death claim, in order that funds would be available for the prompt settlement of the next claim. Later plans adopted the practice of levying assessments at regular intervals—usually, once a year—rather than after each death.

Flat Assessments

The early societies generally levied the same assessment on all members, regardless of age. This "flat assessment" plan was based on the theory that there would be a continual flow of new members at the younger ages, with little variation from year to year in the average age of those in the group. Hence, the total death rate would not increase, and the annual assessments would remain relatively constant over the years.

Unfortunately, this assumption was invalid. It is not true that the total death rate will not increase so long as the average age of the group does not rise. Suppose, for example, that a fraternal society was organized with 2,000 members, all 40 years of age, and that after several years, its membership was composed of 1,000 persons aged 30 and 1,000 aged 50—an admittedly unrealistic assumption. The average age would still be 40, as it was at the society's inception. However, since the death rate increases more rapidly from ages 40 to 50 than it decreases from ages 40 to 30, the number of deaths in the group will be greater under the later distribution of ages than under the original. The 2001 CSO Table shows a male death rate of 1.72 per 1,000 at age 40, 1.14 per 1,000 at age 30, and 3.91 per 1,000 at age 50. With 2,000 members aged 40, the society could expect 3.44 deaths in one year, whereas with 1,000 members aged 30 and 1,000 aged 50, it could expect 5.05 deaths. The disparity would have been even larger if a higher average age had been assumed.

Moreover, the average age was virtually certain to increase. Newly organized societies consisted predominantly of young and middle-aged members. Older aged applicants were not solicited, since their admission to the group would have increased the assessments and placed the younger members at a greater financial disadvantage. As the society grew older, however, there was a tendency for the average age to climb because of the difficulty of offsetting the increase in the age of the current membership by the flow of new entrants.

This difficulty can be explained by a simple example. If a society commenced operations with five members aged 20, 21, 22, 23, and 24, the average age of the group would be 22.

---

character nor organized on the lodge system.

Assume that during the first year of operation the youngest member, aged 20, dies and is replaced by a new member. If the new member is also 20, the average age of the group will be 22.8, since each of the surviving members is now one year older. If any one except the oldest of the original five members dies and is replaced by a member 20 years of age or more, the average age will increase. The practical effect of this phenomenon is that deceased and withdrawing members of a fraternal society have to be replaced by more than an equivalent number of younger members if the average age of the group is not to increase.

Flat Assessment Groups

- Death rates increase with age.

- The rate of increase in the death rate accelerates rapidly after age 50.

- Assessments increase as the group ages.

- Young and healthy members of group drop out, further increasing assessments on group members.

As assessments increased in magnitude and frequency, young and healthy members tended to withdraw from the society, frequently to join a younger society where protection could be obtained at a lower cost, while the old and infirm members remained. This had the obvious effect of increasing the average age even more rapidly, thus further accelerating the withdrawal of the young and healthy members. Under such circumstances it soon became impossible to attract new members. The increase in the proportion of aged and infirm members was accompanied by a corresponding increase in death rates. The inevitable result was an abnormally high rate of assessment and, not infrequently, a collapse of the organization. The attendant loss to those aged members who had all their lives contributed to the benefits of others was disheartening and often tragic.

Graded Assessments

graded assessments

Once the weakness of the flat assessment plan became apparent, many societies began to grade the assessment according to the age at entry, a typical scale ranging from $0.60 at age 20 to $2.50 at age 60. However, the rate for any given member remained fixed and did not increase as the member grew older and constituted a heavier mortality risk. While not as crude as the flat assessment plan, the **graded assessment** arrangement proved unsatisfactory and, like the former, worked a hardship upon the younger members.

adverse selection

A third plan called for assessments that would increase as the member grew older. If based on valid mortality data, such increasing premiums were theoretically sound, but from a practical standpoint, the arrangement was defective because it required low premiums in the younger productive years and high premiums in the older years of lessening productive capacity. More serious, it prompted healthy members to withdraw from the plan as premiums increased, lowering the health level of the residual group and producing an abnormal increase in mortality rates. This process is called either antiselection or **adverse selection** and, while present in many aspects of life insurance and in many different forms, is particularly identified with an insurance plan that has premiums that increase with age.

Finally, some plans provided for a reduction in benefits with advancing age, the assessment rate remaining level. This technique is defensible and is found today in many plans of group life insurance. As a result of the weaknesses explained above, the assessment plan no longer occupies an important place in the field of life insurance. The plans that had been established on that basis have either become insolvent or have been reorganized in accordance with more commonly accepted principles of life insurance management.

YEARLY RENEWABLE TERM INSURANCE

Similar in many respects to assessment insurance is yearly renewable term insurance, a plan widely used in connection with group insurance and reinsurance[6] but having only a limited appeal for individuals needing insurance in the later stages of life. An understanding of its nature and limitations is essential for an appreciation of the more complex forms of insurance.

yearly renewable term insurance

Yearly renewable term insurance is the simplest form of insurance offered by regular life insurance companies. It provides insurance for a period of one year only but permits the policyowner to renew the policy for successive periods of one year each without the necessity of furnishing evidence of insurability. In other words, the policyowner can renew the policy without submitting to a medical examination or providing other evidence of good health. For reasons that will be apparent later, the right to renew is often limited to a specified period or to specified ages. If the insured dies while the policy is in force, the face amount is paid to the designated beneficiaries. If the insured does not die during the

---

6.   See chapter 16.

period of protection, no benefits are payable at the expiration of the policy or upon the insured's subsequent death. Instead, the premiums paid to the insurance company are used to pay the claims of those who die during the period of protection. It should not be inferred, however, that the surviving policyowner did not receive any return on the contributions to the company. The protection enjoyed while the insurance was in force had a definite monetary value that was reflected in the premium charged by the insurance company. It will be demonstrated later that the cost of insurance protection for those who do not die is a most important element in the financial operations of a life insurance company.

Determining the Premium

The premium for yearly renewable term insurance is determined by the death rate for the attained age of the individual involved.[7] This is attributable to the fact that each premium purchases only one year of insurance protection. Moreover, each group of policyowners of a given age is considered to be a separate class for premium purposes; each group must pay its own death claims, the burden borne pro rata by the members of the group. Because the death rate increases with age, the premium for yearly renewable term insurance increases each year.

Example

In a group of 100,000 women aged 25

- Mortality rate for females aged 25—0.55 per 1,000

- Expected deaths from group—55

- $1,000 death benefit per deceased=$55,000 in claims

- Each woman could contribute $0.55 and cover the death benefit amount (ignoring costs of operation)

To illustrate, the female death rate at age 25, according to the 2001 CSO Table, is 0.55 per 1,000. If an insurance company should insure a group of 100,000 women aged 25 for $1,000 each for one year, it could expect 55 death claims, aggregating $55,000. Inasmuch as premiums are paid to the life insurance company in advance, the cost of the anticipated

---

7.   This ignores expenses of operation and interest earned on invested prepaid premiums, but the principle involved is still valid.

death claims would be distributed pro rata over the 100,000 policyowners, and a premium of $0.55 would be exacted from each policyowner. It should be noted that (1) the premium is precisely the same as the death rate applicable to those insured, and (2) those policyowners who, according to the mortality projection, will die during the year contribute on the same basis as those who will survive. The implication of the latter is that each policyowner pays a share of his or her own death claim, a principle that underlies all life insurance contracts. The proportion, however, varies with the type of contract, age at issue, and duration of the protection. The implications of the former are made clear in the following paragraphs.

If the 99,945 survivors of the original group of 100,000 policyowners should be insured for another year, they would be exposed to the death rate for persons aged 26, or 0.58 per 1,000, which would theoretically produce 58 deaths and claims totaling $58,000. That sum divided equally among the 99,945 participants would yield a share, or premium, of $0.58 per person. If the 99,887 survivors should desire insurance for another year, provision would have to be made for $61,000 in death claims, necessitating a premium of $0.6.

For the first several years, the premium would continue to increase slowly, being only $0.70 at age 30, $1.00 at age 35, and $1.34 at age 40. Thereafter, however, the premium would rise sharply, reaching $1.96 at age 45, $3.24 at 50, $5.36 at 55, $8.34 at 60, and $12.33 at 65. If the insurance should be continued beyond age 65, the cost would soon become prohibitive, soaring to $18.63 per $1,000 at age 70, $29.20 at 75, $46.43 at 80, and $77.59 at 85. The premium at 90 would be $124.22 per $1,000; at 95, $203.48. Finally, if a woman aged 119 should want $1,000 of insurance on the yearly renewable term basis, she would have to pay a premium of $1,000, since the 2001 CSO Table assumes that the limit of life is 120 years and that a person aged 119 will die within the year. Under the 1980 CSO Table, the end of life is age 100.

Limiting the Period of Renewability

If the surviving members of the aforementioned group should continue to renew their insurance year after year, the steadily increasing premiums would cause many to question the advisability of continuing the insurance. After a point, there would be a tendency for the healthy individuals to give up their protection, while those in poor health would continue to renew their policies, regardless of cost. This is the adverse selection to which reference has previously been made. The withdrawal of the healthy members would accelerate the increase in the death rate among the continuing members and, unless ample margins were provided in the insurance company's premium rates, could produce death claims in excess of premium income. In this event, the loss would be borne by the

company, because the rates at which the policy can be renewed are guaranteed for the entire period of renewability. It is for this reason that companies offering yearly renewable term insurance on an individual basis often place a limit on the period during which the insurance can be renewed.

Even without restrictions on the period during which the insurance can be renewed, yearly renewable term insurance is not usually feasible for long-term protection. Dissatisfaction with increasing premiums causes many policyowners to discontinue their insurance, often at a time when, because of physical condition or other circumstances, they cannot obtain other insurance. They are also likely to resent that after years of premium payments at increasing financial sacrifice, the insurance protection is lost, with no tangible benefits for the sacrifice involved.

More important, however, is the fact that few, if any, individuals are able and willing to continue their insurance into the advanced ages where death is most likely to occur. Yet the great majority of individuals need insurance that can be continued until death, at whatever age it might occur. This need led to the development of level premium insurance.

Renewable Term Characteristics

- Coverage for a stated period
- Premium based on age at beginning of each new period
- Premiums increase with age
- Rate of premium increases accelerates after age 40
- Can be renewed for a new period without health assessment (up to limiting age specified in policy)
- Additional charges for adverse selection included in premium at advanced ages
- Does not provide living benefits such as cash values, policy loans, and so on

LEVEL PREMIUM PLAN

level premium insurance

Level premium insurance is just what the name implies—a plan of insurance under which premiums do not increase from year to year but, instead, remain constant throughout the

premium-paying period. It does not imply that the insured must pay premiums as long as he or she has insurance protection, only that all premiums required will be of equal size.[8]

It must be apparent that if premiums that have a natural tendency to increase with each passing year are leveled out, the premiums paid in the early years of the contract will be more than sufficient to meet current death claims, while those paid in the later years will be less than adequate to meet incurred claims. This is a simple concept, but it has manifold ramifications and far-reaching significance.

With the level premium technique the redundant premiums in the early years of the contract create an accumulation that is held "in trust"[9] by the insurance company for the benefit and to the credit of the policyowners. This accumulation is called a reserve, which is not merely a restriction on surplus as in the ordinary accounting sense, but an amount that must be accumulated and maintained by the insurance company in order to meet definite future obligations. Because the manner in which the fund is to be accumulated and invested is strictly regulated by law, it is usually referred to in official literature as the legal reserve. Technically the reserve is a composite liability account of the insurance company, not susceptible to allocation to individual policies, but for present purposes it may be viewed as an aggregate of individual accounts established to the credit of the various policyowners.[10]

Term Policies

From the standpoint of an individual policy, the excess portions of the premiums paid in the early years of the contract are accumulated at compound interest and subsequently used to supplement the inadequate premiums of the later years. This process can be explained most simply in connection with a contract that provides protection for only a temporary period, as opposed to one that provides insurance for the policyowner's whole of life. Figure 2-1 shows the level premium mechanism in connection with a term policy issued at age 25, to run to age 65. The level premiums to age 65 are based on the 2001 CSO Female Table and an interest assumption of 4.5 percent. In other words, it is assumed, with respect to the level premium calculations, that the reserves are invested at 4.5 percent, and

---

8. As a matter of fact, arrangements are sometimes found under which the premium for the first few years of the contract is lower than that required for the remainder of the premium-paying period.
9. This is not a trust fund in the legal sense, which would require the insurance company to establish separate investment accounts for each policyowner and render periodic accountings.
10. In practice each policy is credited with a cash value or surrender value, which is not the same as the reserve but has its basis in the redundant premiums of the early years.

with respect to the yearly renewable term premiums, that each premium earns 4.5 percent for one year before being disbursed in the form of death benefits.

In this example no allowance is made for expenses, which makes it easier to understand. It also conforms to the legislative and regulatory approach of setting reserves strictly on the basis of interest and mortality without consideration of other operating costs.

In Figure 2-1 the curve AB represents the premiums at successive ages that would be required to provide $1,000 of insurance from age 25 to age 65 on the yearly renewable term basis. The premium ranges from $0.55 at age 25 to $12.33 at age 65. The line CD represents the level premium that would be required to provide $1,000 of insurance from age 25 to age 65 on the level term basis. The amount of this level premium that would be paid each year through age 64 is $1.79. This exceeds the premiums that would be payable on the yearly renewable term basis prior to age 44 but is smaller than those payable thereafter.

The area AXC represents the excess portions of the level premiums paid prior to age 43; the area BXD represents the deficiency in premiums after that age. It is apparent that the second area is much larger than the first. The disparity in the size of the two areas is attributable to the fact that the sums represented by the area AXC, which constitute the reserve under the contract, are invested at compound interest, and the interest earnings are subsequently used along with the principal sum to supplement the inadequate premiums of the later years. The reserve is completely exhausted at age 65 (the expiration of coverage), having been used to pay the policy's share of death claims submitted under other policies, which is another way of saying that the reserve, including the investment earnings derived therefrom, is gradually used up after age 44 in the process of supplementing the then deficient level premium. The reserve under this particular contract—term to 65, issued at age 25—reaches its maximum size at age 53, diminishing thereafter at an accelerating rate until exhausted at the expiration of the policy.

Figure 2-1
Annual Premium Comparison: Level Term to Age 65 and Yearly Term

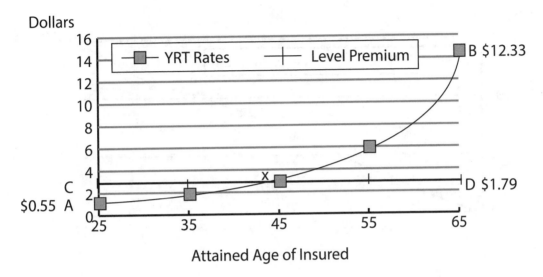

Ordinary Life Policies

The functioning of the level premium plan is even more striking—though more difficult to grasp—when applied to a policy providing insurance for the whole of life. A comparison of the level premium required under an ordinary life policy with that required on the yearly renewable term basis is presented in Figure 2-2. As in the case below, the age of issue is 25, and the premiums are based on the 2001 CSO Female Table and 4.5 percent interest, with no allowance for expenses.

Figure 2-2
Annual Premium Comparison: Whole Life and Yearly Term

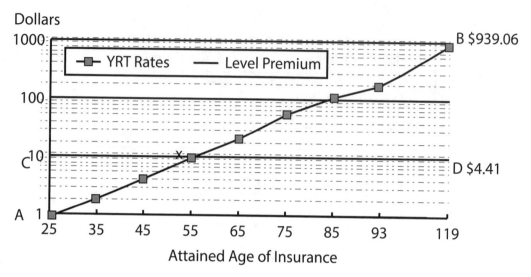

In this case, an annual level premium of $4.41 per $1,000 paid as long as the insured lives would be the mathematical equivalent of a series of premiums on the yearly renewable term basis, ranging from $0.55 per $1,000 at age 25 to $939.06 at age 119.

Yearly Term versus Level Premium for Life for Female Aged 25

- Annual level premium of $4.41 per $1,000 of coverage

- Exceeds yearly term cost of $0.55 per $1,000 coverage at age 25

- Level premium will exceed the yearly term premium until the insured reaches her mid-50's

- Beyond age 55, the level premium of $4.41 per $1,000 of coverage will be less than the cost of yearly term coverage per $1,000

- By age 119, the yearly term premium of $939.06 per $1,000 of coverage greatly exceeds the $4.41 cost per $1,000

The 2001 CSO Female Table assumes that everyone who survives to age 119 will die during the year, producing a net premium on the yearly renewable term basis equal to the face of

the policy, less the interest that will be earned on the premium during the year. In Figure 2-2 line CD bisects the curve AB between the ages of 53 and 54.

The disparity between the areas bounded by AXC and BXD is very much greater in this case than in the figure above. Even more amazing, however, is the fact that the excess premiums (area AXC) in the early years of an ordinary life contract (or, for that matter, any type of insurance contract except term) will not only offset the deficiency in the premiums of the later years when the term premium is in the hundreds of dollars, but with the aid of compound interest will also accumulate a reserve equal to the face of the policy by the time the insured reaches the terminal age in the mortality table. This is in contrast to the level premium term contract, under which the reserve is completely used up at the expiration of the contract. The difference is because the risk (probability of occurrence) under a contract providing protection for the whole of life is one "converging into a certainty," while the risk under a term policy is a mere contingency—one that may or may not occur. Under a whole life contract, provision must be made for a death claim that is certain to occur, the only uncertainty being the time it will occur.

By the time an insured has reached 119, the reserve under his or her policy must have accumulated to an amount that, supplemented by the final annual premium and interest on the combined sums for the last 12 months of the contract, will equal the face amount of the policy. This must be the case if each class of policyowners is to be self-supporting, since there are no other funds for the payment of the claims of the last members to die. In effect, such policyowners pay off their own death claims, in addition to paying their share of the death claims of all other members of the group. It should not be surprising, therefore, that the aggregate premiums paid by long-lived persons can exceed the face amount of the policy.

The manner in which the level premium arrangement makes provision for a risk converging into a certainty is explained more thoroughly in the next section.

Effect of Level Premium Technique on Cost of Insurance

amount at risk

Under a level premium type of contract, the accumulated reserve becomes a part of the face amount payable upon the death of the insured. From the standpoint of the insurance company, the effective amount of insurance is the difference between the face amount of the policy and the reserve. Technically speaking, this is the **amount at risk**. As the reserve increases, the amount at risk decreases. The significance of this relationship under

discussion is that as the death rate increases, the amount at risk (the effective amount of insurance) decreases, producing a cost of insurance[11] within practicable limits.

The true nature of level premium insurance should now be apparent. Under the level premium plan, a $1,000 policy does not provide $1,000 of insurance. The company is never at risk for the face amount of the policy—even in the first year. The amount of actual insurance is always the face amount, less the policyowner's own accumulated excess payments. The accumulation is the reserve for insurance company purposes but the cash value (slightly less in early years) for policyowner purposes. Since the excess payments may be withdrawn by the policyowner at any time through the cash surrender or loan privilege, they may be regarded as an accumulation account. Thus, a level premium policy does not provide pure insurance but a combination of decreasing insurance and increasing cash values, the two amounts computed so that in any year their sum is equal to the face amount of the policy. This is illustrated in the following figure for an ordinary life policy of $1,000 issued at age 25, the calculations are based on the 1980 CSO Female Table and 4.5 percent interest.

The area below the curve represents the reserve under the contract or, as mentioned above, the policyowner's equity in the contract. The area above the curve represents the company's net amount at risk and the policyowner's amount of protection. As the reserve increases, the amount of protection decreases. At any given age, however, the two combined will equal the face amount of the policy. By age 95 the protection element of the contract has become relatively minor, and by age 100—the end of the contract—it has completely disappeared. At age 100, the policyowner will receive $1,000, composed entirely of the cash value element.

---

11. The cost of insurance is an actuarial term referring to the sum obtained by multiplying the death rate at the insured's attained age by the net amount at risk.

Figure 2-3
Proportion of Protection and Savings Elements in Ordinary Life
Contract, Issued at Age 25; 1980 CSO Female Table and 4.5 Percent
Interest

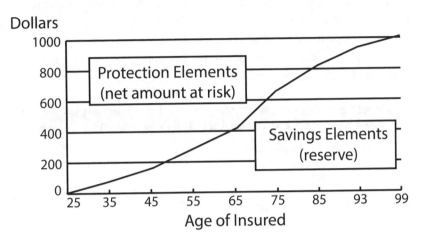

This combination of protection and accumulated cash values is characteristic of all level premium plans with the exception of most term contracts. Fundamentally, one contract differs from another only in the proportion in which the two elements are combined. This basic truth should be kept in mind as the study of contract forms is undertaken.

Yearly term insurance is all protection and has no cash value, while single premium life insurance is at the other end of the spectrum with the highest cash values and lowest proportion at risk. Accumulated cash values should be thought of as some degree of prefunding. Single premium policies are fully prefunded, and lower premium policies that develop cash values are only partially prefunded. The shorter the premium-paying period, the higher the relative proportion of cash value to death benefit.

Further Significance of Level Premium Plan

The impact of the level premium plan is felt by nearly all operations of a life insurance company. It accounts for a major portion of the composite assets of the United States life insurance companies that exceed $3.1 trillion and are increasing at more than $100 billion per year. The other main contributor to this asset growth is the reserve component for annuities and pension plans. The investment of these funds has presented the life insurance institution with one of its most challenging problems but, at the same time, has

enabled the institution to contribute in a most material way to the dynamic expansion of the American economy. The level premium plan underlies the system of cash values and other surrender options that has made the life insurance contract one of the most flexible and valuable contracts in existence. It has caused the life insurance contract to be regarded as one of the most acceptable forms of collateral for credit purposes. Despite these positive contributions-and the complications introduced into company operations-the greatest significance of the plan lies in the fact that it is the only arrangement under which it is possible to provide insurance protection to the uppermost limits of the human life span without the possibility that the cost will become prohibitive.

Major Contributions to Life Insurer Assets From Level Contributions

- Cash values of life insurance

- Annuities

- Pensions and other qualified plans

TAX TREATMENT OF LIFE INSURANCE

Quite often, especially for affluent clients, financial planners recognize that a life insurance purchase can legitimately serve to reduce the client's federal tax burden. In the following discussion we will summarize some of the common tax aspects of individual life insurance.

Income Taxation of Death Proceeds

In general, and subject to some exceptions, proceeds paid under a life insurance contract by reason of the insured's death are excludible from gross income for federal income tax purposes. The basic requirement for the income tax exclusion for life insurance proceeds is that they be paid because of the death of the insured. Current law also extends the exclusion to certain viatical settlements and accelerated death benefits made on behalf of an insured who is terminally ill and expected to die within 24 months.

Transfer-for-Value Rule

transfer-for-value rule

The most important exception to the general rule of exclusion of life insurance death proceeds from federal income taxation is the **transfer-for-value rule**. This rule provides

that if a policy is transferred from one owner to another for valuable consideration, the income tax exclusion is lost. When the insured dies in these cases, the policy beneficiary will recover income tax free only the amount the transferee-owner paid for the policy, plus any premiums subsequently paid. The transfer-for-value rule is not limited to an outright sale of a policy. This rule can also apply when a noncash consideration for a policy transfer can be inferred.

Thus, the transfer-for-value rule is an exception to the general rule of exclusion for policy proceeds. There are also exceptions to the exception (a common phenomenon in tax law). Policy transfers that are not jeopardized by the transfer-for-value rule are as follows:

- transfers in which the transferee-owner is the insured
- transfers to a partner of the insured
- transfers to a partnership in which the insured is a partner
- transfers to a corporation of which the insured is a shareholder or officer
- transfers in which the transferee's tax basis of the policy is determined by reference to its basis to the transferor, as discussed later

Income Tax Definition of Life Insurance

The full exclusion for life insurance death proceeds depends in part on whether the policy itself meets the definition of life insurance under the Internal Revenue Code. A policy qualifies as life insurance for income tax purposes if it satisfies either of two tests. The determination whether a policy qualifies is not performed by the consumer or agent, but rather by the insurance company that makes this information available.

cash value accumulation test

The first test, the **cash value accumulation test**, generally applies to more traditional cash value policies, such as whole life policies. Under this cash value accumulation test, the cash value generally may not exceed the net single premium that would be needed to fund the policy's death benefit. The insurance company calculates the net single premium using an assumed interest rate and certain mortality charges.

guideline premium and corridor test

The second, two-pronged test is the **guideline premium and corridor test**. Policies that are designed to pass the guideline premium and corridor test must meet both of the requirements. The guideline premium requirement limits the total premium that may be

paid into the policy at any given time. This limit varies with each life insurance company based on its own expenses and its own mortality experience. The limit also varies with the insurer's own interest assumptions, subject to specified IRS limits. The policy meets the corridor or death benefit requirement, the second prong of the test, if the contract's death benefit exceeds a specified multiple of its cash value at all times. This multiple varies according to the insured's attained age. Generally, universal life and other similar types of policies are tested under this second, two-pronged test.

Settlement Options

Death proceeds distributed as a series of payments under a settlement option generally include an element of interest earned after the death of the insured, which is taxable. However, the portion of a settlement option payment that represents principal (the policy's face amount) still qualifies for the income tax exclusion.

The portion that represents the death benefit is calculated by prorating the face amount over the option's payment period. This is the excludible portion. Any excess amount of each payment represents interest. If the interest-only option is used, all interest paid or accrued is taxable. If the fixed-amount option is used, the payment period is calculated by determining the number of fixed payments needed to exhaust the policy's face amount at its guaranteed interest rate. If a life-income option is used, the present value of any refund or period-certain feature is subtracted from the excludible amount to be prorated.

Income Taxation of Living Proceeds

inside buildup

The **inside buildup** is the increase in the cash value of a permanent life insurance policy. The inside buildup is not subject to taxation as long as it is left inside the policy. However, amounts taken out of the policy during the insured's life may be subject to taxation, as discussed in this section.

Amounts paid under a life insurance contract while the insured is still living can take several forms. The most common of these are policy loans, policy dividends, proceeds from a cash surrender, and withdrawals from the policy's cash value.

To determine the income tax effect of most of these transactions, the policyowner's tax basis in the policy must be known. A policyowner's basis is initially determined by adding the total premiums paid into the policy and subtracting the dividends, if any, that the

insurer has paid. If nontaxable withdrawals have previously been made from the policy, such amounts also reduce the policyowner's basis.

Policy Loans

Generally policy loans have no effect on basis unless the policy is a modified endowment contract (MEC), as defined later. However, if a policy is surrendered, the principal amount of any outstanding loan is includible in the surrender value of the policy for tax purposes.

Policy Dividends

Policy dividends are treated as a nontaxable return of premium, and they therefore reduce the policyowner's basis. If total dividends exceed total premiums, dividends are taxable to that extent. If dividends are used to reduce premiums or otherwise paid back into the policy (for example, to buy paid-up additions), the basis reduction caused by payment of the dividend is offset by a corresponding basis increase, because the dividend is then treated as an additional premium payment.

Cash Surrender

If a policy is surrendered for cash, the taxable amount is the total surrender value minus the policyowner's current basis in the policy. Dividends left with the insurer to accumulate at interest are not included in the surrender value for tax purposes because they have already reduced the policyowner's basis in the contract.

Example

Aaron Sloan, aged 40, owns a level-premium whole life policy. He has paid $25,000 in premiums and has received $4,000 in dividends from the policy. The face amount of the policy is $100,000. Its total cash value is $29,000. The policy is also subject to an outstanding loan of $15,000. Aaron decides to surrender his policy for cash. The tax effects of Aaron's surrender of his policy are as follows:

<u>Surrender Value</u>

Policy loan	$15,000
Plus net cash value ($29,000 total value minus $15,000 policy loan)	14,000
Total surrender value	$29,000

<u>Basis</u>

Premium paid	$25,000
Minus dividends	4,000
Total basis	$21,000

<u>Taxable Gain</u>

Surrender value	$29,000
Minus basis	21,000
Taxable gain	$ 8,000

Cash Withdrawal

If a policyowner withdraws funds from a policy's cash value, the general rule is that the withdrawal is first treated as a nontaxable return of basis. The excess, if any, of the amount of the withdrawal over the policyowner's current basis is taxable in the year of withdrawal. However, there are important exceptions to this general rule. These exceptions include certain withdrawals from universal life policies and withdrawals from policies classified as modified endowment contracts (MECs).

Universal Life Policies. If a cash withdrawal results in a reduction in the policy's death benefit during the first 15 years of the policy, the withdrawal may first be taxed as income to the extent of income earned within the contract. This income-first, or LIFO (last-in, first-out), method of taxation is the reverse of the general FIFO (first-in, first-out) taxation that life insurance typically enjoys.

modified endowment contract (MEC)

Modified Endowment Contracts (MECs). A policy is treated as a **modified endowment contract** if it fails a test called the 7-pay test. This test is applied at the inception of the policy and again if the policy experiences a material change. A material change generally includes most increases and certain decreases in future benefits. A common example of a material change is an increase in death benefits under the policy, resulting from a flexible premium payment.

The 7-pay test is designed to impose modified endowment contract (MEC) status on policies that take in too much premium during the first 7 policy years, or in the 7 years after a material change. For each policy, a net level premium is calculated. If the total premium

actually paid into the policy at any time during the 7-year testing period is more than the sum of the net level premiums that would be needed to result in a paid-up policy after 7 years, the policy is a MEC. Simply stated, the 7-pay test is designed to discourage a premium schedule that would result in a paid-up policy before the end of a 7-year period.

Any life insurance policy that falls under the definition of a MEC is also subject to an income-first or LIFO tax treatment with respect to loans and most distributions from the policy. A 10 percent penalty tax also generally applies to the taxable portion of any loan or withdrawal from a MEC unless the taxpayer has reached age 59½. With respect to loans (not withdrawals) from a MEC, the policyowner does receive an increase in basis in the policy equal to the amount of the loan that is taxable. However, as shown in the example, the nontaxable portion of a loan from a MEC will not affect the policyowner's basis. A nontaxable portion of a withdrawal, on the other hand, will reduce the basis.

Example

Assume that Aaron Sloan's policy in the previous example is a MEC and that he takes the $15,000 loan from the policy this year. Prior to the loan, Aaron has a total of $8,000 in untaxed gain in the policy. However, the withdrawal of any untaxed gain from the policy triggers a taxable event. Therefore, the loan will first be treated as a taxable event to the extent of $8,000. The remaining $7,000 of the loan is not taxable to Aaron. The $8,000 taxable portion of the loan will also be subject to the 10 percent penalty tax because Aaron is under age 59½. Aaron's basis in the policy will be increased by $8,000 (the taxable portion of the loan). Therefore, Aaron's basis is now $29,000 ($21,000 + $8,000).

1035 Exchanges

A taxable event usually occurs when an existing insurance policy with a cash value is surrendered. However, Sec. 1035 of the Internal Revenue Code provides that replacing one life insurance policy with another is a nontaxable event when certain requirements are met. A policyowner may therefore exchange a life insurance policy for a new policy, insuring the same person, without paying tax on the investment gains earned in the original contract. Only certain exchanges qualify and a qualifying exchange is referred to as a 1035 exchange. Also, the policyowner may not simply receive a check from one insurer and use the proceeds purchase a new contract from another. An actual exchange must take place between the two insurance companies. The old policy is assigned to the new insurer who then surrenders the policy to the old insurer and applies the proceeds of the surrender to the new contract.

Deductibility of Premium Payments

As a general rule, premium payments for individual life insurance policies are not deductible for federal income tax purposes. This rule applies, regardless of who owns the policy and whether it is used for personal or business purposes. In certain situations, however, life insurance premiums can be deductible because they also fit the definition of some other type of deductible expense, not because they are premium payments. For example, a premium payment for a policy on behalf of a charitable organization is deductible by the payor if the charity owns the policy outright. The premium is deductible because it is treated as a charitable contribution, not because it is a life insurance premium. Similarly, in cases where a corporation pays the premium on a policy that covers an employee and the death benefit is payable to the employee's beneficiary, the employer can deduct the premium as compensation paid to the employee. Another situation in which premium payments can fit the definition of a particular deductible expense is when premium payments constitute alimony, made on behalf of an ex-spouse.

Transfer Taxation of Life Insurance

Gift taxes and estate taxes are part of the federal transfer tax system. This section briefly reviews these two transfer taxes, with emphasis on their life insurance implications.

Federal Gift Tax

gift tax

gift

The federal **gift tax** is a tax imposed on transfers of property by gift during the donor's lifetime. The gift taxes are levied on the donor, not the gift's recipient. This tax applies only if both of the following two elements of a **gift** are present:

- a completed transfer and acceptance of property, including money
- a transfer for less than full and adequate consideration

The taxation of a transfer does not require an element of donative intent, only that the transfer be made for less than full consideration. The lifetime amount that a person can gift on a tax-exempt basis in 2013, is $5.25 million. This amount increases with inflation thereafter. annual exclusion Annual Exclusion. Much of the planning and complexity associated with gift tax planning involves the annual exclusion. In 2013, qualifying gifts of $14,000 or less can be made annually by a donor to any number of donees without gift tax. The

exempt amount can be increased to $28,000 if the donor is married and the donor's spouse elects to split gifts on a timely filed gift tax return. With gift splitting, each spouse gives half the gift. The annual exclusion amount is indexed to inflation, and it increases in $1,000 increments. The annual exclusion is in addition to the lifetime tax-exempt amount of $5.25 million described in the previous paragraph.

Nontaxable Gifts. Although most gifts are taxable, the following are not taxable gifts

- gifts that do not exceed the annual exclusion

- gifts to the donor's spouse

- gifts to charities

- tuition paid directly to an educational institution for someone

- medical expenses paid directly to a medical institution for someone

- gifts to a political organization for its use

Federal Estate Tax

estate tax

The federal estate tax is a tax imposed on the transfer of property at death. The most difficult task in calculating the **estate tax** is often the determination of the assets included in the decedent's estate tax base. Some of the included assets are obvious, such as individually owned property, but the estate tax rules often cause the inclusion of property in surprising circumstances. For example, property previously transferred by a decedent can be brought back to the estate tax base by provisions in the statute.

gross estate

Gross Estate. The starting point in the federal estate tax calculation is determining the property included in the decedent's **gross estate**. The gross estate includes the property in the probate estate, which is all property that passes under the deceased's will or, in the absence of a valid will, under the state intestacy law, but it also includes property transferable by the decedent at death by other means. The decedent's gross estate includes, among other things, the following:

- property individually owned by the decedent at the time of death

- (some portion of) property held jointly by the decedent at the time of death

- insurance on the decedent's life if either (1) the decedent held an incident of ownership or transferred it by gift within 3 years of death or (2) the proceeds are deemed payable to the estate

- property transferred by the decedent during his or her lifetime if the decedent retained (1) a life interest in the property, (2) a reversionary interest valued at greater than 5 percent of the property at the time of death, or (3) a right to revoke or amend the transfer at the time of death

Items Deductible from the Gross Estate. Certain items are deductible from the gross estate for estate tax calculation purposes: legitimate debts of the decedent, reasonable funeral and other death costs of the decedent, and the reasonable cost of estate settlement, such as the executor's commission and attorney fees. Moreover, the federal estate tax charitable deduction provides that transfers at death to qualifying charities are fully deductible from the estate tax base.

As with the gift tax, qualifying transfers to a surviving spouse are deductible under the marital deduction rules. Because the marital deduction is unlimited, the usual dispositive scheme (100 percent to the surviving spouse) for married individuals results in no federal taxes for a married couple until the death of the second spouse. As a client's wealth increases, sophisticated planning is needed to make optimal use of the marital deduction. The Taxable Estate. The 2001 Economic Growth and Tax Relief Reconciliation Act significantly revised federal estate taxation. The act increased the exclusion amount, which can pass by death on a tax-exempt basis, to the levels indicated in the following table. The act also reduced the marginal tax rates, which were applied on the amount in excess of the exclusion amount. Furthermore, the exclusion amount increased and the marginal tax rate decreased for larger estates periodically through 2009. In 2010 the estate tax was eliminated.

On January 1, 2013 Congress passed the American Taxpayer Relief Act of 2012. It provided a top federal income tax rate of 39.6 percent, top rate on capital gains & dividends of 20 percent, and a top federal estate tax rate of 40 percent with a $5.34 million exclusion amount for 2013 and 2014. The applicable exclusion amount is adjusted for inflation for future years. The 2012 Act complimented the 2010 Tax Relief Act provides for "portability" of the estate tax applicable exclusion amount, allowing a surviving spouse to elect to take advantage of the unused portion of the estate tax exclusion amount of his or her predeceased spouse.

Table 2-1 Exclusion Amounts for Estate Taxation	
Year of Death	**Exclusion Amount**
2003	$1,000,000
2004–2005	1,500,000
2006–2008	2,000,000
2009	3,500,000
2010	Unlimited
2011	5,000,000
2012	5,120,000
2013	5,250,000
2014	5,300,000
2015	5,430,000

Federal Gift Taxation of Life Insurance

Gifts of life insurance are treated in the same manner as gifts of any other assets as far as the annual exclusion ($14,000 for 2015) is concerned. Sometimes there is an inadvertent gift of life insurance policy proceeds. This can happen when a policy one individual owns on another's life matures by reason of the insured's death and a person other than the policyowner has been named as beneficiary. For example, if a wife purchases a policy on her husband's life and names her children as beneficiaries, the proceeds that otherwise would have been payable to her are payable instead to her children at her husband's death. The transaction is treated as if the policyowner—the wife—had received the proceeds and made a gift in that amount to her children. Moreover, gift splitting will not be allowed because there is no longer a spouse with whom to split the gift.

Federal Estate Taxation of Life Insurance

Estate taxes are payable on property included in a decedent's gross estate if the decedent's estate exceeds the available deductions and credits. Frequently, life insurance is the single largest asset or group of assets in the gross estate. Including life insurance can often mean the difference between a federal estate tax liability and no tax liability. For this reason, it is important to look at the factors that determine when life insurance is included in the decendent-insured's gross estate for federal estate tax purposes:

- Life insurance proceeds payable to the executor, that is, to or for the benefit of the insured's estate, are includible in the estate, regardless of who owned the contract or who paid the premium.

- Life insurance proceeds are included in the estate of an insured if he or she possessed an incident of ownership in the policy at the time of his or her death.

- Life insurance proceeds are included in the gross estate of an insured who transferred incidents of ownership in the policy by gift within 3 years of his or her death.

Life Insurance Payable to the Executor. In general, life insurance should not be made payable to a decedent's estate. There are many reasons in addition to avoiding federal estate taxation why estate planners seldom recommend such a beneficiary designation. These reasons include the following:

- Insurance payable to a decedent's estate subjects the proceeds to the claims of the estate's creditors.

- Insurance payable to a decedent's estate subjects the proceeds to costs of probate administration, such as executor's fees, but provides no corresponding advantages.

incident of ownership

Possession of Incidents of Ownership. When insurance proceeds are paid to a named beneficiary other than the insured's estate, incidents of ownership in the policy at the time of death are the key criteria for determining inclusion. If the insured held an incident of ownership at the time of his or her death, the policy is included in his or her gross estate. An **incident of ownership** is broadly defined as an element of ownership or degree of control over a policy. Incidents of ownership include, but are not limited to, the power to

- change the beneficiary

- assign the policy

- borrow on the policy

- surrender the policy

- exercise any of the other essential contract rights or privileges

Merely being the beneficiary of a policy's death benefit is not an incident of ownership.

Like any other property, a life insurance policy is an asset that a policyowner can freely assign in a gift or sale. Thus, the policyowner may transfer limited interests to others while retaining some of the privileges and rights in the policy. However, to remove the proceeds

from the scope of the federal estate tax, the insured must divest himself or herself of all significant rights and privileges under the contract.

Transfers of Policies within 3 Years of Death. Life insurance policies are often transferred to others so that policy proceeds will not be in the insured's gross estate when he or she dies. Inclusion will still result, however, if the insured dies within 3 years of a gratuitous transfer. Under this 3-year rule, life insurance transferred to a third party for less than full consideration within 3 years of the insured's death is automatically includible in the insured's gross estate. Transfers made more than 3 years before the insured's death are not normally includible in the insured's estate if the insured has retained no incidents of ownership. In addition, a sale to a third party for the full fair market value of the policy will not be included even if the sale occurs within 3 years of the insured's death.

Life Insurance and the Federal Estate Tax Marital Deduction. Life insurance proceeds payable at the insured's death to his or her surviving spouse can qualify for the federal estate tax marital deduction. Because the marital deduction is unlimited, the full value of life insurance proceeds payable in a qualifying manner to the surviving spouse is deductible from the insured's gross estate.

CHAPTER REVIEW

Key Terms and Concepts

risk pooling
assessment insurance
graded assessments
adverse selection
yearly renewable term insurance
level premium insurance
amount at risk
transfer-for-value rule
cash value accumulation test

guideline premium and corridor test
inside buildup
modified endowment contract (MEC)
gift tax
gift
estate tax
gross estate
incident of ownership

Chapter 2 Review Questions

1. Illustrate the insurance principle and show how it applies to life insurance. [1]

2. Explain the problems a fraternal society may encounter if it provides death benefits to its members under a flat assessment plan. [1]

3. How is the premium for yearly renewable term insurance determined? [2]

4. Why is the period of renewability for yearly renewable term insurance sometimes limited? [2]

5. Explain how an ordinary life policy operates from the date of issue until the insured reaches age 119. [3]

6. Explain the importance of the level premium plan to the operation of a life insurance company and to the insured. [3]

Chapter 2 Review Answers

1. *The basic principle involved in insurance can best be illustrated in terms of fire insurance. Suppose that in a certain community there are 1,000 houses, each worth $100,000 and each exposed to approximately the same probability of destruction by fire. The probability that any one of these houses will be destroyed by fire in any particular year is extremely remote, possibly no more than one out of 1,000. Yet if that contingency should occur, the loss to the owner would be staggering—$100,000. If it could be assumed, however, that only one of the 1,000 houses would be destroyed by fire in a particular year, a contribution of only $100 by each homeowner would provide a fund large enough to reimburse in full the unfortunate person whose home was lost. If each homeowner were willing to assume a certain loss of $100, he could rid himself of the risk of a $100,000 loss. In summary, Contribution of each insured = Frequency (chance) of loss x Severity (amount) of loss $100 = (1 house burns/1,000 houses insured) x ($100,000 per house) The principal of loss sharing can be applied in identical fashion to the peril of death. The simplest illustration involves insurance for one year, with all members of the group the same age and possessing roughly similar prospects for longevity. The members of this group might mutually agree that a specified sum, such as $100,000, will be paid to the designated beneficiaries of those members of the group. In its simplest form, this arrangement might envision an assessment upon each member in the appropriate amount as each death would produce an assessment of $100 per member. Among a groups of 10,000 males aged 35, 21 of them could be expected to die within a year, according to the Commissioners 1980 Standard Ordinary Mortality Table (1980 CSO Table); if expenses of operation are ignored, cumulative*

assessments of $210 per person would provide the funds for payment of $100,000 to the beneficiary of each of the 21 deceased persons. Using the formula above, Contribution of each insured = Frequency (chance) of loss x Severity (amount) of loss. $210 = (21 people die/10,000 people insured) x ($100,000 of insurance)

2. *With a flat assessment plan, the same assessment is levied on all members of the fraternal society regardless of age. The assessment is based on the theory that with a continual inflow of new members at the younger ages, there would be little variation from year to year in the average age of those in the group and thus, the total death rate would not increase. Two problems may occur. First, even if the average age of the group members were to stay the same as current members aged but new younger persons joined the group, the fact that the death rate increases more rapidly at older ages than at younger ages would result in greater number of deaths in the membership over time. Second, given the tendency to solicit young and middle-aged members when a fraternal society began operation, it is likely that the average age of the group would also increase because of the difficulty of offsetting the increase in the age of the initial members by the flow of new entrants. As assessments would increase in magnitude and frequency due to these problems, young and healthy members would tend to withdraw from the society to get protection elsewhere. This would leave the society with an increasing proportion of its membership as old and infirm persons and would cause the assessments to become so high that the society might fail.*

3. *Yearly renewable term insurance provides insurance for a period of one year only but permits the policyowner to renew the policy for successive periods of one year each without the necessity of furnishing evidence of insurability. The premium rate for yearly renewable term insurance is determined by the death rate for the attained age of the individual involved. This is attributable to the fact that each premium purchases only one year of insurance protection. Moreover, each group of policyowners of a given age is considered to be a separate class for premium purposes; each group must pay its own death claims, the burden borne pro rata by the members of the group. Because the death rate increases with age, the premium for yearly renewable term insurance increases each year. To illustrate, the female death rate at age 25, according to the 1980 CSO Table, is 1.16 per 1,000. If an insurance company should insure a group of 100,000 women aged 25 for $1,000 each for one year, it could expect 116 death claims, aggregating $116,000. Inasmuch as premiums are paid to the life insurance company in advance, the cost of the anticipated death claims would be distributed pro rata over the 100,000 policyowners. Ignoring interest earned from the date premiums are collected until the date death claims are paid, a premium of $1.16 would be collected from each policyowner (that is, $116,000 in death claims/100,000*

policyowners). Using the formula presented in the answer to the first question, Premium for each policyowner = Frequency (chance) of loss x Severity (amount) of loss $1.16 = (116 death claims/100,000 women insured) x ($1,000 of insurance)

4. As persons renew their yearly renewable term policies, premiums would increase yearly at an increasing rate due to the increasing death rates at older ages. After a point, there would be a tendency for the healthy individuals to give up their protection, while those in poor health would continue to renew their policies, regardless of cost. The withdrawal of the healthy members would accelerate the increase in the death rate among the continuing members and, unless ample margins were provided in the insurance company's premium rates, could produce death claims in excess of premium income. In this event, the loss would be borne by the company, because the rates at which the policy can be renewed are guaranteed for the entire period of renewability. It is for this reason that companies offering yearly renewable term insurance on an individual basis often place a limit on the period during which the insurance can be renewed.

5. An ordinary life policy is a whole life policy where level premiums are paid until the insured dies (or if the insured survives, until age 119, when the insured is assumed to die for premium calculation purposes). In the early years, the net level premiums (the level premiums ignoring expenses) are greater than the amount the insurance company needs each year to pay the policy's share of death claims. The excess premiums in the early years are accumulated at compound interest in a reserve. In the later years, the reserve not only makes up the deficiencies when the net level premiums are less than the policy's annual share of death claims, but also continues to grow to an amount equal to the face of the policy at the end of age 119.

6. The level premium plan is important to the operation of a life insurance company and to the insured in several ways. First, under a level premium type of contract, the accumulated reserve becomes a part of the face amount payable upon the death of the insured. From the standpoint of the insurance company, the effective amount of insurance is the difference between the face amount of the policy and the reserve. Technically speaking, this is the amount at risk. As the reserve increases, the amount at risk decreases. The significance of this relationship is that as the death rate increases, the amount at risk (the effective amount of insurance) decreases, producing a cost of insurance (the policy's annual share of death claims) within practicable limits. Thus, the greatest significance of the plan lies in the fact that it is the only arrangement under which it is possible to provide insurance protection to the uppermost limits of the human life span without the possibility that the cost will become prohibitive. Second, by creating a reserve, the level premium plan underlies

the system of cash values and other surrender options available to policyowners. Finally, the level premium plan accounts for a considerable portion of the composite assets of the United States life insurance companies. The investment of these funds has enabled the life insurance industry to contribute significantly to the expansion of the American economy.

Chapter 3
Basis of Risk Measurement

By Dan M. McGill

Revised by Norma Nielson and Donald Jones

Learning Objectives

An understanding of the material in this chapter should enable the student to

1. **Understand and calculate, using a mortality table, some specific probabilities of living and of dying.**

2. **Understand and explain some of the considerations and adjustments that go into the creation of mortality tables.**

3. **Understand and explain the differences in some specific mortality tables and indicate their uses.**

As stated in an earlier chapter, insurance is a mechanism through which certainty replaces uncertainty. This occurs when many people exposed to loss from a particular hazard contribute to a common fund so those who suffer a loss from that cause can be compensated. The certainty of losing the premium replaces the uncertainty of a larger loss. For a plan of insurance to function, the pricing method needs to measure the risk of loss and determine the amount to be contributed by each participant. The theory of probability provides such scientific measurement.

THEORY OF PROBABILITY

probability

event

The theory of probability develops mathematical representations of uncertainty. A fraction between zero and one, called the **probability**, describes the chance of each possible outcome or collection of outcomes. A set of possible outcomes is called an event. One interpretation of the probability fraction is that its numerator is the number of times we expect an **event** to happen; the denominator is the number of times the event could possibly happen. The probability associated with the combination of all possible outcomes must be one. The probability that a particular event will not happen is one minus the probability that it will happen. These principles can be clarified by a few simple illustrations.

For example, consider the probability associated with tossing a coin. The coin will fall either heads up or tails up when tossed. Two possible outcomes exist, and only one is the

outcome of tossing a head. Therefore the probability of tossing a head is ½. The probability that the coin will fall either heads or tails is ½ + ½ or one.

Another example is drawing a card at random from a deck of 52 playing cards. The chance that the ace of spades will be drawn from the deck is 1/52. Of the 52 cards, only one is the ace of spades. Of the 52 cards, four are aces. Thus, the probability of drawing an ace of any suit is 4/52. The probability that a card drawn randomly will not be an ace is one minus the probability of drawing an ace, or 48/52.

independent event

Sometimes we need to know the probability of a particular combination of events. If the occurrence of one event does not change the probabilities associated with another event, the events are independent. We find the probability that two **independent event**s will happen by multiplying together the separate probabilities that each event will happen. Consider the independent tossing of a nickel and a dime. The probability that both will fall heads up is ½ × ½, or ¼, since the chance is ½ that each separate coin will fall heads up. The probability that at least one of the two coins will fall tails up is 3/4 (1 − 1/4). Confirm these results by looking at Table 3-1 showing the different ways in which the coins may fall. Only these four combinations can be made with the two coins. The first combination is the only one of the four that meets the condition that both coins land heads up. Conversely, the last three of the four meet the condition that at least one of the coins will fall tails up. The probability that three coins tossed simultaneously all fall heads up is found to be ½ × ½ × ½ or 1/8 in this same manner. This same pattern is followed for any number of coins tossed.

Table 3-1 Combinations of Tossing Two Coins	
Nickel	**Dime**
Heads up	Heads up
Heads up	Tails up
Tails up	Heads up
Tails up	Tails up

APPLICATION TO LIFE INSURANCE

mortality table

Probabilities for life insurance are represented in a **mortality table**. Conceptually it is much like drawing cards from a deck. The following table shows portions of the 2008 U.S. Life Table that we can use to illustrate these ideas.

radix

Column (2) in the table shows the number of survivors on each birthday out of 100,000 newborns. We call the number at the youngest age, here 100,000, the **radix** of the table. The number surviving at age one is 99,341. As with a deck of cards, if we draw at random one of the 100,000 members at age zero, the probability is 99,341/100,000 that the newborn will be a survivor at age one. Then the probability of not being a survivor at age one is

$$1 - \frac{99,341}{100,000}$$

This equals 659/100,000, or 0.00659, the probability of dying between age zero and age one. With the probability of dying denoted as q_x in general where the subscript $\times$ represents the age of those dying, q_1 denotes that probability for age one. For the convenience of the user, an alternate method can be used to find q_1 in the mortality tables. Look up the number of lives at age zero who die before attaining age one—659 in column (3)—and divide that number by the number of lives at age zero.

The mortality table is very versatile. It provides enough information to develop probabilities over any age span. For example, the probability that a newborn life will live to age 80 is 55,562/100,000 = 0.55562. Likewise, the probability that a newborn life will die between ages 49 and 50 is 375/100,000 = 0.00375.

Example

1.00 = Probability of death (for a given age) + probability of living (for same age)

1 – probability of death (for a given age) = probability of living (for same age)

1 – probability of living (for a given age) = probability of death (for same age)

If the probability of death for age 80 is 1/10, then the probability of living from age 80 to 81 is 9/10.

1 = 1/10 + 9/10, 1 – 1/10 = 9/10, 1 – 9/10 = 1/10

To find probabilities for anyone older than a newborn, the denominator changes. Consider, for example, the probability of someone aged 45 surviving to age 49 in a population with characteristics similar to those from which Table 3-2 was derived. Again refer to column (2) to find 95,602 lives at age 45. Of these, 94,374 are still living at age 49. The probability of a person aged 45 surviving to age 49 is, therefore, 94,374/95,602, or 0.98715. Then the probability that a person aged 45 will die before age 49 is 1 – 0.98715 = 0.01285. Again, this probability can be found using other numbers from the table. It is the ratio of the number who die between ages 45 and 49 divided by the number alive at age 45. The number of people dying between ages 45 and 49 is the sum of the numbers for four individual ages as found in column (3): 271 + 294 + 318 + 345 = 1,228.

Sometimes a different question can have the same answer. For example, "What is the probability that someone aged 45 will die after age 80?" Following the pattern above, we might first think of adding the numbers from column (3) of those dying at ages greater than 80. This sum would equal exactly the number of lives at age 80 because each life must be in one of the groups dying at a later age. So the answer to the question is 55,562/95,602 = 0.58118. A different way to ask—and solve—the same question is, "What is the probability that a person aged 45 will live until age 80?" Using the number from column (2) of people still living at age 80 (55,562) the answer is the same—0.58118.

Let's summarize the pattern of the reasoning in the symbols shown at the top of the columns of Table 3-2.

- The probability that a life aged x will survive n years to age x + n is

$$\frac{l_x + n}{l_x}$$

Table 3-2				
U.S. Life Table 2008				
Age Interval	Of 100,000 Born Alive		Proportion Dying	Average Remaining Lifetime
(1) Period of Life between Two Ages x to $x + 1$	(2) Number Living at Beginning of Age Interval l_x	(3) Number Dying during Age Interval d_x	(4) Proportion of Persons Alive at Beginning of Age Interval Dying during Interval q_x	(5) Life Expectancy (Average Years of Life Remaining) at Beginning of Age Interval e_x
0–1	100,000	659	0.006593	78.1
1–2	99,341	46	0.000461	77.6
2–3	99,295	28	0.000281	76.7
3–4	99,267	22	0.000219	75.7
4–5	99,245	17	0.000172	74.7
...	...	...	...	...
45–46	95,602	271	0.002833	35.5
46–47	95,331	294	0.003082	34.6
47–48	95,038	318	0.003350	33.7
48–49	94,719	345	0.003647	32.8
49–50	94,374	375	0.003974	31.9
...	...	...	...	...
80–81	55,562	2,918	0.052515	8.9
81–82	52,644	3,037	0.057686	8.4
82–83	49,607	3,153	0.063567	7.9
83–84	46,454	3,278	0.070564	7.3
84–85	43,176	3,378	0.078249	6.9

- The probability that a life aged x will survive n years and die between ages x + n and x + n + 1 is

$$\frac{l_{x+n} - l_{x+n+1}}{l_x}$$

- The mortality rate for the interval x to x+1 is the probability that a life aged x will die within a year. This rate is denoted by the special symbol q_x and is computed as $(l_x - l_{x+1})/l_x$ or, using a simpler notation, d_x/l_x. The mortality rates are in column (4) of the U.S. Life Table:

$$\frac{l_{x+n} - l_{x+n+1}}{l_x} = \frac{d_{x+n}}{l_x}$$

Life Expectancy

life expectancy

An additional column in a mortality table may show the expectation of life or **life expectancy** at each age. Column (5) in Table 3-2 shows this value. The life expectancy at any age is the average number of years remaining once a person has attained that same age. Life expectancy is an average future lifetime for a representative group of persons at the same age. The probable future lifetime of any individual, of course, depends on his or her state of health, among other things, and may be much longer or much shorter than the average.

attained age

For most mortality tables, life expectancy is greatest at age one. It is usually less at age zero due to the high mortality rate in the first year of life. On the other hand, the average age at death, which is the sum of the life expectancy and the **attained age** (or number of years already lived), increases with age. The excerpt in Table 3-3 from the 1979–81 U.S. Life Table illustrates this.

Table 3-3 Life Expectancy		
Attained Age	Life Expectancy	Average Age at Death
0	73.88	73.88
1	73.82	74.82
45	32.27	77.27
80	7.98	87.98

The Law of Large Numbers

Probabilities for coin tossing, card drawing, and mortality tables all depend on the law of large numbers, known more formally as Bernoulli's Law. This law asserts that in a

series of trials, the ratio of the number of occurrences of an event to the number of trials approaches the actual underlying probability of the event as the number of trials increases. In other words, in n tosses of a coin, the number of heads observed divided by n, will be closer to ½ more often when n is large than when n is small. In the extreme, for only one toss, the result will be either zero or one—both of which are far from ½. When n is 2, the ratio will be 0, ½, or one, and it will be zero or one only half the time. Table 3-4 illustrates the idea by showing the pattern for just a few tosses.

law of large numbers

The **law of large numbers** asserts that the probability of the number of heads being near one-half increases to one as the number of tosses increases. In the table you can see that the probability increases from zero to nearly 1.000 as the number of tosses increases from one to 256. This mathematical law forms the basis of the actuarial application of probability to insurance.

Table 3-4 Probabilities			
Number of Tosses	Probability that Proportion of Heads Will Be More than .25 and Less than .75	Probability that Proportion of Heads Will Be More than .40 and Less than .60	Probability that Proportion of Heads Will Be More than .45 and Less than .55
1	0.000	0.000	0.000
2	0.500	0.500	0.500
4	0.375	0.375	0.375
8	0.711	0.273	0.273
16	0.960	0.196	0.196
32	0.993	0.403	0.403
64	1.000	0.618	0.618
128	1.000	0.750	0.750
256	1.000	0.882	0.882

Construction of Mortality Tables

While the application of mortality tables is similar to applications of probabilities in coin tossing and card drawing, the building of the probabilities in mortality tables has a different basis than does the determination of probabilities for coins and cards. For cards and coins we can theorize the probability by physically counting the number of favorable

outcomes compared to the number of total outcomes. In the simple world of coins and cards this is possible.

In the complex and changing world of life and death, actuaries use statistical methods to estimate the probabilities. The first step is to select a sample population representative of the population where the resulting probabilities are to be used. In life insurance this means that both populations should have the same smoking habits and gender, should be buying the same type of contract (insurance or annuity, individual or group, permanent insurance versus term insurance), and that similar underwriting information is available—that is, that medically examined applicants are grouped separate from nonmedical applicants.

The next step is to observe the mortality experience of the representative population for a period of time. The observation period should be as recent as possible, sufficiently long to give adequate data, and free of nonrepresentative events such as war and epidemics.

After following the sample population during the observation period, the data are processed into the number of life-years and the number of deaths observed in each age interval. We will use a one-year interval for our examples here, although in practice the age intervals can be different from one year. Suppose analysis has produced the values in Table 3-5.

Table 3-5 Number of Deaths in Sample Population		
Age	Number under Observation	Number Dying during the Year
1	10,000	60
2	30,000	120
3	80,000	240
4	60,000	180
Etc.	Etc.	Etc.

From these figures, death rates may be computed for the respective ages as shown in Table 3-6. Death rates at the other ages to be included in the table are obtained in like manner.

This illustration assumes the observation of many lives at each age. In practice, such a large "exposure" is not likely to be obtained during any one year. The results of the investigation, if limited to a single year, even in a very large life insurance company, will be subject to considerable distortion because of the small number of lives involved. Therefore, actuaries usually study the experience of several years in deriving the rates to be incorporated in a mortality table. Rates derived for a 5-year period are the ratios for the number of deaths that occur at each age during the 5 years to the total exposure at that age. Each person

who survived the 5-year period would have contributed five years' exposure—one year in each of the 5 one-year intervals. Most mortality tables in use today include the combined experience of several large companies over a period of years. The 1980 CSO (Commissioners Standard Ordinary) Table is based on the experience of several life insurers during the period of 1970 to 1975. The 2001 CSO Table is based on multiple-company experience during the period 1990 to 1995.

Adjustments to Mortality Data

Adjustments of several types occur in converting raw mortality rates into a usable mortality table. Among the most important of these adjustments are smoothing, projections, and safety margins.

Smoothing

For theoretical and practical reasons, actuaries want the schedule of mortality rates to be smooth with respect to age. First, resistance to disease declines and the degeneration of the body system increases in continuous and minute gradations. Thus, sharp changes in the death rates by age should not occur. Second, if the mortality rates are irregular by age, then the premiums and reserves based on them will also be irregular. Such a pattern is not desirable.

Table 3-6		
Death Rates at Respective Ages		
Age	Rate of Death Expressed as a Fraction	Rate of Death Expressed as a Decimal
1	60 / 10,000	0.006
2	120 / 30,000	0.004
3	240 / 80,000	0.003
4	180 / 60,000	0.003

smoothing

graduation techniques

In most mortality studies a smooth set of mortality rates cannot be obtained by the simple procedure described above because sufficient data are not available. Actuaries have developed methods that produce smooth sets of rates from the initial nonsmooth sets (**smoothing**). These methods, called **graduation techniques**, are based on mathematics and statistics and their use requires a high degree of specialized training.

Projections

projections

> **Projections** reflect changes that have occurred in mortality since the observation period. At least 5 years usually pass between the observation period and the publication of a public mortality table. For the table's users, who want current rates for pricing, mortality rates published with projections fill this need. A table of projection factors may be provided as well so that users can adjust the published rates for future use.

Safety Margins

margin of safety

> Another adjustment provides a **margin of safety**. The appropriate adjustment depends on the purpose of the table. In a life insurance mortality table, including a safety margin means increasing the mortality rates above those anticipated. In an annuity table, including a safety margin means lowering the rates of mortality below those expected.

> In early life insurance tables, safety margins occurred implicitly through the use of data from an earlier period known to have had rates of mortality higher than those currently being experienced. In some mortality tables, the margins are provided explicitly. For example, the observed rates for the 1941 CSO Table were increased by use of a mathematical formula. While the adjustment may appear arbitrary, it had a definite objective. Insurance commissioners use this table to monitor solvency of life insurance companies. The adjustment was made in such a way that the table would be appropriate for at least 95 percent of the ordinary insurance business under regulation. On the other hand, the rates entering the GA 1951 Table, an annuity table described in Table 3-7, were reduced by 10 percent at all ages for males and 12.5 percent for females. All subsequent Group Annuity Tables including the GA 1983 are sex distinct.

> The security behind insurance contracts depends on the existence of safety margins in the contract premiums. Savings developed by the use of conservative actuarial assumptions can be returned as dividends to owners of participating policies. For nonparticipating policies, the safety margins must be smaller in order for premium rates to be competitive.

Completing the Table

The previous section describes statistical procedures that transform observations into a smooth series of mortality rates with the needed margins. From that point it is an

arithmetic procedure to prepare the other columns of the mortality tables. The first step is a choice of radix for the number of lives at the first age shown. This number is arbitrary and usually is chosen so the number dying at the end of the life span will not be less than a whole number.

To illustrate we reproduce the construction of Table 3-2. We have derived the q_x column values by the statistical procedures and chosen arbitrarily to set $l_0 = 100,000$. Having determined the radix and the rates of death, the partially complete table appears as Table 3-7.

Now $d_0 = l_0 \times q_0 = 100,000 \times (0.00659) = 659$ and $l_1 = l_0 - d_0 = 100,000 - 659 = 99,341$. With these two values entered in the proper places in the table, we repeat the process at each age. That is, $d_1 = l_1 \times q_1 = 99,341 \times (0.000461) = 46$ and $l_2 = l_1 - d_1 = 99,341 - 46 = 99,295$.

Reflecting Differences in Mortality from Published Tables

Despite the amount of work involved in developing a mortality table, it still falls far short of fitting every situation where mortality rates are needed. As explained below, variations in the published rates are needed to reflect mortality for a group of individuals who are more or less healthy than average, to adjust for the amount of time that has passed since a group of life insurance policies was issued, and to make it easier to consider what events short of death may trigger a policy benefit or other important change.

Table 3-7 Constructing a Mortality Table			
Age Interval	Of 100,000 Born Alive		Proportion Dying
(1) Period of Life between Two Ages x to x + 1	(2) Number Living at Beginning of Age Interval l_x	(3) Number Dying during Age Interval d_x	(4) Proportion of Persons Alive at Beginning of Age Interval Dying during Interval q_x
0–1	100,000	659	0.00659
1–2	99,341	46	0.000461
2–3	99,295	28	0.000281
3–4	99,267	22	0.000219
4–5	99,245	17	0.000172

Nonstandard Mortality

preferred risks

substandard risks

Mortality varies among different types of lives. A life insurance company uses the mortality table that seems most appropriate for its business. For example, a company may use one table for annuitants and another for lives insured, one for men and another for women, and one for smokers and another for nonsmokers. Different tables or adjustments to standard tables are used to estimate the lower mortality of **preferred risks**, those whose personal characteristics suggest better-than-average mortality. Similarly developed tables or adjustments that reflect higher mortality are used for **substandard risks**, those whose personal characteristics suggest worse-than-average mortality.

Select, Ultimate, and Aggregate Mortality

Studies show that the rate of mortality among recently insured lives is lower, age for age, than that among those insured for some years. For example, the mortality rate for a group of 35-year-olds insured 5 years ago will be higher than the mortality rate for a group of newly insured 35-year-olds. Sometimes underwriting—the process of deciding whether to issue a policy and on what terms—includes extensive medical screening. Underwriting screens out applicants suffering from a disease or physical condition likely to prove fatal in the near future. This disparity in death rates is greatest during the first year of insurance, and it diminishes gradually after that but never completely disappears. The difference is measurable for at least 15 years, but for practical purposes actuaries generally assume that the effect of selection "wears off" after approximately 5 years.

To illustrate, the death rate of policyowners insured at age 25 will be substantially lower than that of policyowners now 25 who were insured at age 20. One year later, when these policyowners are age 26, the difference in the death rates will be somewhat smaller. At age 30, death rates for the two groups will be almost the same.

select mortality table

One way to recognize the reduced mortality in the early years of insurance is by a mortality table that shows the rate of mortality not only by age but also by duration of insurance. This recognizes the time passed since an applicant was approved to receive a policy. The result is called a **select mortality table**. While in theory actuaries could create an entire series of mortality tables (one for each age of issue), such extensive effort is not usually necessary. Because the effect of selection is negligible after 5 years, different rates are

needed only for durations below 6 years. Select mortality tables usually are presented in the form shown in Table 3-8.

Table 3-8 gives insight into the mortality reduction due to selection. Column (1) shows the death rate at the various ages during the first year of insurance when the effect of selection is greatest. Column (6) shows the rate after the effect of selection has worn off. Contrast the various death rates for attained age 41 by comparing the six values. All six of these rates apply to a life aged 41; however, the rates apply to six different periods since issue of insurance.

Companies use select tables in developing gross premiums for both participating and nonparticipating insurance and for testing—through asset share calculations described later in this book—the appropriateness of existing or proposed schedules of dividends and surrender values.

Companies also base profit projections for new blocks of nonparticipating business on select tables. Another important use is for tabulating mortality experience for analysis and comparison. Comparisons among companies, or of the experience of different periods within the same company, would be far less valuable unless the comparisons considered the relative proportion of new business and the lower rates of mortality experienced on those recent issues.

ultimate mortality table

If the construction of a mortality table excludes the effects of selection, the table is called an ultimate mortality table. That is, it reflects only the rates of mortality that can be expected after the influence of selection has worn off. Standing alone, column (6) of Table 3-8 is an **ultimate mortality table**.

Table 3-8 Select Mortality Table							
	Deaths per 1,000 Lives Insured						
Issue Age	Policy Year						Attained Age
	(1)	(2)	(3)	(4)	(5)	(5)	
36	1.42	1.64	1.76	1.86	1.94	2.02	41
37	1.56	1.77	1.92	2.07	2.16	2.29	42
38	1.67	1.90	2.10	2.26	2.40	2.56	43
39	1.76	1.99	2.21	2.44	2.63	2.87	44
40	1.79	2.03	2.34	2.61	2.90	3.19	45
41	1.82	2.12	2.51	2.86	3.23	3.55	46

Using an ultimate table during the early years of a life insurance contract provides companies with a source of extra mortality savings. This in turn helps to offset the heavy expenses incurred in placing the business on the books.

aggregate mortality table

A mortality table may be constructed from the experience of insured lives, without regard to the duration of insurance. Such a table is an **aggregate mortality table**. An aggregate table blends in the experience of recently selected lives without segregating it by duration.

Additional Decrements

decrements

In the construction process discussed above for mortality tables, death is the only factor that decreases the number of persons living at each age. Actuaries call such downward reductions **decrements**. For calculation of statutory reserves—those required by state laws or statutes—and cash values, companies use mortality tables that recognize one decrement only. However, operating an insurance company requires more than the basic information required to comply with state laws. Often the actuary combines this additional information with death rates to produce a table that considers more than one decrement.

Several important decrements other than death can be included. For example, the table used to calculate gross premium needs to recognize that policies will lapse before maturity. Calculating the cost of a pension plan needs to include projections for both the number of employees who will die and the number who will leave employment before reaching retirement. If disability benefits are to be provided, accurate projections are needed for the number of covered lives who will become disabled as defined in the policy and the length of time they will remain so disabled. Some pension plans, including the federal Old Age, Survivors, and Disability Insurance (OASDI) program, need to include the probabilities of remarriage in the estimates of the cost of surviving spouse benefits.

multiple-decrement tables

Tables that include rates for more than one decrement are called **multiple-decrement tables**. The construction of multiple-decrement rates is complicated and is beyond the scope of this book. However, once the rates are available, the construction of the multiple-decrement table is very similar to the procedure described above for the single-decrement mortality table.

Example

Both select mortality and ultimate mortality tables are used to determine the two-tiered rate structure for reentry term policies (correctly described as select and ultimate term).

COMMON CHARACTERISTICS OF PUBLIC TABLES

The methods discussed in this chapter for applying the laws of probability to life insurance have produced a multitude of mortality tables for a variety of purposes. Generally, proprietary company tables are used for premium and dividend calculations. Different tables are used for solvency accounting and reporting to regulators. In the remainder of this chapter we describe important and interesting characteristics of some public tables. Table 3-9 provides a summary of these and other tables developed over the past century.

Two principal kinds of public mortality tables exist. First is the set of United States Life Tables published as a by-product of the decennial census. Census data are used to construct a table for the total population and for each of several sub-populations. The purpose of these tables is to display the public health of the country and to provide a general model for the uncertainty of length of life.

statutory table

The other principal kind of public table is required by statute in the various states for use by insurance companies for specific purposes. Sections of these codes, which usually follow model laws developed by the National Association of Insurance Commissioners (NAIC), specify how the assets and liabilities on the annual statements of the insurance companies will be calculated. Insurance and annuity contracts in force create liabilities for life insurers. Valuing these liabilities requires reasonable assumptions about several factors, including mortality. The statute specifies a reasonable assumption for the mortality rates of insureds by naming a specific mortality table—the **statutory table**. Until 1941 the statutes required tables that were selected from among those in existence in the actuarial profession. The 1941 CSO Table was the first constructed at the request of the NAIC for calculating minimum reserves and surrender values. In keeping with this purpose it was also the first to have an explicit margin added to the mortality rates.

Table 3-9
U.S. Mortality Tables

	Name	Purpose	Database	Gender	Type	Margins	Comments
1	79–81 US Life Table	US mortality, general purpose	1979–81	Combined and sex distinct	Aggregate	None	For two centuries, life tables for U.S. population, with sub-populations by sex, race, and geographic region prepared as part of decennial census
2	1941 CSO	Company solvency and minimum nonforfeiture for ordinary insurance	Insurance company experience, 1930–40	Male	Ultimate	Explicit by formula	First table commissioned by the NAIC; first with explicit margins
3	1958 CSO	solvency and minimum nonforfeiture for ordinary insurance	Insurance company experience, 1950–54	Combined female equal to male with 3-year setback	Ultimate	Explicit; sufficient to cover experience of 33 small companies	
4	1958 CET	Company solvency and minimum nonforfeiture for ordinary extended term	58 CSO plus the greater of .00075 or 30% of mortality rate	Combined	Ultimate	Proportional to 58 CSO	First special table for extended term insurance
5	1961 CSG	Company solvency and minimum premiums for group insurance	Insurance company experience, 1950–58	Combined	Aggregate	Explicit	
6	1961 CSI	Company solvency and minimum nonforfeiture for industrial insurance	Insurance company experience on white insureds, 1954–58; US life table for ages > 75	Combined	Aggregate	Explicit and substantial	

Table 3-9
U.S. Mortality Tables

	Name	Purpose	Database	Gender	Type	Margins	Comments
7	1961 CIET	Company solvency and minimum nonforfeiture for industrial extended term	61 CSI plus loading	Combined	Aggregate	Proportional to 61 CET	
8	1980 CSO	Company solvency and minimum nonforfeiture for ordinary insurance	Insurance company experience, 1970–75	Sex distinct	Aggregate policy years 6 and up	Math formula using the life expectancy based on the basic table	10-year selection factors were provided making this the first CSO Table available on a select basis
9	2001 CSO	Company solvency and minimum nonforfeitures for ordinary insurance	insurance company experience, 1990–95	Sex distinct	Aggregate policy year 26 and up	Math formula	25-year selection factor
10	80 CET	Company solvency and minimum nonforfeiture for ordinary extended term	80 CSO plus the greater of .00075 or 30% of mortality rate	Combined	Ultimate	Proportional to 80 CSO	
11	49A	General use for annuities	Group and industrial experience for several years about 1943	Combined	Aggregate	Only to bring it to 1949	First table with projection factors provided to update the table
12	51 GA	For employee annuitants	49A rates for ages < 65; company experience 1946–50 for ages > 65	Male	Aggregate	Margins to make it safe for all occupations	First table for employee annuitants; has projection factors as 49a

Table 3-9
U.S. Mortality Tables

	Name	Purpose	Database	Gender	Type	Margins	Comments
13	71 GAM	For minimum reserves on employee annuitants	Insurance company experience, 1964–68	Sex distinct	Aggregate	8% for males and 10% for females	Had new projection factors
14	71 IAM	For minimum reserves on individual annuitants	Insurance company experience, 1960–67	Sex distinct	Aggregate	10% reduction	
15	83 GAM	For minimum reserves on employee annuitants	Insurance company experience, 1964–68, with projections to 1983	Sex distinct	Aggregate	10% reduction	83 IAM projection factors up age 82; lower reduction factors above
16	83 IAM	For minimum reserves on individual annuitants	Insurance company experience, 1971–76 for ages > 50; 71 IAM for ages < 50	Sex distinct	Aggregate	10% reduction	Had new projection factors
17	Annuity 2000	For minimum reserves on individual annuitants	83 IAM with scale G projection to yr. 2000	Sex distinct	Aggregate	10% reduction	
18	84-UP	Used by PBGC in pension termination cases and general pension work	1965–69 noninsured pension plans and group file	Combined 80% male	Aggregate	Developed by consul. to manage unisex regulations in the 70s	
19	83 Smoker-Nonsmoker	Company solvency and minimum nonforfeiture for ordinary insurance	Various	Sex distinct	Aggregatepolicy years 6 and up	80 CSO margins	Mortality rates for smokers and non-smokers consistent with 80 CSO rates were found for each age

Of the mortality tables listed in Table 3-9, those described in rows 3 through 9 are descendants of the 1941 CSO. The 1958 and 1980 CSOs are updated tables used for ordinary life insurance. The 1980 CSO (see Table 3-10) differs from its predecessors in several ways. It was the first time actuaries developed and published separate rates for men and women. Another difference was in the treatment of the "hump" in the mortality rates for males around age 20. The raw data in most mortality studies show rates for males reaching a low near age 10, then rising to a maximum near age 21, and falling again to a minimum near age 29. After this, they start a long continuous rise to the end of life. In previous mortality tables, the smoothing process eliminated this hump in the initial rates. In the 1980 CSO, however because the hump in the male data was more pronounced than ever (due to auto accidents, homicides, drug overdoses, and suicides) it was not eliminated. An examination of Table 3-10 shows a hump of 1.91 per 1,000 at age 21, then a reduction to the low of 1.70 at age 28, and then a rise back to 1.91 at age 33. The slight hump apparent in the female data was lost in the smoothing process.

The 1980 CSO also was the first to include selection factors in a table developed for regulatory purposes.

The latest CSO table is the 2001 CSO, which is also sex distinct and differentiates between smokers and nonsmokers. It is the first CSO table to go beyond age 100 and stop at age 120. Table 3-11 shows a spreadsheet-derived version of the 2001 CSO table, without rounding or smoothing, starting with a radix of 10 billion persons. A refined version of this crude table was phased in after January 2004, as the states enacted enabling legislation. It is now required by law for reserve valuations of policies sold since 2009 in all states.

The 1958 and 1980 CET Tables, intended for use with extended term insurance, illustrate the need for mortality tables appropriate to their intended use. There were insufficient data to derive mortality rates for extended term coverage at all ages, so the general level of the mortality was determined and then applied to the pattern of mortality for ordinary life insurance. The resulting tables are based on multiples of the ordinary mortality tables rather than being derived directly from the mortality of lives with extended term coverage.

Further illustrations of tables constructed to be appropriate for the relevant population are the 1961 CSG, CSI, and CIET Tables. These are tables constructed at the request of the NAIC for group, industrial, and industrial extended term policies.

The 1983 Smoker-Nonsmoker tables also were constructed at the request of the NAIC. At the time, companies did not possess sufficient experience on insured lives to construct a table in the usual way. The committee that developed their tables estimated the proportion of smokers at each age of the 1980 CSO population and the relative mortality of

smokers versus nonsmokers. Combining this information, the committee estimated mortality rates of the smoking and nonsmoking components of the 1980 CSO populations that were consistent with the overall mortality rates.

The UP-1984 Table was constructed by actuaries to value pension benefits. The Pension Benefit Guarantee Corporation (PBGC) adopted this table to fulfill its mission of protecting defined-benefit pension plan participants with federal guarantees. The PBGC uses this table to value the obligations of pension plans that employers wish to terminate. The table is a unisex table and includes suggestions for complying with laws governing sex discrimination in the distribution of benefits.

Table 3-10
Commissioners 1980 Standard Ordinary (CSO) Table of Mortality
Male Lives

Age (x) at Beginning of Year	Number Living at Beginning of Designated Year (l_x)	Number Dying during Designated Year (d_x)	Yearly Probability of Dying (q_x)
0	10,000,000	41,800	0.004180
1	9,958,200	10,655	0.001070
2	9,947,545	9,848	0.000990
3	9,937,697	9,739	0.000980
4	9,927,958	9,432	0.000950
5	9,918,526	8,927	0.000900
6	9,909,599	8,522	0.000860
7	9,901,077	7,921	0.000800
8	9,893,156	7,519	0.000760
9	9,885,637	7,315	0.000740
10	9,878,322	7,211	0.000730
11	9,871,111	7,601	0.000770
12	9,863,510	8,384	0.000850
13	9,855,126	9,757	0.000990
14	9,845,369	11,322	0.001150
15	9,834,047	13,079	0.001330
16	9,820,968	14,083	0.001510
17	9,806,138	16,376	0.001670
18	9,789,762	17,426	0.001780
19	9,772,336	18,177	0.001860
20	9,754,159	18,533	0.001900

Table 3-10
Commissioners 1980 Standard Ordinary (CSO) Table of Mortality
Male Lives

Age (x) at Beginning of Year	Number Living at Beginning of Designated Year (l_x)	Number Dying during Designated Year (d_x)	Yearly Probability of Dying (q_x)
21	9,735,626	18,595	0.001910
22	9,717,031	18,365	0.001890
23	9,698,666	18,040	0.001860
24	9,680,626	17,619	0.001820
25	9,663,007	17,104	0.001770
26	9,645,903	16,687	0.001730
27	9,629,216	16,466	03001710
28	9,612,750	16,342	0.001700
29	9,596,408	16,410	0.001710
30	9,579,998	16,573	0.001730
31	9,563,425	17,023	0.001780
32	9,546,402	17,470	0.001830
33	9,528,932	18,200	0.001910
34	9,510,732	19,021	0.002000
35	9,491,711	20,028	0.002110
36	9,471,683	21,217	0.002240
37	9,450,466	22,681	0.002400
38	9,427,785	24,324	0.002580
39	9,403,461	26,236	0.002790
40	9,377,225	28,319	0.003020
41	9,348,906	30,758	0.003290
42	9,318,148	33,173	0.003560
43	9,284,975	35,933	0.003870
44	9,249,042	38,753	0.004190
45	9,210,289	41,907	0.004500
46	9,168,382	45,108	0.004920
47	9,123,274	48,536	0.005320
48	9,074,738	52,089	0.005740
49	9,022,649	56,031	0.006210
50	8,966,618	60,166	0.006710

Table 3-10 Commissioners 1980 Standard Ordinary (CSO) Table of Mortality Male Lives			
Age (x) at Beginning of Year	Number Living at Beginning of Designated Year (l_x)	Number Dying during Designated Year (d_x)	Yearly Probability of Dying (q_x)
51	8,906,452	65,017	0.007300
52	8,841,435	70,378	0.007960
53	8,771,057	76,396	0.008710
54	8,694,661	83,121	0.009560
55	8,611,540	90,163	0.010470
56	8,521,377	97,655	0.011460
57	8,423,722	105,212	0.012490
58	8,318,510	113,049	0.013590
59	8,205,461	121,195	0.014770
60	8,084,266	129,995	0.016080
61	7,954,271	139,518	0.017540
62	7,814,753	149,965	0.019190
63	7,664,788	161,420	0.021060
64	7,503,368	173,628	0.023140
65	7,329,740	186,322	0.025420
66	7,143,418	198,944	0.027850
67	6,944,474	211,390	0.030440
68	6,773,084	223,471	0.033190
69	6,509,613	235,453	0.036170
70	6,274,160	247,892	0.039510
71	6,026,268	260,937	0.043300
72	5,765,331	274,718	0.047650
73	5,490,613	289,026	0.052640
74	5,201,587	302,680	0.058190
75	4,898,907	314,461	0.064190
76	4,584,446	323,341	0.070530
77	4,261,105	328,616	0.077120
78	3,932,489	329,936	0.083900
79	3,602,553	328,012	0.091050
80	3,274,541	323,656	0.098840

Table 3-10
Commissioners 1980 Standard Ordinary (CSO) Table of Mortality
Male Lives

Age (x) at Beginning of Year	Number Living at Beginning of Designated Year (l_x)	Number Dying during Designated Year (d_x)	Yearly Probability of Dying (q_x)
81	2,950,885	317,161	0.107480
82	2,633,724	308,804	0.117250
83	2,324,920	298,194	0.128260
84	2,026,726	284,248	0.140250
85	1,742,478	266,512	0.152950
86	1,475,966	245,143	0.166090
87	1,230,823	220,994	0.179550
88	1,009,829	195,170	0.193270
89	814,659	168,871	0.207290
90	645,788	143,216	0.221770
91	502,572	119,100	0.236980
92	383,472	97,191	0.253450
93	286,281	77,900	0.272110
94	146,721	61,660	0.295900
95	146,721	48,412	0.329960
96	98,309	37,805	0.384550
97	60,504	29,054	0.480200
98	31,450	20,693	0.657980
99	10,757	10,757	1.000000

Rows 10 through 15 of Table 3-9 are tables used for annuity contracts. Only the 1971 and 1983 tables were constructed at the request of the NAIC. The mortality experience of lives covered under group annuities and pensions is different from that for lives covered under individually purchased annuities. These differences indicate a need for separate individual annuitant mortality (IAM) tables and group annuitant mortality (GAM) tables.

All public tables, like those described in this chapter, are intended to provide a minimum basis for valuation. Company solvency is the prime concern. For setting premiums and dividend scales, most major life insurance companies rely on their own recent experience. The following tables are the male and female 2001 CSO mortality tables.

Table 3-11 Commissioners 2001 Standard Ordinary (CSO) Table of Mortality Male Lives			
Age (x) at Beginning of Year	Number Living at Beginning of Designated Year (l_x)	Number Dying during Designated Year (d_x)	Yearly Probability of Dying (q_x)
0	10,000,000	9,700	0.00097
1	9,990,300	5,595	0.00056
2	9,984,705	3,894	0.00039
3	9,980,811	2,695	0.00027
4	9,978,116	2,095	0.00021
5	9,976,021	2,096	0.00021
6	9,973,925	2,194	0.00022
7	9,971,731	2,194	0.00022
8	9,969,537	2,193	0.00022
9	9,967,344	2,292	0.00023
10	9,965,052	2,293	0.00023
11	9,962,759	2,690	0.00027
12	9,960,069	3,287	0.00033
13	9,956,782	3,883	0.00039
14	9,952,899	4,678	0.00047
15	9,948,221	6,068	0.00061
16	9,942,153	7,357	0.00074
17	9,934,796	8,643	0.00087
18	9,926,153	9,331	0.00094
19	9,916,822	9,718	0.00098
20	9,907,104	9,907	0.001
21	9,897,197	9,897	0.001
22	9,887,300	10,085	0.00102
23	9,877,215	10,174	0.00103
24	9,867,041	10,360	0.00105
25	9,856,681	10,547	0.00107
26	9,846,134	11,028	0.00112
27	9,835,106	11,507	0.00117
28	9,823,599	11,494	0.00117
29	9,812,105	11,284	0.00115
30	9,800,821	11,173	0.00114

Table 3-11			
Commissioners 2001 Standard Ordinary (CSO) Table of Mortality			
Male Lives			
Age (x) at Beginning of Year	Number Living at Beginning of Designated Year (l_x)	Number Dying during Designated Year (d_x)	Yearly Probability of Dying (q_x)
31	9,789,648	11,062	0.00113
32	9,778,586	11,050	0.00113
33	9,767,536	11,233	0.00115
34	9,756,303	11,512	0.00118
35	9,744,791	11,791	0.00121
36	9,733,000	12,458	0.00125
37	9,720,542	13,026	0.00134
38	9,707,516	13,979	0.00144
39	9,693,537	14,928	0.00154
40	9,678,609	15,970	0.00165
41	9,662,639	17,296	0.00179
42	9,645,343	18,905	0.00196
43	9,626,438	20,697	0.00215
44	9,605,741	22,958	0.00239
45	9,582,783	25,394	0.00265
46	9,557,389	27,716	0.00290
47	9,529,673	30,209	0.00317
48	9,499,464	31,633	0.00333
49	9,467,831	33,327	0.00352
50	9,434,504	35,474	0.00376
51	9,399,030	38,160	0.00406
52	9,360,870	41,843	0.00447
53	9,319,027	45,943	0.00493
54	9,273,084	51,002	0.00550
55	9,222,082	56,900	0.00617
56	9,165,182	63,056	0.00688
57	9,102,126	69,540	0.00764
58	9,032,586	74,699	0.00827
59	8,957,887	80,531	0.00899
60	8,877,356	87,531	0.00986
61	8,789,825	96,161	0.01094

Table 3-11 Commissioners 2001 Standard Ordinary (CSO) Table of Mortality Male Lives			
Age (x) at Beginning of Year	Number Living at Beginning of Designated Year (l_x)	Number Dying during Designated Year (d_x)	Yearly Probability of Dying (q_x)
62	8,693,664	106,497	0.01225
63	8,587,167	117,730	0.01371
64	8,469,437	129,074	0.01524
65	8,340,363	140,535	0.01685
66	8,199,828	151,451	0.01847
67	8,048,377	161,692	0.02009
68	7,886,685	172,324	0.02185
69	7,714,361	182,367	0.02364
70	7,531,994	194,099	0.02577
71	7,337,895	206,562	0.02815
72	7,131,333	223,353	0.03132
73	6,907,980	239,154	0.03462
74	6,668,826	253,949	0.03808
75	6,414,877	268,847	0.04191
76	6,146,030	283,209	0.04608
77	5,862,821	298,535	0.05092
78	5,564,286	314,716	0.05656
79	5,249,570	331,038	0.06306
80	4,918,532	344,986	0.07014
81	4,573,546	357,606	0.07819
82	4,215,940	364,847	0.08654
83	3,851,093	367,818	0.09551
84	3,483,275	367,242	0.10543
85	3,116,033	363,236	0.11657
86	2,752,797	354,863	0.12891
87	2,397,934	341,346	0.14235
88	2,056,588	322,329	0.15673
89	1,734,259	298,084	0.17188
90	1,436,175	269,513	0.18766
91	1,166,662	236,179	0.20244
92	930,483	202,687	0.21783

Table 3-11
Commissioners 2001 Standard Ordinary (CSO) Table of Mortality
Male Lives

Age (x) at Beginning of Year	Number Living at Beginning of Designated Year (l_x)	Number Dying during Designated Year (d_x)	Yearly Probability of Dying (q_x)
93	727,796	170,333	0.23404
94	557,463	140,001	0.25114
95	417,462	112,368	0.26917
96	305,094	87,147	0.28564
97	217,947	66,077	0.30318
98	151,870	48,884	0.32188
99	102,986	35,206	0.34185
100	67,780	24,617	0.36319
101	43,163	16,405	0.38008
102	26,758	10,651	0.39806
103	16,107	6,720	0.41720
104	9,387	4,107	0.43756
105	5,280	2,425	0.45921
106	2,855	1,377	.048222
107	1,478	749	0.50669
108	729	388	0.53269
109	341	191	0.56031
110	150	88	0.58964
111	62	38	0.62079
112	24	16	0.65384
113	8	6	0.68894
114	2	1	0.72618
115	1	1	0.76570
116	0	0	0.80761
117	0	0	0.85207
118	0	0	0.89923
119	0	0	0.94922
120	0	0	1.000000

Table 3-12 Commissioners 2001 Standard Ordinary (CSO) Table of Mortality Female Lives			
Age (x) at Beginning of Year	Number Living at Beginning of Designated Year (l_x)	Number Dying during Designated Year (d_x)	Yearly Probability of Dying (q_x)
0	10,000,000	4,800	0.00048
1	9,995,200	3,498	0.00035
2	9,991,702	2,598	0.00026
3	9,989,104	1,998	0.00020
4	9,987,106	1,898	0.00019
5	9,985,208	1,797	0.00018
6	9,983,411	1,797	0.00018
7	9,981,614	2,096	0.00021
8	9,979,518	2,096	0.00021
9	9,977,422	2,095	0.00021
10	9,975,327	2,195	0.00022
11	9,973,132	2,294	0.00023
12	9,970,838	2,692	0.00027
13	9,968,146	2,990	0.00030
14	9,965,156	3,289	0.00033
15	9,961,867	3,487	0.00035
16	9,958,380	3,884	0.00039
17	9,954,496	4,081	0.00041
18	9,950,415	4,279	0.00043
19	9,946,136	4,575	0.00046
20	9,941,561	4,673	0.00047
21	9,936,888	4,770	0.00048
22	9,932,118	4,966	0.00050
23	9,927,152	4,964	0.00050
24	9,922,188	5,160	0.00052
25	9,917,028	5,355	0.00054
26	9,911,673	5,551	0.00056
27	9,906,122	5,944	0.00060
28	9,900,178	6,237	0.00063
29	9,893,941	6,530	0.00066
30	9,887,411	6,723	0.00068

Table 3-12 Commissioners 2001 Standard Ordinary (CSO) Table of Mortality Female Lives			
Age (x) at Beginning of Year	Number Living at Beginning of Designated Year (l_x)	Number Dying during Designated Year (d_x)	Yearly Probability of Dying (q_x)
31	9,880,688	7,213	0.00073
32	9,873,475	7,603	0.00077
33	9,865,872	8,090	0.00082
34	9,857,782	8,675	0.00088
35	9,849,107	9,554	0.00097
36	9,839,553	10,135	0.00103
37	9,829,418	10,911	0.00111
38	9,818,507	11,488	0.00117
39	9,807,019	12,063	0.00123
40	9,794,956	12,733	0.00130
41	9,782,223	13,499	0.00138
42	9,768,724	14,458	0.00148
43	9,754,266	15,509	0.00159
44	9,738,757	16,751	0.00172
45	9,722,006	18,180	0.00187
46	9,703,826	19,893	0.00205
47	9,683,933	21,983	0.00227
48	9,661,950	24,155	0.00250
49	9,637,795	26,793	0.00278
50	2,611,002	29,602	0.00308
51	9,581,400	32,673	0.00341
52	9,548,727	36,190	0.00379
53	9,512,537	39,953	0.00420
54	9,472,584	43,858	0.00463
55	9,428,726	48,087	0.00451
56	9,380,639	52,813	0.00563
57	9,327,826	57,739	0.00619
58	9,270,087	63,037	0.00680
59	9,207,050	68,040	0.00739
60	9,139,010	73,203	0.00801
61	9,065,807	78,691	0.00868

Table 3-12			
Commissioners 2001 Standard Ordinary (CSO) Table of Mortality			
Female Lives			
Age (x) at Beginning of Year	Number Living at Beginning of Designated Year (l_x)	Number Dying during Designated Year (d_x)	Yearly Probability of Dying (q_x)
62	8,987,116	84,389	0.00939
63	8,902,727	90,274	0.01014
64	8,812,453	96,584	0.01096
65	8,715,869	103,283	0.01185
66	8,612,586	110,413	0.01282
67	8,502,173	118,095	0.01389
68	8,384,078	126,348	0.01507
69	8,257,730	135,097	0.01636
70	8,122,633	144,664	0.01781
71	7,977,969	155,331	0.01947
72	7,822,638	166,622	0.02130
73	7,656,016	178,385	0.02330
74	7,477,631	190,680	0.02550
75	7,286,951	203,306	0.02790
76	7,083,645	216,264	0.03053
77	6,867,381	229,439	0.03341
78	6,637,942	242,816	0.03658
79	6,395,126	256,125	0.04005
80	6,139,001	269,257	0.04386
81	5,869,744	288,263	0.04911
82	5,581,481	306,702	0.05495
83	5,274,779	320,759	0.06081
84	4,954,020	333,257	0.06727
85	4,620,763	344,016	0.07445
86	4,276,747	346,374	0.08099
87	3,930,373	356,839	0.09079
88	3,573,534	361,177	0.10107
89	3,212,357	359,848	0.11202
90	2,852,509	347,778	0.12192
91	2,504,731	317,725	0.12685
92	2,187,006	299,357	0.13688

Table 3-12
Commissioners 2001 Standard Ordinary (CSO) Table of Mortality
Female Lives

Age (x) at Beginning of Year	Number Living at Beginning of Designated Year (l_x)	Number Dying during Designated Year (d_x)	Yearly Probability of Dying (q_x)
93	1,887,649	286,243	0.15164
94	1,601,406	272,736	0.17031
95	1,328,670	257,310	0.19366
96	1,071,360	231,050	0.21566
97	840,310	200,397	0.23848
98	639,913	154,961	0.24216
99	484,952	123,774	0.25523
100	361,178	99,588	0.27573
101	261,590	77,912	0.29784
102	183,678	59,183	0.32221
103	124,495	43,456	0.34906
104	81,039	30,682	0.37861
105	50,357	20,675	0.41057
106	29,682	13,159	0.44333
107	16,523	7,880	0.47689
108	8,643	4,414	0.51065
109	4,229	2,308	0.54581
110	1,921	1,118	0.58177
111	803	495	0.61633
112	308	200	0.64985
113	108	73	0.68037
114	35	25	0.72339
115	10	8	0.76341
116	2	2	0.80493
117	0	0	0.85044
118	0	0	0.89244
119	0	0	0.93511
120	0	0	1.000000

CHAPTER REVIEW

Key Terms and Concepts

probability
event
independent event
mortality table
radix
life expectancy
attained age
law of large numbers
smoothing
graduation techniques

projections
margin of safety
preferred risks
substandard risks
select mortality table
ultimate mortality table
aggregate mortality table
decrements
multiple-decrement tables
statutory table

Chapter 3 Review Questions

1. Using the 2001 CSO mortality table for male lives in the text, calculate the probability that a male living at the beginning of age 30 will: (a) die at age 30 (that is, die before reaching age 31); (b) live to age 31; (c) live to age 34; (d) die before reaching age 34; (e) live to age 40 and then die at age 40; (f) die by age 120 (that is, by the end of age 119). [1]

2. Explain why actuaries do not use the insured's life expectancy in the calculation of life insurance premium rates. [1]

3. List and briefly explain the steps involved in estimating death rates at different ages for use in constructing a mortality table. [2]

4. Explain why actuaries want the schedule of death rates in a mortality table to be smooth with respect to age. [2]

5. Explain how introducing safety margins affects mortality rates in annuity mortality tables differently from the way margins affect mortality rates in life insurance tables. [2]

6. Suppose that after adjusting the data from a mortality study, the actuaries estimate that the probability of a newborn male dying before reaching age one is .004180 and the probability of a one-year-old male dying before age 2 is .001070. Assuming a radix of 10 million newborn males, construct a mortality table showing the numbers living and the numbers dying at ages 0 and 1. [2]

7. Explain how a select mortality table differs from an ultimate mortality table. [2]

8. List the uses of select mortality tables. [2]

9. List and briefly explain several important decrements other than death that may be included in certain mortality tables. [2]

10. Giving several examples, explain how the uses of proprietary company mortality tables differ from the uses of public mortality tables. [3]

11. List the two principal kinds of public mortality tables, and explain the purposes for which they are used. [3]

12. In what ways does the 1980 CSO mortality table differ from its predecessors? [3]

13. What are the maximum ages in each of the 1980 CSO and 2001 CSO mortality tables? [3]

Chapter 3 Review Answers

1. a. *Because there are 9,800,821 men living at the beginning of age 30 and 11,173 of them are expected to die during the year, the probability is 0.00114 (that is, 11,173/9,800,821).*

    b. *Because 9,789,648 of the 9,800,821 men living at age 30 are still living at age 31, the probability is 0.998860 (that is, 9,789,648/9,800,821). The same result can be obtained*

by subtracting the probability of dying at age 30 (calculated above) from one (1 - 0.00114 = 0.99886).

c.   Because 9,756,303 of the 9,800,821 men living at age 30 are still living at age 34, the probability is 0.995458 (that is 9,756,303/9,800,821).

d.   The number of men aged 30 who die before reaching age 34 can be calculated by either (1) adding the numbers of men dying during the years at ages 30, 31, 32, and 33 (11,173 + 11,062 + 11,050 + 11,233 = 44,518 or (2) subtracting the number of men living at age 34 from the number living at age 30 (9,800,821 - 9,756,303= 44,518). Because 44,518 of the 9,800,821 men living at age 30 die before age 34, the probability is 0.004542 (44,518/9,800,821). The same result can be obtained by subtracting the probability of living to age 34 (calculated above) from one (1 - 0.995458 = 0.004542).

e.   Because 15,970 of the 9,800,821 men living at age 30 are expected to die at age 40, the probability is 0.001629 (15,970/9,800,821). The same result can be obtained by subtracting the number of men living at age 41 from the number living at age 40 (9,678,609 - 9,662,639 = 15,970) and then dividing the result by the number living at age 30 (15,970/9,800,821).

f.   Adding the numbers of men dying each year from age 30 through age 119 shows that all 9,800,821 men living at age 30 are expected to die by age 120. Thus, the probability is 1.000000 (9,800,821/9,800,821). An easier way to calculate the number of men dying by age 120 than adding the number dying during all the years from age 30 through 119 is to subtract the number of men living at age 120 (0 because all men living at age 119 are expected to die during the year) from the number living at age 30 (9,800,821 - 0 = 9,800,821). Again, the probability is 1.000000 (9,800,821/9,800,821).

2.   The life expectancy at any age is the average number of years remaining once a person has attained that same age. Life expectancy is an average future lifetime for a representative group of persons at the same age. Life insurance premiums are calculated based on probabilities that persons living at a given age will die during a given interval of time.

3.   The following steps are involved in estimating the death rates at different ages for constructing a mortality table:

a.   The first step is to select a sample population representative of the population where the resulting probabilities are to be used. In life insurance, this means that both populations should have the same smoking habits and gender, should be buying the same type of contract (insurance or annuity, individual or group, permanent insurance versus term insurance), and that similar underwriting information is available-that

   *is, that medically examined applicants are grouped separate from nonmedical
   applicants.*

   b. *The next step is to observe the mortality experience of the representative population
       for a period of time. The observation period should be as recent as possible, sufficiently
       long to give adequate data, and free of nonrepresentative events such as war and
       epidemics.*

   c. *After following the sample population during the observation period, the data are
       processed into the number of life-years and the number of deaths observed in each
       age interval.*

   d. *From these figures, death rates may be computed for the respective ages by dividing
       the number of death in each age interval by the number of life-years observed in each
       corresponding age interval.*

4. *For theoretical and practical reasons, actuaries want the schedule of mortality rates to be
   smooth with respect to age. First, resistance to disease declines and the degeneration of
   the body system increases in continuous and minute gradations. Thus, sharp changes in
   the death rates by age should not occur. Second, if the mortality rates are irregular by age,
   then the premiums and reserves based on them will also be irregular. Such a pattern is not
   desirable. However, in most mortality studies a smooth set of mortality rates cannot be
   obtained because sufficient data are not available. Actuaries use graduation techniques to
   smooth the initial nonsmooth sets of mortality rates.*

5. *In a life insurance mortality table, including a safety margin means increasing the mortality rates above those anticipated. In an annuity table, including a safety margin means
   lowering the rates of mortality below those expected.*

6. *The numbers living and dying at ages 0 and 1 are the numbers shown at those ages in the
   1980 CSO mortality table in McGill's Life Insurance. The radix (10 million) is the number of
   lives at the first age (age 0). The number of males dying at age 0 (41,800) is calculated by
   multiplying the radix by the probability of dying at age 0 (10,000,000 x .004180 = 41,800).
   The number living at the beginning of age one is calculated by subtracting the number
   dying at age 0 from the number living at the beginning of age 0 (10,000,000 – 41,800 =
   9,958,200). The number dying at age one (10,655) is determined by multiplying the number
   living at age one by the probability of dying at age one (9,958,200 x .001070 = 10,655).*

7. *A select mortality table shows the rate of mortality not only by age but also by duration of insurance. This recognizes the time passed since an applicant was approved to receive a policy. Because the effect of selection is generally negligible after 5 years, different rates are usually needed only for durations below 6 years.*

    If the construction of a mortality table excludes the effects of selection, the table is called an ultimate mortality table. That is, it reflects only the rates of mortality that can be expected after the influence of selection has worn off. An ultimate table shows only one rate of mortality at each age.

8. *Companies use select tables in developing gross premiums for both participating and nonparticipating insurance and for testing—through asset share calculations described in later chapters of this book—the appropriateness of existing or proposed schedules of dividends and surrender values. Companies also base profit projections for new blocks of nonparticipating business on select tables. Another important use is for tabulating mortality experience for analysis and comparison. Comparisons among companies, or of the experience of different periods within the same company, would be far less valuable unless the comparisons considered the relative proportion of new business and the lower rates of mortality experienced on those recent issues.*

9. *Other than age, several important decrements can be included in mortality tables:*
   - *The table used to calculate gross premium needs to recognize that policies will lapse before maturity.*
   - *Calculating the cost of a pension plan needs to include projections for both the number of employees that will die and the number who will leave employment before reaching retirement.*
   - *If disability benefits are to be provided, accurate projections are needed for the number of covered lives who will become disabled as defined in the policy and the length of time they will remain so disabled.*
   - *Some pension plans, including the federal Old Age, Survivors, and Disability Insurance (OASDI) program, need to include the probabilities or remarriage in the estimates of the cost of surviving spouse benefits.*

10. *Generally, proprietary company mortality tables are used for premium and dividend calculations. Public mortality tables based on census data are used to display the public health of the country and to provide a general model for the uncertainty of length of life. Another*

group of public mortality tables are those required by state statute for the valuation of insurance company liabilities in connection with solvency accounting and reporting to regulators.

11. Two principal kinds of public mortality tables exist. First is the set of United States Life Tables published as a by-product of the decennial census. Census data are used to construct a table for the total population and for each of several sub-populations. The purpose of these tables is to display the public health of the country and to provide a general model for the uncertainty of length of life.

   The other principal kind of public table is required by statute in the various states for use by insurance companies for specific purposes, such as valuing their liabilities. Valuing liabilities requires reasonable assumptions about various factors, including mortality. The statute specifies a reasonable assumption for the mortality rates of insureds by naming a specific mortality table—the statutory table (for example, the 1980 CSO Table).

12. The 1980 CSO differs from its predecessors in several ways:
   * It was the first time actuaries developed and published separate rates for men and women.
   * Another difference was in the treatment of the "hump" in the mortality rates for males around age 20. The raw data in most mortality studies show rates for males reaching a low near age 10, then rising to a maximum near age 21, and falling again to a previous mortality tables, the smoothing process eliminated this hump in the initial rates. In the 1980 CSO, however, because the hump in the male data was more pronounced than ever (due to auto accidents, homicides, drug overdoses, and suicides), it was not eliminated.
   * The 1980 CSO also was the first to include selection factors in a table developed for regulatory purposes.

13. There are no survivors beyond age 99 under the 1980 CSO, but the 2001 CSO tables go to age 119.

Term Insurance

By Dan M. McGill
Revised by C.W. Copeland & Dave Moon

Learning Objectives

An understanding of the material in this chapter should enable the student to

1. **Describe and understand the nature and features of term life insurance.**

2. **Describe and understand the renewability and conversion provisions.**

3. **Compare term insurance variations and their usefulness.**

There are five basic types of life insurance contracts: term, whole life, universal life, endowment, and annuity. The function of the first four is to create a principal sum or estate, either through the death of the insured or through the accumulation of funds set aside for investment purposes. The function of the annuity, on the other hand, is to liquidate a principal sum in a scientific manner, regardless of how that sum was created. This dissimilarity in the basic functions of life insurance and annuities has caused some to question the propriety of classifying annuities as a type of life insurance contract, but there appear to be enough similarities to justify the practice. This chapter discusses term insurance contracts.

Note: Endowment life insurance policies are still viable and popular in other countries, but United States tax law changes have nearly eliminated endowment sales in this country.

NATURE OF TERM INSURANCE

Term insurance provides life insurance protection for a limited period only. The face amount of the policy is payable if the insured dies during the specified period, and nothing is paid if the insured survives. The period may be as short as one year, or it may run to age 65 or above. The customary terms are one, 5, 10, 15, and 20 years. Such policies may insure for the agreed term only, or they may give the insured the option of renewing the protection for successive terms without evidence of insurability. Applications for term insurance are carefully underwritten; various restrictions may be imposed on the amount of insurance, the age before which it must be obtained, the age beyond which it cannot be renewed, and the like.

Term insurance may be regarded as temporary insurance and, in principle, is more nearly comparable to property and casualty insurance contracts than any of the other life

insurance contracts in use. If a person insures his or her life under a 5-year term contract, no obligation is incurred by the insurance company unless the death of the insured occurs within the term. All premiums paid for the term protection are considered to be fully earned by the company by the end of the term, whether or not a loss has occurred, and the policy has no further value. This is similar to auto and homeowners insurance.

The premium for term insurance is initially relatively low, despite the fact that it contains a relatively high expense loading and an allowance for adverse selection. The reason premiums can be low is that most term contracts do not cover the period of old age when death is most likely to occur and when the cost of insurance is high. In other words, a term policy insures against a contingency only and not a certainty, as do other kinds of policies.

Renewability

renewability

Many term insurance contracts contain an option to renew for a limited number of additional periods of term insurance, usually of the same length (**renewability**). The simplest policy of this type is the yearly renewable term, which is a one-year term contract renewable for successive periods of one year each. Longer term contracts, such as the 10-year term, may also be renewable. The following is a typical renewal provision:

Renewal Privilege. The insured may renew this policy for further periods of 10 years each without medical examination, provided there has been no lapse in the payment of premiums, by written notice to the company at its home office before the expiration of any period of the insurance hereunder and by the payment in each year, on the dates above specified, of the premium for the age attained by the insured at the beginning of any such renewal period in accordance with the table of rates contained herein.

The key to the renewable feature is the right to renew the contract without a medical examination or other evidence of insurability. Where the term policy contains no renewal privilege, or where it can be renewed only upon evidence of insurability satisfactory to the company, the insured may find that coverage cannot be continued as long as needed. Because of poor health, a hazardous occupation, or some other reason, the insured might be unable to secure a renewal of the contract or to obtain any other form of life insurance protection. The renewal feature prevents this situation. Its chief function is to protect the insurability of the named insured.

Under a term insurance the premium increases with each renewal, based on the attained age of the insured at the time of the renewal. The term insurance premium for a person

aged 50 or above, for example, is higher than the premium for a whole life contract acquired before age 35. Within the contract period, however, the premium is level. Over a long period of time, punctuated by several renewals, the premium will consist of a series of level premiums, each series higher than the previous one. Moreover, the rate will continue to increase with each renewal. The scale of rates at which the insurance can be renewed is published in the original contract and cannot be changed by the company as long as the contract remains in force. Evidence of renewal is usually provided in the form of a certificate to be attached to the original contract, although some insurance companies issue a new contract with each renewal.

Insurers have mixed feelings about renewable term insurance. There is no question that, properly used, it fills a real need. However, it presents certain problems to the company that writes it. Whether the policy is on the yearly renewable term plan or a longer term basis, there is likely to be strong selection against the company at time of renewal, and this adverse selection will become greater as the age of the insured—and hence, the renewal premium—increases. Resistance to increasing premiums will cause many of those who remain in good health to fail to renew each time a premium increase takes effect, while those in poor health will tend to take advantage of the right of renewal. As time goes on, the mortality experience among the surviving policyowners will become increasingly unfavorable. While dividend adjustment can provide for adverse mortality experience, it requires substantial margins in the premium rates. As a result, each dollar of protection on the term basis tends to cost middle-aged or older policyowners more than under any other type of contract.

Renewability Features

- Policyowners can renew without medical or other evaluation.

- Premiums change upon renewal.

- Some insurers prohibit renewals beyond a specified age.

As a further safeguard against adverse selection, companies generally do not permit renewals to carry the coverage beyond a specified age such as 65, 70, or 75 (although some insurers guarantee renewability to age 95 or 99). In addition, limitations on yearly renewable term are usually more stringent; coverage is frequently restricted to 10 or 15 years or, occasionally, 15 years or to age 65, whichever is earlier. Renewable term insurance, therefore, is satisfactory for individual coverage to both the policyowner and the company when coverage does not extend into the higher ages.

Convertibility

convertibility

In addition to the renewable privilege, a term policy may contain a **convertibility** provision that permits the policyowner to exchange the term contract for a contract on a permanent plan, likewise without evidence of insurability.[1] In other words, a term insurance policy may be both renewable and convertible. The convertible feature serves the needs of those who want permanent insurance but are temporarily unable to afford the higher premiums required for whole life and other types of cash value life insurance. Convertibility is also useful when the policyowner desires to postpone the final decision as to the type of permanent insurance to be purchased until a later date when, for some reason, it may be possible to make a wiser choice. Thus, convertible term insurance provides a way to obtain temporary insurance and an option on permanent insurance in the same policy.

Insurability is protected by the convertible feature in an even more valuable manner than under the renewable feature because convertibility guarantees access to permanent insurance—not just continuation of temporary protection. The two features together afford complete protection against loss of insurability.

The conversion may be effective as of the date of the exchange or as of the original date of the term policy. If the term policy is converted as of the current date, conversion is usually referred to as the attained age method since the current age determines the premium level. A conversion using the original date of the term policy for the conversion is referred to as the original age method or a retroactive conversion.

Retroactive Conversion

retroactive conversion

Some insurers allow **retroaction conversion** on a policy within the first few years after issue. When the conversion is effective as of the original date, the premium rate for the permanent contract is that which would have been paid had the new contract been taken out originally, and the policy form is that which would have been issued originally. It is these two features that motivate the insured to convert retroactively in most instances. The advantage of the lower premium is obvious, but in many cases, the contract being issued

---

1.   Permanent plan or permanent insurance refers to whole life, universal life, and other cash value types of insurance, as distinguished from the temporary protection afforded by term insurance.

at the original date contains actuarial assumptions or other features more favorable than those being incorporated in current policies.

Offsetting these advantages, however, is the fact that a financial adjustment—involving a payment by the insured to the company—is required, which may be quite substantial if the term policy has been in force for several years. This adjustment may be computed on a variety of bases, but a great number of companies specify that the payment will be the larger of (1) the difference in the reserves (in some companies, the cash surrender values) under the policies being exchanged or (2) the difference in the premiums paid on the term policy and those that would have been paid on the permanent plan, with interest on the difference at a stipulated rate. Under the second type of financial adjustment, an allowance is frequently made for any larger dividends that would have been payable under the permanent form. Some companies require a payment equal to the difference in reserves, plus a charge of up to 8 percent to provide the previously forgone investment return.

The purpose of the financial adjustment, regardless of how it is computed, is to place the insurance company in the same financial position it would have enjoyed had the permanent contract been issued in the first place. Therefore, apart from the possibility of obtaining more favorable actuarial assumptions, there does not seem to be any financial advantage to the insured to convert retroactively. The insured will admittedly pay a smaller premium but—by making up the deficiency in the term premium—will, in effect, pay it over a longer period of time; actuarially, the two sets of premiums are equivalent. Some people are under the mistaken impression that by making the financial adjustment required for conversion as of the original date, they are investing money retroactively and being credited with retroactive interest. The fact is, however, that the insured pays the company the interest it would have earned had the larger premium been paid from the beginning.

Retroactive Conversion

- Premiums after conversion based on earlier age

- Must pay an adjustment to insurer

- Converts term policy to cash value type policy

- Provides level or flexible premiums thereafter

- Conversion must be made before limiting age

The insured should consider many factors in making a choice between the two bases of conversion, one of the most important being the state of his or her health. The insured would be ill-advised to convert retroactively—and pay a substantial sum of money to the insurance company—if his or her health were impaired. The sum the insured pays would immediately become a part of the reserve under the contract and would not increase the amount of death benefits in the event of the insured's early demise—or ever, for that matter. The payment would simply reduce the effective amount of insurance.

In most cases, if the insured has surplus funds to invest in insurance, he or she should consider purchasing additional insurance or perhaps prepaying premiums on existing policies, including the newly converted one. Subject to certain limitations, most companies permit the insured to prepay fixed premiums, either in the form of so-called premium deposits or through discounting of future premiums. The two procedures are very similar. The principal difference is that under the discount method, credit is taken in advance for the interest to be earned on the funds deposited. Under both arrangements, the funds deposited with the company are credited with interest at a stipulated rate and, in some instances, are credited with the interest earned by the company in excess of the stipulated rate. In the event of the insured's death, the balance of any such deposits is returned to the insured's estate or designated beneficiaries in addition to the death benefit of the policy. Some companies permit withdrawal of premium deposits at any time, in which case a lower rate of interest may be credited, while others limit withdrawals to anniversary or premium due dates. A few companies permit withdrawals only in case of surrender or death. Some companies credit no interest or otherwise penalize the insured if the funds are withdrawn.

Time Limit for Conversion

As previously noted, a retroactive conversion must take place within a specified number of years after issue. If the term of the policy is no longer than 10 years, a conversion as of a current date can usually be accomplished throughout the full term. If the term is longer than 10 years, the policy may stipulate that the conversion privilege must be exercised, if at all, before the expiration of a period shorter than the term of the policy. For example, a 15-year term policy must usually be converted, if at all, within 12 years from date of issue, a 20-year term policy within 15 years.

The purpose of a time limit is to minimize adverse selection. There is always a substantial degree of adverse selection in the conversion process. Those policyowners in poor health as the time for conversion approaches are more likely to convert and pay the higher premiums than those who believe themselves to be in good health. If the decision to convert must be made some years before the expiration of the term policy, a higher percentage

of healthy policyowners, uncertain of their health some years hence, will elect to convert. Even so, experience has shown that the death rate among those who convert is higher than normal. This accounts for the fact that premium rates for convertible term insurance are somewhat higher than those for term policies not containing the conversion privilege.

If the policy is renewable, the only time limitation may be that it is converted before age 60 or 65. In other cases, the contract will state that the policy must be converted within a certain period before the expiration of the last term for which it can be renewed. In all cases, conversion may be permitted beyond the time limit, but within the policy term, upon evidence of insurability.

Some companies issue term policies that are automatically converted at the expiration of the term to a specified plan of permanent insurance. It is doubtful that this procedure is effective in reducing adverse selection since healthy individuals may fail to continue the permanent insurance.

Reentry Term (Select and Ultimate Term Insurance)

reentry term insurance

The life insurance industry has developed a term insurance policy intended to charge higher premiums to those in poorer health when they renew their term insurance, thereby reducing the degree of adverse selection. The product is commonly called **reentry term insurance**. It is really a policy subject to two different premium schedules. The lower premium rate is based on select mortality (that applicable to an insured who has recently given evidence that he or she is in good health). The select rates are available as long as the insured is able to provide new evidence of insurability at each renewal date and at other dates specified by the insurer.

The higher premium schedule is based on ultimate mortality rates (that applicable to insureds at least 15 or 20 years after they last provided evidence of insurability). The insureds who cannot provide evidence of insurability acceptable to the insurance company when requested or required must pay the higher premium schedule rates to renew their coverage. They are known to be in poorer health and have to pay for the increased risk right away and probably for each subsequent renewal (unless they experience an improvement in their health).

It is hard to argue with the logic or concept of equity in this approach. In order to get the lower premiums while healthy, the individual should be willing to pay the higher premium when his or her health deteriorates. However, it is questionable whether the policyowner

knows or realizes the full import of a decision to buy reentry term insurance. Young people in good health believe they are immortal and will never have to pay the higher rates. Few of them stop to consider that they may actually end up paying the ultimate rates and that when that happens they will usually be precluded from buying coverage from another insurer. The single premium schedule term insurance they could have bought instead of reentry term might have been a significant bargain. Unfortunately, when that realization sinks in, it is too late to select that option.

Reentry term is economical for those who remain healthy into their retirement years, but it may end up being very costly for anyone whose health deteriorates at about the same rate as that of the general population. On average, people start to experience declining health between the ages of 45 and 55. If they reach their life expectancy (at least 50 percent should), they can live 40 to 50 years in an impaired physical condition—paying the higher term rates for many more years than they enjoyed lower term rates.

Example

Mary purchased a reentry term policy 3 years ago. She saved 10 percent based on the premiums that would have been required for a traditional renewable term policy that guarantees future premium rates. Mary suffered a severe heart attack just before she was required to have her health reassessed for the reentry term. Her new premium is more than double what the renewal premium would have been under the traditional renewable term policy. That difference may get even larger in the future.

It is suggested that the decision to purchase reentry term insurance should involve comparison of the high rates of competing insurers for similar coverage. Once the insured cannot provide satisfactory evidence of insurability, the lower premium schedule is irrelevant. Helpful in making such comparisons are pro forma cash flow simulations of the premiums (both high and low rates) for each policy being considered at a range of premium increase dates. Another important point for evaluation is whether the insurer considers the policy a new contract with a new contestable period after the insured fails a reentry test. Some insurers treat the new premium as an adjustment on continuing coverage, but others impose a new contestable period.

Guarding against Contestability

In general it is a good idea to keep existing coverage in force until after the intended replacement coverage has actually been issued and the policy delivered. It is important for the policyowner to realize that new policies remain contestable for at least one year (and often for 2 years). If the insured dies while the policy remains contestable, the claim will be

investigated much more thoroughly and take longer to settle than one for a policy that is already incontestable.

Long-Term Contracts

While most term contracts provide protection for a relatively short period, subject to renewal for successive periods of the same duration, some term contracts are designed to provide long-period protection in the first instance. These policies often give prospective policyowners the option to purchase waiver-of-premium and accidental death benefits.

A term-to-65 contract, for example, provides protection on a level premium basis from the age of issue to age 65. It is not to be confused with yearly renewable or other forms of term insurance that can be renewed until the insured reaches age 65. The period covered by this contract is normally somewhat shorter than the life expectancy, but its termination date coincides with the age generally regarded as the normal retirement age. Hence it probably comes closest to limiting its protection to the years when the insured's income is derived from personal efforts. Because the term is shorter than that of whole life contracts, the premium will be smaller. It is customary to provide for cash and other surrender values. A conversion privilege may be offered, but if so, it must usually be exercised some time before the expiration of the policy. A typical form requires conversion prior to age 60.

Return of Premium Term

The return of premium term enhancement has been introduced by some life insurance companies to increase demand for the product. Basically, it adds an endowment component to the base term life insurance policy. If the insured lives beyond the end of the term insurance contract and has kept the term insurance in force, the endowment benefit is payable in an amount equal to all prior premium payments. If the insured dies before the end of the term contract, the death benefit will not be increased by the amount of premiums previously paid. The feature seems to be most appealing on 30-year or longer term policies.

The return of premium feature increases the premium level to fund the additional benefit. The increase for a 30-year term policy ranges from 25 to 50 percent of the base premium. For shorter durations the premium increase for the return of premium becomes much more burdensome because of the short time to accumulate the endowment amount. The base term policy does not have a cash value, but the insurance company must reserve for the additional endowment component.

Looking at the return of premium feature as if the additional premium is a side fund, the return ranges between 2 and 9 percent to return the premium at the end of 30 years. There

is a slight tax advantage in the feature in that the return of premium will be free of income tax when received.

Nonlevel Term Insurance

The preceding discussion has presumed that the amount of insurance is level or uniform throughout the term of the policy. This is not necessarily the case since the amount of insurance may increase or decrease throughout the term. As a matter of fact, a substantial—if not predominant—portion of term insurance provides systematic decreases in the amount of insurance from year to year. This type of term insurance, appropriately called decreasing term insurance, may be written in the form of a separate contract, a rider to a new or existing contract, or as an integral part of a combination contract. Mortgage redemption insurance is probably the most familiar form of decreasing term insurance.

Increasing term insurance in the form of a return-of-premium provision has been around for a long time, but in recent years the concept has enjoyed a much wider application in connection with various arrangements, specifically split-dollar plans, which may contemplate borrowing or encumbering the cash value of an underlying policy. In order to provide a uniform death benefit to the insured's personal beneficiaries, contracts developed for these uses frequently make provision for the automatic purchase of an additional amount of term insurance each year in the exact or approximate amount that the cash value increases.

CRITQUE OF TERM INSURANCE

Term insurance has long been a controversial type of insurance. Many people, not familiar with or perhaps not sympathetic to the principle of level premium insurance, advocate the use of term insurance in all situations to the virtual exclusion of permanent insurance. There are certain insurance "consultants" who, when they find permanent plans in an insurance program, will advise their surrender for cash and replacement with term insurance. On the other hand, the insurance companies, mindful of the limitations of term insurance and fearful of possible adverse public reaction, tend to discourage its indiscriminate use. This has given rise to a widespread impression that insurance companies are opposed to term insurance, preferring the higher-premium forms that add more to income and assets. It might be helpful therefore to point out the areas that can legitimately be served by term insurance and to analyze briefly some of the fallacious arguments that have been advanced in favor of term insurance.

Areas of Usefulness

Term insurance is suitable when either (1) the need for protection is purely temporary, or (2) the need for protection is permanent, but the insured temporarily cannot afford the premiums for permanent insurance. In the first case, term insurance is the complete answer, but it should be renewable in the event that the temporary need should extend over a longer period than was originally anticipated. Theoretically the policy need not be convertible, but since relatively few people carry an adequate amount of permanent insurance and since the loss of insurability is a constant threat, it is advisable to obtain a policy with the conversion privilege.

The second broad use of term insurance requires that the policy be convertible. The conversion privilege is the bridge that spans the gap between the need for permanent insurance and the financial ability to meet the need. In this case, since the insured's financial situation might persist longer than anticipated, the policy should be renewable as well as convertible. Thus, the renewable and convertible features serve quite different functions and, ideally, should be incorporated in all term policies.

Temporary Need for Protection

Examples of temporary needs that can—and should—be met through term insurance are encountered daily. One of the most obvious is the need to hedge a loan. A term policy in the amount of the loan payable to the lender not only protects the lender against possible loss of principal but also relieves the insured's estate of the burden of repaying the loan if the insured dies. A mortgage redemption policy serves the same purpose. An individual who has invested heavily in a speculative business venture should protect his or her estate and family by obtaining term insurance in the amount of the investment. If a business firm is spending a considerable sum in an experimental project, the success of which depends on the talents and abilities of one individual or a few individuals, term insurance on the appropriate person or persons will protect the investment. A parent with young children is likely to need more insurance while the children are dependent than he or she will need when they have grown up and become self-sufficient. The additional insurance during the child-raising period can be—and usually is—provided through term insurance. Frequently, decreasing term insurance is superimposed on a plan of permanent insurance.

Example

Tom and Marsha have two very young children and need more life insurance to protect them. However, Marsha will become the recipient of a large trust in 8 years. At that time, they will have a diminished need for life insurance. Term insurance is appropriate for the temporary need.

Lack of Finances for Permanent Insurance

The second function of term insurance is particularly important to young people who expect substantial improvement in their financial situation as the years go by. Young professionals who have made a considerable investment in their education and training, but whose practices must be built up gradually, are likely prospects for term insurance. Young business executives are also good prospects.

Danger of Relying Solely on Group Term Insurance

In these times of fierce competition and corporate downsizing, it can be precarious to rely heavily on employer-provided group life insurance to satisfy all or most of a family's death benefit needs. The need for life insurance usually greatly exceeds the amount of coverage available from group plans. Even if the family has supplemental individual life insurance to provide adequate total coverage, there can be a shortfall of coverage when group coverage ends or is converted at termination of employment. Individuals should find out how much of the employer group coverage can be converted after an involuntary termination of employment—for example, mandatory early retirement, workforce reduction, plant closing, reorganization after a merger or acquisition, employer bankruptcy, statutory banning of a product (freon, for instance), or chronic health impairment resulting from accident or disease. Individual term insurance may be appropriate to cover the potential net reduction in coverage after postemployment conversion of the existing coverage. The safest way for the individual to cover this risk is to purchase an individual policy while he or she is still employed. The cost of such risk aversion is the amount spent on premiums for coverage in excess of the individual's current needs between policy formation and a premature employment termination.

Fallacious Arguments in Favor of Term Insurance

Some of the fallacious arguments in favor of term insurance can just as aptly be described as criticisms of level premium insurance. Upon analysis, most of the arguments can be merged into two sweeping allegations: (1) Level premium insurance overcharges the policyowner, and (2) the accumulation and protection elements should be separated.

The basis for the first allegation is the indisputable fact that if a policyowner dies in the early years of the contract, premium outlay under the level premium plan is considerably larger than it would have been under a term plan. It follows, then, according to the term advocates, that the policyowner paid a larger premium than was necessary. Term advocates question whether it is wise for the insured to pay in advance for something he or she may never need or live to enjoy. They argue that it is better "to pay as you go and get what you pay for."

There is no question that insureds would be far better off financially with term insurance if they could be sure that they would die within a relatively short time. On the other hand, they would be far worse off if they guessed wrong and lived to a ripe old age. Although no one knows whether he or she will die young or live to an excessively old age, the chances of living to an age where the total term premiums exceed the total premiums paid under a level premium plan are relatively high.

The level premium plan protects the insured against the consequences of living too long and having to pay prohibitive premiums for insurance protection. In effect, it shifts a portion of the premium burden of those who live beyond their life expectancy to those who die young and produce an exceedingly large return on their premium outlay. Because at the outset no one can know which group he or she will be in, payment of the level premium by all is an eminently fair and satisfactory arrangement.

Those who argue that level premium insurance overcharges policyowners sometimes assert that the reserve under permanent forms of insurance is forfeited to the company in the event of the insured's death. To correct this "inequity," they contend the normal death benefit should be increased by the amount of the reserve.

It should be apparent that this argument strikes at the very heart of the level premium plan. As stated before, the essence of this plan is a gradual reduction in the net amount at risk as the reserve increases. If the reserve is to be paid in addition to the face amount of the policy, this reduction in the amount at risk does not occur, and premiums that were calculated on the assumption that the risk is to be a decreasing one will clearly be inadequate. Some companies offer a contract that promises to return the reserve in addition to the face amount of the policy, but the premium is increased accordingly.

The second allegation—that the savings and protection elements of the contract should be separated—is based on the proposition that an individual can invest his or her surplus funds more wisely and with a greater return than the life insurance company can. Those who believe this recommend that individuals buy term insurance and then place the difference between the term premium and the premium they would have paid for level

premium insurance in a separate investment program. Some suggest investing this difference in premiums in government bonds, others recommend investment trusts or mutual funds, while others advocate an individual investment program in common stocks. This argument needs to be analyzed in terms of the objectives of any investment program.

Investment Program Objectives

The principal investment program objectives are safety of principal, yield, and liquidity.

Regarding safety of principal, the life insurance industry has compiled a solvency record over the years that is unmatched by any other type of business organization. It has survived wars, depressions, and inflation; composite losses to policyowners have been relatively rare. Even the few companies seized by the regulators in recent years have been able to rescue most of their policyowners' contracts. This exemplary record has been achieved through quality investments and concentration on government bonds—federal, state, and local—high-grade corporate bonds, and real estate mortgages, and through emphasis on diversification. Investments are diversified as to type of industry, geographical distribution, maturity, and size. Many of the larger companies have from 100,000 to 200,000 different units of investment. The individual policyowner's reserve or investment is commingled with all other policyowners' reserves. The insurance company has invested in assets to offset these liabilities (reserves). In effect therefore each policyowner owns a pro rata share of each investment unit in the company's portfolio. The insured may have as little as one cent invested in some units. Such diversification—which is the keystone of safety—is obviously beyond the reach of the individual investor. Only by investing exclusively in federal and state government bonds, with the consequent interest rate risk and sacrifice of yield, could the individual investor hope to match the safety of principal that his or her funds would enjoy with a reputable life insurance company.

Life insurance companies unquestionably obtain the highest possible yield commensurate with the standard of safety that they have set for themselves. As a group, life insurance companies in the United States earned over 9.0 percent of their mean ledger assets during most of the past decade, reaching 9.87 percent in 1985. This figure, which represents the net investment income (but does not reflect capital gains and losses) after deducting all expenses allocable to investment operations but before deducting federal income taxes, is the highest during the 20th century for the United States life insurance industry. Net rates have been declining since 1985 as general investment returns have sagged for all sectors of the economy. Many individuals therefore may be able to secure a higher yield than that provided by a life insurance company by investing in common stocks or other equity investments, especially if unrealized capital appreciation is taken into account, and some

exceptional investors will be able to do it under virtually any circumstances. It is highly questionable, however, that the typical life insurance policyowner can, over a long period, earn a consistently higher yield than a life insurance company, regardless of the type of investment program he or she pursues. Moreover, it should be noted that the annual increases in cash values are not subject to federal income taxes as they accrue,[2] while the earnings from a separate investment program would be taxed as ordinary income.

Principal Investment Program Objectives

- Safety of principal

- Yield

- Liquidity

With respect to the third objective of an investment program, the liquidity of a life insurance contract is unsurpassed. The policyowner's investment can be withdrawn at any time with no loss of cash value unless surrender charges apply. This can be accomplished through surrender for cash or through policy loans. The insured never faces the possibility of liquidating his or her assets in an unfavorable market; nor can the insured's policy loans be called because of inadequate collateral. Certain types of investments' approach the liquidity of life insurance cash values, but no investment whose value depends on the market can match the liquidity of the demand obligation represented by the life insurance contract.

More important perhaps than any of the preceding factors is the question of whether savings under a separate investment program would have been accomplished in the first place. Life insurance that develops cash values is a form of "forced" saving. Not only do its periodic premiums provide a simple and systematic mechanism for saving, but when the savings feature is combined with the protection feature, there is also far more incentive for the insured to save than there would otherwise be. An individual who is voluntarily purchasing a bond a month or setting aside a certain amount per month in some other type of savings account may skip a month or two if some other disposition of money is more appealing. If, however, failure to set aside the predetermined contribution to a savings account would result in loss of highly prized insurance protection that might be irreplaceable, he or she will be far more likely to make the savings effort. The insured saves because it is the only way of preserving his or her protection under a fixed premium policy. The

---

2.   Except in the case of death, most of the earnings on the reserve of a life insurance contract are eventually taxed to the insured but usually at a time when he or she is in a much lower tax bracket.

flexible premiums of universal life policies have removed the compulsory element inherent in whole life policies.

The preceding text is not to disparage other forms of investment. All have their place in an individual's financial program. Level premium life insurance, however, should be the foundation of any lifelong financial program.

CHAPTER REVIEW

Key Terms and Concepts

renewability   retroactive conversion
convertibility   reentry term insurance

Chapter 4 Review Questions

1. What is the basic function of life insurance contracts? [1]

2. Describe the variations of term life insurance that are available. [3]

3. Describe the protection provided by renewability provisions in term life insurance contracts. [2]

4. Compare the attained-age method of converting term insurance with the retroactive conversion method. [2]

5. Explain why there are time limitations on conversion rights for term life insurance, and describe some forms of such limits. [2]

6. Explain how select and ultimate term (reentry term) differs from traditional forms of term life insurance. [3]

7. How do term-to-65 policies differ from shorter duration term life insurance contracts? [3]

8   Describe the most common situations for which term life insurance is suitable. [3]

Chapter 4 Review Answers

1. *The basic function of life insurance contracts is to create a principal sum or estate, either through the death of the insured or through the accumulation of funds set aside for investment purposes.*

2. *Variations of term life insurance include: (a) Renewable term—contains an option to renew for a limited number of additional periods of term insurance, usually of the same length, without evidence of insurability. (b) Convertible term—contains a provision that permits the policyowner to exchange the term contract for a contract on a permanent plan without evidence of insurability. (c) Re-entry term—a term insurance policy intended to charge higher premiums to those in poorer health when they renew their term insurance, thereby reducing the degree of adverse selection. (d) Long-term contracts—term contracts designed to provide long-period protection, such as term to 65. (e) Nonlevel term—the amount of insurance may either increase or decrease throughout the term of the policy.*

3. *Renewable term insurance contracts contain an option to renew for a limited number of additional periods of term insurance, usually of the same length. The key to the renewable feature is the right to renew the contract without a medical examination or other evidence of insurability. Where the term policy contains no renewal privilege, or where it can be renewed only upon evidence of insurability satisfactory to the company, the insured may find that coverage cannot be continued as long as needed. Because of poor health, a hazardous occupation, or some other reason, the insured might be unable to secure a renewal of the contract or to obtain any other form of life insurance protection. The renewal feature prevents this situation. Its chief function is to protect the insurability of the named insured.*

4. *If the term policy is converted as of the current date, conversion is usually referred to as the attained-age method because the current age determines the premium level. A conversion using the original date of the term policy for the conversion is referred to as the original-age method or a retroactive conversion. Retroactive conversion offers both advantages and disadvantages when compared with attained-age conversion.*

    Advantages include (1) the lower premium and (2) the possibility that the contract being issued at the original date contains actuarial assumptions or other features more favorable than those being incorporated in current policies. Offsetting these advantages, however,

is the fact that a financial adjustment—involving a payment by the insured to the company—is required, which may be quite substantial if the term policy has been in force for several years. This adjustment may be computed on a variety of bases, but a great number of companies specify that the payment will be the larger of (1) the difference in the reserves (in some companies, the cash surrender values) under the policies being exchanged or (2) the difference in the premiums paid on the term policy and those that would have been paid on the permanent plan, with interest on the difference at a stipulated rate.

5. *The purpose of a time limit on conversion is to minimize adverse selection. There is always a substantial degree of adverse selection in the conversion process. As the time for conversion approaches, those policyowners in poor health are more likely to convert and pay the higher premiums than those who believe themselves to be in good health. If the decision to convert must be made some years before the expiration of the term policy, a higher percentage of healthy policyowners, uncertain of their health some years hence, will elect to convert. If the term of the policy is no longer than 10 years, a conversion as of a current date can usually be accomplished throughout the full term. If the term is longer than 10 years, the policy may stipulate that the conversion privilege must be exercised, if at all, before the expiration of a period shorter than the term of the policy. For example, a 15-year term policy must usually be converted, if at all, within 12 years from date of issue, a 20-year term policy within 15 years.*

   If the policy is renewable, the only time limitation may be that it is converted before age 60 or 65. In other cases, the contract will state that the policy must be converted within a certain period before the expiration of the last term for which it can be renewed. Some companies issue term policies that are automatically converted at the expiration of the term to a specified plan of permanent insurance.

6. *Unlike traditional forms of term insurance that have a single premium schedule for a given policy, select and ultimate (re-entry) term insurance is a policy subject to two different premium schedules. The lower premium rate is based on the select mortality (that applicable to an insured who has recently given evidence that he or she is in good health). The select rates are available as long as the insured is able to provide new evidence of insurability at each renewable date and at other dates specified by the insurer. The higher premium schedule is based on ultimate mortality rates (that applicable to insureds at least 15 or 20 years after they last provided evidence of insurability). The insured who cannot provide evidence of insurability acceptable to the insurance company when requested or required must pay the higher premium schedule rates to renew their coverage. The rates in*

the higher premium schedule in a re-entry term policy are considerably higher at each age than those in the single premium schedule used in a traditional term insurance policy.

7. *Term to 65 policies (1) are designed to provide long-period protection, (2) often give pro-spective policyowners the option to purchase waiver-of-premium and accidental death benefits, and (3) customarily provide for cash and other surrender values.*

8. *Term insurance is suitable when either (1) the need for protection is purely temporary or (2) the need for protection is permanent, but the insured temporarily cannot afford the pre-miums for permanent insurance. Examples of temporary needs that can—and should—be met through term insurance are encountered daily. A parent with young children is likely to need more insurance while the children are dependent than he or she will need when they have grown and become self-sufficient. The additional insurance during the child-raising period can be—and usually is—provided through term insurance.*

    Term insurance can also be used to hedge a loan. A term policy in the amount of the loan payable to the lender not only protects the lender against possible loss of principal but also relieves the insured's estate of the burden of repaying the loan if the insured dies. A mort-gage redemption policy serves the same purpose. An individual who has invested heavily in a speculative business venture should protect his or her estate and family be obtaining term insurance in the amount of the investment. If a business firm is spending a consid-erable sum in an experimental project, the success of which depends on the talents and abilities of one individual or a few individuals, term insurance on the appropriate person or persons will protect the investment.

    The second function of term insurance is particularly important to young people who expect substantial improvement in their financial situation as the years go by. Young pro-fessionals who have made a considerable investment in their education and training, but whose practices must be built up gradually, are likely prospects for term insurance. Young business executives are also good prospects.

Chapter 5

Whole Life Insurance

By Dan M. McGill

Revised by C.W. Copeland & Dave Moon

Learning Objectives

An understanding of the material in this chapter should enable the student to

1. **Describe and understand the features of whole life insurance policies.**

2. **Explain how joint life policies work and differentiate them from single-life policies.**

3. **Understand how limited-payment whole life policies differ from ordinary life policies.**

4. **Explain how some policies may be considered different because of insurer underwriting.**

5. **Describe and understand the current assumption variations of life insurance.**

6. **Understand the concept of endowment life insurance, and be aware that many endowment policies are still in force.**

7. **Understand the adjustable life policy design.**

ordinary life

limited-payment life

In contrast with term insurance, which pays benefits only if the insured dies during a specified period of years, whole life insurance provides for the payment of the policy's face amount upon the death of the insured, regardless of when death occurs. It is this characteristic—protection for the whole of life—that gives the insurance its name. The expression has no reference to the manner in which the premiums are paid, only to the duration of the protection. If the premiums are to be paid throughout the insured's lifetime, the insurance is known as **ordinary life**; if premiums are to be paid only during a specified period, the insurance is designated **limited-payment life**. Hence there are two principal types of whole life contracts:

- ordinary life insurance
- limited-payment life insurance

PRINCIPAL TYPES OF WHOLE LIFE INSURANCE

Ordinary Life Insurance

Ordinary life insurance (also called continuous premium whole life) is a type of whole life insurance for which premiums are based on the assumption that they will be paid until the insured's death. It is desirable to define ordinary life insurance this way since, in an increasing number of cases, life insurance is purchased with no intention on the policy-owner's part to pay premiums as long as the insured lives. In many cases the insurance is purchased as part of a program that contemplates the use of dividends to pay up the insurance by the end of a period shorter than the life expectancy of the insured. In other cases the plan may be to eventually surrender insurance for an annuity or for a reduced amount of insurance. The point is that ordinary life should not be envisioned as a type of insurance on which the policyowner is irrevocably committed to pay premiums as long as the insured lives or even into the insured's extreme old age. Rather, it should be viewed as a type of policy that provides permanent protection for the lowest total premium outlay and some degree of flexibility to meet changing needs and circumstances for both long-lived persons and those with average-duration lifetimes. It is the most basic lifelong policy offered by any life insurance company, and it enjoys the widest sale. Ordinary life insurance is an appropriate foundation for any insurance program, and in an adequate amount it could well serve as the entire program. Its distinctive features are discussed below.

Permanent Protection

The protection afforded by the ordinary life contract is permanent—the term never expires, and the policy never has to be renewed or converted. If insureds continue to pay premiums or pay up their policy, they have protection for as long as they live, regardless of their health; eventually, the face amount of the policy will be paid. This is a valuable right because virtually all people need some insurance as long as they live, if for nothing more than to pay last-illness and funeral expenses. In most cases the need is much greater than that.

In one sense ordinary life can be regarded as an endowment. As discussed later in this chapter, an endowment insurance contract pays the face amount of the policy, whether the insured dies prior to the endowment maturity date or survives to the end of the period. If age 100 is considered to be the end of the endowment period—as well as the end of the mortality table—then an ordinary life policy is equivalent to an endowment contract that pays the face amount as a death claim if the insured dies before age 100 or as a matured endowment if he or she survives to age 100.

During the years when the American Experience Table of Mortality (which has a terminal age of 96) was being used for new insurance, many insurers labeled their ordinary life contract as an "endowment at 96." For that matter, many companies today offer an "endowment at 95" in lieu of an ordinary life contract. Ironically, many prospects will buy an "endowment at 95" when they will not buy an ordinary life policy. Of course, the ordinary life policy could just as aptly be described as a "level premium term to 100" if it were to be assumed that all individuals who survive to age 99 die before their 100th birthday.

Lowest Premium Outlay

Inasmuch as the premium rate for an ordinary life contract is calculated on the assumption that premiums will be payable throughout the whole of life, the lowest rate is produced. As will be noted later, the net single premium for a whole life policy is computed without reference to the manner in which the periodic premiums will be paid and, at any particular age, is the same for ordinary life insurance and any form of limited-payment life insurance. Naturally, the longer the period over which the single-sum payment is spread, the lower each periodic payment will be.

Thus, the net annual level premium per $1,000 of ordinary life insurance, issued at age 25 and calculated on the basis of the 1980 CSO Male Table and 4.5 percent interest, is only $7.49, while the comparable net annual level premium for a 20-payment life policy is $11.07. The gross annual premiums[1] per $1,000 charged by two life insurance companies for the same two contracts at ages 25 and 35 are shown in Table 5-1.

Limited-payment insurance contracts provide benefits that justify the higher premium rates. If, however, the insured's objective is to secure the maximum amount of permanent insurance protection per dollar of premium outlay, then his or her purposes will be best served by the ordinary life contract. Its moderate cost brings the policy within reach of all people except those in the older age brackets.

Table 5-1				
Sample Gross Annual Premiums per $1,000				
	Ordinary Whole Life		20-Pay Whole Life	
Issue Age	Company A	Company B	Company A	Company B
25	$9.28	$11.90	$13.28	$17.70
35	$ 13.21	$16.90	$19.26	$22.50

---

1. The gross premium is the premium actually paid by the policyowner. It is the net premium increased by an allowance for the insurer's expenses and contingencies.

Cash Value or Accumulation Element

cash value

accumulation element

As level premium permanent insurance, ordinary life accumulates a reserve that gradually reaches a substantial level and eventually equals the face amount of the policy. As is to be expected, however, the reserve at all durations is lower than that of the other forms of permanent insurance. In other words, the protection element tends to be relatively high. Nevertheless, it is the opinion of many that the ordinary life contract offers the optimal combination of protection and savings. The contract emphasizes protection, but it also accumulates a **cash value** that can be used to accomplish a variety of purposes (**accumulation element**).

The cash values that accumulate under an ordinary life contract can be utilized as surrender values, paid-up insurance, or extended term insurance (whose significance will be explained in the next section of this chapter). Cash values are not generally available during the first year or two of the insurance because of the cost to the company of putting the business on the books. Common exceptions are single-premium policies and some durations of limited-payment whole life policies whose first-year premiums are large enough to exceed all first-year expenses incurred to create the policy and maintain policy reserves.

Policy Loans. All level premium life insurance policies that develop cash values (for example, whole life, universal life, adjustable life, variable life, variable universal life, and current assumption whole life) have provisions for policy loans. These policy loans give the policyowner access to the cash value that accumulates inside the policy without having to terminate the policy.

The policyowner merely requests a loan and the life insurer will lend the funds confidentially. The loan provisions in the policy specify what portion of the cash value is available for loans and how interest will be determined on the loan. In most policies over 90 percent of the cash value is available for loans—some policies may restrict the amount of loanable funds to 92 percent of the cash value in recognition of an 8 percent policy loan interest rate—and any portion of the cash value can be borrowed. Policyowners indicate in their requests the amount desired, and they can take out more than one policy loan as long as the aggregate amount of all outstanding loans and accrued interest applicable to those loans does not exceed the policy cash value.

Policy loans do involve interest charged on the borrowed funds. There are two different approaches to setting the policy loan interest rate. The policy will stipulate either (1) a fixed rate as specified in the policy (commonly 8 percent) or (2) a variable interest rate tied by formula to some specified index. One variable approach is to use Moody's composite yield on seasoned corporate bonds or some index that is regularly published in the financial press, such as The Wall Street Journal or The Journal of Commerce. Another index may be the interest rate being credited to the cash value plus a specified spread.

State laws impose changing upper limits on variable policy loan interest rates. These laws require that the rate be lowered whenever the upper limit drops to more than half of 1 percent below the rate being charged. The rate charged can be changed up to four times each year.

The policyowner has the option of paying the policy loan interest in cash or having the unpaid interest charge added to the balance of the outstanding loan(s) so that additional interest charges will be applied to the unpaid interest amount. The policyowner may choose to pay any part of the interest charge he or she desires since there is no repayment schedule or requirement.

The policyowner is not required to pay the interest or repay the policy loan in cash. If any repayments are made, they are totally at the discretion of the policyowner as to both timing and amount.

If the policy loan and accrued interest are not paid in cash, the life insurer can recover the outstanding balance of the loans and accrued interest in the following ways: (1) from the death benefits if the insured dies or (2) from the cash surrender value if the policy is terminated. In fact, the policy will automatically terminate if the policy loan balance plus unpaid interest ever exceeds the policy cash value.

Some whole life policies give policyowners an automatic premium loan option. When this option is selected, a delinquent premium will be paid automatically by a new policy loan. This will keep the policy in force as long as there is adequate cash value to cover each delinquent premium. However, the policy will terminate if the cash value is exhausted.

The automatic premium loan provision does not apply to flexible premium policies because the insurer usually deducts mortality charges and other expenses directly from the cash value. Hence no interest charges are incurred for skipped premium payments.

The creation of a policy loan does have negative consequences on benefits and may reduce the amount credited to the cash value and/or the level of policyowner dividends. The death benefit payable to the beneficiary is reduced by the full amount of outstanding

policy loans and accrued interest under most types of policies. Therefore, an irrevocable beneficiary's consent may be required to obtain a policy loan. A policy loan is really an advance against the death benefit; thus the death benefit is adjusted to reflect the prior disbursement.

Policy loans result in the life insurer's release of funds it would otherwise invest to earn investment income. If the rate of investment return on the insurer's portfolio is greater than the rate being applied to the policy loan, the insurer experiences a reduction in earnings. Therefore the insurance company usually takes steps to offset such loan-induced losses in order to preserve a rough equity between policyowners who leave their cash values invested and those who preclude the insurer from reaping the higher yield. In traditional participating whole life policies, policyowner dividends were not affected by policy loans, but most participating whole life policies being sold today use what is called "direct recognition" to reduce dividends on policies with outstanding loans. This not only adjusts for the differential in earnings but also discourages policy loans. For universal life policies and other non-participating designs, there are no dividends to adjust; insurers compensate for lost earnings by reducing the earnings rate being credited directly to the cash value. If there are no policy loans, the insurer credits its normal crediting rate to the full cash value. However, if there are policy loans, the insurer typically credits the normal rate to the unloaned portion of the cash value and a lower rate (often 2 percent or 200 basis points lower) to the portion of the cash value equal to the loan indebtedness. Once the loan is repaid, the insurer resumes crediting the higher rate to the full cash value. There is no retroactive payment to eliminate the past differential.

Outstanding policy loans reduce both death benefits and nonforfeiture benefits. The net cash value available to provide either extended term insurance or reduced paid-up insurance is lessened by the loan indebtedness. In the case of extended term insurance, the amount of term insurance is reduced from the original amount of coverage by the amount of loan indebtedness as well.

State statutes allow life insurers to delay lending funds for up to 6 months after requested. This is a form of emergency protection in case policyowners' demand for loans accelerates to the point that the insurer is forced to liquidate other assets at significant losses to satisfy the loan demands. In actuality, delaying access to funds is an indication of financial weakness or lack of policyowner confidence that insurers wish to avoid. Those life insurers that have failed in recent years chose not to invoke their right to delay policy loan disbursements. Quick access to cash values was terminated only after the insurance commissioner seized control of the company.

Policy Loan Features

- Available on demand of policyowner

- Interest charges apply

- Depending on the specific contract, interest rates are either fixed or variable

- Variable interest rates tied to a published index

- Unpaid interest charges get added to loan balance

- Repayment of loans is at discretion of policyowner

- Outstanding policy loans plus unpaid interest is recovered from either death benefit or surrender value

- Outstanding loans plus unpaid interest reduce nonforfeiture values

- Policy terminates if loans plus unpaid interest ever exceed the policy cash value

Conversion. A final source of flexibility is the right to convert to other forms of insurance. It is customary to include a provision in all whole life policies giving the insured the right to exchange the policy for another type of contract, sometimes subject to certain conditions. Whether this privilege is specifically granted or not, an exchange can usually be negotiated. Virtually all companies will permit any form of permanent insurance to be converted to another form without evidence of insurability, as long as the new contract calls for a larger premium.

Most companies, however, will not permit a higher-premium contract to be exchanged for a lower-premium contract without evidence of insurability. Such an exchange not only reduces future premiums but also requires the company to return a portion of the reserve to the insured, thereby increasing the actual amount at risk. Moreover, insurers always suspect an impairment of health under such circumstances.[2] If the insured is converting to a higher-premium form, however, the net amount at risk will be reduced more rapidly, and the company does not have to fear adverse selection.

The ordinary life contract has a unique advantage in this regard because it is the lowest-premium form of fixed-premium permanent insurance and hence can be converted to any other form of permanent insurance without evidence of insurability. Therefore the

---

2.   Some companies are willing to issue a policy on a lower-premium plan without evidence of insurability if the amount of insurance is increased to such an extent that the company is relieved of the obligation to refund a portion of the reserve and suffers no reduction in premium income.

insured, whose savings objective may entail substantial amounts of limited-payment insurance but whose current financial situation limits the funds available for insurance, might well inaugurate his or her insurance program with ordinary life, with the idea of converting it later to higher-premium forms. If feasible, ordinary life is preferable to term insurance under such circumstances since, if the more ambitious program is never realized, the insured will still have permanent protection and a modest cash surrender value. Moreover, if conversion is ultimately effected, the financial adjustment involved—whether it be the lump-sum payment of the difference in reserves or merely a shift to the higher-premium basis—will not be so drastic.

Participating versus Nonparticipating

Whole life policies can be issued on a nonparticipating basis with fixed and guaranteed premiums. This version of whole life does not pay any policyowner dividends. The insurance company retains all gains from favorable experience. Historically, nonparticipating policies were associated with stock life insurance companies (owned by stock holders).

Whole life policies issued on a participating basis anticipate charging a small extra margin in the fixed premium with the intent to return part of the premium in the form of policyowner dividends. This approach allows the insurer to maintain a stronger contingency margin and still adjust the cost downward after periods of coverage have been evaluated. Policyowner dividends are based on favorable experience such as higher than expected investment returns or lower than expected expenses for operations and/or mortality.

Although participating policies were originally offered by mutual life insurers (owned by policyowners), the appeal of policyowner dividends prompted stock life insurance companies to offer participating policies. Most stock life insurance companies offer a choice of both participating and nonparticipating policies. Almost all policies sold by mutual companies are participating policies.

Policyowner dividends are generally declared annually based on the insurance company experience. Investment results usually account for the largest portion of dividends. The amount of dividends cannot be guaranteed and it is illegal for an agent to present projections of future dividends as if they were guaranteed or certain. If insurance company experience turns unfavorable, policyowner dividends may decline or even cease altogether. Dividend reductions have been common during the 1990s.

Policy Dividends

- Payable on participating policies issued by either mutual or stock companies

- Primarily influenced by investment results

- Future dividend levels cannot be guaranteed

- May decline or even cease

The policyowner chooses the dividend option to which actual dividends are applied. In addition to direct payment, dividends can be (1) used to reduce premium payment, (2) used to purchase additional fully paid-up insurance (often called paid-up additions), (3) accumulated by the insurance companies to earn interest on behalf of the policyowner (similar to a savings account), (4) used to purchase term insurance, and (5) used to increase premiums and make the policy paid up at an earlier age than originally anticipated.

Dividend Forms

- Cash

- Applied to premium

- Used to purchase more insurance (fully paid up)

- Left with insurer to earn interest

- Used to purchase more insurance (term)

- To overpay premiums until policy is fully paid up

Limited-Payment Life Insurance

Limited-payment life insurance is a type of whole life insurance for which premiums are limited by contract to a specified number of years. The extreme end of the limited-payment policies spectrum is the single-premium whole life policy. However, few people can afford the premium or are willing to pay that much in advance.

The limitation in limited-payment policies may be expressed in terms of the number of annual premiums or of the age beyond which premiums will not be required. Policies whose premiums are limited by number usually stipulate 1, 5, 7, 10, 15, 20, 25, or 30 annual payments, although some companies are willing to issue policies calling for any desired number of premiums. The greater the number of premiums payable, naturally, the more

closely the contract approaches the ordinary life design. For those who prefer to limit their premium payments to a period measured by a terminal age, companies make policies available that are paid up at a specified age—typically, 60, 65, or 70. The objective is to enable the insured to pay for the policy during his or her working lifetime. Many companies issue contracts for which premiums are payable to an advanced age, such as 85, but for all practical purposes, these contracts can be regarded as the equivalent of ordinary life contracts.

Since the value of a limited-payment whole life contract at the date of issue is precisely the same as that of a contract purchased on the ordinary life basis, and since it is presumed that there will be fewer premium payments under the limited-payment policy, it follows that each premium must be larger than the comparable premium under an ordinary life contract. Moreover, the fewer the guaranteed premiums specified or the shorter the premium-paying period, the higher each premium will be. However, the higher premiums are offset by greater cash and other surrender values. Thus the limited-payment policy will provide a larger fund for use in an emergency and will accumulate a larger fund for retirement purposes than will an ordinary life contract issued at the same age. On the other hand, if death takes place within the first several years after issue of the contract, the total premiums paid under the limited-payment policy will exceed those payable under an ordinary life policy. The comparatively long-lived policyowner, however, will pay considerably less in premiums under the limited-payment plan than on the ordinary life basis.

There is no presumptive financial advantage between forms. The choice depends on circumstances and personal preference. The limited-payment policy offers the assurance that premium payments will be confined to the insured's productive years, while the ordinary life contract provides maximum permanent protection for any given annual outlay. The limited-payment policy contains the same surrender options, dividend options, settlement options, and other features that make for significant flexibility.

An extreme form of limited-payment contract is the single-premium life insurance policy. Under this plan the number of premiums is limited to one. The effective amount of insurance protection is, of course, substantially less than the face amount of the policy, and the investment element is correspondingly greater. Such contracts therefore are purchased largely for accumulation purposes. They offer a high degree of security, a satisfactory interest yield, and ready convertibility into cash on a basis guaranteed by the insurer for the entire duration of the contract. Since the single premium represents a substantial amount of money and since it is computed on the basis that there will be no return of any part of it in the event of the insured's early death, it has only limited appeal for protection purposes.

The limited-payment principle is applicable to any type of contract and is frequently used in connection with endowment contracts. However, it is important to differentiate between a limited-payment policy (in which paid-up status is guaranteed at the end of the premium-paying period) and a premiums-paid-by-dividend approach (which uses policyowner dividends to pay all of the premiums after they are adequate to do so). Premiums-paid-by-dividend approaches have been sold much more frequently than limited-payment policies over the last decade under the misnomer of vanishing premium. The notable difference between the two is that under the misnamed vanishing-premium approach dividends are not guaranteed and may decline in the future. If dividends turn out to be inadequate to pay the premiums, the policyowner will have to resume actual premium payments out of pocket or let the policy lapse. There is no guarantee that so-called vanishing premiums will actually vanish or that if they do vanish, they will never reappear.

JOINT LIFE INSURANCE

joint-life policy

The typical life insurance contract is written on the life of one person and is technically known as single-life insurance. A contract can be written on more than one life, however, in which event it is known as a joint life contract, also called a first-to-die **joint life policy**. Strictly speaking, a joint life contract is one written on the lives of two or more persons and payable upon the death of the first person to die. If the face amount is payable upon the death of the last of two or more lives insured under a single contract, it is called either a survivorship policy or a second-to-die policy. Such policies have become quite popular as a means of funding federal estate taxes of wealthy couples whose wills make maximum use of tax deferral at the first death. Joint life policies are fairly common for funding business buy-sell agreements.

The joint life policy may cover from two to 12 lives, but because of expense and other practical obstacles, most companies limit the number to three or four lives. (Theoretically there is no limit on the number of lives that can be insured under a joint contract. A few insurers will issue policies on more than 12 lives if they all have related business interests.) The contract is most often written on the whole life plan, either ordinary life, limited-payment or universal life. It is seldom written on the term plan since separate term policies on each life for the same amount would cost little more than a joint policy and would offer the advantage of continued protection to the survivor or survivors.

The premium for a joint life policy is somewhat greater than the combined premiums on separate policies providing an equivalent amount of insurance. In other words, the

premium for a $200,000 joint life policy covering two lives is larger than the sum of the premiums on two separate contracts providing $100,000 each. This is because only $100,000 is payable upon the death of the first of the two insureds to die with separate policies, while $200,000 is payable under a joint life policy. Moreover, since two lives are covered, the cost of insurance is relatively high, and cash values are relatively low. However, a joint life policy costs less than two separate policies providing $200,000 each.

The provisions of the joint life contract closely follow those of the single-life contract. The clause allowing conversion to other policy forms differs in that it allows conversion policies on separate lives as follows: (1) conversion to single-life policies on the same plan as that of the joint policies upon divorce or dissolution of business, (2) division of the amount of insurance among the insured lives either equally or unequally, and (3) dating of the new policies as of the original date of issue of the joint policy.

Business partners sometimes take out a joint policy covering the lives of all partners and written for an amount equal to the largest interest involved. Upon the death of the first partner, the surviving partners receive funds with which to purchase the deceased's partnership interest. Stockholders in a closely held corporation may follow the same practice. Because the insurance usually terminates upon the first death of the partners or stockholders, the remaining members of the firm will not only be without insurance but—of greater consequence—may also be uninsurable. Some life insurers have introduced joint life policies that are designed specifically for business buy-sell funding. Some of them offer a short period of extended coverage for the surviving partners or shareholders and guarantee their insurability under a new joint life policy similar to the previous one. A few insurers have even introduced joint life policies that allow allocations of unequal amounts of death proceeds to match actual unequal ownership interests.

Joint Life Features

- Insure more than one life with one policy

- Pay only one death benefit

- First-to-die policies pay death benefit when the first death of the insureds occurs

- Survivorship or second-to-die policies pay death benefit when the second insured person dies (no benefit at first death)

- Survivorship policies often used to prefund federal estate taxes of husband and wife

- May be converted to single-life policies if insureds divorce or dissolve their business relationship

A joint life policy may be suitable for a husband and wife when the death of either will create a need for funds, as would be true if death taxes were involved. Even here, dissatisfaction sometimes arises when the survivor faces the fact that he or she no longer has any coverage under the contract.

"SPECIAL" WHOLE LIFE INSURANCE

One of the most controversial recent developments in the life insurance industry is the widespread introduction and vigorous promotion of "special" policies. Usually on the ordinary life plan, these policies carry a premium rate lower than those of the regular forms. Such policies have long been offered by many companies, but in recent years many more companies have begun to offer them to meet the growing price competition.

preferred risks

A company may justify a special low rate on a particular policy—which, in all other respects, is identical to the regular policy—by limiting the face to a specified minimum amount or by limiting its issue to **preferred risks**—that is, to groups that should experience a lower rate of mortality than that among insured lives generally because of more rigorous underwriting requirements. In some cases, both practices are factors.

The purpose of the minimum amount is to reduce the expense rate per $1,000 of insurance. Many items of expense reflected in a policy's gross premium are not affected by the policy's face amount—for example, the medical examiner's fee, inspection fee, accounting costs, and general overhead. If the average size of the policy can be increased, therefore, the expense rate per $1,000 will be lower. A class of policies in which the minimum face amount is $50,000 can be expected to develop an average face amount double that of the regular classes in which the minimum is $10,000. Some companies do not offer their special policy in less than a specified amount ($50,000, $100,000, $250,000, $500,000, or $1 million, for example). The savings in the expense rate alone can be quite substantial. Then, because the gross premium is lower, expenses that vary directly with the size of the premium—notably, commissions and premium taxes—will also be less per $1,000 of insurance. In fact, in many companies the commission rate on special policies is lower than that on other whole life policies.

The savings realized by superior selection depend on the nature of the standards imposed, the test of which is actual mortality experience. The potential savings are fairly large since selection standards have a significant impact on mortality rates. Furthermore, preferred-risk policies are almost always issued on a minimum-amount basis and thus reap the

expense savings described above. At most ages and in most companies, the difference in premiums between a special whole life policy and a regular ordinary life policy ranges from $2 to $3 per $1,000. On a multimillion-dollar policy, the savings can be very attractive.

The case for special policies is based largely on the grounds of equity. If a policyowner takes out a policy of such size that its expense rate is lower than average, or if he or she is a better risk than average, the policyowner should be given the benefit of the savings in the form of a lower premium.

The principal argument against bargain policies is the arbitrary nature of the underlying classification. For example, the reasons that justify a lower expense loading per $1,000 for a policy of $200,000 than for one of $50,000 argue just as forcefully for an even lower rate for a $1 million policy, a $2 million policy, and so on. In fact, the logical conclusion is that premium rates per $1,000 should decrease as the size of the policy increases. However desirable such a practice might be from the standpoint of equity, it would tremendously complicate the operation of the business and might, in fact, be impractical. Furthermore, limiting the expense discount to policies of $50,000 or over, or limiting it to any other arbitrary amount, is only partial recognition of the relatively lower expenses on large policies.

By the same token, if the principle of granting a lower rate to superior risks is sound, it should be extended to all other kinds of policies and not be limited to the whole life variety.[3] The soundness of the principle has been questioned in some quarters, however, on the grounds that it is contrary to the basic insurance principle of averaging. It is argued that to get average results, coverage of large groups is essential—which, from a practical standpoint, requires including people with widely varying prospects of longevity in the same group. Some insureds must bear more than their theoretically accurate share of mortality costs, while others will contribute less than their true share.

While not a part of the argument for or against special policies, it should be observed that placing larger policies or superior risks in a separate class with a lower premium rate inevitably results in a higher cost of insurance for smaller policies and insureds who cannot qualify as preferred risks.

FUNCTIONS OF WHOLE LIFE INSURANCE

At this point, the purposes served by whole life insurance should be clear. In summary, the whole life policy

---

3.   As a matter of fact, this is now being done on an increasingly broader basis through a system of graded premiums.

- provides protection against long-range or permanent needs
- accumulates a savings fund that can be used for general purposes or to meet specific objectives

The protection function is particularly applicable to a surviving spouse's need for a life income, last-illness and funeral expenses, expenses of estate administration, death taxes, philanthropic bequests, and the needs of dependent relatives other than the surviving spouse. The general savings feature of the whole life policy is useful in a financial emergency or as a source of funds to take advantage of an unusual business or investment opportunity. The policyowner may use the policy for the specific purpose of accumulating funds for his or her children's college education, to set a child up in business, to pay for a child's wedding, or to supplement the insured's retirement income.

CURRENT ASSUMPTION WHOLE LIFE

current assumption whole life

Current assumption whole life is a variation of traditional whole life that lies somewhere between adjustable life and universal life. Its cash value development is more like that of universal life than any other policy. It has a redetermination feature that essentially recasts the premium amount, and in some instances the death benefit, in reaction to the most recent interval of experience. That interval varies from one company to another but is frequently 5 years, although it can be as short as 2 years or as long as 7 years. The main feature that differentiates current assumption whole life from universal life is the absence of total premium flexibility in the renewal years (see figure below).

Current assumption whole life is sometimes described as universal life with fixed premiums. This is an oversimplification since premiums can and will be restructured at specified policy anniversary dates. However, the analogy is probably useful in getting a mental image of this type of policy and how it differs from the traditional whole life policy, the adjustable life policy, and the universal life policy. It is just another example of refinements in policy design that fill in some of the missing points along a continuum of possibilities between both extremes—all fixed components and guarantees at one end and all flexible and nonguaranteed components at the other.

interest-sensitive whole life policy

There are still quite a few guaranteed elements in current assumption whole life policies. There is a guaranteed death benefit and a minimum guaranteed interest rate to be

credited on policy cash values. Some companies guarantee the mortality charge and the expense charges. When mortality and expense charges are guaranteed, the policy is often referred to as an **interest-sensitive whole life policy** because excess interest (credited interest minus guaranteed interest) credited to the cash value becomes the only nonguaranteed element in the contract. However, the bulk of the current assumption whole life policies have some degree of flexibility in the expense elements. Because many of these designs periodically recast the premium amount based on recognition of the most recent interval of experience, some of these policies are referred to as indeterminate premium whole life policies. The idea is that there is a guaranteed maximum possible premium that could be charged, but the actual mortality, interest, and expenses give rise to lower premium amounts actually being assessed as a result of favorable experience under the policy.

Current assumption whole life policies are nonparticipating policies that have some after-the-fact adjustment mechanisms without actually creating explicit policyowner cash dividends. These adjustment mechanisms allow the insurer to constantly fine-tune its policy and keep it competitive in the marketplace, based on actual company experience underlying the particular blocks of policies. From a company standpoint one of the big advantages of this policy design is its ability to eliminate the need for any deficiency reserve for the block of policies. Policy reserves can be calculated on the basis of the maximum chargeable premium and the minimum interest rate guarantee. Reserves will always be based on these factors even though the premiums actually collected are lower than the premium assumption underlying the reserve and, more important, are less than the guideline premium for reserve valuation.

Figure 5-1
Current Assumption Whole Life Type I or A
Premiums Changed at Policy Redetermination Anniversary Date

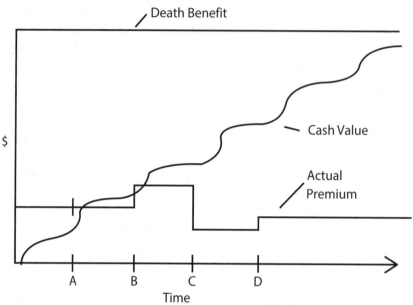

For competitive purposes in the marketplace, current assumption whole life gives the insurance company a product with a mechanism for sharing favorable investment returns with policyowners. These policies take away the advantage that participating whole life policies had over nonparticipating whole life policies. They are not so rigid that a change in market conditions automatically renders them obsolete, as was the unfortunate case with nonparticipating whole life policies before 1980. Most of the insurance companies offering current assumption whole life policies are stock insurance companies that sold mainly nonparticipating whole life contracts prior to 1980.

Most current assumption whole life policies base their maximum possible mortality rate on one of the Commissioners Standard Ordinary (CSO) Table rates (1980 or 2001). Because most insurance companies experience mortality significantly less costly than indicated by the CSO rates, the differential provides a very large safety margin for the insurer if it is later necessary to increase mortality rates and possibly even increase premiums on policy anniversaries when redetermination occurs.

Cash Value Illustrations

There are some variations in the way insurance companies approach the illustration of current assumption whole life policies. As with every other type of illustration, an insurance company tries to have its illustration be enough different from any other company's that the illustrations are not directly comparable. Nevertheless, it is possible to classify these variations into two basic categories.

The first basic category has a guaranteed cash value column and a separate column for excess accumulations (or some other descriptive title indicating that these values supplement the guaranteed cash value amounts). The total cash value for the policy is the sum of the guaranteed cash value and the accumulation supplements. The most complete representation tends to have three different columns for cash values—one for the guaranteed amount, one for the excess accumulations, and one representing the total of the two components. Any insurance company has wide discretion in how it depicts this approach in its illustrations. For example, illustrations often depict only the total cash value column and may or may not explicitly indicate that the cash value depends on projections of nonguaranteed amounts.

The second basic category merely has a single column titled "Enhanced Cash Value" (or an equivalent thereof). There is rarely any inclusion of the guaranteed cash value amount. This approach makes the policy look more like the cash value accumulation account reported under most universal life policies: premiums are shown as an incoming item that is reduced by expense charges before being added to the cash value account. Interest on the account balance is usually credited before any mortality charges are deducted. After mortality charges are deducted, the end-of-year fund balance is derived. The significant difference between the accumulation accounts in current assumption whole life and universal life is that universal life policies tend to charge off both expenses and mortality before crediting investment earnings. Current assumption whole life policies tend to deduct expenses from premiums but then credit that amount to the cash value and reflect a credit for investment earnings before deducting a mortality charge.

This approach has led many people to describe current assumption whole life as a hybrid of universal life and traditional whole life because it has cash value accumulations of excess interest crediting but still maintains a rigid level premium structure that can be changed on redetermination anniversaries.

Low Premium/High Premium Designs

The proportion of excess accumulations under these policy designs is highly dependent on the premium level in the base design.

Some insurance companies use a relatively low-premium current assumption whole life design. Adjustments on redetermination dates are more likely to involve an adjustment of the death benefit to make the policy compatible with the premium level being paid. However, sometimes adjustments are to the premium (up or down) which may or may not change the death benefit. At the other end of the spectrum some insurers utilize a high-premium design of current assumption whole life, where the premium paid is usually more than adequate and normally does not ever require an upward adjustment on a redetermination date. The high-premium design is more likely to involve projections of how long premiums may be needed until the policy is expected to be self-supporting without further contributions from the policyowner. It is a form of misnamed vanishing premium design. The caution, however, is that excess accumulations are not guaranteed; nor is the projected period of premium payments guaranteed to make the policy fully paid up at the end of that period. The policy will be paid up only if the future experience under the policy from that date forward is such that the interest credited and the accumulated account generate enough funds to meet all mortality charges and expenses over the entire remainder of the contract. There are no guarantees that this accumulation account might not have to be supplemented at some point if mortality charges and expenses cost more than the accumulation account can provide.

On the optimistic side, the policy could continue to exceed expectations even after it reaches paid-up status. If the investment returns on the accumulated fund keep the balance in that account more than adequate to pay all mortality charges and expenses, the policy could continue to enhance the benefits on each redetermination date. This would most likely involve an increase in death benefits since there are no further premiums to reduce at that point.

Redetermination

redetermination

The level of premiums influences the frequency of **redetermination**. The lower the premium design, the more frequent the policy's redetermination dates. In some of the more recent policy designs redetermination can be every year; more often the redetermination frequency is every 2 years or every 5 years. On policy anniversaries when redetermination is applicable, the insurance company looks at its actual experience for the block of policies

since the previous redetermination date and decides what adjustments, if any, are necessary, based on the assumption that past experiences are indicative of what to expect in the period before the next redetermination.

Policyowner Options

The policyowner generally selects the method he or she prefers to adjust the policy from an available group of options when redetermination occurs. For example, if the redetermination results in a potentially lower premium, the policyowner usually has the option of continuing the past level of premiums and having the favorable results applied to enhance the policy's cash value or increase the death benefit (assuming the insured can provide satisfactory evidence of insurability), or the policyowner may choose to pay the lower policy premium amount.

When past experience is less favorable than expectations, the policyowner again has a range of options, including lowering the death benefit, increasing the premium amount, or maintaining the status quo and allowing the policy accumulation account to decrease as the mortality and expense charges exceed the investment earnings on the accumulated fund. This last choice, if available, may have restrictions on its use.

Uses of Current Assumption Whole Life

In a current assumption whole life policy current interest rates are used to enhance the accumulation account, but the policy does not provide the premium flexibility of a universal life policy. Current assumption whole life is an appropriate policy choice for individuals who need the discipline imposed by its fixed-premium design but want to participate at least in part in the positive investment returns beyond the guaranteed interest rate in the policy. Under this type of policy, the policyowner assumes some of the investment risk and a limited portion of the mortality risk. If actual experience turns out to be poor, the policy may be periodically downgraded on each redetermination date. If actual experience is positive, the policyowner participates in the upside as the quid pro quo for assuming those risks or a portion thereof. Costs in the long run may turn out to be much less than the original projections if experience is favorable enough over the duration of the contract. The real challenge with this and many other life insurance products in which policyowners assume some of the risk is to make sure policyowners understand the nature and extent of the risk being assumed.

ENDOWMENT POLICIES

As mentioned previously, level premium term insurance to age 100 is identical to whole life insurance. There is also another type of life insurance that is identical to whole life insurance—endowment at age 100. However, the majority of endowment contracts mature at ages less than 100. At earlier maturity dates they are not identical to whole life policies.

endowment life insurance

Endowment life insurance policies are a variation of whole life insurance. They not only provide level death benefits and cash values that increase with duration so that a policy's cash value equals its death benefit at maturity but they also allow the purchaser to specify the policy's maturity date.

A whole life contract provides a survivorship benefit at age 100 (120 under the 2001 CSO mortality table) that is equal to the death benefit that would have been payable prior to the insured's age 100 (see figure below). Endowment contracts merely make the same full survivorship benefit payable at younger ages. The wide variety of endowments that were available included 10-, 15-, 20-, 25-, 30-, 35-, and 40-year endowments (or longer), or the maturity date could have been a specific age of the insured, such as 55, 65, 70, or older.

The endowment contract was designed to provide a death benefit during an accumulation period that is equal to the target accumulation amount. Purchasing an endowment policy with a face amount equal to the desired accumulation amount assures that the funds will be available regardless of whether the insured survives the target date. The policy was popular with purchasers who were beyond the chronological midpoint of their careers and sought accumulation for retirement or other objectives. As Dr. Solomon S. Huebner often pointed out, young people prefer term life insurance; with more experience and age, purchasers prefer whole life because of its level premiums; the mature market prefers endowments with the earlier cash value accumulations that they can use during their own lifetimes.

With the advent of double-digit inflation rates during the late 1970s and early 1980s, most consumers were moving away from long-term fixed-dollar contracts including nearly all forms of life insurance and particularly endowment policies. This happened in an economy where tax-sheltered investment in real estate had taken on a frenzied pitch as consumers turned to much shorter maturity contracts and investments. This was a reasonable reaction to runaway inflationary expectations. The tax law changes in 1986 affected endowment life insurance contracts by classifying them outside of the tax code definition of life insurance. Subsequently, few companies offer endowment contracts for sale in the United States.

Some endowment contracts are still in force in this country and endowment contracts are still sold in many other countries.

Figure 5-2
One-Year Level Term

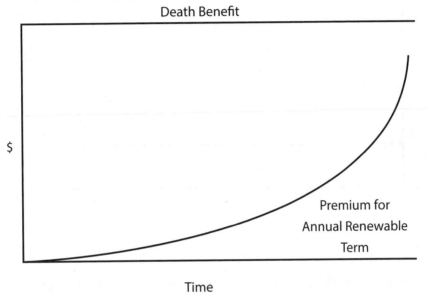

Figure 5-3
Whole Life

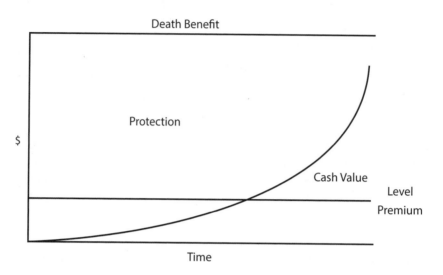

Sec. 7702

Although endowment contracts were readily available, sales were declining in the United States even before the federal income tax law was changed in 1984 to take away the tax-free buildup of flexible-premium endowment policies' cash value. Congress was concerned that life insurance policies (especially endowment and universal life) with high cash values relative to their death benefit amounts were being used as a tax-advantaged accumulation vehicle by the wealthy. Congress had, by then, developed a dislike for any form of real or perceived tax shelter. The legislators, therefore, developed a test for flexible-premium life insurance. This so-called corridor test—Sec. 101(f) of the Internal Revenue Code—took away the tax preference that flexible premium endowments previously enjoyed, although it retained the preference for policies in force before 1985. Subsequently, adding **Sec. 7702** to the Internal Revenue Code extended the corridor test to all life insurance policies (repealing Sec. 101(f), including fixed-premium endowments, entered into after October 22, 1986. (See Table 2.)

Since 1984, sales of new endowment contracts have been very limited. While contracts are still available from a few insurers, most new sales are for policies used in tax-qualified plans where the tax treatment is controlled by other factors.

Outside of the United States, especially in countries with high savings rates, however, the endowment policy is still quite successful and widely purchased to accumulate funds for a

variety of purposes. It is frequently purchased to fund retirement and sometimes to fund children's higher education.

It is interesting to note that endowment policies purchased in other countries are usually bought for the same reasons permanent life insurance policies are purchased in the United States. Regardless of the society or its tax laws, the primary factor motivating life insurance sales is an individual's concern about financial security for his or her children, spouse, parents, and/or business partners. The individual's particular needs tend to change in predictable ways over a normal life cycle.

ADJUSTABLE LIFE INSURANCE

adjustable life policy

Families' changing needs for life insurance over long durations prompted some insurers to introduce whole life insurance that can be adjusted when needed to accommodate life cycle shifts. The **adjustable life policy,** which can be configured anywhere along the spectrum from short duration term insurance through single premium whole life insurance, gives the policyowner the right to request and obtain a reconfiguration of the policy at specified intervals. It appeals to purchasers who want the ability to restructure their coverage without assuming any of the investment or mortality risks. Adjustable life insurance policies offer all of the same guarantees regarding cash values, mortality, and expenses as traditional whole life policies do. The elements subject to change are the premium, face amount, and cash value (see figure below). Most changes can be made without evidence of insurability, but the insurer can require such evidence if the proposed change increases the amount at risk.

Events that frequently prompt policy adjustments include dependent children's starting private school or entering college, the self-sufficiency of the youngest child(ren), loss of employment, the start of a new business venture, failure of a business, change of career, or retirement. As you might surmise, a large proportion of adjustments involve lowering the premium level to lessen the cash flow burden during prolonged reductions in income, increases in expenses, or both. Empty nesters, on the other hand, may request a change that increases premiums because they can often redirect their income after their children are grown.

Figure 5-4
Adjustable Life

Policy Recast at Policyowner's Request at A, B, and C

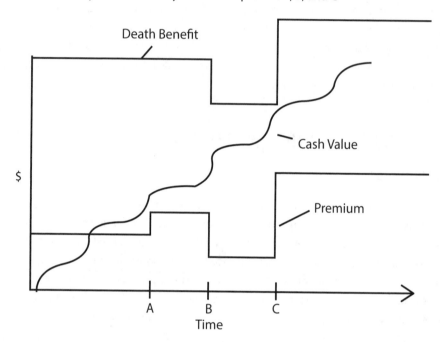

One important aspect of adjustable life is that it is a whole life policy with fixed premiums. Although premiums can be changed, such a change requires a formal adjustment agreed to by both insurer and policyowner before it can be made. The premium remains fixed and inflexible between formal adjustments.

This policy was introduced in the mid-1970s and had gained modest success with a few insurers before the advent of universal life policies (to be discussed in another chapter). Interest in adjustable life waned after the runaway success of universal life in the 1980s. Some of the insurers that maintained adjustable life as part of their product line, however, found that it had renewed acceptability after universal life lost its predominant share of new product sales in the low-interest environment since the 1990s.

Unfortunately, the terminology that has developed to describe adjustable life and universal life has been confusing. Many insurers have used the word adjustable in the title or name for their universal life policies. Consequently, many agents have come to regard adjustable

life as simply an alternate name for universal life. Many of them are unaware that generic adjustable life policies predate universal life.

CHAPTER REVIEW

Key Terms and Concepts

ordinary life
limited-payment life
cash value
accumulation element
joint-life policy
preferred risks

current assumption whole life
interest-sensitive whole life policy
redetermination
endowment life insurance
Sec. 7702
adjustable life policy

Chapter 5 Review Questions

1. Describe the general features of whole life insurance policies. [1]

2. Describe how limited-payment life insurance differs from ordinary life insurance policies. [1]

3. Explain why endowment life insurance policies have nearly disappeared in the United States marketplace. [1]

4. Describe the two distinct types of joint life insurance policies, and indicate what they are commonly used for. [2]

5. Explain how a policy loan changes the rights of (1) the beneficiary and (2) the policyowner. [1]

6. What factors can be used to separate "special" whole life policies from standard-issue whole life? [4]

7. Explain the functions of whole life insurance. [1]

8. Explain how endowment life insurance differs from whole life insurance and why endowment policies have nearly disappeared from new policy sales. [1]

9. Describe current assumption whole life insurance, and explain why some of its variations have different names in the marketplace. [5]

10. Describe the redetermination concept as it applies to current assumption whole life insurance. [5]

11. Describe current assumption whole life insurance, and explain why some of its variations have different names in the marketplace. [5]

12. Describe the redetermination concept as it applies to current assumption whole life insurance. [5]

Chapter 5 Review Answers

1. The general features of whole life insurance policies include

- *Permanent protection—whole life insurance provides for the payment of the policy's face amount upon the death of the insured, regardless of when death occurs*

- *Reserve and cash value—increase over the duration of the policy and eventually equal the face amount at the end of the policy period (usually age 100)*

- *Policy loans—give the policyowner access to the cash value that accumulates inside the policy without having to terminate the policy. Policy loans do involve interest charged on the borrowed funds. The policyowner has the option of paying the policy loan interest in cash or having the unpaid interest charge added to the balance of the outstanding loan(s) so that additional interest charges will be applied to the unpaid interest amount. If the policy loan and accrued interest are not paid in cash, the life insurer can recover the outstanding balance of the loans and accrued interest in the following ways: (1) from the death benefits if the insured dies or (2) from the cash surrender value if the policy is terminated. In fact, the policy will automatically terminate if the policy loan balance plus unpaid interest ever exceeds the policy cash value.*

- *Automatic premium loan—when this option is selected, a delinquent premium will be paid automatically by a new policy loan. This will keep the policy in force as long as*

there is adequate cash value to cover each delinquent premium. However, the policy will terminate if the cash value is exhausted.

- *Nonforfeiture or surrender options—the surrender value may be taken in cash, a reduced amount of paid-up insurance, or paid-up term insurance*
- *Annuity or retirement income—the surrender value can be used to purchase an annuity or retirement income*
- *Participating versus nonparticipating—can be purchased on a participating (pay policyowner dividends) or nonparticipating (do not provide for policyowner dividends) basis*

2. *Unlike ordinary life policies where premiums are paid until the insured's death, limited-payment life insurance is a type of whole life insurance for which premiums are limited by contract to a specified number of years. The limitation may be expressed in terms of the number of annual premiums (for example, 20-pay life) or of the age beyond which premiums will not be required (for example, life paid up to 65).*

3. *United States tax law changes have nearly eliminated endowment sales in this country.*

4. *In a broad sense, a joint-life contract is one written on the lives of two or more persons. There are two types of joint-life policies that differ in terms of when the death benefit is paid. First, in a strict sense of the term, a joint-life policy pays the death benefit upon the death of the first insured to die. These policies are used commonly to fund business buy-sell agreements. The second type, typically referred to as a survivorship policy or a second-to-die policy, pays the face amount upon the death of the last of two or more lives insured under a single contract. Such policies have become quite popular as a means of funding federal estate taxes of wealthy couples whose wills make maximum use of tax deferral at the first death.*

5. *A policy loan changes the right of the beneficiary because the outstanding balance of the loan and accrued interest are deducted from the death benefits if the insured dies. A policy loan changes the right of the policyowner since the outstanding balance of the loan and accrued interest are deducted from the cash surrender value if the policy is terminated. The latter also leads to a reduction in the extended term insurance and reduced paid-up insurance benefits available on lapse.*

6. "Special" whole life policies carry a premium rate lower than those of the standard-issue forms. A company may justify a special low rate on a particular policy—which, in all other respects, is identical to the standard-issue policy—by limiting the face to a specified minimum amount in order to reduce the expense rate per $1,000 of insurance, or by limiting its issue to preferred risks—that is, to groups that should experience a lower rate of mortality than that among insured lives generally because of more rigorous underwriting requirements. In some cases, both practices are factors.

7. The key functions of whole life insurance are (1) to provide protection against long-range or permanent needs and (2) to accumulate a savings fund that can be used for general purposes or to meet specific objectives.

8. While a whole life insurance contract provides a survivorship benefit at age 100 that is equal to the death benefit that would have been payable prior to the insured's age 100, endowment contracts make the same full survivorship benefit payable at younger ages. Among the wide variety of endowments that have been sold are 10-, 15-, 20-, 25-, 30-, 35-, and 40-year endowments (or longer), or the maturity date can be a specific age of the insured, such as 55, 65, 70, or older.

    Endowment policies have nearly disappeared from new policy sales, because changes in the federal income tax laws in the mid-1980s took away the tax preference for newly sold endowments. Interest earned on the cash value of a newly sold endowment would now be taxed annually rather than tax deferred as with other life insurance policies.

9. A current assumption whole life policy has a guaranteed death benefit and at any point in time, a premium that must be paid by the end of the grace period or the policy will lapse. Premiums paid are charged for mortality and expense and credited with interest to produce the policy cash value. In low premium plans, premiums are guaranteed for several years and then redetermined periodically (every 2 or 5 years). Depending upon current assumptions and the amount already accumulated in the cash value, premiums for the next period may go up or down. In the high premium version of current assumption whole life, favorable experience may increase the cash value to a level where the policy becomes self-supporting. There is, however, no guarantee that premiums will ever vanish or if they do, that they will not have to be paid again in the future if experience worsens.

    There are still quite a few guaranteed elements in current assumption whole life policies. There is a guaranteed death benefit and a minimum guaranteed interest rate to be credited

on policy cash values. Beyond this, there are design variations that lead to different names in the marketplace. Some companies guarantee the mortality charge and the expense charges. When mortality and expense charges are guaranteed, the policy is often referred to as an interest-sensitive whole life policy because excess interest (credited interest minus guaranteed interest) credited to the cash value becomes the only nonguaranteed element in the contract, However, the most current assumption whole life policies have some degree of flexibility in the expense elements. Because many of these designs periodically recast the premium amount based on recognition of the most recent interval of experience, some of these policies are referred to as indeterminate premium whole life policies. The idea is that there is a guaranteed maximum possible premium that could be charged, but the actual mortality, interest, and expenses give rise to lower premium amounts actually being assessed as a result of favorable experience under the policy. Finally, as mentioned above, the high premium version of current assumption whole life insurance uses favorable experience to increase the cash value and as a result, the policy may become self-supporting. These high premium policies are commonly referred to as vanishing premium whole life policies.

10. In low-premium plans, premiums are guaranteed for several years and then periodically redetermined (recalculated). The level of premiums influences the frequency of redetermination. The lower the premium design, the more frequent the policy's redetermination dates. In some of the more recent policy designs, redetermination can be every year; more often the redetermined frequency is every 2 years or every 5 years. On policy anniversaries when redetermination is applicable, the insurance company looks at its actual experience for the block of policies since the previous redetermination date and decides what adjustments, if any, are necessary, based on the assumption that past experiences are indicative of what to expect in the period before the next redetermination.

The policyowner generally selects the method he or she prefers to adjust the policy from an available group of options when redetermination occurs. For example, if the redetermination results in a potentially lower premium, the policyowner usually has the option of continuing the past level of premiums and having the favorable results applied to enhance the policy's cash value or increase the death benefit (assuming the insured can provide satisfactory evidence of insurability), or the policyowner may choose to pay the lower policy premium amount.

When past experience is less favorable than expectations, the policyowner again has a range of options, including lowering the death benefit, increasing the premium amount, or maintaining the status quo and allowing the policy accumulation account to decrease

as the mortality and expense charges exceed the investment earnings on the accumulated fund. This last choice, if available, may have restrictions on its use.

11. *A current assumption whole life policy has a guaranteed death benefit and at any point in time, a premium that must be paid by the end of the grace period or the policy will lapse. Premiums paid are charged for mortality and expense and credited with interest to produce the policy cash value. In low premium plans, premiums are guaranteed for several years and then redetermined periodically (every 2 or 5 years). Depending upon current assumptions and the amount already accumulated in the cash value, premiums for the next period may go up or down. In the high premium version of current assumption whole life, favorable experience may increase the cash value to a level where the policy becomes self-supporting. There is, however, no guarantee that premiums will ever vanish or if they do, that they will not have to be paid again in the future if experience worsens. There are still quite a few guaranteed elements in current assumption whole life policies. There is a guaranteed death benefit and a minimum guaranteed interest rate to be credited on policy cash values. Beyond this, there are design variations that lead to different names in the marketplace. Some companies guarantee the mortality charge and the expense charges. When mortality and expense charges are guaranteed, the policy is often referred to as an interest-sensitive whole life policy because excess interest (credited interest minus guaranteed interest) credited to the cash value becomes the only nonguaranteed element in the contract, However, the most current assumption whole life policies have some degree of flexibility in the expense elements. Because many of these designs periodically recast the premium amount based on recognition of the most recent interval of experience, some of these policies are referred to as indeterminate premium whole life policies. The idea is that there is a guaranteed maximum possible premium that could be charged, but the actual mortality, interest, and expenses give rise to lower premium amounts actually being assessed as a result of favorable experience under the policy. Finally, as mentioned above, the high premium version of current assumption whole life insurance uses favorable experience to increase the cash value and as a result, the policy may become self-supporting. These high premium policies are commonly referred to as vanishing premium whole life policies.*

12. *In low-premium plans, premiums are guaranteed for several years and then periodically redetermined (recalculated). The level of premiums influences the frequency of redetermination. The lower the premium design, the more frequent the policy's redetermination dates. In some of the more recent policy designs, redetermination can be every year; more often the redetermined frequency is every 2 years or every 5 years. On policy anniversaries when redetermination is applicable, the insurance company looks at its actual experience*

for the block of policies since the previous redetermination date and decides what adjustments, if any, are necessary, based on the assumption that past experiences are indicative of what to expect in the period before the next redetermination. The policyowner generally selects the method he or she prefers to adjust the policy from an available group of options when redetermination occurs. For example, if the redetermination results in a potentially lower premium, the policyowner usually has the option of continuing the past level of premiums and having the favorable results applied to enhance the policy's cash value or increase the death benefit (assuming the insured can provide satisfactory evidence of insurability), or the policyowner may choose to pay the lower policy premium amount. When past experience is less favorable than expectations, the policyowner again has a range of options, including lowering the death benefit, increasing the premium amount, or maintaining the status quo and allowing the policy accumulation account to decrease as the mortality and expense charges exceed the investment earnings on the accumulated fund. This last choice, if available, may have restrictions on its use.

Chapter 6
Universal Life Insurance

Revised by C.W. Copeland & Edward E. Graves

Learning Objectives

An understanding of the material in this chapter should enable the student to

1. **Describe the universal life policy, and explain how its features differ from whole life policies.**

2. **Learn the methods of comparing life insurance policies and some strengths and weaknesses of each.**

UNIVERSAL LIFE INSURANCE

universal life insurance

Universal life insurance was introduced in 1979 as a revolutionary new product. It was the first variation of whole life insurance to offer truly flexible premiums. It also included adjustment provisions similar to those contained in the adjustable life contract. These policies shifted some of the possibility of investment fluctuations to the policyowner because the cash value can be increased by credited interest rates in excess of the guaranteed interest rate, but they did not give the policyowner any option to direct the investment portfolio. Two other features initiated with universal life policies: (1) the policyowner's ability to withdraw part of the cash value without having the withdrawal treated as a policy loan and (2) the choice of either a level death benefit design or an increasing death benefit design.

The economic conditions of the early 1980s were a perfect incubator for the universal life variation of whole life. The economy was experiencing extremely high inflation rates and very high nominal rates of investment return. The real rate of return, however (nominal rate of return minus inflation rate), was quite low. Inflationary expectations were so rampant that investors were avoiding long-term investments, and the demand for short-term investments was outstripping the supply of funds, leading to what is known as a reverse yield curve (the cost of borrowing short-term funds is actually higher than the cost of borrowing for long-term mortgages). During more normal economic conditions, higher rates for borrowing are associated with longer-term investments, and lower rates are associated with the shortest investment durations.

disintermediation

Both short-term investment returns and inflation were hovering near 20 percent annual rates. This prompted many policyowners with traditional life insurance contracts to pull the cash value out of their existing life insurance contracts via policy loans or policy surrenders and invest the funds directly in these new high-yield investments. This process is commonly referred to as **disintermediation**.

Example

Whenever the short-term investment yields exceed both policy loan interest rates and long-term investment yields, life insurers suffer from disintermediation. Policyowners withdraw funds in the form of policy loans and/or policy surrenders. This prevents insurers from investing in the current high yields and in extreme cases can force liquidation of investments at a loss to pay out the funds.

Life insurance companies were looking for a way to stem this outflow of funds that was forcing many of them to liquidate some of their long-term investments at a loss in order to honor policyowner requests. In such an inflationary environment the traditional fixed-dollar life insurance contract lost much of its appeal.

Stock insurance companies were the first ones to introduce universal life policies. Mutual insurance companies were concerned that federal income tax law precluded them from offering universal life insurance policies; mutual insurance companies that introduced universal life insurance usually formed a downstream subsidiary stock insurance company with the parent mutual insurance company controlling the subsidiary. The real advantage was that nearly every insurance company introducing a universal life policy did so through a brand-new company that invested all of its assets into a new money portfolio and earned very high short-term investment yields. These yields seemed astronomical when compared with the yields being earned by traditional life insurance companies with long-term investment portfolios. Although the tremendous immediate advantage of higher yields could not persist over the entire duration of the life insurance contract, it was successfully exploited in the marketplace for the few years it lasted.

After normal investment conditions returned and yields dropped to lower levels, the universal life policies decreased in popularity. Insurers selling universal life insurance started investing in longer term assets to increase their returns, and the total portfolios associated with universal life policies became very similar to those of seasoned insurance companies with large blocks of traditional whole life policies in force.

Flexible Premiums

The true innovation of universal life insurance was the introduction of completely flexible premiums after the first policy year, the only time a minimum level of premium payments for a universal life policy is rigidly required. As usual, the first year's premium can be arranged on a monthly, quarterly, semiannual, or annual basis. The insurance company requires only that a minimum specified level of first-year premium payments be equaled or exceeded. After the first policy year, it is completely up to the policyowner as to how much premium to pay and even whether or not to pay premiums.

Of course this sounds too good to be true. If only one year's premium needs to be paid and the policyowner can skip all other premium payments, life insurance would be free for all years after the first. To the contrary, the aggregate premiums paid, regardless of their timing, must be adequate to cover the costs of maintaining the policy. Consider the analogy of an automobile's gas tank, where premium payments are synonymous with filling the tank. Premium payments (tank refills) can be made frequently to keep the tank nearly full at all times. With that approach the automobile is never likely to run out of gas. The same automobile, however, can operate on a just-in-time philosophy, where premium payments of minimal amounts are made only as frequently as necessary to keep the car from running out of gas. The vehicle operator has full discretion in deciding how to maintain an adequate amount of gasoline in the car. If the operator fails to keep enough gas in the tank, the vehicle may run out of gas and be inoperable until the tank can be refilled. Likewise, under a universal life insurance policy, if the policy cash value is allowed to drop too low (the cash value is inadequate to cover the next 60 days of expense and mortality charges), the policy will lapse. If an additional premium payment is made soon enough, the policy may be restarted without a formal reinstatement process. However, if an injection of additional funds comes after the end of the grace period, the insurance company may force the policyowner to request a formal reinstatement before accepting any further premium payments.

Prefunding

With the advent of universal life insurance the insurance company shifted the degrees of risk to the policyowner by asking the policyowner to determine the amount, if any, of prefunding. The policyowner can pay maximum premiums and maintain a very high cash value (keeping the automobile gas tank full at all times). On the other hand, the policyowner can pay minimal premiums and just barely cover the mortality and expense charges because there is little or no prefunding (constantly running near empty).

The higher the amount or proportion of prefunding, the more investment earnings will be utilized to cover policy expenses. This gets down to the basic adage that there are two sources of money: people at work and money at work. By putting money into the policy early, the money starts earning money and therefore reduces the amount of premium payments needed from people at work at later policy durations. The ultimate extreme of prefunding is the single-premium approach, where an adequate fund is created at the inception of the policy to cover all future costs. The more common approach is a level premium structure in which partial prefunding creates an ever-increasing cash value that in turn generates increasing investment returns to offset mortality and administrative costs.

All premium suggestions are based on some assumed level of investment earnings and the policyowner bears the risk that actual investment earnings will be less than that necessary to support the suggested premium. Even though investment earnings cannot go below the guaranteed rate, a long-term shortfall may necessitate either an increase in premiums or a reduction in coverage at some future point.

At the other end of the spectrum is the minimum-premium approach, which is virtually synonymous with annual renewal term insurance. There is minimal, if any, prefunding, and premium payments barely cover the current mortality and expense charges. Under this approach the premiums must increase as the insured ages since mortality rates increase with the age of the insured. Premiums increase rapidly at advanced ages because there is still a maximum amount at risk (the cash value is very low, and the mortality rate must be applied to nearly the full death benefit amount). Under the partial prefunding approach, however, cash value increases make the amount at risk decrease (amount at risk equals the policy's face amount minus its cash value) as the insured ages, and the increasing mortality rate is applied to a smaller at-risk amount.

Under traditional whole life insurance policies insurance companies designed a wide range of level premium contracts, each with a different level of fixed premiums. Contracts with a higher level premium tended to develop larger cash values at earlier policy durations. Once the policy cash value was adequate to prefund the policy totally, the policy could be converted to a guaranteed paid-up status. Under participating designs, dividends could exceed the premiums once the policy had developed a large enough cash value to prefund all future policy elements.

A lot of the misunderstanding of life insurance stems from the investment component of policy prefunding. A one-half percent increase in investment earnings at each policy duration is sufficient to justify a discernible lower gross premium. The difficulty comes in trying to predict what level of investment earnings will actually be developed. It is highly unlikely that investment earnings rates will always increase. The only safe thing to predict is

that future investment earnings rates will change. Some of those changes will be downward, and no one knows for sure what the actual pattern will be. As noted earlier, in the past, policies have generally done much better than the guaranteed amounts. However, because few policyowners discuss life insurance with their friends, the general public is not aware of how much actual performance has exceeded guaranteed or expected levels. In a recent article about the 50th policy year of a whole life policy issued by a company that charges high premiums and generates high early cash values, a policyowner observed that his policy now provides more than five times the original death benefit. The cash value in the policy is more than four times the value of all premiums paid over the 50 years. This particular policy is a participating policy, and the policyowner dividends are now greater than 13 times the annual premium.

It is unlikely that the positive deviations from the guarantees over the next 50 years will be as strong as those mentioned here for the last 50 years. The intense competition and resulting premium reductions have drastically decreased the cash value build-up in the early policy years.

Prudent insurance management requires insurers to seek maximum prefunding before granting any sort of premium reduction or elimination. This is necessary to ensure that the insurance company has adequate funds on hand to honor the promises under the contract even in the worst possible economic conditions in the future. Otherwise, the insurance company will not have enough funds if that worst-case scenario actually occurs.

Insurance companies are no better than economists (or any other group) at predicting future interest rates and investment returns. But every type of life insurance contract that develops a cash value is highly dependent on those returns. If they are high enough, the insurance company can return part of the premiums. If they are not, the insurer may need all of the investment returns and still have difficulty meeting the promises in the contract. Philosophically and economically, it is justifiable to have more premium money collected up front rather than delaying the collection of funds in the hope that rosy economic conditions will prevail in the future.

Under the traditional contracts with cash values, the only mechanism for returning any policy overfunding in the early years was policyowner dividends. With universal life policies, however, the accumulations from prefunding are credited to the policy's cash value and are quite visible to the policyowner. The earnings rates applied to those accumulations are also clearly visible as they fluctuate with current economic conditions. This open disclosure for universal life policies eliminates some of the doubts about fair treatment often directed at whole life insurance.

Withdrawal Feature

As noted above, another new feature introduced with universal life policies is the policy-owner's ability to make partial withdrawals from the policy's cash value without incurring any indebtedness. In other words, money can be taken out of the policy cash value just like a withdrawal from a savings bank, and there is no obligation to repay those funds; nor is there any incurring interest on the amount withdrawn. Withdrawals do affect the policy's future earnings because the fund still intact to earn interest for future crediting periods is reduced by the amount of the withdrawal. Its effect on the death benefit depends on the type of death benefit in force. (This will be discussed later in the chapter.)

Target Premium Amount

target premium amount

Nearly every universal life policy is issued with a target premium amount. The **target premium amount** is the suggested premium to be paid on a level basis throughout the contract's duration or for a shorter period of time if a limited-pay approach was originally intended to fund the policy. The target premium amount is merely a suggestion and carries no liability if it is inadequate to maintain the contract to any duration, much less to the end of life.

In some insurance companies that target premium is actually sufficient to keep the policy in force (under relatively conservative investment return assumptions) through age 95 or 100 and to pay the cash value equivalent to the death benefit amount if the insured survives to either age 95 or 100 (120 under the 2001 mortality table). On the other hand, some companies with a more aggressive marketing stance have chosen lower target premiums, which are not adequate to carry the policy in force to advanced ages even under more generous (and of questionable validity) assumptions of higher investment returns over future policy years. If in fact the investment return credited to the policy cash value falls short of the amounts assumed in deriving the target premium, the policy may essentially run out of gas before the maximum contract age.

In cases where the policy does run out of gas, the policyowner will be faced with two options: (1) to increase the premium level or (2) to reduce the death benefit amount. Neither one of these options is necessarily desirable, but they are the only acceptable ways under the contract's provisions to correct for unfulfilled optimistic assumptions about investment returns in the contract's early years.

Example

Bert is now 70 years old. He has paid the target premium on his universal life policy for the last 15 years. He was not told, and he did not realize, that the target premium was only intended to keep coverage in force to age 65. Bert wants to keep his coverage, but the target premium he is paying is not adequate to support it. He will have to increase premium payments by more than 20 percent to keep the same amount of coverage, or else he will have to reduce the amount of coverage to a level where the target premium is adequate to support the reduced coverage.

Some insurance companies have introduced a secondary guarantee associated with their target premium. These companies have pledged contractually to keep the policy in force for, say, 15 or 20 years and to pay the full death benefit as long as the premium has been paid in an amount equal to or greater than the target premium amount at each suggested premium-payment interval. Even these guarantees do not extend to the maximum contract age, but they are at least a guarantee that the premium suggested as a target will be adequate to provide the coverage at least as long as the guarantee period. Probably the best indication of whether or not the target premium is adequate to keep the policy in force up through the maximum contract age is to compare it with premiums for a traditional whole life policy of a similar face amount and issue age. Universal life policy target premiums less than premiums for a comparable whole life policy should be suspect; they may be low by design because the insurance company does not expect the policy to remain in force until the very end of life in the majority of cases. The only people who will ever really find out whether or not their policy target premiums are adequate are those who pay the premiums religiously throughout the duration of the contract and live to be an age that is old enough to test the target premium.

Additional Premium Payments

The flexible features of universal life premiums allow policyowners to make additional premium payments above any target premium amount at any time the policyowner desires without prior negotiation or agreement with the insurance company. (The only limitation on paying excess premiums is associated with the income tax definition of life insurance.) However, the insurance company reserves the right to refuse additional premium payments under a universal life policy if the policy's cash value is large enough to encroach upon the upper limit for cash values relative to the level of death benefit granted in the policy.

Skipped Payments or Payments Lower than Target Premium

The premium flexibility also allows the policyowner to skip premium payments, again without any prior negotiation or notification, or to pay premium amounts lower than the target premium suggested at the time of purchase. The lower limitations on premium payments have two constraints. The first is that nearly every company specifies a minimum acceptable amount for any single payment. This is easy to understand in that a check for $.50 is likely to generate $5 to $10 (or more) in processing costs. Insurance companies usually set this minimum amount per transaction at a level above their estimated cost of processing such a transaction.

The other constraint for minimum premium payments has to do with whether or not there is enough cash value in the contract to meet the mortality and administrative charges for the next 60 days. This can include potential surrender charges in early policy years. In other words, if the tank is running on empty, more premium is required. This constraint is also easily justified.

No-Lapse Guarantee

The flexible premium feature of universal life policies has increased the risk that the policy may terminate due to inadequate premium payments. The insurers have introduced guarantees that the coverage will stay in force if the actual premiums paid meet the requirement specified in the no-lapse guarantee provision. This provision guarantees that the coverage will continue as long as the premium requirement has been complied with. There are two different approaches to the associated premium requirement.

The first approach requires that at least the target premium amount be paid on time for every month or other specified interval. The payments may not be delayed into the grace period or be less than the target amount. Such delay or underpayment will negate the no-lapse guarantee. This approach takes away the flexibility to completely skip a premium payment or to make a payment for less than the target amount if the no-lapse guarantee is to be preserved. But the guarantee continues coverage even if the cash value account drops to zero because the target premium turns out to be inadequate under this approach.

The second approach to the no-lapse guarantee is intended to allow the flexibility of skipping premiums or paying smaller than target premiums. The criteria for maintaining the guarantee is that the policy cash value must equal or exceed a specified schedule of accumulation. The required schedule is often called a shadow cash value amount. In order to be able to skip premiums and maintain the guarantee, adequately large prior premiums will have to be paid to build up the cash value in excess of the required schedule. Failure

to maintain a cash value that equals or exceeds the required schedule will negate the guarantee.

Death Benefit Type

As mentioned earlier, universal life insurance gives policyowners a choice between level death benefits and increasing death benefits. The level death benefit design is much like the traditional whole life design (see Figures 6-1 and 6-2). When the death benefit stays constant and the cash value increases over the duration of the contract, the amount at risk or the protection element decreases. The one new aspect of a level death benefit designed under universal life policies is not really a function of universal life itself but a function of a tax law definition of life insurance that was added to the Tax Code shortly after the introduction of universal life insurance policies, requiring that a specified proportion of the death benefit is derived from the amount at risk. Whenever the cash value in the contract gets high enough that this proportion is no longer satisfied, the universal life policy starts increasing the death benefit even though the contract is called a level death benefit contract. This phenomenon does not occur until ages beyond normal retirement, and it is not a significant aspect of this design.

The increasing death benefit design is a modification that was introduced with universal life policies (see Figures 6-3 and 6-4). Put quite simply, under this approach there is always a constant amount at risk that is superimposed over the policy's cash value, whatever it may be. As the cash value increases, so does the total death benefit payable under the contract. A reduction in the cash value will reduce the death benefit. This design pays both the policy's stated face amount and its cash value as benefits at the insured's death. Policies with an increasing death benefit design overcome the criticism of whole life policies that the death benefit is partially made up of the contract's cash value portion. By selecting the increasing death benefit option under a universal life policy the policyowner is ensuring that the death benefit will be composed of the cash value and an at-risk portion equal to the original face value of the contract.

Death Benefit Type Mortality Charges

- Mortality charges for level death benefit type apply to a decreasing amount at risk.

- Mortality charges for increasing death benefit type apply to a constant amount at risk.

There is nothing magical about this larger death benefit amount. As is said often, there is no free lunch. A higher portion of the premium is needed for the larger amount at risk under this design.

There are similarities between the increasing death benefit design for universal life and the paid-up additions option under a participating whole life policy. Under a whole life policy, dividends are used to purchase single-premium additions to the base policy. In both types of policies the excess investment earnings are used to increase the cash value and the death benefit.

Because the mechanics of the two death benefit designs in the universal life policies are slightly different, the effect of partial withdrawals on the mortality charges differs even though the death benefit is reduced by the amount of the partial withdrawal under both designs. Under the level death benefit design, partial withdrawals reduce the death benefit by the amount of the withdrawal. They decrease the amount of the policy's cash value and consequently increase proportionately the mortality charge.

Under the increasing death benefit design, partial withdrawals will reduce the death benefit payable because the withdrawal decreases the cash value that constitutes part of the death benefit amount. However, such withdrawals will not increase the mortality charges because the amount at risk remains the same. The cash value decreases and has a negative impact on the amount of investment earnings credited to the cash value after the withdrawal.

Effect of Policy Loans

Another aspect of policy design ushered in with universal life policies is the differential crediting rate on the cash value, depending on whether there are policy loans outstanding. Most universal life policies credit current interest rates on the cash value as long as there are no outstanding policy loans. Once the policyowner borrows funds from the cash value, the insurance company usually credits a lower interest rate or earnings rate to the portion of the cash value associated with the policy loan. This is another effort to curb disintermediation.

Outstanding policy loans at the time the insured dies will reduce the death benefit by the amount of the loan plus any unpaid interest on the loan. This is the same for universal life policies as it is for any life insurance policy that has policy loans.

Some of the earliest universal life policy designs had several different bands with different crediting rates. In other words, the first $500 or $1,000 of policy loan interest rate may have been credited with one interest rate and each successively larger band would have carried a higher policy loan interest rate. This structure still exists in a few universal life policies offered in the marketplace today, but by and large, many insurance companies have dropped the multiple-rate, banded approach to premium loan interest charges. It had such

a complex structure that it was hard to explain to policyowners, and tracking it required much more complex computer software. Many universal life policies sold today credit the cash value with the current rate for nonborrowed funds and a lower rate, which is often 2 percent (200 basis points) lower than the current rate, for borrowed funds.

Figure 6-1
Universal Life Type I, Type A, and so on
Level Death Benefit (If Target Premium Is Always Paid)

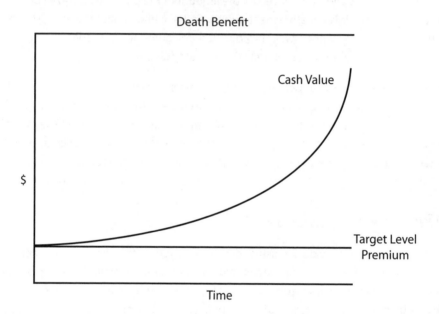

Figure 6-2
Universal Life Type I, Type A, and so on
Level Death Benefit (but Premium Payment Waived)

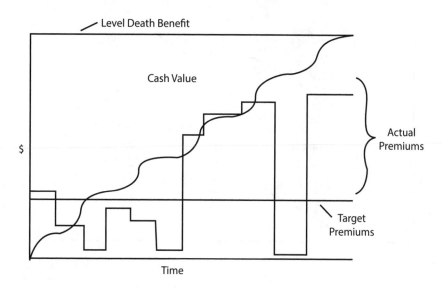

Figure 6-3
Universal Life Type II, Type B, etc.
Target Premium Paid

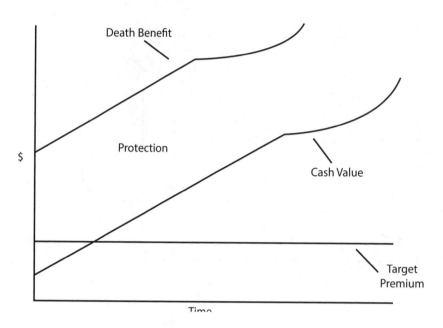

Figure 6-4
Universal Life Type II, Type B (Uneven Premium Paid)
Death Benefit = Level Amount at Risk + Cash Value

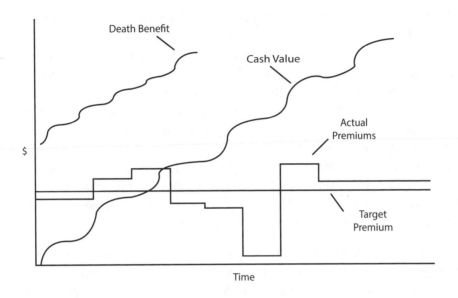

Internal Funds Flow

Although universal life insurance policies are still relatively young in the overall realm of life insurance products, some policies are already in their eighth or ninth generation of policy series from the company that introduced them. As with all products, the individual policy designs constantly evolve in response to the economy, competitive pressures, and innovative zeal. As previously noted, most of the first generation of universal life policies were heavily front-end-loaded products. They took a significant proportion of each premium dollar as administrative expenses, and the remaining portion was then credited to the policy cash value account.

After the funds had reached the policy cash value account, they were subject to charges for current death benefits in the form of a mortality charge based on the amount at risk. In most insurance companies the mortality rate actually charged was often in the neighborhood of 50 percent of the guaranteed maximum mortality rate set forth in the policy contract for each attained age of the insured. The difference in the mortality rate actually being charged and the maximum permitted mortality rate published in the policy represents the safety margin the life insurance company is holding in reserve. If the future mortality costs

for the block of policies turn out to be more expensive than initially assumed, the insurance company can increase the mortality rate as long as it does not exceed guaranteed maximum rates specified in the contract itself.

After deductions for expenses and mortality, the universal life cash value account is then increased at the current crediting rate to reflect investment earnings on that cash value. These are the dollars at work for the policyowner to help reduce his or her current and future out-of-pocket premium expenses. The actual rate credited is a discretionary decision on the part of the insurance company, and it tends to fluctuate freely, reflecting current economic conditions. There have been times when some insurers were reluctant to credit the current interest rate to the policy's cash value. As interest rates were dropping gradually and steadily over the last decade, many insurance companies were hesitant to allow their current interest crediting rate to drop below 10 percent, and interest crediting rates seemed to stick around that point. Eventually, the economic folly of crediting interest rates in excess of actual earnings on the invested assets became apparent, and single-digit interest rates replaced double-digit rates in the crediting formula.

Interest crediting rates have been the focal point of most of the competition among companies selling universal life policies. There has been very little emphasis on the mortality rates charged or the expense charges levied against incoming premiums. In reality all three concepts constitute the total cost of insurance. Interest rates can be (and have been) intentionally elevated to a level above what the investment portfolio actually supported, but they are still viable because of compensating higher levels of mortality charges and expense deductions. When consumers choose to focus only on one of the three elements, it is not surprising that the marketing efforts zero in on that element. The assessment of overall policy efficiency requires that all factors be considered in concert.

As the universal life insurance policies evolved, more of them moved to a back-end loading design. In other words, they lowered or eliminated the up-front charge levied against incoming premium amounts and instead imposed new or increased surrender charges applicable to the cash value of a policy surrendered during the contract's first 7 to 15 years. Surrender charges are usually highest during the first policy year and decrease on a straight-line basis over the remaining years until the year in which the insurance company expects to have amortized all excess first-year expenses. At that point the surrender charge is reduced to zero and will not be applicable at later policy durations. The actual surrender charge itself can be based on either the cash value amount or on the target premium level. Some insurers have developed a hybrid that depends on both approaches to generate the full surrender charge. The surrender charge usually decreases by the same percentage on each policy anniversary until the applicable charge reaches zero. The net amount payable

for a surrendered policy is determined by deducting any applicable surrender charge from the policy cash value minus any unpaid policy loans and interest.

Companies with the highest surrender charges tend to have little or no front-end expenses charged against premiums. Some companies have policies that combine moderate front-end loading and moderate surrender charges. There seems to be a discernible preference for higher surrender charges and little or no front-end loading in most universal life policies being marketed today.

The actual component of the front-end loading can be a flat annual charge per policy plus a small percentage of premium dollars actually received, and a charge of a few cents per each $1,000 of coverage in force under the policy. The charges applicable to the premiums and the amount of coverage are usually deducted monthly from the policy cash value account. Similarly, the current interest crediting rate is also usually applied monthly. These are the deposits and withdrawals from our gas tank.

Some companies have actually eliminated charges based on the amount of coverage in force. Competitive pressures have also caused many insurance companies to minimize front-end loading in order to emphasize that nearly all premium dollars go directly into the cash value account. The actual expenses are still being exacted internally, but the manner in which they are handled is not easily discernible by the consuming public. For example, expenses can be embedded in the spread between actual mortality costs and actual mortality charges or in the spread between investment earnings and the interest rate credited to the cash value accounts.

It is important to realize that no insurance company is able to operate without generating legitimate costs of operations above the amount needed to pay death benefits only. These expenses must be covered somehow, and the method of allocating them is nothing more or less than a cost-accounting approach. The exact allocation formula is always arbitrary and to some extent guided by the philosophy of the insurance company management team. It must address such issues as equity among short-term and long-term policyowners, the appropriate duration for amortizing excess first-year expenses, and how much investment and operations gains to retain for company growth and safety margins and how much to distribute to policyowners.

Flexibility to Last a Lifetime

The astonishing flexibility of premiums under universal life policies and the ability to adjust death benefits upward and downward have created life insurance policies that can literally keep pace with the policyowner's needs. The policy can be aggressively funded when the

premium dollars are available, and premium payments can be intentionally suspended during tight budget periods, such as the formation of a new business or while children are attending college. The policy death benefit can be increased (sometimes requiring evidence of insurability) if the need exists, and once any temporary needs have expired, the policy can be adjusted downward to provide lower death benefits if that is what the policyowner wants. The ability of a universal life contract to fit constantly changing policy-owner needs and conditions has led some companies to label this coverage irreplaceable life insurance. Some see it as the only policy ever needed because its versatility will allow it to compensate for any necessary changes.

Probably the most serious drawback to universal life policies is the competitive forces insurance marketers use to try to convince the prospect that their own version of universal life is better than anyone else's. In reality all universal life policies are similar, and only future investment performance will really determine which one turns out to be slightly more efficient than its competitors. Consumers will be better off seeking a policy that does well over the long haul than looking for a policy that wins every short-term contest because no policy can be best in all facets at every duration. Sometimes focusing on a single competitive advantage prompts insurance companies to make short-term adjustments that are not necessarily in their own or the policyowner's best interest in the long-term scenario.

Indexed Universal Life

The indexed product phenomenon started with fixed annuities, spread to universal life policies, and is now making inroads into whole life policies. The indexed universal life policies have all of the normal features of nonindexed universal life contracts but also have a minimum interest crediting rate guarantee, and are classified as fixed rather than variable life insurance contracts.

So far, these products are not subject to securities regulation by the SEC or FINRA. The indexed feature adds the possibility of enhanced crediting rates linked to the performance of a specific stock index such as the Standard & Poor's 500. The contract specifies which particular or composite index applies. All of the indexes measure stock market performance. Increases in the specified index are applied to a formula set forth in the policy to determine if there will be an increase in the crediting rate for the measured time interval. The formula is designed to reduce the interest enhancement to significantly less than the change in the stock index. The specific formula varies significantly from one company to another and often has many components. Frequently there is a cap for any single performance period which puts an upper limit on the amount of interest enhancement permitted. Some formulas utilize a participation rate applicable to the index, which can further

dampen the results if the rate is less than 100 percent. There are many different approaches to determining the high and low points for the index during the measurement interval.

Because the universal life policy is a fixed contract, 90 percent of the investments in the portfolios must be bonds and mortgages. Insurance regulations limit the investment portfolio to less than 10 percent in stocks and equities. Consequently, the interest enhancement component is derived from a very small portion of the overall invested funds. The applicable formula must keep the enhancements in line with what can actually be delivered by the relatively small proportion of equity portfolio. None of the formulas recognize dividend income from the stock portfolio. In 2008, the New York Insurance Department mandated that indexed insurance product sales be accompanied by a report showing the difference between the index portfolio performance when dividends are and are not included. Agents are also required to emphasize that the indexed policy does not include dividends.

It is common for an insurance company to provide a lower guaranteed interest rate under indexed universal policies than for standard universal life policies. The reduction may range from 50 to 150 basis points. Thus, the indexed enhancements must overcome this reduction before the policyowner derives a positive net benefit from the contract. During periods of poor stock market performance, the indexed universal life policy will most likely underperform the standard universal life policy.

The marketing promotions for the indexed products emphasize the interest guarantee plus the potential enhancement of the crediting rate from stock index increases. This is often described as the best of both worlds, a guaranteed minimum performance with the chance to participate on the upside with stock market increases. This kind of promotion creates an expectation that generally exceeds the maximum possible performance from these contracts. Anyone marketing these contracts must guard against exuberant expectations. At best, in a strong bull market indexed universal life policies will provide crediting rates only slightly above the guaranteed rate.

Indexed annuities have already created a pool of dissatisfied contract owners who expected more than the contracts were able to deliver. The Securities and Exchange Commission has argued that these contracts should be regulated as investment contracts, because the enhancements are based on stock market performance. However, legislative changes have resulted in the SEC dropping the efforts to regulate the contracts as investments.

CHAPTER REVIEW

Key Terms and Concepts

universal life insurance
disintermediation
target premium amount

Chapter 6 Review Questions

1. Describe universal life insurance, and explain why it was so successful in the 1980s. [1]

2. Describe universal life insurance's flexible premium feature. [1]

3. Explain how partial withdrawals of cash value from a universal life policy differ from a policy loan from that policy. [1]

4. Explain the target premium concept applicable to universal life insurance. [1]

5. Describe both of the death benefit options commonly available to universal life insurance purchasers. [1]

6. Explain how policy loans affect universal life insurance's cash value and death benefit. [1]

7. Describe the explicit loading charges and surrender charges in universal life insurance policies. [1]

8. Describe interest-adjusted indexes, and explain how they differ from the traditional net-cost method of comparing life insurance policy costs. [2]

9. Describe the cash-accumulation method of policy comparison, and explain its strengths and weaknesses. [2]

Chapter 6 Review Answers

1. *Universal life insurance was introduced in 1979 as a revolutionary new product. It was the first variation of whole life insurance to offer truly flexible premiums. The policy death benefit can be adjusted upward (sometimes requiring proof of insurability) or downward to meet the policyowner's needs. Two other features also were initiated with universal life policies: (1) the policyowner's ability to withdraw part of the cash value without having the withdrawal treated as a policy loan and (2) the choice of either a level death benefit design or an increasing death benefit design.*

    The economic conditions of the early 1980s were a perfect incubator for the universal life variation of whole life. The economy was experiencing extremely high inflation rates and very high nominal rates of investment return. Inflationary expectations were so rampant that investors were avoiding long-term investments, and the demand for short-term investments was outstripping the supply of funds, leading to what is known as a reverse yield curve (the cost of borrowing short-term funds is actually higher than the cost of borrowing for long-term mortgages). Both short-term investment returns and inflation were hovering near 20 percent annual rates. This prompted many policyowners with traditional life insurance contracts to pull the cash value out of their existing life insurance contracts via policy loans or policy surrenders and invest the funds directing in these new high-yield investments. Life insurance companies were looking for a way to stem this outflow of funds that was forcing many of them to liquidate some of their long-term investments at a loss in order to honor policyowner requests. In such an inflationary environment, the traditional fixed-dollar life insurance contract lost much of its appeal. Nearly every insurance company introducing a universal life policy did so through a brand-new company that invested all of its assets into a new-money portfolio and earned very high short-term investment yields. These yields seemed astronomical when compared with the yields being earned by traditional life insurance companies with long-term investment portfolios. Although the tremendous immediate advantage of higher yields could not persist over the entire duration of the life insurance contract, it was successfully exploited in the marketplace for the few years it lasted.

2. *The true innovation of universal life insurance was the introduction of completely flexible premiums after the first policy year, the only time a minimum level of premium payments for a universal life policy is rigidly required. As usual, the first year's premium can be arranged on a monthly, quarterly, semiannual, or annual basis. The insurance company requires only that a minimum specified level of first-year premium payments be equaled*

or exceeded. After the first policy year, it is completely up to the policyowner the amount of premium to pay (limited only by the maximums contained in the income tax definition of life insurance) and even whether or not to pay the premiums. Of course, premiums can be skipped altogether only if the policy cash value is at least adequate to cover the next 60 days of expense and mortality charges. Otherwise, the policy would lapse if no additional premium were paid by the end of the grace period.

3. *A universal life policy permits the policyowner to make partial withdrawals from the policy's cash value without incurring any indebtedness. In other words, money can be taken out of the policy cash value, but no interest is charged on the amount withdrawn as there would be with a policy loan. Withdrawals do affect the policy's future earnings because the fund still intact to earn interest for future crediting periods is reduced by the amount of the withdrawal. Its effect on the death benefit depends on the type of death benefit in force. Partial withdrawals do not reduce the death benefit amount under the level death benefit design. They do, however, decrease the amount of the policy's cash value and correspondingly increase the amount at risk. Partial withdrawals under the increasing death benefit design will, in fact, reduce the death benefit payable because the withdrawal decreases the cash value that constitutes part of the death benefit amount.*

4. *Nearly every universal life policy is issued with a target premium amount. The target amount is the suggested premium to be paid on a level basis throughout the contract's duration or for a shorter period of time if a limited-pay approach was originally intended to fund the policy. The target premium amount is merely a suggestion and carries no liability if it is inadequate to maintain the contract to any duration, much less to the end of life.*

   Some insurance companies have introduced a secondary guarantee associated with their target premium. These companies have pledged contractually to keep the policy in force for, say, 15 or 20 years and to pay the full death benefit as long as the premium has been paid in an amount equal to or greater than the target premium amount at each suggested premium-payment interval.

5. *Universal life insurance gives policyowners a choice between level death benefits and increasing death benefits. The level death benefit design is much like the traditional whole life design. When the death benefit stays constant and the cash value increases over the duration of the contract, the amount at risk or the protection element decreases.*

The one new aspect of a level death benefit design under universal life policies results from a tax law definition of life insurance that was added to the Code shortly after the introduction of universal life insurance policies, requiring that a specified proportion of the death benefit is derived from the amount at risk. Whenever the cash value in the contract gets high enough that this proportion is no longer satisfied, the universal life policy starts increasing the death benefit even though the contract is called a level death benefit contract.

The increasing death benefit design is a modification that was introduced with universal life policies. Under this approach, there is always a constant amount at risk that is superimposed over the policy's cash value, whatever it may be. As the cash value increases, so does the total death benefit payable under the contract. A reduction in the cash value will reduce the death benefit. This design pays both the policy's stated face amount and its cash value as benefits at the insured's death. There is nothing magical about this larger death benefit amount. A higher portion of the premium is needed for the larger amount at risk under this design.

6. *Most universal life policies credit current interest rates on the cash value as long as there are no outstanding policy loans. Once the policyowner borrows funds from the cash value, the insurance company usually credits a lower interest rate or earnings rate to the portion of the cash value associated with the policy loan. Many universal life policies sold today credit the cash value with the current rate for nonborrowed funds and a lower rate, which is often 2 percentage points (or 200 basis points) lower than the current rate, for borrowed funds.*

    Any outstanding debt will reduce any death benefit proceeds or cash value proceeds otherwise payable under a universal life policy.

7. *Universal life policies cover expenses through front-end loads and/or back-end loads (surrender charges). Most of the early universal life policies were heavily front-end-loaded products. They took a significant proportion of each premium dollar as administrative expenses, and the remaining portion was then credited to the policy cash value account. As the universal life insurance policies evolved, more of them moved to a back-end loading design. In other words, they lowered or eliminated the up-front charge levied against incoming premium amounts and instead imposed new or increased surrender charges applicable to the cash value of a policy surrendered during the contract's first 7 to 15 years. Surrender charges are usually highest during the first policy year and decrease on a*

straight-line basis over the remaining years until the year in which the insurance company expects to have amortized all excess first-year expenses. At that point, the surrender charge is reduced to zero and will not be applicable at later policy durations.

After the premiums less any front-end load reach the policy cash value account, they are subject to charges for current death benefits in the form of a mortality charge based on the amount at risk. In most insurance companies, the mortality rate actually charged is often considerably less than the guaranteed maximum mortality rate set forth in the policy contract for each attained age of the insured.

After deductions for expenses and mortality, the universal life cash value account is then increased at the current crediting rate to reflect investment earnings on that cash value. These are the dollars at work for the policyowner to help reduce his or her current and future out-of-pocket premium expenses. The actual rate credited is a discretionary decision on the part of the insurance company, and it tends to fluctuate freely, reflecting current economic conditions.

Competitive pressures have caused many insurance companies to minimize front-end loading in order to emphasize that nearly all premium dollars go directly into the cash value account. The actual expenses are still being enacted internally, but the manner in which they are handled is not easily discernible by the consuming public. For example, expenses can be embedded in the spread between actual mortality costs and actual mortality charges or in the spread between investment earnings and the interest rate credited to the cash value accounts.

8. *There are two interest-adjusted cost indexes—the surrender cost index and the payment cost index. The logic of using interest-adjusted indexes is similar to that of the traditional net-cost approach with the exception that interest-adjusted indexes explicitly take into account the time value of money. Essentially, the interest-adjusted methods take all payments for premiums and treat them as if they had been put into interest-bearing accounts to accumulate interest (usually assumed to be 5 percent) until the end of the interval for evaluation (usually 20 years). In a like manner, all dividend payments are carried as if they are deposited in an interest-bearing account, and that account balance is calculated for the end of the interval of evaluation. For the surrender cost index, the policy cash value at the end of the evaluation period and the amount of accumulated dividends are subtracted from the accumulated value of all the premiums paid, and the result is divided by the future value of an annuity due of $1 for the length of the evaluation period at the assumed rate*

of interest. Determining the payment cost index is similar to calculating the surrender cost index except that there is no recognition of the end-of-period cash value.

9. The cash accumulation comparison method involves accumulating the premium differences between the policies being compared, while holding the death benefits of both policies constant and equal. For example, to compare a cash value contract with a term contract, set the death benefits equal at the beginning of the period, and use the yearly premium difference between the cash value contract and the term policy to determine the amount to deposit into a side fund to accumulate at interest. The calculation is basically a buy-term-and-invest-the-difference approach to comparing the policies. At the end of the interval being evaluated, the side fund accumulation amount can be compared to the cash value in the whole life or other form of cash value insurance policy. The policy with the greater accumulation at the end of the comparison interval is considered the preferable of the two contracts.

Chapter 7

Variable Life & Variable Universal Insurance

By Dan M. McGill

Revised by C.W. Copeland, Edward E. Graves, and Joseph W. Huver

Learning Objectives

An understanding of the material in this chapter should enable the student to

1. **Describe the features of variable life, and understand its dual regulation status.**

2. **Be aware of the variable adjustable life policy and its features.**

3. **Describe and understand variable life insurance policies.**

4. **Describe and understand variable universal life insurance policies.**

VARIABLE LIFE INSURANCE

variable life insurance

Adjustable life insurance was one of two major life insurance variations introduced in the decade before universal life insurance. The other, which was introduced in 1976, is **variable life insurance**, the first life insurance policy designed to shift the investment risk to policyowners. This product had a long and expensive gestation period. It not only had to run the gauntlet of state insurance department approvals but it also needed (and finally acquired after many years of negotiations) approval by the Securities and Exchange Commission (SEC).

A variable life insurance policy provides no guarantees of either interest rate or minimum cash value. Theoretically, the cash value can go down to zero, and if so, the policy will terminate unless all required premiums have been paid and there is a guaranteed minimum death benefit applicable. As the SEC pointed out, in order for policyowners to gain the additional benefit of better-than-expected investment returns, they also have to assume all of the downside investment risk. Consequently, the SEC required variable life policies to be registered with the SEC and all sales to be subject to the requirements applicable to other registered securities. In other words, policy sales can be made only after the prospective purchaser has a chance to read the policy prospectus. The SEC also requires that the insurance company be registered as an investment company and that all sales agents be registered with the SEC for the specific purpose of variable life insurance policy sales.

Agents who sell variable life insurance policies must be licensed as both life insurance agents and securities agents.

SEC Objections to Variable Life

There were two main stumbling blocks in gaining SEC approval of variable life products. The first one was the maximum compensation to agents for the sale of this product. The SEC wanted the sales load not to exceed 8 percent of the sale price. Keeping in mind that most securities are sold on a cash-sale basis rather than on an installment-sale basis, this presented some serious drawbacks from the insurance companies' standpoint. The insurance companies and the SEC finally compromised on a 20 percent load on the first year's premiums. This was argued to be the equivalent of an 8 percent load over the lifetime of the policy. The other major stumbling block had to do with whether or not insurance companies would be permitted to allow flexible-premium payments under these policies. Initially the SEC did not relent on this issue. Therefore the first generation of variable life insurance products were fixed-premium products (see figure below). The only real innovation was the variable investment aspect—that is, the policyowner was permitted to select among a limited number of investment portfolio choices, with the death benefit amount varying as a function of the portfolio's investment performance.

Investment Choices

Generally, the first generation of variable life insurance policies gave the purchaser three investment options into which the funds could be directed. The policyowner was free to put all of the funds into one of these choices or to distribute the funds in whatever proportions he or she desired among the three options. There was usually a minimum requirement of at least 5 or 10 percent of incoming funds that had to be allocated to any investment option the policyowner selected. The purpose of this minimum requirement was to eliminate the possibility that administrative costs would exceed the amount of money being directed into a particular option.

Very often the options were a stock fund, a bond fund, and either a treasury fund or a money market fund. The funds were essentially mutual funds run by the insurance company and set aside as separate accounts (required by the SEC) that do not constitute part of the insurance company's general investment fund and put such assets beyond the claims of its general creditors. These separate funds have to be reported as separate items on the insurance company's financial statements for both statutory purposes and generally accepted accounting purposes. (Stock insurance companies must issue both types of reports; mutual companies are only required to issue statutory reports.)

**Figure 7-1
Variable Life
Fixed Premium**

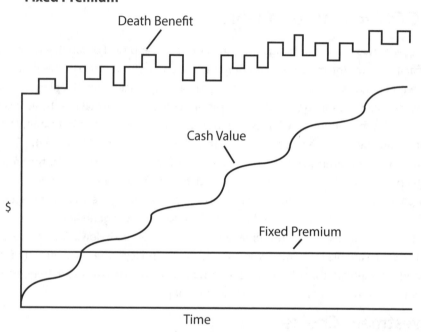

By allowing the policyowner to direct the funds backing the policy, the policyowner becomes the portfolio director, within limits. Obviously, the policyowner has no control over what assets are purchased and sold by the individual funds that can be selected. That portion of the investment decision process is still within the hands of the insurance company's portfolio management team. The important thing is that the policyowner plays a participative role in portfolio management and consequently can benefit directly from better-than-expected results or bear the full brunt of poor investment performance. The results of the investment performance are credited directly to the policy cash values.

Ability to Tolerate Risk

Individuals who are already experienced in equity investments are quite comfortable with the variable life insurance policy. However, this policy is subject to daily portfolio fluctuations and can provoke great anxiety in individuals who are not used to or comfortable with such market value fluctuations.

Part of the challenge of marketing variable life policies is this volatility. Many life insurance agents are reluctant to try to sell any policy whose success depends on the investment

decisions of the policyowner. They are afraid that some purchasers will expect the life insurance agent to give them investment advice.

A variable life policy is a market-driven phenomenon, and to some extent its popularity is influenced by general investment market conditions. The policy becomes more acceptable to consumers after a long period of market increases and falls out of favor when the market experiences a general decline in prices. In the early 1990s when interest rates dropped to very low levels, people used to higher yields on bonds and other investment instruments turned to variable life insurance contracts as one alternative to reinvesting in certificates of deposit.

Insurance Charges

Assuming the right investment choices are made, variable life insurance allows the policyowner's money to work harder for him or her. But variable life insurance contracts are not exclusively investments. They are in fact life insurance contracts, and they sustain mortality charges for the death benefits they provide. Consequently, the return on the invested funds within a variable life insurance contract will never equal that of a separate investment fund that does not provide death benefits but invests in assets of a similar type and quality.

Variable life insurance should not be purchased as a short-term investment vehicle. The combination of sales load, mortality charges, and surrender charges will significantly reduce any potential gains in the policy's early years.

Linkage of Death Benefits with Investment Performance

Because the primary reason for life insurance is to provide death benefits, it makes sense to link superior investment performance with increases in the death benefit level. Theoretically, this is a way of keeping up with inflation. In fact, studies indicate that such a linkage would more than keep pace with inflation. However, there is an important caveat. Although investment performance in equities tends to equal or exceed inflation in the economy over the long term, the correlation is not perfect in the short term. In other words, it is possible for inflation to exceed increases in the investment performance for short durations of time (possibly 2 or 3 years). This is another reason why life insurance should be looked at as a long-term financial security purchase and not a short-term investment.

There is more than one way to link the policy's death benefit to the associated portfolio's investment performance. In the early generation of fixed-premium variable life insurance

contracts, insurance companies settled on two different approaches—the level additions method or the constant ratio method. Regardless of which linkage design was chosen, all of the early contracts had the purchaser select a target level of investment performance as a benchmark against which actual investment performance would be measured. Performance in excess of the target level would be used to fund incremental increases in the death benefit; performance below the target amount would require downward adjustments in the death benefits to make up for the deficit.

Level Additions Model

The level additions model uses excess investment returns (returns in excess of the target rate) to purchase a level single-premium addition to the base policy. The face amount or death benefit will rise as long as investment performance equals or exceeds the target rate. This model does not cause as rapid an increase or decrease as the constant ratio method of linking the policy's death benefit to investment performance. The strength of the level addition design is that it does not require an ever-increasing investment return to support incremental increases in death benefits. Additional coverage is added more slowly, but it is more easily supported once it is added. Similarly, downward adjustments in death benefits are less rapid, and they are less likely to accelerate in future years. Furthermore, policies using the level additions design provide a minimum base value guarantee equal to the amount of coverage when the policy was first purchased.

Constant Ratio Method

The constant ratio method also uses the excess investment earnings as a net single premium to purchase a paid-up additional amount of coverage. The difference is that under this method the paid-up additional coverage is not a level benefit amount but a decreasing benefit amount because it is designed to maintain a ratio between the death benefit and the policy reserve that satisfies the corridor test. Under this policy design more volatile increments are added to or subtracted from the contract as investment performance differs from the target amount.

Like the level addition model, this design has a minimum death benefit guarantee equal to the initial face amount of the policy. If the initial stage of the contract has lower returns than the target level, the policy reserves will drop below the level necessary to sustain the guaranteed death benefit amount. The policy will have to remain in force for a long enough period for the investment returns to exceed the target rate to bring the reserve back up to a level capable of supporting incremental increases in coverage before the policyowner will see increases in the death benefit.

Usually variable life policies have positive excess investment earnings in the early years of the contract and do provide incremental increases in the death benefit before the investment earnings drop below the target rate. Looking at variable life insurance policies since 1976, most policies have experienced investment earnings over the target rate more frequently and for longer durations than they have experienced investment earnings below the target rate. There is no guarantee that this will always be true, but the expectation is that overall investment earnings will exceed the target amount over the bulk of the policy duration. Many variable life policyowners have been pleasantly surprised at how well their policies have done over two decades.

In the long run, regardless of the policy design, the excess investment earnings over the target level must support any incremental additions to the policy. If investment earnings are negative (the actual earnings are lower than the target rate), then the adjustments will have to be downward from any previously attained levels above the policy's initial face value. If investment earnings are positive (the actual earnings are above the target rate), the adjustments will be upward.

Increased Number of Investment Fund Options

Variable life insurance designs have not been static since their introduction in the mid-1970s. Life insurance companies are now offering many more investment fund options than they made available in the early stages of this product's development. Some insurance companies have more than 4 dozen funds to choose from in their current product offering. There are usually a variety of stock funds, including growth stock funds, income stock funds, balanced stock funds, and international stock funds. Bond fund offerings are likewise more robust and include different durations and different types of issuers (large corporations, small corporations, state governments, and the federal government) as well as Government National Mortgage Association (GNMA) funds and collateralized mortgage obligations (CMOs).

In addition, many insurance companies offer a managed fund as one of the portfolio choices. The policyowner can put all of the policy funds in a managed portfolio fund and have the investment allocation decisions made by a professional money manager working for the insurance company. This appeals to policyowners who do not want to spend a lot of time studying the market and making investment decisions. With a managed portfolio policyowners can reap all of the long-term advantages of a variable insurance contract without having to perform the investment allocation function themselves.

Some insurance companies have even formed alliances with large mutual fund groups that make their entire range of mutual funds available by offering copycat funds to the insurer.

Such alliances make it possible for smaller life insurance companies to gain access to the administrative services already in place in these large mutual fund family groups. (Separate account funds cannot be available directly to the public.)

Policy Cash Values

Policy premiums paid under variable life insurance contracts are often subject to an administrative charge; the balance of the premium payment goes into the cash value account. The actual value of the cash component is determined by the net asset value of the separate account funds that make up the policy portfolio. The cash value of a variable life policy fluctuates daily. Each day's net asset value is based on the closing price for the issues in the portfolio on that trading day. Cash value accounts are further diminished by mortality charges to support the death benefits.

As with traditional life insurance contracts, the policyowner has access to the cash value via policy loans. Variable life insurance policies usually limit maximum policy loans to a slightly smaller percentage of the total cash value than is traditionally available in whole life policies.

The earnings on the cash value are obviously affected by any outstanding policy loans. The policyowner accrues indebtedness at the applicable policy loan interest rate, and that is the yield applicable to the assets associated with the portion of the cash value offset by the outstanding loan. Whenever the policy loan interest rate is lower than the portfolio investment earnings rate, the insurance company experiences a lower effective investment return. The only time the insurance company experiences a financial gain from policy loans is when the policy loan interest rate exceeds that earned by the portfolio backing the policies. Policy loans can be repaid at any time in part or in full, but there is no requirement that policy loans be repaid in cash at any time during the existence of the life insurance contract. For any portion of the loan not repaid interest accrues on a compound basis. Just as in any other form of whole life policy, outstanding policy loans under a variable life insurance policy reduce the death benefit payable. The policy loan is always fully secured by the remaining cash value in the policy. Whenever the outstanding loans plus accrued interest equal the remaining cash value, the net cash value becomes zero and the policy terminates.

The net cash value in the contract is also closely related to the nonforfeiture options available under the policy. Variable life insurance contracts provide the same range of nonforfeiture options as do traditional whole life policies. The net cash surrender value can be obtained by surrendering the contract to the insurance company, or the net cash value can be applied as a single premium to purchase either a reduced amount of paid-up insurance

or the same amount of extended term insurance. The duration of the extended term insurance will be the longest period of coverage for the same death benefit amount that can be obtained from the insurance company for the policy's net cash value.

Variable life insurance policies also contain the usual form of reinstatement provisions, including a specific prohibition on reinstatements if the policy has been surrendered for its cash value. Contracts also have the standard waiver-of-premium option since premiums are fixed and the policy will lapse if they are not paid.

The Prospectus

prospectus

Variable life insurance policies cannot be sold without an accompanying **prospectus**. The prospectus mandated by the SEC is similar in many respects to the prospectus required of new stock issues. It is a full disclosure of all of the provisions of the contract, including expenses, investment options, benefit provisions, and policyowner rights under the contract. It is a lengthy and detailed document. Most purchasers are reluctant to read the entire document, but it is an important source of information that is not available anywhere else. In fact, one of the authors of this book has observed that the prospectus for a variable life insurance contract offers more information to prospective purchasers than even very aggressive information seekers can obtain for traditional life insurance contracts.

Primary Focus of Prospectus Disclosure

- Operating expenses

- Marketing expenses

- Taxes and fees

- Cost of insurance charge

- Surrender charges

- Investment charges

- Investment performance

As always, the SEC focus is on providing thorough and accurate information. The prospectus for a new stock issue from a stock life insurance company therefore provides more information about the company to potential investors than would ever be available

to purchasers of life insurance products (except for SEC registered variable and variable universal life).

Expense Information

The prospectus has very thorough information about all of the expense charges levied by the insurance company against variable life insurance contracts. This includes commissions paid to soliciting agents, state premium taxes, administrative charges, collection charges, and possibly fees for specific future transactions.

Administrative charges usually differ between the first year of the contract and all renewal years. It is common for first-year administrative charges to run in the neighborhood of $15 to $50 per month. The same administrative charges in the second policy year and there-after drop to a lower level, perhaps $5 to $10 per month. The prospectus also indicates whether or not there is any maximum guarantee on those administrative fees over the duration of the contract.

cost-of-insurance charge

In addition, the prospectus sets forth the manner in which charges are made against the asset account to cover the cost of insurance under the contract. This is usually referred to in the prospectus as the **cost-of-insurance charge**. The prospectus specifies exactly what rate will be used to determine cost-of-insurance charges and explicitly specifies if there is any maximum rate above the intended rate. It also explains the manner in which charges are levied against the separate account itself—essentially the fees associated with man-aging the various mutual fund type of accounts from which the policyowner can choose. Part of that charge is always some specified percentage (usually less than one full percent) of the assets in the separate accounts themselves. There also may be specific charges to establish and maintain trusts necessary in managing those assets. These charges are very similar to the charges levied by mutual fund administrators on investors in the fund.

Surrender Charges

One very important item that is clearly spelled out in the prospectus and should always be considered important information when considering the purchase of any life insurance policy—variable or traditional—is the surrender charge applicable to policy surrenders. In most cases this information is set forth in a tabular form, giving the policy year and the applicable percentage for the surrender charge in that year. Under some contract designs the surrender charge is specified in terms of percentage of premiums; under other contracts it is specified in terms of the aggregate account balance in the separate funds.

Surrender charges are applicable only if the policy is surrendered for its cash value, allowed to lapse, or under some contracts if the policy is adjusted to provide a lower death benefit. Surrender charges are commonly levied during the first 10 to 15 years of the contract. The actual number of years and specific rates are always set forth in the prospectus. The maximum duration of surrender charges is usually a good indicator of how long the insurer intends to amortize excess first-year acquisition costs. The surrender charge is applicable only to policies surrendered before the insurance company's front-end expenses have been recovered. Sometimes these surrender charges are called contingent deferred sales charges.

Investment Portfolio Information

The prospectus sets forth the investment objectives of each of the available investment funds and a record of their historical performance. There is detailed information on the current holdings of each of the available portfolios, usually supplemented by information about purchases and sales of individual equities or debt instruments by the fund over the previous 12 months. Further information is given about earnings during that same period of time and usually for longer intervals of prior performance if those portfolio funds have been in existence long enough to give investment results for trades over 5 or 10 years. Any investment restrictions applicable to these portfolios as indicated in the trust instruments themselves are fully disclosed.

There are also projections of future performance under the contract if portfolio funds generate a fixed level of investment earnings over the projected interval. All illustrations must show a hypothetical zero percent gross rate of return, and may show any additional combinations of rates of return up to and including a gross rate of 12 percent, though members are cautioned to choose a rate that is reasonable given current market conditions.

Much of the detailed information in the prospectus concerns ownership and voting rights regarding procedures to change any of the trust documents or restrictions. These elements are very similar to those found in self-standing mutual funds not associated or affiliated with life insurance policies or protection.

Risks the Policyowner Assumes

As mentioned earlier, fixed-premium variable life insurance contracts are very similar to whole life insurance contracts; the main difference is that the policyowner assumes the investment risk and therefore can participate in favorable investment returns. The fixed-premium provision does not allow the policyowner to increase or decrease the death

benefit by negotiated adjustment; favorable results automatically translate into increased death benefit amounts.

One unique benefit is that the policy does guarantee a minimum death benefit level equal to the original face amount of the contract if the required premiums are paid, regardless of how badly the investment performance turns out to be. In other words, if all of the required premiums are paid, the insurance company guarantees that the death benefit equal to the original face amount of the policy will be paid even if the investment funds are otherwise inadequate to support the policy. Therefore, the variable feature of this contract can provide additional coverage if investment experience warrants, but the policyowner will never be required to pay more or permitted to pay less than the guaranteed premium.

A fixed-premium variable life insurance policy provides more guarantees to the policyowner than its more recently developed cousins with truly flexible provisions, such as universal life and variable universal life.

VARIABLE ADJUSTABLE LIFE INSURANCE

The same companies that developed adjustable life contracts subsequently developed a variation on that contract—variable adjustable life. As its name suggests, this coverage is an adjustable life policy that can be negotiated to change the death benefit level up or down, or to increase or decrease premium amounts to a new fixed level, which can shorten or lengthen the premium-paying period. The new feature is, of course, the policyowner's ability to choose the investment portfolio, within limits. This contract actually overcomes one of the shortcomings of the fixed-premium variable life contract by allowing the policyowner to negotiate with the insurance company a changed policy configuration that more closely fits the policyowner's changed circumstances.

The policyowner does not have the unilateral right to skip premium payments or vary the amount of any one premium payment at will without prior negotiation with the insurance company. As with the first generation of variable life insurance contracts, the death benefit is tied to investment performance but guaranteed never to be less than the original amount of coverage under the policy.

variable adjustable life insurance

Most of the insurance companies offering variable adjustable life coverage chose not to enter the universal life market. In fact, they introduced **variable adjustable life insurance**

as a defensive move to enhance their competitiveness after the marketing success of universal life with its flexible-premium design.

VARIABLE UNIVERSAL LIFE

variable universal life insurance

Variable universal life insurance is one of the most recently developed variations of whole life. This policy incorporates all of the premium flexibility and policy adjustment features of the universal life policy with the policyowner-directed investment aspects of variable life insurance. Obviously this design discards the fixed-premium features of the variable life insurance contract (see figures below).

One of the most interesting aspects of variable universal life insurance is that it eliminates the direct connection between investment performance above or below some stated target level and the corresponding formula-directed adjustment in death benefits. Instead variable universal life insurance adopts the death benefit designs applicable to universal life policies, namely, either a level death benefit or an increasing death benefit design where a constant amount of risk is paid in addition to the cash accumulation account. Under the first of those options, the death benefit doesn't change, regardless of how positive or negative the investment performance under the contract turns out to be. If the policyowner wants to have the death benefit vary with the performance of the investments under the contract, he or she must choose the increasing death benefit design. All of the increase or decrease is a direct result of the accumulation account balance, rather than the result of purchasing paid-up additions (or some form of modified premium addition) as is the case under fixed-premium variable life insurance.

Variable universal life policies offer the policyowner a choice among a specified group of mutual fund types of separate accounts that are usually created and maintained by the insurance company itself. Some insurance companies have made arrangements with other investment companies to utilize separate account portfolios created and maintained by those investment management firms. Some of these separate funds are copies of popular mutual funds available to retail investors.

Figure 7-2
Variable Universal Life Type I or A
Level Death Benefit

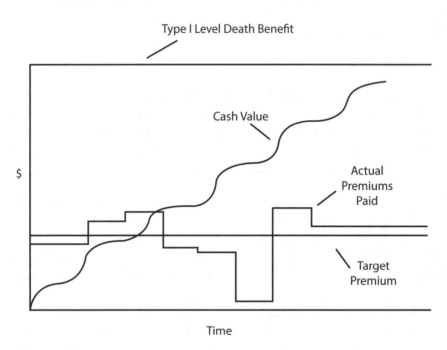

Like variable life insurance, variable universal life insurance policies are technically classified as securities and are subject to regulation by the SEC. The SEC requires registration
of agents marketing the product, the separate accounts supporting the contracts, and
the contracts themselves. In addition, policies must conform with the SEC requirements
that the investment funds be separate accounts that are segregated from the insurance
company's general investment portfolio and therefore not subject to creditors' claims
applicable to the insurer's general portfolio in times of financial difficulty. Variable universal
life contracts are also subject to regulation by the state insurance commissioners. Nearly 80
percent of the states have adopted the National Association of Insurance Commissioners
(NAIC) model variable life insurance regulation in its modified form (which is less restrictive
than the original model regulation).

Figure 7-3
Variable Universal Life Type II or B
Increasing Death Benefit

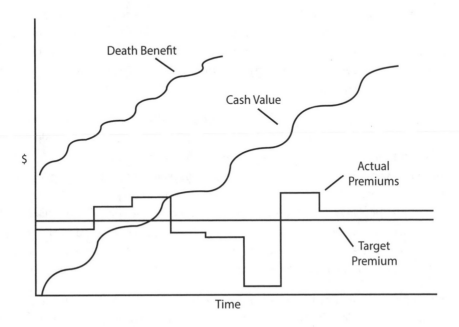

Because variable universal life is a registered investment product, policies must be accompanied by a prospectus, which is governed by the same rules applicable to prospectuses for variable life policies. The prospectus provides the necessary information for a meaningful evaluation and comparison of policies.

Ultimate Flexibility

Probably the easiest way to describe variable universal life insurance is to say that it is a universal life insurance policy with the added feature that the policyowner gets to choose the investments, as under fixed-premium variable life insurance contracts. Variable universal life offers the ultimate in both the flexibility afforded to the policyowner and the amount of risk shifted to the policyowner. There are no interest rate or cash value guarantees and very limited guarantees on the maximum mortality rates applicable. Policyowners have wide-open premium flexibility under this contract and can choose to fund it at whatever level they desire as long as it is at least high enough to create coverage similar to yearly renewal term and not in excess of the amount that would drive the cash accumulation account

above the maximum threshold set forth in I.R.C. Sec. 7702. Policyowners do not need to negotiate with the insurance company or inform the insurer in advance of any premium modification or cessation.

These contracts permit partial withdrawals that work just like those under universal life policies. Early partial withdrawals may be subject to surrender charges, and surrender charges are applicable to total surrenders in the policy's early years when the insurance company is still recovering excess first-year acquisition costs. The surrender charges vanish at a specified policy duration.

Variable universal life can be aggressively prefunded so that the policy can completely support itself from its cash value. If adequate premiums are contributed to the contract, this can be accomplished in a relatively short number of years. As with universal life and current assumption whole life, variable universal life policies have no guarantee that once the cash value is large enough to carry the policy it will always be able to do so. The policyowner assumes the risk of investment return and, to a limited extent, some of the risk of mortality rate charges. Consequently, the policyowner has to make adjustments and either pay more premiums or reduce the death benefit at some future time if in fact the cash value subsequently dips below the level needed to totally prefund the remaining contract years.

By choosing the increasing death benefit option under this contract policyowners are afforded an automatic hedge against inflation. This inflation protection is general in nature and subject to a timing mismatch in that investment experience may not keep pace with short-term bursts of inflation. Over the long haul, however, the investment-induced increases in coverage should equal, if not exceed, general increases in price levels.

Many variable universal life policies offer an additional cost-of-living adjustment rider to further assure timely death benefit increases associated with increases in the consumer price index. These riders trigger death benefit increases paid for by term charges against the policy's cash value.

As with variable life, the policyowner is able to switch investment funds from one of the available choices to any other single fund or combination thereof whenever desired. Some insurance companies put a limit on how many fund changes can be made without incurring explicit costs for those changes. Some companies allow one change of funds per year at no cost, others allow one change per open fund per year with no explicit charges, and others specify in the prospectus a given number of fund changes that can be accomplished during any given time interval (usually annually but sometimes other intervals such as quarterly or monthly) without incurring additional charges. Within some companies there is a banding of charges, depending on the number of fund reallocations or redirections

during the specified period of time. The cost per transaction goes up as the number of transactions increases in the time interval. Theoretically, policyowners could redirect funds on a daily basis, but such aggressive reallocation could generate significant internal expenses and would probably be a strong indication that the policyowner is attempting to be more aggressive than warranted for this type of contract.

Switching investment funds is accomplished without any internal or external taxation of inherent gains in the funds. The internal buildup of the cash value is tax deferred at least as long as the policy stays in force and will be federal income tax free if the policy matures as a death claim.

Variable universal life insurance policies are still primarily life insurance contracts that generate cash value as part of the prefunding level premium mechanism. They are not strictly investment contracts and should not be viewed as such. Philosophically there seems to be a conflict when policyowners manage variable life or variable universal life policies for maximum aggressive growth when in fact the reason for the contracts is to provide a financial safety net for beneficiaries. If the primary coverage is for its death benefits, it seems more appropriate that the investment allocations not pursue the most aggressive growth objectives. A more conservative growth approach is suggested.

On the other hand, if the primary objective for acquiring the contract is for its cash value and the policyowner intends to use the policy's cash values prior to the insured's death, perhaps the more aggressive growth stance is acceptable. In this case the policyowner is likely to be the beneficiary and the risk bearer.

Income Tax Burdens for Early Depletion

Variable universal life policies should not be utilized as short-term investment vehicles. There are two potential traps for policyowners who significantly deplete the policy's cash values at various intervals during the first 15 policy years. These income tax burdens are in addition to any surrender charges that may be applicable within the policy itself.

One potential trap is the modified endowment contract provisions of the Tax Code, which treat all cash value distributions as taxable income until all investment returns have been taxed before the remainder of the distribution is treated as recovery of basis. Such treatment is possible whenever material policy changes are made and the policy fails the seven-pay test (reaching the cash value amount for a policy paid up after 7 years). If the policy fails the seven-pay test, not only will the distributed amounts be subject to income tax (up to the extent of the gain) but there may also be a 10 percent penalty tax applicable to those taxable gains if the policyowner is younger than 59 1/2 years of age. High cash value/

high premium configuration variable universal life policies are the most likely candidates for this tax trap. Making sure that the cash value before and after any material change is lower than what it would be if the policy were fully paid up after 7 years will, in most cases, avoid this potential problem.

The other potential trap again deals with high levels of cash value approaching the upper limits permitted under the Tax Code. If a reduction in the death benefit level forces a distribution of the cash value in order to retain life insurance status under the Code, those distributions may be taxable income to the extent that they represent gain in the policy. The most stringent constraints apply to such "forced out" withdrawals during the first 5 years of the policy's existence. Slightly less binding constraints are applicable for policy years 6 through 15. Any policyowner contemplating a switch from the increasing death benefit design to the level benefit design during the policy's first 15 years should consider these rules before making the switch. As long as there is no forced distribution or concurrent request by the policyowner for a discretionary distribution of cash value funds, there will be no problem.

Conversely, if the increasing death benefit form of the contract is already prefunded near the maximum limitations, there is the possibility that some cash value will be forced out to maintain compliance with the Tax Code limitations on life insurance policies.

Neither of these tax traps has any consequence if there are no gains in the contract (premiums paid exceed cash value) when distributions are made. Also, under Modified Endowment Contract (MEC) provisions the taxation will be applicable only if there are distributions of the cash value. If the funds are left in the contract and allowed to remain part of the cash value, there will be no taxation even though the potential still exists for any distribution once the policy has become classified as a MEC.

Variable universal life contracts are not desirable for policyowners who do not wish to assume the investment risk under the contract. Potential policyowners who say they want to assume the investment risk but become extremely anxious over any short-term fall in the value of the selected investment portfolio funds should also be cautioned. A successful life insurance agent once facetiously suggested that anyone purchasing variable life or variable universal life insurance should cancel his or her subscription to the Wall Street Journal to minimize the likelihood of daily assessments of the investment fund performance. Realistically, maybe the best prospects for variable life contracts and variable universal life contracts are those who do in fact have a subscription to the Wall Street Journal and are more attuned to the daily fluctuations in fund values. Policyowners are not likely to find asset value information regarding the specific funds backing their policies in the Wall Street Journal anyway. The separate account requirements imposed by the SEC have

prompted most insurance companies to use funds that are not available to the general public. These funds are very rarely publicly traded and therefore not included in the Wall Street Journal's daily listing of funds.

Variable universal life insurance has become a viable contract for corporate-owned life insurance. Its flexibility is compatible with the constantly changing needs of the corporation owning the policy. Corporate management is usually fairly sophisticated in understanding the investment process and the short-term upward and downward fluctuations in portfolio holdings.

CHAPTER REVIEW

Key Terms and Concepts

variable life insurance
prospectus
cost-of-insurance charge
variable adjustable life insurance
variable universal life insurance

Chapter 7 Review Questions

1. Explain why variable life and variable universal life insurance policies are subject to Securities and Exchange Commission (SEC) regulation, and describe the requirements that regulation imposes on the insurers, agents, and policies. [3]

2. Describe the link between investment performance and death benefits under variable life insurance policies. [1]

3. Explain how investment options have changed under many variable universal life policies over the past two decades. [4]

4. Explain how the cash value of a variable life policy differs from that of a whole life policy. [3]

5. Describe the type of information in a variable life insurance or variable universal lifein-surance prospectus. [3]

6. Describe the risks the policyowner assumes under a variable life or variable universal life policy. [3, 4]

7. Compare variable adjustable life insurance with adjustable life insurance. [2]

8. Describe variable universal life insurance, and explain how it differs from: (a) universal life; (b) variable life. [3, 4]

Chapter 7 Review Answers

1. *A variable life insurance policy provides no guarantees of either interest rate or minimum cash value. As the SEC pointed out, in order for policyowners to gain the additional benefit of better-than-expected investment returns, they also have to assume all of the downside investment risk. Consequently, the SEC required variable life policies to be registered with the SEC and all sales to be subject to the following requirements applied to other registered securities. Policy sales can be made only after the prospective purchaser has a chance to read the policy prospectus. An insurance company issuing a variable life insurance policy must be registered as an investment company and all sales agents must be registered with the SEC for the specific purpose of variable life insurance policy sales. Agents who sell variable life insurance policies must be licensed as both life insurance agents and securities agents.*

2. *Because the primary reason for life insurance is to provide death benefits, it makes sense to link superior investment performance with increases in the death benefit level. A variable life insurance policy has a minimum death benefit equal to the initial face amount when the policy was first purchased. However, if the policy's actual investment performance exceeds a target level of investment performance, the excess investment return is used to purchase additional life insurance under either the level additions method or the constant ratio method. Under both methods, the amount of additional coverage in excess of the initial face amount will fluctuate depending on actual investment performance. If invest-ment earnings are negative (the actual earnings are lower than the target rate), then the adjustments will have to be downward from any previously attained levels above the policy's initial face value. If investment earnings are positive (the actual earnings are above the target rate), the adjustments will be upward.*

3. Life insurance companies are now offering many more investment fund options than they made available in the early stages of the variable life product's development. Some insurance companies have more than a dozen funds from which to choose in their current product offering. There are usually a variety of stock funds, including growth stock funds, income stock funds, balanced stock funds, and international stock funds. Bond fund offerings are likewise more robust and include different durations and different types of issuers (large corporations, small corporations, state governments, and the federal government) as well as Government National Mortgage Association (GNMAs) funds and collateralized mortgage obligations (CMOs). In addition, many insurance companies offer a managed fund as one of the portfolio choices. Some insurance companies have even formed alliances with large mutual fund groups that make their entire range of mutual funds available.

4. Unlike a whole life policy where the cash value increases over time due to the crediting of at least the guaranteed interest rate, the cash value of a variable life policy fluctuates daily depending on the net asset value of the separate account funds that make up the policy portfolio.

5. The prospectus is a full disclosure of all of the provisions of the contract, including expenses, investment options, benefit provisions, and policyowner rights under the contract. The prospectus has very thorough information about all of the expense charges levied by the insurance company against variable life insurance contracts. This includes commissions paid to soliciting agents, state premium taxes, administrative charges (which usually differ between the first year of the contract and all renewal years), collection charges, and possibly fees for specific future transactions. In addition, the prospectus sets forth the manner in which charges are made against the asset account to cover the cost of insurance under the contract. It also explains the manner in which charges are levied against the separate account itself-essentially the fees associated with managing the various mutual fund type of accounts from which the policyowner can choose. Part of that charge is always some specified percentage (usually less than one full percent) of the assets in the separate accounts themselves. One very important item that is clearly spelled out in the prospectus is the surrender charge applicable to policy surrenders. In most cases, this information is set forth in a tabular form, giving the policy year and the applicable percentage for the surrender charge in that year. Surrender charges are commonly levied during the first 10 to 15 years of the contract. The actual number of years and specific rates are always set forth in the prospectus. The prospectus sets forth the investment objectives of each of the available investment funds and a record of their historical performance. Any investment restrictions applicable to these portfolios, as indicated in the trust instruments

themselves, are fully disclosed. There are also projections of future performance under the contract if portfolio funds generate a fixed level of investment earnings over the projected interval. Under SEC regulations, the permissible rates of return that can be projected are the gross annual rates after tax charges but before any other deductions at 0, 4, 8, 10, or 12 percent. The insurance company can decide the permissible rates it chooses to project. Finally, much of the detailed information in the prospectus concerns ownership and voting rights with regard to procedures to change any of the trust documents or restrictions.

6. With a variable life insurance policy, the policyowner assumes the investment risk and, therefore, can participate in favorable investment returns. The fixed-premium provision does not allow the policyowner to increase or decrease the death benefit by negotiated adjustment; favorable results automatically translate into increased death benefit amounts. One unique benefit is that the policy does guarantee a minimum death benefit level equal to the original face amount of the contract, regardless of how negative the investment performance. In other words, if all of the required premiums are paid, the insurance company guarantees that the death benefit equal to the original face amount of the policy will be paid even if the investment funds are otherwise inadequate to support the policy. Therefore, the variable feature of this contract can provide additional coverage if warranted by investment experience, but the policyowner will never be required to pay more or permitted to pay less than the guaranteed premium.

7. Both the variable adjustable life policy and the adjustable life policy permit the policyowner to negotiate changes in the death benefit level up or down, or to negotiate an increase or decrease in the premium amount to a new fixed level, which can shorten or lengthen the premium-paying period. However, with the variable adjustable life policy, the policyowner also has the ability to choose the investment portfolio, within limits.

8. Variable universal life insurance (VUL) incorporates all of the premium flexibility and policy adjustment features of the universal life policy with the policyowner-directed investment aspects of variable life insurance.

    a. VUL differs from universal life in providing no minimum interest rate guarantee. Premium net of mortality and expense charges are invested in separate accounts chosen by the policyowner and the VUL cash value depends solely on the investment results achieved. Also, like variable life insurance, variable universal life insurance policies are technically classified as securities and are subject to regulation by the SEC. The SEC requires registration of agents marketing the product, the separate accounts supporting the contracts, and the contracts themselves. In addition, policies must

conform with the SEC requirements that the investment funds be separate accounts that are segregated from the insurance company's general investment portfolio and, therefore, not subject to creditors' claims applicable to the insurer's general portfolio in times of financial difficulty. Because variable universal life is a registered investment product, policies must be accompanied by a prospectus, which is governed by the same rules applicable to prospectuses for variable life policies.

b. *VUL discards the fixed-premium features of the variable life insurance contract and also, unlike variable life insurance, offers a choice of level or increasing death benefits.*

Settlement Agreements, Settlement Options, & Surrender Values

By Dan M. McGill

Revised by C.W. Copeland & Edward E. Graves

Learning Objectives

An understanding of the material in this chapter should enable the student to

1. Describe and understand each of the surrender options required in policies with cash values.

2. Explain how policy loans affect surrender options, especially extended term insurance.

3. Understand the underlying concepts and rules of settlement options.

4. Describe the basic settlement option choices available to policyowners and policy beneficiaries.

5. Explain the settlement agreement provisions concerning contract and current rates, rights of withdrawal and commutation, and minimum-amount requirements.

6. Describe the structure, characteristics, and functions of the four fundamental settlement options.

7. Understand the use of settlement options to meet family needs, such as estate liquidity, mortgages, emergencies, education, and income.

8. Describe the possible approaches to a withdrawing policyowner's equitable treatment, including any adjustments that might be made to a policy's asset share in implementing those approaches.

9. Describe the requirements the Standard Nonforfeiture Law imposes on surrender values.

10. Explain the philosophy underlying the adjusted-premium method, how a surrender value is computed with that method, and how the adjusted-premium method and its resulting surrender values differ from the full net level premium reserve valuation method and its resulting prospective terminal reserves.

11. Calculate policy surrender values using the adjusted-premium method, and interpret the results in terms of the extent to which first-year expenses have been amortized.

12. Explain how surrender values are determined for nontraditional

products such as universal life insurance.

SURRENDER OPTIONS

The surrender values provided under the Standard Nonforfeiture Law can be taken by the policyowner in one of three forms:

- cash
- paid-up cash value life insurance
- extended or (paid-up) term insurance

These forms are properly referred to as surrender benefits, but since the policyowner has the option or privilege of choosing the form under which the surrender value is to be paid, the benefits are usually referred to as surrender options.

The Standard Nonforfeiture Law requires that a surrender benefit be granted whenever a value appears under the formula. This may be as early as the end of the first year under some policies and later than 3 years under other policies. Under most plans and at most ages of issue, a surrender value will appear in the second policy year. Formerly, no cash or other surrender benefits were required in the case of term insurance policies of 20 years or less. Under the current law a level-premium term policy for more than 15 years[1]—or one that expires after age 65, regardless of its duration—must provide surrender benefits if the mandated formula indicates that one exists. The nature and significance of the various standard forms of surrender benefits are discussed in the following sections.

surrender options

Nonforfeiture or Surrender Options. Ordinary life, in common with other forms of whole life insurance, provides a limited degree of flexibility. This flexibility is derived from several different contract provisions, but one of the most significant is the set of provisions referred to as nonforfeiture or **surrender options**. Designed originally to preserve the policyowner's equity in the policy reserve, surrender provisions are increasingly being used to adapt policy coverage to changing circumstances and needs. Most policies stipulate that the surrender value may be taken in one of three forms: cash, a reduced amount of paid-up whole life insurance, or paid-up term insurance.

---

1.   Twenty years in some states.

Cash Value. The policy may be surrendered at any time for its cash value. In that event the protection terminates and the company has no further obligation under the policy. While this privilege provides a ready source of cash to meet a financial emergency or to take advantage of a business opportunity, it should be exercised with restraint since it diminishes the further usefulness of the policy. A policy that has been surrendered for cash cannot be reinstated except by special permission of the company, which is usually withheld unless the insured can provide evidence of insurability that would satisfy the criteria for issuing a new policy to a first-time applicant.

reduced amount of paid-up whole life

Reduced Amount of Paid-Up Whole Life. The second option permits the insured to take a **reduced amount of paid-up whole life** insurance, payable upon the same conditions as the original policy. The amount of the paid-up insurance is the amount that can be purchased at the insured's attained age by the net cash value (cash value, less any policy indebtedness [policyowner loans plus accrued interest], plus any dividend accumulations) applied as a net single premium. Note that the paid-up insurance is purchased at net rates, which constitutes a sizable saving to the purchaser. According to the 1980 CSO Table and a 4.5 percent interest assumption, the cash value at the end of 20 years on an ordinary life contract issued at age 30 is $220, which is sufficient, as a net single premium, to purchase $615 of paid-up whole life insurance. The protection continues in the reduced amount until the insured's death unless the reduced policy is surrendered for cash, and no further premiums are called for under this plan.

paid-up term

Paid-Up Term. The third option provides **paid-up term** insurance in an amount equal to the original face amount of the policy, increased by any dividend additions or deposits and decreased by any policy indebtedness. The length of the term is what can be purchased at the insured's attained age with the net cash value applied as a net single premium. At age 50 the aforementioned cash value of $220 would purchase $1,000 of term insurance for about 16.5 years. If the insured fails to elect an option within a specified period after default of premiums, this option automatically goes into effect.

If the financial status of the policyowner makes it impracticable to continue premium payments, or if the need for insurance protection undergoes a change, the policyowner may wish to elect one of the surrender options. After his or her dependents have become self-supporting, for example, the policyowner may elect to discontinue premium payments and continue the protection on a reduced scale for the remainder of the insured's life. If, on the other hand, the need for insurance continues, he or she may elect to eliminate

premium payments but continue the full amount of protection for a definite period of time. The elimination of fixed payments may be particularly attractive as the insured approaches retirement and anticipates a reduction in income.

Example

Donald, aged 50, has a $300,000 policy with a $66,000 cash value. His wife, Janet, and their only child, Betty, were severely injured in an auto accident and had many uninsured medical expenses before Betty died. Donald and Janet have the following nonforfeiture options:

- to surrender policy for $66,000 cash

- to continue the $300,000 coverage for 16.5 years as paid-up term insurance with no more premiums

- to reduce the coverage to $184,000 of paid-up whole life coverage with no more premiums

Annuity or Retirement Income. Another use of surrender values that is growing in popularity is applying them to the purchase of an annuity or retirement income. If the life insurance policy does not specifically give the insured the right to take the cash value in the form of a life income (purchased at net rates), the insurer will grant the privilege upon request. More and more insureds are purchasing ordinary life insurance to protect their families during the child-raising period with the specific objective of eventually using the cash values for their own retirement. The cash value of an ordinary life policy purchased at age 25 will usually be in the range of 50 percent to 60 percent of the face amount at age 65. The comparable percentage range for an ordinary life policy purchased at age 35 is 40 percent to 55 percent, and even a policy issued as late as age 40 will accumulate a cash value at age 65 only slightly less than one-half of the face amount (35 percent to 50 percent). Therefore if an individual procures $50,000 of ordinary life insurance at age 35, for example, he or she would have approximately $24,000 in cash value at 65, which at net rates would provide a life income somewhere in the range of $140 to $165 per month. Supplemented by federal OASDI (Old-Age, Survivors, and Disability Insurance) benefits, private retirement plan benefits, and income from other savings, this could provide the insured with an adequate retirement income.

Some people might feel that the interruption of premium payments on an ordinary life policy would in some way amount to failure to complete the program. There are, of course, situations where this might be the case. However, if the ordinary life plan is deliberately selected with the idea of discontinuing premiums at an advanced age, there can be no suggestion of failure to complete the undertaking. Neither should an insured be reluctant

to convert ordinary life insurance to reduced paid-up insurance if a change of circumstance makes the reduced amount adequate for his or her needs, particularly if retirement status makes paying life insurance premiums an unjustified burden. Life insurance is designed to provide protection where the need exists. If it becomes a burden and represents a very real sacrifice on the part of the insured, the burden can be lightened when the need for protection ceases. This is an advantage of the ordinary life contract that should be recognized at the outset and utilized as the occasion arises.

Cash

The simplest form in which the surrender value may be taken is cash. After the policy has been in force long enough to have no surrender charges, there is an exact equivalence between the surrender value of a policy and the cash that can be obtained upon its surrender, leading many persons to refer to the surrender value generically as the cash surrender value. The new law requires that the surrender value of a policy be made available in the form of cash, but it does not compel a company to grant cash values until the end of 3 years in the case of ordinary insurance. This limitation on cash values was provided in order to relieve the companies of the expense of drawing checks for the relatively small values that might have developed during the first and second policy years. It does not, however, relieve the company of the obligation to make available in some noncash form of benefit any surrender value that might accumulate during the first 2 years. Most companies waive this statutory provision and provide a cash value as soon as any value develops under the policy.

delay clause

The law permits a company to postpone payment of the cash surrender value for a period of 6 months after demand thereof and surrender of the policy. This **delay clause** was given statutory sanction in order to protect companies against any losses that might otherwise arise from excessive demands for cash during an extreme financial emergency. The law has made the inclusion of a delay clause mandatory and has made the delay period of 6 months uniform. It is contemplated that the clause would be invoked only under the most unusual circumstances. Mutual Benefit Life Insurance Company was already experiencing a run on its assets from demand for policy surrenders and maximum policy loans before it sought both the protection of the delay clause and intervention by the state insurance commissioner. Even though the company was in poor financial shape, it was reluctant to impose the delay clause until loss of confidence was so widespread that it had no other choice.

As might be expected, provision is made for deduction of any policy indebtedness (policy loans plus accrued interest) from the cash value that would otherwise be available.

Impact of Electing Surrender Benefits

The impact of the election of each surrender benefit on the structure of the underlying insurance contract is illustrated in Figures 8-1 through 8-4. In each case the underlying contract will be assumed to be a whole life policy, but the principle involved is applicable to any type of contract, with some modification. Figure 8-1 shows the change produced in cash value life insurance contracts by the exercise of the cash surrender option. The figure indicates that up to the point of surrender, the contract is a combination of protection and cash value. By surrendering the policy for cash, however, the policyowner takes the cash value element of the contract and, in so doing, terminates the protection element as well. Subject only to any reinstatement privilege that might exist, the company has no further obligations under the contract. Generally, the reinstatement rights are available only to policies that have terminated for reasons other than a cash surrender.

Reduced Paid-Up Insurance

This form of surrender benefit is referred to as reduced paid-up insurance, in recognition of the fact that under this option, the withdrawing policyowner receives a reduced amount of paid-up cash value insurance, payable upon the same conditions as the original policy. If the original policy was either an ordinary life or a limited-payment life policy, the insurance under this option will be paid-up whole life insurance. If the original policy was an endowment contract, this option will provide an endowment with the same maturity date but in a reduced amount. Some companies make this option available under a term policy, in which case an appropriately reduced amount of term insurance is paid up to the expiry date of the original term policy.

The amount of paid-up insurance provided under this option is the sum that can be purchased at the insured's attained age by the net surrender value (cash value, less any policy indebtedness, plus the cash value of any dividend additions or deposits) applied as a net single premium computed on the mortality and interest bases specified in the policy for the calculation of the surrender value. The amount of paid-up insurance available at various durations under an ordinary life and under a 20-payment life policy, issued at age 35, is shown in the table below.

Figure 8-1
Effect of Cash Surrender on Structure of Several Types of
Life Insurance Contracts

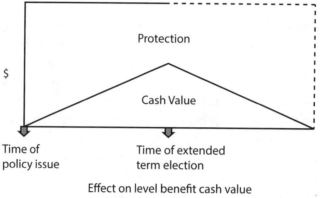

Effect on level benefit cash value
life insurance contracts

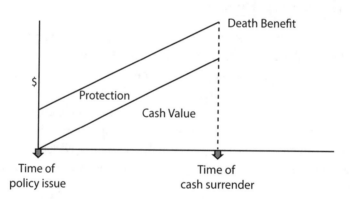

Effect on increasing death benefit type of
universal life or variable universal life policies

Paid-up insurance is provided under this option at net premium rates, despite the fact that maintenance and surrender or settlement expenses will be incurred on the policies.[2] The law made no specific allowance for expenses on the theory that the margins in the mortality and interest assumptions underlying the net rates are sufficient to absorb any

---

2.   It should be noted that certain other types of expenses–for example, commissions, premium taxes, underwriting expenses, and service fees—are not incurred.

expenses that will be involved. In the case of participating insurance, however, any margins available for this purpose are reduced by the payment of dividends on the paid-up insurance.

Table 8-1 Example of Surrender Benefits at Selected Durations for Ordinary Life and 20-Payment Life (Issue Age 35, Male 1980 CSO Mortality, 4.5 Percent Interest)								
Ordinary Life					20-Payment Whole Life			
Policy Year	Cash Value	Reduced Paid-up Insurance	Extended Term Insurance		Cash Value	Reduced Paid-up Insurance	Extended Term Insurance	
			Yrs.	Days			Yrs.	Days
3	6	28	1	297	7	29	2	42
5	28	122	6	261	40	157	9	216
10	92	331	13	211	142	468	20	318
15	168	498	16	15	266	743	25	145
20	250	630	16	170	420	1,000	27	242
25	336	721	15	186	487	1,000	22	175
30	429	794	14	9	558	1,000	18	88
35	523	850	12	119	629	1,000	14	300
All values are per $1,000 of insurance.								

It is interesting to note that there is a surrender privilege under reduced paid-up whole life and endowment policies. The law states that such policies can be surrendered for cash within 30 days after any policy anniversary, provided the original policy was in force long enough to grant a cash value. In other words, the cash surrender privilege of the paid-up policy cannot be used to subvert the provision in the law that cash values need not be granted until the end of 3 years.

The effect of the reduced paid-up insurance option on the structure of the whole life policy is illustrated in Figure 9-2. It is readily apparent that the most important impact is on the protection element of the contract. In the example, the cash value before surrender had accumulated to a sum half the face of the policy, which at age 60, for instance, would purchase a paid-up whole life policy in an amount approximately 75 percent of the original face. The entire shrinkage comes out of the protection element, however, since the investment element continues to increase until it equals the reduced face at the end of the mortality table. The same phenomenon occurs with a surrender at any duration. As was pointed out, this cash value element of a reduced paid-up policy can be converted into cash by surrendering the policy pursuant to its terms.

Universal life insurance and variable universal life policies provide a nonguaranteed form of reduced paid-up option. The policyowner can reduce the death benefit so that the existing cash value is sufficient to cover all future charges, helped by the future earnings credited to the cash value. The nonguaranteed element is the fact that the variable universal policyowner bears the investment risk, and if the earnings on the cash value drop below the level anticipated when the policy benefit was reduced, further adjustment(s) may be needed.

The policyowner has to explicitly request a death benefit reduction to create the equivalent of a reduced paid-up surrender option for a universal or variable universal life policy.

Extended Term Insurance

The extended term insurance option provides paid-up term insurance in an amount equal to the original face of the policy, increased by any dividend additions or deposits and decreased by any policy indebtedness. The length of the term is that which can be purchased at the insured's attained age by the application of the net surrender value as a net single premium. This gives effect to the statutory requirement that the present value at the time of surrender of any paid-up surrender benefit must be at least the equivalent of the surrender value. The period for which term insurance is provided for various durations under an ordinary life policy, and under a 20-payment life policy, issued at age 35, is shown in Table 8-1.

Universal and variable universal life insurance policies do not have a guaranteed extended term surrender option. However, they are automatically configured to work similarly to extended term insurance. These policies have no fixed or required premiums, and the viability of the contract depends on the account balance of the policy's cash value. The policy will remain in force as long as the cash value is sufficient to cover the next 60 days of charges for mortality (term charges) and administration, and until these charges consume the cash value.

It is readily apparent that the policy loan should be deducted from the surrender value to determine the net single premium, since it is only the net value that is available for the purchase of extended insurance, but many persons do not understand why it is also necessary to deduct the policy loan from the face of the policy. The requirement is founded on underwriting considerations. If the policy indebtedness is not deducted from the face of the extended policy, the companies will be exposed to a virulent form of antiselection.

Figure 8-2
Effect of Reduced Paid-up Insurance on Structure of Several Types of Life Insurance Contracts

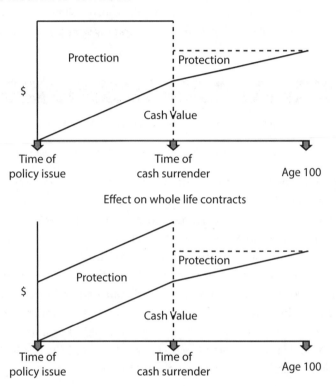

Effect on whole life contracts

Effect on increasing death benefit universal
and variable universal life insurance contracts

Consider the case of a person suffering from an incurable illness who has a $200,000 life insurance policy with a $100,000 cash value. If, to meet the cost of medical treatment or for any other reason, he or she borrows the maximum amount against the cash value, say $95,000, and then dies shortly thereafter, the company will be obligated to pay only $105,000, since the policy loan is an encumbrance against both the cash value and the death proceeds. The total return will thus equal the face of the policy, or $200,000. If, on the other hand, he or she borrows $90,000, for example, surrenders the policy, and applies the remaining equity, $10,000, to the purchase at net rates of $200,000 of extended term insurance, death within the next few years will result in a total payment—the face plus the loan—of $290,000. Under present practice as required by law, the ill policyowner can extend only $110,000, thus limiting the total obligation of the company to $200,000, as was the original intent.

The deduction of policy loans is based on the theory that the cancellation of an unliqui-dated policy loan constitutes a prepayment of a portion of the face amount. To ignore policy indebtedness in determining the face amount of extended insurance would be to make available, without medical or other evidence of insurability, additional term insur-ance equivalent to the policy indebtedness. This strategy would violate all the tenets of sound underwriting.

Extended Term Insurance Surrender Options

- Amount of coverage is reduced by the amount of policy loans

- Surrender value available to purchase extended coverage is reduced by policy loans

The effect of deducting the policy loan from both the surrender value and the amount of extended insurance is to produce a shorter period of term insurance than would be available if no loan existed. This is a natural consequence of the fact that the deduction is a much greater proportion of the cash value than it is of the face amount of the policy. Theoretically the amount of term insurance should not be the face amount less the loan, as required by law, but should be the face amount less the portion thereof having a cash value equal to the loan; in other words, a proportionate part of the policy would be sur-rendered to pay the loan, and only the remainder would be continued as term insurance. If this method were used, a lower amount of coverage would be extended and the period of term insurance would not be affected by policy indebtedness. The rule laid down by law in effect increases the total insurance extended and thus reduces the term, since the net cash value remains the same.

Thus, if a policy of $1,000 has a cash value of $500 and policy indebtedness of $200, the net cash value of $300 will theoretically support a $600 extended term benefit (a propor-tionate reduction in both the benefit and the cash value). Seen from the loan perspective, a $400 reduction in coverage will be required to offset $200 of loan forgiveness. However, the actual amount of extended insurance is $800, instead of the theoretical $600. In other words, the actual amount of the term insurance is reduced by 20 percent, whereas the cash value available to purchase it is reduced by 40 percent. The period of insurance, therefore, must be less than it would be if no indebtedness existed in order to make the benefit reduction proportionate to the cash value reduction.

From the standpoint of the companies, paid-up term insurance is a more attractive sur-render benefit than paid-up whole life or endowment insurance. The companies consider the favorable features of extended term insurance to be (1) the relatively large amount of insurance involved, with the correspondingly low expense rate; (2) the definite date of

expiry, which limits the maintenance expenses and minimizes the problem of tracing policyowners; (3) the uninterrupted continuation of the original amount of coverage, as modified by dividend additions and policy loans, for those persons who contemplate eventual reinstatement; and (4) its adaptability to liberal reinstatement requirements, which stems from the fact that the amount at risk is normally decreased by reinstatement, in contrast to the increase in the amount at risk that occurs on the reinstatement of reduced paid-up insurance.

The only real disadvantage of extended term insurance from the insurer's standpoint is the adverse mortality selection encountered, and this can be hedged through the use of the higher mortality assumptions authorized by law or minimized through making the extended term option the automatic paid-up benefit. All things considered, the extended term option is so attractive that most companies designate it as the option to go into effect automatically if the insured does not elect another available option within 60 days after the due date of the premium in default.

The change produced in the structure of a whole life insurance policy by its surrender for extended term insurance is plotted in Figure 8-3. This diagram reveals that, in direct contrast to the situation under reduced paid-up insurance, the protection element grows progressively larger, and the investment element progressively smaller, until the policy finally expires. The investment element is at a peak at the time of surrender but is gradually used up in the payment of term insurance premiums, being completely exhausted at the point of expiry. Because of the complementary nature of the protection and investment elements in any insurance contract, the protection element becomes constantly larger, eventually equaling the face of the extended insurance. This explains why the amount at risk is reduced through the reinstatement of a policy that has been running under the extended term option.

The investment element of a paid-up term insurance policy can be obtained by surrendering the insurance for cash, subject to the same conditions governing the surrender of reduced paid-up insurance. Extended term insurance is normally nonparticipating with respect to dividends.

AUTOMATIC PREMIUM LOANS

A policy provision found in some—but not all—policies that bears a close resemblance to the paid-up term insurance option but is technically not a surrender option (because the policy is not surrendered) is the automatic premium loan feature. It grew out of the conventional premium loan clause, which states that at the request of the policyowner

any premium may be paid by means of a loan against the surrender value, provided that a surrender value is then available and large enough to cover the loan. Such a loan usually bears interest at the rate applicable to all policy loans.

Figure 8-3
Effect of Extended Term Insurance Option on Structure of Several Types of Life Insurance Contracts

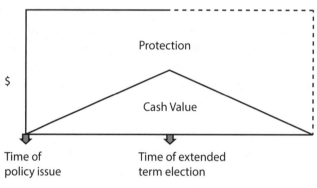

Effect on level benefit cash value
life insurance contracts

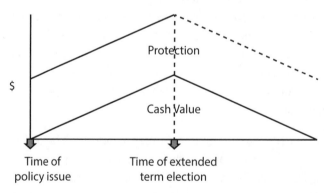

Effect on increasing death-benefit designs of
universal and variable universal policies

automatic premium loan clause

The **automatic premium loan clause** provides that any defaulted premium will be auto-matically paid and charged against the cash value without request from the policyowner

unless he or she elects to surrender the policy for cash or one of the paid-up insurance options.

The effect of the premium loan clause is to extend the original plan of insurance for the original face amount decreased by the amount of premiums loaned with interest. Such extension will continue as long as the cash value at each premium due date is sufficient to cover another premium. It should be noted that each premium loan increases the cash value, lengthening the period during which the process can be continued. At the same time, however, the indebtedness against the cash value is growing, not only by the granting of additional premium loans but also by the accrual of interest. Eventually a premium due date will be reached when the unencumbered cash value is no longer large enough to cover another full premium.

The principal advantage to the policyowner of an automatic premium loan provision is that in the event of inadvertent nonpayment of the premium or temporary inability to pay the premium, the policy is kept in full force. Several collateral advantages flow from this basic fact. First, premium payments can be resumed at any time (as long as the equity in the policy remains sufficient to pay premiums as they become due) without furnishing evidence of insurability. This is in contrast to the reinstatement of policies surrendered for paid-up insurance, in which case evidence of insurability is almost invariably required. Second, special benefits—such as waiver of premium, disability income, and accidental death or double indemnity—remain in full force, contrary to the situation under the paid-up insurance options. Finally, if the policy is participating, the policyowner continues to receive dividends, which is usually not true of paid-up term insurance and might not be true under reduced paid-up insurance.

On the other hand, unless the provision is used only as a temporary convenience, as intended, it may prove disadvantageous to the policyowner. If premium payments are not resumed, not only will the period during which the policy is kept in force usually be less than under extended insurance, but the amount payable in the event of death will be less, and the disparity will become greater with each passing year.

In the event of the insured's death during the period covered, the insurer is better off financially under the automatic premium loan arrangement than under extended term insurance, because the former receives additional premiums by way of deduction from the policy proceeds, but offsetting this advantage to some extent are the additional outlays for commissions, premium taxes, and dividends (if participating).

The effect of the automatic premium loan feature on the structure of a whole life policy is shown in Figure 8-4. Upon default of the first premium the effective amount of protection

is reduced by the amount of the gross premium. Each year thereafter that the feature is permitted to operate, the amount of protection is reduced by the gross premium due that year, plus interest on that premium and all unpaid premiums of previous years. Hence, the protection element will decline at a constantly increasing rate. The surrender value will be exhausted, however, before the protection element is reduced to zero.

Figure 8-4
Effect of Automatic Premium Loans on Structure of Cash Value Whole Life Insurance Contracts

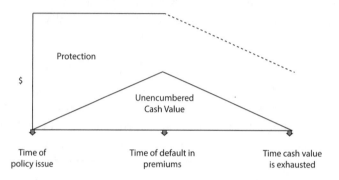

The effective or unencumbered investment element also turns downward, but not immediately, and it never declines at the same rate as the protection element, so the solid and broken lines are not parallel. The nominal investment element—cash value—increases with the payment of each gross premium (regardless of the source of the funds) by the amount of the net premium, plus interest at the contractual rate and benefit of survivorship, less the cost of insurance.

lump sum

Most life insurance policies provide that upon maturity the proceeds shall be payable to the designated beneficiary in one sum, generally referred to as a **lump sum**. Many life insurers now make the lump-sum death benefit payable through an interest-bearing account against which the beneficiary can draw checks. The way these accounts work is similar to the way a money market fund works. The beneficiary can withdraw the total proceeds in one transaction or make partial withdrawals as funds are needed merely by writing checks. The balance in the account continues to earn interest until withdrawn. Even though the beneficiary can leave the benefits in the account and earn more investment income, over 90 percent of beneficiaries still choose a single lump-sum withdrawal and take possession of all the proceeds.

SETTLEMENT OPTIONS

settlement options

Life insurance companies have a wide range of periodic income options available to beneficiaries and policyowners. These alternatives are varied enough to fit nearly every set of circumstances that beneficiaries encounter. Collectively, these contractual choices are known as **settlement options**. They constitute an important feature of a life insurance contract and can play a vital role in the protection of the insured's dependents. Knowledge of the settlement options characteristics and the manner in which they can be used is essential to successful life underwriting.

Death proceeds from a life insurance policy can be paid out in many different options: lump-sum, life income, interest only, fixed period, and fixed amount.

1. **Lump-sum**—The death benefit is paid out all at once to the beneficiary.

2. **Life income**—Income payments continue as long as the beneficiary is alive, regardless of the length of time (Note: It is important to recognize that if the beneficiary dies before all of the principal is paid out, the insurer retains the balance).

3. **Interest only**—Interest earned on the proceeds that are held in trust by the insurer is paid to the beneficiary at stated intervals. Typically, the death proceeds are then payable under a life income plan.

4. **Fixed period**—Equal payments are made until the principal and interest are exhausted by the end of the fixed period. [Note: When the specified period ends, payments end]

5. **Fixed amount**—A specified amount of income is paid at regular intervals until the proceeds are exhausted. [Note: When the specified amount is reached, payments cease]

GENERAL CONCEPTS AND RULES

settlement agreement

When the proceeds of a life insurance policy are payable in a lump sum, the company's liability under the policy is fully discharged with the payment of such sum. If, however, the company retains the proceeds under one of the optional methods of settlement, its liability

continues beyond the maturity of the policy and must be evidenced by some sort of legal document. That document is the **settlement agreement**.[3]

The settlement agreement contains the designation of the various classes of beneficiaries and a detailed description of the manner in which the proceeds are to be distributed. During the early development of deferred-settlement arrangements, settlement agreements were tailored to fit the insured's exact specifications and were typewritten in their entirety. As the requests for deferred settlements multiplied, it became necessary, for reasons of economy and administration, to standardize the various arrangements and privileges that the company would make available. As a result, the modern settlement agreement is composed primarily of preprinted provisions, some of which are general in scope and apply to any option that might be elected, and some of which pertain to only one specific option. All of the rights, privileges, and restrictions that the company is willing to make available are included and become effective by appropriate action of the policyowner (usually by making a check mark in a box opposite the provision in question). The only portion of the agreement that must be filled in concerns beneficiary designations and any modifications of the printed provisions that are acceptable to both parties.

The typical settlement agreement is one entered into between the insurance company and the insured, or policyowner, to control the distribution of the policy proceeds to third-party beneficiaries after the insured's death. Depending on company practice, the agreement may be a basic part of the insurance policy, or it may be separate and distinct from the policy. It can be drawn up at the time the policy goes into effect or at any time prior to the insured's death. Although the insured can revoke the agreement at any time and substitute a new agreement, he or she can revoke the beneficiary designation only if such right has been specifically reserved. The policyowner may or may not give the primary beneficiary the right to set aside the prior agreement after the insured dies. Upon the insured's death, the insurance company's obligation under the original contract terminates, and it assumes a new obligation, which is defined by the terms of the settlement agreement.

The insured may also enter into a settlement agreement with the insurer to provide payments to himself or herself from a surrendered policy's cash value. If the agreement relates to the proceeds of an endowment policy, it can be entered into at the policy's inception or at any time prior to the policy's maturity.

---

3.   Such a document may also be referred to as a supplementary contract, supplementary agreement, or settlement statement. Some companies do not use a special agreement; the beneficiary simply retains the policy, possibly with an endorsement, as evidence of the company's continuing obligation.

If the insured did not elect a deferred settlement or did elect one but gave the primary beneficiary the right to set it aside, under the rules of most companies the beneficiary may elect a settlement option and enter into an agreement with the company to govern the distribution of the proceeds. The beneficiary is usually given 6 months after the insured's death in which to elect a settlement option, provided the check proffered by the insurer in full settlement of the death claim has not been cashed. Insurers pay interest on the portion of proceeds still held by the insurer after the insured dies. The interest starts accruing from the date of death (even if the election of the specific option is made long after the insured dies) and continues accruing until the underlying proceeds are distributed to the beneficiary.

spendthrift clause

When a beneficiary elects the settlement option or when the policyowner elects a deferred settlement for his or her own benefit, a spendthrift clause cannot be included in the settle-ment agreement (if it is included, it will not be enforceable). A **spendthrift clause** states that the proceeds will be free from attachment or seizure by the beneficiary's creditors. This clause may properly be embodied in a life insurance policy or settlement agreement procured by one person for the benefit of another, but it cannot be incorporated into an agreement at the behest of the party for whose benefit the agreement is being drawn up.[4] This offers an argument for having the insured elect the settlement option on behalf of the beneficiary, especially if the beneficiary has credit problems (or may be expected to have them in the future).

Parties to Settlement Agreements
• Insurance company
• Policyowner
• Beneficiary may have the option of becoming a contracting party after the insured dies (if so provided by the policyowner)

revocable contingent beneficiaries

Under the rules of many companies, a settlement agreement entered into between the company and the beneficiary must provide that any proceeds unpaid at the time of the beneficiary's death will be paid either to his or her estate in a lump sum or in a single sum

---

4. However, the beneficiary's election of a deferred settlement does not necessarily deprive him or her of the protec-tion of this clause.

or installments to irrevocably designated contingent beneficiaries. In other words, the beneficiary cannot designate **revocable contingent beneficiaries**.

Companies that impose this limitation fear that designating revocable contingent beneficiaries to receive proceeds that are already in existence at the time the designation is made might be construed as a disposition of property to take effect at the primary beneficiary's death. If the beneficiary's action should be so construed, the settlement agreement would be ineffectual as to the residual proceeds unless the agreement had been executed with all the formalities of a will—which, of course, is not the practice. Some insurance companies, however, feel that such a construction of the settlement agreement is a remote contingency and they, therefore, permit the beneficiary to designate contingent beneficiaries with the right of revocation.

Contract Rates versus Current Rates

rate of income

contract rates

As pointed out earlier, the liability of the insurer at the maturity of a life insurance policy is generally stated in terms of a single-sum payment. In making other modes of settlement available, the company promises a set of installment benefits, based on various patterns of distribution, that have a present value precisely equal to the lump-sum payment. The policy contains tables that show the amount of periodic income that will be payable under the different options for each $1,000 of proceeds left with the company. Under each option a specified **rate of income** per $1,000 of proceeds is guaranteed in the policy; these are referred to as **contract rates**. It is important to note that insurers can and often do credit investment earnings in excess of the guaranteed contract rate to the funds supporting settlement options.

current rates

From time to time, a company will modify the actuarial assumptions underlying the benefits provided under the optional modes of settlement, which means that the amount of periodic income per $1,000 of proceeds will change. Historically, because of declining interest yields and growing longevity, these modifications have produced lower benefits per $1,000 of principal. Such benefit modifications are, of course, reflected only in those policies and settlement agreements issued after the change. The benefits under existing agreements cannot be modified without the specific consent of the policyowner. (Consequently, insurers rarely take steps to modify existing settlement agreements.) In

order to distinguish the rates of income available under existing policies and settlement agreements from rates that are applicable to contracts currently being issued, the latter are referred to as **current rates**. For policies and agreements issued since the latest rate changes there is, obviously, no difference between the contract and current rates. For all others, however, the distinction can be significant.

Contract rates are always available to the policyowner, except for options that can be "negotiated"—that is, options not contained in the original policy. If a policyowner wants the proceeds to be distributed in a manner not provided for in the original policy and his or her request is granted, the benefits will almost invariably be based on the rates in effect at the time the option was requested. Thus, if a policy does not contain all the options that the applicant thinks he or she might want to utilize, the applicant should try to have them added to the policy by endorsement at the time the policy is issued or as soon thereafter as possible.

Under most companies' rules, a beneficiary who is entitled to a lump-sum payment can choose to leave the proceeds with the company under the interest option or elect one of the liquidating options at contract rates. Contract rates are usually available to the beneficiary if a liquidating option (any option other than the interest option) is elected within a specified period after the insured's death—usually somewhere in the range of 6 months to 2 years. If within the 6-month period, the beneficiary elects the interest option, he or she can switch to a liquidating option at contract rates up to 2 years after the insured's death. Moreover, if—during the prescribed period of 6 months to 2 years—the beneficiary elects to have a liquidating option go into effect at some specified date beyond the 2-year period, contract rates will apply. On the other hand, if the beneficiary requests a change of option after the permissible period, the requested benefits will be made available only at current rates, if at all.

Interest Rates in Settlement Options

- Contract interest rates are guaranteed (such as 3.5 percent) as a lower limit on current rates when interest rates in the economy drop below the guaranteed rate

- Contract interest rates remain fixed for the entire contract duration.

- Current rates are rates actually being paid under the settlement agreements (such as .3.9 percent).

- Current rates usually exceed contract rates.

- Current rates fluctuate along with economic conditions.

It is important to grasp the rationale of the restrictions on contract rates. They are not designed primarily to prevent an indefinite projection of contract rates into an uncertain future. Rather, they are intended to protect the insurance company from adverse mortality and financial selection. For example, if a beneficiary could elect a life income option at any time, his or her attitude toward that right would be influenced by the condition of his or her health. If, after the insured's death, the beneficiary's health deteriorated, he or she would not consider a life income option appropriate, unless it were the cash refund type. On the other hand, if the beneficiary's health over the years were excellent, he or she might elect a life income option. Because beneficiaries as a group could be expected to react in this manner, without a time limit or option selection the company would find itself with an undue proportion of healthy annuitants.

Likewise, if a beneficiary has the choice of withdrawing the proceeds and placing them in some other type of investment or leaving them with the company to be liquidated under one of the installment options, he or she would probably place the investment burden on the insurer if it provided a higher return than could be obtained in the open market. The reverse would be true if the market yield were higher than that provided by the insurer. While the behavior of one or a few beneficiaries has little impact on the insurance company, the adverse action of tens of thousands could be financially devastating to the insurer.

Right of Withdrawal

unlimited right of withdrawal

limited right of withdrawal

As stated earlier, the beneficiary may be given the right to withdraw all or a portion of the proceeds held by the insurer under a deferred-settlement arrangement. If the beneficiary can withdraw all of the proceeds at any one time, subject only to a delay clause, he or she is said to have an **unlimited right of withdrawal**. However, if the privilege is subject to restrictions, it is generally identified as a **limited right of withdrawal**.

The right of withdrawal may be limited as to the following:

- the frequency with which it can be invoked
- the minimum amount that can be withdrawn at any one time
- the maximum amount that can be withdrawn at any one time
- the maximum amount that can be withdrawn in any one year

- the maximum amount that can be withdrawn in the aggregate

The first two types of limitations are imposed by the insurers to control the cost of administration, while the last three are imposed by the policyowner (often a parent of the beneficiary) to prevent dissipation or too rapid exhaustion of the proceeds by the beneficiary. The right of withdrawal can usually be invoked only on dates when regular interest or liquidation payments are due. Most companies permit withdrawals on any such dates, but some restrict the privilege to a stated number of withdrawals per year, such as three, four, or six. Although some insurers have no minimum requirement, the minimum amount that can usually be withdrawn at any one time ranges from $10 to $1,000.

Most policies reserve the right to delay cash withdrawals under settlement options for a period of up to 6 months. This is a counterpart to the delay clause required by law in connection with loan and surrender requests.

cumulative right of withdrawal

noncumulative right of withdrawal

Cumulative right of withdrawal. The policyowner may provide that the right of withdrawal will be cumulative. This means that any withdrawable amounts that are not withdrawn during a particular year can be withdrawn in any subsequent year, in addition to any other sums that can be withdrawn pursuant to the terms of agreement. Thus if the settlement agreement permits the beneficiary to withdraw up to $1,000 per year in addition to the periodic contractual payments and provides that the right will be cumulative, the beneficiary's failure to withdraw any funds during the first year would automatically give him or her the right to withdraw $2,000 during the second year. No withdrawals during the first or second years would bestow the right to withdraw $3,000 during the third year, and so on. A **noncumulative right of withdrawal**, whether exercised or not, expires at the end of the period to which it pertains. Most limited rights of withdrawal are noncumulative.

A right of withdrawal is included in a settlement agreement in order to provide flexibility. It can be invoked to obtain funds for unexpected emergencies or to meet the problem of a rising price level. It is especially desirable during the period when the beneficiary is caring for dependent children. In most cases, however, the right should be hedged with reasonable restrictions in order to prevent premature exhaustion of the proceeds.

Right of Commutation

commutation

The right of **commutation** is related to the right of withdrawal. To commute, in this sense, is to withdraw the present value of remaining installment payments in a lump sum. The term is properly applied only to a right attaching to proceeds distributed under a liquidating option. Hence it does not apply to proceeds held under the interest option. For all practical purposes, however, the right of commutation is identical to an unlimited right of withdrawal.

The right of commutation is not implicit in an installment arrangement; in order to be available, it must be specifically authorized in the settlement agreement. Commutation is specifically and intentionally denied the beneficiary in the spendthrift clause that is sometimes made part of the settlement agreement.

Minimum-amount Requirements

To hold down the cost of administering proceeds under deferred-settlement arrangements for which there is no specific charge, life insurance companies will not accept a sum less than a specified amount (such as $2,000 or $10,000) under a settlement option and will not provide periodic installments in amounts less than $25 or $50. If the proceeds of a policy are split into two or more funds with different options, the foregoing requirements apply to each fund. The minimum-payment requirement also applies to each beneficiary. Thus, a policy large enough to satisfy the requirements if payable to the widow(er) alone might have to be paid in a lump sum if several children become payees as contingent beneficiaries.

These requirements are usually referred to in the policy as rules subject to change. Because of the anticipated variation, the specific dollar amounts are rarely stated in the policy.

There is usually a special requirement for proceeds held under the installment amount option. Most companies will not make monthly payments of less than $5 or $6 per $1,000 under this option. The requirement is sometimes stated as a percentage; the minimum is usually 4, 5, or 6 percent liquidation per year. This special rule is designed to assure liquidation of all proceeds and interest within a reasonable period of time.

STRUCTURE AND FUNCTIONAL CHARACTERISTICS OF SETTLEMENT OPTIONS

Life insurance settlement options, as a group, embody these three basic concepts:

- retention of proceeds without liquidation of principal
- systematic liquidation of the proceeds without reference to life contingencies
- systematic liquidation of the proceeds with reference to one or more life contingencies

A number of options have evolved from this conceptual foundation, but they can be reduced to these four fundamental options:

- the interest option
- the installment time option or fixed-period option
- the installment amount option or fixed-amount option
- the life income option

(These four options will be discussed under the conceptual classifications mentioned above.)

Retention of Proceeds at Interest

Structure of the Interest Option

The simplest and most flexible of all settlement options is the interest option. The fundamental concept underlying this option is that the proceeds will be maintained intact until the expiration of a specified period or until the occurrence of some specific event. It is an interim option; it postpones the ultimate disposition of the proceeds and must be followed by a liquidating option or a lump-sum distribution.

The company guarantees a minimum rate of interest on the proceeds, which is payable at periodic intervals, usually monthly. If the policy was participating, the proceeds will be credited with the actual rate of interest earned by the company or, more likely, a rate approximately equal to the interest factor in the dividend formula. Excess interest is usually paid once a year on one of the normal interest payment dates.

The interest on proceeds left with the company may constitute a significant portion of the primary beneficiary's income. Indeed, it is sometimes adequate for all the beneficiary's

income needs. Frequently, a life income is provided to the primary beneficiary (usually, the insured's spouse) through the interest option, with the proceeds at the primary beneficiary's death applied to the needs of the contingent beneficiaries (often the insured's children). To determine how much principal must be left with the company to provide an interest income of a desired amount, see the following tables.

The following tables are based on the assumption that the proceeds will yield even percentages between 3 percent and 8 percent annual interest. Thus, the annual income per $1,000 is assumed to be $30, $40, $50, $60, $70, or $80. However, if payments are to be made monthly rather than annually, the amount of each payment will be somewhat less than a proportionate share of the annual interest, owing to an adjustment made for loss of interest. If, instead of paying interest at the end of the year, the company pays at the end of the first and each subsequent month, it loses 11 months' interest on the first payment, 10 months' interest on the second, 9 on the third, and so on. Altogether it loses 11/24 of one year's interest. At 3 percent, the interest on $30 is $0.90, 11/24 of which is $0.41. Thus, the effective amount of interest earned is $29.59, which divided by 12, yields $2.47 as the proper monthly payment, rather than $2.50 (30 ÷ 12). Such adjustments are preprogrammed into financial calculators' solutions.

Table 8-2 Amount of Principal Needed to Provide a Specified Annual Interest Income at Various Rates of Interest

Annual Income Desired	Annual Interest Rate					
	3%	4%	5%	6%	7%	8%
$100	$3,350*	$2,500	$2,000	$1,700	$1,450	$1,250
250	8,350	6,250	5,000	4,200	3,600	3,150
500	16,700	12,500	10,000	8,350	7,150	6,250
750	25,000	18,750	15,000	12,500	10,750	9,400
1,000	33,350	25,000	20,000	16,700	14,300	12,500
2,000	66,700	50,000	40,000	33,350	28,600	25,000
10,000	333,350	250,000	200,000	166,700	142,900	125,000
20,000	666,700	500,000	400,000	333,350	285,750	250,000
100,000	3,333,350	2,500,000	2,000,000	1,666,700	1,428,600	1,250,000

The values above are interest-only payments; payments would continue without change and without liquidating the principal. Assumes end-of-year payments.
*All numbers have been rounded up to the nearest $50.

Table 8-3 Amount of Principal Needed to Provide a Specified Monthly Income at Various Rates of Interest						
Monthly Income Desired	Equivalent Annual Interest Rate					
	3%	4%	5%	6%	7%	8%
$100	$40,000*	$30,000	$24,000	$20,000	$17,150	$15,000
250	100,000	75,000	60,000	50,000	42,900	37,500
500	200,000	150,000	120,000	100,000	85,750	75,000
750	300,000	225,000	180,000	150,000	128,600	112,500
1,000	400,000	300,000	240,000	200,000	171,450	150,000
2,000	800,000	600,000	480,000	400,000	342,900	300,000
3,000	1,200,000	900,000	720,000	600,000	514,300	450,000
4,000	1,600,000	1,200,000	960,000	800,000	685,750	600,000
5,000	2,000,000	1,500,000	1,200,000	1,000,000	857,150	750,000

The values above are interest-only payments; payments would continue without change and without liquidating the principal.
*All numbers have been rounded up to the nearest $50.

Functional Characteristics

The primary beneficiary can be given varying degrees of control over proceeds held by the company under the interest option. If the policyowner wants the proceeds to go intact to the contingent beneficiaries eventually, he or she will give the primary beneficiary no rights in the proceeds other than the right to receive the interest for a lifetime or for some other specified period. If the policyowner wants to provide flexibility to meet unforeseen needs, he or she may grant the primary beneficiary a limited right of withdrawal. This creates no complications for the insurance company and is generally permitted.

Further flexibility and control may be provided by giving the primary beneficiary the right to elect a liquidating option within a specified period or at any time. Most insurance companies permit this flexibility, but as explained earlier, unless the liquidating option is elected within a stipulated period after the insured's death, the benefits will be provided on the basis of current rather than contract rates. The settlement agreement itself may stipulate that after a specified period of time, or upon the occurrence of a stipulated contingency, the proceeds will be applied under a liquidating option for the benefit of either the primary beneficiary or the contingent beneficiaries, or both. In that event, contract rates will apply.

Interest-Only Option

- The interest-only option is frequently used for the primary beneficiary (keeping the proceeds intact for liquidation on behalf of a contingent beneficiary).

- Most often the interest-only option is payable to a surviving spouse. Frequently, the contingent beneficiaries are the children.

The beneficiary may be given complete control over the proceeds by receiving an unlimited right of withdrawal during his or her lifetime, as well as the right to dispose of the proceeds after his or her own death. One or the other of these rights must be present if the proceeds are to qualify for the marital deduction, which can be very important if the insured has a large enough estate to create a federal estate tax liability. As mentioned, the only forms of disposition by the beneficiary that many insurance companies will permit are payment to the beneficiary's estate or payment to irrevocably designated contingent beneficiaries. If the primary beneficiary is given an unlimited right of withdrawal, the guaranteed rate of interest may be lower than would otherwise be the case. If the beneficiary is entitled to a lump-sum settlement but chooses to leave the proceeds with the insurer under the interest option, she or he can retain any privileges the insurance company is willing to grant.

Most companies are willing to retain proceeds under the interest option throughout the remaining lifetime of the primary beneficiary or for 30 years, whichever is longer. Thus, the interest option may be available to contingent beneficiaries. A few companies will hold the proceeds throughout the lifetime of the primary beneficiary and the first contingent beneficiary. From the company's standpoint, some limit is necessary to control the cost of administration and to avoid an indefinite projection of contract rates. (If the insured or the beneficiary elects a liquidating option for the contingent beneficiaries to commence upon termination of the interest option, contract rates will be applicable.)

As a general rule, a company will not accumulate the interest credited to proceeds retained under the interest option. In other words, it insists upon paying out the interest at least annually. This is to avoid any conflict with the laws in several states that forbid the accumulation of trust income except that payable to a minor beneficiary. By analogy, these laws can be applied to proceeds held by a life insurance company. Most—but not all—companies will therefore permit the accumulation of interest income payable to a minor beneficiary; otherwise, a guardian might have to be appointed to receive the interest distributions.

Insurance companies' unwillingness to accumulate interest has a profound impact on the technique of programming, as will be apparent later.

Systematic Liquidation without Reference to Life Contingencies

Proceeds left with a life insurance company to be liquidated at a uniform rate without reference to a life contingency must be paid out either over a specified period of time, with the amount of each payment being the variable, or at a specified rate, with the period of time over which the liquidation is to take place being the variable. [If the period over which the liquidation is to be made, and the interval between payments.] If the amount of each payment is fixed in advance, the period over which the liquidation is to take place depends on these same factors. An option is available for each situation. The fixed-period option (also called an installment time option) provides payments over a stipulated period of time, while the fixed-amount option (also called an installment amount option) provides payments of a stipulated amount. The two options are based on the same mathematical principles and differ only as to whether emphasis is attached to the duration of the payments or to the level of payments. If the insured or the beneficiary wants the assurance of some income, however small, over a specified period, he or she should select the fixed-period option. If, however, the need is for temporary adequacy of income, irrespective of its duration, the insured or the beneficiary should choose the fixed-amount option. In some situations, the decision will turn on the flexibility under the two options.

Fixed-period Option

Structure of the Fixed-Period Option. If a given principal sum is to be liquidated at a uniform rate over a specified period of years, the amount of each annual payment can be derived from a financial calculator or from compound discount tables. For example, if $1,000 is to be liquidated in annual installments over a 20-year period and the undistributed proceeds are assumed to earn interest at the rate of 3.5 percent, the amount of each payment due at the beginning of the year will be $1,000 ÷ $14.71 = $67.98. In other words, the present value of a series of annual payments of $1, at 3.5 percent interest, due at the beginning of the year, for a period of 20 years, is $14.71. If $14.71 will provide $1 per year for 20 years, then $1,000 will provide an annual payment equal to 67.98 times $1 since it takes $14.71 to support each series of $1 payments, and $1,000 will support 67.98. The monthly payment for 20 years at 3.5 percent interest from $1,000 is $5.78.

The amount of annual, semiannual, quarterly, or monthly payment for each $1,000 of proceeds at the beginning of any period of years can be computed using a financial calculator. The $1,000 amount is entered as the present value using the PV key (clear the financial section of the calculator before starting to calculate). For annual payments enter the number of payments (20) using the n key and enter the annual interest rate (3.5 percent) using the

i key. The calculation of payments on a monthly basis requires changing the number of payments (in our example 20 × 12 = 240 total payments) for the n key and changing the annual interest rate to a monthly rate equivalent to the annual rate (in our example 3.5 ÷ 12 = .29166) for the i key. Remember to set the calculator in a beginning of period mode (or due mode) before solving for the payment amount using the PMT key.

The following table shows the guaranteed installments for each $1,000 of proceeds at 3.5 percent interest. Obviously, the numbers in the table would change if a different interest rate were used.

Functional Characteristics. The essence of the fixed-period option is the certainty of the period over which the proceeds will be distributed. Hence, any developments that increase or decrease the amount of proceeds available are reflected by variation in the size of the monthly payments and not in the duration of the payments. Additional proceeds payable by reason of the insured's accidental death increase the amount of the monthly payments. Dividend accumulations and paid-up additions have the same effect. If prepaid or discounted premiums are considered part of the proceeds, they can be applied under a settlement option and, in the case of the fixed-period option, raise the level of payments. (Under the provisions of some policies, however, such premium deposits are treated as belonging to the insured's estate and do not become part of the proceeds payable to third-party beneficiaries.) Policy loans, if still outstanding at the policy's maturity reduce the proceeds available and, hence, the size of the monthly benefits. Some companies permit the beneficiary to repay a policy loan after the insured's death in order to have the full amount of proceeds payable under a settlement option. Excess interest, if any, may be paid in one sum at the end of each year or added in pro rata proportions to each of the regular benefit payments during the following year.

The fixed-period option is a very inflexible arrangement. The only flexibilities are to permit the beneficiary to choose the date on which the option becomes operative, rather than having it go into effect automatically at the policy's maturity, and to grant the beneficiary the right of commutation. If the option is designed not to go into operation automatically upon maturity of the policy, the proceeds are held under the interest option until such time as the beneficiary indicates that liquidation should commence. Limited withdrawals are not permitted, presumably because of the administrative expense involved in recomputing the benefits and recasting the agreement after each withdrawal. Insurers are willing, however, to permit the settlement agreement to be terminated by the beneficiary's withdrawal of all proceeds remaining with the company.

Fixed-Amount Option

Structure of the Fixed-Amount Option. The fixed-amount option is based on the simple proposition of distributing a specified sum each month, or at some other periodic time interval, until the proceeds are exhausted. Mathematically, it is based on the same compound discount function that underlies the fixed-period option. The application is different, however. The principle can be explained in terms of $1,000 to be distributed in equal annual payments of $100, the first payment being due immediately. It is obvious that the liquidation will extend over a minimum period of 9 years because the principal alone will provide payments for that period of time. The problem is to determine how much longer the payments can be continued because of crediting compound interest to the unliquidated portion of the principal.

The first step is to use a financial calculator and enter the known information; then solve for the number of periodic payments that will be made (find n).

Table 8-4 Guaranteed Installments per $1,000 of Proceeds (3.5 Percent Interest, Beginning-of-period Payments)				
Number of Years Payable	Annually	Semiannually	Quarterly	Monthly
1	$1,000.00	$504.34	$253.30	$84.67
2	508.60	256.54	128.84	43.08
3	344.86	173.98	87.41	29.22
4	263.04	132.72	66.69	22.29
5	213.99	107.99	54.27	18.14
6	181.32	91.51	45.99	15.37
7	158.01	79.76	40.09	13.40
8	140.56	70.96	35.67	11.92
9	127.00	64.12	32.24	10.78
10	116.18	58.66	29.50	9.86
11	107.34	54.21	27.26	9.11
12	99.98	50.50	25.40	8.49
13	93.78	47.37	23.83	7.96
14	88.47	44.70	22.49	7.52
15	83.89	42.39	21.33	7.13
16	79.89	40.37	20.32	6.79
17	76.37	38.60	19.43	6.49
18	73.25	37.03	18.64	6.23
19	70.47	35.63	17.94	5.99
20	67.98	34.37	17.31	5.78
21	65.74	33.24	16.74	5.59
22	63.70	32.26	16.23	5.42
23	61.85	31.28	15.76	5.26
24	60.17	30.43	15.33	5.12
25	58.62	29.65	14.94	4.99
26	57.20	28.94	14.58	4.87
27	55.90	28.28	14.25	4.76
28	54.69	27.67	13.95	4.66
29	53.57	27.11	13.67	4.56
30	52.53	26.59	13.40	4.48

Example

Assume that $50,000 is available to be paid out in monthly installments of $3,020 each and the interest earned on the undistributed balance is 4 percent annually. After clearing the financial calculator and setting it in beginning-of-period (due) mode, the entries are as follows: $50,000 is the PV; – $3,020 (note: the sign of the PV must be the opposite of the sign of the payment for the calculator to work) is the PMT; 4 ÷ 12 = 0.3333% is the monthly interest rate. Then the duration of payments can be found by solving for n. In this example n = 17, indicating that the payments will continue for 17 months. The aggregate amount of payments is $51,340, indicating that $1,340 of interest is earned on the $50,000 capital base before the last benefit payment is made.

Functional Characteristics. Because the amount of each payment is fixed under this option, any augmentation in the volume of proceeds or interest lengthens the period over which payments will be made; any diminution in the amount of proceeds shortens the period. Thus, dividend accumulations, paid-up additions, accidental death benefits, and excess interest extend the period of liquidation, whereas loans outstanding at the insured's death and withdrawals of principal by the beneficiary shorten the period. This is true even though the payments are to terminate at a specified date or at the occurrence of some specified event, with the balance of the proceeds being distributed in some manner.

The fixed-amount option offers a great deal of flexibility. As with the fixed-period option, the beneficiary can be given the right to indicate when the liquidation payments are to begin. In the meantime, the proceeds will be held at interest, with the interest payments going to the primary beneficiary. Unlike the fixed-period option, the beneficiary can be given either a limited or an unlimited right of withdrawal. Under this option, withdrawals will merely shorten the period of installment payments and will not necessitate recomputing benefit payments.

The beneficiary can also be given the right to accelerate or retard the rate of liquidation. That is, he or she can be given the privilege of varying the amount of the monthly payments, subject to any limitations the policyowner might wish to impose. For example, the policyowner might direct the company to liquidate the proceeds at the rate of $3,000 per month, while giving the beneficiary the option of stepping up the payments to $5,000 per month or reducing them to any level acceptable to the company. Under such circumstances, the insured is not likely to prescribe any minimum rate of liquidation.

Furthermore, the beneficiary can be given the privilege of discontinuing payments during particular months of the year or from time to time. For example, when the proceeds of an educational endowment policy are being paid out to a beneficiary who is enrolled in a college or university, payments can be discontinued during the summer vacation months. Similarly, larger-than-usual payments can be provided for months in which tuition and

other fees are payable. Such flexibility stems from the fact that the fixed-amount option basically creates a savings account from which withdrawals can be made to suit the beneficiary's convenience.

Finally, this option can include a provision for transferring the remaining proceeds to another liquidating option. If the transfer is to take place at a specified date or age, contract rates will be available. If the beneficiary has the right to transfer the proceeds at any time, the conversion will be subject to current rates.

Systematic Liquidation with Reference to Life Contingencies

The proceeds of a life insurance policy may be liquidated at a uniform rate over the lifetime of one or more beneficiaries. This type of arrangement, peculiar to life insurance companies, is of very great value. It protects a beneficiary against the economic hazard of excessive longevity—that is, it protects the beneficiary against the possibility of outliving his or her income.

Structure of the Life Income Options

life income option

Any settlement option based on a life contingency is called a **life income option**. The principle underlying a life income option is identical to that underlying an annuity. As a matter of fact, a life income option is nothing more than the annuity principle applied to the liquidation of insurance proceeds (each payment is composed partly of principal and partly of income on the unliquidated principal). Hence, there are as many variations of the life income option as there are types of immediate annuities. Among the single-life annuities, there are the pure or straight life annuity, life annuity with guaranteed installments, the installment-refund annuity, and the cash-refund annuity. There are similar annuities based on two or more lives.

While there is a counterpart among the life income options for every type of immediate annuity, it is not customary for a company to include the whole range of annuity forms in its life insurance policies. The typical policy provides for a life income with payments guaranteed for 10, 15, and 20 years and the installment-refund option. Some companies include the joint-and-last-survivor annuity, and a few show the straight life annuity. Virtually all will make additional options available upon request.

Mathematically, the straight life income option is equivalent to a pure immediate annuity. To be precisely accurate, it is the same as a life annuity due because the first payment is due immediately upon maturity of the policy or upon election of the option, whichever is later. The monthly income provided per $1,000 of proceeds depends on the age and sex of the beneficiary and the insurer's assumptions as to mortality and interest. Although the schedules of income guaranteed under various insurers' policies are similar, there is currently little uniformity among companies as to the combination of mortality and interest assumptions used to calculate the income payments. Benefits are provided at net rates, and there is no charge for the use of the life income settlement.

deferred life annuity

The life income option with a specified period of guaranteed payments is mathematically a combination of a fixed-period installment option of appropriate duration and a pure **deferred life annuity**.[5] For example, a life income option that promises to provide payments of a specified amount to a beneficiary aged 45 throughout his or her remaining lifetime, and in any event for 20 years, is a combination of a fixed-period installment option running for 20 years and a pure life annuity deferred to the beneficiary's age 65. If the beneficiary does not survive to age 65, the portion of the proceeds allocated to the deferred life annuity is retained by the insurance company without further obligation.

Because the life income settlement options are essentially annuity contracts available without any applicable sales commissions or other expense loadings, they often provide more benefits for the same contribution than do separate annuity contracts. The only way to be certain that the settlement option is less costly is to make price and benefit comparisons with the annuity contracts available from other insurers. If an annuity contract is found to be more advantageous than the settlement option, that life insurer should be carefully scrutinized to determine its long-term financial strength.

The installment refund option is a combination of a pure immediate life annuity and decreasing term insurance in an amount sufficient to continue payments until the proceeds, without interest, have been paid out in full. (As indicated in chapter 6, this option promises to continue the monthly payments beyond the annuitant's death until the purchase price of the annuity or, in this case, the proceeds of the life insurance policy have been returned.) At the inception, the term insurance is in an amount equal to the proceeds, less the first payment due immediately, but it decreases with each periodic payment and

---

5. Such an option may also be viewed as a combination of a pure deferred life annuity and decreasing term insurance, the latter being represented by the guaranteed payments.

expires altogether when the cumulative benefit payments equal or exceed the life insurance proceeds committed to the installment-refund option.

The cash-refund option is likewise a combination of a pure immediate life annuity and decreasing term insurance. Since the refund is payable in cash rather than payable in installments, however, a slightly larger amount of term insurance is required.

To use a life income option in planning a client's estate, the life underwriter needs two types of tables. The first type enables the life underwriter to compute the amount of insurance required to meet the life income needs of the beneficiary or beneficiaries. It shows the amount of principal needed to provide $10 a month under the various life income options for a wide range of male and female ages. The values for such a table, based on one set of actuarial assumptions, are presented in Tables 8-5 and 8-6.

The second type of table shows the amount of monthly income that will be provided for each $1,000 of proceeds under the life income options and ranges of ages. After the life underwriter determines how much insurance in multiples of $1,000 is needed, he or she can demonstrate to the client, through the second type of table, exactly how much income can be provided with the actual and contemplated insurance. The values for this type of table, calculated on the same basis as the values for Tables 8-5 and 8-6, are shown in Tables 8-7 and 8-8.

Functional Characteristics

Because the life income option contemplates the complete liquidation of the proceeds during the beneficiary's lifetime, it follows that any circumstances that enlarge the volume of proceeds will increase the amount of each periodic payment, while shrinkages in the proceeds will decrease the size of the payments. In this connection, it is interesting to note that excess interest is usually payable only under the annuity form calling for a guaranteed number of payments and, even then, only during the period of guaranteed installments. This is another way of saying that excess interest is payable on the portion of the proceeds applied under the fixed-period installment option but is not payable on that portion of the proceeds allocated to the deferred life annuity. Some companies guarantee a lower rate of interest on the fixed-period option portion of the arrangement than under the deferred life annuity.

Table 8-5 Principal Amount Needed to Provide Life Income of $10 per Month at Selected Male Ages			
Age	Life Annuity	10-Year Certain + Life	20-Year Certain + Life
50	$2,074.72	$2,092.4386	$2,151.0323
51	2,043.45	2,062.7682	2,126.4265
52	2,011.56	2,032.5134	2,101.7083
53	1,979.00	2,001.6522	2,076.9307
54	1,945.73	1,970.1663	2,052.1523
55	1,911.70	1,938.0465	2,027.4383
56	1,876.88	1,905.2949	2,002.8620
57	1,841.21	1,871.9240	1,978.5044
58	1,804.65	1,837.9573	1,954.4541
59	1,767.18	1,803.4327	1,930.8080
60	1,728.77	1,768.4122	1,907.6737
61	1,689.46	1,732.9815	1,885.1662
62	1,649.31	1,697.2468	1,863.4048
63	1,608.41	1,661.3293	1,842.5077
64	1,566.86	1,625.3595	1,822.5883
65	1,524.77	1,589.4676	1,803.7493
66	1,482.26	1,553.7817	1,786.0778
67	1,439.45	1,518.4284	1,769.6418
68	1,396.43	1,483.5328	1,754.4876
69	1,353.31	1,449.2195	1,740.6381
70	1,310.18	1,415.6112	1,728.0929
71	1,267.12	1,382.8293	1,716.8311
72	1,224.21	1,350.9933	1,706.8147
73	1,181.51	1,320.2200	1,697.9912
74	1,139.07	1,290.6243	1,690.2966
75	1,096.96	1,262.3231	1,683.6587
76	1,055.28	1,235.4283	1,677.9980
77	1,014.12	1,210.0381	1,673.2300
78	973.61	1,186.2301	1,669.2662
79	933.85	1,164.0560	1,666.0169
80	894.98	1,143.5380	1,663.3935
81	857.11	1,124.6717	1,661.3114
82	820.36	1,107.4297	1,659.6907
83	784.85	1,091.7671	1,658.4572
84	750.68	1,077.6228	1,657.5428
85	717.92	1,064.9197	1,656.8857
Male 1983 Individual Annuity Table (4 percent interest net rates)			
Editor's Note: The 1983 Individual Annuity Mortality is still used for settlements, even though there is a 2000 Annuity Table used for reserves.			

Table 8-6 Principal Amount Needed to Provide Life Income of $10 per Month at Selected Female Ages			
Age	Life Annuity	10-Year Certain + Life	20-Year Certain + Life
50	$2,237.91	$2,244.7293	$2,272.6161
51	2,208.92	2,216.6597	2,247.8142
52	2,179.14	2,187.8547	2,222.5817
53	2,148.53	2,158.3038	2,196.9426
54	2,117.07	2,127.9981	2,170.9289
55	2,084.73	2,096.9326	2,144.5825
56	2,051.51	2,065.1151	2,117.9610
57	2,017.38	2032.5550	2,091.1317
58	1,982.33	1,999.2603	2,064.1720
59	1,946.35	1,965.2489	2,037.1739
60	1,909.45	1,930.5356	2,010.2380
61	1,871.65	1,895.1533	1,983.4812
62	1,832.98	1,859.1360	1,957.0284
63	1,793.45	1,822.5286	1,931.0152
64	1,753.15	1,785.3961	1,905.5879
65	1,712.08	1,747.7927	1,880.8914
66	1,670.28	1,709.7883	1,857.0756
67	1,627.71	1,671.4403	1,834.2483
68	1,584.36	1,632.8252	1,812.6609
69	1,540.18	1,594.0268	1,792.3413
70	1,495.16	1,555.1662	1,773.4541
71	1,449.38	1,516.4019	1,756.1091
72	1,402.92	1,477.9123	1,740.3840
73	1,355.91	1,439.8962	1,726.3185
74	1,308.52	1,402.5704	1,713.9114
75	1,260.89	1,366.1510	1,703.1193
76	1,213.21	1,330.8508	1,693.8614
77	1,165.59	1,296.8726	1,686.0267
78	1,118.20	1,264.4172	1,679.4831
79	1,071.14	1,233.6701	1,674.0847
80	1,024.57	1,204.8069	1,669.6856
81	978.63	1,177.9807	1,666.1476
82	933.48	1,153.3068	1,663.3430
83	889.29	1,130.8537	1,661.1568
84	846.23	1,110.6411	1,659.4863
85	804.47	1,092.6360	1,658.2403

Female 1983 Individual Annuity Table (4 percent interest net rates)

Editor's Note: The 1983 Individual Annuity Mortality is still used for settlements, even though there is a 2000 Annuity Table used for reserves.

Table 8-7 Monthly Lifetime Benefit for Male per $1,000 Annuity Purchase (Net Rates)			
Age	Life Annuity	10-Year Certain + Life	20-Year Certain + Life
50	$4.82	$4.78	$4.65
51	4.89	4.85	4.70
52	4.97	4.92	4.76
53	5.05	5.00	4.81
54	5.14	5.08	4.87
55	5.23	5.16	4.93
56	5.33	5.25	4.99
57	5.43	5.34	5.05
58	5.54	5.44	5.12
59	5.66	5.54	5.18
60	5.78	5.65	5.24
61	5.92	5.77	5.30
62	6.06	5.89	5.37
63	6.22	6.02	5.43
64	6.38	6.15	5.49
65	6.56	6.29	5.54
66	6.75	6.44	5.60
67	6.95	6.59	5.65
68	7.16	6.74	5.70
69	7.39	6.90	5.75
70	7.63	7.06	5.79
71	7.89	7.23	5.82
72	8.17	7.40	5.86
73	8.46	7.57	5.89
74	8.78	7.75	5.92
75	9.12	7.92	5.94
76	9.48	8.09	5.96
77	9.86	8.26	5.98
78	10.27	8.43	5.99
79	10.71	8.59	6.00
80	11.17	8.74	6.01
81	11.67	8.89	6.02
82	12.19	9.03	6.03
83	12.74	9.16	6.03
84	13.32	9.28	6.03
85	13.93	9.39	6.04

Male 1983 Individual Annuity Table (4 percent interest net rates)

Editor's Note: The 1983 Individual Annuity Mortality is still used for settlements, even though there is a 2000 Annuity Table used for reserves.

Table 8-8 Monthly Lifetime Benefit for Female per $1,000 Annuity Purchase (Net Rates)			
Age	Life Annuity	10-Year Certain + Life	20-Year Certain + Life
50	$4.47	$4.45	$4.40
51	4.53	4.51	4.45
52	4.59	4.57	4.50
53	4.65	4.63	4.55
54	4.72	4.70	4.61
55	4.80	4.77	4.66
56	4.87	4.84	4.72
57	4.96	4.92	4.78
58	5.04	5.00	4.84
59	5.14	5.09	4.91
60	5.24	5.18	4.97
61	5.34	5.28	5.04
62	5.46	5.38	5.11
63	5.58	5.49	5.18
64	5.70	5.60	5.25
65	5.84	5.72	5.32
66	5.99	5.85	5.38
67	6.14	5.98	5.45
68	6.31	6.12	5.52
69	6.49	6.27	5.58
70	6.69	6.43	5.64
71	6.90	6.59	5.69
72	7.13	6.77	5.75
73	7.38	6.94	5.79
74	7.64	7.13	5.83
75	7.93	7.32	5.87
76	8.24	7.51	5.90
77	8.58	7.71	5.93
78	8.39	7.91	5.95
79	9.34	8.11	5.97
80	9.76	8.30	5.99
81	10.22	8.49	6.00
82	10.71	8.67	6.01
83	11.24	8.84	6.02
84	11.82	9.00	6.03
85	12.43	9.15	6.03

Female 1983 Individual Annuity Table (4 percent interest net rates)

Editor's Note: The 1983 Individual Annuity Mortality is still used for settlements, even though there is a 2000 Annuity Table used for reserves.

The life income option is extremely inflexible. Benefits are calculated on the basis of the age and sex of the primary beneficiary, and once the payments have begun, no other person can be substituted for the designated beneficiary, even with an adjustment in the benefits. No right of withdrawal is available and no commutation privilege exists for benefits payable under a deferred life annuity. Otherwise, persons in poor health would be inclined to withdraw the proceeds. When the benefits are guaranteed for a specified period of time, however, a few companies will permit the proceeds payable under the fixed-period installment option to be commuted. If the commutation privilege is exercised, the beneficiary is usually given a deferred life annuity certificate. This certificate provides for life income payments to the beneficiary if he or she survives the period during which the guaranteed payments were to have been made.

SURRENDER VALUES

Under their terms, valid contracts of life insurance cannot be canceled by the insurer except for nonpayment of premiums. However, a policyowner may end the arrangement at any time. Depending on the amount of time the policy has been in force and the method by which premiums have been paid, a substantial value may have accumulated in the policy. This occurs when the life insurance is purchased with a premium that prepays some of the funds a company will need to pay future claims and expenses.

This content addresses the question of how value accumulated within a policy is divided if a policy ends before the death of the insured. The following terms used to describe a policy's discontinuation require some clarification:

lapse

surrender

termination

- **Lapse** refers to termination of a life insurance policy through nonpayment of premiums before surrender values are available.
- **Surrender** refers to termination of a life insurance policy through nonpayment of premiums after surrender values are available.
- **Termination** refers to both lapses and surrenders. Typically, terminations during the first year or two are lapses and later ones are surrenders.

None of these terms applies to an action or inaction by the policyowner before the policy's grace period has expired.

GUIDING PRINCIPLES

Defining Equity

Experts offer three possible approaches to equitable treatment of a withdrawing policy-owner. WEach approach produces different costs for the insurance. At one extreme, the policyowner receives no refund of any amount. According to this view, the function of life insurance is viewed solely as providing benefits upon the death of the insured. Those who "drop out" of the venture forfeit all payments and all interest in the contract. This view generally has not been accepted since the early days of life insurance.

At the other extreme, it might be argued that terminating policyowners should receive a refund of all premiums paid, plus interest at the contractual rate, less a pro rata contribution toward death claims and the premium loading. A contract with such generous surrender values implicitly assumes that expenses occur evenly throughout the policy's premium-paying period and that the premium is sufficient to absorb expenses that arise each year. A separate process to find surrender values is not needed; withdrawing policy-owners receive exactly the reserve under the policy. When higher expenses occur in early policy years, this approach leaves persisting policyowners to pay those costs that remain unpaid when a policy ends during its early years.

Supporters of this view argue that the healthy growth of a company benefits all policy-owners and therefore the cost of acquiring new business should be charged to all policies. Strictly applied, this approach charges all acquisition expenses to the entire body of policy-owners. A modified approach charges existing policyowners some acquisition costs of new policies.

The third and prevailing approach holds that a withdrawing policyowner should receive a surrender benefit—either cash or some form of paid-up insurance—approximately equal to the amount contributed to the company, minus the cost of the protection received, minus the expenses of establishing and maintaining the policy. Ideally, a policyowner's withdrawal should neither benefit nor harm continuing policyowners. The maximum benefit to a withdrawing policyowner would be a pro rata share of the assets accumulated by the company for the block of policies—that is, by definition, the policy's asset share. The actual surrender benefit should be reduced below the asset share, however, for several reasons.

Deductions from Asset Share

A company will usually reduce the surrender benefit to an amount less than the asset share of a surrendered policy. Five possible explanations for this include the following:

- adverse mortality selection
- adverse financial selection
- contribution to a contingency reserve
- contribution to profits
- cost of surrender

In addition, it could be argued that surrender benefits may need to be limited to prevent their payment from threatening the solvency of the insurance company.

Adverse Mortality Selection

Over the years actuaries have speculated about the effect of voluntary withdrawals on the mortality of those persisting in the insured group. Some actuaries maintain that most voluntary terminations result either from a reduced need for insurance protection or from a change in the insured'sfinancial circumstances. They reason that termination occurs with little regard for the state of the insured's health, and they see little adverse mortality selection in withdrawals.

Other actuaries argue that persons in extremely poor health are not likely to surrender their policies and will instead borrow to maintain their protection. Many believe that those who do surrender are, on the average, in better health and can be expected to live longer than those who do not surrender. If surrender values are too high, the accumulated funds may not be sufficient to pay the death claims of the remaining policyowners. In view of a lack of conclusive data on the subject, some companies withhold a small portion of the asset shares from surrendering policyowners in order to offset any adverse selection that might occur.

Adverse Financial Selection

It has been observed that many terminations, particularly cash surrenders, tend to increase sharply during periods of economic crises and depressions. In addition, many cash surrenders occur when market interest rates are higher than those provided on life insurance cash values. Terminations reduce the inflow of cash to the company and, if cash is demanded, increase the outflow of cash. A company may be adversely affected (1) if it has

fewer funds to invest at what might be an attractive rate of interest, and (2) if it is forced to liquidate assets at depressed prices. The policyowner's right to demand the cash value of a policy at any time forces the company to maintain a more liquid investment portfolio than would otherwise be necessary.[6] This adverse financial selection reduces the yield on the portfolio. Most companies charge terminating policyowners with the resulting loss of investment earnings by reducing surrender values below what would be otherwise available.

Contribution to Contingency Reserve

Sound life insurance management demands that each group of policies ultimately pay its own way, including a provision for adverse contingencies like wars and epidemics. Newly issued policies depend on prior accumulations to provide these protective margins. Later, those same policies leave the company with something less than the actual accumulations as a surrender value.

The difference between a policy's accumulation and its surrender value varies with the size of the company. The law of large numbers tells us that predictability increases with greater numbers. Applying the law of large numbers to contingency reserves means that a larger contingency reserve is needed per policy on a small block of business than would absorb the same financial variation in a larger block of business. The primary objective, as always, is safeguarding the security of the policies remaining in the group.

Contribution to Profits

Little needs to be said on this point, except that in a stock company, a deduction may be made from the asset share of the surrendering policyowner to compensate stockholders for the risk borne by capital funds. The size of the deduction varies depending on the level of profits already distributed to stockholders.

Cost of Surrender

All companies incur expenses to process the surrender of a policy. Some companies estimate aggregate expenses for surrenders and include them as part of the loading in the premium for all policies. Other companies charge the cost of the transaction to the

---

6. As mentioned elsewhere, all policies give the company the legal right to postpone payment of the cash surrender value for a period of 6 months. Enforcing this contractual provision has a serious effect on the company's position compared to the competition and on customer relations, and few companies choose to do so.

particular policies involved by deducting it from the surrender value that would otherwise be available. Under the latter practice, the cost of surrender is a deduction from the asset share.

Assuring Company Solvency

In practice, surrender benefits must be limited if their payment might impair the security of remaining policyowners. When balancing the interests between terminating and continuing policyowners, conflicts are resolved in favor of continuing policyowners. Placing higher priority on the interests of continuing policyowners is consistent with general contract law. The party to a contract who is willing to continue under its original terms is not made to suffer through the inability or unwillingness of another party to honor the contract. On the other hand, modern insurance contracts include surrender value as part of the policy's benefits. A policyowner who chooses to withdraw the surrender value arguably acts within the terms of the contract as much as the policyowner who keeps a policy in effect until it matures. Nonetheless, the argument justifies favoring policyowners who wish to continue under the original terms of the contract.

NONFORFEITURE LEGISLATION

Standard Nonforfeiture Law

Early United States insurance policies made no provision for refunds upon termination before maturity. Forfeiture of all accumulated funds was still prevalent in the mid-1850s. Gradually companies recognized, with varying degrees of liberality, the withdrawing policyowner's right to such funds. Interest in the issue grew, and Massachusetts enacted the first nonforfeiture law in 1861. It evolved into the **Standard Nonforfeiture Law**, the first modern nonforfeiture legislation, which became effective in 1948 in most jurisdictions. Policies issued since that date have provided at least the minimum surrender values prescribed by law.

nonforfeiture laws

nonforfeiture values

Laws to assure policyowners who voluntarily terminate their contracts a fair share of the value built up inside some policies are called **nonforfeiture laws**. Refunds required by such laws are called **nonforfeiture values**. Unless it refers to legislation, the adjective "surrender" is synonymous with "nonforfeiture" and is generally used in this text.

The Standard Nonforfeiture Law does not require specific surrender values. The only requirement is that surrender values are at least as large as those that would be produced by the method the law prescribes. In addition, each policy must contain a statement of the method used to find the surrender values and benefits provided under the policy at durations not specifically shown. This permits companies to use alternate formulas by describing them in their policies.

Rationale of the Standard Nonforfeiture Law

Minimum surrender values under the Standard Nonforfeiture Law reflect these two important principles:

- Surrender values should be derived independently of a policy's reserve
- Such values should reflect approximate asset shares accumulated under the policies.

The technique used to accomplish these two objectives is called the "adjusted-premium" method.[7] This method reflects the philosophy that each group of policies issued on the same plan and at the same age should pay its own way, including the costs of acquisition. It recognizes that expenses are concentrated heavily in the first year and that first-year loading is not sufficient to absorb these expenses. The basic assumptions and techniques underlying the preliminary term method of reserve valuation described in chapter 14 are adopted. The difference between adjusted premiums used to derive reserves and surrender values is simple but subtle.

adjusted-premium method

adjusted premium

The **adjusted-premium method** derives its name from the manner in which surrender values reflect unamortized acquisition expenses. First-year expenses beyond normal recurring expenses are treated as an additional obligation under the policy. This amount is amortized over the premium-paying period in precisely the same manner as the present value of policy benefits is amortized. The amount that must be added to the net level premium to amortize this additional obligation is determined by dividing the excess

---

7.　The term adjusted premium is usually used to represent only the premium defined in the Standard Nonforfeiture Law, which produces minimum values. Any other modified premium used to compute surrender values is usually called a nonforfeiture factor. A nonforfeiture factor is employed to produce larger values than those required by law. In more complex methods of computing surrender values, several nonforfeiture factors may be used in the same policy.

first-year expenses by the present value of an appropriate life annuity due. The result, when added to the net level premium, produces the **adjusted premium**. In short, the net level annual premium is adjusted to reflect the annual cost of liquidating the initial acquisition expenses. The actuary finds the surrender value at any duration by taking the difference between the present value of the benefits under the policy and the present value of future adjusted premiums.

The similarity between the adjusted-premium method and the prospective reserve should be apparent. The only difference is the use of adjusted premiums in one case and net level premiums in the other. With the same mortality and interest assumptions, the present value of future benefits is identical under either calculation. Therefore, the present value of future adjusted premiums is larger than the present value of future net level premiums because the adjusted premium is larger than the net level premium. This means that the surrender value is smaller than the reserve.

With identical mortality and interest assumptions, the difference between the reserve and the surrender value at any particular point in time is the unamortized first-year expenses. This difference decreases with each premium payment and disappears with the last payment.

It is important to note, however, that the mortality and interest assumptions employed by a company to calculate surrender values need not be the same as those used by the company to calculate premiums and reserves. The actual values promised may be computed on any basis that produces values at or above the statutory minimum values.

Illustration of the Adjusted-Premium Method

There are three steps in deriving surrender values under the Standard Nonforfeiture Law. Step one is to find the special first-year expense allowance. The law safeguards terminating policyowners' interests by limiting the amount of first-year expenses that may be considered in computing the surrender values.[8] The permitted values provide ample expense margins for a well-managed company.

---

8.   The maximum special first-year expense allowance that may be used in finding the adjusted premium is the sum of 125 percent of the lesser of the policy's net level premium or $40 per $1,000 of insurance. For a policy with a nonlevel benefit amount and/or premiums, a more complex method is used. The percentage factors in the expense limitation formula consider expenses that depend on the amount of the premium and the plan of insurance. The constant factor of $20 per $1,000 reflects those expenses that depend on the number of policies or the amount of insurance.

Step 2 in the process is to calculate the adjusted premium. This may be either (1) the level annual premium required to amortize a principal sum equal to the present value of the benefits under the policy and the special first-year expense allowance or (2) the sum obtained by adding to the net level premium the annual increment needed to amortize the special acquisition expenses over the premium-paying period.

The former approach is illustrated here with an ordinary life policy issued at age 32. Assume that the maximum special first-year expense allowance for such a policy, calculated according to the prescribed formula, is $20.64 per $1,000. That amount is added to $140.28, the assumed net single premium for an ordinary life policy issued at age 32, to obtain the amount needed at the inception of the contract to meet the obligations under the contract—namely, $160.92. To obtain the equivalent annual sum, $160.92 is divided by $16.49, the present value of a whole life annuity due of $1 as of age 32, based on an interest rate of 5.5 percent. The result, $9.76, is the adjusted premium.

The second approach is equally simple. To find the amount that must be set aside out of each gross annual premium—including the first—to amortize the special costs of acquisition, divide $20.64 by $16.49. The answer, $1.25, is the amount that must be added to the net level premium for an ordinary life policy issued at 32—$8.51—to arrive at the same adjusted premium obtained above, $9.76.

Step 3 entails substituting the adjusted premium for the net level premium in the formula for prospective reserves. Recall from chapter 18 that the 10th-year terminal reserve for an ordinary life policy issued at age 32 is determined as follows[61]: $214.82 − ($8.51 × $15.06) = $86.66. The first element in the equation, $214.82, represents the net single premium for a whole life policy issued at age 42; the second element, $8.51, represents the net level premium for an ordinary life policy issued at age 32 (rounded to two digits after the decimal); the last element, $15.06, is the present value of a whole life annuity due of $1 calculated at age 42. All values are based on the 1980 CSO Table and 5.5 percent interest. To find the surrender value under this policy at the end of 10 years, substitute the adjusted premium, $9.76, for the net level premium, $8.51. The result, $214.82 − ($9.76 × $15.06) = $67.83, is the surrender value.

The difference between the reserve at the end of 10 years and the surrender value for the same period, $86.66 − $67.83, or $18.83, represents a form of surrender charge assessed to cover unamortized first-year expenses. The surrender value under the same policy at the end of 20 years is calculated as follows: $319.53 − ($9.76 × $13.05) = $192.16. Because the 20th-year terminal reserve for an ordinary life policy issued at 32 is $208.50, the unamortized acquisition expenses are reduced to $16.34. The disparity disappears completely when all premiums have been paid.

Summary of Steps

The detailed steps in the calculation of the 10th-year surrender value for an ordinary life policy issued at age 32, with all computed values based on the 1980 CSO Table and 5.5 percent interest, can be summarized as follows:

Example

Calculation of the 10th-year surrender value for a policy issued at age 32.

1. Find net single premium for ordinary life policy at age 32 ($140.28).
2. Find allowance for special first-year expenses ($20.64).
3. Add (1) and (2) ($160.92).
4. Find present value at age 32 of whole life annuity due of $1 ($16.49).
5. Divide (3) by (4) to find adjusted premium ($9.76).
6. Find net single premium for ordinary life policy at age 42 ($214.82).
7. Find present value at age 42 of whole life annuity due of $1 ($15.06).
8. Multiply (5) by (7) to find present value at age 42 of future adjusted premiums ($146.99).
9. Subtract (8) from (6) to find 10th-year surrender value ($67.83).

The surrender value under the adjusted-premium method also may be found retrospectively by accumulating the annual adjusted premiums (less the excess first-year expenses) at the assumed rate of interest and deducting death claims at the tabular rate. The process is identical to the calculation of retrospective reserves except that adjusted premium is used to reflect excess first-year expenses. The retrospective approach is particularly useful in considering modifications of the adjusted-premium method.

Modifications of the Adjusted-Premium Method

The illustration above computes minimum surrender values under a 5.5 percent interest assumption. Many companies offer surrender values greater than those required by law if such adjustments are supported by the company's expense rates, by competitive pressures, or by other considerations. Higher values are obtained by assuming lower first-year expenses than the maximum permitted by law or by assuming the maximum expenses and amortizing them over a shorter period than the number of years for which premiums are payable (or at an uneven rate over the entire period of premium payments).

Surrender Dividends

surrender dividend

For a well-managed company, the asset share of a particular policy will, after a few years, exceed its surrender value and eventually will exceed the reserve. If the policy goes off the books, equity suggests that the withdrawing policyowner should be permitted to take some share of the surplus created. Such a final settlement with a withdrawing policyowner can be accomplished through a **surrender dividend**. The surrender dividend, because it is not guaranteed, provides more flexibility to the insurer than surrender values of the same amount.

RELATIONSHIP BETWEEN SURRENDER VALUES AND OTHER VALUES

The following table illustrates the relationship between surrender values, asset shares, and reserves, both level premium and modified. This table presents an asset share calculation for a participating ordinary life policy issued at age 32.

Death rates are based on varying percentages of the rates of tabular mortality. Specifically the rates assumed in Table 8-9 for the first 6 policy years are 42, 52, 60, 66, 70, and 72.5 percent of the corresponding rates in the 1980 CSO Male Table. From age 38 the mortality rate is assumed to increase one-half percentage point for each year of attained age after that, reaching 79.5 percent of 1980 CSO male rates at the 20th policy year. After the first 5 years, these are the same mortality rates used in calculating dividends for this policy. Mortality rates for the first 5 years below those in the dividend formula reflect the influence of selection. The rates used in calculating dividends usually do not reflect the savings from selection. Instead the savings are applied to amortize excess first-year expenses.

Table 8-9 Asset-share Calculation $100,000 Ordinary Life Policy Issued to a Male Aged 32 Gross Premium = $1,301							
(1)	**(2)**	**(2a)**	**(3)**	**(4)**	**(5)**	**(6)**	**(7)**
Policy Year	Surviving and Per-sisting	Expenses	Effective Premium	Total Effective Premium (2) × (3)	Initial Fund (13) n - 1 + (4)	Initial Fund + Interest (5) × (1.0625)	Death Claims + Expenses and Interest
1	10,000.00	$1,867	($566)	($5,661,200)	($5,661,200)	($6,015,025)	$793,839
2	7,993.85	136	1,165	9,312,277	1,847,287	1,962,742	820,021
3	6,708.17	136	1,165	7,814,544	6,830,900	7,257,832	831,414
4	5,762.10	136	1,165	6,712,443	11,260,574	11,964,360	828,780
5	5,006.05	136	1,165	5,831,693	15,095,556	16,039,028	810,724
6	4,348.43	136	1,165	5,065,617	18,051,288	19,179,494	781,473
7	3,819.96	136	1,165	4,449,987	20,420,055	21,696,308	743,077
8	3,355.23	136	1,165	3,908,613	22,251,261	23,641,964	710,635
9	2,946.55	136	1,165	3,432,526	23,634,176	25,111,312	680,119
10	2,616.57	136	1,165	3,048,121	24,823,217	26,374,668	662,395
11	2,349.14	66	1,235	2,901,142	26,064,036	27,693,038	647,817
12	2,132.01	66	1,235	2,632,991	27,258,309	28,961,954	643,398
13	1,955.72	66	1,235	2,415,274	28,441,867	30,219,483	643,230
14	1,813.03	66	1,235	2,239,052	29,660,266	31,514,033	651,792
15	1,698.31	66	1,235	2,097,383	30,949,211	32,883,537	664,516
16	1,590.37	66	1,235	1,964,071	32,132,636	34,140,925	677,240
17	1,488.78	66	1,235	1,838,614	33,222,028	35,298,405	688,445
18	1,393.19	66	1,235	1,720,560	34,228,367	36,367,640	701,461
19	1,303.21	66	1,235	1,609,442	35,160,381	37,357,905	713,505
20	1,218.53	66	1,235	1,504,856	36,027,832	38,279,572	730,394

(8)	(9)	(10)	(11)	(12)	(13)	(14)	(15)	(16)
Minimum Cash Value	Number of Surren-ders	Amount Paid on Surrender	Divi-dend per $100,000	Total Dividend Paid (11) × (2)	Fund Balance [(6)-(7)-(10)- (12)]	Asset share (13)/[(2) n+1]	1980 CSO 5.50% NLP Reserve	1980 CSO 5.50% CRVM Reserve
$0	1998	$0	$82	$656,126	($7,464,990)	($934)	$716	$0
0	1278	0	266	2,126,364	(983,643)	(147)	1,464	754
0	938	0	280	1,878,286	4,548,131	789	2,247	1,542
230	748	171,897	295	1,699,819	9,263,863	1,851	3,063	2,364
1,063	650	690,759	310	1,551,874	12,985,671	2,986	3,914	3,221
1,931	521	1,006,016	327	1,421,937	15,970,068	4,181	4,798	4,112
2,834	458	1,296,517	344	1,314,066	18,342,648	5,467	5,716	5,036
3,771	402	1,515,085	362	1,214,595	20,201,650	6,856	6,667	5,995
4,742	323	1,533,461	381	1,122,636	21,775,096	8,322	7,653	6,987
5,747	261	1,500,135	401	1,049,245	23,162,893	9,860	8,671	8,012
6,786	211	1,430,913	421	988,988	24,625,319	11,550	9,723	9,073
7,861	170	1,336,822	448	955,141	26,026,593	13,308	10,810	10,168
8,970	136	1,224,117	476	930,922	27,421,215	15,125	11,933	11,299
10,116	108	1,096,647	504	913,765	28,851,829	16,989	13,092	12,465
11,299	102	1,146,953	532	903,502	30,168,565	18,970	14,288	13,670
12,519	95	1,189,666	560	890,605	31,383,414	21,080	15,521	14,912
13,778	89	1,225,261	589	876,892	32,507,807	23,333	16,795	16,195
15,078	83	1,254,249	618	860,990	33,550,939	25,745	18,107	17,517
16,418	78	1,276,941	648	844,482	34,522,977	28,332	19,460	18,880
17,799	73	1,293,726	679	827,379	35,428,072	31,111	20,850	20,280

Withdrawals shown in Table 8-9 approximate those in a study of ordinary insurance conducted by the Life Insurance Marketing Research Association (LIMRA) in the United States from 1983 to 1987. Combined with the assumed rates of mortality and applied to a radix of 10,000 insureds at age 32, these withdrawal rates determine the number of living and persisting policyowners shown in column (2).

A gross premium of $13.01 per $1,000 of coverage is assumed for $100,000 of insurance. This is the net premium, based on the 1980 CSO Male Table and 5.5 percent interest, loaded by 16 percent plus $2.50. Expenses are assumed to occur as shown in Table 8-9.

The effective first-year premium is $566.12. The effective premium for the 2d through the 10th policy years is $1,164.93. Table 8-9 reveals that the only expenses after the 10th year are the premium tax, maintenance expenses, and the cost of settlement. The first two types of expenses occur annually. The cost of settlement is incurred only once per policy and is included in the death claims. These reduced costs mean that for each year after the 10th, the effective premium is $1,234.98.

Effective premiums are assumed to accumulate at the rate of 6.25 percent, a rate that is higher than the rate of interest currently used in premium and reserve calculations, but one that realistically measures the interest being earned on long-term interest-bearing investments.

Cash values are assumed to be the minimum cash values computed on a 5.5 percent interest basis. Dividends are assumed to be paid according to the scale derived in Table 8-9 with the full amount of the dividend for any particular year going to all persons who enter that year even if they fail to survive or persist to the end of the year. First-year dividends, however, are assumed to be paid only to those policyowners who either have survived and persisted or have died during the year. In other words, first-year dividends are not paid to those who withdraw during the year.

Column (14) of Table 8-9 shows the asset share developed from these assumptions. Note that the asset share is negative the first and 2d years. This is normal for a policy of this type and premium. The asset share is also less than the net level premium reserve until the 8th year. This shows that the company does not recover its acquisition expenses for this group of policies until the 9th year. This is perhaps normal for mutual companies, but stock companies usually amortize their first-year expenses over a shorter period. As can be seen by comparing columns (14) and (15) of Table 8-9, the excess of the asset share over the net level premium reserve—an amount that, by the end of the 20th year, amounts to $102.61 per $1,000—measures the contribution of each $1,000 policy to the surplus of the company. In later years, the asset share can be reduced through an increase in the dividend scale.

NONTRADITIONAL INSURANCE PRODUCTS

surrender charge

This chapter has discussed surrender values under ordinary life insurance products. Non-traditional products that were developed during the 1980s, such as universal life insurance, have an explicit accumulated value on which the contract's rate of interest is paid. The

surrender value is the accumulated value minus an explicit surrender charge. Typically the **surrender charge** begins at 100 percent of the accumulated value for termination during the first year of the contract. Then it declines steadily until it disappears, usually at least 7 years after policy issue and sometimes as many as 20 years after policy issue.

Surrender Value Equals

- Cash value (or accumulated value) minus surrender charge

The removal of the mysterious "black box" operation typical of surrender values in traditional life insurance is a defining characteristic of many modern nontraditional insurance contracts. The distinct surrender charge clearly displays the cost to consumers of purchasing permanent insurance only to cancel it after a short period.

USE OF SETTLEMENT OPTIONS

Adaptation of Settlement Options to Basic Family Needs

The opening chapter of this book described the basic family needs that life insurance can meet.

CHAPTER REVIEW

Key Terms and Concepts

surrender options	cumulative right of withdrawal
reduced amount of paid-up whole life	noncumulative right of withdrawal
paid-up term	commutation
delay clause	life income option
automatic premium loan clause	deferred life annuity
lump sum	lapse
settlement options	surrender
settlement agreement	termination
spendthrift clause	Standard Nonforfeiture Law
revocable contingent beneficiaries	nonforfeiture laws
rate of income	nonforfeiture values
contract rates	adjusted-premium method
current rates	adjusted premium
unlimited right of withdrawal	surrender dividend
limited right of withdrawal	surrender charge

Chapter 8 Review Questions

1. Explain why the cash available to the policyowner when surrendering a policy may be less than the reported cash value (assume there have been no policy loans). [3]

2. Why are life insurers reluctant to invoke the protections of the delay clause that is included in every life insurance policy developing cash values? [3]

3. A policyowner intends to surrender her policy with a reported $60,000 cash value. She took out a $10,000 policy loan 2 years ago that has an 8 percent fixed policy loan rate. None of the loan has been repaid, and there are no applicable surrender charges. How much will she receive as a result of surrendering the policy? [4]

4. Explain what reinstatement rights are normally available to a policyowner after surrendering a policy for cash. [4]

5. What type of coverage is provided when the reduced paid-up insurance nonforfeiture option is elected? [4]

6. Why do life insurers prefer the extended term insurance nonforfeiture option to other surrender options? [4]

7. Explain how the automatic premium feature works on fixed-premium policies. [4]

8. How is the amount of reduced paid-up insurance determined when that nonforfeiture option is elected? [4]

9. How does the reduced paid-up insurance nonforfeiture provision in a whole life policy differ from a similar reduction under a variable life or a universal life policy? [4]

10. Describe the extended term insurance nonforfeiture option. [4]

11. A policyowner elects the extended term insurance option for a policy having a $30,000 cash value, a $100,000 face amount, and indebtedness of $10,000. (a) How much extended term insurance will be provided? (b) How much will be available to purchase the extended term coverage? [4]

12. Why do life insurers prefer the extended term insurance nonforfeiture option to other-surrender options? [4]

13. Explain how the automatic premium feature works on fixed-premium policies. [4]

14. Compare insurance company liability when policy proceeds are paid in a lump sum and when an optional method of settlement is selected. [1]

15. Explain when a spendthrift clause in a settlement agreement is enforceable. [2]

16. Explain the difference between contract rates and current rates. [3]

17. Martin, an applicant for life insurance, discovers that the policy does not contain a settlement option he thinks he will want to use. Why should Martin request to have the desired settlement option added to the policy by endorsement at the time the policy is issued? [3]

18. Describe the ways a beneficiary's right of withdrawal of proceeds held by the insurer under a deferred-settlement arrangement may be limited. [3]

19. Describe how a cumulative right of withdrawal differs from a noncumulative right of withdrawal. [3]

20. Cathy is the beneficiary of her father's life insurance policy. Under a settlement option, the policy provides that Cathy has a cumulative right to withdraw $4,000 each year in addition to periodic contractual payments. During the next 5 years, Cathy exercises the right of withdrawal according to the following pattern: year one, a $1,500 withdrawal; year 2, no withdrawal; year 3, a $2,000 withdrawal; year 4, no withdrawal; year 5, a $2,500 withdrawal. Ignoring other sums that can be withdrawn pursuant to the terms of agreement, what is the maximum amount Cathy can withdraw under the cumulative right of withdrawal in year 6? [3]

21. Describe the three basic concepts of life insurance settlement options. [4]

22. Describe the four fundamental settlement options that have evolved from settlement option concepts. [4]

23. Explain why the interest option is simple and flexible. [4]

24. Define the fixed-period option (also called an installment time option) and the fixed-amount option (also called an installment amount option). [4]

25. What factors must be taken into account to determine the amount of each payment when the liquidation period is a fixed period of time or if the amount of each payment is fixed in advance? [4]

26. Describe developments that may increase or decrease the amount of proceeds available under the fixed-period option. [4]

27. Describe the flexibility features available with the fixed-amount option. [4]

28. Explain the underlying principle of a life income option. [4]

29. Describe the following life income options: (a) straight life income option; (b) life income with guarantee (period certain); (c) installment-refund option; (d) cash-refund option. [4]

30. Explain why life income options are considered to be inflexible. [4]

31. Discuss the advantages of having a life insurance trust own the policy when the insured's estate is substantial. [5]

32. Describe how an election of the fixed-period option and the fixed-amount option can be used to provide a mortgage cancellation fund for the mortgage on the insured's home. [5]

33. Greta and Hal are 33 and 35 years old, respectively, and have been married for 8 years. They have two children, Jimmy, aged 6, and Joanie, aged 2. At this time in their lives, Hal is the only income provider. Although all family members are currently in excellent health, Hal wants his family to be provided for in the event that he dies while his children are young. Discuss what Greta and Hal should consider in selecting a settlement option that will provide income during the dependency period for Greta and their children. [5]

34. Describe three possible approaches to equitable treatment of a withdrawing policy-owner. [9]

35. List and briefly explain the reasons a company may reduce the surrender benefit to an amount less than a surrendered policy's asset share. [9]

36. What requirements does the Standard Nonforfeiture Law impose on surrender values? [10]

37. Explain how a surrender value is derived with the adjusted-premium method and how this method differs from prospective reserve valuation. [11]

38. Compute the 10th-year surrender value per $1,000 of insurance for a life insurance policy with actual first-year expenses of $30 per $1,000, a maximum first-year expense

allowance permitted by the nonforfeiture law of $25 per $1,000, a net single premium at issue of $240, and a net single premium at valuation (end of the 10th policy year) of $250. Assume that the present value of a life annuity due of $1 per year for the policy's full premium-paying period is $20 and the present value of a life annuity due of $1 per year for the remainder of the premium-paying period calculated at valuation is $10. [12]

39. For a life insurance policy with a maximum first-year expense allowance permitted by the nonforfeiture law of $25 per $1,000, a net level annual premium at issue of $12, and a net single premium at valuation (end of the 15th policy year) of $270, and assuming that the present value of a life annuity due of $1 per year for the policy's premium-paying period is $20 and the present value of a life annuity due of $1 per year for the remainder of the premium-paying period calculated at valuation is $7, do the following:

(a) Compute the 15th-year surrender value per $1,000 of insurance.

(b) Explain why the 15th-year surrender value is less than the 15th-year terminal reserve computed with the full net level premium valuation method if the same mortality and interest assumptions are used, and indicate when the surrender value will become equal to the reserve.

(c) Explain why the 15th-year surrender value is greater than the 10th-year surrender value computed in question 6. [12]

40. Explain the difference between the adjusted premium and a nonforfeiture factor. [11]

41. Explain how the surrender value under the adjusted-premium method may be found retrospectively. [11]

42. Explain what adjustments can be made to produce surrender values with the adjusted-premium method that are higher than the minimum values required by law. [11]

43. Why does a surrender dividend give an insurer more flexibility than surrender values enhanced by the same amount? [11]

45. Explain what each of the following indicates: (a) A policy's asset share is less than its net level premium reserve. (b) A policy's asset share is equal to its net level premium reserve. (c) A policy's asset share is greater than its net level premium reserve. [9]

46. Explain how surrender values are determined for nontraditional products such as universal life insurance. [13]

Chapter 8 Review Answers

1. *The current law requires that the surrender value of a policy be made available in the form of cash, but it does not compel a company to grant cash values until the end of 3 years in the case of ordinary insurance. This limitation on cash values was provided in order to relieve the companies of the expense of drawing checks for the relatively small values that might have developed during the first and second policy years. It does not, however, relieve the company of the obligation to make available in some noncash form of benefit any surrender value that might accumulate during the first 2 years. Most companies waive this statutory provision and provide a cash value as soon as any value develops under the policy.*

2. *To maintain policyowner confidence, insurers do not invoke the delay clause until they are already experiencing an excessive demand for cash due to a widespread loss of confidence.*

3. *Solution:*

$10,000	loan
800	first-year interest ($10,000 x 0.08)
+ 864	second-year interest ($10,800 x 0.08)
$11,664	policy indebtedness
$60,000	cash value
−11,664	indebtedness
$48,336	cash upon surrender

4. *Normally, there are no reinstatement rights available to a policyowner after surrendering a policy for its cash value.*

5. *When the reduced paid-up option is elected, the policyowner receives a reduced amount of paid-up cash value insurance, payable upon the same conditions as the original policy.*

6.   *From the standpoint of the companies, paid-up term insurance is a more attractive sur-
     render benefit than paid-up whole life insurance. The companies consider the favorable
     features of extended term insurance to be (1) relatively large amount of insurance involved,
     with the correspondingly low expense rate; (2) the definite date of expiry, which limits the
     maintenance expenses and minimizes the problem of tracing policyowners; (3) the uninter-
     rupted continuation of the original amount of coverage, as modified by dividend additions
     and policy loans, for those persons who contemplate eventual reinstatement; and (4) its
     adaptability to liberal reinstatement requirements, which stems from the fact that the
     amount at risk is normally decreased by reinstatement, in contrast to the increase in the
     amount at risk that occurs on the reinstatement of reduced paid-up insurance. The only
     real disadvantage of extended term insurance from the insurer's standpoint is the adverse
     mortality selection encountered, and this can be hedged through the use of the higher
     mortality assumptions authorized by law or minimized through making the extended term
     option the automatic paid-up benefit.*

7.   *The automatic premium loan clause provides that any defaulted premium will be auto-
     matically paid and charged against the cash value without request from the policyowner
     unless he or she elects to surrender the policy for cash or one of the paid-up insurance
     options. The effect of the automatic premium loan clause is to extend the original plan of
     insurance for the original face amount decreased by the amount of premiums loaned with
     interest. Such extension will continue as long as the cash value at each premium due date
     is sufficient to cover another premium.*

8.   *The amount of paid-up insurance provided under the reduced paid-up option is the sum
     that can be purchased at the insured's attained age by the net surrender value (cash value,
     less any policy indebtedness, plus the cash value of any dividend additions or deposits)
     applied as a net single premium computed on the mortality and interest bases specified in
     the policy for the calculation of the surrender value.*

9.   *The reduced paid-up option is provided by a benefit provision in a whole life policy and
     is a guaranteed option upon lapse. For a variable universal life policy or universal life
     policy, there is no option providing for reduced paid-up insurance. The policyowner has to
     explicitly request a death benefit reduction to create the equivalent of a reduced paid-up
     surrender option. Moreover, because the policyowner bears the investment risk with
     variable universal life insurance, further adjustments may be needed if the earnings on the
     cash value drop below the level anticipated when the policy benefit was reduced.*

10. The extended term insurance option provided paid-up term insurance in an amount equal to the original face of the policy, increased by any dividend additions or deposits and decreased by any policy indebtedness. The length of the term is that which can be purchased at the insured's attained age by the application of the net surrender value as a net single premium.

11. a. $90,000 of extended term ($100,000 – $10,000)

    b. $20,000 as a net single premium purchase ($30,000 – $10,000)

12. From the standpoint of the companies, paid-up term insurance is a more attractive surrender benefit than paid-up whole life insurance. The companies consider the favorable features of extended term insurance to be (1) relatively large amount of insurance involved, with the correspondingly low expense rate; (2) the definite date of expiry, which limits the maintenance expenses and minimizes the problem of tracing policyowners; (3) the uninterrupted continuation of the original amount of coverage, as modified by dividend additions and policy loans, for those persons who contemplate eventual reinstatement; and (4) its adaptability to liberal reinstatement requirements, which stems from the fact that the amount at risk is normally decreased by reinstatement, in contrast to the increase in the amount at risk that occurs on the reinstatement of reduced paid-up insurance. The only real disadvantage of extended term insurance from the insurer's standpoint is the adverse mortality selection encountered, and this can be hedged through the use of the higher mortality assumptions authorized by law or minimized through making the extended term option the automatic paid-up benefit.

13. The automatic premium loan clause provides that any defaulted premium will be automatically paid and charged against the cash value without request from the policyowner unless he or she elects to surrender the policy for cash or one of the paid-up insurance options. The effect of the automatic premium loan clause is to extend the original plan of insurance for the original face amount decreased by the amount of premiums loaned with interest. Such extension will continue as long as the cash value at each premium due date is sufficient to cover another premium.

14. When the proceeds of a life insurance policy are payable in a lump sum, the company's liability under the policy is fully discharged with the payment of such sum. If, however, the company retains the proceeds under one of the optional methods of settlement, its liability continues beyond the maturity of the policy and must be evidenced by some sort of legal document. That document (called the settlement agreement) contains the designation of

the various classes of beneficiaries and a detailed description of the manner in which the proceeds are to be distributed.

15. *When either the policyowner of beneficiary elects the settlement option and the settlement option is to benefit the party who elected it, a spendthrift clause (if included in the settlement agreement) will not be enforced. A spendthrift clause is generally enforceable when the party procures the life insurance policy or settlement agreement for the benefit of someone else.*

16. *Under each settlement option, a specified rate of income per $1,000 of proceeds is guaranteed in the policy; these are referred to as contract rates. The benefits under existing agreements cannot be modified without the specific consent of the policyowner. In order to distinguish the rates of income available under existing policies and settlements agreements from rates that are applicable to contracts currently being issued, the latter are referred to a current rates.*

17. *If Martin's request for the particular settlement option is granted, a specified rate of income per $1,000 is guaranteed in the policy. These rates are referred to as contract rates. This means that the issuing company cannot later modify the actuarial assumptions underlying the benefits provided under this optional mode of settlement.*

18. *The right of withdrawal may be limited as to the following: • the frequency with which it can be invoked • the minimum amount that can be withdrawn at any one time • the maximum amount that can be withdrawn at any one time • the maximum amount that can be withdrawn in any one year • the maximum amount that can be withdrawn in the aggregate The first two types of limitations are imposed by the insurers to control the cost of administration, while the last three are imposed by the policyowner (often a parent of the beneficiary) to prevent dissipation or too rapid exhaustion of the proceeds by the beneficiary. The right of withdrawal can usually be invoked only on dates when regular interest or liquidation payments are due.*

19. *A cumulative right of withdrawal means that if any or all of withdrawable amounts are not withdrawn during a particular year, they can be withdrawn in a later year along with any other amounts withdrawable that (later) year. A noncumulative right of withdrawal means that at the end of the time period allowed for withdrawal, the right to withdraw that time period's amounts ends and is not carried over into later periods.*

20. Cathy can withdraw a maximum of $20,000 (5 x $4,000) during the 5-year period. Because she withdrew $6,000 during that time, she has a maximum amount of $18,000 that she can withdraw in year 6. This is the cumulative sum, less the withdrawals over the 5 years, plus the $4,000 right-of-withdrawal amount attributed to year 6.

21. Life insurance settlement options, as a group, embody these three basic concepts:
     •   retention of proceeds without liquidation of principal
     •   systematic liquidation of the proceeds without reference to life contingencies (that is, without reference to how long the primary beneficiaries live)
     •   systematic liquidation of the proceeds with reference to one or more life contingencies (that is, with reference to how long the primary beneficiaries live)

22. The four fundamental settlement options are: • the interest option • the installment time option or fixed-period option • the installment amount option or fixed-amount option • the life income option

23. The interest option is a simple option because the insurance company maintains the proceeds intact until a stated period of time has expired or a stated occurrence has taken place. Afterwards, a method of ultimate disposition of the proceeds commences. The interest option is flexible because of the varying degrees of control over proceeds held by the company that a primary beneficiary can be given. For example, if a policyowner wants the beneficiary to have access to money for emergencies, he or she may give the primary beneficiary a limited right of withdrawal. The policyowner may also give the primary beneficiary the right to elect a liquidating option if additional flexibility is desired.

24. The fixed-period option (also called an installment time option) provides payments over a stipulated period of time, while the fixed-amount option (also called an installment amount option) provides payments of a stipulated amount. The two options are based on the same mathematical principles and differ only as to whether emphasis is attached to the duration of the payments or to the level of payments.

25. When the fixed-period option, the amount of each payment during the liquidation period depends on several factors: the size of the fund, the rate of interest assumed to be earned, the time when the first payment is to be made, and the interval between payments. If the amount of each payment is fixed in advance, the period over which the liquidation is to take place depends on these same factors.

26. *Additional proceeds payable because of the accidental death benefits, dividend accumulations, paid-up additions, increased investment earnings during payout period, or prepaid or discounted premiums that are considered to be part of the proceeds can increase the amount of proceeds available. Outstanding policy loans at the insured's death, however, may decrease the proceeds available and, therefore, reduce the size of the monthly benefits.*

27. *The fixed-amount option offers a great deal of flexibility. The beneficiary can be given the right to indicate when the liquidation payments are to begin. In the meantime, the proceeds will be held at interest, with the interest payments going to the primary beneficiary. Unlike the fixed-period option, the beneficiary can be given either a limited or an unlimited right of withdrawal Under this option, withdrawals will merely shorten the period of installment payments and will not necessitate recomputing benefit payments.*
The beneficiary can also be given the right to accelerate or retard the rate of liquidation. That is, he or she can be given the privilege of varying the amount of the monthly payments, subject to any limitations the insured might wish to impose. Furthermore, the beneficiary can be given the privilege of discontinuing payments during particular months of the year or from time to time. Finally, this option can include a provision for transferring the remaining proceeds to another liquidating option.

28. *The principle underlying a life income option is identical to that underlying an annuity. As a matter of fact, a life income option is nothing more than the annuity principle applied to the liquidation of insurance proceeds. At a minimum, all life income options guarantee benefit payments as long as the primary beneficiary (beneficiaries) lives (live). Other HS 323 138 guarantees can be added such as a minimum number of benefit payments (that is, payments for at least a specified period of time) or return of at least the amount of proceeds placed under the option.*

   In the case of a life income option, the annuity principle works as follows:
   If the primary beneficiary is willing to pool his or her death proceeds with those of other people in the same situation, the administering agency, relying on the laws of probability and large numbers, can provide each of the participants with an income of a specified amount as long as he or she lives—regardless of longevity. No one would outlive his or her income. Such an arrangement, however, implies a willingness on each participant's part to have all or a portion of his or her unliquidated principal and/or interest at the time of death used to supplement the exhausted principal of those who live beyond their expectancy.

29. *There are several life income options available in a life insurance policy:*

    a. *The straight life income option is equivalent to a pure immediate annuity. The first payment is due one payment period (usually, one month) after maturity of the policy or after election of the option, whichever is later. The monthly income provided per $1,000 of proceeds depends on the age and sex of the beneficiary and the insurer's assumptions as to mortality and interest. The monthly income benefit is paid as long as the primary beneficiary lives, but ceases upon his or her death.*

    b. *The life income option with a specified period of guaranteed payments is mathematically a combination of a fixed-period installment option of appropriate duration and a pure deferred life annuity. For example, a life income option that promises to provide payments of a specified amount to a beneficiary aged 45 throughout his or her remaining lifetime, and in any event for 20 years, is a combination of a fixed-period installment option running for 20 years and a pure life annuity deferred to the beneficiary's age 65. If the beneficiary does not survive to age 65, the portion of the proceeds allocated to the deferred life annuity is retained by the insurance company without further obligation. The primary beneficiary receives a monthly income benefit as long as he or she lives, but if the primary beneficiary were to die during the 20-year period certain, the monthly income benefit would be to due during the 20-year period certain, the monthly income benefit would be continued to the contingent beneficiary for the remainder of the period certain.*

    c. *The installment refund option is a combination of a pure immediate life annuity and decreasing term insurance in an amount sufficient to continue payments until the proceeds, without interest, have been paid out in full. (In addition to promising monthly benefit payments as long as the primary beneficiary lives, this option promises to continue the monthly payments beyond the primary beneficiary's death until the proceeds of the life insurance policy have been returned.) At the inception, the term insurance is in an amount equal to the proceeds, less the first payment due immediately, but it decreases with each periodic payment and expires altogether when the cumulative benefit payments equal or exceed the life insurance proceeds committed to the installment-refund option.*

    d. *Like the installment refund option, the cash-refund option is a combination of a pure immediate life annuity and decreasing term insurance. Because the refund is payable in cash rather than payable in installments, however, a slightly larger amount of term insurance is required.*

30. *Because benefits are calculated according to the primary beneficiary's age and sex, once the payments have started, there are no substitutions allowed. Rights of withdrawal and commutation are not available.*

31. *When life insurance proceeds are payable to an irrevocable life insurance trust, funds can be made indirectly available to the insured's estate for liquidity purposes, either by the trustee's purchase of noncash assets from the estate or by loans of money to the estate. If the insurance proceeds are more than sufficient to meet the insured's estate liquidity needs, the excess may be made available for the insured's dependents without the delay and expense associated with probate.*

32. *If the mortgage has no prepayment privilege or can be prepaid only with a heavy penalty, an income settlement can be arranged to provide funds in the required amount and frequency for the mortgage payments. Either the fixed-period option or the fixed-amount option is generally satisfactory.*

33. *The actual dependency period is considered to be the period of time from the end of the readjustment period following Hal's death until the youngest child's (Joanie's) 18th birthday, assuming Joanie remains in generally good health. If Social Security survivorship benefits in conjunction with the interest on retained life insurance proceeds are inadequate during this period, additional income can be provided through the fixed-period or fixed-amount options. If the fixed-amount option is elected, Greta can also be granted the right of withdrawal for even greater flexibility in meeting family needs.*

34. *Experts offer three possible approaches to the equitable treatment of a withdrawing policyowner.*

    - *At one extreme, the policyowner receives no refund of any amount. According to this view, the function of life insurance is viewed solely as providing benefits upon the death of the insured. Those who "drop out" of the venture forfeit all payments and all interest in the contract. This view generally has not been accepted since the early days of life insurance.*

    - *At the other extreme, it might be argued that terminating policyowners should receive a refund of all premium paid, plus interest at the contractual rate, less a pro rata contribution toward death claims and the premium loading. A contract with such generous surrender values implicitly assumes that expenses occur evenly throughout the*

policy's premium-paying period and that the premium is sufficient to absorb expenses that arise each year.

- The third and prevailing approach holds that a withdrawing policyowner should receive a surrender benefit—either cash or some form of paid-up insurance—approximately equal to the amount contributed to the company, minus the cost of the policy. Ideally, a policyowner's withdrawal should neither benefit nor harm continuing policyowners. The maximum benefit to a withdrawing policyowner would be a pro rata share of the assets accumulated by the company for the block of policies—that is, by definition, the policy's asset share. The actual surrender benefit should be reduced below the asset share, however, for several reasons discussed in the answer to question 26.35.   A company will usually reduce the surrender benefit to an amount less than the asset share of a surrendered policy for the following reasons:

- adverse mortality selection—Some actuaries argue that persons in extremely poor health are not likely to surrender their policies and will instead borrow to maintain their protection. Many believe that those who do surrender are, on the average, in better health and can be expected to live longer than those who do not surrender. If surrender values are too high, the accumulated funds may not be sufficient to pay the death claims of the remaining policyowners. In view of a lack of conclusive data on the subject, some companies withhold a small portion of the asset shares from surrendering policyowners in order to offset any adverse selection that might occur.

- adverse financial selection—Many terminations, particularly cash surrenders, tend to increase sharply during periods of economic crises and depressions, as well as when market interest rates are higher than those provided on life insurance cash values. Also, the policyowner's right to demand the cash value of a policy at any time forces the company to maintain a more liquid investment portfolio than would otherwise be necessary, which reduces the yield on the portfolio. Thus, terminations may adversely affect a company (1) if it has fewer funds to invest at what might be an attractive rate of interest and (2) if it is forced to liquidate assets at depressed prices. Most companies charge terminating policyowners with the resulting loss of investment earnings by reducing surrender values below what would otherwise be available.

- contribution to a contingency reserve—Sound life insurance management demands that each group of policies ultimately pays its own way, including a provision for adverse contingencies such as wars and epidemics.

- contribution to profits—In a stock company, a deduction may be made from the asset share of the surrendering policyowner to compensate stockholders for the risk borne

by capital funds. The size of the deduction varies depending on the level of profits already distributed to stockholders.

- cost of surrender—All companies incur expenses to process the surrender of a policy. Some companies estimate aggregate expenses for surrenders and include them as part of the loading in the premium for all policies. Other companies charge the cost of the transaction to the particular policies involved by deducting it from the surrender value that would otherwise be available.

- assuring company solvency—In practice, surrender benefits must be limited if their payment might impair the security of remaining policyowners. When balancing the interests between terminating and continuing policyowners, conflicts are resolved in favor of continuing policyowners. Placing higher priority on the interests of continuing policyowners is consistent with general contract law.

36. The Standard Nonforfeiture Law does not require specific surrender values. The only requirement is that surrender values are at least as large as those that would be produced by the method the law prescribes. In addition, each policy must contain a statement of the method used to find the surrender values and benefits provided under the policy at durations not specifically shown. This permits companies to use alternate formulas by describing them in their policies.

37. First-year expenses beyond normal recurring expenses are divided by the present value of a life annuity due of $1 for the number of years in the premium-paying period to obtain the amount that must be added to the net level premium to obtain the adjusted premium. Then, the surrender value is derived with the adjusted premium method by subtracting the present value of future adjusted premiums from the present value of benefits. The adjusted-premium method differs from prospective reserve valuation that subtracts the present value of future net level premiums, rather than the present value of future adjusted premiums, from the present value of benefits. Also, it is important to note that the mortality and interest assumptions employed by a company to calculate surrender values need not be the same as those used by the company to calculate premiums and reserves.

38. The 10th-year surrender value is $117.50. The first step in calculating the 10th-year surrender value is to find the special first-year expense allowance. Because the policy's actual firstyear expenses ($30 per $1,000) are greater than the maximum permitted by law for this policy, $25 per $1,000 is the largest amount of first-year expense than can be included in the adjusted-premium calculation. The second step involves calculating the adjusted premium ($13.25) by adding the special first-year expense allowance ($25) to the policy's

net single premium at issue ($240) and dividing the resultant sum ($265) by the present value of a life annuity due of $1 per year for the policy's premium-paying period ($20). This determines the level annual premium required to amortize the present value of the policy's benefits and the special first-year expense allowance over the premium-paying period. The final step is substituting the adjusted premium for the net level premium in the formula for prospective reserves. As such, the adjusted premium ($13.25) is multiplied by the present value of a life annuity due of $1 per year for the remainder of the premium-paying period calculated at valuation ($10) to obtain the present value of future adjusted premiums ($132.50). That amount is subtracted from the present value of future benefits (the net single premium at valuation of $250) to obtain the 10th-year surrender value ($117.50).

39. a. *The 15th-year surrender value is $177.25. The first step in calculating the 15th-year surrender value is to find the special first-year expense allowance. The maximum permitted by law ($25 per $1,000) is the largest amount of first-year expense that can be included in the adjusted-premium calculation. The second step is to calculate the adjusted premium ($13.25) by first dividing the special first-year expense allowance ($25) by the present value of a life annuity due of $1 per year for the policy's premium-paying period ($20) to determine the level annual premium that is needed to amortize the special first-year expense allowance over the premium-paying period calculated at valuation ($7) to obtain the present value of future adjusted premiums ($92.75), which is subtracted from the present value of future benefits (the net single premium at valuation of $270) to obtain the 15th-year surrender value ($177.25).*

    b. *If the same mortality and interest assumptions are used, the 15th-year surrender value is less than the 15th-year terminal reserve computed with the full net level premium valuation method because the adjusted premium ($13.25) covering special first-year expenses as well as benefits, rather than the net level premium ($12) covering only benefits, is used to calculate the present value of future premiums, which is subtracted from the present value of future benefits in both cases. Thus, the 15th-year surrender value ($270 –[$13.25 x $7] = $177.25) is less than the 15th-year terminal reserve ($270 – [$12 x $7] = $186). The difference of $8.75 is a form of surrender charge assessed to cover unamortized first-year expenses. This disparity decreases over time (as first-year expenses are amortized) and disappears completely when all premiums have been paid.*

    c. *The 15th-year surrender value is greater than the 10th-year surrender value computed in question 6 because the present value of future benefits (the net single premium at valuation) is larger at the end of the 15th year ($270) than at the end of the 10th year ($250), and the present value of future adjusted premiums is smaller at the end of the 15th year ($92.75) than at the end of the 10th year ($132.50). Because a smaller*

present value of future adjusted premiums is subtracted from a larger present value of future benefits to compute the surrender value, the 15th-year surrender value is greater than the 10th-year surrender value.

40. *The term adjusted premium is usually used to represent only the premium defined in the Standard Nonforfeiture Law, which produces minimum values. Any other modified premium used to compute surrender values is usually called a nonforfeiture factor. A nonforfeiture factor is employed to produce larger values than those required by law.*

41. *The surrender value under the adjusted-premium method can be found retrospectively by accumulating the annual net premiums less the unamoritized excess first-year expenses at the assumed rate of interest and deducting death claims at the tabular rate.*

42. *Higher surrender values are obtained by assuming lower first-year expenses than the maximum permitted by law or by assuming the maximum expenses and amortizing them over a shorter period than the number of years for which premiums are payable (or at an uneven rate over the entire period of premium payments).*

43. *The surrender dividend, because it is not guaranteed, provides more flexibility to the insurer than surrender values of the same amount.*

45. a. *When the policy's asset share is less than its net level premium reserve, the company does not recover its acquisition expenses if the policy matures as a death claim.*

    b. *When the policy's asset share is equal to its net level premium reserve, the company will recover its acquisition expenses if the policy matures as a death claim.*

    c. *When the policy's asset share is greater than it net level premium reserve, the policy will contribute to the surplus of the company if it matures as a death claim or is surrendered.*

46. *Nontraditional products, such as universal life insurance, have an explicit accumulated value on which the contract's rate of interest is paid. The surrender value is the accumulated value minus an explicit surrender charge. Typically, the surrender charge begins at 100 percent of the accumulated value for termination during the first year of the contract. Then it declines steadily until it disappears, usually at least 7 years after policy issue and sometimes as many as 20 years after policy issue.*

Policy Provisions

Revised by: C.W. Copeland, Dave Moon, & Burke A. Christensen

Learning Objectives

An understanding of the material in this chapter should enable the student to

1. **Understand and explain the standard policy provisions in a life insurance contract.**

2. **Identify the provisions that are required by law in life insurance policies.**

3. **Identify and explain the types of provisions from which insurers are prohibited, including those in life insurance policies.**

4. **Explain the concepts of waiver and estoppel.**

5. **Briefly describe the provisions: accidental death, guaranteed purchase option, and waiver of premium.**

contract of adhesion

Contract of Adhesion

A contract of adhesion is one that is not negotiated. It is drafted entirely by one party. The other party to the contract is not permitted to alter the terms of the contract but may only accept or reject the contract. Because the drafting party has the freedom to choose the words of the contract, the law requires that party to abide by the words it has chosen. This means any ambiguities are interpreted in favor of the other party.

A life insurance contract is a **contract of adhesion**. This means that the policyowner and the insurer do not negotiate the terms of the contract. The prospective policyowner performs only these two functions in the creation of a life insurance contract:

*   He or she applies for the policy (the contract) by filling out the application and supplying any medical information required by the insurer. This is not a negotiation. The applicant is merely specifying what type of contract he or she would like to be offered. Based on this information, the insurer will make an offer by issuing a policy.

*   The applicant is then asked to accept or reject the contract as offered by the insurer. The applicant accepts the offer by paying the initial premium. If a partial premium has been paid and a premium receipt has been issued by the insurer's agent, only temporary coverage under the terms of the receipt is in effect. The contract is

accepted by the applicant and binding on the insurer under the particular terms of the receipt and the policy. The applicant rejects the offered contract by refusing delivery of the policy. Even after the applicant accepts the insurer's offer of coverage and a contract is binding on the insurer, the policyowner may, in effect, reject the contract and get a full refund based on the 10-day free look provision (which is explained later in this chapter). New York and about half of the other states require this provision, so it is now included in most contracts.

- The language in the application for coverage stresses the fact that the contract cannot be altered by the agent. Applicants must accept the language in the policy as it is or else choose not to contract with that company.

- Possibly another insurance company may have policies containing more acceptable language.
    - Life insurance is a contract of adhesion.
    - Applicants for coverage must accept the contract as it is without change or modification.

Because the prospective policyowner can only accept or reject the contract offered by the insurer, the contract of adhesion rules provide that all ambiguities in the contract of insurance will be resolved in favor of the policyowner and against the insurer. This rule of law is not entirely fair to insurance companies because there are substantial limitations on the insurer's freedom to draft the insurance contract as it wishes. Insurers are required by law to include many types of provisions and in some cases are required to use or not use certain words. Thus, it is not entirely correct to state that since the insurers are free to select the contract language, they have to give the benefit of ambiguity to the applicant.

Many states require that the contract avoid complex sentences and arcane legal terminology. The goal is to make the contracts easier for the consumer to read and understand. This goal, while laudable, conflicts with the goal of lawyers to be certain that a contract is interpreted exactly as the drafter intended. Over many years, courts have given certain legal terms specific meanings upon which lawyers have come to rely in drafting contracts. This "legalese" may be hard for the uninitiated to understand, but it offers a certainty that lawyers prefer. Nevertheless, it has become the policy of this country to prefer less technical language over the certainty of interpretation. Lawyers will have to rely on current and future cases developing new standard meanings as the simplified language of modern contracts is interpreted by the courts.

There are a number of required, prohibited, and optional provisions that are controlled by state law. Before a policy may be sold in a particular jurisdiction, its provisions must be filed with that state's insurance department for approval.

POLICY FACE PAGE

Although the placement of the provisions may vary from company to company, the face pages of most life insurance contracts are quite similar. The face page of the contract usually has the following information:

- the name of the insurance company

- some specific details for that policy—for example, the name of the insured and the name of the policyowner, the face amount of the policy, the policy number, and the policy date or issue date (some include both dates)

- a general description of the type of insurance provided by that policy contract. For example, the face page of a traditional participating whole life policy might read as follows:

  - Whole Life—Level Face Amount Plan. Insurance payable upon death. Premiums payable for life. Policy participates in dividends. Dividends, dividend credits, and policy loans may be used to help pay premiums.

- statement about the policy's free look provision. This is a provision that gives the policyowner a period of time, usually 10 days, to return the policy after acceptance. The following is an example of such a provision:

  - Not later than 10 days after you get this contract, you may return it tous. Allyouhavetodoistakeitormailittooneofourofficesor to the agent who sold it to you. The contract will be canceled from the start, and a full premium refund will be made promptly.

- the insurer's promise to pay. This is the heart of the insurance contract.

- the signatures of the officers (usually the president and the secretary) of the company, which binds the company to the terms of the contract

The remainder of the required and optional provisions are not usually included on the face page.

Example

Typical promise-to-pay statements

- We will pay the beneficiary the sum insured under this contract promptly if we receive due proof that the insured died while this policy was in force. We make this promise subject to all the provisions of this contract.

- We will pay the benefits of this policy in accordance with its provisions.

- We agree to pay the death benefits of this policy to the beneficiary upon receiving proof of the insured's death; and to provide you with the other rights and benefits of this policy.

STANDARD POLICY PROVISIONS

The standard policy provisions laws of the various states require that life insurance policies include certain provisions but allow the insurance companies to select the actual wording. However, the wording must be submitted to and approved by the state insurance department. The standard provisions laws do not apply to group life insurance. For some insurance contracts, such as term, single premium, and nonparticipating policies, some of the standard provisions may not be applicable. To that extent, those contracts are excused from compliance with the law. Note: Term life insurance will not have cash value. Therefore, policy loan and nonforfeiture provisions will not be included in the term policy.

Prior to 1900, life insurance contracts were not regulated as they are today. After the Armstrong Investigation of 1905 in New York, the number of restrictions on the language and form of life insurance contracts was drastically increased. In fact, the state of New York enacted statutes that prescribed exactly how term life, ordinary life, and endowment contracts could be written. This inflexible statutory solution proved to be impractical almost immediately, and it was soon repealed. In its place, New York enacted legislation that merely required that certain kinds of provisions be included in the contract. Insurers were permitted to draft their own contractual language for these provisions. The language the insurers selected was subject to state approval, which would be granted so long as (1) the minimum intent of the required statutory provision was obtained or (2) the insurer's language was more favorable to the policyowner than the statutory intent.

The state insurance codes generally impose a requirement that unless specifically exempted from the law, all life insurance policies delivered or issued for delivery in the state must contain language substantially the same as certain specified provisions. Insurers are also generally given the option to insert different provisions than those specified in the

statute if the language in the insurer's provisions is more favorable to policyowners. The insurance department determines whether an alternative provision is more favorable to consumers.

REQUIRED PROVISIONS

Grace Period

grace period clause

The **grace period clause** grants the policyowner an additional period of time to pay any premium after it has become due. While the clause is now required by law, it was a common practice among insurers before the existence of laws compelling the inclusion of the provision in the contract. Because of the provision, a policy that would have lapsed for nonpayment of premiums continues in force during the grace period. The premium remains due, however, and if the insured dies during the grace period, the insurer may deduct one month's premium from the death benefit.

Note that although insurers could charge interest on the unpaid premium for the late period, they do not normally do so. If the insured survives the grace period but the premium remains unpaid, the policy lapses (except for any nonforfeiture options).

As with all renewal premiums, the policyowner has no obligation to pay the premium for the insurance coverage provided under the grace period provision. Thus, it might be said that the insured has received "free" insurance during that time. This is an accurate conclusion only if the insured does not die within the grace period.

The standard length of the grace period is 31 days. If the last day of the grace period falls on a nonbusiness day, the period is normally extended to the next business day.

> **Example**
>
> A sample grace period provision reads as follows:
> We allow 31 days from the due date for payment of a premium. Your insurance coverage continues during this grace period. Note: If the insured dies during the grace period, the past due premium will be deducted from the death benefit.

Late Remittance Offers

It is important to make a distinction between the grace period rules and a late remittance offer; they are not the same. There is usually no provision in the contract concerning late remittance offers. Such offers are made solely at the insurer's option. The late remittance offer is not a right of the policyowner or an obligation of the insurer that is included in the insurance contract under the requirements of the law.

Some insurers will make a late remittance offer to a policyowner whose coverage has lapsed after the grace period has expired. This is not an extension of the grace period and coverage is not continued as a result of the offer. Late remittance offers are intended to encourage the policyowner to reinstate the policy; they do not extend coverage. The inducement from the insurer is that coverage can be reinstated without having to provide evidence of insurability. The policyowner accepts the late remittance offer by paying the premiums that are due and meeting any other conditions imposed by the insurer. The most common condition is that the insured must have been alive when the late premium payment was made.

Policy Loans

The law requires that the insurance contract permit policy loans if the policy generates a cash value. To understand this requirement it is necessary to make a distinction between loans, policy loans, and advancements.

> Loan—a transfer of money (or other property) with an obligation to repay the money plus interest (or to return the asset transferred) at a certain time

> Policy loan—an advance of money available to the policyowner from a policy's cash values. Interest is accrued on the amount borrowed from the policy. Although there is no fixed time for repayment of the money to the insurer, the amount of the loan plus any unpaid interest will be deducted from any policy values payable under the policy.

> Advancement—money or other property transferred to someone prior to the anticipated time of payment or delivery

From the definitions above it can be seen that the term policy loan is a misnomer. A policy loan is actually an advancement against the policy's cash surrender value or death benefit. It is not technically a loan because the policyowner assumes no obligation to repay the money taken from the policy. Thus, it is not technically correct to say that the policyowner borrows from the insurer and the loan is secured by the policy cash values. It is more

accurate to say that the policyowner makes an advance withdrawal of cash values otherwise available when the policy is surrendered or when the insured dies. However, this distinction is really only of academic interest because the universal practice is to call it a *loan*.

Example

Ms. Policyowner obtains a policy loan of $8,000; it is subject to an 8 percent interest rate. Her repayment options are to

- repay none of it

- repay interest only

- repay some of balance due

- repay all $8,000 plus interest due

(Note: the timing and amount of any repayments are totally at the discretion of Ms. Policyowner unless either the insured dies or the policy is terminated.)

After 2 years at an 8 percent policy loan interest, the loan balance will be $9,331.20 if no repayments have been made.

$$\$8,000 + \$640 + \$691.20 = \$9,331.20$$

If Ms. Policyowner pays the $640 interest charge each year, the loan balance will remain level at $8,000. Death benefits will be reduced by the loan balance, plus any unpaid interest, such as the $9,331.20.

One might ask, if it is not a loan, why is the insurer permitted to assess an interest rate against the amount borrowed? The policyowner is expected to pay interest on the "loan" because he or she has withdrawn assets from the insurer that were intended to support the level premium concept. If the policyowner withdraws those assets, it is fair to expect him or her to pay an interest rate that would approximate what the insurer would earn if the money was left with the insurer to invest.

Automatic premium loans are another type of policy loan. These loans are advances the insurer makes from policy cash values to pay any unpaid premiums.

Incontestable Clause

incontestable clause

The National Association of Insurance Commissioners Standard Policy Provisions Model Act and the laws based upon it require that the policy contain an **incontestable clause**, a provision that makes the life insurance policy incontestable by the insurer after it has been in force for a certain time period. This provision was originally introduced in New York in 1864 by the voluntary action of insurers. By 1906, the clause had become so firmly entrenched and was so obviously beneficial to the public that it was made mandatory by New York law. Other states followed New York's example, and now the incontestable clause is required by statute in all states. The laws of the states differ as to the form of the clause prescribed, but no state permits a clause that would make the policy contestable for more than 2 years.

Example

A sample incontestable clause:
Except for nonpayment of premium, we will not contest this contract after it has been in force during the lifetime of the insured for 2 years from the date of issue.

After a policy has been in effect for the period of time prescribed by the incontestable clause (normally 2 years), the insurance company cannot have the policy declared invalid. The courts have generally recognized three exceptions to this rule. If there was no insurable interest at the inception of the policy, if the policy had been purchased with the intent to murder the insured, or if there had been a fraudulent impersonation of the insured by another person (for example, for purposes of taking the medical exam), then the incontestable clause is deemed not to apply because the contract, which includes the incontestable clause, was void from its inception.

Example

Abigail and Diane were identical twins, but they had different states of health. Diane had a heart murmur for the decade prior to her death. Four years prior to her death, she purchased a life insurance policy by concealing her heart problem and having healthy Abigail take the physical examination the insurance company requested.

The insurance company discovered the impersonation when they investigated for the death claim, but the policy had been in force for 4 years.

Will the insurer be liable for the death claim?

No. The contract was void from the inception because of the fraudulent impersonation at the physical examination. But if there had not been any fraudulent impersonation and merely concealment, then the policy would have been voidable until the end of the contestable period. After 4 years, the policy would be incontestable in the absence of fraudulent impersonating.

Divisible Surplus

divisible surplus provision

The **divisible surplus provision** applies only to participating provision policies. It requires the insurer to determine and apportion any divisible surplus among the insurer's participating policies at frequent intervals.

A typical divisible surplus provision from an insurance contract reads as follows:

> While this policy is in force, except as extended term insurance, it will be entitled to the share, if any, of the divisible surplus that we shall annually determine and apportion to it. This share is payable as a dividend on the policy anniversary.

In addition, some contracts provide that payment of a dividend is conditioned upon payment of all premiums then due. The provision in most contracts notes that a dividend is not likely to be paid before the second anniversary of the policy.

Entire Contract

Ordinarily we expect that a contract of any type includes all the provisions that are binding on the parties. However, this is not always the case. Sometimes one contract will include the terms of another document without actually including that second document in the contract. This is done by referring to the other document and incorporating it into the contract by that reference. This is known as incorporation by reference. Entire contract statutes grew out of an attempt to prohibit insurers' use of incorporation by reference and to make life insurance contracts more understandable by consumers. One goal was to assure that the policyowner was given a copy of all documents that constitute the contract. Another was to preclude any changes in the contract after it had been issued.

The various state statutes impose different requirements. Some states require a provision disclosing that the contract and the application constitute the entire contract; other states simply provide that the contract and the application are the contract regardless of what the policy may say.

Example

A sample provision is as follows:

This policy and any attached copy of an application form the entire contract. We assume that all statements in an application are made to the best of the knowledge and belief of the persons who make them; in the absence of fraud, they are deemed to be representations and not warranties. We rely on those statements when we issue the contract. We will not use any statement, unless made in an application, to try to void the contract, to contest a change, or to deny a claim.

Reinstatement

reinstatement provisions

Reinstatement provisions allow a policyowner to reacquire coverage under a policy that has lapsed. This right is valuable to both the policyowner and the insurer. The various state laws and the insurance contracts impose certain requirements that the policyowner must meet to reinstate the policy. New York law requires that life insurance policies contain a provision granting the policyowner the right to reinstate the policy ". . . at any time within three years from the date of default, unless the cash surrender value has been exhausted or the period of extended term insurance has expired, if the policyholder makes application, provides evidence of insurability, including good health, satisfactory to the insurer, pays all overdue premiums with interest at a rate not exceeding six per centum per annum compounded annually, and pays or reinstates any other policy indebtedness with interest at a rate not exceeding the applicable policy loan rate or rates determined in accordance with the policy's provisions. This provision shall be required only if the policy provides for termination or lapse in the event of a default in making a regularly scheduled premium payment."[1]

A typical reinstatement provision might provide the following:

This policy may be reinstated within 3 years after the due date of the first unpaid premium, unless the policy has been surrendered for its cash value. The conditions for reinstatement are that (1) you must provide evidence of insurability satisfactory to us, (2) you must pay all overdue premiums plus interest at 6 percent per year, and (3) you must repay or reinstate any policy loan outstanding when the policy lapsed, plus interest.

---

1.   N.Y. Ins. Law Sec. 3203(a)(10) McKinney 1985.

Normally, insurers do not permit reinstatement of a policy that has been surrendered for its cash value, and this prohibition is often included in the contractual definition of the requirements for reinstatement.

Misstatement of Age or Sex

The age and sex of the insured are fundamentally important factors in the evaluation of the risk the life insurance company assumes. Inaccurate statements about the insured's age or sex are material misrepresentations. Rather than voiding the contract based on such misrepresentations, the practice after discovering the inaccuracy is to adjust the policy's premium or benefits to reflect the truth. Adjustments in the policy's premiums or benefits based on misstatements of age or sex are not precluded by the incontestability clause. This is because incontestability clauses preclude contests of the validity of the policy. If a misstatement of age or sex clause appears in the contract, an adjustment based on that clause would be an attempt to enforce the terms of the contract, not invalidate it.

A sample provision might read as follows:

> If the age or sex of the insured has been misstated, we will adjust all benefits payable under this policy to that which the premium paid would have purchased at the correct age or sex.

Example

Janet understated her age when she purchased a life insurance policy. The premium she paid was $900 annually but would have been $1,000 annually for her correct age. The policy face amount will be adjusted down to the amount of coverage she could have purchased with a $900 annual premium based on her true age.

Note that if the insured is still alive when it is discovered that the insured's age or sex has been misrepresented, it may be that the parties will elect to adjust the premium to the correct amount rather than to adjust the benefits.

The New York insurance code requires insurance contracts to contain a provision stipulating that if the age of the insured has been misstated, any amount payable or benefit accruing under the policy will be what the premium would have purchased at the correct age.[2] This clause is ambiguous for flexible premium policies, because it does not specify

---

2.   N.Y. Ins. Law Sec. 3203(a)(5).

how to calculate the correct charges. A minority of states have a provision requiring a reference to misstatement of sex.

Nonforfeiture Provisions

nonforfeiture provisions

Nonforfeiture provisions. When insurers developed the concept of level premium insurance policies, the goal was to make life insurance more affordable to older policyowners. This was accomplished by charging a lifetime level premium. In the earlier years of the policy this level premium was higher than necessary to cover the mortality costs. The excess portion of the premium in the policy's early years (and the interest it earned) built up a cash reserve that was used to pay the mortality costs at older ages, which then exceeded the level premium being charged. A question soon arose concerning who was entitled to those reserves when a policy lapsed in the early years. Initially, these reserves were forfeited by the policyowner and kept by the insurer. This was clearly inequitable, and the practice was soon modified. Today that question has been answered by the nonforfeiture laws.

The states require that insurers assure policyowners who voluntarily terminate their contracts a fair return of the value built up inside some policies. These laws are known as the nonforfeiture laws. As late as the middle of the nineteenth century, insurance policies in the United States made no provision for refunds of excess premiums paid on cash value policies upon the policyowner's termination of the policy before maturity. However, in 1861 Massachusetts recognized that the policyowner had a right to at least a portion of those funds, and the first nonforfeiture law was enacted in that state. By 1948 that idea had evolved into the Standard Nonforfeiture Law, and subsequent versions of the law have become effective in all jurisdictions. Policies issued since that date have provided at least the minimum surrender values prescribed by the version of the law in effect when the policy was put in force. Modifications of the Standard Nonforfeiture Law do not apply retroactively to insurance policies that are already in force when the new law is adopted.

The Standard Nonforfeiture Law does not require specific surrender values. The only requirement is that surrender values are at least as large as those that would be produced by the method the law prescribes. In addition, each policy must contain a statement of the method used to find the surrender values and benefits provided under the policy at durations not specifically shown. This permits life insurance companies to use alternate formulas by describing them in their policies.

These laws require that after a cash value policy has been in effect for a minimum number of years—usually 3—the insurer must use part of the reserved excess premium to create a guaranteed minimum cash value. In addition, the insurer must make that value available to the policyowner in cash as a surrender value and must give the policyowner a choice of two nonforfeiture options: (1) extended term insurance for the net face amount of the policy or (2) paid-up insurance at a reduced death benefit amount. If the policyowner has not elected between them, the policy must provide that one of these two options will be effective automatically if the policy lapses.

Example

Standard Nonforfeiture Law
100,000 whole life policy.

$10,000 = cash value
$ 6,000 = outstanding policy loan

This policy has been in effect the minimum number of years and the Company has given Marshall his choice of

- Extended term insurance—$94,000 of coverage would be extended for as long as the $4,000 net cash value will purchase as a single premium.

- Paid-up insurance—a paid-up whole life policy will be provided for whatever face amount can be purchased with the $4,000 net cash value (based on the age of the insured). The face amount will be significantly less than $94,000

Settlement Options

The standard policy provisions of the various states require that a life insurance policy must include certain settlement options tables if the settlement options include installment payments or annuities. These tables must show the amounts of the applicable installment or annuity payments.

PROHIBITED PROVISIONS

Although the state laws are not uniform, most states prohibit insurers from including certain provisions in their policies. For various reasons, courts or state legislatures have determined that these prohibited contract provisions violate public policy. There are five generally prohibited provisions:

- The insurance producer, who is the agent of the insurance company, cannot be made the agent of the insured for purposes of filling out the application for insurance. If the producer could be made the insured's agent rather than the company's agent, then the insurance company could not be charged with knowing facts presented to the agent but not communicated to the insurance company by the agent. Note that this restriction against making the producer the agent of the insured is confined to taking the application. The producer is sometimes held to be the agent of the insured for other purposes after the policy is in force.

- Nonpayment of a loan cannot cause a forfeiture. The state laws generally provide that so long as the cash value of the policy exceeds the total indebtedness on the policy, the policyowner's failure to repay the loan or to pay interest on the loan cannot cause a forfeiture of the policy.

- Less value statutes preclude an insurer from promising something on the face of the policy and taking it away in the fine print. These laws are called less value statutes because the insurer is prohibited from providing a settlement option of less value than the death benefit of the policy.

- There are limitations on the time for filing lawsuits against the insurer. All states have statutes of limitation that control how long a person may wait before bringing a lawsuit of any type against another party. These statutes are designed to force people to sue in a timely fashion rather than waiting in the hope that evidence favorable to the other side will be lost. Once the time period specified in the statute has expired, the courts will not hear the lawsuit.

The statutes of limitation have different lengths for different types of lawsuits. Ordinarily, the time period during which a lawsuit based on a contract must be brought is quite long; 10 years is not an unusual length. Sometimes the parties to a contract will agree to a shorter time period for initiating a lawsuit (based on a breach of that contract) than the period prescribed by the state law. The insurance codes of several states prohibit insurers from issuing policies that greatly reduce the length of the statute of limitations on contract actions. These statutes permit insurers to shorten the period to a reasonable length but not to eliminate it entirely. The permissibly shorter periods range from one to 6 years. Some states do not permit insurers to reduce the statute of limitations period at all.

These laws protect the interests of the insurers and the public. Insurers are protected because the laws allow them to impose shorter limitation periods than otherwise permitted in the state. This benefits insurers because it requires plaintiffs to sue while information relevant to the insurance policy is still easy to obtain.

The public is protected because the statutes do not allow insurers to shorten the limitation period so much that the public does not have sufficient time to determine whether a lawsuit is worthwhile.

- No lengthy backdating to save age is allowed. Backdating a policy means issuing the policy as if it had been purchased when the insured was younger. This practice has an advantage and a disadvantage. The advantage is that the insured will pay lower annual premiums for each increment of the policy because the premium will be based on the younger age. The disadvantage is that the insured must pay the premium applicable to the length of the backdating. This means that the insured will have paid for insurance protection during a period of time before the policy was issued when no coverage was provided. The statutes generally limit backdating to no more than 6 months.

OPTIONAL PROVISIONS

In addition to the required provisions and the prohibited provisions, there are numerous other provisions that are neither required nor prohibited:

- suicide provision. An insurer may elect to include suicide as a covered risk from the day the policy is issued. However, this is not normally the case, and as a general rule most insurance contracts do not provide coverage for a death by suicide within the first one or 2 years after the policy is issued. If the policy does not contain a suicide exclusion provision, then a death by suicide is covered by the policy and the death benefit is payable to the beneficiary regardless of when the suicide occurs.

Example

A typical insurance contract suicide provision

Suicide of the insured, while sane or insane, within 2 years of the issue date, is not covered by this policy. In that event, we will pay only the premiums paid to us less any unpaid policy loans.

- ownership provision. Ordinarily the insured is the applicant and owner of the policy. The ownership provision in the life insurance contract describes some of the rights of the owner. The typical ownership provision stipulates that the owner of the policy is the insured unless the application states otherwise. The provision also usually states that the policyowner may change the beneficiary, assign the policy to another party, and exercise other ownership rights. If these powers are

described, the provision will also define how such powers are to be exercised in order to be recognized by the insurance company.

- assignment provision. As with most contracts and most interests in property, the policyowner has, as a matter of law, the right to transfer some or all of his or her rights to another person. In contract law this is generally known as the right to assign. The act of transferring a property right is an assignment. The right to assign an ownership interest in an insurance policy exists even without an assignment provision in the contract. However, most contracts include an assignment clause because it sets out clearly the conditions upon which an assignment can be made. If the policy contains a provision prohibiting an assignment, any attempted assignment by the policyowner will not be binding on the insurer. If the policy sets conditions for an assignment, the policyowner must comply with these restrictions.

Example

A sample assignment clause might provide the following:

You may assign this policy if we agree. We will not be bound by an assignment unless it has been received by us in writing at our home office. Your rights and the rights of any other person referred to in this policy will be subject to the assignment. We assume no responsibility for the validity of an assignment. An absolute assignment will be the same as a change of ownership to the assignee.

- plan change. This provision simply asserts that the parties may agree to change the terms of the contract. It does not add anything that does not already exist under the law.

Example

A sample contract change provision might read as follows:

Subject to our rules at the time of a change, you may change this policy for another plan of insurance, you may add riders to this policy, or you may make other changes if we agree.

- accelerated benefits. As a result of the AIDS epidemic and public concern about other terminal illnesses, some insurers have added a provision that permits the insured to withdraw policy death benefits under certain circumstances. These accelerated benefits or living benefits provisions state that if the insured develops

a medical condition that renders the insured terminally ill, then he or she may withdraw a portion of the policy's death benefit.

The 1990 NAIC Accelerated Benefits Model Regulation was designed to regulate accelerated benefit provisions of individual and group life insurance policies and to provide required standards of disclosure. (See Section 1 below of the model regulation.)

Accelerated benefits are defined as benefits payable during the lifetime of the insured under a life insurance contract to a policyowner (or certificate holder for group insurance) upon the occurrence of life-threatening or catastrophic conditions that are specified in the policy. To qualify as accelerated benefits, the lifetime payments must reduce the death benefit otherwise payable under the contract.

The model regulation prescribes that the condition that permits the payment of the accelerated benefits must be a medical condition that drastically limits the insured's normal life span expectation (for example, to 2 years or less). The regulation also lists several diseases as examples of a qualifying medical condition: acute coronary artery disease, a permanent neurological deficit resulting from a cerebral vascular accident, end-stage renal failure, HIV (AIDS), or such other medical condition as the commissioner may approve.

Twenty-five states have adopted regulations or statutes similar to the NAIC model. The first two sections of the model regulation are as follows:[3]

Section 1. Purpose

The purpose of this regulation is to regulate accelerated benefit provisions of individual and group life insurance policies and to provide required standards of disclosure. This regulation shall apply to all accelerated benefits provisions of individual and group life insurance policies except those subject to the Long-Term Care Insurance Model Act, issued or delivered in this state, on or after the effective date of this regulation.

Section 2. Definitions

1. "Accelerated benefits" covered under this regulation are benefits payable under a life insurance contract:

    a. To a policyowner or certificateholder, during the lifetime of the insured, in anticipation of death or upon the occurrence of specified

---

3. Accelerated Benefits Model Regulation. Copyright NAIC 2001.

life-threatening or catastrophic conditions as defined by the policy or rider; and

b.   Which reduce the death benefit otherwise payable under the life insurance contract; and

c.   Which are payable upon the occurrence of a single qualifying event which results in the payment of a benefit amount fixed at the time of acceleration.

2.   "Qualifying event" shall mean one or more of the following:

a.   A medical condition which would result in a drastically limited life span as specified in the contract, for example, twenty-four (24) months or less; or

b.   A medical condition which has required or requires extraordinary medical intervention, such as, but not limited to, major organ transplant or continuous artificial life support, without which the insured would die; or

c.   Any condition which usually requires continuous confinement in an eligible institution as defined in the contract if the insured is expected to remain there for the rest of his or her life; or

d.   A medical condition which would, in the absence of extensive or extraordinary medical treatment, result in a drastically limited life span. Such conditions may include, BUT ARE NOT LIMITED TO, one or more of the following:

(1)   Coronary artery disease resulting in an acute infarction or requiring surgery;

(2)   Permanent neurological deficit resulting from cerebral vascular accident;

(3)   End stage renal failure;

(4)   Acquired Immune Deficiency Syndrome; or

(5)   Other medical conditions which the commissioner shall approve for any particular filing; or

e.   Other qualifying events which the commissioner shall approve for any particular filing.

WAIVER AND ESTOPPEL

waiver

The concepts of waiver and estoppel are quite similar and easy to confuse. Some courts treat waiver and estoppel as two parts of the same theory.

Waiver—the voluntary and intentional surrender of a known right. By a waiver, a party relinquishes a right. For example, if an insurer issues a policy even though the medical questionnaire has not been completed and was not signed by the applicant, the insurer will have waived the right to have that information.

Nevertheless, the law is clear that some waivers are forbidden. No party to an insurance contract may waive a right that also partly benefits the general public. For example, the insurable interest requirement benefits the public as well as the insurer; thus an insurer may not waive its right to demand that the applicant have an insurable interest in the life of the insured at the time the policy is applied for. Similarly, a policyowner may not waive his or her rights to nonforfeiture values or premium notices.

Granting a waiver is not necessarily permanent. An insurer may elect to waive a particular right for one time and one purpose only. If so, the waiver will have no effect on future actions between the parties. If a party has repeatedly waived a contractual right in the past, it can reclaim that right simply by notifying the other party that it intends to reassert that right in the future.

estoppel

Estoppel—the loss of the ability to assert a defense because the party has acted in a manner inconsistent with that defense. For example, if an insurer has repeatedly accepted payment of late premiums after the end of the grace period without requiring the insured to comply with the reinstatement process, the insurer may be prohibited (estopped) from requiring a reinstatement for future late premiums. This may be the result even if the prior late premiums were accepted by mistake and without recognizing that they were late.

There is a fine distinction between the example above and the rule that the concept of estoppel may not be used to create coverage or to extend coverage beyond that assumed by the insurer in the contract.

> **Example**
>
> A classic case is Pierce v. Homesteaders Life Association.[4] The policy in that case provided that the death benefit was payable only if the insured died before age 60. The policyowner paid and the insurer accepted premium payment through the end of September of the year in which the insured turned 60. The insured's 60th birthday was on March 3, and she died on March 11. The insured's beneficiary filed a claim for the death benefit asserting that because the insurer had accepted a premium payment for a period beyond the insured's 60th birthday, the insurance company had waived that contractual limitation and should, therefore, be estopped from denying coverage. The court held for the insurer and asserted that coverage cannot be created by waiver.

The essence of the distinction between the example and the case is narrow but clear. In the case, no coverage was to be provided after the insured reached age 60. Estoppel could not be invoked to create something that never existed. In the example, coverage existed for the insured subject to the condition that premiums be paid on time. The insurance company's actions were inconsistent with the existence of that timely premium payment condition; thus, the insurance company was estopped from asserting it.

ADDITIONAL COMMON PROVISIONS

Other common policy provisions are those concerning accidental death benefits, the guaranteed purchase option (also known as the guaranteed insurability option), and the waiver of premium in the event of the insured's disability.

Accidental Death Benefits

This optional policy provision is added to some insurance contracts in the form of a rider, or amendment, to the policy. It is also known as the double indemnity provision because it normally doubles the standard death benefit if the insured dies accidentally.

accidental death

Because this benefit is payable only in the event of the insured's accidental death, that term requires definition. In the absence of a specific definition in the rider, the word accident means an unintentional event that is sudden and unexpected. An **accidental death** is one that is caused by an accident. This statement seems quite clear, but it is not always easy to apply. There have been cases where an insured has been mortally injured in an

---

4.   *Pierce v. Homesteaders Life Association,* 272 N.W. 543 (Iowa 1937).

accident, but the actual cause of death is a disease. Is the accidental death benefit payable? The answer is yes only if the accident was the cause of death. If the insured is in an automobile accident but dies from a heart attack, the accidental death benefit will be payable only if the accident can be proven to have triggered the heart attack. The insurance company is usually successful in positing the heart attack caused the accident.

Example

The insured died when driving an automobile. The car was severely damaged in an accident associated with the death. The cause of death was determined to be a heart attack.

The policy had a face amount of $50,000 and included an accidental death benefit rider.

The insurance company claims the heart attack occurred first and caused both the death and the accident.

The beneficiary spouse with minor children thinks the auto accident occurred first and was the cause of the heart attack. The burden of proving this in order to collect the accidental death benefit is almost impossible to satisfy.

The most likely outcome is that the insurer will only pay a $50,000 death benefit. Money spent by the beneficiary trying to collect the accidental death benefit usually results in squandering part of the basic benefit on legal costs.

The problems caused by cases in which there is potentially more than one cause of death are mitigated somewhat by the standard practice of putting a time limit in the accidental death benefit provision. In the most common type the death must occur within 90 days of the accident that is said to have caused the injury.

These basic definitions preclude coverage for any death that is the natural and probable result of a voluntary act. It is an unchallenged principle of law that people are presumed to expect and intend the probable or foreseeable consequences of their actions. This concept is sometimes described by the term assumption of the risk. If one plays Russian roulette, jumps off buildings, or runs with the bulls in Pamplona, Spain, his or her death as a result of those activities cannot be described as accidental.

There are two types of accidental death clauses: (1) the accidental result type and (2) the accidental means type.

Example 1

A sample accidental result death benefit provision is as follows:

We will pay this benefit to the beneficiary when we have proof that the Insured's death was the result, directly and apart from any other cause, of accidental bodily injury, and that death occurred within one year after that injury and while this rider was in effect.

Example 2

An accidental means death benefit provision would be only slightly different such as

We will pay this benefit to the beneficiary when we have proof that the Insured's death was caused directly, and apart from any other cause, by accidental means, and that death occurred within one year after that injury and while this rider was in effect.

The most common type of provision that insurers use is the accidental result type. This is because the accidental result clause is more favorable to the consumer. It is also because most courts have recognized that the difference between the two clauses is too difficult for many consumers to understand and have therefore ceased to recognize a distinction between the two types of clauses.

The distinction can be explained as follows: under an accidental means clause both the cause (means) of the death and the result must be unintentional. Under an accidental result clause, only the result must be unintentional. For example, assume that an insured is participating in an obstacle course race at a family reunion, and the race requires the racers to dive over a barrel, do a somersault, and run to the next event. The insured breaks her neck and is killed doing the somersault. Because she was doing exactly what she intended to do, the means was not accidental although the result was certainly an accident. The accidental means clause would not require the payment of the benefit, but the accidental result clause would.

There is another factor that has made accidental means clauses less attractive to insureds and thus less frequently used by insurers. This is the provision requiring that, in addition to being accidental, the means (cause) of death must also be violent and caused by an external agency. Courts have been liberal in their interpretation of these limitations in favor of the public.

Most accidental death benefit clauses do not provide coverage in the event of the insured's death by suicide. If suicide of the insured (whether sane or insane) is excluded, then an examination of the insured's mental state at the time of the suicide is avoided. If the insured is sane at the time of the suicide, then it is an intentional act that would not qualify

as an accident. If the insured is insane, the suicide might be classified as unintentional because the insured may be presumed not to have been able to intend the consequences of his or her act.

Guaranteed Purchase Option

guaranteed purchase option

Another popular policy provision is the **guaranteed purchase option**, which is also called the guaranteed insurability option. Although it is quite common now, this is a relatively new option for insureds. It was developed during the 1950s, but it did not become widely available for many years.

The guaranteed purchase option provision helps to protect policyowners against the possibility that they might become uninsurable. Under the typical provision, the policyowner receives the right to acquire additional insurance in specified amounts at specified times or ages. Typically, this provision allows additional purchases every 3 years and after the birth of a child, provided the events occur before the insured reaches a specified maximum age (often 45). The right to purchase additional insurance can be very valuable because the insured does not have to provide evidence of insurability to exercise the option. Another benefit of this option is that the new coverage is normally not subject to a new suicide provision or a new incontestability clause.

Example

Larry purchased a policy with a guaranteed purchase option when he was age 27. He exercised his right to purchase more coverage every 3 years until his 39th birthday. Because his children had entered college and the costs of tuition were squeezing his budget severely, he did not purchase more coverage when he was 42. Unfortunately, he was found to have cancer at age 44. Consequently, he wants to exercise his guaranteed purchase option at age 45.

The insurance company informed Larry that the option lapsed when he did not use it at age 42.

There is a ceiling on the maximum amount of insurance available under the guaranteed purchase option and a maximum age at which the option may be exercised. Once the insured passes an age or event that triggers the right to purchase additional insurance but he or she does not exercise that option, the option lapses.

Waiver of Premium

A waiver-of-premium provision in the event of the insured's disability is another extremely valuable coverage.

According to a typical waiver-of-premium provision, if the insured becomes totally disabled as defined in the life insurance contract, the insurance company will waive payment of premiums on the policy during the continuance of the insured's disability.

The disability waiver of premium has some limitations. For example, the waiver will not be granted if the insured's disability begins after a specified age. In addition, the provision in the sample below will not waive premiums if the disability is self-inflicted or the result of an act of war. As with all contracts, it is important to pay close attention to the language used. Seemingly small differences in the language of the provision can make large differences in the obligations the insurer incurs.

The following is a sample disability waiver-of-premium rider:

Disability Waiver-of-Premium Rider

Waiver of Premiums. We will start to waive the premiums for this policy when proof is furnished that the Insured's total disability, as defined in this rider, has gone on for at least 6 months in a row.

If a total disability starts on or prior to the anniversary on which the Insured is age 60, we will waive all of the premiums which fall due during that total disability. If it goes on until the anniversary on which the Insured is age 65, we will make the policy fully paid-up as of that date, with no more premiums due.

If a total disability starts after the anniversary on which the Insured is age 60, we will waive only those premiums which fall due during that total disability and prior to the anniversary on which the Insured is age 65.

Premiums are waived at the interval of payment in effect when the total disability started. While we waive premiums, all insurance goes on as if they had been paid. We will not deduct a waived premium from the policy proceeds.

Definition of Total Disability. "Total Disability" means that, because of disease or bodily injury, the Insured cannot do any of the essential acts and duties of his or her job, or of any other job for which he or she is suited based on schooling, training, or experience. If the Insured can do some but not all of these acts and

duties, disability is not total and premiums will not be waived. If the Insured is a minor and is required by law to go to school, "Total Disability" means that, because of disease or bodily injury, he or she is not able to go school.

"Total Disability" also means the Insured's total loss, starting while this rider is in effect, of the sight of both eyes or the use of both hands, both feet, or one hand and one foot.

Total Disabilities for Which Premiums Not Waived. We will not waive premiums in connection with any of these total disabilities.

1. Those that start prior to the fifth birthday of the insured, or start at a time when this rider is not effect.

2. Those that are caused by an injury that is self-inflicted on purpose.

3. Those that are caused by any kind of war, declared or not, or by any act incident to a war or to an armed forces of one or more countries while the Insured is a member of those armed forces.

Proof of Total Disability. Written notice and proof of this condition must be given to us, while the Insured is living and totally disabled, or as soon as it can reasonably be done. As long as we waive premiums, we may require proof from time to time. After we have waived premiums for 2 years in a row, we will not need to have this proof more than once each year. As part of the proof, we may have the Insured examined by doctors we approve.

Payment of Premiums. Premiums must be paid when due, until we approve a claim under this rider. If a total disability starts during a grace period, the overdue premium must be paid before we will approve any claim.

Refunds of Premiums. If a total disability starts after a premium has been paid, and if it goes on for at least 6 months in a row, we will refund the part of that premium paid for the period after the policy month when the disability started. Any other premium paid and then waived will be refunded in full.

Values. This rider does not have cash or loan values.

Contract. This rider, when paid for, is made a part of the policy, based on the application for the rider.

Incontestability of Rider. We have no right to contest this rider after it has been in force during the lifetime of the insured for 2 years from its date of issue, unless the Insured is totally disabled at some time within 2 years of the date of issue.

Dates and Amounts. When this rider is issued at the same time as the policy, we show the rider premium amount on the front page of the policy. The rider and the policy have the same date of issue.

When this rider is added to a policy that is already in force, we also put in an add-on-rider. The add-on-rider shows the date of issue. The rider premium amount is shown in a new Premium Schedule for the policy.

When Rider Ends. You can cancel this rider as of the due date of a premium. To do this, you must send the policy and your signed notice to us within 31 days of that date. If this rider is still in effect on the anniversary on which the Insured is age 65, it will end on that date.

This rider ends if the policy ends or is surrendered. Also, this rider will not be in effect if the policy lapses or is in force as extended or paid-up insurance.

Policy Filing and Approval

It is the rule that if a policy is sold in a state but does not include a required provision or has not been filed with the state for approval, the courts will treat the policy as if it did include all the required provisions under the law of that jurisdiction. The policyowner or beneficiary will be permitted to enforce the policy against the insurer as if it complied in all respects with the applicable state law. The state insurance commissioners are charged with the responsibility to see that the insurance companies doing business in their state are complying with that state's law regarding the permitted and prohibited policy provisions. To enable the insurance department to do its job, a policy may not be issued or delivered in a state until it has been approved by the department. In some states, the insurer may assume that the policy has been approved if it has not been advised otherwise within a fixed period of time, such as 30 days, after it has been submitted to the state insurance department. In other states, the insurer may not issue the policy until it has received notice of approval from the department.

If an insurer issues a policy that has not been approved by the insurance department, the policyowner may seek a refund of premiums paid or seek to enforce the policy. If suit is brought, the courts will enforce the unapproved contract against the insurer on behalf of the beneficiary. If the unapproved policy does not include a provision that would have

been required for approval, the policy will be treated by the courts as if it does contain such a provision. Furthermore, if a required provision is more favorable to the policyowner than one actually included in the contract, the courts will treat the contract as if it included the more favorable provision. The insurer that violates the laws requiring filing of the policy and approval of its provisions by the state will also be subject to fines or other penalties (such as revocation of the insurer's right to do business in that state).

CHAPTER REVIEW

Key Terms and Concepts

contract of adhesion

grace period clause

incontestable clause

divisible surplus provision

reinstatement provisions

nonforfeiture provisions

waiver

estoppel

accidental death

guaranteed purchase option

Chapter 9 Review Questions

1. Describe the two functions the prospective policyowner plays in the creation of a life insurance contract. [1]

2. Explain how ambiguities in a life insurance contract are generally resolved by the courts. [1]

3. List the types of information generally found on the face page of a life insurance policy. [1]

4. Explain why standard policy provisions might be more accurately called required provisions. [1]

5. What benefit does the grace period provide for the policyowner? [1]

6. How do the rules applicable to late remittance offers differ from the grace period rules? [1]

7. Because a policy loan is not technically a loan because the policyowner is not obligated to pay it back, why is the insurer allowed to assess an interest charge against the amount borrowed? [2]

8. List the goals of entire contract statues. [2]

9. List the typical requirements that must be met for a policyowner to reinstate a life insurance policy. [2]

10. When Jim purchased $100,000 of life insurance, he told the company he was 35 years old and was charged $1,500 per year. When Jim died 20 years later, it was discovered that he had understated his age and was 38 at the time he purchased the policy. The premium for a 38-year-old would have been $1,667 per year. Explain how this situation would be handled? [2]

11. List the key requirements of the Standard Nonforfeiture Law. [2]

12. Explain why certain policy provisions are prohibited. [3]

13. List the five generally prohibited policy provisions. [3]

14. Explain how statutes that prohibit insurers from contractually reducing the period for filing a lawsuit against them to a period shorter than that specified in the statute protect the interests of both insurers and the public. [3]

15. Explain how the backdating of a life insurance policy provides both an advantage and disadvantage for the policyowner. [3]

16. Sally purchased a $250,000 life insurance policy containing a one-year suicide provision. How much would the insurer have to pay if Sally committed suicide: (a) during the first year of coverage; (b) during the fifth year of coverage. [1]

17. Explain why the assignment provision is included in a life insurance policy. [4]

18. Describe how the 1990 NAIC Accelerated Benefits Model Regulation: (a) defines accelerated benefits; (b) defines qualifying medical conditions. [2]

19. What limitations are typically found in accidental death benefit coverage? [5]

20. Explain the difference between the two types of accidental death clauses. [5]

21. Why does the accidental death provision most commonly use the accidental result type terminology? [5]

22. Explain how the guaranteed purchase option helps policyowners protect themselves against the possibility that they, as insureds, may become uninsurable. [5]

23. Describe the possible consequences if an insurer issues a policy that has not been filed and approved by the insurance department as required by state law. [3]

Chapter 9 Review Answers

1. *The prospective policyowner performs only these two functions in the creation of a life insurance contract:*

    • *He or she applies for the policy (the contract) by filling out the application and supplying any medical information required by the insurer.*

    • *The applicant is then asked to accept or reject the contract as offered by the insurer. The applicant accepts the offer by paying the initial premium. If a partial premium has been paid and a premium receipt has been issued by the insurer's agent, only temporary coverage under the terms of the receipt is in effect. The contract is accepted by the applicant and binding on the insurer under the particular terms of the receipt and the policy. Even after the applicant accepts the insurer's offer of coverage and a contract is binding on the insurer, the policyowner may, in effect, reject the contract and get a full refund based on the 10-day free look provision.*

2. *Because the prospective policyowner can only accept or reject the contract offered by the insurer, the contract-of-adhesion rules provide that all ambiguities in the contract of insurance will be resolved in favor of the policyowner and against the insurer.*

3. The face page of the contract usually has the following information:

   - the name of the insurance company

   - some specific details for that policy

   - a general description of the type of insurance provided by that policy contract

   - a statement about the policy's free look provision

   - the insurer's promise to pay

   - the signatures of the officers (usually the president and the secretary) of the company, which binds the company to the terms of the contract

4. The standard policy provisions laws of the various states require that life insurance policies include certain provisions but allow the insurance companies to select the actual wording. However, the wording must be submitted to and approved by the state insurance department.

   The state insurance codes generally impose a requirement that unless specifically exempted from the law, all life insurance policies delivered or issued for delivery in the state must contain language substantially the same as certain specified provisions. Insurers are also generally given the option to insert different provisions than those specified in the statute if the language in the insurer's provisions is more favorable to policyowners. The insurance department determines whether an alternative provision is more favorable to consumers.

5. Because of the provision, a policy that would have lapsed for nonpayment of premiums continues in force during the grace period. The premium remains due, however, and if the insured dies during the grace period, the insurer may deduct one month's premium from the death benefit.

6. There is usually no provision in the contract concerning late remittance offers. Such offers are made solely at the insurer's option. The late remittance offer is not a right of the policy-owner or an obligation of the insurer that is included in the insurance contract under the requirements of the law.

   With a late remittance offer, coverage is not continued as a result of the offer. Late remittance offers are intended to encourage the policyowner to reinstate the policy; they do not extend coverage. The inducement from the insurer is that coverage can be reinstated without having to provide evidence of insurability.

7.   *The policyowner is expected to pay interest on the "loan" because he or she has withdrawn assets from the insurer that were intended to support the level premium concept. If the policyowner withdraws those assets, it is fair to expect him or her to pay an interest rate that would approximate what the insurer would earn if the money was left with the insurer to invest.*

8.   *The goals of the entire contract statutes are*

   •   *to assure that the policyowner is given a copy of all documents that constitute the contract*

   •   *to preclude any changes in the contract after it has been issued*

9.   *The typical requirements that must be met for a policyowner to reinstate a life insurance policy are as follows:*

   •   *Normally, insurers do not permit reinstatement of a policy that has been surrendered for its cash value.*

   •   *The reinstatement must occur within a specified period of time from the date of lapse-for example, 3 or 5 years.*

   •   *The policyowner must provide evidence of insurability satisfactory to the insurer.*

   •   *The policyowner must pay or reinstate any other policy indebtedness with interest at a specified rate.*

10. *Rather than voiding the contract based on misrepresentation of age, the practice after discovering the inaccuracy is to adjust the policy's premium or benefits to reflect the truth. Because Jim is already dead, the benefits would be adjusted. Adjustments in the policy's premiums or benefits based on misstatements of age or sex are not precluded by the incontestable clause. This is because incontestability clauses preclude contests of the validity of the policy.*

   The typical policy would provide that if the age of the insured has been misstated, the insurer will adjust all benefits payable under this policy to that which the premium paid would have purchased at the correct age or sex. In this case, the death benefit would be reduced from $100,000 to approximately $90,000 (that is, $100,000 x [$1,500/$1,667]).

11. *The Standard Nonforfeiture Law does not require specific surrender values. Rather it requires the following:*

   • *surrender values must be at least as large as those that would be produced by the method the law prescribes*

   • *each policy must contain a statement of the method used to find the surrender values and benefits provided under the policy at durations not specifically shown*

   • *after a cash value policy has been in effect for a minimum number of years—usually 3—the insurer must use part of the reserved excess premium to create a guaranteed minimum cash value*

   • *the insurer must give the policyowner a choice of two nonforfeiture options: (1) extended term insurance for the net face amount of the policy or (2) paid-up insurance at a reduced death benefit amount*

   • *if the policyowner has not elected between them, the policy must provide that one of these two options will be effective automatically if the policy lapses.*

12. *Certain policy provisions are prohibited because they violate public policy.*

13. *The five generally prohibited policy provisions are as follows:*

   • *The insurance producer, who is the agent of the insurance company, cannot be made the agent of the insured for purposes of filling out the application for insurance.*

   • *Nonpayment of a loan cannot cause a forfeiture.*

   • *Less-value statutes preclude an insurer from promising something on the face of the policy and taking it away in the fine print.*

   • *Insurers may not contractually reduce the period for filing a lawsuit against them to a period shorter than that specified in the statute.*

   • *No lengthy backdating to save age is allowed.*

14. *Insurers are protected because the laws allow them to impose shorter limitation periods than otherwise permitted in the state. This benefits insurers because it requires plaintiffs to sue while information relevant to the insurance policy is still easy to obtain. The public is protected because the statutes do not allow insurers to shorten the limitation period so much that the public does not have sufficient time to determine whether a lawsuit is worthwhile.*

15. *The advantage of backdating is that the insured will pay lower annual premiums for each increment of the policy because the premium will be based on the younger age. The disadvantage is that the insured must pay the premium applicable to the length of the backdating. This means that the insured will have paid for insurance protection during a period of time before the policy was issued when no coverage was provided.*

16. *Answers:*

    a. *If Sally committed suicide during the first year of coverage, the company would pay the amount described in the suicide provision-typically, only the premiums paid less any unpaid policy loans.*

    b. *If Sally committed suicide during the fifth year of coverage, the company would pay the $250,000 (less any unpaid policy loans).*

17. *As with most contracts and most interests in property, the policyowner has, as a matter of law, the right to transfer some or all of his or her rights to another person. In contract law, this is generally known as the right to assign. The right to assign an ownership interest in an insurance policy exists even without an assignment provision in the contract. However, most contracts include an assignment clause because it sets out clearly the conditions upon which an assignment can be made.*

18. *Answers:*

    a. *Accelerated benefits are defined as benefits payable during the lifetime of the insured under a life insurance contract to a policyowner (or certificate holder for group insurance) upon the occurrence of life-threatening or catastrophic conditions that are specified in the policy. To qualify as accelerated benefits, the lifetime payments must reduce the death benefit, otherwise payable under the contract.*

    b. *The model regulation prescribes that the condition that permits the payment of the accelerated benefits must be a medical condition that drastically limits the insured's normal life span expectation (for example, to 2 years or less). The regulation also lists several diseases as examples of a qualifying medical condition; acute coronary artery disease, a permanent neurological deficit resulting from a cerebral vascular accident, end-stage renal failure, HIV (AIDS), or such other medical condition as the commissioner may approve.*

19. The following limitations are typically found in accidental death benefit coverage:

    - This benefit is payable only in the event of the insured's accidental death; not if the cause of death is disease.

    - There is a standard practice of putting a time limit in the accidental death benefit provision—most commonly, the death must occur within 90 days of the accident that is said to have caused the injury.

    - Basic definitions preclude coverage for any death that is the natural and probable result of a voluntary act.

    - Most accidental death benefit clauses do not provide coverage in the event of the insured's death by suicide.

20. There are two types of accidental death clauses: (1) the accidental result type and (2) the accidental means type. Under an accidental means clause, both the cause (means) of the death and the result must be unintentional. Under an accidental result clause, only the result must be unintentional.

21. This is because the accidental result clause is more favorable to the consumer. It is also because most courts have recognized that the difference between the two clauses is too difficult for many consumers to understand and here, therefore, ceased to recognize a distinction between the two types of clauses.

22. Under the typical provision, the policyowner receives the right to acquire additional insurance in specified amounts at specified times or ages. Typically, this provision allows additional purchases every 3 years and after the birth of a child, provided the events occur before the insured reaches the specified maximum age (often 45). This right to purchase additional insurance may be very valuable because the insured does not have to provide evidence of insurability in order to exercise the option.

23. It is the rule that if a policy is sold in a state but does not include a required provision or has not been filed with the state for approval, the courts will treat the policy as if it did include all the required provisions under the law of that jurisdiction. The policyowner or beneficiary will be permitted to enforce the policy against the insurer as if it complied in all respects with the applicable state law.

    If an insurer issues a policy that has not been approved by the insurance department, the policyowner may seek a refund of premiums paid or seek to enforce the policy. If suit is

brought, the courts will enforce the unapproved contract against the insurer on behalf of the beneficiary. If the unapproved policy does not include a provision that would have been required for approval, the policy will be treated by the courts as if it does contain such a provision. Furthermore, if a required provision is more favorable to the policyowner than one actually included in the contract, the courts will treat the contract as if it included the more favorable provision.

The insurer that violates the laws requiring filing of the policy and approval of its provisions by the state will also be subject to fines or other penalties (such as revocation of the insurer's right to do business in that state).

Chapter 10
Net Premiums

By Dan M. McGill

Revised by Norma Nielson and Donald Jones

Learning Objectives

An understanding of the material in this chapter should enable the student to

1. **Understand and explain the important elements and steps in making life insurance premium calculations.**

2. **Understand and describe the net single premium calculation process.**

3. **Explain and calculate some net single premiums.**

4. **Explain and calculate some present values for life annuities.**

5. **Explain and calculate some net level premiums.**

premium

The **premium** is the price charged by a life insurance company for an insurance or annuity contract. This term arises from the very first insurance arrangements. In the Middle Ages a lender, for an additional payment—or "premium"—over the interest charge, would waive repayment of the loan should the insured vessel or cargo be lost at sea. The expression has survived the practice and is still used to designate the monetary consideration for an insurance company's promise.

rate

single premium

To calculate a premium the first step is to develop a number that equates to the value of benefits promised under the contract. The premium for a life insurance contract is usually expressed as a **rate** per $1,000 of face amount. On the other hand, the premium for an annuity contract normally is expressed as a rate per specified amount of income, such as $100 per year or $10 per month. If the premium is paid in one sum, it is called a **single premium**. Alternatively, the premium may be paid more frequently with annual, semiannual, quarterly, or monthly frequencies occurring most often. In fact, life insurance companies often use the equivalent of daily premiums when adjusting a policy's death benefit payment either up or down. A downward adjustment reflects any unpaid fractional premiums; an increase reflects the refund of premium amounts paid to cover any period after the insured's death.

The computation of premiums requires three fundamental assumptions:

- a rate of mortality
- a rate of interest
- a rate of expense

net premium

The expense rate may provide a margin for contingencies. Only the first two factors—the rate of mortality and the rate of interest—enter the calculation of the **net premium**. The net premium is sufficient to provide all benefits owed under the contract, whether payable because of death or survival. If the actual experience conforms to the projected experience, the net premiums will be exactly equal to the total of all claims.

loading

gross premium

The amount added to the net premium to cover expenses of operation, to provide for contingencies, and to allow any profit is called **loading**. The net premium increased by the loading is called the **gross premium**, which is the premium payable by the policyowner. This chapter describes how actuaries derive net premiums. Chapter 13 extends this discussion to illustrate the development of gross premiums.

NET SINGLE PREMIUM

net single premium

The first step in deriving any premium is to find the **net single premium** for that policy. Then a set of more frequent premiums that are equivalent to the single premium may be developed if needed, as is usually the case. Finally, an amount is added for expenses and contingencies. This section describes how to calculate the net single premium.

An important feature of premium calculation develops because mortality tables display annual rates. Calculations start with the assumption that premiums are paid at the beginning of each policy year and benefits are paid at the end of the policy year. Annuity contract calculations also start with payments made annually. Then premiums for contracts with benefits and payments more than once yearly are computed by assuming that deaths occur uniformly throughout the policy year.

Concept of the Net Single Premium

rate making

The objective of life insurance **rate making** is to assure that the company collects enough from each group of insureds to pay the benefits promised under the contract. If the contract is purchased with a single or lump sum, that sum is the present value of future benefits. Rate making, the process of valuing the promises in the contract, involves three steps.

The first step is to learn the benefits promised under the contract and the length of time that the promise remains in effect. Life insurance benefits take two basic forms: (1) a death benefit that is the company's promise to pay a specified amount—called the face amount—if the insured dies while he or she is covered and (2) an endowment benefit that is the company's promise to pay a specified amount if the insured should survive to the end of the covered period. Some contracts contain both promises, while most contain only the first.

The second step is to select a mortality table to use in measuring the probabilities involved. Whether the company's promise is to pay upon death, survival, or both, the rate of mortality determines the value of the promise. Unless otherwise stated, this book uses the 2001 Commissioners Standard Ordinary (CSO) Mortality Tables to illustrate premium computations. In practice, however, a company must adopt the most appropriate mortality table for the group of persons insured. The CSO Mortality Table is usually revised at approximately 20-year intervals and then phased into use for regulatory purposes.

The third step is to select an interest rate to be used in adjusting for the time value of money. The fact that premiums are paid in the present while the benefits to be received from the company must be fulfilled in the future significantly reduces the cost of all forms of insurance. (See chapter 10 for discussions of the time value of money.) The rate at which expected benefits are discounted greatly influences the size of the net single premium. The lower the rate, the higher the premium, and vice versa. All calculations in this section assume 5.5 percent interest.

Major Components of Net Single Premium
• Benefits
• Mortality
• Interest

Two Techniques of Calculation

individual approach

aggregate approach

The net single premium is always the sum of the present values of all the expected benefits. It may, however, be computed according to either of two techniques. The first uses probabilities for each insured and is called the **individual approach**. The second assumes a large group of insureds and is called the **aggregate approach**.

The individual approach incorporates the necessary three steps by finding the product of these three factors for each year of the contract:

1. the amount (which is defined in the contract)

2. the discount factor (as discussed in chapter 10)

3. the probability of payment (as shown in the mortality table)

The probability of dying, factor (3), is a scientific estimate that will always contain an element of uncertainty. That uncertainty is acceptable, however, if a company sells a sufficiently large number of policies. As discussed in chapter 13, the law of large numbers assures that the average of many such payments actually made will be near the value expected—that is, $(1) \times (2) \times (3)$.

The individual approach can be illustrated with the calculation of the net single premium for a one-year term policy issued to a male at age 32. This contract pays the $1,000 face of the policy if the insured dies during the year of coverage and nothing if he survives. The three factors are as follows:

1. the possible amount of $1,000

2. the discount factor 1/$1.055 = $0.947867 that reflects the fact that any payment will be made at the end of one year

3. the probability that a 32-year-old male will die within one year. According to the 2001 male CSO Table, 11,050 out of 9,778,586 males aged 32 will die within the year. Thus the probability is 11,050/9,778,586 = 0.001130.

The expected present value of this uncertain payment is

$$(\$1,000) \times (.94787) \times (0.001130) = \$1.07$$

The aggregate approach, on the other hand, uses the large numbers shown in a mortality table directly and requires less proficiency with combining decimal numbers. The process begins by assuming that the number of persons shown in the mortality table as living at the issue age is the starting population for the insurance arrangement. The rates in the table predict how many payments are expected to occur at each subsequent age. A discount factor reduces the aggregate payments at each age to the present value. In the final step, the total of these present values is divided by the number of lives at issue age.

The two methods give identical premiums. This is demonstrated by recalculating, using the aggregate method, the net single premium for the same policy as was shown earlier. To apply the 2001 male CSO Table using the aggregate approach, 9,778,586 males aged 32 are assumed to apply for a one-year term policy for $1,000. Of those, 11,050 die during the following year. Therefore, the company must have $11,050,000 on hand at the end of the year to pay claims. Some of that money can come from interest earned during the policy's one-year term. The insurance company needs to collect only the present value of this amount from the policyowners at issue. Therefore, the amount that must be collected from the group is $11,050,000 divided by $1.055, or $10,473,934. Because it is not known at the beginning of the year which persons will die, each must pay the same amount into the fund. That is the total contribution divided by the 9,778,586 receiving coverage:

$$\$10,473,934 \div 9,778,586 = \$1.07$$

Because both techniques have educational value, their use will be alternated in this chapter's illustrations.

[Editor's note: The above $1.07 premium based on 2001 CSO mortality is significantly lower than the $1.73 premium derived from 1980 CSO mortality and the same interest rate.]

Term Insurance

Term insurance policies that provide protection on a level premium basis for several years are important in practice and for illustration. The net single premium for a 5-year term policy for $1,000 issued to a female aged 32 will be calculated by the individual approach.

The individual approach was defined earlier for one uncertain future payment. The 5-year term policy has five uncertain future payments. The present value of each expected future payment is calculated. The net single premium for the term insurance is the sum of these expected present values. Stated differently, the net single premium, developed using the individual approach, is the sum of the following five products:

1.   For the possible payment at the end of the first policy year, the amount is $1,000, the discount factor for one year is 1/1.055, and the probability of payment is, according to the 2001 female CSO Table, 7,603 out of 9,873,475, or 0.00077. The expected present value is the product of these factors:

$$\$1,000 \times 0.947867 \times 0.00077 = \$0.73$$

2.   For the possible payment at the end of the second policy year, the amount is $1,000, the discount factor for 2 years is (1/1.055)2, and the probability of payment is, according to the 2001 female CSO Table, 8,090 out of 9,873,475, or 0.000819. The expected present value is the product of these factors:

$$\$1,000 \times 0.898452 \times 0.000819 = \$0.74$$

3.   For the possible payment at the end of the third policy year, the amount is $1,000, the discount factor for one year is 1/(1.055)3, and the probability of payment is, according to the 2001 female CSO Table, 8,675 out of 9,873,475, or 0.000879. The expected present value is the product of these factors:

$$\$1,000 \times 0.851614 \times 0.000879 = \$0.75$$

4.   For the possible payment at the end of the fourth policy year, the expected present value is

$$\$1,000 \times 0.807217 \times \frac{9,554}{9,873,475} = \$0.78$$

5.   For the fifth policy year, the expected present value is

$$\$1,000 \times 0.765134 \times \frac{10,135}{9,873,475} = \$0.79$$

In summary, the net single premium for the 5 years of coverage is

$$0.73 + 0.74 + 0.75 + 0.78 + 0.79 = \$3.79$$

Example

The net single premium for a 32-year-old female for $1,000 of term insurance covering 5 years is the sum of the expected present values of the benefit costs in each of the 5 years. (2001 CSO mortality and 5.5 percent interest):

$0.73	(expected present value of 1st year benefit cost)
0.74	(expected present value of 2nd year benefit cost)
0.75	(expected present value of 3rd year benefit cost)
0.78	(expected present value of 4th year benefit cost)
+0.79	(expected present value of 5th year benefit cost)
$3.79	= net single premium

If each policyowner contributed $3.79 and there were no costs of operation, the fund created plus the interest it earns should be sufficient to pay all of the $1,000 death benefits during the 5 years of coverage. The last death benefit payment will exhaust the fund.

The aggregate approach achieves this same result by adding the terms before dividing by the number of policyowners who are alive to share the costs at issue, 9,873,475.

Whole Life Insurance

An insurance policy that provides protection for the whole of life is called whole life insurance. The face amount of the policy is payable upon the insured's death, whatever the insured's age. Eventual payment of the face is certain. The only uncertainty is the year in which the policy will become a claim. However, because whole life also can be viewed as a term insurance policy for the remaining life span, the techniques for computing the net single premium are the same as for a term policy.

Under the individual approach, the net single premium for a whole life insurance policy issued to a male aged 32 is the sum of the expected payments at the end of his 33d year, his 34th year, and every year up to and including his "last age" according to the table being used for the calculation. Because this is age 120 in the 2001 CSO Tables, the example involves 88 separate probabilities. For the sake of brevity, the following table shows only the equations for the first 5 years.

Adding the results of these 88 computations produces a sum of $109.49. That number represents the expected present value of possible payments at the end of each year from age 32 to 119, inclusive.

Table 10-1
Calculating Net Single Premium for Whole Life Insurance Policy Issued to Male Aged 32

Cost of 1st year's mortality:

$$\text{Age 32: } \$1,000 \times 0.947867 \times \frac{11,050}{9,778,586} = \$1.07$$

Cost of 2rd year's mortality:

$$\text{Age 33: } \$1,000 \times 0.898452 \times \frac{11,233}{9,778,586} = \$1.03$$

Cost of 3rd year's mortality:

$$\text{Age 34: } \$1,000 \times 0.851614 \times \frac{11,512}{9,778,586} = \$1.00$$

Cost of 4th year's mortality:

$$\text{Age 35: } \$1,000 \times 0.807217 \times \frac{11,791}{9,778,586} = \$0.97$$

Cost of 5th year's mortality:

$$\text{Age 36: } \$1,000 \times 0.765134 \times \frac{12,458}{9,778,586} = \$0.97$$

One interesting and significant result arises from the fact that a whole life policy inevitably will become a claim. The net single premium at any age of issue would be $1,000 per $1,000 of insurance except for the interest earnings on the advance deposit. The entire process of calculating the probability that death will occur at each of the possible ages is important only to help find the amount of interest that will be earned on the advance premium before the death claim must be paid.

Endowment Insurance

An endowment insurance contract promises to pay a death benefit if the insured should die during the term of the contract or to pay an endowment amount (usually equal to the death benefit) if the insured should survive to the end of the term. Endowment contracts have been dropped by United States life insurers as a result of federal income tax law changes. These policies do not satisfy the tax code definition of life insurance if they endow

at ages below 95. Endowment policies that were issued before 1985 and have been kept in force continue to be treated as life insurance under the transition provisions of the tax code.[1] Endowment policies are still available in many countries. They are even the most frequently purchased types of life insurance in some countries where high savings rates are common.

pure endowment

An endowment insurance contract is a combination of a **pure endowment** and term insurance. The former pays only if the insured survives the specified period of years, and the latter pays only if the insured does not survive the specified period. The net single premium for the endowment insurance contract is then the sum of the respective net single premiums for the pure endowment and term insurance contracts.

Life Annuities

annuities certain

life annuities

life annuity due

life annuity immediate

deferred life annuity

With **annuities certain**, certain means that payments occur unconditionally for a known term without regard to any contingencies. With **life annuities**, the adjective life defines the payments as occurring only upon survival of a designated life. The terminology used to describe life annuities is consistent with the terminology used for annuities certain. A **life annuity due** has its first payment due at issue or contract date; a **life annuity immediate** has its first payment due at the end of one payment interval; a **deferred life annuity** has its first payment due after the completion of a deferment period.

Life annuities play dual roles for any insurance company. The company can be on the paying end or on the receiving end of a life annuity. The company pays annuities to annuitants, beneficiaries, and retirees; these are usually annuities immediate. It receives premiums from policyowners in the form of annuities; these are usually annuities due. As

---

1.   IRC Sec. 7702(j).

we calculate the net single premiums for life annuities, remember that these concepts are applied to value both benefit payments and premium receipts.

The appropriate mortality rates differ between computations for annuities and for insurance policies. This important difference occurs simply because annuitants live longer. The table must be chosen to reflect the experience of annuitants or insured lives. Example calculations are based on the 1983 Individual Annuity Mortality table.

Calculating Life Annuity Present Values

To compute the net single premium for a life annuity, view the annuity as a series of pure endowments. Just as the pure endowment pays only if the insured survives to the end of a specified period, a life annuity pays only if the annuitant is alive on the date the payment is due.

Calculating the present value of the life annuity requires three dates: (1) the contract or issue date, (2) the due date of the first payment, and (3) the due date of the last possible payment. Consider each payment a pure endowment payable on its due date. The net single premium of the annuity is the sum of the net single premiums on the contract date for the payments or "pure endowments" specified by the annuity.

The dates for the net single premium of a life annuity immediate payable to a 70-year old male are as follows: (1) The contract date is at age 70, (2) the first payment is at age 71, and (3) the last possible payment is at the end of the mortality table. When using the 1983 Individual Annuity Mortality (IAM) Table for Males, the payments could extend to age 115. While the table (not included in this book) ends at age 115, the payments would, of course, continue after age 115 if the annuitant survives. The following discussion uses the individual method to illustrate this calculation for annual $100 payments.[2]

The probability that the first payment of $100 will be made is 7,747,886 ÷ 7,917,081 = 0.97863. The numerator is the number of persons alive at age 71; the denominator is the number alive at age 70. Because one year will elapse before the payment, if it occurs at all, the sum set aside at the time of purchase can be discounted at 5.5 percent. The present value of the first payment, therefore, is figured as follows:

$$\frac{7,747,886}{7,917,081} \times \$100 \times 0.947867 = \$92.76$$

---

2.   Although the great majority of annuity contracts provide monthly income, the premiums derived here use the rates per $100 of annual income. In practice, this rate is derived first and then computed to a monthly equivalent.

The probability that the second payment occurs is the probability that a person now aged 70 will be alive at age 72. Again discount the contingent payment, this time for 2 years. The present value of the second payment is determined as shown in the following equation:

$$\frac{7,564,671}{7,917,081} \times \$100 \times 0.898452 = \$85.85$$

The denominator in the first term does not change in these equations or any of the other 43 separate equations. The first five and last four equations needed to compute the net single premium for the entire series of contingent payments are shown in the next example.

The present value of all payments is $901.82; the present value at age 70 of a payment at extreme ages, such as 111, is zero when rounded to the nearest cent. We show the figures to six decimals to emphasize that only the last computation produces an answer that is literally zero.

Thus, in consideration of $901.82 paid in a single sum at the inception of the contract, an insurance company could afford to pay a 70-year-old man an income of $100 per year as long as he lives, the first payment being made at age 71. The computation of the net single premium for such an annuity can also be viewed on an aggregate basis. Either premium computation presumes that the company enters into sufficient contracts to experience average results.

immediate annuity with guaranteed payments

The net single premium for an **immediate annuity with guaranteed payments** for a specified number of years, whether the annuitant survives or not, is similar to the immediate annuity above. Simply replace the probability of payment with 1.00 for each year during the certain period. Because no contingency is involved, the discount factor is the only cost-reducing factor during this period.

Example

Calculations of the net single premium for a life annuity immediate payable to a male aged 70.

$$\text{Age 71: } \times \frac{7,747,886}{7,917,081} \times 100 \times .947867 = \$92.76$$

Present value of first annuity payment

$$\text{Age 72: } \times \frac{7,547,886}{7,917,081} \times 100 \times .898452 = \$85.85$$

Present value of second annuity payment

$$\text{Age 73: } \times \frac{7,366,999}{7,917,081} \times 100 \times .851614 = \$79.24$$

Present value of third annuity payment

$$\text{Age 74: } \times \frac{7,154,571}{7,917,081} \times 100 \times .807217 = \$72.95$$

Present value of fourth annuity payment

$$\text{Age 75: } \times \frac{6,927,099}{7,917,081} \times 100 \times .765134 = \$66.95$$

Present value of fifth annuity payment

$$\bullet \quad \bullet \quad \bullet$$

$$\text{Age 111: } \times \frac{487}{7,917,081} \times 100 \times .111134 = \$0.000685$$

Present value of 41st annuity payment

$$\text{Age 112: } \times \frac{148}{7,917,081} \times 100 \times .105535 = \$0.000197$$

Present value of 42d annuity payment

$$\text{Age 113: } \times \frac{35}{7,917,081} \times 100 \times .100033 = \$0.000044$$

Present value of 43d annuity payment

$$\text{Age 114: } \times \frac{6}{7,917,081} \times 100 \times .094818 = \$0.000007$$

Present value of 44th annuity payment

To take a simple example, consider an immediate annuity purchased at age 70 to provide an income of $100 per year with the payments guaranteed for 5 years. Using the 1983 IAM Table for Females and the aggregate method, 8,837,346 payments are assumed to be

payable at the end of each of the first 5 years instead of the number of persons shown as living in the mortality table at those ages. The mortality table values are used as before beginning with the sixth payment. Determining the net single premium for the entire series of payments involves 45 separate equations. The sum of the present values of these 45 payments is $1,045.88.

temporary life annuity

The net single premium for a **temporary life annuity** is calculated using the same underlying principles. Because the promised payment is zero after the term of the annuity, the computations end with that age. For a 10-year life annuity issued to a male at age 70, for instance, the first probability would be the chance of survival to age 71, or

$$\frac{7,747,886}{7,917,081} = 0.97863$$

and the last probability would be the chance that the annuitant would survive to age 80, or

$$\frac{5,560,108}{7,917,081} = 0.70229$$

Deferred Whole Life Annuity

The amount that must be on hand at age 70 to provide a life income of $100 per year, with no payments guaranteed, was shown in the previous example to be $901.82. This amount may be paid to the insurance company in a single sum at the purchaser's age 70. Alternatively, the present value of that amount may be deposited with the company years before the time the income is to commence. More likely still, the present value may be accumulated through a series of periodic deposits before the income is to begin. If the funds are deposited with the company before annuity payments begin, a smaller premium is required.

nonrefund annuity

The adjustment can be most clearly explained in terms of a **nonrefund annuity** purchased with a single premium some years before the annuity starting date. Assume that a male aged 30 purchases an annuity contract that will pay him an annual income of $100 for life beginning at age 70. Under the contract's terms, nothing is paid or refunded in the event of his death before age 70. Note that in this example the income is to begin one year earlier than the earlier example that derived the premium for an immediate annuity.

Example

Calculations of the net single premium for an immediate annuity with payments guaranteed for 5 years for a female aged 70.

$$\text{Age 71: } 1 \times 100 \times .947867 = \$94.76$$

Present value of first year's payment

$$\text{Age 72: } 1 \times 100 \times .898452 = \$89.85$$

Present value of 2d year's payment

$$\text{Age 73: } 1 \times 100 \times .851614 = \$85.16$$

Present value of 3d year's payment

$$\text{Age 74: } 1 \times 100 \times .807217 = \$80.72$$

Present value of 4th year's payment

Present value of 5-year annuity certain – $427.03

$$\text{Age 76: } \times \frac{8{,}046{,}977}{8{,}837{,}346} \times 100 \times .725246 = \$66.04$$

Present value of 6th year's payment

$$\text{Age 77: } \times \frac{7{,}864{,}680}{8{,}837{,}346} \times 100 \times .6874368 = \$61.18$$

Present value of 7th year's payment

$$\text{Age 78: } \times \frac{7{,}664{,}060}{8{,}837{,}346} \times 100 \times .65159887 = \$61.18$$

Present value of 8th year's payment

$$\text{Age 79: } \times \frac{7{,}443{,}971}{8{,}837{,}346} \times 100 \times .617629 = \$52.02$$

Present value of 9th year's payment

$$\text{Age 80: } \times \frac{7{,}203{,}323}{8{,}837{,}346} \times 100 \times .585431 = \$47.02$$

Present value of 10th year's payment

$$\text{Age 111: } \times \frac{2{,}640}{8{,}837{,}346} \times 100 \times .11134 = \$47.02$$

Present value of 41st year's payment

$$\text{Age 112: } \times \frac{922}{8{,}837{,}346} \times 100 \times .105535 = \$0.00$$

Present value of 42d year's payment

$$\text{Age 113: } \times \frac{254}{8{,}837{,}346} \times 100 \times .100033 = \$0.00$$

Present value of 43d year's payment

$$\text{Age 114: } \times \frac{49}{8,837,346} \times 100 \times .094818 = \$0.00$$

Present value of 44th year's payment

$$\text{Age 115: } \times \frac{5}{8,837,346} \times 100 \times .089875 = \$0.00$$

Present value of 45th year's payment

Pure Endowment and General Annuity Approaches

The premium for this deferred annuity can be calculated in two different ways. First is the "pure endowment approach." It consists of calculating the net single premium for an immediate life annuity providing $100 per year, with the first payment at 70, and considering this net single premium to be the amount of a pure endowment promised at age 70. Next, the net single premium at age 30 for this pure endowment due at age 70 is calculated.

To illustrate the pure endowment approach recall that $901.82 for a male at age 70 will provide a life income of $100 per year beginning at age 71. With $100 added to this sum, the $100 payments could begin at age 70, the additional $100 taking care of the payment to be made on the effective date of the contract. Because no time elapses, no interest is earned and no life contingency is involved. Therefore, the net single premium at age 70 for an annuity that will provide $100 immediately and $100 per year thereafter as long as the annuitant lives is $1,001.82.

A sum less than $1,001.82 deposited with the company at age 30 will provide that same payment stream commencing at age 70. Two reasons justify a substantial reduction: First, funds deposited at age 30 will earn interest for 40 years. Second, a substantial probability exists that the purchaser will not survive to age 70 to receive payments. The sums forfeited by those who fail to survive to that age reduce, through the benefit of survivorship, the amount that each annuitant must pay at the outset. Therefore, the sum that must be deposited with the company at age 30 is

$$\frac{7,917,081}{8,878,453} \times \$1,001.82 \times 0.117463 = \$94.31 \text{ (the net single premium)}$$

The second method available to determine the net single premium for an annuity is the "general annuity" method. Using the same example as above, each payment is treated as a separate pure endowment to be discounted to age 30. The first payment of $100 is discounted for 40 years and multiplied by the probability of the annuitant's surviving to age

70. The second payment is discounted for 41 years and is multiplied by the probability of survival to 71, and so on to age 114 when the 1983 IAM Table is used.

The sum of the present values of all 45 payments is $117.96. This compares with a value of $94.31 developed earlier for males. The difference illustrates vividly the spread between male and female mortality; females live longer. The net single premium can also be obtained by using the aggregate approach as shown in the following example. As usual, only the first five and last five equations appear in the table.

Example

Calculate the net single premium for a deferred whole life annuity for a female aged 30 (the aggregate approach).

1st	payment:	8,837,346	×	$100	×	.117463	=	103,806,117.30
2d	payment:	8,733.975	×	$100	×	.111339	=	97,243,204.25
3d	payment:	8,621,263	×	$100	×	.105535	=	90,984,499.07
4th	payment:	8,497,815	×	$100	×	.100033	=	85,006,192.79
5th	payment:	8,362,020	×	$100	×	.094818	=	79,287,001.24
			•	•	•			
41st	payment:	2,640	×	$100	×	.013078	=	3,452.59
42d	payment:	922	×	$100	×	.012396	=	1,142.91
43d	payment:	254	×	$100	×	.011750	=	298.45
44th	payment:	40	×	$100	×	.011138	=	54.28
45th	payment:	5	×	$100	×	.010557	=	5.28

Present Value of payments = 1,172,546,028.40

$$\text{Net single premium} = \frac{1{,}172{,}546{,}028.4}{9{,}939{,}983} = \$117.96$$

NET LEVEL PREMIUM

Few life insurance contracts are purchased with single premiums. Few persons have sufficient savings to buy adequate life insurance on a single-premium basis. This would also run counter to the prevailing practice in consumer finance, where installment purchases have become the pattern.

Apart from the trends of the times, financing life insurance on an installment basis is appropriate. Because the fundamental purpose of life insurance is to provide protection against the loss of future earnings—which by definition are received in periodic installments—paying the cost of that protection over a similar time frame is logical.

Another reason most people prefer installment financing of life insurance is the lower total cost if the insured dies early. One monthly premium purchases as much life insurance protection as a single premium—only the period of coverage is reduced. If the insured dies within a few years after the single-sum purchase of a life insurance policy, the cost will be many times greater than if annual (or more frequent) installment payments are made. On the other hand, if policyowners live beyond the period, the total amount of the annual premiums paid will exceed the single premium, and with each passing year the disparity will become greater.

Concept of the Level Annual Premium

actuarially equivalent pricing

Policyowners must be given a fair choice between paying for insurance with a single premium and with a set of level annual premiums. The prices must be determined in a manner that leaves the financial position of the company unaffected by the policyowner's decision. Such pricing is referred to as **actuarially equivalent pricing**. To be the actuarial equivalent of a policy's net single premium, its net level premiums must reflect (1) the possibility that the insured may die having made only some of the payments and (2) the smaller amount invested that will reduce the investment earnings to the company. Expressed in positive terms the net level premium must reflect (1) the probability that the insured will survive to pay premiums and (2) the period during which the premiums will earn investment income.

Deriving the net level annual premiums integrates two computations described earlier in this chapter. No new computational skills are required. The rule for determining net level annual premiums is this: divide the net single premium for the policy in question by the present value of a life annuity due of $1 for the premium-paying period. The process is illustrated on the following pages using net single premiums derived above.

Net Level Premium

$$\text{NLP} = \frac{\text{NSP}}{\text{PVLAD}}$$

where:

NLP = net level premium

NSP = net single premium

PVLAD = present value of a life annuity due of $1 for the premium paying period

Hypothetical example:

NSP = 25,000

PVLAD = 16

$$\text{NLP} = \frac{25,000}{16} = \$1,562.50$$

Term Insurance

The earlier example found the net single premium for a $1,000 5-year term policy issued to a female aged 32 to be $3.79. What level annual premium paid at the beginning of the contract and on each of the next four anniversary dates, if the insured is then living, is the equivalent of $3.79? The answer to this question, following the rule stated above, requires that one know the present value of a temporary life annuity due of $1 for a term of 5 years for a female aged 32. The female 2001 CSO Table is used for this calculation since that is the table used to derive the $3.79 premium. In other words, the same mortality and interest assumptions must be used to determine the present value of the annual premiums as are used to determine the present value of benefits. The present value is computed as shown in Table 10-2.

The sum of the five payments, the present value of a 5-year temporary annuity due of $1 for a female aged 32, is $4.50. This means that a premium of $1 for each period will purchase a policy with a net single premium of $4.50. The net single premium for the 5-year term policy, however, is $3.79. Hence, to determine the size of five level annual premiums payable beginning at age 32 that are equivalent to $3.79, divide $3.79 by $4.50. The net level annual premium for a 5-year $1,000 term policy issued to a female aged 32 is $3.79 ÷ $4.50 = $0.84. The maximum amount any policyowner might pay is $4.20—five annual premiums of $0.84 each. This exceeds the net single premium of $3.79.

Example

Calculate the net level premium for $1,000 5-year term for 32-year-old female (2001 CSO, 5.5 percent interest).

NSP = $ 3.79

PVLAD = 4.50

$$NLP = \frac{3.79}{4.50} = \$0.84$$

[Editor's note: The above premium of $0.84 is significantly lower than the NLP of $1.50 derived from 1980 CSO mortality and the same interest rate.]

See the calculation of PVLAD in Table 10-3.

The difference reflects (1) the loss of interest and (2) the chance that the insured will die before making all the installment payments contemplated. If the net single premium is paid, the company has $3.79 on which to earn interest from the beginning. Under the net level premium arrangement, however, only $0.84 is available at the outset. The longer the period involved, the greater the disparity between the net single premium and the sum potentially payable by the insured under the annual premium arrangement.

Ordinary Life Insurance

whole life annuity

Ordinary life insurance is whole life insurance for which premiums will be paid throughout the lifetime of the insured. To obtain the net level annual premium for an ordinary life policy, the net single premium for a whole life policy is divided by the present value of a **whole life annuity** due of $1. Because the whole of life is the longest premium-paying period contemplated under any whole life insurance policy, the present value of $1 per annum is greater than for any shorter premium-paying period. This produces the lowest level annual premium of any whole life policy because the net single premium for a whole life policy at any particular age is the same, regardless of the premium-paying period. The longer the period over which the premiums are spread, the smaller each periodic premium will be.

Earlier in this chapter the net single premium for a whole life insurance policy for a 32-year-old male was determined. Here the present value of a life annuity due of $1 for the

whole of life for a male aged 32 is calculated by the aggregate approach. Then the level annual premium for an ordinary life insurance policy can be determined.

Table 10-2
Calculating Present Value of a Life Annuity Due for a 5-year Term Policy Issued to Female Aged 32

$$\text{Age 32:} \frac{9,873,475}{9,873,475} \times 1.00 = \$1.00$$

Present value of first annuity payment

$$\text{Age 33:} \frac{9,865,872}{9,873,475} \times .947867 = \$1.00$$

Present value of 2nd annuity payment

$$\text{Age 34:} \frac{9,857,782}{9,873,475} \times .898452 = \$0.90$$

Present value of 3rd annuity payment

$$\text{Age 35:} \frac{9,849,107}{9,873,475} \times .851614 = \$0.85$$

Present value of 4th annuity payment

$$\text{Age 36:} \frac{9,839,553}{9,873,475} \times .807217 = \$0.80$$

Present value of 5th annuity payment

$$\text{Total} = 1.00 + 0.95 + 0.90 + 0.85 + 0.80 = 4.50$$

The present value of the life annuity due must recognize the possibility that the insured may not be alive at age 33 (and each age thereafter to the end of the mortality table) to pay the second and subsequent premiums. The probability of survival is the probability of a payment occurring. The first five computations are shown in Table 10-3.

The present value of the last payment is very slight. Still, it must be taken into account. The sum of all the payments' present values is $17.08. Dividing this number into the net single premium of $109.49 for a whole life policy issued at age 32 produces a net level annual premium of $6.41. Stated differently, the $1,000 whole life policy that costs $109.49 if

purchased with a single-sum payment can also be purchased with premium payments of $6.41 annually.

Table 10-3
Calculating the Present Value of a Life Annuity Due (PVLAD) for Whole Life Policy Issued to Male Aged 32

$$\text{Age 32:} \frac{9,778,586}{9,778,586} \times 1 \times 1.00 = \$1.00$$

$$\text{Age 33:} \frac{9,767,536}{9,778,586} \times 1 \times .947867 = \$0.95$$

$$\text{Age 34:} \frac{9,756,303}{9,778,586} \times 1 \times .898452 = \$0.90$$

$$\text{Age 35:} \frac{9,744,791}{9,778,586} \times 1 \times .851614 = \$0.85$$

$$\text{Age 36:} \frac{9,773,000}{9,778,586} \times 1 \times .807217 = \$0.80$$

This continues in the same manner to the end of the mortality table. The present value of the life annuity due (PVLAD) is, thus, the sum of all the individual years calculated amounts.

Limited-Payment Life Insurance

The net single premium for a whole life policy can be spread over any number of years by means of the appropriate life annuity due. Suppose a male policyowner, aged 32, wants to pay for his policy in 20 annual installments. Then the present value of a 20-year temporary life annuity due of $1 per annum is determined. This annuity's first payment is at age 32 and its last possible payment is at age 51. The present value of such an annuity is $12.45. This number is smaller than the corresponding whole life annuity due and divided into the same net single premium, $109.49, produces a larger level annual premium. The level annual premium for a 20-payment life policy issued at age 32 is

$$\$109.49 \div \$12.45 = \$8.79$$

For a 10-payment life policy, end the computations at age 41. Following the formula previously given, this yields a present value for the temporary life annuity due of $7.91. Dividing $7.91 into $109.49 gives a 10-payment life premium of $13.84.

Finally, if the whole life policy is to be paid up at age 65, the annuity value needed for the denominator is the present value of a series of payments of $1 per year, extending from age 32 to 64 and contingent on the insured's survival. This value is $15.51 and, when divided into the single premium of $109.49, gives a level premium of $7.06.

Endowment Insurance

The net level premium for an endowment insurance policy is derived in exactly the same manner as that of any other policy. Once again, the procedure to determine the net level annual premium is to divide the net single premium by the present value of a temporary life annuity due of $1 for the premium-paying period. All endowment policies, of course, are limited-payment policies in the sense that the premium is not payable for the whole of life. Usually premiums are payable for the full term of an endowment insurance contract.

Deferred Annuity

Deferred annuities usually are financed with annual—rather than single premiums. Premiums may be paid throughout the period of deferment or may be limited to a shorter period of years. The annuity contract may promise to return the annuitant's premiums with or without interest. The annual premium in this case does not involve life contingencies but rather is a sum of money that must be set aside annually to accumulate at an assumed rate of compound interest to a predetermined amount at a specified date. For example, $1,151.88 must be on hand at age 65 to provide an income of $100 per year to a male. How much would a male aged 40 have to set aside each year, including a payment on his 40th birthday, to accumulate a sum of $1,151.88 by his 65th birthday, assuming such annual payments earn compound interest at the rate of 5.5 percent? Such a program includes 25 payments, the first at age 40 and the last at age 64. The period of accumulation is 25 years. At the end of 25 years $1 per year earning 5.5 percent interest will accumulate to $53.9660. Dividing $1,151.88 by $53.9660 shows that $21.34 must be set aside during each of 25 years to accumulate the required single premium. This computation presumes that premiums are to be returned if the annuitant dies before age 65.

Alternatively, the contract may provide that the company retains all premiums paid in the event of death before the annuity income commences. If premiums will not be refunded, the net level annual premium for a deferred annuity is determined by the same methods as life insurance. Again, however, the premium annuity's present value must be computed using the same mortality rates as those used for the benefit annuity. Using the 1983 Individual Annuity Mortality Table, the net level premium for a nonrefund deferred annuity purchased by a female aged 40, with income to begin at 65, is computed as a temporary

life annuity due. That annuity makes one payment immediately with 24 subsequent payments due. The net single premium for that annuity is $311.38. The net level premium is $311.38 ÷ $13.95198, or $22.32.

THE EFFECT OF GENDER-DISTINCT MORTALITY ON PREMIUMS

Lower mortality rates exist among females. Historically this has resulted in higher rates for annuities and periodic settlements under life insurance policies. The corresponding rate reductions for life insurance on females arose more recently. The differential premiums reflect the use of separate mortality rates for female lives. Such rates may be found, for example, in the 1980 and 2001 CSO Tables or in special reports on intercompany mortality experience.[3] Despite differences in premiums, the policy reserves, surrender values, and dividend scales are usually the same as those used for males.

---

3. These reports have separated the data for male and female lives since 1957.

CHAPTER REVIEW

Key Terms and Concepts

premium
rate
single premium
net premium
loading
gross premium
net single premium
rate making
individual approach
aggregate approach
pure endowment

annuities certain
life annuities
life annuity due
life annuity immediate
deferred life annuity
immediate annuity with guaranteed
   payments
temporary life annuity
nonrefund annuity
actuarially equivalent pricing
whole life annuity

Chapter 10 Review Questions

1. List the three fundamental assumptions required for the computation of premiums, and indicate which of these are used in calculating net premiums. [1]

2. What are the three basic steps in deriving any premium? [1]

3. Rate making is the process of valuing the promises in a life insurance contract. (a) What is the objective of life insurance rate making? (b) Describe briefly the three initial steps in rate making. [1]

4. What are the three factors that are multiplied for each year of a life insurance contract to determine the contract's net single premium using the individual approach? [1]

5. Describe the process of calculating the net single premium for a life insurance contract using the aggregate approach. [2]

6. Using the values in the 2001 CSO table in the text and the appropriate table(s) for future and/or present values in chapter 23 of the text, calculate the net single premium, assuming 4.5 percent interest, for a 3-year term policy for $1,000 issued to a male aged 40 under: (a) the individual approach; (b) the aggregate approach. [3]

7. Explain how the calculation of the net single premium for a $1,000 whole life policy issued to a male aged 40 differs from the calculation of the net single premium for the $1,000 3-year term policy issued to a 40-year-old male in question 6 above (again assuming 2001 CSO mortality rates and 4.5 percent interest). [2]

8. Explain how the calculation of the net single premium for a $1,000 3-year endowment policy issued to a male aged 40 differs from the calculation of the net single premium for the $1,000 3-year term policy issued to a 40-year-old male in question 6 above (again assuming 2001 CSO mortality rates and 4.5 percent interest). [2]

9. In what sense are the premiums for an endowment policy a limited payment stream? [2]

10. List the dual roles that life annuities play for life insurance companies, and give an example of each. [2]

11. What are the three dates required to calculate the present value of a life annuity? [4]

12. Explain how the mortality and benefit factors used to calculate the net single premium with the individual approach for a life annuity immediate of $100 per year purchased by a 60-year-old male differ from those used to calculate the net single premium for a $1,000 whole life policy issued to a male aged 60. [4]

13. Assuming the same interest rates and the same annuity mortality tables, how does the computation of the net single premium for each of the following annuities differ from the calculation of the net single premium of a life annuity immediate of $100 per year payable to a female aged 65? (a) an immediate annuity of $100 per year with payments guaranteed for 5 years purchased by a female aged 70; (b) a temporary life annuity of $100 per year payable for 10 years to a female aged 70 (that is, a 10-year life annuity). [3]

14. Explain how the net single premium for a deferred annuity of $100 per year purchased by a male aged 35 with the first payment to be received at age 65 is calculated under each of the following approaches: (a) the pure endowment approach; (b) the general annuity approach. [3]

15. What are the reasons that most people prefer to purchase life insurance on an install-ment, rather than a single premium, basis? [5]

16. Why is it necessary to divide a life insurance policy's net single premium by the present value of a life annuity due of $1 per year for the premium-paying period to determine the policy's net level premium, instead of simply dividing the net single premium by the number of years in the premium-paying period? [5]

17. Suppose the net single premium for a $1,000 whole life policy issued to a male aged 45 is $196.68. Explain why the net level premium is smaller if this is an ordinary life policy than if it is a 20-pay life policy. [5]

18. How does the calculation of the net level premium of a deferred annuity that does not refund the annuitant's premiums if the annuitant dies before annuity income com-mences differ from the calculation of the net level premium of a deferred annuity that does return the premiums in the event of death? [5]

Chapter 10 Review Answers

1. The computation of premiums requires three fundamental assumptions:
    - *a rate of mortality*
    - *a rate of interest*
    - *a rate of expense*

2. The three basic steps in deriving any premium are:
    - *first, find the net single premium for the policy*
    - *then (if needed), develop a set of more frequent premiums that are equivalent to the single premium*
    - *finally, add an amount for expenses and contingencies*

3. a. The objective of life insurance rate making is to assure that the company collects enough from each group of insureds to pay the benefits promised under the contract.

    b. The three initial steps in rate making are:

        •   The first step is to learn the benefits promised under the contract and the length of time that the promise remains in effect. Life insurance benefits take two basic forms: (1) a death benefit that is the company's promise to pay a specified amount—called the face amount—if the insured dies while he or she is covered and (2) an endowment benefit that is the company's promise to pay a specified amount if the insured should survive to the end of the covered period. Some contracts contain both promises, while others contain only the first.

        •   The second step is to select a mortality table to use in measuring the probabilities involved. Whether the company's promise is to pay upon death, survival, or both, the rate of mortality determines the value of the promise.

        •   The third step is to select an interest rate to be used in adjusting for the time value of money. The fact that premiums are paid in the present while the benefits to be received from the company must be fulfilled in the future significantly reduces the cost of all forms of insurance.

4. The following three factors are multiplied for each year of life insurance to determine the contrast's net single premium using the individual approach:

    •   the amount (which is defined in the contract)

    •   the discount factor (at the assumed rate of interest)

    •   the probability of payment (as shown in the mortality table)

5. The aggregate approach, on the other hand, uses the large numbers shown in a mortality table directly and requires less proficiency with the combining decimal numbers. The process begins by assuming that the number of persons shown in the mortality table as living at the issue age is the starting population for the insurance arrangement. The numbers dying during each year in the table predict how many payments are expected to occur at each subsequent age. A discount factor reduces the aggregate payments at each age to the present value. In the final step, the total of these present values is divided by the number of lives at issue age.

6. a. With the individual approach, the expected future payment is first calculated for each year of the contract (that is, ages 40, 41, and 42) by computing the product of the

benefit amount, the discount factor, and the probability of payment for each year of the contract. The expected future payments for the 3 years of the contract are then added to obtain the net single premium.

The benefit amount for each year of the contract is $1,000. The discount factors (present values) from Table 23-2 are .9569, .9157, and .8763 for the first, second, and third contract years, respectively. (Alternatively, the future values at 4.5 percent interest for one, 2, and 3 years in Table 23-1 can each be divided into 1 to get these present values.) According to the 2001 CSO mortality table, the probabilities of a male aged 40 dying at ages 40, 41, and 42 are 0.00165 (that is 15,970/9,678,609), 0.00179 (that is, 17,296/9,678,609), and 0.00195 (that is, .18,905/9,678,609), respectively. The expected future payments for each of the 3 years and the net single premium are calculated as follows:

Year	Age	Benefit	x	Discount Factor	x	Probability of Payment	=	Expected Future Payment
1	40	$1,000	x	.9569	x	0.00165	=	$1.58
2	41	1,000	x	.9157	x	0.00179	=	1.64
3	42	1,000	x	.8763	x	0.00195	=	1.71
						Net Single Premium	=	$4.93

b. With the aggregate approach, the expected future aggregate payments are first calculated for each year of the contract (that is, ages 40, 41, and 42) by computing the product of the number of men expected to die each year, the benefit amount, and the discount factor. The expected future aggregate payments for the 3 years of the contract are then added, and the sum is divided by the number of men living at age 40 to obtain the net single premium.

Year	Age	Number of Men Dying	x	Benefit	x	Discount Factor	=	Future Aggregate Payment
1	40	15,970	x	$1,000	x	.9569	=	$15,281,693
2	41	17,296	x	1,000	x	.9157	=	15,837,947
3	42	18,905	x	1,000	x	.8763	=	16,566,451
				Total Expected Payments			=	$47,686,091

Net Single Premium = Total Expected Payments/Number of Men Living at Age 40

 = $47,686,091/9,678

 = $4.93

Note that both the individual approach and the aggregate approach produce the same result ($8.99) for the net single premium of this 3-year contract.

7. Whether the individual or aggregate approach is used, the only difference is the number of years for which the expected future (aggregate) payments are calculated. Instead of calculating the expected future (aggregate) payments for only 3 years (ages 40–42) as was done for the 3-year term policy in question 6, the calculation of the net single premium for a $1,000 whole life policy issued to a male aged 40 involves computing the expected future (aggregate) payments for 80 years—from age 40 to age 119—because the whole life policy provides protection for the whole of life (assumed to be until the end of age 119 in the 2001 CSO mortality table).

8. The net single premium for the $1,000 3-year endowment issued to a male aged 40 is equal to the sum of (1) the net single premium for the $1,000 3-year term policy issued to a male aged 40 in question 6 and (2) the net single premium for a 3-year pure endowment of $1,000 issued to a male aged 40. Thus, the difference between the net single premiums of the 3-year endowment and the 3-year term policies is the net single premium for a 3-year pure endowment of $1,000 issued to a male aged 40. The net single premium for a 3-year pure endowment of $1,000 issued to a male aged 40 is $873.29. With the individual approach, the net single premium for the 3-year pure endowment is calculated by computing the product of the benefit ($1,000), the 3-year discount factor at 4.5 percent interest (.8763), and the probability of a male aged 40 surviving to age 43 ([9,645,343/9,678,609] = 0.996563). With the aggregate approach, the net single premium for the 3-year pure endowment is calculated by computing the product of the benefit ($1,000), the number of men living at age 43 (9,645,343), and the 3-year discount factor at 4.5 percent interest (.8763), and dividing the result 8,452.241,071) by the number of men living at age 40 (9,678,609).

9. The premiums are not payable for life. They will terminate at or before the endowment date for the coverage.

10. Life annuities play dual roles for any insurance company.

    •   The company can be on the paying end of a life annuity. The company pays annuities to annuitants, beneficiaries, and retirees; these are usually annuities immediate.

    •   The company can be on the receiving end of a life annuity. It receives premiums from policyowners in the form of annuities; these are usually annuities due.

11. The three dates required to calculate the present value of a life annuity are:

   • the contract or issue date

   • the due date of the first payment

   • the due date of the last possible payment

12. The mortality factors differ in several ways. First, the mortality factors for the life annuity immediate are based on a mortality table reflecting the experience of annuitants, rather than the experience of insured lives. Second, the probability used at each age (n) for the life annuity immediate is the probability of a male aged 60 living to age (n+1), rather than the probability of male aged 60 dying at age (n). Finally, because annuity mortality tables extend different ages than life insurance tables (for example, ages 99 or 119. The benefit factor for the life annuity immediate calculation is $100 instead of $1,000.

13. a. Begin the calculations at age 70, rather than age 65. Also, for each of the first 5 years (the certain period) replace the probability of payment with 1.00.

    b. Begin the calculations at age 70, rather than age 65. End the computations after 10 years because the promised payment is zero after the term of the annuity.

14. a. The pure endowment approach consists of calculating the net single premium for an immediate life annuity providing $100 per year, with the first payment at 65, and considering this net single premium to be the amount of a pure endowment promised at age 65. Next, the net single premium at age 35 for this pure endowment due at age 65 is calculated.

    b. The second method available to determine the net single premium for an annuity is the general annuity method. Each payment is treated as a separate pure endowment to be discounted to age 35. The first payment of $100 will be discounted for 30 years and multiplied by the probability of the annuitant's surviving to age 65. The second payment will be discounted for 31 years and multiplied by the probability of survival to 66, and so on to age 115 (the end of the annuity mortality table). The sum of the present values of all the yearly payments is the net single premium.

15. *The reasons most people prefer installment financing of life insurance include:*

    - *Few persons have sufficient savings to buy adequate life insurance on a single-premium basis.*

    - *Because the fundamental purpose of life insurance is to provide protection against the loss of future earnings—which by definition are received in periodic installments—paying the cost of that protection over a similar time frame is logical.*

    - *Most people prefer installment financing of life insurance because it produces a lower total cost if the insured dies early.*

16. *Simply dividing the net single premium by the number of years in the premium-paying period understates the net level premium because this approach does not take into account the possibility that the insured may die having made only some of the premium payments. Moreover, with only the net level premium, rather than the larger net single premium, paid the first year, the insurance company will have lower investment earnings. Dividing the net single premium by the present value of a life annuity due of $1 per year for the premium-paying period produces a net level premium that reflects both the probability that the insured will live to pay premiums and the period during which the premiums are investment income. As such, the net level premiums are the actuarial equivalent of the net single premium.*

17. *In both cases, the net level premium is calculated by dividing the net single premium of $196.68 by the present value of a life annuity due of $1 per year for the premium-paying period. Because the premium-paying period is longer for the ordinary life policy (ages 45-119) than for the 20-pay life policy (ages 45-64), the life annuity due of $1 and, thus, the present value of the life annuity due of $1 is larger for the ordinary life policy than for the 20-pay life policy. Dividing a larger present value of a life annuity due of $1 into the same net single premium produces a smaller net level premium for the ordinary life policy.*

18. *If a deferred annuity contract promises to return the annuitant's premiums with or without interest, the annual premium does not involve life contingencies, but rather is a sum of money that must be set aside annually to accumulate at an assumed rate of compound interest to a predetermined amount at a specified date.*

    On the other hand, if a deferred annuity contract provides that the company retains all premiums paid in the event of death before the annuity income commences, the net level annual premium for the deferred annuity is determined by the same methods as

life insurance. However, the premium annuity's present value must be computed using the same mortality rates as those used for the benefit annuity. For example, the net level premium for a nonrefund deferred annuity purchased by a female aged 40, with income to begin at 65, is computed as a temporary life annuity due. That annuity makes one payment immediately with 24 subsequent payments due. The net single premium for that annuity is divided by the present value of a life annuity due of $1 for 25 years (from age 40 to age 64) to obtain the net level premium.

Chapter 11
Gross Premiums

By Dan M. McGill

Revised by Norma Nielson and Donald Jones

Learning Objectives

An understanding of the material in this chapter should enable the student to

1. **Describe the considerations that guide a life insurance company in setting its loading.**

2. **Explain the key components of a typical loading, including the types of operating expenses related to each.**

3. **Describe the ways in which companies deal with per-policy expenses.**

4. **Explain how the methods typically used for deriving gross premiums differ for participating and nonparticipating policies**

5. **Explain how gross premiums are tested for adequacy using an asset-share test, how various assumptions affect asset shares, and how the results of an asset-share test are interpreted.**

6. **Compute the gross premium for a participating policy, given the net level premium and the loading factors.**

7. **Describe the steps that might be taken in developing a schedule of competitive premiums.**

The previous discussion of rate making explains the derivation of net premiums, which, when interest is added, are sufficient to pay the assumed benefits under the life insurance contract. Furthermore, the policy should contribute to profit or surplus. The gross premium for "traditional products" is the amount that, when interest is added, will be sufficient to pay both benefits and expenses. It is the gross premium that policyowners pay.

loading

dividend

Gross premium may be regarded in either of two ways. The gross premium is the net premium plus an amount called **loading**. Alternatively, the gross premium is an amount, independent of the net premium, found using realistic factors for mortality, interest, expenses, contingency allowances, and profit. The former method is typically used to find gross premiums for participating policies; the latter is typically used for nonparticipating policy

premiums. Loading in participating policies, usually greater than is likely to be needed, includes an amount the company expects to return to the policyowner later as a **dividend**.

These three considerations guide the company in setting its loading:

- Total loading from all policies should cover the company's total operating expenses, provide a margin of safety, provide a margin for a minimum dividend for participating policies, and contribute to profits or surplus.

- Company expenses and safety margins should be apportioned equitably over the various plans and ages of issue. In other words, each class of policies should pay its own costs.

- Resulting gross premiums should enable the company to maintain or improve its competitive position.

This chapter describes the manner in which a company attempts to fulfill these objectives and to resolve the conflict that may exist among them.

GENERAL CONSIDERATIONS

Nature of Insurance Company Expenses

investment expenses

A life insurance company's operating expenses fall into the two broad categories of **investment expenses** and insurance expenses. Investment expenses include all costs to make, service, and safeguard the company's investments. Accountants recognize these expenses as a reduction of gross investment income. (Because these expenses are not covered by an explicit loading of the net premium, they are not considered in the remainder of this chapter.)

insurance expenses

Insurance expenses include all items of costs not related to the investment function. Among the various expense classifications insurers use, the most meaningful for calculating gross premiums organizes insurance expenses into those that

- vary with the rate of premium

- vary with the amount of insurance

- are the same for all policies

Items that vary with the premium rate are commissions to agents, state premium taxes, acquisition expenses other than commissions, and agency expenses. The first two items are defined directly as percentages of the gross premium involved, while the last two items may be expressed as percentages of either the premiums collected or the commissions paid. Some agency expenses and acquisition expenses other than commissions may be charged on a per-policy basis. Agency renewal expenses may be assessed entirely per policy, as illustrated later in this chapter.

Several expenses relate to the amount of insurance. Selection costs are the most sensitive to the size of the policy. For example, companies issue policies for less than a certain size without a medical examination. If an application warrants, a paramedic exam for small and moderate-size policies will usually run from $50 to $100. When a larger amount of insurance is involved, the company requires an electrocardiogram, X-rays, blood tests, and other expensive diagnostic procedures. In this event the examiner's fee may be $200 or more. Occasionally, the company may require two or more independent medical examinations. Investigation of the applicant's other characteristics, such as lifestyle, financial status, and character, is also more thorough for larger policy sizes. Therefore, a larger policy often incurs a larger inspection fee. Other expenses that may vary with the size of the policy include those associated with the issue, maintenance, and settlement of the policy.

Examples of expenses assessed per policy include the costs of issuing policies, establishing the necessary policy records, sending premium notices, accounting for premium remittances, settling routine claims, and general overhead. As indicated above, certain agency and acquisition expenses may also be assessed per policy.

Nature of the Loading Formula

Based on this classification scheme, the typical loading to a net premium has three parts:

- a percentage of the premium

- a constant amount for each $1,000 of insurance

- a constant amount for each policy

grading of premiums

bands

Using all three of these elements produces a premium rate per $1,000 that decreases with an increase in the face amount of the policy. This happens because per-policy expenses, by definition the same for each contract, are smaller for each $1,000 of the face amount. Called **grading of premiums**, such prices that decline with policy size are a general practice today. Grading can be accomplished by setting broad amount classifications called **bands** and setting a uniform rate of expense loading per $1,000 within each band. To assess per-policy expenses on a band basis, the actuary must assume an average size policy within each band.

policy fee

A more commonly used method for dealing with per-policy expenses—and the one illustrated in this chapter—is the policy-fee approach. The **policy fee** is designed specifically to cover expenses that are roughly constant per policy. The resulting composite rate varies incrementally with each $1,000 of insurance.

A common modification of the policy-fee system is to charge a smaller fee on policies below a certain size, such as $50,000, in the interest of minimizing the expense charge on small policyowners.[1] Above the specified size, the per-policy charge is constant, ranging from about $25 to $75. A combination of the two methods uses bands for policies below some level, such as $1 million, and a policy fee for policies over that amount.

LOADING OF PARTICIPATING PREMIUMS

The theoretical basis for the loading formula is the same as that for computing net premiums. The present value of income must equal the present value of payments. Specifically, the present value of policy expenses, margins for contingencies, and anticipated dividends should be divided by the present value of an appropriate life annuity due.

A key difference lies in the certainty of the two sets of present values. The contract specifies benefits with certainty. Policy expenses, on the other hand, are estimates at best. They are found only after a painstaking analysis of operating costs and the probable future trend of such costs. Allocating costs to the various policies and ages at issue also presents one of

---

1.   When a policy fee is smaller than the constant expense per policy, the excess per-policy cost must be allocated based on an assumed average size policy.

the actuary's most difficult tasks—and one that cannot be accomplished with complete equity.

Computation of Present Values

Cost studies usually precede adoption of a loading formula. Expenses are reduced to a unit basis and allocated among the various policy plans and ages at issue. Each unit expense rate is expressed either as a percentage of the premium, an amount per $1,000 of face value, or an amount per policy. While the first of these types is straightforward, the latter two require sophisticated cost studies to achieve valid rates.

To calculate the present value of these expenses, the time of their occurrence must be known. One must know whether the expenses occur at the inception of the contract, at periodic intervals after that, or only upon the occurrence of some particular event in the future. A typical formula might contain values for the following elements:

- expenses expressed as a percentage of the premium

  - those incurred only at time of issue
  - those incurred only during a definite number of renewal years
  - those incurred every year, including the first

- expenses expressed as an amount per $1,000 of insurance

  - those incurred only at time of issue
  - those incurred each year
  - those incurred only in the year of death

- expenses expressed as an amount per policy

  - those incurred only at time of issue
  - those incurred only during a definite number of renewal years
  - those incurred each year
  - those incurred only in the year of death

Expenses Incurred Only at Time of Issue

Under the first bulleted item expenses incurred only at time of issue include first-year commissions, agency expense allowances, and other acquisition costs. First-year commissions to the soliciting agent vary widely among companies and, to a lesser extent, among

policy plans of the same company. A typical first-year commission on an ordinary life policy issued at age 32 might be 55 percent or more of gross premium. Additional expenses, including inspection reports, medical exam, administration, reserve establishment, and the override commission to the general agent or agency might also amount to as much as 55 percent of gross premium. Thus the total of all the expenses incurred at the time of issue may be substantially more than 110 percent of the first year's premium.

These costs are paid by the company during the first policy year while the policyowner pays only a level gross premium plus perhaps a modest policy fee. Consequently, these first-year expenses must be amortized over the entire premium-paying period of the policy. To do this the actuary finds the level percentage of the gross premium that amortizes this first-year expense. If premiums are payable throughout the insured's lifetime and first-year expenses equal 110 percent of the premium, the actuary divides 110 percent by the present value of a whole life annuity due of $1 as of age 32. Based on the previously determined value of $16.49, a level 6.67 percent (1.10 ÷ 16.49) of each premium payment is available to amortize the acquisition expenses.

Expenses Incurred Only during a Definite Number of Renewal Years

Items of expense here include renewal commissions to the soliciting agent and agency expense allowances. Recent compensation agreements show many patterns of renewal commissions. Some provide a minimum commission or service fee throughout the life of the policy. For a simple illustration, assume a renewal commission of 5 percent payable for 9 years. Because these commissions will be paid only if the policy's premiums are paid, the actuary discounts for the probability that the insured dies or the policyowner lapses or surrenders the policy. Discounts also could apply for termination of the agent without vested rights to the renewal commissions. In practice, however, companies do not discount these expenses for termination of the policy or the agent. With a discount for mortality only, based on the 1980 CSO Male Table and 5.5 percent interest, the present value at issue of the 5 percent renewal commissions is 33.97 percent of the annual gross premium. This must also be spread over the entire premium-paying period of the policy, here assumed to be the lifetime of the insured. The percentage of the annual premium necessary to amortize these commissions is obtained by dividing 33.97 percent by 16.49, which yields 2.06 percent.

Expenses Incurred Every Year

State premium taxes are the only significant item of expense that occurs every year, including the first. These taxes vary somewhat among states, but they average about 2

percent. No computation of present value is required since the tax applies equally to each year. It adds 2 percent to the loading formula.[2]

Table 11-1 summarizes the assumptions and calculations for our illustration. Beside the type of expense or loading factor are two major columns. The first column shows the expense rates assumed; the second shows what must be added to the annual net premiums to recover expenses. Each of these major columns is subdivided into three subcolumns, one for each type of expense: percent of gross premium, per policy, and per $1,000 of insurance.

The previous discussion explains how the actuary finds the amount that must be added to the premium to recover the assumed expenses—but just for the percent-of-gross-premium expenses. Similar calculations are made for per-policy and per-$1,000 expenses.

Expenses Incurred at Year of Death

We must introduce one more increment—premium additions—to handle settlement costs at the policy's maturity. Premium additions to pay expenses at death are calculated in the same way as finding the present value of the death benefit, as explained earlier. To find the amount to add to the annual premium, divide this present value by the appropriate annuity-due factor. The lower right-hand corner of Table 11-1 displays the results. The expenses expressed as a percentage of the gross premium total 10.76 percent. Those expressed as an amount per $1,000 are $0.31 per $1,000. Those expressed as an amount per policy are $36.25. If no other factors were considered, this would be the loading formula. Other factors must be considered, however.

Adding of Margins

Most fixed-premium life insurance policies are long-term contracts with premiums that cannot be changed after issue. Many unforeseen developments may occur, however, before the company discharges its contractual obligations. Possible developments unfavorable to the company include epidemics, heavy investment losses, lower-than-anticipated interest rates, adverse tax legislation, and unexpected increases in operating expenses. A specific increment to the loading enables the company to accumulate funds to meet such contingencies if and when they arise. Since overcharges in a participating

---

2.　Some companies now ignore premium taxes on annuity considerations in computing the basic gross premium for individual annuity contracts. Then the rates for annuities in states that tax annuity considerations are increased by the amount of the tax.

policy can be returned through the dividend formula, the company usually allows a generous amount for contingencies. An addition of 3 percent of the gross premium would be reasonable.

Table 11-1
Hypothetical Expense and Other Loading Factors for $100,000 Ordinary Life Policy Issued to a Male Aged 32

Type of Expense of Loading Factor	When Incurred	Expense Rate at Time of Occurrence			Annual Amount That Amortizes the Exposure		
		Percent of Gross Premium	Per Policy	Amount Per $1,000	Percent of Gross Premium	Per Policy	Amount per $1,000
First-year commission	At issue	55%	$60.00		3.33%		
Agency expense allowance	At issue	44	10.00		2.67 / 0.67	$3.64 / 0.61	
Other acquisition expenses	At issue	11			2.09		
Renewal commissions	2d to 10th policy year	5	5.00			X 2.06	
Agency expense taxes	2d to 10th policy year		100.00	$1.50	2.00	6.06	$0.09
State premium taxes	Annually	2	50.00	0.20		3.03	0.01
Selection	At issue		20.00	0.20		20.00	0.20
Issue	At issue		100.00	1.00		.85	0.01
Maintenance	Annually						
Settlement costs	At maturity						
Total Expenses					10.76%	$36.25	$0.31
Allowance for contingencies					3.00		0.50
Allowance for dividends					2.40	3.00	x1.25
Grand Total					16.16%	$39.25	$2.06

Mutual companies also usually load the premium intentionally to create surplus from which dividends can be paid. To provide these anticipated dividends, the company adds safety margins to the mortality and interest assumptions. The extent to which the expense-loading formula is used to create dividends depends on managerial viewpoints. The company decides where it wants to be along the spectrum between high-premium, large-dividend companies and low-premium, small-dividend companies. If management

leans in the former direction, the addition to the loading formula will be large; if it favors the latter approach, the increment will be at a minimum level. The example in the table above includes a loading for contingencies of 3 percent of the premium plus $.50 per $1,000 of the policy's face amount and a loading for dividends that consists of 2.40 percent of gross premium plus $3 per policy plus $1.25 per $1,000 of face amount.

Testing the Loading Formula

Before a formula is adopted, the company tests it at various pivotal issue ages, such as 15, 25, 35, 45, and 55. These tests show whether realistic assumptions about mortality, interest earnings, expenses, and cancellations produce a workable set of gross premiums. The premiums "work" if the group of policies is anticipated to develop sufficient assets to provide the surrender values promised under the contract, to meet the reserve requirements imposed by law or adopted by the company, to support a reasonable dividend scale, and to provide the desired addition to the company's surplus. Gross premiums are also compared to those of competing companies to see whether they meet the competition. Of course, these two objectives are often in conflict.

Asset Shares

asset share

Adequacy tests for loading, as well as other aspects of product pricing, use **asset share** calculations. To understand the asset share, first think of a block of identical policies all issued on the same day and on different lives. As time passes, the assets accumulated for these policies could be measured and the share belonging to each allocated. This stream of actual asset shares would be of interest only historically. For them to be of value at the time of pricing, the actuary projects (forecasts) asset shares based on a set of actuarial assumptions. These assumptions may range from simple to complex. In the extreme, if one assumes no expenses other than benefits and no terminations other than for death or maturity, asset shares would equal the net level premium reserves described in chapter 12. For pricing purposes, however, the assumptions also include expenses and rates of termination.

The asset share calculation traces the share from the end of one policy year to the end of the next. Assumptions reflect the timing of the payment of premiums, expenses, and benefits. For premiums and expenses paid at the beginning of the year and benefits paid at the end of the year, the actuary would perform the following steps:

- Start with the total asset share at the end of a year.

- Add the premiums and subtract the expenses at the beginning of the next year.

- Add the investment income and subtract the benefits paid at the end of this new year.

- Allocate this total to each surviving and persisting policy.

To test the adequacy of participating premiums, the actuary compares the asset shares year by year to the policy surrender values and reserve. In a policy's early years, the asset shares are less than the surrender values because of the insurer's high first-year expenses. Therefore, a loss occurs any time a policy terminates in the early years. When the asset share is larger than the surrender value but less than the reserve the insurance company experiences a gain if the policy lapses, but it experiences a loss if the policy matures then as a death claim. At later durations, the asset shares usually exceed the reserve, and the policy contributes to surplus when it is surrendered or matures. If, in the opinion of management, too many years pass before these crossover points are reached, then the loading should be increased. The converse would be true if the crossovers are too early.

The percentages and factors in Table 11-1 were set for a policy issued to a male aged 32. Similar elements would be developed for other issue ages. In the process of adjusting the loading to balance the various factors involved, such as competitive considerations, the percentage and constant factors will be modified and may lose all linkage to the cost studies on which they were initially based. Frequently, the only logic supporting the percentage and constant factors that evolve is that they represent the only combination that will produce a satisfactory result at all ages of issue.

In that spirit, we simplify our example here by adopting the following loading factors:

Percent-of-gross-premium expenses	16%
Constant expenses per $1,000	$2.00
Per-policy expenses	$42.00

Example

Loading for a $100,000 ordinary life policy issued to a 32-year-old male would be as follows:

$100,000 policy	
net premium	$8.51 per $1,000
constant expense	$2.00 per $1,000
per policy expense	$42.00
percent-of-gross-premium expense	16%
Net premium	100 x $8.51 = $851
Loading	100 x $2.00 = $200
	+ 1 x $42.00 = $42
	+ 0.16 gross premium

$$\begin{array}{r} \$851 \\ 200 \\ \underline{42} \\ \$1,093 \end{array} \qquad = 84\% \text{ of gross premium}$$

gross premium = $1,093/0.84 = $1,301 (rounded to nearest $1)

16% of gross premium - $208

Full loading $200 + $42 + $208 = $450

$$\begin{array}{l} \$851 \text{ net premium} \\ \underline{+\ 450} \text{ loading} \\ \$1,301 \text{ gross premium} \end{array}$$

This procedure for gross premiums is not followed by all mutual companies. Some mutual companies calculate their gross premiums using a process similar to the one that follows for nonparticipating premiums.

GROSS NONPARTICIPATING PREMIUMS

The chief difference between deriving gross participating premiums and gross nonparticipating premiums is the set of actuarial assumptions used. Conservative assumptions produce higher margins. In participating premiums these margins can be returned as dividends when they emerge. In nonparticipating premiums the lack of dividends may make high premiums particularly noncompetitive. Asset share calculations test for this possibility.

Two Basic Approaches

Two basic approaches are available to derive a gross nonparticipating premium. Under the first, the actuary computes the premium based on the most probable assumptions about mortality, interest, expenses, and terminations, plus a specific addition for profit. The

principal advantage of this approach is the explicit provision for profits for each plan of insurance and each age of issue.

The second approach uses assumptions that are more conservative than the most probable, but it makes no specific allowance for profit. Profits must emerge from more favorable experience than was assumed. Profit that varies widely among the various plans and issue ages is regarded as an advantage by some on the grounds that profit depends on the risk assumed. This second method is sometimes used alongside the first to show how large a profit margin is needed to assure the company a minimum return if deviations from the most probable assumptions occur.

The premium computation shown in the following pages uses the first approach.

Selecting the Most Probable Assumptions

Of the four assumptions affecting asset shares—mortality, interest, expenses, and terminations—only the impact of interest increases with duration. The impact of interest increases with the size of reserves and thus has its biggest impact at later durations, when the reserve increases.

The impact of mortality and terminations decreases over time when the amount at risk decreases as the duration increases. The impact of expenses decreases because they occur primarily in the early years. While current mortality rates are easy to find, favorable and unfavorable changes in the future due to medical advances, underwriting changes, and social changes are difficult to project. To ignore the impact of medical advances is conservative for insurance rates but careless for annuity rates.

Economic changes greatly affect policy termination. For example, changes in unemployment and alternative investment opportunities can influence termination. Termination rates also vary from company to company, from plan to plan, and with issue age.

Illustrative Premium Calculation

tentative premium

We illustrate the process of setting gross nonparticipating premiums by calculating and testing the gross premium for a 10-payment ordinary life policy issued to a woman aged 32. This illustration uses an asset share calculation to test a **tentative premium**. The principles involved apply equally to the testing of a tentative participating premium.

The tentative premium can be quite arbitrary. When calculations are part of a general rate revision, the tentative premium is usually the current premium. Alternatively, it may be the premium charged by a competing company. For our illustration, the tentative premium is the 10-pay net level premium based on 1980 CSO Female Table mortality and 5.5 percent interest. For $100,000 of insurance, this is $1,451.57.

Our illustration (see Table 11-2) uses expense factors consistent with those in Table 11-1.

Table 11-2			
Expense Factors Used in Illustration			
Policy Year	Percent of Premium	Per Policy	Per $1,000
1	54	$220	$1.70
2–10	4	25	.20
At settlement		100	1.00

Table 11-3		
Deaths per 1,000 Lives Select and Aggregate Mortality		
Age	1975–80 Select Table	1980 CSO Female Table
32	0.38	1.45
33	0.44	1.50
34	0.54	1.58
35	0.65	1.65
36	0.76	1.76
37	0.86	1.89
38	0.97	2.04
39	1.08	2.22
40	1.19	2.42
41	1.31	2.64

Mortality rates used to test a trial or tentative gross premium should be the most realistic available. This example uses death rates from the 1975–80 select table.[3] Those select rates per 1,000 lives at ages 32 through 41 are compared with the 1980 CSO Female Table (which are aggregate rates) in Table 11-3.

Withdrawals, expressed as a rate per 1,000 policyowners, are assumed to occur according to the pattern in Table 11-4.

---

3.   See Claude Y. Paquin, "An Extension of the 1975–80 Basic Select and Ultimate Mortality Tables, Male and Female-Actuarial Note," Transactions of the Society of Actuaries , vol. 38, 1986, pp. 205–224.

Table 11-4			
Withdrawals per 1,000 Policies			
First year	200	Sixth year	8
Second year	100	Seventh year	42
Third year	80	Eighth year	36
Fourth year	66	Ninth year	30
Fifth year	55	Tenth year	25

Applying the death and withdrawal rates in Table 11-3 and Table 11-4 to an arbitrary number of persons allows us to prepare a table showing the number of persons living and persisting at the beginning and end of each year after that. That table enables us to predict the premium revenue that will be received at the beginning of each policy year and the number of persons entitled to a share of the group's fund at the end of each policy year. Table 11-5 presents these values, based on 10,000 persons and the death and withdrawal rates given in Table 11-3 and Table 11-4.

Table 11-5						
Number Living and Persisting the First 10 Policy Years						
Policy Year	Number Living and Persisting First of Year	Rate of Death	Number Dying during Year	Rate of Termination	Number Terminating End of Year	Number Living and Persisting End of Year
1	10,000	0.00038	3.8	0.200	1999.2	7,997
2	7,997	0.00044	3.5	0.100	799.3	7,194
3	7,194	0.00054	3.9	0.080	575.2	6,615
4	6,615	0.00065	4.3	0.066	436.3	6,174
5	6,174	0.00076	4.7	0.055	339.3	5,830
6	5,830	0.00086	5.0	0.048	279.6	5,546
7	5,546	0.00097	5.4	0.042	232.7	5,308
8	5,308	0.00108	5.7	0.036	190.9	5,111
9	5,111	0.00119	6.1	0.030	153.1	4,952
10	4,952	0.00131	6.5	0.025	123.6	4,822
Implicit in the calculation of this table is the assumption that withdrawals occur only at the ends of the policy years. This might be the case for annual-premium business, but for more frequently paid premiums the withdrawals occur at other times during the policy year.						

One additional set of values is needed before we begin the asset share calculation—the surrender values available each year to terminating policyowners. These values for the first

10 policy years under a $100,000 10-payment life policy issued at age 32 are assumed to be as shown in Table 11-6.

Table 11- 6 Surrender Values Used in Illustration			
First year	$0	Sixth year	$8,175
Second year	483	Seventh year	10,349
Third year	2,262	Eighth year	12,632
Fourth year	4,136	Ninth year	15,028
Fifth year	6,105	Tenth year	17,544

Assumptions about the following provide the raw materials to calculate the asset share:

- the number and volume of premiums to be received each year

- the number of death claims of $100,000 each plus settlement expenses and interest to the end of the policy year that will be incurred each year (based on the same death rates as those used to learn the number of premiums to be received)

- the number and amount of surrender payments that will be disbursed each year

- the rate of interest that will be earned on accumulated funds (5.5 percent)

These assumptions combine as shown in Table 11-7 to produce the asset share per $100,000 at each duration.

According to Table 11-7, 10,000 policyowners will pay a total of $2,777,222 in effective premiums at the beginning of the first year. These funds earn interest throughout the year at 5.5 percent and grow to $2,929,969 at the end of the year. Death claims will diminish this amount by $391,091 – $380,000 in claim payments, $760 in settlement expenses, and $10,331 in loss of assumed interest. The loss of interest arises because we have assumed that the total effective premiums will accrue interest to the end of the policy year. On average, however, claims will be paid at mid-year, so the company loses interest earnings on these payments. It is also assumed that 1,999 54. These are the minimum values required under the Standard Nonforfeiture Law on a 5.5 percent interest basis. Chapter 15 discusses the Standard Nonforfeiture Law in greater detail. policyowners surrender their policies at the end of the first year, receiving $0 individually and in total.

Table 11-7
Asset Share, $100,000 10-Pay Life, Issue Age 32

Policy Year	(1) Surviving and Persisting	(2) Expenses Per Policy	(3) Effective Premium Per Policy	(4) Total Effective Premium (1) x (3)	(5) Initial Fund $(11)_{n-1}+(4)$	(6) Initial Fund + Interest (5) × (1.055)
1	10,000	$1,174	$278	$2,777,222	$2,777,222	$2,929,969
2	7,997	103	1,349	10,783,958	13,322,837	14,055,593
3	7,194	103	1,349	9,701,292	23,008,665	24,274,142
4	6,615	103	1,349	8,920,369	31,493,551	33,225,696
5	6,174	103	1,349	8,326,209	39,304,820	41,466,585
6	5,830	103	1,349	7,862,288	46,774,293	49,346,879
7	5,546	103	1,349	7,478,461	54,023,427	56,994,715
8	5,308	103	1,349	7,157,416	61,190,336	64,555,805
9	5,111	103	1,349	6,892,297	68,447,083	72,211,672
10	4,952	103	1,349	6,677,573	75,961,751	80,139,647

(7) Death Claims + Expenses and Interest	(8) Minimum Cash Value	(9) Number of Surrenders	(10) Amount Paid on Surrender	(11) Fund Balance (6)-(7)-(10)	(12) Asset Share $(11) \div (1)^{n+1}$	(13) 1980 CSO 5.5% NLP Reserve
$391,091	$0	1,999	$0	$2,538,878	$317	$1,388
362,136	483	799	386,083	13,307,374	1,850	2,851
399,820	2,262	575	1,301,141	22,573,182	3,412	4,388
442,524	4,136	436	1,804,561	30,978,611	5,017	6,005
482,949	6,105	339	2,071,630	38,912,005	6,674	7,704
516,046	8,175	280	2,285,867	46,544,966	8,393	9,489
553,636	10,349	233	2,408,159	54,032,920	10,180	11,361
589,957	12,632	191	2,411,062	61,554,785	12,043	13,325
625,967	15,028	153	2,301,527	69,284,178	13,992	15,384
667,622	17,544	124	2,169,026	77,302,999	16,032	17,544

Net premiums based on 1980 CSO Table and 5.5 percent interest.

At the end of the year a fund of $2,538,878 is assumed to be on hand. Dividing this pro rata among the 7,997 surviving and persisting policyowners gives each $317. That is the asset share per $100,000 at the end of the first year. The terminal reserve at each duration is shown for comparison. Observe that at the end of the first year the reserve exceeds the asset share by $1,071 and the asset share exceeds the surrender value by $317.

At the beginning of the second year, 7,997 surviving and persisting policyowners pay a total of $10,783,958 in premiums. When added to the fund from the end of the first year, this produces a total fund at the beginning of the second year of $13,322,837. At 5.5 percent interest, this fund amounts to $14,055,593 at the end of the second year before deduction of death and surrender claims. Death claims and settlement expenses, adjusted for loss of interest, and surrender payments reduce the fund to a net balance of $13,307,374. Divided pro rata among the 7,194 surviving and persisting policyowners, this fund yields an asset share of $1,850. This falls short of the second-year terminal reserve by $1,001 per $100,000, and surpasses the surrender value by $1,367.

This process continues through the next 8 years. By the end of the 10th policy year, the fund is seen to have grown to $77,302,999, an amount sufficient to provide $16,032 to each of the 4,822 surviving and persisting policyowners. This is $1,512 less than the full net level premium reserve and the surrender value at that point.

Evaluating the Trial Premium

By comparing the asset share at each duration with the comparable surrender value and reserve, the company can evaluate the appropriateness of the trial gross premium. Until the asset share equals or exceeds the surrender value, each termination is a direct drain on the company's surplus. In other words, the company gives back to each withdrawing policyowner more money than that policyowner has contributed to the company. This situation may prevail for several years under many plans and ages at issue. The asset share is usually negative during the first few years of a continuous premium whole life policy. It takes several years to exceed the cash value and takes even more years to exceed the reserve. However, under a high-premium policy, such as the 10-payment life shown in Table 11-7, the asset share normally should exceed the surrender value by at least a small amount even at the end of the first year.

validation period

A more fundamental test companies use is the period required for the asset share to equal or exceed the full net level premium reserve. Until that occurs, the company has not recovered its acquisition expenses and is still showing a book loss for the block of business represented in the asset share calculation. Once the asset share exceeds the reserve, acquisition expenses have been recovered in full and that block of policies is contributing to the company's surplus. Based on many considerations a company decides how long it can afford—and is willing—to wait before recovering its outlay. That period of time is called the policy's **validation period** (see Figure 11-1). If the company can wait 10 years to recoup its

acquisition expenses, it uses gross premiums that accumulate asset shares exactly equal to the reserves at the end of the 10th policy year.

It would be sheer accident if a trial gross premium produced an asset share precisely equal to the full net level premium reserve at the end of the validation period. Variation will exist in one direction or the other. To eliminate the variation, the trial gross premium is adjusted either upward or downward. The amount of this adjustment is found by dividing the difference between the asset share and the reserve at the end of the validation period by the future value of a $1 premium increase, and adding (or subtracting) the result to the trial gross premium.

The technique is illustrated, continuing with the example of the 10-payment life policy, by assuming a validation period of 10 years. A 10-pay life policy will have settlement costs and maintenance expenses after premiums have ceased. The present value of these costs, $350, is added to the 10th year reserve when determining a gross premium. The fact that the asset share is $1,512 less than the reserve at the end of the validation period means that the trial gross premium is high enough to make the policy profitable by the end of the second year. To find the required correction, the effect of changing the trial gross premium by $1 upon the accumulation at the end of 10 years is measured. Then, by simple proportion, the exact change in the premium that would increase (or decrease) the accumulation by the desired amount can be found.

It is helpful at this stage to visualize the change in the trial gross premium as an increase of $1, whatever the direction of the adjustment needed. (See Table 11-8.) Then it will be apparent that this additional annual $1 payment will not have to bear any share of the death and surrender claims, since these were met through the original premium payments. However, the additional $1 should bear its proportionate share of expenses that vary directly with the size of the premium. Since these expenses were earlier assumed to be 54 percent of the first-year premium and 4 percent of the renewal premium, the effective additional premium will be $0.46 the first year and $0.96 for each of the other 9 years. The number of surviving and persisting policyowners at each duration remains the same, and so does the assumed rate of interest earnings. Therefore, the additional premium of $1 will bring in an additional sum of $4,600 the first year. At 5.5 percent interest, that additional amount accumulates to $4,853 by the end of the first year.

Figure 11-1
Break Even When Asset Share ≥ Policy Reserve

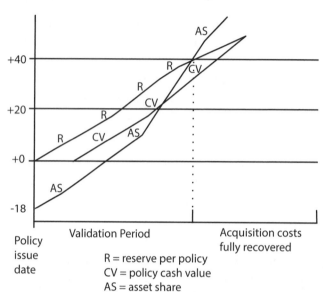

Policy issue date

Validation Period

Acquisition costs fully recovered

R = reserve per policy
CV = policy cash value
AS = asset share

Because of lower renewal expenses, the additional effective premiums for the second year will aggregate $7,677, which, when supplemented by the fund at the end of the first year and interest at 5.5 percent on the composite fund, amounts to $13,219 at the end of the second year. By the end of the 10th year, the additional premium of $1 paid each year by the surviving and persisting policyowners will accumulate to $78,667. Divided pro rata among the 4,822 policyowners surviving and persisting at that point, this sum would provide an additional $16.32 increment to the asset share for each policy. In other words, increasing the trial gross premium by $1 increases the asset share at the end of 10 years by $16.32.

For the 10-pay life policy in our illustration, at the end of the 10th policy year we need an asset share equal to the net level premium reserve (which for this example is also the net single premium for policy year 10 and later) plus $350 to cover the future expenses for a total of $17,894. The trial premium of $1,451.57 provided an asset share of $16,032–$1,512 less than is needed. Since each $1 increase in premium increases the asset share by $16.32 at the end of the 10th year, the tentative premium needs to be increased by $92.65 ($1,512/16.32) to $1,544.22. This premium will accumulate an asset share at the end of 10 years exactly equal to the net level premium reserve if actual results conform precisely to the assumptions.

Table 11-8 presents the calculations supporting this adjustment.

Table 11-8 Accumulation of Annual Premium of $1							
	(1)	(2)	(3)	(4)	(5)	(6)	(7)
Policy Year	Surviving & Persisting	Expenses	Effective Premium	Total Effective Premium (1) x (3)	Initial Fund $(6)_{n-1}$ + (4)	Fund at Year End (5) x 1.055	Asset Share (6)/ $(1)^{n+1}$
1	10,000.00	$0.54	$0.46	$4,600	$ 4,600	$ 4,853	$ 0.61
2	7,996.96	0.04	0.96	7,677	12,530	13,219	1.84
3	7,194.10	0.04	0.96	6,906	20,126	21,232	3.21
4	6,615.00	0.04	0.96	6,350	27,583	29,100	4.71
5	6,174.39	0.04	0.96	5,927	35,027	36,954	6.34
6	5,830.36	0.04	0.96	5,597	42,551	44,891	8.09
7	5,545.73	0.04	0.96	5,324	50,215	52,977	9.98
8	5,307.66	0.04	0.96	5,095	58,072	61,266	11.99
9	5,111.06	0.04	0.96	4,907	66,173	69,813	14.10
10	4,951.83	0.04	0.96	4,754	74,566	78,667	16.32
11	4,822.00						

model office

When constructing a set of gross premium rates, the detailed study just outlined would not be done for each policy and issue age. This would be too much work and would probably produce inconsistent rates. Rather, the procedure would be used for rates at quinquennial or decennial ages. These rates would be tested for adequacy for a simplified portfolio using policies with only these ages. The simplified book of business is selected to represent the company's overall book of business and is called a **model office**.

The asset share calculation is concerned only with the adequacy of the proposed gross premiums. Once this has been established, the gross premiums at the representative ages are compared with those of other companies operating in the same territory to learn whether the rates are competitive. A company whose rates are clearly out of line will have trouble holding its agents and obtaining new business. If the survey of other companies' rates shows the test set to be competitive, the company proceeds to derive the complete set of rates by formula or interpolation. If rates appear to be too high relative to those of the competition, the company considers adjusting its rates.

Developing a Schedule of Competitive Premiums

If the "most probable" mortality, interest, expense, and termination rates have been used in calculating gross premiums, there is little possibility that the competitive situation can be improved by changing any of those assumptions. Even with the same basic assumptions, however, the premiums can be reduced by extending the period over which acquisition expenses are amortized. This increases the drain on surplus, but it may be the most practical solution. If a specific allowance for profit has been made in the calculations, shaving this margin may reduce premiums slightly. If extending the validation period and narrowing the profit margin do not produce competitive premiums, more fundamental adjustments may be needed. Such adjustments might include more stringent underwriting requirements, less conservative (and thus higher yielding) investments, greater operating economies, or elimination of less persistent policies.

The final step in deriving a set of gross premium rates is to review the results for consistency among the various plans and ages at issue. Identical premiums should always be charged for identical benefits. The premium scale should contain no "bargain rates" since such rates are likely to attract an undue volume of business for certain plans and ages of issue, which may indicate the presence of a high level of adverse selection.

Participating Gross Premiums Derived through Tentative Gross Premiums

As mentioned earlier, the technique underlying the calculation of nonparticipating gross premiums in larger stock companies is used by some mutual companies. It is modified to reflect the payment of policyowner dividends. In using this technique, a mutual company

- computes a set of tentative gross premiums at quinquennial or decennial ages, based on the most probable assumptions about mortality, interest, and expenses

- tests such premiums for adequacy by means of asset share calculations

At this stage, the computation does not allow for dividend distributions. The margins in the basic assumptions are so narrow that no funds are presumed to be available for distribution to policyowners. Trial gross premiums, adjusted to reflect the redundancy or deficiency in the asset share, are compared with the gross premiums (after dividends, in the case of participating gross premiums) of competing companies. Once the premiums have been fitted to the best competitive advantage, the company considers its dividend policy.

A dividend scale of any desired level and pattern can be developed without relating the resulting dividends to any particular sources of surplus. Margins to support the proposed dividend scale are added directly to the gross premiums. Usually several sets of premium rates, based on various assumed margins, are constructed and compared before the final set of representative gross premiums—with the built-in dividend scale—is selected. Gross premiums for all ages of issue usually are computed by loading the valuation net premiums in accordance with a formula that experimentation has found to develop rates approximately equivalent to the desired gross premiums when applied to net premiums. As pointed out earlier, such a formula usually is the sum of a percentage of the gross or net premium, a constant amount per $1,000 of insurance, and a policy fee.

Some companies vary the procedure by calculating the trial gross premiums on a nonparticipating basis and then adding the margin for a predetermined dividend scale before running the various asset-share tests. Dividend distributions operate as a decrement in such a procedure, along with death claims and surrender payments. Each approach produces the same results.

Premiums Paid at Intervals of Less than One Year

So far the calculations have assumed premiums to be paid annually. Theoretically, premiums paid more frequently than once per year could be calculated in precisely the same manner by using probability and interest functions based on shorter time units. To derive true monthly premiums, a mortality table that shows the rate of mortality month by month, rather than annually, is needed. Similarly, claim payments could be discounted monthly instead of yearly. Such precise computations are not used in practice, however, because mortality studies produce annual rates. Instead, actuaries calculate monthly, quarterly, and semiannual net premiums in a way that distributes deaths uniformly between whole ages. That technical procedure, which must include loadings for the expense of additional premium processing, is not covered here.[4]

---

4.   For a detailed discussion see Newton L. Bowers, Hans S. Gerber, James C. Hickman, Donald A. Jones, and Cecil J. Nesbitt, Actuarial Mathematics (Chicago, IL: Society of Actuaries, 1986).

CHAPTER REVIEW

Key Terms and Concepts

loading   policy fee
dividend   asset share
investment expenses   tentative premium
insurance expenses   validation period
grading of premiums   model office
bands

Chapter 11 Review Questions

1. Explain how the methods typically used to find the gross premiums for participating and nonparticipating policies differ from one another. [1]

2. Describe three considerations that guide a life insurance company in setting its loading. [1]

3. List the two broad categories of life insurance company operating expenses, and give examples of the types of expenses in each category. [2]

4. List the three elements in the typical loading to a net premium, and explain why they produce a premium rate per $1,000 that decreases with an increase in the policy's face amount. [2]

5. Describe the methods insurers use to deal with per-policy expenses (that is, to grade premiums). [3]

6. What is the key difference between computing the present value of policy expenses, margins for contingencies, and anticipated dividends, and computing the present value of benefits for a participating policy? [4]

7. Give examples of each of the following types of policy expenses, and explain how the amount that must be added to the premium to cover them is determined: (a) expenses incurred only at the time of issue; (b) expenses incurred only during a definite number

of renewal years; (c) expenses incurred every year; (d) expenses incurred at the year of death. [3]

8. What are the reasons that life insurance companies include margins in the loading? [5]

9. What steps are involved in calculating the asset share for a block of policies and for a given policy within that block? [5]

10. Explain what each of the following indicates: (a) A policy's asset share is less than its surrender value. (b) A policy's asset share is larger than its surrender value but less than its reserve. (c) A policy's asset share is larger than its reserve. [5]

11. Suppose the net level premium per $1,000 for a participating ordinary life policy is $10 and the loading factors adopted by the insurer are 20 percent of the gross premium, plus a constant of $2.00 per $1,000, and a constant of $40 per policy. Calculate the gross premium for a $200,000 policy. [6]

12. What is the chief difference between deriving gross participating premiums and gross nonparticipating premiums? [4]

13. Describe the two approaches available for deriving a gross nonparticipating premium. [4]

14. List the four assumptions that affect the asset shares of nonparticipating policies, and note the impact of each on the asset share as duration increases. [5]

15. Explain how a company wanting to recoup acquisition expenses in 8 years determines the adjustment to make to a nonparticipating life insurance policy's tentative gross premium if an asset share test for the tentative gross premium indicates that the asset share does not equal the policy's reserve until the end of the 10th policy year. [5]

16. What steps might a company take to develop a schedule of competitive premiums? [7]

17. Describe the procedures that some mutual companies use to derive participating gross premiums through tentative gross premiums. [7]

Chapter 11 Review Answers

1. *The gross premium for a participating policy is typically determined by adding a loading to the net premium. Alternatively, the gross premium for a nonparticipating policy is determined as an amount, independent of the net premium, found using realistic factors for mortality, interest, expenses, contingency allowances, and profit. Also, loading in participating policies includes an amount the company expects to return to the policyowner as a dividend. Nonparticipating policies do not pay dividends.*

2. *These three considerations guide the company in setting its loading:*

   - *Total loading from all policies should cover the company's total operating expenses, provide a margin of safety, provide a margin for a minimum dividend for participating policies, and contribute to profits or surplus.*

   - *Company expenses and safety margins should be apportioned equitably over the various plans and ages of issue. In other words, each class of policies should pay its own costs.*

   - *Resulting gross premiums should enable the company to maintain or improve its competitive position.*

3. *A life insurance company's operating expenses fall into the two broad categories of investment expenses and insurance expenses.*

   - *Investment expenses include all costs to make, service, and safeguard the company's investments.*

   - *Insurance expenses include all items of costs not related to the investment function. Among the various expense classifications insurers use, the most meaningful for calculating gross premiums organizes insurance expenses into*

     a. *those that vary with the rate of premium such as commissions to agents, state premium taxes, acquisition expenses other than commissions, and agency expenses*

     b. *those that vary with the amount of insurance such as selection costs*

     c. *those that are the same for all policies such as costs of issuing policies, establishing the necessary policy records, sending premium notices, accounting for premium remittances, settling routine claims, and general overhead, as well as some agency expenses and acquisition expenses other than commissions*

4. *The typical loading to a net premium has three elements:*

    •   *a percentage of the premium*

    •   *a constant amount for each $1,000 of insurance*

    •   *a constant amount for each policy*

    Using all three of these elements produces a premium rate per $1,000 that decreases with an increase in the face amount of the policy. This happens because per-policy expenses, by definition the same for each contract, are smaller for each $1,000 of the face amount.

5. *Grading can be accomplished in several ways:*

    •   *The actuary sets broad-amount classifications called bands and sets a uniform rate of expense loading per $1,000 within each band.*

    •   *A more commonly used method for dealing with per-policy expenses is the policy-fee approach. The policy fee is designed specifically to cover expenses that are roughly constant per policy. The resulting composite rate varies incrementally with each $1,000 of insurance.*

    •   *A common modification of the policy-fee system is to charge a smaller fee on policies below a certain size, such as $50,000, in the interest of minimizing the expense charge on small policyowners. Above the specified size, the per-policy charge is constant.*

    •   *A combination approach uses bands for policies below some level, such as $1 million, and a policy fee for policies over that amount.*

6. *A key difference between computing the present value of benefits and the present value of policy expenses, margin for contingencies and anticipated dividends lies in the certainty of the two sets of present values. The contract specifies benefits with certainty. Policy expenses, on the other hand, are estimates at best. They are found only after a painstaking analysis of operating costs and the probable future trend of such costs. Likewise, the margin for contingencies and the factor for anticipated dividends are also estimates.*

7. *Answers:*

   a. *expenses incurred only at the time of issue*

      *   *examples—first-year commissions, agency expense allowances, and other acquisition costs*

      *   *how amount is determined—These costs are paid by the company during the first policy year while the policyowner pays only a level gross premium plus perhaps a modest policy fee. Consequently, these first-year expenses must be amortized over the entire premium-paying period of the policy. To do this, the actuary finds the level percentage of the gross premium that amortizes this first-year expense by dividing (1) the first year expense expressed as a percent of the first year's gross premium by (2) the present value of a life annuity due of $1 for the number of years in the premium-paying period.*

   b. *expenses incurred only during a definite number of renewal years*

      *   *examples—renewal commissions to the soliciting agent and agency expense allowances*

      *   *how amount is determined—Because these commissions will be paid only if the policy's premiums are paid, the actuary discounts for the probability that the insured dies. The present value of the renewal commissions (discounted for mortality) at issue is then spread over the entire premium-paying period by dividing it by the present value of a life annuity due of $1 for the number of years in the premium-paying period.*

   c. *expenses incurred every year*

      *   *example—state premium tax*

      *   *how amount is determined—No computation of present value is required because the tax applies equally to each year. The premium tax percentage is added to the loading formula.*

   d. *expenses incurred at the year of death*

      *   *example—premium additions—to handle settlement costs at the policy's maturity*

      *   *how amount is determined—Premium additions to pay expenses at death are calculated in the same way as finding the present value of the death benefit. To find the amount to add to the annual premium, divide this present value by the appropriate annuity-due factor.*

8. Life insurance companies include margins in the loading for the following reasons:

   - Many life insurance policies are long-term contracts with premiums that cannot be changed after issue. Many unforeseen developments may occur, however, before the company discharges its contractual obligations. Possible developments unfavorable to the company include epidemics, heavy investment losses, lower-than-anticipated interest rates, adverse tax legislation, and unexpected increases in operating expenses. A specific increment to the loading enables the company to accumulate funds to meet such contingencies if and when they arise.

   - Mutual companies also usually load the premium intentionally to create surplus from which dividends can be paid. To provide these anticipated dividends, the company adds safety margins to the mortality and interest assumptions. The extent to which the expense-loading formula is used to create dividends depends on managerial viewpoints.

9. The following steps are involved in calculating the asset share for a block of policies for a given year:

   - Start with the total asset share at the end of the previous year.

   - Add the premiums and subtract the expenses at the beginning of this new year.

   - Add the investment income and subtract the benefits paid at the end of this new year.

   To calculate the asset share for a given policy within the block, the asset share calculated for the block of policies using the three steps above is allocated to each surviving and persisting policy by dividing it by the number of policyowners surviving and persisting at the end of the year under consideration.

10. Answers:

   a. When a policy's asset share is less than its surrender value, a loss occurs if the policy is terminated.

   b. When a policy's asset share is larger than its surrender value but less than its reserve, the insurance company experiences a gain if the policy lapses, but it experiences a loss if the policy matures as a death claim.

   c. When a policy's asset share is larger than its reserve, the policy contributes to surplus when it is surrendered or matures.

11. *Eighty percent of the gross premium must provide $2,000 for benefits (200 x $10) and $440 for expenses ([200 x $2] + $40). Because 80 percent of the gross premium must be $2,440 to cover benefits and these expenses, the gross premium for the $200,000 ordinary life policy is $3,050, which is calculated by dividing $2,440 by .80.*

12. *The chief difference between deriving gross participating premiums and gross nonparticipating premiums is the set of actuarial assumptions used. Conservative assumptions produce higher margins. In participating premiums, these margins can be returned as dividends when they emerge. In nonparticipating premiums, the lack of dividends may make high premiums particularly noncompetitive. Asset share calculations test for this possibility.*

13. *Two basic approaches are available to derive a gross nonparticipating premium:*

    •   *Under the first approach, the actuary computes the premium based on the most probable assumptions about mortality, interest, expenses, and terminations, plus a specific addition for profit.*

    •   *The second approach uses assumptions that are more conservative than the most probable, but it makes no specific allowance for profit. Profits must emerge from more favorable experience than was assumed.*

14. *The following four assumptions affect the asset shares of nonparticipating policies:*

    •   *Interest—impact increases with duration when the size of the reserve increases over time*

    •   *Mortality—impact decreases over time when the amount at risk decreases with duration*

    •   *Terminations—impact decreases over time when the amount at risk decreases with duration*

    •   *Expenses—impact decreases with duration because expenses occur primarily in the early years*

15. *First, accumulate an additional premium of $1 paid in each of the 8 years by the surviving and persisting policyowners and divide the total by the number of policyowners surviving and persisting at the end of 8 years. This is the additional increment to the 8th asset share for each policy that would result from a $1 increase in the policy's tentative gross premium.*

Next, add any future expenses beyond the 8th year to the policy's reserve at the end of the 8th year to determine the amount the asset share needs to equal at the end of 8 years. Then subtract the policy's asset share at the end of the 8th year from the amount the asset share needs to equal after 8 years to find the amount the asset share calculated with the tentative premium is less than is needed at the end of the 8th year.

Finally, divide the amount the asset share calculated with the tentative premium is less than is needed at the end of the 8th year by the additional increment to the 8th asset share for each policy that would result from a $1 increase in the policy's tentative gross premium to determine the amount that needs to be added to the tentative premium so the asset share will equal the reserve at the end of the 8th year.

16. *Competitive premiums can be developed by*
    - *extending the period over which acquisition expenses are amortized*
    - *reducing the profit margin*
    - *introducing more stringent underwriting requirements*
    - *undertaking a less conservative (and thus higher yielding) investment strategy*
    - *introducing greater operating economies*
    - *eliminating less persistent policies*

17. *Some mutual companies derive participating gross premiums through tentative gross premiums by modifying the procedure to reflect the payment of policyowner dividends. In using this technique, a mutual company*
    - *computes a set of tentative gross premiums at quinquennial or decennial ages, based on the most probable assumptions about mortality, interest, and expenses*
    - *tests such premiums for adequacy by means of asset-share calculations*
    - *considers its dividend policy with margins to support the proposed dividend scale added directly to the gross premiums, once the premiums have been fitted to the best competitive advantage*

Usually several sets of premium rates, based on various assumed margins, are constructed and compared before the final set of representative gross premiums-with the built-in dividend scale—is selected.

Some companies vary the procedure by calculating the trial gross premiums on a nonparticipating basis and then adding the margin for a predetermined dividend scale before running the various asset-share tests. Dividend distributions operate as a decrement in such a
procedure, along with death claims and surrender payments.

Surplus— An Insurance Company's Capital

Norma Nielson and Donald Jones

Learning Objectives

An understanding of the material in this chapter should enable the student to

1. **Identify and explain the factors that top management must consider in managing surplus—that is, monitoring the surplus accumulated within the insurance company and deploying it in the best possible directions.**

2. **List and explain the sources of surplus (capital) for a life insurance company.**

3. **Describe the several competing needs among which a company's board of directors must allocate newly earned surplus.**

4. **Explain the considerations and techniques involved in equitably distributing a company's divisible surplus to its policyowners in the form of dividends.**

surplus

Preceding chapters stress the long-term obligations of life insurance companies. The premiums an insurer charges its customers cover the expected claims of those customers. The purpose of capital in any insurance company is to absorb unexpected upward fluctuations in claims and unexpected downward fluctuations in investment results. To meet long-term obligations, then, an insurance company needs capital that, in the terminology of insurance accounting, is called **surplus**.

Suppose, for example, that a medium-sized life insurer expects claims to be $7.5 million during an upcoming period. Uncertainties are inherent in any such projection. This means that the situation is more accurately represented by a distribution than by a single number. Figure 12-1 illustrates one possible distribution, where aggregate claims for each quarter are plotted on the horizontal axis and the probability that each level of aggregate claims will occur is depicted on the vertical axis. The company expects claims of $7.5 million, but losses in excess of $16 million are theoretically possible, although highly improbable. Sophisticated statistical analysis beyond the scope of this book suggests that for this specific distribution the company should not expect aggregate claims to exceed $9 million in a bad year.

Figure 12-1 Distribution of Quarterly Claims

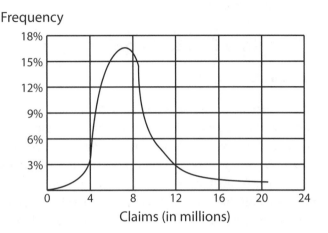

An epidemic or natural disaster that produces bad life insurance results in one quarter is also likely to affect subsequent quarters. Life insurers are particularly vulnerable to changes in claims caused by an epidemic or natural disaster because many of their contracts involved fixed premiums that cannot be adjusted upward.

One way to explain capital adequacy is by expressing how many quarters of bad experience a company's financial position can absorb. Based on the statistical analysis mentioned above, this insurer could have actual claims exceed expected claims by $1.5 million in a bad quarter. A firm with exposures illustrated by Figure 12-1's distribution and capital of $3 million can remain solvent only through two consecutive poor quarters. An insurer with $6 million in capital can be confident of its ability to remain solvent through four consecutive poor quarters, and so forth.

MANAGING SURPLUS

The fundamental charge of top managers in insurance companies is to monitor the surplus accumulated within the company and deploy it in the best possible directions. This means

- assuring that the company meets the minimum statutory capital requirements in the states where it operates
- assessing the need for capital beyond those regulatory minimum requirements
- understanding the relationship between surplus and the investment function
- evaluating how much surplus is needed and available from various sources

Growing out of this surplus management process is the need for a system to distribute some surplus back to policyowners.

Minimum Statutory Capital Requirements

risk-based capital standards

Because regulators understand the role of adequate capital in a company's solvency, each state has minimum capital requirements. Historically, these requirements took the form of a law specifying a minimum amount of capital for a company to become licensed in that state, (often between $1 million and $2 million). These fixed-dollar requirements have been relegated to history. The National Association of Insurance Commissioners (NAIC) developed new capital standards that vary depending on the level of insurance and investment risk maintained by individual companies. All states have risk-based capital standards for life insurers. The NAIC is already implementing the new standard by mandating that the standardized annual statement contain the information and ratios needed for **risk-based capital evaluation**.

The Need for Capital Beyond Minimum Requirements

Companies have always needed capital beyond the statutory minimum amounts. The amount of capital required depends on the type of business a life insurer writes and the willingness of the company's owners and managers to take risks. The move by regulators toward risk-based capital requirements imposes a limit on how much risk the companies can choose to assume.

Traditionally, most life insurance policies were issued for long terms and sold at fixed prices. These circumstances remove all possibility of future price adjustments and force an insurer to calculate its premiums conservatively. The degree of conservatism needed depends somewhat on the type of policies being sold. For example, a life insurance company writing participating insurance usually assigns its highest priority to the adequacy of gross premiums and can incorporate ample margins of safety into each basic assumption. The premiums of nonparticipating policies and policies paying market rates of interest must also meet the test of adequacy. However, contracts that include no provisions to adjust future costs in light of actual experience require careful consideration in order to develop premiums that will prove adequate over the long run and be competitive in the marketplace. The margins in such premiums will be narrower.

Relationship to Investment Function

An insurance company invests its capital in financial instruments whose values move with interest rates and equities markets. The straight line labeled duration in Figure 12-2 illustrates an asset whose value declines 25 percent (from $80 to $60) when interest rates rise from 6 percent to 8 percent.

immunization

When a life insurance company's assets and liabilities move in the same direction and at the same pace in response to interest rate changes, the company is said to have immunized its portfolio against interest rate risks. **Immunization** means that a financial risk has been effectively neutralized—that is, the losses expected in one part of the business are offset by gains somewhere else when market conditions and interest rates change. For example, an immunized portfolio will offset a decrease in income due to lower interest rates by increases in the market value of the bonds held in that portfolio. This requires a very precise combination of bonds, mortgages, and stock of the appropriate durations to accomplish this balance and maintain it over a wide range of interest rate environments.

duration

asset duration

liability duration

duration matching

surplus duration

convexity

Two somewhat more sophisticated concepts measure the sensitivity of the insurer's assets and liabilities to changes in interest rates. **Duration** is a representative time interval somewhat similar to the average holding period. **Asset duration** is the average time after acquisition until assets (investments) mature; **liability duration** is the average period after policy issuance until a claim is paid. Optimal durations are affected by changes in interest rates. Liability durations also depend on events—like lapse, death rates, and policy loan demand—that are beyond the control of the insurer. **Duration matching** is an attempt to select asset durations that will closely match the cash flows from assets to the flows required by the insurer's liabilities. **Surplus duration** is related to asset duration, liability duration, and the firm's leverage. **Convexity** measures the relative rate of change in the outside market and inside the company as interest rates change. As shown by the curved

line in Figure 12-2, price changes are much greater for lower interest rate changes than they are around high interest rates.

Understanding the confounding effects of interest rate changes permits management to protect a firm's surplus during unfavorable economic and underwriting cycles by implementing safeguards, such as constraints on asset duration compared to liability duration. Ideally, the effect of external events on a company's assets and liabilities will be matched in such a way that the company can remain solvent—preferably profitable—in a wide range of interest rate environments.

Figure 12-2 Value/Interest Rate Relationship Duration versus Convexity

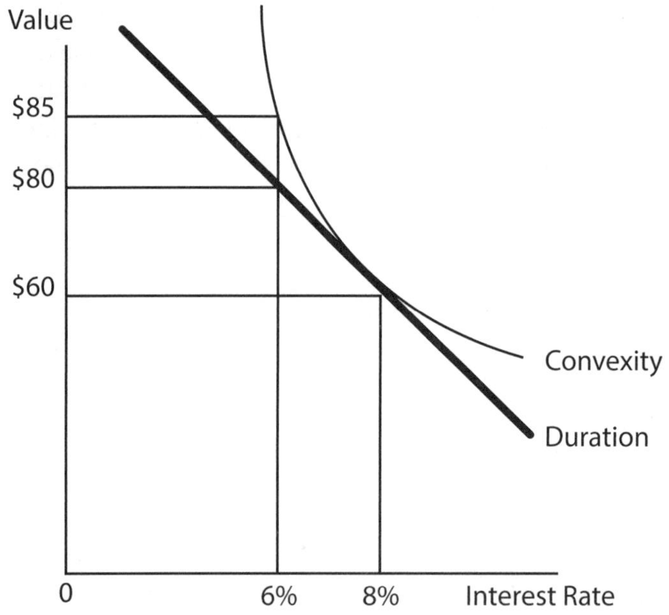

Sources of Surplus

To maintain its financial strength a growing insurance company needs regular additions to its capital. This is particularly true during periods of rapid growth because the costs of establishing a new policy exceed the premium collected in the first year. The primary source of capital is internal and comes from favorable deviations of actual experience from assumed experience on seasoned life insurance policies. External sources of surplus include traditional capital markets and reinsurance.

Matching Asset and Liability Durations

- Objective is to have assets mature when funds are needed to pay liabilities.

- A shortened liability duration may force liquidating assets prematurely at a loss.

- Lengthening the liability duration may result in reinvesting assets at lower returns than would have been available if originally invested for a longer period.

- Both asset and liability durations are subject to forces beyond the control of the insurance company.

- Volatility increases at lower interest rates.

Insurance Operations

savings

The immediate result of profitable operations is an increase in the company's surplus—that is, the company's assets grow more than its liabilities. The primary sources of insurance gains are mortality **savings**, excess interest, and expense savings. The word savings, while somewhat misleading, refers to the amount remaining from more efficient and economical operations than were assumed when setting the premiums. Often the savings reflect margins built intentionally into the premiums to produce surplus. Interest earnings greater than the assumed rate usually contribute the largest portion of insurer gains for policies that develop a cash value. This includes the realization of capital gains—that is, the sale of an asset for more than its book value. Any transaction that increases assets more than liabilities or decreases liabilities to a greater extent than assets—voluntary policy terminations at early durations,[1] for example—is a source of surplus. Supplementary features of the insurance contract, such as disability income and accidental death provisions, are examples of other sources of surplus.

---

1. Surrender values are usually less than reserves during the early years of a policy. Under the Standard Nonforfeiture Law, they may be less until the end of the premium-paying period. A policy termination before the surrender value equals the reserve increases surplus since a liability item (reserves) is decreased more than an asset item (cash). The creation of surplus by the termination of policies does not mean that a termination is financially beneficial to the insurer. This is a mismatch of income and expense items of the statutory accounting system mandated by regulators. If the accounting rules required amortization of most acquisition expenses (rather than dealing with those expenses on a cash basis), the reverse might be true.

Insurers also make assumptions about future expense levels (including anticipated inflation) when setting premium rates. If actual expenses remain lower than the assumed level this savings will contribute to surplus.

It is possible, of course, that a company will experience a loss with respect to one or more of the assumptions that enter the gross premium. For example, while AIDS deaths in the 1990s have not been sufficient in number to seriously affect the solvency of the life insurance industry, they have produced higher than expected mortality rates in some geographic regions and age categories, particularly for group insurance. These increased death rates, combined with generally declining interest rates during the last few years, make it much harder for life insurance companies to earn the profits anticipated.

Traditional Capital Markets

Financing sources for noninsurance companies usually include debt and equity (the corporation issues bonds or stock). Theoretically these same options are available for some insurance companies. Insurance companies usually buy bonds, however, rather than issue them. The issuance of new stock, a common approach to raising capital, is available only to stock insurance companies. Because mutual companies do not have stock, they cannot raise capital by issuing stock.

demutualization

In recent years, converting a mutual insurance company to stock form has become an option for mutual insurance companies wishing to expand their access to capital markets. This process is called **demutualization**. In 1986 Union Mutual Life Insurance Company completed the first demutualization by a healthy life insurance company. The company—now called UNUM Life Insurance Company—raised about $580 million in new capital, roughly doubling its surplus. In 1988 a New York law permitting domestic mutual life insurance companies to convert to stock form took effect. This law addressed many formerly unanswered procedural and regulatory concerns. The Equitable Life Assurance Society of the United States became the first major company to use that law, announcing in the last days of 1990 its intent to pursue demutualization. Equitable obtained the required policyowner approvals for conversion during the first half of 1992. A French insurance company provided a large increase in surplus through the purchase of a large block of the Equitable stock. A more recent example is the demutualization of John Hancock Insurance Company.

Some new developments for insurers in the capital markets are (1) the issuance of unsecured corporate bonds by a mutual company and (2) the sale of part of real estate holdings

to a newly formed real estate investment trust (REIT) sponsored by the insurer and financed by a public sale of the REIT.

Other Sources of Surplus

Reinsurance can serve as a major source of (it is perhaps more accurate to say substitute for) capital in the insurance business. Some studies show that the availability of reinsurance diminishes the importance of organizational form (stock or mutual) that a company uses, primarily because it equalizes access to capital. Annual renegotiation of reinsurance treaties can be used to transfer more of a company's financial risk to outsiders when adequate internal capital is not available to support that risk. From a financial perspective, the company buying reinsurance is "borrowing" the use of the reinsurance company's capital. (See chapter 20 for a discussion of reinsurance arrangements.) While the analogy is imperfect, reinsurance serves a function similar to a line of credit. In the aggregate, the capacity of the insurance industry is enhanced by an amount up to the total capital available through the reinsurance market.

DISTRIBUTION OF SURPLUS

A profitable insurance operation produces a company with increasing surplus. The board of directors must determine how to allocate newly earned surplus among several competing needs. The most important of these are as follows:

- the need to finance company growth
- the need in some companies to provide investors with an acceptable return on their investment
- the need to remain competitive by returning a portion of premiums to policyowners whose policies generated those profits or retained surplus

Surplus to Meet A Company's Capital Needs

Unless the board of directors takes specific action, contributions to surplus remain in the company's surplus account. This increases the company's net worth (defined as the difference between the total assets and the total liabilities) and strengthens its financial position. From the surplus account, monies can be used to pay off debts or to pay the expenses associated with writing new business. Financing company growth undoubtedly presents the life insurer's largest internal demand for capital, regardless of whether it is a mutual or a stock company.

Return for Financial Investment

The shareholders in a stock company expect financial rewards for their investments. Rewards can take the form of dividends on the stock increases, increases in the market price per share, or some combination of the two. Only a portion of an insurance company's profits is normally distributed to stockholders in cash. The remainder stays in the company's capital account to finance the acquisition of new business and to provide a financial buffer against adverse contingencies. Such additions also tend to increase the share price of the company's stock.

Return of Premium Overcharge

dividend

A portion of the earnings from an insurance operation (stock and mutual companies) results from the company's deliberate overcharge for its participating products. The policy **dividend** refunds this amount to the customers who paid the higher price for participating insurance. It is important to differentiate between stockholder dividends and policyowner dividends.

divisible surplus

No predetermined relationship exists between the surplus gains in a particular year and the dividends returned to policyowners. The gains enhance the appropriate surplus account as they accrue, and at the end of the calendar year the directors of the company, based on information then available and in light of a number of factors, decide what portion of the total surplus should be distributed in dividends the following year and what portion should be retained as an increase in contingency reserves. The board of directors earmarks the amount as divisible surplus, and paying that sum becomes a formal obligation of the company. Once set aside by action of the directors, the **divisible surplus** becomes a liability and is no longer part of the company's surplus.

The decision to set aside funds for dividends requires an insurance company's managers to balance the need for a general contingency fund against the advantages of pursuing a liberal dividend policy. In any well-managed company the share of the total surplus to be distributed always involves careful consideration of the impact on the company's safety cushion. In some companies the importance attached to this component of financial operations is such that needed surplus is decided upon first, and the remainder becomes the divisible surplus.

given set of gross premiums, surrender values, and dividends with realistic assumptions about mortality, interest earnings, expenses, and voluntary policy terminations. The result shows whether the accumulated asset shares for the various plans, ages at issue, and durations meet the requirements of both adequacy and equity. An existing dividend scale should be tested periodically to assure that it meets the same objectives.

Over the life of any block of policies the aggregate dividends distributed will be somewhat less than the amount contributed to surplus. This is necessary if the company is to accumulate and maintain a contingency reserve sufficient to protect it from its liabilities. That is an objective of well-managed companies. As reserves increase, whether from the sale of new policies or the natural progression under old policies, the absolute size of the contingency reserve must also increase. Apart from interest earnings on the contingency reserve or "free surplus,"[3] the only source of such funds is the current earnings from policies. Therefore, even over the long term, something less than the net additions to surplus from all blocks of policies will be returned to policyowners as dividends. Equity demands that each group of policies bear a share of this cost. This is just another way of saying that a policy's asset share should eventually exceed the reserve and that management expects each policy to make a permanent contribution to the company's surplus.

Other Issues

The dividend process described here is simplified to deal with only the major sources of surplus. Some elements of cost and price—such as policy size, smoking behavior, and gender—are commonly included today in premium computations. Should experience vary for these populations, some adjustment may be needed in the dividend scale. Furthermore, this discussion ignores several refinements that may be introduced in the interest of equity or under the pressures of competition.

Ordinary (immediate) annuities present unique problems in pricing and dividend policy. First, expense loading from any single premium contract can arise only in the first year. Second, as reserves under such policies decline with duration, excess earnings are likely to diminish each year. Finally, unless an actuary provides for future improvement in annuitant mortality, as with the use of projection factors, declining death rates among annuitants erode any margins in the mortality assumptions and may eventually produce mortality losses, offsetting the declining gain from excess interest.[4] Thus, unless the margins in the

---

3. In many companies interest on these funds is taken into account in determining the excess interest factor.

4. The mortality element of an annuity dividend formula involves another complication, this one being philosophical in nature. Within a given class of life insurance policies, mortality gains are created by the surviving members of the group, who are credited with the dividends. With a given group of annuitants, the mortality gains, if any,

actuarial assumptions are very conservative, which might produce noncompetitive rates, dividends are seldom used in annuity contracts. When they do appear, they are likely to be small and to become smaller over time.

CHAPTER REVIEW

Key Terms and Concepts

surplus

risk-based capital standards

immunization

duration

asset duration

liability duration

duration matching

surplus duration

convexity

savings

demutualization

dividend

divisible surplus

extra dividends

terminal dividends

surrender dividends

postmortem dividend

contribution plan

three-factor contribution plan

direct recognition dividend scales

Chapter 12 Review Questions

1. What is the purpose of capital (surplus) in any insurance company? [1]

2. Describe top management's key considerations in monitoring the surplus accumulated within a company and deploying it in the best possible directions. [1]

3. Describe the following sources of surplus: (a) internal sources (insurance operations); (b) external sources (traditional capital markets and reinsurance). [2]

4. List and explain the competing needs among which a company's board of directors must determine how to allocate newly earned surplus. [3]

---

are created by those who die, while the dividends are payable to the surviving annuitants. This suggests that mortality gains should be discounted in advance and passed along to all members of the original group by means of a lower premium.

5. Describe the principles that should guide the apportionment of divisible surplus among groups of policyowners. [3]

6. Explain the considerations involved in a company's efforts to maintain its current dividend scale over time. [3]

7. Describe the two patterns that extra dividends may follow and the reasons each may be used. [4]

8. Explain the difference between a terminal dividend and a postmortem dividend. [4]

9. Explain how each of the following components of a dividend is calculated: (a) the mortality contribution; (b) the interest contribution; (c) the loading contribution. [4]

10. Explain why, in reality, total equity cannot be attained in the distribution of divisible surplus and how, in practice, systems of computing dividends aim to provide equity. [1]

11. Explain how proposed and existing dividend scales are tested. [4]

12. What unique problems in pricing and dividend policy do immediate (ordinary) annuities present? [4]

Chapter 12 Review Answers

1. *The purpose of capital (surplus) in any insurance company is to absorb unexpected upward fluctuations in claims and unexpected downward fluctuations in investment results.*

2. In carrying out their fundamental charge to monitor the surplus accumulated within the company and deploy it in the best possible direction, top managers consider the following processes:

    • assuring that the company meets the minimum statutory capital requirements in the states in which it operates

    • assessing the need for capital beyond those regulatory minimum requirements

    • understanding the relationship between surplus and the investment function

    • evaluating how much surplus is needed and available from various sources

    Growing out of this surplus-management process is the need for a system to distribute some surplus back to policyowners.

3. a. The primary sources of insurance gains are mortality savings, excess interest, and expense savings. The word savings refers to the amount remaining from more efficient and economical operations than were assumed when setting the premiums. Often the savings reflect margins built intentionally into the premiums to produce surplus. Interest earnings greater than the assumed rate usually contribute the largest portion of insurer gains for policies that develop a cash value. This includes the realization of capital gains—that is, the sale of an asset for more than its book value. Any transaction that increases assets more than liabilities or decreases liabilities to a greater extent that assets—voluntary policy terminations at early durations, for example— is a source of surplus. Supplementary features of the insurance contract, such as disability income and accidental death provisions, are examples of other sources or surplus. Insurers also make assumptions about future expense levels (including antici-pated inflation) when setting premium rates. If actual expenses remain lower than the assumed level, this savings will contribute to surplus.

    b. In terms of the traditional capital markets, stock insurance companies can raise capital by issuing new stock. Because mutual companies do not have stock, they cannot raise capital by issuing stock. In recent years, converting a mutual insurance company to stock form (demutualization) has become an option for mutual insurance companies wishing to expand their access to capital markets. Also, some new developments for insurers in the capital markets are (1) the issuance of unsecured corporate bonds by a mutual company and (2) the sale of part of real estate holdings to a newly formed real estate investment trust (REIT) sponsored by the insurer and financed by a public sale of the REIT.

        Reinsurance can serve as a major source of (it is perhaps more accurate to say substi-tute for) capital in the insurance business. Annual renegotiation of reinsurance treaties

between classes and among individual policies within classes. As a minimum standard of equity, surplus distribution should consider the sources from which surplus arises and should not be oversimplified to cause injustice to any group of policyowners.

| | | | Mortality Return per $100k Amount at Risk | Loading Return Factors | | | | | Loading Return (5) × 1,301 + (6) + (7) | Total Divi-dend (8) + (9) + (10) |
| | | | | Percent of Gross Premium $1,301 | Per Policy | Per $100k Face | Interest Return 0.0075× | Mortality Return (3) × (4) / 100k | | |
Year	Initial Reserve	Amount at Risk								
(1)	(2)	(3)	(4)	(5)	(6)	(7)	(8)	(9)	(10)	(11)
1	$851	$99284	$64	0.0%	$2.00	$10	$6.38	$63.70	$12.00	$82
2	1567	98536	66	0.5	2.50	180	11.75	64.86	189.01	266
3	2315	97753	68	1.0	3.00	180	17.36	66.64	196.01	280
4	3098	96937	71	1.5	3.50	180	23.24	68.68	203.02	295
5	3914	96086	74	2.0	4.00	180	29.36	70.95	210.02	310
6	4765	95202	78	2.5	4.50	180	35.74	74.10	217.03	327
7	5649	94284	83	3.0	5.00	180	42.37	77.76	224.03	344
8	6567	93333	88	3.5	5.50	180	49.25	81.90	231.04	362
9	7518	92347	94	4.0	6.00	180	56.39	86.49	238.04	381
10	8504	91329	100	4.5	7.00	180	63.78	91.50	245.55	401
11	9522	90277	107	5.0	8.00	180	71.42	96.30	253.05	421
12	10574	89190	114	6.0	9.00	180	79.31	101.78	267.06	448
13	11661	88067	122	7.0	10.00	180	87.46	107.01	281.07	476
14	12784	86908	130	8.0	11.00	180	95.88	112.58	295.08	504
15	13943	85712	138	9.0	12.00	180	104.57	118.16	309.09	532
16	15139	84479	146	10.0	13.00	180	113.54	123.48	323.10	560
17	16372	83205	155	11.0	14.00	180	122.79	129.06	337.11	589
18	17646	81893	165	12.0	15.00	180	132.35	134.89	351.12	618
19	18958	80540	174	13.0	16.00	180	142.19	140.40	365.13	648
20	20311	79150	186	14.0	17.00	180	152.33	147.39	379.14	679

Table 12-1 Dividends for First 20 Years of Ordinary Life Policy, Male Aged 32, Net Premium Based on 1980 CSO Table and 5.5% Interest

Testing the Dividend Scale

Just as gross premiums and surrender values are tested by asset share calculations prior to adoption, so are proposed and existing dividend scales tested. Such a test combines a

The interest factor of the dividend formula seeks to credit each policy with its share of a company's investment earnings above the sum needed to meet its obligations. The evolution of computer technology has expanded the extent to which a particular policy's interest contribution can be traced. The strict equity of considering the different times of premium payments and different interest rates apportioned to the cash value portion of premiums paid under universal life contracts is approximated in participating whole life contracts. For example, because policy loans can cost the insurance company much of the investment return it could otherwise earn, some companies vary the dividend on an individual policy depending on whether a policy loan was outstanding over the dividend year. Loans are very popular during periods of high interest rates, and they can be particularly costly at those times because they preclude the insurer from reinvesting the funds at the higher yields available. Thus, if each policyowner receives dividends according to identical scales, those who do not borrow subsidize those who do borrow.

direct recognition dividend scales

The growing use of **direct recognition dividend scales** since the late 1970s is an excellent example of attempts to increase the equity of dividend distributions. Direct recognition means that policy choices made by an individual policyowner are reflected in the policy dividends returned to that policyowner.

However, total equity cannot be attained in reality. Mortality experience, for example, varies widely with duration, occupation, amount of insurance, and plan of insurance. It is impractical to distinguish among these factors in computing the individual contributions to surplus from favorable mortality. Many factors affect the rate of expense, including the size of the policy and the variation in the premium tax rates among the different states. Recognizing all these factors would unduly complicate the dividend formula. Also, the divisible surplus will not, except by accident, equal the total "profits" or aggregate contributions to surplus. It is affected by considerations unconnected to the sources of surplus that cannot be related to individual policies or even to classes of policies. Therefore, a method of distribution that calls for the computation of individual contributions to surplus would require modification to equal the sum available for distribution. Such modification is likely to disturb the relationship between the assumed contributions from different sources.

Thus, under practical conditions it is not possible to refund the excess payments of individual policyowners exactly. In such matters policies must be dealt with as groups or classes. The system of computing refunds or dividends aims to approximate equity

---

reserved for the method described herein as the three-factor contribution plan.

Table 12-1 shows how dividends might be determined for the first 20 years of an ordinary life policy issued to a 32-year-old male. The following experience factors have been chosen arbitrarily:

• The mortality return is based on actual mortality being 65 percent of the table value at age 32 and increasing one-half point per year of attained age up to age 75. The mortality savings then range from 35 percent at age 32 to 24.5 percent at age 51, the 20th year. (These same assumptions were used in the example earlier in this chapter.)

• The interest return reflects an excess interest factor of 0.75 percent times the initial reserve for each of the durations.

• The loading return is composed of the three factors, each graded by duration to illustrate the heavier expenses at early durations. For example, the 16 percent of gross premium loading is assumed to be released at the rate of .5 percent per year up to the 11th year and then increases by a full percent each year thereafter. These patterns have been chosen arbitrarily to illustrate the development of the dividend scale pattern. The pattern may vary by company, policy, or trends of the times.

Note that the rates used in the dividend computation represent actual experience of the company. They will always differ from the assumptions that were used to compute premiums, reserves, and surrender values.

GENERAL EQUITY OF DIVIDEND SCALE

contribution plan

three-factor contribution plan

Experts generally agree that a system of surplus distribution should, to the extent possible, be equitable. As explained earlier, equity is best served by a dividend formula that allocates to each policy its share of surplus in the proportion it has contributed to that surplus. To attain equity most companies in the United States and Canada employ a system of surplus distribution called a **contribution plan**. For reasons of simplicity noted above, consideration is usually limited to the three major sources of surplus: mortality savings, excess interest, and loading savings. A distribution plan that recognizes only these sources of surplus is called a **three-factor contribution plan**.[2]

---

2.   There are three other methods of apportioning surplus that are based on the contribution concept: experience premium method, asset share method, and fund method. In common usage, the term contribution method is

net amount at risk, multiplied by the 1980 CSO Male Table rate at age 41, 3.29 per 1,000, which yields $301. The actual mortality charge is the percentage of actual to expected mortality for age 41 multiplied by the tabular cost of insurance. The rate of mortality used in the calculation of an actual dividend varies by attained age and reflects the company's own mortality experience during recent years. If we assume the actual rate of mortality at age 32 is 65 percent of the 1980 CSO Male Table rate and that the percentage increases by one-half point for each year of attained age, the assumed actual rate of mortality at age 41 would be 69.5 percent of the rate reflected in the table. The mortality saving at attained age 41 is 30.5 percent of the tabular rate. Therefore, the mortality charge would be $209, which, deducted from $301, gives a mortality saving for the year of $92.

The interest contribution at all durations is calculated by multiplying the initial reserve for the year in question plus the net level premium by the difference between the assumed rate of interest and the so-called dividend rate of interest. While the latter will bear a close relationship to the actual rate of interest the company earned in recent years, it might deviate in either direction in any particular year. In the illustration, the dividend rate of 6.25 percent produces an excess interest factor of 0.75 percent when compared to the assumed rate of 5.5 percent. Applying this factor to the sum of the initial reserve of $7,653 produces an excess interest contribution of $64 for the year.

The loading in our example is 16 percent of the gross premium, $2.00 per $1,000 of insurance, and a per-policy expense of $42. Of this, 2.4 percent of the gross premium, $1.25 per $1,000 of insurance, and $3.00 per policy were included intentionally to provide future dividends. The difference between actual expenses and the policy's loading for our $100,000 example policy provides a savings of $245. This amount is available for dividend distribution, a portion of which may well have been included in the loading formula for that specific purpose. The assumptions described in this dividend illustration result in a total dividend of $401—that is, $92 from mortality savings plus $64 from excess interest, plus $245 from expense savings.

Example

Dividend Elements

$ 92 mortality savings

64 excess interest

+ 245 expense savings

$401 total dividend

the year, thus giving effect to the arbitrary assumption that a company pays death claims at the end of the year. The loss of interest involved in this assumption is charged to surplus.

ILLUSTRATIVE DIVIDEND COMPUTATION

This section illustrates the principles explained earlier in this chapter through a hypothetical dividend calculation. Details of computing the 10th-year dividend of a $100,000 ordinary life policy issued to a male aged 32 are shown in the following example.

Example

Illustrative dividend calculation for a $100,000 ordinary life policy issued to a male aged 32 (reserve basis: full net level premium reserves, 1980 CSO Male Table, and 5.5% interest).

(1)	Gross premium: $12.51 × 100 + $50 policy fee	$1,301
(2)	Net level premium: 100 × 8.51	851
(3)	Loading: (1) – (2)	450
(4)	Mortality contribution to 10th-year dividend	
	(a) 9th-year terminal reserve	7,653
	(b) 10th-year terminal reserve	8,671
	(c) Tabular cost of insurance:	301
	{[100,000 – 4(b)]/1,000} × 3.29	
	(d) Mortality charge: 0.695 × 4(c)	209
	(e) Return of tabular mortality: 4(c) – 4(d)	92
(5)	Interest contribution: (0.0625 – 0.055) × [(2) + 4(a)]	64
(6)	Loading contribution	
	(a) Expense charge: 0.115 × (1) + 35.00 + 20.00	205
	(b) Return of loading: (3) – 6(a) 245	
(7)	Total dividend for the 10th-year: 4(e) + (5) + 6(b)	401

The steps in the calculation are as follows: The gross premium for the policy in this example is $12.51 per $1,000, plus a policy fee of $50. This premium is the net level premium ($8.51 per $1,000), computed using mortality from the 1980 CSO Male Table and 5.5 percent interest, plus loading. The loading—developed in Table 13-1 of chapter 13 and used in this example—is 16 percent of the gross premium, plus $2 per $1,000, plus the policy fee of $50.

The mortality contribution to the 10th-year dividend is the tabular cost of insurance minus the actual mortality charge for the 10th year. The tabular charge in this example is the

Periodic extra dividends, at every 5th year for example, have little justification in theory. Perhaps the only valid reason is that regular dividends are calculated on such a conservative basis that additional surplus remains even after annual dividends are paid. Extra dividends, while improving illustrative net-cost figures over a period of years, are paid only on those policies that remain in force. This is particularly true of a special dividend payable only at the end of 20 years. The 20-year extra dividend is further suspect when used to improve a company's showing in net-cost comparisons.

In Canada companies issue policies under which dividends are apportioned only every 5 years, but the amount of surplus set aside for deferred dividends during each 5-year period must be carried as a liability until paid. Under Canadian practices, it is customary for the company to pay an interim dividend when a policyowner dies during the period of deferral but not upon lapse or surrender.

surrender dividends

Terminal Dividends. Terminal dividends refer to special dividends paid upon termination of a policy through maturity, death, or surrender. Such dividends are normally paid only after the policy has been in force for a specified period of years. **Surrender dividends** are usually a percentage of the surrender value, while mortality and maturity dividends may be a percentage of the face amount of the policy or of the reserve, the percentage varying by plan and duration.

Terminal dividends are available only from companies that subscribe to the philosophy that a withdrawing policyowner should receive back all or a portion of his or her contribution to surplus. Those companies that do not provide terminal dividends—and they are in the majority—either feel that each policyowner should make a permanent contribution to the company's surplus or they view any attempt to allocate the contingency fund to individual policies or classes of policies as impractical. However, the Standard Nonforfeiture Law requires the payment of surrender dividends whenever the rate of interest used in the calculation of reserves is more than .5 percent less than the rate used in the calculation of surrender values.

postmortem dividend

A terminal dividend payable at death should not be confused with a postmortem dividend. A **postmortem dividend** is payable at death and covers the period between the preceding policy anniversary and the date of death. It may be computed in various ways, but the most common practice is to provide a pro rata portion of the dividend that would have been payable for the full year. Most companies pay postmortem dividends and add the amount to the death proceeds under the policy. A few companies pay the full dividend for

The Desirability of a Nonreducing Dividend Scale

The minimum objective of most companies is to continue the current dividend scale. This usually implies a larger absolute distribution of surplus each year than that of the preceding year. Current additions to surplus historically have been sufficient to support the existing dividend scale. In years when adverse fluctuations in experience do not produce gains, the company may draw on funds accumulated in previous years to avoid reducing the scale. Similarly, in a year when additions to surplus are more than adequate to support the existing dividend scale, the excess often is added to existing surplus in order to avoid the expense and other complications of changing the scale. If, however, a significant disparity develops between the funds needed to maintain the existing scale and those currently available for distribution, and if the disparity is expected to continue over a long period, the board of directors must consider a change in the scale.

Determining whether a change in mortality or interest rates is permanent or temporary normally requires several years. The nature and magnitude of modifying the dividend scale will reflect the directors' judgment about the duration and future course of the relevant trends.

Special Forms of Surplus Distribution

extra dividends

terminal dividends

In most states divisible surplus must be apportioned and distributed annually. However, sufficient theoretical and practical justifications exist for some degree of deferral that most states permit limited departures, under proper safeguards, from the general requirement of annual distributions. These departures take the form of either **extra dividends** or **terminal dividends**.

Extra Dividends. Extra dividends may follow one of two patterns. One is a single payment made after a policy has been in force a specified number of years, usually 5. Another is periodic additional dividends distributed at stated intervals. The single extra payment is usually a substitute for a first-year dividend. From a practical standpoint, this procedure has some distinct advantages and can be justified to some extent on equitable grounds. It reduces the strain of initial expenses and deters voluntary terminations during the early years. It also serves as a special system to assess a larger part of excess first-year expenses against policies that cancel during the first few years.

Guiding Principles in the Distribution of Divisible Surplus

The apportionment of the divisible surplus among the various groups of policyowners is a complex matter and one that should measure up to a set of guiding principles established over many years. The system of distribution should be reasonably simple in operation, equitable, flexible, and understandable by policyowners and the agency force.

Simplicity. For practical reasons the method of distribution should be simple. A complicated formula is troublesome, expensive, and difficult to explain to policyowners and others. A small increase in accuracy may also be more apparent than real. Complicated refinements have only minor significance and are of questionable value.

Equity. The distribution of surplus should be equitable by allocating dividends to each policy on the basis of the proportion it has contributed to the insurer's surplus. Policies cannot be considered individually but must be dealt with on the basis of groups or classes, and the system of computing dividends or other distributions of surplus should be one that aims at approximate equity between classes and among individual policies within classes.

Flexibility. To say that the system of distribution must be adaptable to changing conditions is merely an extension of the statement that the method must be equitable. An insurer attains flexibility by separately recognizing as many sources of surplus as possible, using a formula that permits proper adjustments to the factors involved, and avoiding arbitrary expedients in annual adjustments to dividend scales.

Comprehensibility by Policyowners and Agents. This is a minor consideration, but policyowners occasionally ask about their dividends, particularly if a company has reduced its dividend scale. Such an inquiry may be addressed to the home office or to a field representative. In the interest of good public relations, the formula should afford policyowners an understandable explanation. Certainly the field force should have a general understanding of the sources of surplus and how they combine to produce a dividend scale.

Example

The price competition during the 1980's and early 1990's reduced premium levels and cut back the likelihood of future dividend increases. However, many agents still expected dividend increases to continue as they had in previous decades. When dividends were actually reduced in the 1990's, some policyowners filed lawsuits against life insurers for misleading and deceptive sales practices.

Unrealistic expectations can have costly results.

5. The following principles should guide the apportionment of divisible surplus among groups of policyowners:

    •   Simplicity—For practical reasons, the method of distribution should be simple. A complicated formula is troublesome, expensive, and difficult to explain to policyowners and others.

    •   Equity—The distribution or surplus should be equitable by allocating dividends to each policy on the basis of the proportion it has contributed to the insurer's surplus. Policies cannot be considered individually but must be dealt with on the basis of group or classes, and the system of computing dividends or other distributions of surplus should be one that aims at approximate equity between classes and among individual policies within classes.

    •   Flexibility—To say that the system of distribution must be adaptable to changing conditions is merely an extension of the statement that the method must be equitable. An insurer attains flexibility by separately recognizing as many sources of surplus as possible, using a formula that permits proper adjustments to the factors involved, and avoiding arbitrary expedients in annual adjustments to dividend scales.

    •   Comprehensibility by policyowners and agents—In the interest of good public relations, the formula should afford policyowners an understandable explanation of their dividends. Also, the field force should have a general understanding of the sources of surplus and how they combine to produce a dividend scale.

6. The minimum objective of most companies is to continue the current dividend scale. This usually implies a larger absolute distribution of surplus each year than that of the preceding year. Current additions to surplus historically have been sufficient to support the existing dividend scale. In years when adverse fluctuations in experience do not produce gains, the company may draw on funds accumulated in previous years to avoid reducing the scale. Similarly, in a year when additions to surplus are more than adequate to support the existing dividend scale, the excess often is added to existing surplus in order to avoid the expense and other complications of changing the scale. If, however, a significant disparity develops between the funds needed to maintain the existing scale and those currently available for distribution, and if the disparity is expected to continue over a long period, the board of directors must consider a change in the scale.

can be used to transfer more of a company's financial risk to outsiders when adequate internal capital is not available to support that risk. From a financial perspective, the company buying reinsurance is "borrowing" the use of the reinsurance company's capital. In the aggregate, the capacity of the insurance industry is enhanced by an amount up to the total capital available through the reinsurance market.

4. *The board of directors must determine how to allocate newly earned surplus among several competing needs. The most important of these are as follows:*

   - *the need to finance company growth—Unless the board of directors takes specific action, contributions to surplus remain in the company's surplus account. This increases the company's net worth (defined as the difference between the total assets and the total liabilities) and strengthens its financial position. From the surplus account, monies can be used to pay off debts or to pay the expenses associated with writing new business. Financing company growth undoubtedly presents the life insurer's largest internal demand for capital, regardless of whether it is a mutual or a stock company.*

   - *the need in some companies to provide investors with an acceptable return on their investment. The shareholders in a stock company expect financial rewards for their investments. Rewards can take the form of dividends on the stock, increases in the market price per share, or some combination of the two. Only a portion of an insurance company's profits is normally distributed to stockholders in cash. The remainder stays in the company's capital account to finance the acquisition of new business and to provide a financial buffer against adverse contingencies. Such additions also tend to increase the share price of the company's stock.*

   - *the need to remain competitive by returning a portion of premiums to policyowners whose policies generated those profits or retained surplus. At the end of the calendar year, the directors of the company, based on information then available and in light of a number of factors, decide what portion of the total surplus should be distributed in dividends the following year and what portion should be retained as an increase in contingency reserves. The board of director earmarks the amount as divisible surplus, and paying that sum becomes a formal obligation, a liability, of the company. The decision to set aside fund for dividends requires an insurance company's managers to balance the need for a general contingency fund against the advantages of pursuing a liberal dividend policy. In any well-managed company, the share of the total surplus to be distributed always involves careful consideration of the impact on the company's safety cushion.*

7. *Extra dividends can follow one of two patterns:*

    - *One pattern is a single payment made after a policy has been in force a specified number of years, usually 5. The single extra payment is usually a substitute for a first-year dividend. From a practical standpoint, this procedure has some distinct advantages and can be justified to some extent on equitable grounds. It reduces the strain of initial expenses and deters voluntary terminations during the early years. It also serves as a special system to assess a larger part of excess first-year expenses against policies that cancel during the first few years.*

    - *Another pattern is periodic additional dividends distributed at stated intervals. Periodic extra dividends, at every 5th year, for example, have little justification in theory. Perhaps the only valid reason is that regular dividends are calculated on such a conservative basis that additional surplus remains even after annual dividends are paid.*

8. *Terminal dividends refer to special dividends paid upon termination of a policy through maturity, death, or surrender. Such dividends are normally paid only after the policy has been in force for a specified period of years.*

    A postmortem dividend is payable at death and covers the period between the preceding policy anniversary and the date of death. It may be computed in various ways, but the most common practice is to provide a pro rata portion of the dividend that would have been payable for the full year. Most companies pay postmortem dividends and add the amount to the death proceeds under the policy.

9. a. *The mortality contribution to the dividend for a given year is the tabular cost of insurance for the year minus the actual mortality charge for the year. The tabular cost of insurance is the net amount at risk during the year ([policy face amount—terminal reserve for the year]/1,000) multiplied by mortality rate for the insured's age in that year that is found in the mortality table used in computing the reserve. The actual mortality charge is the percentage of actual-to-expected mortality for the insured's age in that year multiplied by the tabular cost of insurance.*

    b. *The interest contribution at all durations is calculated by multiplying the initial reserve for the year in question (that is, the terminal reserve for the prior year plus the net level premium) by the difference between the assumed rate of interest and the so-called dividend rate of interest.*

    c. *The loading contribution is calculated by subtracting an expense charge reflecting actual expenses from the loading included in the gross premium.*

10. *Total equity cannot be attained in reality for several reasons. Mortality experience, for example, varies widely with duration, occupation, amount of insurance, and plan of insurance. It is impractical to distinguish among these factors in computing the individual contributions to surplus from favorable mortality. Many factors affect the rate of expense, including the size of the policy and the variation in the premium tax rates among the different states. Recognizing all these factors would unduly complicate the dividend formula. Also, the divisible surplus will not, except by accident, equal the total "profits" or aggregate contributions to surplus. It is affected by considerations unconnected to the sources of surplus that cannot be related to individual policies or even to classes of policies. Therefore, a method of distribution that calls for the computation of individual contributions to surplus would require modification to equal the sum available for distribution. Such modification is likely to disturb the relationship between the assumed contributions from different sources.*

  Thus, under practical conditions it is not possible to refund the excess payments of individual policyowners exactly. In such matters, policies must be dealt with as groups or classes. The system of computing refunds or dividends aims to approximate equity between classes and among individual policies within classes. As a minimum standard of equity, surplus distribution should consider the sources from which surplus arises and should not be oversimplified to cause injustice to any group of policyowners.

11. *Proposed dividend scales are tested by combining a given set of gross premiums, surrender values and dividends with realistic assumptions about mortality, interest earnings, expenses, and voluntary policy terminations. The result shows whether the accumulated asset shares for the various plans, ages at issue, and durations meet the requirements of both adequacy and equity. An existing dividend scale also should be tested periodically in this manner to assure that it meets the same objectives.*

12. *Ordinary (immediate) annuities present unique problems in pricing and dividend policy. First, expense loading from any single premium contract can arise only in the first year. Second, as reserves under such policies decline with duration, excess earnings are likely to diminish each year. Finally, unless an actuary provides for future improvement in annuitant mortality, as with the use of projection factors, declining death rates among annuitants erode any margins in the mortality assumptions and may eventually produce mortality losses, offsetting the declining gain from excess interest. Thus, unless the margins in the actuarial assumptions are very conservative, which might produce noncompetitive rates, dividends are seldom used in annuity contracts. When they do appear, they are likely to be small and to become smaller over time.*

Chapter 13

Selection and Classification of Risks—Part I

By Dan M. McGill

Revised by Jeremy S. Holmes and James F. Winberg

Learning Objectives

An understanding of the material in this chapter should enable the student to

1. **Describe the fundamental guiding principles that govern the selection process.**

2. **Describe the various factors that affect proper risk selection.**

surplus

Surplus. The essence of the insurance principle is the sharing of losses by those exposed to a common hazard. This is made possible by contributions to a common fund by those exposed to loss from the common hazard. If the plan is to be scientific and equitable, however, each participant must pay into the fund a sum of money reasonably commensurate with the risk that the insured places on the fund. To accomplish this objective, an insurance company prepares a schedule of premiums that represents its judgment as to the risk inherent in each category of applicants acceptable to the company. The function of the selection process is to determine whether an applicant's degree of risk for insurance is commensurate with the premium established for people in the same classification being considered. If within each broad risk category, various graduations of risk have been established, as would be true of a company that offers either preferred risk or substandard insurance, the evaluation of an application for insurance involves not only selection but also classification.

RISK CLASSIFICATION

It is neither possible nor desirable to establish risk categories in which each component risk represents a loss potential that is identical to that of all the other risks in the category. For practical reasons, the categories must be broad enough to include risks with substantial differences in loss potential. In life insurance the primary basis for the risk classification is the age of the applicant. Yet within each age group, the probability of death is greater for some than for others. These differences in risk stem from physical condition, occupation, sex, and other factors. Some persons in the group might be near death, while others might confidently look forward to a long lifetime comparatively free of bodily ailments. The relative frequencies of mortality expectation represented in any randomly selected group

of people who are the same age approximates the curve shown in Figure 13-1, with 100 percent representing average mortality for the group. The graph reveals a wide range of mortality expectations for a group of persons falling within a risk category measured by age alone. Clearly, all should not be offered insurance on the same terms. Considerations of equity would suggest that those persons subject to the lowest degree of mortality should pay a lower premium than those who represent an average risk; those with greatly impaired longevity expectations should be charged more than the standard premium or even declined altogether.

Figure 13-1
Relative Frequency of Mortality Expectations for a Group of People at Any Particular Age

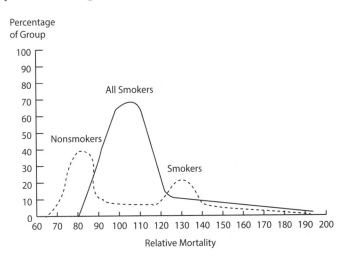

The insurance company must establish a range of mortality expectations within which applicants will be regarded as average risks and hence entitled to insurance at standard rates or, conversely, the limits beyond which applicants will be considered either preferred or substandard and subject to a discount or surcharge. The insurance company should be guided by the principles set forth below.

After the limits for the various risk categories have been established, the company must adopt selection and classification procedures that will enable it to place applicants for insurance into the proper categories. This process is complicated by the fact that applicants for insurance may not fit the curve illustrated in Figure 13-1. That curve depicts the mortality expectations of a randomly selected group, whereas applicants for insurance do not constitute such a group. The observation has frequently been made that a life insurance

company could safely insure the life of everyone who passes by any designated location in a typical American city, so long as the practice does not become public knowledge. Unfortunately, the applications received by a life insurance company do not reflect such randomness. Instead, they are biased by antiselection (or adverse selection). Many who seek insurance have knowledge of an impairment that might be expected to shorten their life span or at least suspect that they have such an impairment that they may conceal. A company's underwriting procedures must either screen out such applicants or classify them into appropriate substandard groups. Thus, it might be argued that the primary purpose of risk selection is to protect the company from antiselection. If there were no antiselection, there would be no need for the underwriting process except to separate and classify substandard risks.

GUIDING PRINCIPLES

There are certain fundamental principles that must govern the selection procedures of an insurance company if it is to operate on a sound basis. Some of these principles are mutually inconsistent, which means that a company must fashion its selection in such a manner as to balance these opposing principles.

Predominance of the Standard Group

The range of mortality expectations within which applicants will be regarded as average and hence entitled to insurance at standard rates should be broad enough to encompass the great percentage of applicants.[1] This is particularly important if the company does not offer substandard insurance. An excessive number of rejections undermines the morale of the agency force, increases the cost of doing business, and causes a loss of goodwill among the insurable public.[2] A disproportionate number of substandard policies may have similar effects. Apart from the practical considerations just mentioned, the broader the base of standard risks, the more stable the mortality experience of the group is likely to be. On the other hand, considerations of equity and competition prevent an unwarranted extension of the standard class.

---

1.   That this principle is being observed in practice is evidenced by the fact that approximately 90 percent of the applicants for ordinary insurance in the United States are currently being accepted at standard rates. Only 3 percent are declined, the remaining 6 to 7 percent being insured at substandard rates.

2.   For the industry as a whole, an excessive number of rejections deprives the insurable public of avaluable economic service and could give rise to demands for governmental intervention.

Balance within Each Risk or Rate Classification

A company must obtain and maintain a proper balance among the risks in each rate classification. This is especially important within the classification of standard risks, which, in view of the principle stated above, is likely to have broad limits. If the overall mortality of the risks in the standard category is to approximate the theoretical average for the group—the goal of most companies—every risk that is worse than average must be offset by one that is better than average. If the range is broad, the margin by which the inferior risk fails to meet the norm for the group should be counterbalanced by the margin by which the offsetting superior risk exceeds the norm. Such precise offsetting or balancing of risks is more of an ideal than an attainable reality. A rough approximation is feasible, however, for a company using the numerical rating system, under which, as explained later, the mortality expectation of individual applications is expressed as a percentage of the average expectation, which is assumed to be 100 percent.

A recent development has constricted the standard range. Companies have developed varying degrees of preferred mortality classes based on such factors as smoking status, tobacco usage in any form, cholesterol level, family history, sports and avocation participation, and other factors. This further refinement of the traditional standard class serves to narrow the remaining standard range not only by removing the superior risks, but also, theoretically at least, by limiting the inferior higher risks allowed in the standard class.

Irrespective of the underwriting procedures used by a company, if each risk classification is overbalanced with risks whose longevity prospects are less favorable than the assumed average for the classification, the company will end up with excessive mortality costs and—unless it enjoys offsetting advantages in other areas of operations—will have difficulty in maintaining its competitive position. The force of this factor will not be diminished by further improving the overall mortality experience of the company unless the rate of improvement is greater than that of its competition—an unlikely situation.

Equity among Policyowners

The manner in which applicants are grouped for rating purposes should not unduly violate considerations of equity. Some discrimination among insureds is unavoidable since all risk classifications must be broad enough to include risks of varying quality. Nevertheless the spread between the best and worst risks within a classification should not be so great as to produce rank injustice.

There is a practical side to this matter. If the spread is too great, the better risks may seek insurance with competing companies whose classification system is more equitable,

leaving the first company with a disproportionate number of inferior risks. Consequently, the first company will have to respond since its premium could be inadequate for the residual group of risks.

Compatibility with Underlying Mortality Assumptions

The foregoing considerations tend to be relative matters, concerned primarily with equity and competition. There is another factor, however, that operates as an absolute regulator of a company's underwriting standards—the mortality assumptions entering into the company's premiums. All mortality tables used by life insurance companies today reflect the experience of insured lives—lives that were subject to some degree of selection. A company's underwriting standards must be at least as effective as those utilized by the companies that supplied the data for the mortality table. Furthermore the companies that pool their mortality experience for the construction of modern mortality tables employ rather rigorous standards of selection. This is a factor of some importance to companies that, in a desire to capture a larger share of the life insurance market, might be tempted to lower their selection standards. The general improvement in mortality that has been such a prominent feature of the insurance scene during recent decades cannot be expected to nullify the long-run consequences of lax underwriting standards.

FACTORS AFFECTING RISK

In order to place an applicant for insurance into the proper risk classification, an insurance company needs reliable information about every factor that might significantly affect an applicant's longevity. As a matter of practice, companies seek applicant information about the following:

- age
- build
- physical condition
- personal history
- family history
- occupation
- residence
- habits

- morals
- sex
- plan of insurance
- economic status
- aviation activities
- avocation
- military service

Age

The applicant's age is the most important single factor on individual mortality expectations. Except for the first few years of life, resistance to disease and injury weakens with the passage of time, and the probability of death increases with age. Age is such a significant measure of the likelihood of death that it is the point of departure in classifying applicants for insurance. Each applicant is placed within the proper age classification and is then compared to the norm for that age to determine insurability.

One might assume that such a vital underwriting factor as age would be subject to verification at the time submitted. Ideally, verification of age is desirable in all cases, but practical considerations mitigate against it. To require proof of age at the time of application would inevitably delay the policy's issue and would be a source of irritation to the applicant. The agency force would object to the requirement, since many applicants would be unable or unwilling to submit documentary proof of their dates of birth. Therefore, it is customary to accept the life insurance applicant's statement of age unless there is reason to believe that it is a misstatement.

Neither is it customary to require documentation of age at the time of a claim settlement unless the company has reason to question the accuracy of the stated date of birth. A typical circumstance in which a company would require verification of age would be if there are conflicting dates of birth on two or more documents. If a misstatement is discovered after the policy has become a claim, the amount of the proceeds is adjusted in accordance with the misstatement-of-age clause.

The situation is different with an immediate annuity. Under such a contract, the relationship between the annuitant's age and the amount of the periodic payments is so direct and immediate that proof of age is required at the time the annuity is purchased.

Age Documentation

- Proof of age is not generally required for underwriting life insurance.

- Persons who purchase immediate annuities may be required to prove their age at the time of purchases.

The age of the applicant enters into a company's underwriting considerations in another respect. For reasons that will be explained later in this chapter, all companies have upper age limits beyond which they will not write insurance on any basis and somewhat lower limits for writing certain types of policies, such as term insurance. The absolute limit may be as low as 60 or as high as 95 or more. Under such circumstances, the age of the applicant

may bar acceptability to the company on any basis. In other words, age alone—regardless of the other facts of the case—may render a person uninsurable. For that reason, a mis-statement of age that induces a company to issue a policy it would not otherwise issue is grounds for rescission if discovered by the company during the contestable period. Companies also have special underwriting rules for children and seniors, under which age may be an absolute determinant of insurability.

Build

The applicant's build—the relationship between height, weight, and girth—is one of the basic determinants of mortality expectation. This was one of the first discoveries in the area of medical selection. The earliest attempts to arrive at the ideal relationship between height and weight were rather crude, some drawing their inspiration from the physical proportions of certain ancient Greek athletes as revealed by statues dating back to the third century BC. Two statues in particular were considered to represent ideal proportions: The Gladiator and *Bronze Tumbler*.

The first comprehensive statistical study of the relationship between build and mortality covered the experience on policies issued by prominent life insurance companies from 1885 through 1908 and was published in 1913 as the *MedicoActuarial Mortality Investigation*. The findings of this study, as refined and supplemented by subsequent investigations, served as the basis for the build tables used by life insurance companies in this country for the next several decades. These tables were eventually supplanted by the Build and Blood Pressure Study of 1959, derived from findings of an investigation by the Society of Actuaries that encompassed the ordinary policy issues of 26 leading companies from 1935 through 1953. These tables remained in use until 1980 when most companies adopted tables based on the Build Study of 1979 (see Table 13-1).

Compared to the 1959 tables, the 1980 tables raised the ranges of acceptable weight for shorter men and women. The lower portion of the table shows various combinations of height and weight, along with the average weight for each height. The upper portion of the table shows the mortality debits associated with each combination of height and weight in intervals of 25 points. As a group, people can be expected to experience mortality 25 percent higher than normal if they fall within the first overweight column. Thus an applicant in that classification would be assigned a debit of 25 points for purposes of the numerical rating system described in chapter 18. Build becomes a neutral factor when the weight is average or only slightly underweight or overweight. Beyond the average classification, debits are assessed, and the maximum debit for the age category in Table 13-1 is 300 points. There is a special juvenile build table for people under 15. (There are also other build tables in common use that differ in both format and substance from the one presented here.)

Table 1 Adult Build Table											
Ht.	Avg. Male Weight	Avg. Female Weight	+25	+50	+75	+100	+125	+150	+200	+250	+300
Ft. In.	Lbs.	Lbs.	Lbs.	Lbs.	Lbs.	Lbs.	Lbs.	Lbs.	Lbs.	Lbs.	Lbs.
4'8"	121	105	180	190	200	215	220	230	240	245	255
4'9"	124	108	185	195	205	215	225	235	245	255	260
4'10"	127	112	190	200	210	220	230	240	250	255	265
4'11"	130	116	195	205	215	225	235	245	255	260	270
5'0"	133	118	195	205	220	230	240	250	255	265	275
5'1"	136	122	205	210	225	235	245	250	260	270	280
5'2"	139	125	205	215	230	235	245	255	265	275	285
5'3"	143	129	210	220	230	245	255	265	275	280	290
5'4"	147	132	220	225	240	250	260	270	280	290	300
5'5"	151	135	225	235	245	255	265	275	285	295	305
5'6"	155	138	230	240	250	260	270	285	295	305	315
5'7"	159	143	235	245	255	270	280	290	300	310	320
5'8"	163	146	240	250	265	275	285	300	310	320	330
5'9"	167	151	250	260	270	285	295	305	320	330	340
5'10"	172	154	255	265	280	290	305	315	325	335	345
5'11"	176	158	260	275	285	300	310	325	335	345	355
6'0"	181	162	270	280	295	305	320	330	340	355	365
6'1"	185	166	275	290	300	315	325	340	350	360	370
6'2"	190	169	285	300	310	325	335	345	360	370	380
6'3"	195	173	290	305	320	330	345	355	365	380	390
6'4"	201	177	300	315	325	340	350	365	375	390	400
6'5"	207	180	305	320	335	345	360	370	385	400	410
6'6"	213	184	315	330	340	355	365	380	395	405	415
6'7"	219		320	335	350	365	375	390	405	415	425
6'8"	225		330	345	360	370	385	400	410	425	435
6'9"	231		335	350	365	380	395	410	425	435	450
6'10"	237		345	360	375	385	400	415	430	440	460
6'11"	243		355	370	385	390	410	420	435	450	465

With overweight male applicants, the company is also interested in the distribution of the excess weight. This involves a comparison of the chest (expanded) with the abdominal girth. Among well-built men of average height, the chest measurement (expanded) normally exceeds the abdominal measurement by two inches; this relationship is likely to be reversed among overweight persons. Insurance companies have prepared charts that assign debits for abdominal measurements in excess of chest measurements. The number of points depends on the person's age, the percentage he is overweight, and the number of inches by which the one measurement exceeds the other. Credits, derived the same way, are assigned when chest measurements are in excess of the abdominal girth. Under the numerical rating system, it is possible for an applicant to be credited with 20 points for a favorable relationship between his chest and girth or debited 70 points for an unfavorable one. Taking chest and abdominal measurements also enables a company to check on the accuracy of reported weights.

Physical Condition

Next in general importance is the applicant's physical condition. In the short run, this factor may outweigh all others in importance. In evaluating an application for insurance, the company wishes to know whether there are any impairments of body or mind that would tend to shorten the life expectancy of the applicant. Questions designed to elicit information on the applicant's physical status are included in the application. If a sizable amount of insurance is involved, the information is also confirmed and supplemented by a medical examination and laboratory testing. The primary purpose of the medical examination is to detect any malfunctioning of vital organs. The heart and other parts of the circulatory system are subjected to special scrutiny.

Tests for Heart Disease or Impairment

Impairment of the heart may be evidenced by subjective symptoms—shortness of breath or pain in the chest—or by objective symptoms—changes in the quality of the heart sounds, murmurs, enlargement of the heart, persistently rapid or slow pulse, irregular pulse, poor reaction to exercise, abnormal blood pressure, or abnormalities revealed by X ray and electrocardiogram.[3]

---

3.   Contrary to the general impression, a normal tracing on an electrocardiogram cannot be accepted as conclusive proof of the nonexistence of a heart irregularity since the valves, and even the muscles, of the heart may be defective without affecting the transmission of the electrical impulses recorded on the electrocardiogram.

One of the most common manifestations of heart impairment is murmurs. A murmur is any sound other than those associated with the normal closing of the heart valves. Functional murmurs are considered harmless and are consequently of no significance to the underwriter; organic murmurs indicate damage to some part of the heart tissue. The problem is distinguishing between the two. Organic murmurs are regarded as serious and may cause the applicant to be rated highly or declined altogether. True functional murmurs are not rated, but if there is any doubt about their cause or origin, provision may be made for some extra mortality.

Enlargement of the heart (cardiomegaly) is a condition of underwriting significance, since it is nature's way of compensating for damages to valves or other sections of the heart mechanism. Before 1979, extra mortality of 50 to 100 percent had been anticipated from an enlarged heart, without any other evidence of disease. The fallacy of that rule was demonstrated by the Blood Pressure Study of 1979, which is the basis for blood pressure underwriting by most companies. This study covered about 4.35 million policies issued from 1950 through 1971 that were traced from 1954 policy anniversaries to 1972 policy anniversaries.

The findings of the study indicated lower extra mortality associated with hypertension than did the study published 20 years earlier. Specifically, among men with borderline blood pressures, regardless of treatment, the mortality ratios in the Blood Pressure Study of 1979 were about 20 percentage points lower than in the Build and Blood Pressure Study of 1959. The corresponding mortality ratios for high blood pressures were from 30 to 50 percentage points lower than in the earlier study. Among women with borderline hypertension, regardless of treatment, the mortality ratios were generally not much different from those in the 1959 study, but the corresponding mortality ratios for the upper range of high blood pressure were more than 50 percentage points lower than in the earlier study. This is believed to reflect the effects of antihypertensive treatment after issue of insurance.

High blood pressure may be a symptom of a condition that impairs longevity. It is particularly associated with kidney ailments. A combination of overweight and hypertension is always regarded seriously. Low blood pressure can usually be disregarded unless it is abnormally low or associated with some definite impairment, such as tuberculosis or congestive heart failure. High blood pressure that responds to treatment by returning to normal levels may receive favorable underwriting consideration, provided normal blood pressure levels are maintained for a reasonable period (one to two years).

Low Blood Pressure

- Low blood pressure by itself is not generally considered a high risk factor.

- Low blood pressure associated with either congestive heart failure or tuberculosis is considered a high risk factor.

The systolic pressure is more susceptible to emotion than the diastolic, so diastolic pressure is considered to be a better measure of the constant strain on the heart. (Systolic pressure is the higher pressure created by heart contractions, and the lower diastolic pressure is the residual reading created by blood in the body without the added pressure of a heart contraction.) Insurance experience indicates that both should be taken into consideration, and if both are higher than normal, the mortality rate will be greater than if only one of the two is out of line. For people at advanced ages, however, the systolic reading assumes more significance.

The condition of the circulatory system can also be evaluated by the pulse rate, normally 60 to 80 beats per minute. A rapid pulse is unfavorable, because it indicates that the heart has to work harder than usual to meet the body's needs. This may be a sign of an inefficient or impaired heart, an infection, or any other abnormal condition within the body that demands an extra supply of blood. An occasional rapid pulse can be overlooked for underwriting purposes, but a pulse rate that is persistently over 90 is regarded as significant. A rate persistently between 90 and 100 indicates mortality about 50 percent above normal, while a rate between 100 and 110 results in almost 200 percent above normal mortality. In general, a slow pulse is a sign of an efficient heart and is viewed as a favorable sign. An irregular pulse, or one that is slow to return to normal after exercise, is regarded unfavorably.

Blood Tests

Blood profile tests have gained added importance with the discovery of Acquired Immune Deficiency Syndrome (AIDS). The bleak outlook for those infected with the Human Immunosuppressive Virus (HIV) has mandated extensive random testing of insurance applicants. In turn this nearly universal blood testing has provided insurers with additional useful information regarding applicants' renal and liver function and blood lipids (fats, oils and waxes). The availability of this additional information has facilitated the proliferation of products offering preferred premium classifications.

Urinalysis

A standard feature of all medical examinations is the urinalysis. This important diagnostic procedure has a three-fold purpose: (1) to measure the functional capacity of the kidneys, (2) to detect infections or other abnormal conditions of the kidneys, and (3) to discover impairments of other vital organs of the body.[4] The ability of the kidneys to concentrate liquids is revealed by the amount of water in the urine, which is measured by the specific gravity test. Other tests, not a part of the standard urinalysis, measure the ability of the kidneys to excrete. The urine is examined chemically and microscopically for the presence of albumin, pus, casts, or red blood cells, which would indicate a diseased condition of the kidneys.

The presence of an undue amount of sugar in the urine suggests the possibility of diabetes, a condition characterized by an inability to metabolize carbohydrates and caused by a deficiency of insulin. The urinalysis may also reveal abnormalities of the bladder, prostate, and other sections of the urinary tract. A kidney condition revealed by an urinalysis may point to a circulatory ailment, such as heart disease or arteriosclerosis, since there is ample evidence that a close relationship exists between kidney and circulatory impairments. The urinalysis is also used to screen for the use of illicit drugs such as cocaine and marijuana. Urine testing for the presence of antibodies to HIV is also available.

In addition to the foregoing tests, the medical examiner carefully checks the other organs of the body for evidence of disease or functional disturbance, giving special attention to any factor or condition that might be related to any previous impairment disclosed by the applicant's medical history.

---

4.   The urinalysis is considered to be such a significant diagnostic procedure that the medical examiner is required to certify as to the authenticity of the specimen; for certain combinations of age and amount of insurance, the specimen may have to be forwarded to the home office for chemical analysis and microscopic examination.

Urinalysis Can Detect

- kidney problems

- infections

- sugar in the urine (possible diabetes)

- marijuana

- cocaine

- HIV antibodies

- tobacco

Personal History

The applicant's personal history sheds important light on his or her acceptability to the company. Consequently, the person to be insured is asked to provide details about his or her health record, past habits, previous environment, and insurance status on the application for insurance.

The applicant's health record is usually the most important of the personal history factors. Complete information about previous illnesses, injuries, and operations may indicate the necessity for special additional tests or examinations. Particular emphasis is placed on recent illnesses and operations, and it is customary for the company to contact the attending physician or physicians for the medical details that normally would not be known to the applicant and might have a bearing upon insurability. The medical examination findings need to be supplemented by the subjective feelings and symptoms of the applicant. It is not the practice to consider an application from any person who is scheduled for diagnostic testing or surgery, currently under treatment for any condition, or not fully recovered from any illness.

The company also wants to know whether the applicant has ever been addicted to the use of drugs or alcohol, because there is always a possibility that the "cure" will prove to be only temporary. The past abuse may have caused irrevocable damage to one or more body systems. The personal history may reveal that the applicant has only recently left a hazardous or unhealthful occupation, raising the possibility that he or she may retain ill effects from the job or might return to the job in the future. It may also disclose that the applicant has changed residence to improve his or her health or has had intimate association with a person who has a contagious disease such as tuberculosis.

Finally, the company wants to know whether the applicant has ever been refused insurance by any other company or offered insurance on rated terms. An affirmative answer would indicate a prior impairment that might still be present. Information as to existing insurance also enables the company to judge whether the amount of insurance, existing and proposed, bears a reasonable relationship to the applicant's needs and financial resources.

Family History

Family history is considered significant because certain characteristics are hereditary. Build follows family lines, and to some extent, so do structural qualities of the heart and other organs. A greater than average susceptibility to infectious diseases may also be inherited. Hence, the applicant is asked to provide information about the ages and state of health of parents and brothers and sisters if they are living, or if deceased, their ages at death and the causes of death.

Long-lived parents and siblings at one time were looked at as assuring a long life for an applicant, even though he or she was somewhat overweight or had some other impairment that would normally have been placed in the category of borderline risks. On the other hand, an applicant from a short-lived family, unless the deaths resulted from accidents, had to be better than average in other respects in order to be insured at standard rates. Except for cardiovascular-renal diseases and to a lesser (and declining) degree, tuberculosis, considerably less emphasis is now placed on family history with the exception of preferred-risk programs. This is because of the unreliability of family history details recited by the applicant and the difficulty of tracing the influence of heredity.

There is a tendency, which can be demonstrated statistically, for the applicant to exaggerate the ages of family members when they died. Unless his or her parents and siblings are dead or dying, the applicant generally reports them to be in good health; instances of hypertension, diabetes, and other impairments that would be regarded as significant by the home office underwriters are usually not disclosed. Furthermore, it is not feasible to follow up on the applicant's family record. Even if the facts were accurately reported, there would still be insufficient evidence to measure the true impact of heredity on longevity. Only data concerning parents and siblings are usually required, whereas hereditary influences may extend back to grandparents and great-grandparents. Moreover, the influence of heredity may not have an impact until an individual is aged 60 or older, which is too late to be useful in evaluating the application of a younger person whose family record is relatively immature.

Despite the foregoing inadequacies, it has been determined that if a group of applicants—all free of any known personal qualities that would adversely affect their longevity—is divided into classes on the basis of their family histories as revealed in their applications, the lowest mortality will be found in the class with the most favorable record, and the highest mortality will be found in the class with the poorest record. The best group shows a mortality of about 85 percent of the average for all classes, while the poorest group reflects a mortality of about 115 percent. Therefore companies usually give a credit of 15 points for a very good family history and a debit of 15 points for a very poor history.

Occupation

There are many occupations that are known to have an adverse effect on mortality, and insurance companies must impose an extra charge on applicants engaged in such occupations. The higher mortality rate associated with these occupations may be attributable to a greater than normal accident hazard, unhealthful working conditions, or "socioeconomic" hazards.

Accident Hazards

Accidents, if not the most common hazard, are probably the most obvious. All people working with machinery are exposed to some accident hazard. Construction workers are exposed to the hazard of falling. Underground miners—in addition to the hazard of machinery—run the risk of explosions, rock falls, fire, and lung disease. Some electrical workers are exposed to high voltages and some to the danger of falling from high places. Laborers handling heavy materials run the risk of having the materials fall on them. Railroad workers, particularly those around heavy rolling equipment, are subject to a high accident rate. Other groups subject to a higher than normal accident rate include fishermen, lumbermen, and farmers.

Dusts and Poisons

Many health hazards arise from the processes associated with a complex industrial civilization, but some of the more important were known to early civilizations. Dust is probably the most serious health hazard. It arises out of such industrial processes as grinding, drilling, and crushing, and is associated particularly with the mining industry. Organic dusts, which are largely derived from substances of animal and plant origin and are identified especially with the textile industry, produce irritation of the upper air passages and may lead to tuberculosis and other respiratory infections. Inorganic dusts, which are primarily metallic and mineral, will give rise to silicosis if they contain free silica and, in

any event, increase the possibility of diseases of the respiratory organs. The lasting effects of exposure to dust make previous employment in the dusty trades an important underwriting factor. Asbestos exposure has also proven to be a serious health hazard.

The hazard from poisons exists in many industries, the number of which has been considerably increased by the expanding use of chemicals in industry. Lead poisoning—largely identified with the mining and smelting of lead but also found in printing, painting, file-cutting, and other processes—is one of the major hazards. Other health hazards include abnormalities of temperature, dampness, defective illumination, infections, radiant energy, and repeated motion, pressure, or electrical shock.

Socioeconomic Hazards

The socioeconomic hazard is associated with occupations that employ unskilled and semi-skilled labor and pay commensurately low wages. The extra mortality that occurs among such people is attributable primarily to their unsatisfactory living and working conditions and to inadequate medical care. Their low economic status may reflect substandard physical or mental capacity.

There are some occupations that are thought to have a socioeconomic hazard not because of low wages but because of the environment in which the people work. Bartenders, liquor salespeople, and cab drivers, for example, are believed to represent a hazard purely because of environment.

All insurance companies have occupational manuals in which they list the occupations that are deemed to have adverse effects on mortality. An applicant employed in one of the listed occupations will be required to pay an additional premium, even though all other factors are favorable. Previous employment in such an occupation may be the basis for an additional premium if there is reason to suspect that the applicant may return to the occupation. Because of greater emphasis on industrial safety and public health measures, the number of such occupations is declining steadily.

If an applicant is placed in a substandard classification because of an unfavorable current occupation, the rating is usually removed and the premium reduced upon a subsequent change to an unrated occupation. The company cannot, of course, increase the premium if a policyowner changes from an unrated to a rated occupation after the policy has been issued, and it is not customary for such differences to be recognized for underwriting purposes.

Residence

The applicant's residence—present or prospective—is important, since mortality rates vary throughout different geographical regions of the United States and throughout the world. If the applicant is contemplating foreign travel or residence, the insurance company wants to know about it. It also wants to know whether the applicant has recently traveled or resided in a foreign country, particularly in the tropics. Differences among countries as to climate, living standards, sanitary conditions, medical care, political stability, and terrorist risk can be expected to have a decided effect on mortality.

Generally speaking, policies are not issued by United States companies to applicants whose permanent residence is in a foreign country, even though that country may have a climate and living conditions similar to those of the United States. Unless an insurance company has an organization and representatives in another country, it may not be able to get full information about applicants, and practical difficulties may arise in settling claims. Policies are freely issued to persons who plan to be abroad temporarily, provided they do not contemplate visiting crisis areas or making an extended stay in tropical countries. A small but growing number of American and Canadian companies do business in foreign countries and use special premium rates to account for the different mortality rates.

Habits

habits

The term **habits**, for underwriting purposes, refers to the use of alcohol and drugs. The company is concerned about an applicant's habitual use of alcohol because of the impairment of judgment and reactions during intoxication; it is concerned about the use of drugs because of the effect on the applicant's health and behavior. Of course, prolonged immoderate use of alcohol may also be harmful to a person's health.

An insurance company is not concerned about a prospective insured who uses alcoholic beverages in moderate amounts on social occasions. It is concerned about the applicant who drinks to the point of intoxication. All investigations of the effect of drinking on longevity indicate that there is substantial mortality increase among heavy drinkers. Successful completion of an in-house alcohol treatment program, combined with several years of total abstinence, will render prior abusers insurable on some basis with most life insurers. There is still a substantial relapse rate among abusers, however.

A person who is known to be a drug addict cannot obtain insurance on any basis. Even after treatment, a former drug user may be considered uninsurable for as long a period as 5

years and, at best, will be rated heavily for a long period of years because of the possibility of resuming the habit. Former addicts may remain uninsurable or be charged extremely high rates only after many years of proven drug-free living. For example, a former drug addict may be rated up to 200 percent of standard mortality for the first 5 or 10 years after taking the cure; a rating of 150 percent thereafter is not unusual.

Morals

It is surprising to many people that an insurance company would concern itself with an applicant's morals. It seems like an unnecessary intrusion into the applicant's personal life. Actually, the company is interested in the moral fiber of the applicant, not because it wants to sit in judgment, but because it has been clearly established that departures from the commonly accepted standards of ethical and moral conduct involve extra mortality risks.

Marital infidelity and other kinds of behavior that are considered immoral are regarded seriously, partly because they are frequently found in combination with other types of risky behavior, such as overindulgence in alcoholic beverages, gambling, and the use of drugs. The hazards to longevity are the impairment of health and the possibility of violence.

Unethical business conduct is another form of moral hazard. Companies do not care to insure persons who have a record of numerous bankruptcies, operate businesses that are just within the law, or have a general reputation for dishonesty. The companies fear the applicant's misrepresentation and concealment of material underwriting facts on the application. A person who is dishonest in general business dealings is not likely to make an exception for insurance companies, which have always been prime targets for unscrupulous schemes.

Sex

The superior longevity of women is the basis for offering women life insurance coverage at lower premiums. It is also the basis for higher annuity premiums and lower benefits under life-income options for women. Under the 1980 CSO mortality table—sex distinct—males face a higher probability of dying during the late teens and early twenties than between ages 28 and 30. Females do not yet show elevated rates for the early adult years. Suicide, drug overdose, AIDS, and auto accidents are rising causes of death among young men and women.

Example

Gender-based Life Expectancy

Life expectancy at birth in

	2012	2001
Male	76.4 years	75.7
Female	81.2 years	79.9

Plan of Insurance

The plan of insurance is taken into account because policies differ not only as to the amount at risk but also as to mortality rates. All other things being equal, the smaller the amount at risk, the more liberal the underwriting standards of the company. Thus, companies tend to be somewhat more liberal in underwriting single premium and limited payment policies, particularly when the extra mortality from a known impairment is not expected to be felt until middle or later life.

The higher initial premium discourages antiselection in connection with single premium and limited payment policies. The amount of antiselection is believed to be particularly great in connection with term insurance. The plan of insurance can be especially important in the consideration of substandard risks.

Economic Status

In the eyes of the law every person has an unlimited insurable interest in his or her own life. Thus, the burden of preventing overinsurance is placed on the insurance company. The company carefully investigates the applicant's financial status in order to make sure that family and business circumstances justify the amount of insurance applied for and carried in all companies. This investigation also reveals whether the amount of insurance applied for bears a reasonable relationship to the applicant's income. The company is interested not only in preventing too much insurance on the life of the applicant but also in keeping the insurance in force once issued.

Aviation Activities

In the early days of aviation, any form of flying was considered to be so hazardous—and rare—that the risk was either excluded altogether (through an exclusion clause) or made subject to a substantial extra premium. As technical developments and improvements in pilot skills reduced the hazards of flying, underwriting restrictions were gradually relaxed.

Today, the risk has been reduced to such a low level and air travel has become so common that companies do not consider it necessary to impose any underwriting restrictions on passenger travel on any type of nonmilitary aircraft, whether it is a commercial airliner, a company plane, or a personal aircraft. Furthermore, no occupational rating or restriction is applied to crew members on regularly scheduled commercial aircraft.

The treatment of private pilots depends on the person's age, experience, training, and amount of flying. For example, most companies will treat as a standard risk an applicant between the ages of 27 and 60 who has at least 100 hours of pilot experience and does not fly more than 200 hours per year. A person who flies between 200 and 400 hours annually might be charged an extra premium of $3 per $1,000; flying in excess of 1,400 hours per year might involve an extra premium of $5 per $1,000. An applicant under age 27 who is otherwise qualified as a standard risk might be charged an extra premium of $5 per $1,000. Credits are commonly allowed for advanced training, such as attaining the Instrument Flight Rated (IFR) designation. The underwriting treatment of a crew member of a military aircraft depends on the applicant's age and type of duty. Service with combat aircraft is regarded the least favorably, as one would naturally suppose. Accidental death benefit riders often exclude aviation deaths if the insured was the pilot or crew member of any type of aircraft.

When there is an indication that the applicant will be involved in any aeronautical activity that might present a special hazard, the applicant is usually required to complete a supplementary form that gives the company full details of past, present, and probable future aviation activities. In recent years there has been a proliferation of flying in ultralight aircraft, for example, which are not nearly as regulated as regular aircraft. Based on mortality experience to date, this activity requires ratings in the range of $5 or more per $1,000.

In the absence of a specific restriction, all basic policies cover the aviation hazard in full. In other words, there is no presumption that the hazard is not covered or is subject to a limitation of liability. It is only when the company is put on notice, usually through the applicant's own disclosure, that an unusual aviation hazard exists that it takes any special underwriting action.

Avocation

Certain avocations are sufficiently hazardous to justify an extra premium, at least under given circumstances. Among the avocations that may entail an extra premium are automobile, motorcycle, scooter, and speedboat racing; sky diving; skin diving (to depths over 50 feet); and mountain climbing. Most of these avocations involve a flat extra premium of

$3.50 to $10.00 per $1,000. An extra premium of $3.00 (or more) per $1,000 is required for hang gliding.

Military Service

For more than 100 years—at least as far back as the Civil War—American life insurance companies have taken special underwriting cognizance of the extra mortality risk associated with applicants engaged in or facing military service during a period of armed conflict. The underwriting action has taken three principal forms: outright rejection of the applicant, limitation on the face amount of insurance issued, or the attachment of a so-called war clause that limits the insurer's obligation to return of premiums, less dividends, with interest, if the insured dies under circumstances as defined in the war clause.

"status" war clause

"results" war clause

The use of a war clause has been the most common method of dealing with the extra hazard of military or naval service. Some companies have also used a **"status" war clause**, which limits the insurer's obligation to return of premium if the insured should die while in military service outside the territorial boundaries of the United States, whether or not the cause of death can be attributed to military service. Other companies have used a rider, referred to as a **"results" war clause**, which limits the insurer's obligation only if the insured's death is the result of military service. While regarded as more liberal to the insured than the status clause, this provision limits liability even though the insured is no longer in a war zone at the time of death. Most companies have been willing to waive these clauses for an appropriate extra premium.

War clauses were widely if not universally used during both World Wars (especially World War II) in policies that were issued to persons of military age. After the cessation of hostilities, the clauses were generally revoked by the insurance companies without request from the insureds. During the Korean conflict, war clauses were again inserted in policies that were issued to young men facing military service. With the termination of hostilities, use of the clauses was again discontinued, and such clauses in outstanding policies were voluntarily cancelled by the companies.

With the American involvement in Vietnam, life insurance companies were again confronted with the problem of assessing the risk in military service. There was no consensus among the companies as to the best approach to the problem, and a variety of practices were followed. One approach used by a number of companies was to refuse to write

any coverage on military personnel at the lower ranks but to issue insurance in normal amounts to all other military persons, attaching a "results" type of war clause to policies written. Generally applications were not accepted on persons in combat units or on orders to combat zones.

The American-led action to expel the Iraqi military presence from Kuwait triggered the most recent challenge to the industry's risk classification practices. Once again, with the exception of the general demise of the war exclusion clause,[5] company practices were characterized by a lack of uniformity. During the military buildup, while some companies continued to issue unrestricted insurance, others sought to withdraw from the sale of insurance to military personnel in or under orders to report to the Persian Gulf. These companies cited their long-standing philosophies of not insuring any applicant (civilian or military) residing in or traveling to areas of political instability. Others simply defended their practice based on the extra risk of military duty in the Persian Gulf. However, what differentiated the Persian Gulf conflict in terms of its impact on insurer practices was the significant role of political pressure. Faced with the avowed threat by a number of state insurance department commissioners to label companies as unpatriotic in press conferences and to suspend their licenses for discriminatory practices (even companies described above who maintained nondiscriminatory restrictions on military or civilian applicants in areas of political instability), companies generally provided such coverage with normal restrictions on insurance face amounts.

CHAPTER REVIEW

Key Terms and Concepts

surplus
habits
"status" war clause
"results" war clause

Chapter 13 Review Questions

1. What is the function of the selection process? [1]

---

5.   A number of companies maintained war exclusion clauses on their accidental death benefit and premium-waiver-for-disability provisions.

2. Jimmy and Johnny were both born on the same date. Does this mean that they will always pay the identical premium if they both purchase the same type of life insurance policy on the same day? Explain. [1]

3. What is the potential result if each risk classification used in the selection process is overloaded with risks whose longevity prospects are less favorable than the assumed average for the classification? [1]

4. Why should a company's underwriting standards be at least as effective as those utilized by the companies that supplied the data for the mortality table used in risk classification? [1]

5. Why is age considered an important factor in classifying applicants for life insurance? [2]

6. How are build tables used in determining an applicant's mortality expectation? [2]

7. (a) Why is physical condition important in the selection process?

    (b) What kinds of information can be obtained from (i) tests for heart disease or impairment; (ii) blood tests? [2]

8. What is the purpose of the urinalysis diagnostic procedure? [2]

9. What information can be acquired by completing the applicant's personal history questionnaire? [2]

10. Why is family history significant in the selection process? [2]

11. How do the following factors associated with various occupations have an adverse effect on mortality and therefore result in modifications in the selection and/or premium charge for applicants engaged in such occupations?

    (a) accident hazards

    (b) dusts and poisons

    (c) socioeconomic hazards. [2]

12. What relevance does an applicant's residence have in the life insurance selection process? [2]

13. Why should an applicant's morals concern an insurance company? [2]

14. How can aviation activities affect the risk classification of an applicant for life insurance? [2]

15. (a) What three principal forms of underwriting action have historically been associated with applicants engaged in or facing military service during a period of armed conflict?

    (b) How does the "status" clause differ from the "results" cause? [2]

Chapter 13 Review Answers

1. *The function of the selection process is to determine whether an applicant's degree of risk for insurance is commensurate with the premium established for people in the same classification being considered.*

2. *Even though they would be in the same age group and are the same sex, differences stemming from physical condition, occupation, avocations, smoking, and other factors might result in them being placed in different rate categories and, thus, paying different premiums for the same policy.*

3. *Irrespective of the underwriting procedures used by a company, if each risk classification is overbalanced with risks whose longevity prospects are less favorable than the assumed average for the classification, the company will end up with excessive mortality costs*

and—unless it enjoys offsetting advantages in other areas of operations—will have diffi-culty in maintaining its competitive position.

4.   *If a company's underwriting standards are not at least as effective as those utilized by the companies that supplied the data for the mortality table, its actual mortality experience will likely be worse than that assumed in calculating its premium rates, and unless it enjoys offsetting advantages in other areas of operations, it will suffer an underwriting loss.*

5.   *The applicant's age is the most important single factor on individual mortality expecta-tions. Except for the first few years of life, resistance to disease and injury weakens with the passage of time, and the probability of death increases with age. Age is such a significant measure of the likelihood of death, that it is the point of departure in classifying applicants for insurance. Each applicant is placed within the proper age classification and is then compared to the norm for that age to determine insurability.*

The age of the applicant enters into a company's underwriting considerations in another respect. All companies have upper-age limits beyond which they will not write insurance on any basis and somewhat lower limits for writing certain types of policies, such as term insurance. The absolute limit may be as low as 60 or as high as 75 or more. Under such cir-cumstances, the age of the applicant may bar acceptability to the company on any basis. In other words, age alone—regardless of the other facts of the case—may render a person uninsurable.

6.   *The applicant's build—the relationship between height, weight, and girth—is one of the basic determinants of mortality expectation. Build tables containing debits for various combinations of height and weight are used to determine an applicant's debit (if any) for purposes of the numerical rating system.*

With overweight male applicants, the company is also interested in the distribution of the excess weight. This involves a comparison of the chest (expanded) with the abdominal girth. Insurance companies have prepared charts that assign debits for abdominal mea-surements in excess of chest measurements. The number of points depends on the person's age, the percentage he is overweight, and the number of inches by which the one measure-ment exceeds the other. Credits, derived the same way, are assigned when chest measure-ments are in excess of the abdominal girth. Under the numerical rating system, it is possible for an applicant to be credited with 20 points for a favorable relationship between his chest

and girth or debited 70 points for an unfavorable one. Taking chest and abdominal measurements also enables a company to check on the accuracy of reported weights.

7. a. *In evaluating an application for insurance, the company wishes to know whether there are any impairments of body or mind that would tend to shorten the life expectancy of the applicant. In the short run, the applicant's physical condition may outweigh all other factors in importance. Questions designed to elicit information on the applicant's physical status are included in the application. If a sizable amount of insurance is involved, the information is also confirmed and supplemented by a medical examination and laboratory testing. The primary purpose of the medical examination is to detect any malfunctioning of vital organs.*

    b. *(1) Tests for heart disease or impairment can provide a number of kinds of information. One of the most common manifestations of heart impairment is murmurs. A murmur is any sound other than those associated with the normal closing of the heart valves. Functional murmurs are considered harmless and are, consequently, of no significance to the underwriter; organic murmurs indicate damage to some part of the heart tissue. The problem is distinguishing between the two. Organic murmurs are regarded as serious and may cause the applicant to be rated highly or declined altogether. True functional murmurs are not rated, but if there is any doubt about their cause or origin, provision may be made for some extra mortality.*

Enlargement of the heart (cardiomegaly) is a condition of underwriting significance, because it is nature's way of compensating for damage to the valves or other sections of the heart mechanism. High blood pressure may be a symptom of a condition that impairs longevity. It is particularly associated with kidney ailments. A combination of excess weight and hypertension is always regarded seriously.

The condition of the circulatory system can also be evaluated by the pulse rate, normally 60 to 80 beats per minute. A rapid pulse is unfavorable, because it indicates that the heart has to work harder than usual to meet the body's needs. This may be a sign of an inefficient or impaired heart, an infection, or any other abnormal condition within the body that demands an extra supply of blood.

(2) Blood profile tests have gained added importance with the discovery of Acquired Immune Deficiency Syndrome (AIDS). Nearly universal blood testing for HIV has also provided insurers with additional useful information regarding applicants' renal and liver function and blood lipids (fats, oils, and waxes). The availability of this additional information has facilitated the proliferation of products that offer preferred-premium classifications.

8.   Urinalysis has a three-fold purpose: (1) to measure the functional capacity of the kidneys, (2) to detect infections or other abnormal conditions of the kidneys, and (3) to discover impairments of other vital organs of the body.

9.   The applicant's personal history provides several types of information. Complete information about previous illnesses, injuries, and operations can indicate the necessity for special additional tests or examinations.

The company also wants to know whether the applicant has even been addicted to the use of drugs or alcohol, because there is always a possibility that the "cure" will prove to be only temporary. The past abuse may have caused irrevocable damage to one or more body systems. The personal history may reveal that the applicant has only recently left a hazardous or unhealthful occupation, raising the possibility that he or she may retain ill effects from the job or might return to the job in the future. It may also disclose that the applicant has changed residence to improve his or her health or has had intimate association with a person who has a contagious disease such as tuberculosis.

Finally, the company wants to know whether the applicant has even been refused insurance by any other company or offered insurance on rated terms. An affirmative answer would indicate a prior impairment that might still be present. Information about existing insurance also enables the company to judge whether the amount of insurance, existing and proposed, bears a reasonable relationship to the applicant's needs and financial resources.

10.   Family history is considered significant because certain characteristics are hereditary. Build follows family lines, and to some extent, so do structural qualities of the heart and other organs.

11.   a.   All people working with machinery are exposed to some accident hazard. Construction workers are exposed to the hazard of falling, Underground miners—in addition to the hazard of machinery—run the risk of explosions, rock falls, fire, and lung disease. Some electrical workers are exposed to high voltages and some to the danger of falling from high places. Laborers handling heavy materials run the risk of having the materials fall on them. Railroad workers, particularly those around heavy rolling equipment, are subject to a high accident rate. Other groups subject to a higher-than-normal accident rate include fishermen, lumbermen, and farmers.

      b.   Dust is probably the most serious health hazard. It arises out of such industrial processes as grinding, drilling, and crushing, and is associated particularly with the

mining industry. Organic dusts, which are largely derived from substances of animal and plant origin and are identified especially with the textile industry, produce irritation of the upper air passages, and may lead to tuberculosis and other respiratory infections. Inorganic dusts, which are primarily metallic and mineral, can give rise to silicosis if they contain free silica and, in any event, increase the possibility of diseases of the respiratory organs. The lasting effects of exposure to dust make previous employment in the dusty trades an important underwriting factor. Asbestos exposure has also proven to be a serious health hazard.

The hazard from poisons exists in many industries, the number of which has been considerably increased by the expanding use of chemicals in industry. Lead poisoning-largely identified with the mining and smelting of lead but also found in printing, painting, file-cutting, and other processes—is one of the major hazards. Other heath hazards include abnormalities of temperature, dampness, defective illumination, infections, radiant energy, and repeated motion, pressure, or electrical shock.

c.   *The socio-economic hazard is associated with occupations that employ unskilled and semi-skilled labor and pay commensurately low wages. The extra mortality that occurs among such people is attributable primarily to their unsatisfactory living and working conditions and to inadequate medical care. Their low economic status may reflect substandard physical or mental capacity.*

There are some occupations that are thought to have a socio-economic hazard not because of low wages but because of the environment in which the people work. Bartenders. liquor salespeople, and cab drivers, for example, are believed to represent a hazard purely because of environment.

12. *The applicant's residence—present or prospective—is important, because mortality rates vary throughout different geographical regions of the United States and throughout the world. If the applicant is contemplating foreign travel or residence, the insurance company wants to know about it. It also wants to know whether the applicant has recently traveled or resided in a foreign country, particularly in the tropics. Differences among countries as to climate, living standards, sanitary conditions, medical care, political stability, and terrorist risk can be expected to have a decided effect on mortality.*

Generally speaking, policies are not issued by United States companies to applicants whose permanent residence is in a foreign country, even though that country may have a climate and living conditions similar to those of the United States. Policies are freely issued to persons who plan to be abroad temporarily, provided they do not contemplate visiting crises areas or making an extended stay in tropical countries.

13. An insurance company is interested in the moral fiber of the applicant, not because it wants to sit in judgment, but because it has been clearly established that departures from the commonly accepted standards of ethical and moral conduct involve extra mortality risks. Marital infidelity and other kinds of behavior that are considered immoral are regarded seriously, partly because they are frequently found in combination with other types of risky behavior, such as overindulgence in alcoholic beverages, gambling, and the use of drugs. The hazards to longevity are the impairment of health and the possibility of violence.

Unethical business conduct is another form of moral hazard. Companies do not care to insure persons who have a record of numerous bankruptcies, operate businesses that are just within the law, or have a general reputation for dishonesty. The companies fear the applicant's misrepresentation and concealment of material underwriting facts on the application. A person who is dishonest in general business dealings is not likely to make an exception for insurance companies, which have always been prime targets for unscrupulous schemes.

14. The treatment of private pilots depends on the person's age, experience, training, and amount of flying with extra premium charged or credits allowed based on these factors. The underwriting treatment of a crew member of a military aircraft depends on the applicant's age and type of duty. Service with combat aircraft is regarded the least favorably, as one would naturally suppose. Accidental death benefit riders often exclude aviation deaths if the insured was the pilot or crew member of any type of aircraft. In recent years, there has been a proliferation of flying in ultralight aircraft that are not nearly as regulated as regular aircraft and, thus, may require an extra premium.

15. a. American life insurance companies have taken special underwriting cognizance of the extra mortality risk associated with applicants engaged in or facing military service during a period of armed conflict. The underwriting action has taken three principal forms: outright rejection of the applicant, limitation on the face amount of insurance issued, or the attachment of a war clause that limits the insurer's obligation to return of premiums, less dividends, with interest, if the insured dies under circumstances as defined in the war clause.

     b. A status clause limits the insurer's obligation to return of premium if the insured should die while in military service outside the territorial boundaries of the United States, whether or not the cause of death can be attributed to military service. A results war clause limits the insurer's obligation only if the insured's death is the result of military service. While regarded as more liberal to the insured than the status clause, the results

provision limits liability even though the insured is no longer in a war zone at the time of death.

Selection and Classification of Risks — Part 2

Dan M. McGill

Revised by Jeremy S. Holmes and James F. Winberg with contribution by Ronald F. Duska

Learning Objectives

An understanding of the material in this chapter should enable the student to

1. **Identify the sources of information regarding an applicant, and describe the role that each plays in the selection process.**

2. **Explain two methods of risk classification.**

3. **Describe the special considerations in the selection process when nonmedical insurance is available.**

4. **Explain the insurability option.**

5. **Describe the concerns regarding the issuance of life insurance at extremes of age.**

The preceding chapter reviewed the type of information an insurance company's underwriting department needs when considering an application for insurance. This chapter briefly describes the sources from which it obtains this information. Much of it comes from more than one source. This gives the company the means of verifying information that it considers critical to the underwriting decision and serves as a deterrent to collusion or fraud by any of the parties to the transaction.

SOURCES OF INFORMATION

The Agent

A company's field force is the foundation of the selection process. The other parts of the selection mechanism can go into operation only after the field force has acted. The home office can exercise its underwriting judgment only on the risks submitted by the agents and brokers. A company's overall selection process can be no stronger than its agency force. If agents submit consistently good business, the underwriting results will be favorable; if they submit consistently below-average risks, the underwriting results will be no better.

Most companies give their agents explicit instructions about the types of risks that will or will not be acceptable, and they instruct the agents to solicit only those risks they believe

to be eligible under the company's underwriting rules. Where eligibility for insurance is doubtful in any way, some companies, in order to save unnecessary expense and trouble, require the agent to submit a preliminary statement setting forth the facts of the case and the grounds upon which the doubt as to insurability is based. Some companies require a preliminary statement in all cases where an application for insurance in any company has been declined, postponed, or accepted at other than standard rates.

The agent is asked to supply a variety of information in the certificate, the details varying with the company. The information typically includes the following: how long and how well the agent has known the applicant; an estimate of the applicant's net worth and annual income; the applicant's existing and pending insurance, including any plans for the lapse or surrender of existing insurance; whether the applicant sought the insurance or whether the application was the result of solicitation by the agent; and whether the application came through another agent or broker.

Information Often Asked of An Agent

- How long have you known the applicant?

- How well do you know the applicant?

- What do you estimate as the applicant's income/net worth?

- What is the applicant's insurance in force?

- Are there other applications for coverage pending

- Does the applicant plan to terminate any existing coverage?

- Did the applicant initiate request for coverage?

- Was there another agent or broker involved in the origination of the application?

The degree of selection exercised at the field level depends on the integrity and reliability of the agents and brokers. There is clearly some selection involved, since self-interest would cause the agent not to solicit insurance from persons who—because of obvious physical impairments, moral deficiencies, or unacceptable occupations—manifestly could not meet the underwriting standards of the company. Beyond that, the amount of selection practiced by the agent is rather limited. Since the agent's compensation depends on the amount of insurance he or she sells, the motive exists to submit any application, even though it is borderline, that stands a chance of being accepted. Hence the responsibility for

applying the company's underwriting standards falls to the home office underwriters, who do not labor under the same conflicts of interest.

The agent is usually the only company representative to see an applicant face-to-face and make a visual assessment. If there is anything unusual about the applicant that requires an explanation, it is up to the agent to convey that information to the home office. For example, a person whose weight is high for the given age and height could be very muscular rather than obese. The agent can include this information with the report that accompanies the application.

Experienced agents know what types of additional information the home office under-writers are likely to request when the application reveals specific health problems. These agents can expedite the process by asking for the supplemental reports at the same time the application is completed. Otherwise, the reports will not be generated until the home office staff has made a preliminary evaluation of the case and forwarded a request to the agent for the needed information. In some cases, the first supplemental report triggers a request for additional supplemental reports.

The home office evaluation is usually very expeditious if all the information needed to make the evaluation accompanies the application. The time needed to approve, reject, or rate the case can be extended by months if there is difficulty in obtaining reports, such as attending physician statements. Another advantage that some experienced agents have is a reputation with the home office underwriters for thoroughness, accuracy, and attention to detail in furnishing applications and supporting documents. This reputation can benefit applicants who are on the borderline between classifications and can be rated either way. They may get the benefit of the lower premium class because of their agent's reputation. Borderline cases from agents who always argue with the home office evaluation and send applications with less than complete information are more likely to be classified under the higher premium category when it is strictly a judgment call at a borderline.

The Applicant

Much of the information a company needs to underwrite a case is supplied by the appli-cant. This information is contained in the application, which constitutes an important part of the offer and acceptance process and will become part of the contract if the policy is issued. Application blanks vary in their content and design, but they usually consist of two parts—the first containing nonmedical questions and the second including questions to be asked by the medical examiner. (Many companies permit the agent to ask the medical questions subject to age and amount limitations under "nonmedical" programs, which are discussed later in this chapter.)

Statements made by the applicant in the first part of the application cover the particulars of identification, such as name, address, former and prospective places of residence, and place and date of birth. If the applicant has recently moved, including previous places of residence enables the company, through reporting services, to interview the applicant's former acquaintances. (The importance of obtaining the correct date of birth was explained in the previous chapter.)

Additional questions in the first part of the application relate to the applicant's occupation, including any changes within the last 5 years or any contemplated changes of occupation; aviation activities other than passenger travel on regularly scheduled airlines (if there is any unusual aviation hazard, details must be provided in a supplementary form); and the possibility of foreign residence. The application also elicits information about the applicant's insurance history including details of all insurance already in force, as well as declinations and other insurance company actions of underwriting significance.

The foregoing information—together with a statement of the amount of insurance applied for, the plan upon which it is to be issued, the names of the policy beneficiary and policyowner, and the respective rights of the insured, beneficiary, and policyowner as to control of the policy—completes the first part of the application. This section is usually filled out by the agent on behalf of the applicant, who must sign it and certify the correctness of the information. The applicant's signature is generally witnessed by the agent.

The answers to questions in the second part of the application normally must be recorded in the medical examiner's handwriting, and the applicant must sign the form to attest to the completeness and accuracy of its contents. This part of the application asks several groups of related questions. The first group seeks the details of the applicant's health record, including illnesses, injuries, and surgical operations, usually within the last 10 years. The applicant is also required to give the name of every physician or practitioner consulted within a specified period of time (usually the last 5 years) in connection with any ailment whatsoever. The second group of questions elicits information about the applicant's present physical condition. There are questions about the applicant's use of alcohol and drugs, and other questions concerning the applicant's family history.

Information Often Requested of an Applicant

- Identification

- Age

- Medical history

- Occupation and recent work history

- Amount and type of insurance applied for

- Existing insurance

- Intended policyowner

- Intended beneficiary

- Physicians consulted within last 5 years

- Use of alcohol and drugs

- Family health history

The Medical Examiner

In addition to recording the answers to part 2 of the application, the medical examiner is required to file a separate report or certificate, which accompanies the application but is not seen by the applicant. The first portion of the report contains a description of the applicant's physical characteristics, which not only provides useful underwriting information but also guards against substituting a healthy person for an unhealthy applicant in the medical examination. Some companies ask the examiner to review the applicant's driver's license or other form of identification to establish conclusive identification. The examiner is also usually asked to indicate whether the applicant looks older than the age stated.

The basic purpose of the medical examiner's report is to transmit the findings of the physical examination. The medical examiner's comments are specifically required regarding any abnormalities of the applicant's arteries or veins, heart, respiratory system, nervous system, abdomen, genitourinary system, ears, eyes, and skin. The examiner also reports the urinalysis result, certifies that the urine examined is authentic, describes the applicant's build, and indicates the applicant's blood pressure.

In the final section of the report, the examiner may be requested to indicate any knowledge or suspicion that the applicant abuses alcohol or narcotics or has any moral

deficiencies that would affect his or her insurability. The examiner is also asked about the prior patient/doctor relationship that has existed between the two of them, if any.

The medical examiner's report is considered to be the property of the insurance company and is carefully safeguarded at all times.

Attending Physicians

Attending physicians are a source of information on applicants who have undergone medical treatment prior to applying for insurance. When it appears that the information in the attending physician's files might influence the insurance company's underwriting decision, such information is sought as a matter of routine. After the application has been signed, because the application gives the insurer consent to seek medical and personal information. Insurance companies have enjoyed a remarkable degree of cooperation from the medical profession regarding inquiries of this nature, with physicians normally providing all of the relevant information in their files. However, their response is not always prompt, and their delay suspends the policy issuance process. To expedite the physician's response, insurers usually send a check along with the letter of inquiry to cover the physician's expenses incurred to supply the information.

Inspection Report

Insurance companies attempt to verify all information from the previously mentioned sources, generally in one of two ways. The first method is through telephone interviews conducted by insurance company staff, which allows the insurer to structure the questions to best serve its purposes. The second alternative is to employ the services of an independent reporting agency. The unique advantage of these independent investigations is that they provide an evaluation of the applicant by a source having no interest in the outcome of the application.

The insurer's home office or its local agency may make the request for an inspection report. In either case, the report is filed directly with the insurance company's home office. Under provisions of the Fair Credit Reporting Act the applicant has the right to review the contents of the report at the offices of the agency that produced it.

The thoroughness of the inspection depends on the amount of insurance involved. When the amount of insurance is not large, the report is rather brief, commenting in a general way on the applicant's health, prescription usage, habits, finances, environment, and reputation. When a large amount has been applied for, the report tends to be comprehensive. It reflects the results of interviews with the applicant's neighbors, employer, pharmacist,

banker, business associates, and others. The inspection focuses particularly on the applicant's business and personal ethics. The report calls attention to any bankruptcies and fire losses, and it comments on the applicant's use of alcohol, drugs, and other departures from "normal" social behavior. The inspection also occasionally uncovers physical impairments that were not revealed in the medical examiner's report.

The Medical Information Bureau

A final source of information is the Medical Information Bureau (MIB). This organization is a clearinghouse for confidential medical data on applicants for life insurance. The information is reported and maintained in code symbols to help preserve its confidentiality.

Companies that are members of the Bureau are expected to report any impairments designated on the official list. The designated impairments are related primarily to the applicant's physical condition but also include hereditary characteristics and addiction to alcohol and narcotics. If they have a bearing on insurability, any suspicious tendencies revealed in an examination are reported in order to bring the matter to the notice of all companies using the Bureau's records. All impairments must be reported whether the company accepts, postpones, or declines the risk, or offers a modified plan of insurance. In no event does the company report its underwriting decision to the Bureau.

Example

Paula Harried of ABC Insurance Company would like to use MIB files to evaluate the underwriting standards of QRS Insurance, Inc., a prime competitor. She quickly discovers that MIB files do not include information about acceptance or rejection of applicants. The files, therefore, are of no use to Paula. (Note: Information concerning an applicant's impairments is reported to MIB regardless of whether the insurer issues coverage or rejects the application.)

A company normally screens all of its applicants against the MIB file of reported impairments. If the company finds an impairment and wants further details, it must submit its request through the MIB, but only after it first conducts its own complete investigation from all known sources. The company that reported the impairment is not obligated to supply further information, but if it agrees to do so, it provides the requested information through the MIB.

It should be emphasized that there is no basis for the widespread belief that a person who is recorded in the MIB files cannot obtain insurance at standard rates. The information contained therein is treated like underwriting data from any other source and, in the final analysis, may be outweighed by favorable factors. In many cases, it will enable a company

to take favorable action, since favorable medical test results are reported as well as unfavorable ones. In any case, the rules of the MIB stipulate that a company cannot take unfavorable underwriting action solely on the basis of the information in the MIB files. In other words, the company must be in possession of other unfavorable underwriting facts or else determine through its own channels of investigation that the condition of impairment recorded in the MIB files is substantial enough to warrant an unfavorable decision.

CLASSIFICATION OF RISKS

Once all available underwriting information about an insurance application has been assembled, the data must be evaluated and a decision reached as to whether the applicant is to be accepted at standard rates, placed in one of the various substandard classifications, or rejected entirely. This is clearly the focus of the vitally important selection process. Ideally the evaluation and classification system used by a company should (1) accurately measure the effect of each of the factors, favorable and unfavorable, that can be expected to influence an applicant's longevity; (2) assess the combined impact of multiple factors, including the situations in which the factors are conflicting; (3) produce consistently equitable results; and (4) be simple and relatively inexpensive to operate.

The Judgment Method of Rating

The earliest rating system used in the United States was the "judgment method." Routine cases were processed with a minimum of consideration by clerks trained in the review of applications, and doubtful or borderline cases were resolved by supervisors relying on their experience and general impressions. The method is still used, particularly by smaller companies, and in all insurance companies, the element of judgment plays an important role.

The judgment method of rating functions very effectively when there is only one unfavorable factor to consider or when the decision is simply one of accepting the applicant at standard rates or rejecting the application altogether. It leaves something to be desired when there are multiple unfavorable factors (offset perhaps by some favorable factors) or when the risk, if it does not qualify for standard insurance, must be fitted into the proper substandard classification. To overcome the weaknesses of the judgment method of rating, the numerical rating system, devised over a half century ago, is used today by most insurers.[1]

---

1. The system was developed in 1919 by Arthur H. Hunter and Dr. Oscar H. Rogers, actuary and medical director, respectively, of the New York Life Insurance Company. It is described in a paper by Hunter and Rogers, titled "The

The Numerical Rating System

The numerical rating system is based on the principle that a large number of factors enter into the composition of a risk and that the impact of each of these factors on the longevity of the risk can be determined by a statistical study of lives possessing that factor. It assumes that the average risk accepted by a company has a value of 100 percent and that each of the factors that enter into the risk can be expressed as a percentage of the whole. Favorable factors are assigned negative values, called credits, while unfavorable factors are assigned positive values, called debits. The summation of the debits and credits, added to or deducted from the par value of 100, represents the numerical value of the risk.

Assigning Weights to Risk Factors

Naturally, it would be impossible to assign weights to all the factors that might influence a risk. In practice, values are generally assigned to the following 10 factors: (1) build, (2) physical condition, (3) medical history, (4) family history, (5) occupation, (6) aviation and avocation, (7) residence, (8) habits, (9) morals, and (10) plan of insurance.

The values assigned to the various factors are derived from mortality studies among groups of people possessing those characteristics or, in some cases, from estimates of what such mortality studies might be expected to show. For example, if the mortality experience of a group of insured lives with a particular medical history has been found to be 135 percent of that among all standard risks, a debit (addition) of 35 percentage points might be assigned to that medical history. The degrees of extra mortality cited in connection with many of the impairments discussed in the preceding chapter is the basis for the debits under the numerical rating system.

Example

The operation of the system can be illustrated with the following hypothetical case. The applicant is a married man, aged 32, living in Philadelphia, Pennsylvania, with two children. He is 6 feet one inch tall and weighs 290 pounds. He is in good physical condition except that, in addition to being overweight, his build is unfavorable—that is, his expanded chest measurement is one inch less than the girth of his abdomen (see chapter 17). His personal health record shows no operations, broken bones, ulcers, or other ailments that would have an adverse effect on longevity. His family is long-lived, and the family history reveals no tuberculosis, insanity, cardiac conditions, malignancies,

---

or diabetes. He has been employed for several years as a warehouseman in an industrial plant. His habits and morals are good. The plan of insurance is 20-payment whole life insurance.

The company might evaluate the facts as follows: The applicant is overweight, which calls for a debit of 50 points according to Table 17-1 (see chapter 17). The unfavorable build (girth greater than chest expanded) is the basis for an additional debit of 20 points. The favorable family history receives a credit of 15 points, and the plan of insurance, 20-payment whole life, calls for an additional credit of 10 points. The residence is a neutral factor (only debits are assigned to residence, and debits are usually assessed only for a foreign or tropical residence). Regarding habits and morals, there is no credit for good behavior, only debits for bad behavior. The occupation is also a neutral factor with no debits or credits. Thus, the debits add up to 70 points and the credits add up to only 25. Hence, the numerical value of the risk is 145.

The analysis is summarized below:

Base = 100

Factor	Debit	Credit
Weight: overweight	50	—
Physical condition: favorable	—	—
Build: unfavorable	20	—
Family history: superior	—	15
Occupation: favorable	—	—
Residence: normal	—	—
Habits and morals: favorable	—	—
Plan of insurance: 20-payment whole life	—	10
	70	25

Rating = 145

It should be noted that credits are generally not allowed when there are other ratable physical impairments or debits for blood pressure or other cardiovascular-renal impairments.

The ratings obtained by this method may go as low as 75 and as high as 500 or more. The ratings that fall between 75 and 125 are usually classified as standard, although some companies, especially those that do not write substandard insurance, may include risks that produce a rating of 130 (or if the applicant is below age 30, even 140) in the standard category. Risks that produce ratings beyond the standard limit are either assigned to appropriate substandard classifications or declined. The risk is rejected if the company does not write substandard insurance or if the rating is higher than that eligible for the highest substandard classification. Many companies are willing to accept risks that indicate

a mortality rate up to 500 percent of normal.[2] Most companies feel that assessing mortality beyond 500 percent will yield results too erratic to price accurately.

Substandard Classifications

As will be explained in the following chapter, the broad category of substandard risks is subdivided into several classifications, each with its own scale of premiums. There may be as few as three or as many as 12 substandard classifications. The full significance of the earlier statements concerning the balancing of risks within each classification should now be apparent. With a spread of 50 percentage points in the standard classification, which comprises the great bulk of accepted risks, it is vitally important that each risk that falls within the 100 to 125 range be balanced (in percentage points) by one that falls in the 75 to 100 category. Otherwise, the average mortality for the entire group will exceed the norm of 100. With a rating of 145, the hypothetical case illustrated above would have fallen into a substandard classification.

The numerical rating system follows much the same procedure as systems that judge a risk without the benefit of numerical values. The same factors are considered, and the final decision is based on the relationship of the various favorable and unfavorable features of the risk. The numerical method, however, sets up objective standards that assist in the final valuation of the risk and allow for greater consistency of treatment. Lay underwriters can process all applications other than those requiring detailed medical analysis and the inevitable borderline cases. This not only expedites the handling of cases but also helps to hold down the expense of the selection process. Underwriters can consult with their home office medical directors on complex medical situations.

Criticisms against the System

Various criticisms, however, have been leveled against the numerical rating system. It has been alleged, for example, that (1) the system is too arbitrary, (2) there are many impairments concerning which knowledge is too limited to permit the assignment of numerical values, (3) the interrelated factors are nonadditive in so many cases that it nullifies the value of the numerical process, and (4) too many minor debits and credits are taken into account in evaluating risk. Supporters of the system recognize its flaws but feel that it is still superior to any other method that has been devised. They stress that the procedure must be—and, in practice, is—applied with common sense. They admit that there are many impairments whose effect on longevity cannot be expressed numerically, but they point

---

2.   Some companies are willing to accept risks that appear to be subject to mortality up to 1,000 percent of normal.

out that this constitutes a handicap under any method. They argue that under any system, the cases with interrelated impairments require the expert judgment of the insurer's medical staff and actuarial staff. Whether too many debits and credits are taken into account is a matter of opinion, of course; some companies have modified the numerical rating system to take only major impairments into account.

NONMEDICAL INSURANCE

In citing the medical examiner as a source of underwriting information, the preceding section implies that a medical examination is mandatory with any life insurance application. That is not the case.

nonmedical insurance

A substantial portion of all new insurance is written without a medical examination. For example, neither group nor industrial life insurance ordinarily requires a medical examination. Furthermore, an increasing amount of ordinary life insurance is being sold without a medical examination. While any type of insurance sold without a medical examination might logically be called **nonmedical insurance**, the expression usually refers to ordinary insurance sold in that manner.

History of Nonmedical Insurance

Nonmedical life insurance is not a recent innovation. The first life insurance was sold without medical examination. In the early days of life insurance in England, each applicant appeared before the directors of the company, who made their decision largely on the basis of personal appearance. Personal inspection by the company directors was later supplemented by recommendations of the applicant's friends and associates and eventually a medical examination was introduced. The medical examination quickly established its usefulness and was soon regarded as essential.

In about 1886, companies in Great Britain began to experiment with nonmedical underwriting. To protect the companies against adverse selection, the policies, which were limited in amount, contained liens during the early years of the contract, or they were issued at advanced premium rates. Some companies offered only double endowments on a nonmedical basis.

Nonmedical underwriting as it is practiced today, however, began in 1921 in Canada. The immediate motivation for its development was the shortage of medical examiners,

particularly in the rural areas. The desire to reduce expenses on the predominantly small policies issued in Canada at that time was also a strong influence.

Nonmedical underwriting spread to the United States around 1925 after the success of the Canadian experiment seemed assured. It gained increasing acceptance during the 1930s as American experiences proved favorable and enjoyed its greatest growth when a shortage of medical examiners developed during World War II. The practice of nonmedical underwriting is firmly entrenched today in both Canada and the United States.

Underwriting Safeguards

Because nonmedical insurance is subject to higher than normal mortality, at least for the first several policy years, insurance companies have adopted certain underwriting safeguards.

Limiting the Amount of Insurance

Perhaps the most important safeguard is a limit on the amount that will be made available to any one applicant. As explained more fully below, the limit is determined by the extra mortality that can be expected from eliminating the medical examination and the savings in selection expenses that will be available to absorb the extra mortality costs.

In the early days of nonmedical insurance, the limit was placed at $1,000. When the extra mortality turned out to be lower than expected, the limits were gradually raised. Today, most companies will provide up to $100,000 on a nonmedical basis, subject to appropriate age restrictions, while many will issue up to $200,000 or $250,000 on that basis. The limit generally varies by age groups; the largest amounts are available to the younger age groups. A few companies are willing to write up to $500,000 at the younger ages.

The foregoing limits are for any one application for nonmedical insurance. Some companies will issue additional amounts, subject to an aggregate limit, after a specified period of time has elapsed. Most companies are willing to reinstate the original limits for any insured who, subsequent to obtaining one or more policies on a nonmedical basis, undergoes a medical examination satisfactory to the company. In other words, all nonmedical insurance issued to the person prior to the medical examination will be disregarded and additional amounts made available up to the applicable limits.

Limiting the Age of Issue

A second safeguard companies impose is a limit on the ages at which insurance will be issued. Studies have shown that the extra mortality resulting from waiving the medical examination increases with age and after a point will exceed any savings in selection expense. The point at which the extra mortality costs will exceed the expense savings is obviously a function of the underwriting age limit, but most companies place it around age 45 or 50. There is usually no lower age limit; most companies offer nonmedical insurance down to age zero.

Limiting Insurance to Standard Risks

A third safeguard is the general limitation of nonmedical insurance to standard risks. As a broad class, substandard risks must submit to medical examinations. Exceptions are commonly made, however, for risks that are substandard because of an occupational, aviation, or avocational hazard.

Relying on Other Sources of Information

A final safeguard, which is more general and pervasive in nature, is the intensive cultivation of the sources of underwriting information other than the medical examiner. Insurance companies place a heavier burden on the applicant, agent, and inspector to offset in some measure the absence of a medical examiner's findings. The application form used in connection with nonmedical insurance is elaborate, containing all the questions usually contained in an application blank as well as those normally asked by a medical examiner. A urine specimen and blood profile may be required for home office analysis. If the applicant has recently been under the care of a physician, a statement may be necessary from the attending physician (at the expense of the company). If any adverse medical information is revealed by the applicant's statement, the inspection report, or other source, the company may demand a complete medical examination.

A particularly heavy responsibility is placed on the agent, with great reliance on the agent's judgment and integrity. Agents may submit nonmedical applications only from applicants who appear to meet the company's underwriting requirements from a physical, medical, occupational, and moral standpoint. The agent must elicit from the applicant and accurately document most of the information that a medical examiner would seek. A detailed agent's certificate that records the agent's underwriting impressions of the applicant is also required. It is understandable that the privilege of submitting nonmedical business is not bestowed indiscriminately on the field force. Inspection reports are sometimes ordered to

supplement the larger nonmedical insurance applications, even though such information would not be requested for medically underwritten cases for the same or larger amounts of coverage.

Economics of Nonmedical Insurance

Several advantages are associated with nonmedical insurance. It lessens the demands on the time and talents of the medical profession, it eliminates the delays and inconvenience connected with medical examinations, and it removes one of the greatest psychological barriers to the sale of insurance. Important as these advantages are, insurers could not enjoy them if nonmedical insurance did not rest on a solid economic foundation. It must justify itself on a dollars-and-cents basis.

As mentioned earlier, nonmedical insurance is subject to a higher rate of mortality than medically examined business. This extra mortality is believed to stem from (1) impairments known to the applicant but deliberately concealed and (2) impairments not known to the applicant that could have been discovered by a medical examination. This extra mortality can be measured and expressed as a dollar amount per $1,000 of insurance.

The procedure customarily used to measure the extra mortality is to compare the mortality experience on nonmedical business with the mortality at the same ages, years of issue, and durations on business that was subject to a medical examination. This does not give a direct answer to the question of what the mortality on the nonmedical applicants would have been had they been selected by medical examination, since the two groups may not be comparable in all respects. For example, they might differ as to ratio of males to females, income level, and size of policies. Nevertheless, this method is the best available and is deemed satisfactory.

Studies reveal that most of the extra mortality occurs during the first 10 years after issue, although some extra mortality is observable up to 15 years after the policy is issued. The disparity between nonmedical and medical mortality increases with age of issue, both in absolute amount and as a percentage of the base mortality rate. This seems to indicate that up to a point at least, the importance and effectiveness of the medical examination grow greater with age. Extra death claims are offset by the savings in medical examiners' fees and incidental home office expenses, less the increase in expenditures for inspection reports and attending physicians' statements. This net saving, it should be noted, is realized on every application that does not involve a medical examination, while the extra mortality is experienced only on those policies that remain in force until they become claims—a much smaller number because of lapses and surrenders. The savings in selection expenses are expressed as an amount per policy and range from $30 to $100.

Example

Trade-off between extra mortality costs and savings in underwriting expense

Once the extra mortality per $1,000 and the expense savings per policy are known, it is a matter of simple arithmetic to determine the proper limits for nonmedical insurance. If, at ages below 30, the extra mortality cost per $1,000 is $0.75 and the expense savings per policy is assumed to be $100, the company could safely offer about $133,000 of nonmedical insurance to applicants under 30 ($100 ÷ 0.75 = $133 rounded to nearest whole number). With the same expense savings and an extra mortality cost of $1.50 per $1,000 at ages 30 to 34, the proper limit for persons in that age group would be $67,000 ($100 ÷ 1.50 = $67 rounded). By the same logic, the limit for applicants aged 35 to 39 might be about $30,000. Thus, the need for age limits and the equity of variable limits are apparent.

In practice, companies are inclined to offer larger amounts of nonmedical insurance than the above figures suggest. While the amount made available to any one applicant might seem excessive, all applicants do not request the maximum. Because the company's objective is to break even on its nonmedical business in the aggregate, it may safely set its limits higher than the precise relationship between the expected extra mortality and expense savings would support.

Furthermore, at ages under 30, the absolute rate of mortality is so low and the probability of finding impairments on examination so small that the nonmedical rules can be greatly relaxed. A particular company may also set its nonmedical limits on the basis of its own mortality experience and expense assumptions or in response to competitive factors. The increased use of blood and urine screening tests also allows for increased nonmedical limits.

Special Branches of Nonmedical Insurance

There are certain special situations in which policies may be issued on a nonmedical basis even when the company does not follow a general practice of issuing nonmedical policies. Three of the most common instances are discussed in this subsection.

Policyowner Nonmedical

Most companies are willing to issue insurance up to a stated limit on the basis of the applicant's declaration of good health if, within a short period prior to issuance—such as 3 to 6 months—standard insurance has been obtained from the company on the basis of a satisfactory medical examination. The reasoning behind this practice, of course, is that the

policyowner's health is not likely to have deteriorated within such a short period of time, and any serious affliction would probably be apparent to the agent.

Some companies have extended this privilege to policyowners who apply for additional insurance within a much longer period, such as one to 5 years. Under such circumstances, however, the applicant is required to bring physical and medical histories up to date, and the case is underwritten on the basis of both the old and the new information. The general experience under this type of nonmedical insurance has not been very favorable and indicates some adverse selection among applicants.

This category of insurance without medical examination goes under the name of policyowner nonmedical, because it is limited to applicants who are already policyowners of the company.

Guaranteed Issue

guaranteed issue

Traditionally, if individual contracts were used, each employee had to furnish evidence of insurability—a satisfactory medical examination. Current practice, however, includes underwriting such plans on a nonmedical basis. In fact, the arrangement frequently goes beyond the conventional concepts of nonmedical insurance. If the group is acceptable, the insurance company dispenses with individual underwriting and agrees in advance to accept all applications for insurance up to a formula-determined limit. This practice is known as **guaranteed issue**. There is no underwriting beyond a screening of the group and the person's being a member of the group.

A higher than normal mortality is anticipated on these products. The mortality rate is higher than that associated with ordinary nonmedical insurance, not only because of the absence of individual underwriting but also because the age distribution of the employees is likely to be higher than that of normal nonmedical groups.

In order to offset the anticipated extra mortality under guaranteed issue plans, most companies pay lower than normal commissions and separately classify the policies for dividend purposes.

Paramedical Examination

Somewhere between the medical examination and nonmedical evidence is another alternative—the paramedical examination. This examination is conducted by nurses or other medical technicians and consists of securing basic examination from measurements:

height, weight, blood pressure, pulse rate and waist measurement. Blood and urine specimens may also be taken.

The chief advantages of paramedical examinations are their reduced cost compared to a physician's fees and their convenience for the client since most services offer traveling examiners. The paramedical examinations, however, do not include the heart and other detailed reports typically provided by an insurance medical examiner.

Example

The convenience of paramedical examiners coming to the home or workplace of the applicant eliminate potential delays in the process that scheduling a medical examination might impose. These traveling examiners have expedited the evaluation process and reduced some of the costs.

INSURABILITY OPTION

With all new policies except those issued on a substandard basis and short-duration term policies, most insurance companies are now offering an option that permits the policyowner, at stated intervals and below a specified age, to purchase specified amounts of additional insurance without evidence of insurability. The additional insurance need not be on the same plan as the basic policy to which the option is attached; the option is exercisable in favor of any standard whole life or other cash value insurance policies offered by the company. Premiums for the new insurance are payable at standard rates on the basis of the insured's attained age on the option date. If the original policy contains a waiver-of-premium provision and accidental death benefits, the new policies will, at the insured's option, contain the same features. If premiums are being waived on the original policy at the time an option for additional insurance is exercised, premiums on the new policy will be waived from the beginning (and will continue to be waived if the insured is totally disabled).

The insurability options vary as to details, but the first provision of this type,[3] which was introduced in the 1950s and has served as a pattern for most of those introduced later, permitted the insured to purchase up to $10,000 of additional insurance at 3-year intervals beginning with the policy anniversary nearest the insured's 25th birthday and terminating with the anniversary nearest the insured's 40th birthday. Under current policies, the amount of insurance that can be obtained on each specified policy anniversary is usually

---

3.   This option was first introduced by the Bankers Life Insurance Company of Des Moines, Iowa, under the name of guaranteed purchase option.

limited to some percentage of the original face amount up to a specified maximum dollar amount, such as $60,000. Some policies also specify an aggregate limit (for example, two times the original face amount) on the amount of coverage that can be purchased under this option without evidence of insurability. Option amounts vary from company to company but may be as high as $100,000 per exercise option with some insurers.

Some contracts also permit the purchase of additional insurance upon the insured's marriage or following the birth of the insured's first child or subsequent children. Some contracts even provide coverage automatically for 60 to 90 days after each option date.

The option is available only for an extra premium that varies, not in proportion to the number of option dates remaining, as might be supposed, but with the age of issue. The schedule of annual premiums charged for the option by one company begins at $0.50 per $1,000 at age 0 and increases to approximately $2.00 per $1,000 at age 37. These premiums reflect the company's estimate of the average amount of extra mortality that it will experience on policies issued without evidence of insurability and, from the standpoint of the insured, may be regarded as the cost of "insuring" his or her insurability. Premiums for the option are payable to the last anniversary at which it can be exercised—usually age 40—or to the end of the premium-paying period of the basic policy, whichever is earlier.

Many insurers also offer guaranteed insurance under cost-of-living adjustments that increase policy amounts based on rises in economic inflation indicators, such as the Consumer Price Index. The insured typically can accept or refuse this offer, but if the insured refuses, the provisions may terminate. Guaranteed insurance under cost-of-living adjustments is typically offered at 3-year intervals from the issue date of the policy.

INSURANCE AT EXTREMES OF AGE

Applications for insurance at both extremes of age must be carefully underwritten. In both cases, the basic obstacle is limited insurable interest—which, if not recognized, may lead to speculation and excessive mortality.

In some families, there is a demand for juvenile insurance, and most companies will write insurance on the lives of very young children, even down to 15 days old. These insurers attempt to cope with the lack of insurable interest in three ways: (1) by limiting the coverage to amounts much smaller than those available to adults, particularly at the early ages, (2) by seeing that the insurance on the child bears a reasonable relationship to the amounts in force on the other members of the family, especially the breadwinner, and (3) by seeking a large volume of juvenile insurance applications to minimize adverse selection.

From the standpoint of the basic mortality risk, juvenile risks are very attractive. With the exception of the first few weeks after birth, the death rate is very low and does not begin to climb until around age 10. The death rate is high immediately after birth because of the hazards of childbirth to the child, congenital defects, and the naturally delicate physique of a newborn infant. This period of heavy mortality can be avoided by limiting coverage to children who have attained the age of one, 3, or perhaps 6 months. Family economic circumstances seem to have greater influence on mortality at the younger ages than later in life, which makes it necessary to inquire about family finances. In general, juvenile insurance is sold without a medical examination.

At the other extreme—that is, at the older ages—the lack of insurable interest is only one of the complicating factors. In the first place, the volume of insurance issued at ages above 70 or 75 is not large enough to yield predictable mortality results. The restricted demand for insurance at those ages reflects the high cost of the insurance, the general inability to satisfy the medical requirements, and the limited need for new insurance. In the second place, a high degree of adverse selection is associated with applications received at those ages. Low volume in itself is suggestive of adverse selection, but when it is accompanied by burdensome premium payments, the environment is even more conducive to adverse selection. This antiselection may be exercised by the insureds themselves, aware of a serious impairment, or by a third party, perhaps a relative, who seeks insurance on the life of an elderly person for speculative reasons. A third factor, related to the others, is the relative ineffectiveness of the medical examination for elderly people. A routine medical examination does not reveal many conditions of a degenerative nature that can materially shorten the life of the elderly applicant.

Estate tax law changes of the 1980s have led to a dramatic expansion of the marketing of life insurance, particularly joint-life and survivorship products, to applicants of advanced age. This has resulted in the extension of insurable ages to 90 or 95 by some insurers.

ETHICAL ISSUES OF CLASSIFYING RISK

Morality has been aptly described[4] as a social system of rules created to allow people to adjudicate disputes rationally without resorting to physical force so that the relationships affected by the dispute can endure and, perhaps, even flourish. Because most disputes are generated over the question of who is entitled to certain goods, the pursuit of goods and the avoidance of harm are at the core of any moral system. Hence, we can claim that the

---

4.   Stanley Cavell, The Claims of Reason , p. 119.

creation of some benefit or the avoidance of harm is the goal of any activity. The first prong of the ethical approach then is to determine what counts as goods and harms. The second part of the approach is that such goals should be achieved fairly, that is, without doing an injustice to others.

Thus, we can say that ethics deals primarily with enhancing, not diminishing, the quality of life on the one hand, and the issues of fairness and justice on the other. The basic ethical rule can be summarized: pursue your interests fairly and unselfishly. Fair treatment means "the same should be treated the same." Consequently, a difference in treatment is justified only when there are relevant differences. Selfish behavior is behavior in which the pursuit of self-interest is without regard for the interests of, or at the expense of, others. This rule is required in any society that claims to be rational to prevent life in that society from being, as characterized by Thomas Hobbes, "nasty, brutish and short."

To illustrate why fairness is the rational way in which to proceed, imagine how irrational it is to treat two identical things differently. For example, if there are two identical paintings and we think one has superb composition, it is illogical to think the other painting, which is identical, does not also have superb composition. Similarly, if two people are identical in all relevant ways and one is entitled to something, so is the other. Children recognize this concept at an early age. For them it is unfair if one of their siblings, who they see as essentially the same as themselves, is given a bigger share of some good. Of course, if it is the sibling's birthday, that constitutes a relevant difference which underlines the lack of identity. Thus, when children begin to use reason, they clearly see the basic principle of fairness—"the same should be treated the same." If we believe that most human beings are alike in most morally relevant respects, then they should be treated the same in most respects.

This notion of fairness and rational thinking underlies the principle of the Golden Rule: "Do unto others as you would have others do unto you." This principle reinforces the notion that others are the same as you in most relevant respects.

Reflecting on the principle of fairness helps us see the unethical nature of selfishness. By "selfishness" we do not mean just the pursuit of self-interest. The pursuit of self-interest is a perfectly natural and acceptable activity. Selfishness is the pursuit of self-interest at the expense of another when one is not entitled to the good pursued. When a person is being selfish, he or she puts their own interest first in a situation where pursuing that interest will hurt another. For example, if there is one piece of cake allotted to each person at a party, and I take two pieces, I have deprived someone of their share of the cake. The question, of course, to be asked is why is one person entitled to more than another. If two people need or want the same thing and only one can have it, how is it to be decided who will get it? In such a case whoever pursues his own interest will do so at the expense of the other. It is

for situations like this that society has created rules of fair distribution. If two people have a desire or need for the good, why should it go to one and not to the other? We need rules to decide. These are the ethical rules of society.

Adam Smith, a famous eighteenth century philosopher, ethicist, and economist indicated in his work, The Wealth of Nations, that what motivated a great deal of activity was self-interest. He thought that the free pursuit of self-interest without concern for societal benefits would bring about more social benefit than if government tried to intervene to bring about just results. (This is his famous "doctrine of the invisible hand.") Still, Smith always cautioned that such a pursuit of self-interest must be limited by considerations of justice and fairness. Further, he noted that there are two great motivators of humans—self-interest and a concern for others which he called "sympathy." This concern (sympathy) for the benefit of others allows us to check our self-interest when it is at the expense of others and justice or fairness demands it.

The demands for justice and enhanced quality of life require a set of ethical rules for appropriate behavior that govern any existing society. How are such rules established? Basically, they are established through a process of trial and error, and the assigning of responsibilities, all of which aim at a type of social stability that will allow the individuals of the society to flourish.

Societies in the Greco-Roman-Judeo-Christian tradition developed these general principles into more specific rules, such as the Ten Commandments, which include prohibitions against murder, stealing, lying, adultery, and so forth. They indicate what counts as proper behavior toward others.

It is easy to see how those specific Commandments rest on the more general prohibitions against selfishness and unfairness. For example, stealing is wrong because it is fundamentally unfair or selfish. If a person has acquired property through a process the society deems fair only to have it taken by another who is not entitled to it (has no right to it) because they have not acquired it through an approved process, such stealing violates fairness and involves selfishness.

One of the processes for distribution of goods that our society has set up is the process of market acquisition. Smith said human beings have a natural propensity to barter and to trade, which is driven by the desire to be better off because of the trade. The free exchange of goods in a market requires the informed consent of both parties. Neither party would give consent if their information on the proposed trade indicated they would not benefit. For example, if we view a life insurance sale as a market transition, we can see that certain types of fraud that misrepresent the product or withhold significant information do not

allow informed consent, so they constitute misappropriation of the buyer's goods. Such a sale involves a type of stealing that is unfair and unjust.

To be fair or just requires society to work out procedures for the distribution of the benefits and burdens of the world. Entitlement to the benefits are rights, and burdens are obligations or responsibilities. What is due another as a right is generally determined by the relationship to the person with the obligation. For example, if I have a right to liberty that means all those who have a relationship with me which could impede my liberty have an obligation to respect my autonomy. Further, if I have a right to an education, certain individuals have an obligation to provide it. Some relationships exist simply because we share the same world. Other relationships exist because we have entered into a type of relationship with another that involves a commitment to them. In societies there are various relationships, some natural and some conventional (literally based on agreements), that help in the smooth functioning of those societies. Many of those conventional relationships are based on promises made, implicit or explicit contracts to which people are committed. For example, if I become a parent, I have implicitly committed—and my society expects me—to meet certain obligations to care for and educate my child. As another example, societies set up various jobs (the division of labor); people who, more or less freely, take on one or more of those jobs, commit to do what the job requires. Commitment to jobs and relationships automatically carries responsibilities.

Assuming most of the social rules or jobs we take on are beneficial to society, we want to take a look at the various relationships that are the result of a division of labor in society. This will help us to see what responsibilities fall on those who take up certain positions within society. In this section we will apply the ethics of relationships to the insurance industry, and specify the rights and responsibilities of the various individuals and constituencies in the world of insurance. We will look at some particular practices that are ethically suspect and try to show why they are inappropriate and, if they are problematic, show the reasons both for and against them.

Insurance is first of all a cooperative enterprise hence a social system created to minimize the risk of financial loss from specific unforeseen future events. It minimizes the risk of financial loss both to oneself and to others, depending on the beneficiary. To enter into a private insurance contract is, in effect, to enter into a group of one's own free will in order to collectively help one another minimize the risks involved. (This applies to private insurance; public insurance is a compulsory group.) The collective nature of insurance immediately raises ethical questions about the fairness or unfairness of discriminating for some and against others who wish to join a group. For example, if a group of healthy people join together to insure their lives, the cost of insurance would be much cheaper if they could exclude people with unhealthy characteristics, histories, and/or lifestyles.

Applying our ethical concepts, one could ask if it is "fair" for such a group to be exclusionary. If someone significantly more unhealthy than the others wants to pay, what is the fair price for entrance? In this case, ethics and morality are at work. There is a dispute about whether someone should be allowed to join a group. The joining would be at the expense of the others. Under what conditions would causing that harm to others be justified by the benefit of including the unhealthy person? What reasons can be given in answer to such questions? The reasons that can be given constitute the fundamental ethical concepts.

When we consider life insurance in particular, as opposed to property and casualty insurance, a relevant difference arises. Life insurance is primarily designed to provide support for dependents. Property and casualty insurance is meant to minimize the risk to oneself rather than benefit survivors. Life insurance was originally designed to respond to an ethical belief that people have a moral responsibility for the support and maintenance of their children during the children's dependent years. Given that fact, life insurance is a rare financial instrument whereby the benefit goes to a person other than the one who makes the investment and the sacrifice. In its earliest form, before the use of life insurance as an investment or a viatical tool, or a source of long-term care, it required the setting aside of one's self-interest for the sake of others. That is the very essence of unselfish behavior, and selfishness is paradigmatic of unethical behavior. Consequently, a life insurance salesperson becomes a promoter of this type of altruistic behavior.

However, while the original concept of insurance is remarkably simple—a group of people joining to pool their resources to protect themselves from risk—the products and their distribution have gotten quite complex over the years. Questions of what is fair and right and beneficial to whom, all-important ethical issues, have gotten similarly complex. We will now take a look at some of the ethical issues and responsibilities that face the various actors in the drama of the life insurance industry.

Recently there has been intense interest in the ethics of market behavior, essentially focused on the misrepresentation of the values of certain products, or on the unnecessary replacement of policies to further the interests of the agent, thereby helping the agent meet quotas to further the profits of the company. But this is only one type of ethical difficulty present in the field of life insurance. Other problems involve the ethics of underwriting or conflicts between the demands of the company and the demands of the client. Some of the issues are merely matters of selfishness or greed on the part of the agent, while others involve conflicts of obligations where the agent is in a no-win situation.

There are at least three groups of people (four if we distinguish between the insured and the insured's beneficiaries) involved in the ethics of insurance: the insurer (the company), the insured (the client or beneficiary), and the agent. Each of these has a relationship to

the other and, as we have seen, relationships carry ethical responsibilities. Some of these relationships occur as a given in life, some are taken on freely and are the result of implied or explicit commitments. The remainder of the chapter will investigate those relationships and the moral responsibilities that arise from them.

The three relationships we will examine are:

1. the agent/client relationship

2. the agent/insurer relationship

3. the insured/insurer relationship.

Before examining the three relationships, we need to expand upon what we have said so far about the ethics of relationships. Every human being is involved in an indefinite, if not infinite, number of relationships of varying degrees of proximity. We can view each person as somehow in relation to the whole universe and, in a sense, we could say everyone and everything is interdependent. There are numerous discussions of our relationships to the universe, to the world, to ecological systems, to other animals, and to all other humans in a brother- and sisterhood of persons. But the obligations and responsibilities that arise from those relationships are quite amorphous and undefined. We can certainly claim that people ought to respect whatever exists and treat all things with care, and we can argue for a general rule that stipulates no one should do harm to anything. By narrowing our concentration, we can move from a focus on all beings; to all living beings; to all animals; to all sentient animals; to the human race; to the citizens of our country; to the members of our immediate community; to our schools, neighborhoods, churches, clients, and families. In doing so, our responsibilities and obligations progressively become more narrowly defined and delineated. More narrow responsibilities are the result of more specific commitments. For example, as we have seen, when I take a job I commit to do those things required by that specific job. When I become a friend, I commit to do the things required by that particular friendship. When I commit to be a parent, which I do when I have a child—which does not take an explicit commitment of marriage—I commit to do the things necessary to bring that child up well. Finally, when I commit to be an insurance agent, I commit to meet certain responsibilities toward my clients and the company. Focusing on these responsibilities is to adopt an approach to ethics that has been called role morality. Role morality means that one's situation in life, which results from commitments to others, brings with it specific duties.

At this point let's turn our attention to the three specific relationships that exist in the insurance industry (agent/client, agent/insurer, and insured/insurer) and examine the specific ethical responsibilities of the partners in each relationship.

The Agent/Client Relationship

The Agent's Responsibility to the Client

Analyzing the ethical aspects of the agent/client relationship without reference to the insurer is somewhat problematic because, in insurance, there is really a three-part relationship in which the agent is a mediator between the company and the client. However for purposes of discussion we will focus on the various two-part relationships that exist and take cognizance of the added dimensions as necessary.

In the agent/client relationship it is important to note that the responsibilities change toward the client during the course of the relationship. For example, the client is technically only a prospective client before the policy goes into effect. In the early stages of contact between agent and client, the client is a customer and the agent is a salesperson. In that context, the ethics of marketing hold. In a marketing situation the agent is obliged to adhere to the requirements of honest marketing, such as necessary disclosure and the avoidance of undue pressure which could limit the client's freedom to buy or not to buy. Once the insurance goes into effect the customer is then an "insured" and a client, and new obligations emerge. The agent's responsibilities now include servicing, helping with claims, and updating policies.

The differences can be obviated by the adoption of a general principle to cover all phases of the relationship. Most people would agree that the agent should follow the Golden Rule and treat clients as the agent would like to be treated. The professional pledge to which all CLU and ChFC designees commit specifically applies that Golden Rule when it states: "I shall, in light of all conditions surrounding those I serve, which I shall make every conscientious effort to ascertain and understand, render that service which, in the same circumstances, I would apply to myself." This rule exists and needs to be followed because insurance agents, like everyone else, are subject to the conflict between self-interest and the interests of others.

Agents should make recommendations based on their client's needs, but obviously they need to sell policies to make a living and their company needs to sell policies to stay in business. Consequently, from time to time, there can be pressure based on the agent's personal financial situation or from the agent's company and manager to sell the client what he or she does not need. According to The Market Conduct Handbook for Agents, "The insurer may say it wants the field force to provide a careful needs analysis but, in fact, the reward system for the agent is based on sales—not service. If an agent discovers that less service and needs analysis can result in quicker sales, then the agent faces the ethical

conflict of whether to make more sales and more money at the expense of the clients' needs."[5] Of course, for the agent to act in his own self-interest at the expense of another is the very core of selfishness; it is an attitude universally condemned.

Other than the avoidance of selfishness, and the refusal to sell what does not need to be sold, what other responsibilities does an agent have to a client by virtue of his or her role as an agent? That agent certainly has an obligation to ascertain a client's needs for life insurance. It is unethical to sell a client an unnecessary insurance policy. The attempt to sell a client an unnecessary policy would tend to involve lying and/or deception, practices universally considered unethical.

There might be times when such a sale does not involve deception but is the result of the agent's ignorance about the product. The agent might not have known what the client needed and subsequently recommended an unsuitable product. If the agent does not know but could reasonably be expected to know, that agent has an obligation to divulge the ignorance and to learn more. If the agent thinks he knows but does not, we might hold the agent responsible for his ignorance. Whatever the resolution of these issues, we can see that the obligation to do an analysis of needs puts the further requirement of product knowledge on the shoulders of the agent. In addition to adherence to the Golden Rule in selling and looking out for the client's best interests, other obligations are inherent in the agent/client relationship.

Confidentiality. In the course of writing a policy and doing a needs evaluation, the agent acquires a great deal of private information about the client. It is an obligation of the agent to keep such client information confidential, which means it should only be shared with those who have a legitimate right to such information after the client has authorized a release.

Obligations Associated with Delivering the Policy. "The agent is responsible for delivering the insurance policy to the insured and (many times) also collects any premium which may be due at the time of policy delivery. Since some coverages do not take effect until the policy is delivered, timely delivery is crucial."[6] Obviously, the agent should take the time to explain all the policy provisions, including riders and exclusions, to see one more time if the policy meets the needs of the client, and to explain how the agency handles ongoing service. Finally, the agent needs to explain any changes that have been made to the policy that were not in the original application.

---

5. Cynthia Davidson, The Market Conduct Handbook for Agents , p. 29.
6. Cynthia Davidson, The Market Conduct Handbook for Agents , p. 45.

Claims Handling. When the situation arises for the owner or beneficiary to make a claim, the agent has a responsibility to help in various ways: explaining what the beneficiary is obliged to do in order to collect on a claim, helping the beneficiary expedite the claim settlement, mediating between the beneficiary and the insurer, and explaining the final settlement if the settlement is not what the owner or beneficiary expected.

Other Servicing. The agent should review the client's policies to see if they are up to date with reference to beneficiaries, and more importantly, to see if they provide the coverages currently needed.

Ethics of Market Conduct. Thus far we have looked at what the agent should do. All the above aside, most attention to ethics in the insurance industry is paid to market misconduct and the most notorious examples of unethical behavior on the part of agents comes under the heading of unfair trade.

One unfair trade practice is misrepresentation, including misrepresenting the benefits or terms of a policy; misrepresenting dividends as guaranteed when they are not; misrepresenting the financial condition of the insurer; misrepresenting a life insurance policy as other than what it is; or, finally, misrepresenting oneself by perhaps claiming to be a financial planner when one is not.

Coercion that restricts free choice of products is also unethical. For example, for a bank to coerce one of its clients into buying the mortgage insurance it is selling rather than a competitor's insurance as a condition of granting a loan is clearly unethical. This obviously violates the conditions of a free market exchange and informed consent as discussed.

Other well-known types of unethical behavior are twisting and churning. Twisting occurs when a policyowner is induced to discontinue and replace a policy through agent or insurer distortion or misrepresentation of the facts. When a policy is replaced unnecessarily it is known as churning. These practices are obviously unethical to the extent they exemplify the agent pursuing self-interest at the expense of the client. If the replacement were really beneficial to the client, it would be the ethically correct thing to do. There is also the practice of rebating, which is usually considered unethical, although there is some argument. "Rebating is defined as any inducement in the sale of insurance that is not specified in the insurance contract."[7] An offer to share a commission with an applicant is an example of such an inducement, and is illegal in most states except California and Florida. Rebating is generally considered wrong because it gives one agent an unfair advantage over other agents, or is seen as unfair to those clients who are not given a rebate. Defenders of

---

7.   Cynthia Davidson, The Market Conduct Handbook for Agents , p. 49.

rebating argue that it is not unfair, but rather should be viewed simply as a competitive market ploy.

"It is also generally unethical, as well as illegal, for an agent to charge fees in addition to a policy premium for services that are not 'truly' extra."[8] Currently there is a good deal of argument concerning the proper way to compensate agents. Because of recent abuses in the replacement of policies in order to take advantage of front-end-loaded commissions, the question is raised about the appropriateness of front-end-loaded commission-based selling as opposed to levelized commissions or fee-based selling.

It goes without saying that the agent owes the client the truth. Knowing that, we see that it is unethical to do what is called company bashing. It is clearly unethical to tell lies or to misrepresent the strengths and weaknesses of the competition whether it is another agent or another company. Yet there are numerous examples of agents who suggest that another agent or company is disreputable. Certainly if a product is not meeting a client's needs, or if clients are being misguided by another agent, the first agent has an obligation to disclose that fact, but it should be based on facts, not the needs and desires of the agent to replace the company business of another agent.

Discrimination against clients for reasons other than sound actuarial principles is unethical. Discrimination—which used to be a neutral term to describe the process of choosing to include or exclude people on the basis of some relevant characteristic(s)—has become a pejorative term. Unethical discrimination is exclusion committed on the basis of some unjustified bias or hatred toward a person or group. Hence, discrimination committed on the basis of such considerations as race, sex, religion, nationality, or ethnic group is unethical when those considerations are irrelevant and when they are done from motivations such as sexism, racism, or antireligious bias. There are, of course, insurance companies that are tied to a particular religious or national group. Their exclusion of nonmembers is not unethical. But if a company is not an exclusive company from its inception, then such exclusionary policies are unethical. There are, however, legitimate reasons in underwriting for exclusion. A famous case of whether the discrimination was permissible concerned granting of premiums to young women drivers that were lower than the premiums applied to men. Actuarially, as a group, young women had safer driving records than their male counterparts. Was this sexist? Because it was not based on denigrating women, and in fact favored them, it was not deemed discriminatory in the unethical sense.

It is unethical for the agent to discriminate against a client based on considerations such as race, for this violates one of the first principles of a market economy: in any exchange only

---

8.   Cynthia Davidson, *The Market Conduct Handbook for Agents*, p. 40.

relevant economic factors should apply. Questions that should be asked are: Is the person worth the risk? Does the person have the ability to pay?

These, in brief, are the ethical responsibilities an agent has toward his or her client. We now need to consider the responsibilities the client has toward his agent or the company.

Client Responsibilities. The agent/client relationship is not a one-way street. Thus far we have talked mainly of the agent's responsibilities to the client. The client has ethical responsibilities to the agent as well. Again the principle is simple: the client should do nothing that is deceitful, unfair, or harmful to the agent or the company. The insured owes the company the truth. The chief examples of a client's unethical behavior include fraudulent claims, lying to the agent and withholding information on an application.

There is a widespread practice involving fraudulent claims, particularly in the disability income area where back injuries are faked in order to collect compensation. The fact that such practices exist does not make them ethically acceptable. They are fraudulent and unfair because their cost is borne by those who pay premiums and/or by those who receive less return on their investments. Another type of unethical practice is lying or withholding information on an application. There are a number of stories told in which a client, while smoking a cigarette, has told the agent he is a nonsmoker. What should an agent do? There are agents who write the policy the way the applicant wants. The honest agent will not do this, but the client puts that agent in an uncomfortable situation by asking him to violate his obligation to the company. In this case we are focusing on the ethics of the client. It is unethical to put an agent into that kind of situation and it is unethical to lie.

Once again, as in the fraudulent claims case, the fact that many people lie on their applications does not make it right.

The following example shows the subtle kind of unethical behavior engaged in by the client when he puts the agent into a conflict of interest situation. Consider the following example.

Example

Your brother-in-law, Sam, an attorney, is undergoing treatment for an inoperable malignant brain tumor. Because of the aggressive nature of the treatment, he may live for up to 3 years. On the other hand, he may not make it 3 months.

Sam feels he is woefully underinsured. He is concerned for his family's financial welfare after his death. So are you.

Sam has always been a bit of a spendthrift. He has lived the good life, spending everything he has earned over the course of the years—and then some. You know that you will probably have to help support his family if he dies without adequate life insurance.

Sam comes to you, an experienced, professional life insurance agent and asks for your help and understanding. Sam wants to apply for life insurance—not a big policy, but $100,000 of annual renewable term, which he feels is just enough to guarantee his children's college education. He plans to deny his medical history when he is examined for the policy. He will claim that he has no attending physician.

Sam is prepared to take his chances that he will live beyond the policy's contestable period. As an attorney, he believes that he fully understands the implications of what he is about to do, at least as far as those implications may affect his beneficiaries.

He does not however seem to have given much thought to how they may affect you and your career.

What are your ethical obligations to Sam, to Sam's family, to your company (if you give it the business), and to yourself?[9]

The example is interesting because selfishness on the agent's part is not involved, rather there is a conflict of loyalty. Sam, as a member of the agent's family, puts a claim on the agent in the name of family loyalty and, in this situation, the family's interest conflicts with the company's interest.

There are other cases in which the self-interest of an agent is involved. For example, when an agent knows the applicant is a smoker, or has cancer, and also knows that if he does not write the policy, someone else will. So the agent is losing a client and the commission that goes with it. What is the ethical thing to do in that case? What does the agent owe the company? Because honesty in filling out the application will cost the agent the commission, there is great temptation to submit false data on the application. There is also a conflict between the agents, clients, and companies interest (the interests of the shareholders and other policyowners of the company). Clearly misrepresenting the fact of smoking on

---

9.   Taken from Alan Press, "Ethical Standards for General Agents and Managers."

an application is unfair as well as dishonest because it lets the current applicant play on an uneven field.

What these examples show is that clients have at least three obligations: 1) to tell the truth on an application, 2) to file honest claims, and 3) to not put the agent into an unnecessary conflict-of-interest situation. Acquiescence by the agent is essentially collusion against the insurer and the other policyowners.

We turn now to the relationship of the agent to the insurer (company).

The Agent/Insurer Relationship

The Agent's Responsibilities to the Company

An agent (and, in some cases, a broker) serves as an agent of the company in accord with agency law. That means the agent is empowered to act on behalf of the company (known in law as the principal) and acts performed by the agent bind the company. Thus, in certain situations and under certain conditions, when the agent signs an application or binds an insurance contract, he or she binds the company to that contract. However, because an agent is expected to act in the best interests of the company, there are times the agent's interests are expected to be subordinated to those of the company. There is a proviso here, however. An agent is never required to do anything illegal for the sake of the company. Many would expand upon that to say an agent is never required to do anything illegal or unethical for the sake of the company. It is an interesting phenomenon that a vital ethical issue among office assistants is whether they are required to lie on behalf of their bosses. Something as seemingly innocuous as telling a caller with relevant business that the boss is not in—when he or she is—takes on moral import.

If the agent is bound to look out for the best interest of the principal, part of defining the responsibilities of the agent to the company will require a look at the interests of the company. In insurance there are three types of companies: mutual, publicly owned for profit, and state run. The mutual company is theoretically a group of individual insureds with a mutual interest who pool their resources in order to protect themselves from undue risk. The publicly owned for profit company is a business set up with a pool of resources that allows one to purchase protection from risk at a price. State funded insurance programs may or may not be considered insurance companies depending on one's definition of risk management. Nevertheless, the purpose of the state-run program is to provide public services for private individuals who, in some cases, do not enter the program voluntarily but are required to belong. The focus here will be on the mutual and for profit companies.

It has been said (by such as Milton Friedman) that the primary and only responsibility of for profit businesses is to maximize profit for the shareholders. Hence, as an agent for the company, the agent must act on behalf of the company, and act in ways that will make money for the company, not cost the company money.

There is a popular hypothetical case in which a husband cancels a life insurance policy covering himself. His wife had encouraged him to purchase the policy, and he had reluctantly agreed. The cancellation took place late on a Friday. The agent did the paper work and gave the client a cancellation slip, but did not send the requisite paperwork to the company because the mail had already been collected for the weekend. The husband was killed in a hunting accident on Saturday and his wife called the agent on Sunday because she was unable to find the policy, all she had found was the cancellation memorandum. This scenario raises many questions. What should the agent do? What obligations does the agent have to the company? What obligations does the agent have to the wife?

If we concentrate on the obligation to the company we can state that though sympathy favors ripping up the return receipt and the paperwork, that is not fair to the company. The agent's first loyalty is to the company. As harsh as it sounds, it is nonetheless true that giving the money to the wife is tantamount to giving stockholder's money to her. Of course, considerations of good public relations and a compassionate image might persuade the company to pay the benefit if they knew the truth. But that raises the question of what obligations companies have to clients or former clients.

Some people would argue that the agent should withhold the information from the company while others would argue that as an agent, committed to looking out for the best interests of the company, he would be obliged to inform the company of the cancellation. The law clearly maintains the latter position. The courts hold that a company is aware of all information known by any of its agents. When polled on this issue, agents are likely to be split in their response as to which course of action is ethical.

Not all situations are as difficult to resolve as the one above. In most situations the obligations are clear. The agent's contract or agency agreement spells out many of the agent's (or broker's) responsibilities to the company.

The Company's Responsibilities to the Agent

Agent Support and Training. Companies have two obligations with respect to training their agents. First, they owe it to their agents to insure that they have the competence to do adequate analyses of the various needs of their clients. Secondly, they owe it to their agents to teach them what behavior is ethically acceptable and what is not. One might

expect young recruits to be able to distinguish between the acceptable and the unacceptable, but a young, inexperienced person might be more easily swayed into thinking that a somewhat shady practice is standard operating procedure. I have experienced a company (not an insurance company) that taught its young salespeople to slip a contract and a pen into the hands of a prospective client on the premise that only 5 percent of people would have enough fortitude to hand back a contract without signing it if the sales presentation were handled correctly. That is a real hard sell technique. What is valued by such a hard-sell artist is not whether the client's needs have been met but whether the sale is made. The sales manager who trains his recruits that such behavior is intolerable meets his ethical obligation; the hard-sell artist does not.

Provide Clear Sales Materials. In addition to offering the agent training, the company should provide the agent with good tools—sales material that is clear and nondeceptive.

Fair Commission Structures. One cannot pick up literature about how to influence ethical behavior without sooner or later encountering the question of the effects of commission structures on ethical behavior. The move to levelized commissions and/or fee for services is a direct result of the attempt to dissuade purely commission-driven sales. We can see why when we look at the next obligation, the obligation to reward ethical behavior.

Reward Ethical Behavior. Abraham Lincoln once threw a man out of his office, angrily refusing a substantial bribe. "Every man has his price," Lincoln explained, "and he was getting close to mine."[10] Human beings are self-interested and subject to temptations. Consequently, they can be motivated by the rewards their companies choose to put in place. If the only behavior rewarded is productivity, not honesty, the company is not meeting its responsibility to encourage ethical behavior. Richard O. Lundquist of the Equitable Life Assurance Society once said, "Most companies give numerous awards for achievement and accomplishment for sales, for growth, for longevity and loyalty; but there are no medals in the business world for honesty, compassion, or truthfulness."[11] Numerous studies have shown the significant correlation between behavior and rewards. Common sense tells us that what the boss rewards is what the boss expects. To the extent that a company needs to promote ethical behavior, it has a responsibility to set up systems that reward that behavior. Many of the unethical practices of the past can be traced to undue pressure from the home office to do business without regard for how that business was done.

---

10. From the lunchtime collection of Tom Steward, as quoted by Bob Solomon in The New World of Business, page 117.

11. Ibid., p. 115.

The Insured/Insurer Relationship

Company's Responsibility to the Insured

Many of the following considerations concerning the relationship of the agent to the insured have been discussed in the previous sections. As the company's agent, the agent is responsible for acting on behalf of the company. His responsibilities therefore are inherent in the fact that he is an agent. Now we will focus on the company's responsibilities.

The company's responsibilities are based on the various functions it fulfills. The company develops and markets the product. After the product is applied for, the company must underwrite the product. This underwriting makes the company the custodian of a great deal of sensitive private information about the insured. Finally, the company promises to meet the insured's legitimate claims. Each of these relationships carries ethical responsibility.

Product Creation

As with all products, insurance policies should be quality products that are dependable and not harmful. More than most products, the insurance policy is an ethical instrument because it is a promise, a promise to pay compensation given the occurrence of a specific harmful event. This places a moral burden on the company to be fiscally sound so it is able to meet its payment obligations. The product should not be excessively risky and should be fairly priced. The product is generally too complicated for the average lay person to adequately determine its value, hence, the company is responsible for giving fair value to the client.

Marketing

It should be clear that there are many ethical constraints on the marketing of the product. The utilization of the principle of caveat emptor (buyer beware) should no longer guide corporate philosophy. Products today—from pharmaceuticals, to electronics, to automobiles, to food, to insurance policies—are far too complicated for the average buyer to know their quality, safety factors, or fair market value. Liability laws indicate that society has moved from favoring caveat emptor (buyer beware) to favoring caveat vendor (seller beware). The burden to be open and honest in marketing has shifted to the producer.

An insurance company owes the client whatever any company owes a prospective customer: truth in advertising. As we have seen, the basis of the market is ideal exchange, and

ideal exchange requires full information and autonomous individuals making the choice to exchange freely. In medical ethics the operative ideal is known as informed consent. For a client to give informed consent requires there be no misleading, coercive or manipulative advertising. Such advertising takes the decision out of the hands of the client. An ad that says "guaranteed renewable" when in reality it is not, is deceptive and unethical.

Underwriting

Knowledge of health risks are relevant for underwriting purposes. One of the classic ethical conundrums is whether a company should underwrite a client who is a known health risk, such as in the case of a prospective client who has AIDS. Should insurance companies insure those with AIDS? Obviously they are not a good health risk. But most risks can be insured. So the question is not so much should companies insure people with AIDS, but rather into what insurance pool should they be placed? More humanitarian, egalitarian groups might insist on putting the AIDS group into the general pool. Of course those in that pool might call it unfair for they would, in a sense, be subsidizing the AIDS policy-owner. On the other hand, if we were to create a pool only for those who have AIDS, the cost of the premiums would be prohibitive. Some people might argue that this is an area where the insurance needs to be social insurance and, therefore, be funded through taxes.

A different problem for insurance companies is whether—and to what extent—to engage in genetic testing and/or genetic screening. This results in an actuarial paradox because the more we can predict about the future health and time of death of a person, the greater the role the risk factor plays in the decision of who gets covered and for how much. If I knew a client would cost X number of dollars to care for by a certain date, then should I not in all fairness to the other policyholders and the owners of the company, underwrite a policy in such a way that there is no loss of revenue? Companies make promises to deliver money upon certain contingencies. They have a responsibility therefore to stay in sound fiscal shape so they can deliver on those promises. The inclusion of people with known and highly predictable health risks into an insurance group at premiums that cannot be soundly underwritten is a violation of the company's trust to others who depend on its soundness. What looks hard-hearted may be the ethical path.

It could be said that the company has the right—possibly even the duty—to be discriminatory, but not unfairly discriminatory, and this involves fair underwriting. A company is obliged to treat its constituency fairly, with requirements set forth in the canons of fairness that govern marketplace transactions.

One practice that is prohibited by the NAIC's Unfair Trade Practices Act is the practice of redlining. At one time realtors drew red lines around a geographic area on a map to keep

certain people out of that area. Redlining is a form of unfair discrimination and is more common in auto insurance than in life insurance. There are companies that do not want to insure in certain geographic areas. This is not to say there are not genuine underwriting issues involved, but one must look carefully at the exclusion of anyone to see that it occurs on legitimate grounds and not on the basis of racist or sexist biases. Of course, there can be lively debate as to what counts as legitimate grounds.

As a result of the underwriting process, and given the amount of information required on insurance applications, insurance companies receive an extraordinary amount of private information about people, particularly in life insurance contracts where physical examination may be required. Thus the company is obliged to practice due care that this private information—the disclosure of which could be harmful to the client—does not become available to anyone without a reason to possess it. It is a very important responsibility for a company to keep confidentialities, including the maintenance of privacy and the protection of confidential health records.

What constitutes the proper use of health records? Clearly, only those with legitimate claims to such knowledge should have access to it. Does a pharmaceutical company have a right to access the list of a Health Maintenance Organization's client records so it can push its prescription drugs? No matter what the case, to have information on someone is to hold that information in trust and it is unethical to divulge it except to those who are legitimately entitled to it—those the client has authorized to receive the information.

Claims Settlement Practices

The insured has a right to prompt, fair, and equitable settlement. Prompt settlement is the efficient processing and payment of a claim within a reasonable time. Fair settlement means paying what a claim is worth. If a company attempts to settle a claim for less than what a reasonable person could expect, the company is acting unethically. The company also has an obligation to give reasons for any compromise claims settlement and the company has the responsibility to make known when and where appeals procedures are available.

Fair Cancellations and Nonrenewals

Suppose a company that sells guaranteed renewable disability insurance finds that such a policy is not profitable and discontinues the line. On the policy there is an automatic reinstatement period following the expiration of the contractual thirty-one day grace period, so if a policyowner missed the end of the grace period, he could get identical coverage

automatically reinstated. Suppose as a result of poor financial conditions, the company changes its procedure and requires policyowners to apply and qualify for reinstatement. That reinstatement however, when granted, is on a modified basis. Beneficial riders are dropped in some cases and some promises of return of premiums are discontinued.

In this case it would appear that the company is adopting a policy that harms policy-holders in order to minimize loss. What is the responsibility of a company that finds itself with commitments that are far more costly than they seemed originally? To what extent can the pursuit of profit override obligations to the insured? What should happen when circumstances change so that the terms of a contract now benefit one party and injure another far more than was foreseen? If the purpose is to make contracts as a hedge against those times, shouldn't they be honored? Should the insurer's main concern be profit or the benefit of the client? On the other hand, if a company needs to make adjustments to long-standing agreements in order to stay in business, aren't those adjustments ethically defensible? In our system one cannot benefit the client without remaining competitive in the marketplace.

Due Diligence in Hiring, Firing, and Retaining Agents

As mentioned, another responsibility of the company is to practice due diligence in the hiring and firing of agents. It has been said that one of the problems with retention is recruitment. If you don't recruit well, you will not retain your agents. We could add that if you don't recruit well, you may acquire unethical agents. Along with the responsibility of diligence in the hiring of agents, the company also has an obligation to provide for the training of its agents.

On another issue, should a company keep a top producer if it becomes clear that top producer writes business by cutting ethical corners? Recently a CEO of a major insurance company that had recently ceased commission payments on internal replacements con-templated offering no commissions for external replacements. The reason was simple— such a move would disincentivize replacements. Clearly, this was an insurance executive who took the company's responsibility to its clients very seriously. But is such a plan fair to the agents who also had to work hard on replacements? Would it be fair to the share-holders of the company if it forced productive agents to look for another company? This example shows that responsibilities are not simply one-sided but involve a multitude of responsibilities, some of which may be in conflict.

This concludes the discussion of the various relationships and obligations that arise among the agent, client, and insurer. We have seen in the course of this discussion that the rela-tionships are multidimensional and involve a wide range of stakeholders, that is, anyone

who has a stake in an action or a situation. When there is a multitude of stakeholders, inevitably and occasionally conflicts of obligation with respect to two or more of those stakeholders will occur. The CEO mentioned above has duties to many stakeholders: his stockholders (or policyowners in the case of a mutual company), his agents, his clients, his family, and himself. What should be done when these duties conflict? The ethical course of action would be to try to resolve the difficulty without hurting someone in the process, and to try to be fair and true to yourself.

CHAPTER REVIEW

Key Terms and Concepts

nonmedical insurance
guaranteed issue

Chapter 14 Review Questions

1. (a) What is the role of the agent or broker in the selection process?

   (b) Why is it important that the agent or broker furnish applications and supporting documents in a thorough, accurate, and efficient manner? [1]

2. (a) What information is provided by the applicant in the first part of the application?

   (b) What information does the applicant attest to in the second part of the application? [1]

3. (a) What is the basic purpose of the medical examiner's report?

   (b) What information is requested in the medical examiner's report? [1]

4. What is the Medical Information Bureau (MIB), and what function does it perform? [1]

5. What characteristics should a company include in its evaluation and classification system? [2]

6. Under what circumstances will the judgment rating method function effectively? [2]

7. What is the basic assumption on which the numerical rating system is based? [2]

8. (a) What are the various factors that are assigned weights when the numerical rating system is used to evaluate and classify risks? (b) How are the values assigned to these factors derived? [2]

9. What criticisms have been leveled against the numerical rating system? [2]

10. How does each of the following work as an underwriting safeguard in the issuance of nonmedical insurance?

    (a) limiting the amount of insurance;

    (b) limiting the age of issue;

    (c) limiting insurance to standard risks;

    (d) relying on other sources of information. [2]

11. What factors might contribute to a higher rate of mortality for nonmedical insurance than for medically examined applicants? [2]

12. Although they do not follow a general practice of issuing nonmedical policies, some companies may issue policies on a nonmedical basis. How does each of the following support this statement?

    (a) policyowner nonmedical;

    (b) guaranteed issue;

    (c) paramedical examination. [3]

13. The insurability option permits the policyowner to purchase specified amounts of additional insurance without evidence of insurability.

(a) When can these purchase options be exercised?

(b) What type of policy can be purchased?

(c) What is the basis for the premium for the newly purchased insurance?

(d) How is the premium for this option determined? [4]

14. How do insurers attempt to cope with the lack of insurable interest in writing insurance on the lives of very young children? [5]

15. What are the problems associated with writing life insurance for elderly applicants? [5]

Chapter 14 Review Answers

1. a. *A company's field force is the foundation of the selection process. The other parts of the selection mechanism can go into operation only after the field force has acted. The home office can exercise its underwriting judgment only on the risks submitted by the agents and brokers. Most companies give their agents explicit instructions about the types of risks that will or will not be acceptable, and they instruct the agents to solicit only those risks they believe to be eligible under the company's underwriting rules.*

   The agent is asked to supply a variety of information in the certificate, the details varying with the company. The information typically includes the following: how long and how well the agent has known the applicant; an estimate of the applicant's net worth and annual income; the applicant's existing and pending insurance, including any plans for the lapse or surrender of existing insurance; whether the applicant sought the insurance or whether the application was the result of solicitation by the agent; and whether the application came through another agent or broker.

   The degree of selection exercised at the field level depends on the integrity and reliability of the agents and brokers. There is clearly some selection involved, since self-interest would cause the agent not to solicit insurance from persons who—because of obvious physical impairments, moral deficiencies, or unacceptable occupations— manifestly could not meet the underwriting standards of the company. Beyond that, the amount of selection practiced by the agent is rather limited.

could not meet the underwriting standards of the company. Beyond that, the amount of selection practiced by the agent is rather limited.

The agent is usually the only company representative to see an applicant face-to-face and make a visual assessment. If there is anything unusual about the applicant that requires an explanation, it is up to the agent to convey that information to the home office. The agent can include this information with the report that accompanies the application.

Experienced agents know what types of additional information the home office underwriters are likely to request when the application reveals specific health problems. These agents can expedite the process by asking for the supplemental reports at the same time the application is completed.

b. Some experienced agents have a reputation with the home office underwriters for thoroughness, accuracy, and attention to detail in furnishing applications and supporting documents. This reputation can benefit applicants who are on the borderline between classifications and can be rated either way. They may get the benefit of the lower premium class because of their agent's reputation. Borderline cases from agents who always argue with the home office evaluation and send applications with less than complete information are more likely to be classified under the higher premium category when it is strictly a judgment call.

2. *a. Application blanks vary in their content and design, but they usually consist of two parts—the first containing nonmedical questions and the second including questions to be asked by the medical examiner. Statements made by the applicant in the first part of the application cover the particulars of identification, such as name, address, former and prospective places of residence, and place and date of birth. If the applicant has recently moved, including previous places of residence enable the company, through reporting services, to interview the applicant's former acquaintances. Additional questions in the first part of the application relate to the applicant's occupation, including any changes within the last 5 years or any contemplated changes of occupation; aviation activities other than passenger travel on regularly scheduled airlines (if there is any unusual aviation hazard, details must be provided in a supplementary form); and the possibility of foreign residence. The application also elicits information about the applicant's insurance history including details of all insurance already in force, as well as declinations and other insurance company actions of underwriting significance. The foregoing information—together with a statement of the amount of insurance applied for, the plan upon which it is to be issued, the names of the policy*

beneficiary and policyowner, and the respective rights of the insured, beneficiary, and policyowner as to control of the policy—completes the first part of the application.

b. The answers to questions in the second part of the application normally must be recorded in the medical examiner's handwriting, and the applicant must sign the form to attest to the completeness and accuracy of its contents. This part of the application asks several groups of related questions. The first group seeks the details of the applicant's health record, including illnesses, injuries, and surgical operations, usually within the last 10 years. The applicant is also required to give the name of every physician or practitioner consulted within a specified period of time (usually the last 5 years) in connection with any ailment whatsoever. The second group of questions elicits information about the applicant's present physical condition. There are questions about the applicant's use of alcohol and drugs, and other questions concerning the applicant's family history.

3. a. The basic purpose of the medical examiner's report is to transmit the findings of the physical examination.

b. In addition to recording the answers to part 2 of the application, the medical examiner is required to file a separate report or certificate, which accompanies the application but is not seen by the applicant. The first portion of the report contains a description of the applicant's physical characteristics, which not only provides useful underwriting information but also guards against substituting a healthy person for an unhealthy applicant in the medical examination. Some companies ask the examiner to review the applicant's driver's license or other form of identification to establish conclusive identification. The examiner is also usually asked to indicate whether the applicant looks older than the age stated.

The medical examiner's comments are specifically required regarding any abnormalities of the applicant's arteries or veins, heart, respiratory system, nervous system, abdomen, genitourinary system, ears, eyes, and skin. The examiner also reports the urinalysis result, certifies that the urine examined is authentic, describes the applicant's build, and indicates the applicant's blood pressure.

In this final section of the report, the examiner may be requested to indicate any knowledge or suspicion that the applicant abuses alcohol or narcotics or has any moral deficiencies that would affect his or her insurability. The examiner is also asked about the prior patient/doctor relationship that has existed between the two of them, if any.

4. The Medical Information Bureau (MIB) is a clearing house for confidential medical data on applicants for life insurance. The information is reported and maintained in code

symbols to help preserve its confidentiality. Companies that are members of the Bureau are expected to report any impairments designated on the official list. All impairments must be reported whether the company accepts, postpones, or declines the risk, or offers a modified plan of insurance. In no event does the company report its underwriting decision to the Bureau.

A company normally screens all of its applicants against the MIB file of reported impairments. If the company finds an impairment and wants further details, it must submit its request through the MIB, but only after it first conducts its own complete investigation from all known sources. The company that reported the impairment is not obligated to supply further information, but if it agrees to do so, it provides the requested information through the MIB.

The rules of the MIB stipulate that a company cannot take unfavorable underwriting action solely on the basis of the information in the MIB files. In other words, the company must be in possession of other unfavorable underwriting facts or else determine through its own channels of investigation that the condition of impairment recorded in the MIB files is substantial enough to warrant an unfavorable decision.

5. *Ideally, the evaluation and classification system used by a company should (1) accurately measure the effect of each of the factors, favorable and unfavorable, that can be expected to influence an applicant's longevity; (2) assess the combined impact of multiple factors, including the situations in which the factors are conflicting; (3) produce consistently equitable results; and (4) be simple and relatively inexpensive to operate.*

6. *The judgment method of rating functions very effectively when there is only one unfavorable factor to consider or when the decision is simply one of accepting the applicant at standard rates or rejecting the application altogether.*

7. *The numerical rating system is based on the principle that a large number of factors enters into the composition of a risk and that the impact of each of these factors on the longevity of the risk can be determined by a statistical study of lives possessing that factor.*

8. a. *In practice, weights are generally assigned to the following 10 factors when the numerical rating system is used to evaluate and classify risks: (1) build, (2) physical*

        condition, (3) medical history, (4) family history, (5) occupation, (6) aviation and avocation, (7) residence, (8) habits, (9) morals, and (10) plan of insurance.

    b.   The values assigned to the various factors are derived from mortality studies among groups of people possessing those characteristics or, in some cases, from estimates of what such mortality studies might be expected to show.

9.   Among the criticisms leveled against the numerical rating system are (1) the system is too arbitrary, (2) there are many impairments for which knowledge is too limited to permit the assignment of numerical values, (3) the interrelated factors are nonadditive in so many cases that it nullifies the value of the numerical process, and (4) too many minor debits and credits are taken into account in evaluating risk.

10. a.   Perhaps the most important safeguard in the issuance of nonmedical insurance is a limit on the amount made available to any one applicant. The limit is determined by the extra mortality that can be expected from eliminating the medical examination and the savings in selection expenses that will be available to absorb the extra mortality costs. Today, most companies will provide up to $100,000 on a nonmedical basis, subject to appropriate age restrictions, while many will issue up to $200,000 or $250,000 on that basis. The limit generally varies by age groups; the largest amounts are available to the younger age groups.

    b.   A second safeguard companies impose is a limit on the ages at which insurance will be issued. Studies have shown that the extra mortality resulting from waiving the medical examination increases with age and after a point, will exceed any savings in selection expense. The point at which the extra mortality costs will exceed the expense savings is obviously a function of the underwriting age limit; most companies offer nonmedical insurance down to age zero.

    c.   A third safeguard is the general limitation of nonmedical insurance to standard risks. As a broad class, substandard risks must submit to medical examinations. Exceptions are commonly made, however, for risks that are substandard because of an occupational, aviation, or avocational hazard.

    d.   A final safeguard, which is more general and pervasive in nature, is the intensive cultivation of the sources of underwriting information other than the medical examiner. Insurance companies place a heavier burden on the applicant, agent, and inspector to offset in some measure the absence of a medical examiner's findings. The application form used in connection with nonmedical insurance is elaborate, containing all the questions usually contained in an application blank, as well as those normally asked by a medical examiner. A urine specimen and blood profile may be required for

home office analysis. If the applicant has recently been under the care of a physician, a statement may be necessary from the attending physician (at the expense of the company). If any adverse medical information is revealed by the applicant's statement, the inspection report, or other source, the company may demand a complete medical examination.

A particularly heavy responsibility is placed on the agent, with great reliance on the agent's judgment and integrity. Agents may submit nonmedical applications only from applicants who appear to meet the company's underwriting requirements from a physical, medical, occupational, and moral standpoint. The agent must elicit from the applicant, and accurately document, most of the information that a medical examination would seek. A detailed agent's certificate that records the agent's underwriting impressions of the applicant is also required.

Inspection reports are sometimes ordered to supplement the larger nonmedical insurance applications, even though such information would not be requested for medically underwritten cases for the same or larger amounts of coverage.

11. Nonmedical insurance is subject to a higher rate of mortality than medically examined business. This extra mortality is believed to stem from (1) impairments known to the applicant but deliberately concealed and (2) impairments not known to the applicant that could have been discovered by a medical examination.

12. a. Most companies are willing to issue insurance up to a stated limit on the basis of the applicant's declaration of good health if, within a short period prior to issuance—such as 3 to 6 months—standard insurance has been obtained from the company on the basis of a satisfactory medical examination. The reasoning behind this practice, of course, is that the policyowner's health is not likely to have deteriorated within such a short period of time, and any serious affliction would probably be apparent to the agent. This category of insurance without medical examination goes under the name of policyowner nonmedical, because it is limited to applicants who are already policyowners of the company.

   b. One of the important contractual agreements under which retirement benefits are provided to superannuated employees is the individual contract pension trust. Under this arrangement, the benefits are provided through retirement annuity contracts or retirement income contracts that are purchased by the employer, through a trustee, for each of the employees who is eligible to participate in the pension plan. Current practice includes underwriting such plans on a nonmedical basis. In fact, the arrangement frequently goes beyond the conventional concepts of nonmedical insurance. If the

group is acceptable, the insurance company dispenses with individual underwriting and agrees in advance to accept all applications for insurance up to a formula-determined limit. This practice is known as guaranteed issue. There is no underwriting beyond a screening of the group.

c. Somewhere between the medical examination and nonmedical evidence is another alternative—the paramedical examination. This examination is conducted by nurses or other medical technicians and consists of securing basic examination from measurements: height, weight, blood pressure, pulse rate, and waist measurement. The chief advantages of paramedical examinations are their reduced cost compared to a physician's fees and their convenience for the client because most services offer traveling examiners. The paramedical examinations, however, do not include the heart and other detailed reports typically provided by an insurance medical examiner.

13. a. The insurability option permits the policyowner to purchase specified amounts of additional insurance without evidence of insurability at stated intervals and below a specified age-for example, at 3-year intervals beginning with the policy anniversary nearest the insured's 25th birthday and terminating with the anniversary nearest the insured's 40th birthday. Some contracts also permit the purchase of additional insurance upon the insured's marriage or following the birth of the insured's first child or subsequent children. Some contracts even provide coverage automatically for 60 to 90 days after each option date.

b. The additional insurance need not be on the same plan as the basic policy to which the option is attached; the option is exercisable in favor of any standard whole life or other cash value insurance policies offered by the company.

c. Premiums for the new insurance are payable at standard rates on the basis of the insured's attained age on the option date. If the original policy contains a waiver-of-premium provision and accidental death benefits, the new policies will, at the insured's option, contain the same features. If premiums are being waived on the original policy at the time an option for additional insurance is exercised, premiums on the new policy will be waived from the beginning (and will continue to be waived if the insured is totally disabled).

d. The insurability option is available for an extra premium that varies with the age of issue. The schedule of annual premiums charged for the option by one company begins at $0.50 per $1,000 at age 0 and increases to approximately $2.00 per $1,000 at age 37. These premiums reflect the company's estimate of the average amount of extra mortality that it will experience on policies issued without evidence of insurability and, from the standpoint of the insured, may be regarded as the cost

of "insuring" his or her insurability. Premiums for the option are payable to the last anniversary at which it can be exercised—usually age 40—or to the end of the premium-paying period of the basic policy, whichever is earlier.

14. *Insurers writing insurance on the lives of very young children attempt to cope with the lack of insurable interest in three ways: (1) by limiting the coverage to amounts much smaller than those available to adults, particularly at the early ages, (2) by seeing that the insurance on the child bears a reasonable relationship to the amounts in force on the other members of the family, especially the breadwinner, and (3) by seeking a large volume of juvenile insurance applications to minimize adverse selection.*

15. *At the older ages, the lack of insurable interest is only one of the complicating factors. In the first place, the volume of insurance issued at ages above 70 or 75 is not large enough to yield predictable mortality results. The restricted demand for insurance at those ages reflects the high cost of the insurance, the general inability to satisfy the medical requirements, and the limited need for new insurance. In the second place, a high degree of adverse selection is associated with applications received at those ages. Low volume in itself is suggestive of adverse selection, but when it is accompanied by burdensome premium payments, the environment is even more conducive to adverse selection. This antiselection may be exercised by the insureds themselves aware of a serious impairment, or by a third party, perhaps a relative, who seeks insurance on the life of an elderly person for speculative reasons. A third factor, related to the others, is the relative ineffectiveness of the medical examination for elderly people. A routine medical examination does not reveal many conditions of a degenerative nature that can materially shorten the life of the elderly applicant.*

Chapter 15
Insurance of Substandard Risks

By Dan M. McGill

Revised by Jeremy S. Holmes and James F. Winberg

Learning Objectives

An understanding of the material in this chapter should enable the student to

1. **Explain the group concept applied to substandard risks.**

2. **Identify the broad additional hazard groups into which most companies assume substandard risks fall, and give examples of additional hazards that would cause life insurance applicants to fall into each of these groups.**

3. **Identify the various methods life insurers use to deal with substandard risks, explain how each method works, describe the types of risks for which each method is appropriate, and explain what effect, if any, each method has on policy surrender values and dividends.**

4. **Explain the reasons (both theoretical and practical) for and against removing the substandard rating when a person a company has classified as a substandard risk is subsequently found to be a standard risk by another life insurance company.**

substandard risks

Using the numerical rating system or some other method of rating, an insurance company classifies certain risks as **substandard risks**. A group or classification of risks rated substandard is expected to produce a higher mortality rate than a group of normal lives. The group concept must be emphasized, because—as with insuring standard risks—there is no certainty about any one individual's longevity expectations. All calculations, therefore, are based on the anticipated average experience of a large number of individuals, and the experience of any one individual is merged into that of the group.

This is an elementary concept, but it needs to be reiterated in any consideration of substandard risk insurance, involving, as it does, extra cost to or restricted benefits for the policyowner or beneficiary. It is commonly supposed that if an individual is placed in a substandard classification and subsequently lives to a ripe old age, the company erred in its treatment of the case. However, if 1,000 persons, each of whom is suffering from a particular physical impairment, are granted insurance, it is certain that the death rate among them will be greater than the death rate among a group of people the same age who are free from of any discernible impairments. To allow for the higher death rates that

will certainly occur within the substandard group, the company must collect an extra premium from—or impose special terms on—all who are subject to the extra risk since it is not known which of the members of the group will be responsible for the extra mortality. It is not expected that every member of the group will survive for a shorter period than the normal life expectancy. In fact, it is a certainty that this will not be the case; it is known merely that a larger proportion of people in a normal group will attain normal life expectancy.

The fact that certain members of the impaired group reach old age is, therefore, no indication that an error was made in their cases. If they had paid no extra premium, a still higher premium would have been required from the others. Generally speaking, nothing could—or should—be refunded to members of a substandard group who live beyond the normal life expectancy, provided that the extra premiums charged (or other special terms imposed) were a true measure of the degree of extra hazard represented by the group.

INCIDENCE OF EXTRA RISK

If a group of substandard risks is to be fairly treated, the degree of extra mortality represented by the group and the approximate period in life when the extra mortality is likely to occur must both be known within reasonable limits. It makes a great deal of difference financially whether the extra claims are expected to occur primarily in early life, middle age, old age, or at a level rate throughout the individuals' lifetimes. If the extra mortality occurs during the early years of the policies when the amount at risk is relatively large, the burden on the company will be greater than if it occurs later when the amount at risk is relatively small. Hence, between two substandard groups representing the same aggregate amount of extra mortality, the group whose extra mortality is concentrated later in life should pay a smaller extra premium than the group whose extra mortality occurs earlier.

There are innumerable variations in the distribution of the extra risk among different classes of substandard risks. It is impractical, however, for companies to recognize all the many patterns of risk distribution. The majority of companies therefore proceed on the assumption that each substandard risk falls into one of three broad groups. In the first group, the additional hazard increases with age; in the second group, it remains approximately constant at all ages; in the third, it decreases with age.

Examples of each type of hazard are easy to find. High blood pressure presents an increasing hazard. Occupational hazards represent a constant hazard, as do certain types of physical defects. (Even though most constant hazards tend to increase somewhat with age, they are treated as if they remain constant.) Impairments attributable to past illnesses

and surgical operations are hazards that decrease with time, although not all illnesses and operations fall into this category.

TREATMENT OF SUBSTANDARD RISKS

Several methods have been devised to provide insurance protection to people with impaired health. With the exception of the lien, most United States life insurance companies utilize all the available methods. In general, companies make an effort to adapt the method to the type of hazard represented by the impaired risk, but departures from theoretically correct risk treatment are frequently made for practical reasons.

Increase in Age

One method of treatment, widely used in the past and still favored by many companies for joint-and-survivor products, is to "rate up" the age of the applicant. Under this method, the applicant is assumed to be a number of years older than his or her real age, and the policy is written accordingly. The number of years older is usually determined by adding the amount estimated as necessary to provide for the extra mortality to the net premium for the applicant's actual age, and then finding the premium in the standard table that most closely matches that total, and deriving the rate-up from the standard age in the table. For example, assume the net level premium for an ordinary life contract issued at age 25 is $12.55 per $1,000. If a male applicant for such a contract, aged 25, should be placed in a substandard classification that is expected to produce an extra mortality equivalent to $3.67, the correct net premium for the applicant would be $16.22 per $1,000. The net level premium in the standard table closest to this amount is $16.43, which is the premium for age 33. Therefore, the applicant is rated up 8 years and is thereafter treated in all respects as if he were 33 years of age.

His policy would contain the same surrender and loan values and would be entitled to the same dividends, if any, as any other ordinary life contract issued at age 33.

Example

<u>Increased-in-Age Method</u>

In some substandard cases, the estimated extra mortality charge will be added to the net premium for the applicant's actual age to determine the appropriate net premium level. Then the insurer will offer a policy for the age associated with the higher net premium.

The policy will have higher premiums and build cash values (if any) faster than a policy based on actual age. For example, an extra mortality charge of $10 per $1000 of coverage for someone aged 30 might be the equivalent of a net premium for a 35-year-old for a specific insurer. The insurer would propose a policy and premiums based on age 35 instead of age 30.

This method of dealing with substandard risks is suitable only when the extra risk is a decidedly increasing one and will continue to increase indefinitely at a greater rate. Although few impairments give rise to such a consistent and rapid increase in the rate of mortality as provided in the rated-up age method, the method is considered to be appropriate for all types of substandard risks where the extra mortality, in general, increases with age.

The chief appeal of the method for the insurance company is its simplicity. Policies can be dealt with for all purposes as standard policies issued at the assumed age. No separate set of records is required; no special calculations of premium rates, cash and other surrender values, reserves, and dividends are involved. For the applicant, the method is attractive because the higher premium is accompanied by correspondingly higher surrender values and dividends (if participating). Thus, a portion of each extra premium is refunded as a dividend, and another portion is applied to the accumulation of larger surrender values than would be available under a policy issued at the applicant's true age. If the policy is surrendered for cash, the additional cash value is equivalent to a refund of a portion of the extra premium paid. To protect themselves against the use of the surrender privilege for this purpose, some companies add a slight loading to the original extra premium.

Extra Percentage Tables

extra percentage tables

The most common method of dealing with risks that present an increasing hazard is to classify them into groups based on the expected percentage of standard mortality and to charge premiums that reflect the appropriate increase in mortality. The number of substandard classifications may vary from three to 12, depending to some extent on the degree of extra mortality the company is willing to underwrite. Some companies are unwilling to

underwrite substandard groups whose average mortality is expected to exceed 200 percent of standard, and they usually establish three substandard classifications with expected
average mortalities of 150, 175, and 200 percent, respectively. Table 15-1 shows a scale of
substandard classifications widely used by companies offering coverage up to 500 percent
of standard mortality.

Table 15-1 Scale of Substandard Classifications			
Class	Mortality (Percent)	Class	Mortality (Percent)
1	125	6	250
2	150	7	275
3	175	8	300
4	200	10	350
5	225	12	400
		16	500

In effect, a special mortality table reflecting the appropriate degree of extra mortality is
prepared for each substandard classification, and a complete set of gross premium rates is
computed for each classification. The gross premium rates at quinquennial ages quoted by
one company for an ordinary life contract under substandard tables A, B, C, and D, are set
forth in Table 15-2. For purposes of comparison the rate for a standard risk at each quinquennial age is also given.

Perhaps the most notable feature of these premiums is that they do not increase in proportion to the degree of extra mortality involved. The rates under substandard table D, for
example, are not double the rates at which insurance is made available to standard risks.
Neither are the rates under table B one-and-one-half times the standard rates. There is a
twofold explanation of this apparent inconsistency. In the first place, the rates illustrated
in Table 15-2 are gross premium rates, and the amount of loading does not increase from
one rate classification to the other, except for commissions and premium taxes but remains
constant (with minor exceptions). In the second place, the percentage of extra mortality
is computed on the basis of actual—rather than tabular—mortality. The premiums for
standard risks are calculated on the basis of the 1980 CSO Table (on which the majority
of existing policies are based), which contains a considerable overstatement of mortality
at the young and middle ages, but additions to standard premiums to arrive at the substandard rates reflect only the excess mortality for the substandard classifications over

the actual standard mortality. Hence, the rates for the substandard classifications are not proportionally greater than even the net premiums for the standard risks.

Table 15-2
Illustrative Gross Annual Premium Rates at Quinquennial Ages for Ordinary Life Contract under Substandard Tables A, B, C, and D

Age	Rate for Standard Risks	Substandard Tables			
		A 125 Percent	B 150 Percent	C 175 Percent	D 200 Percent
15	$14.46	$15.74	$16.67	$17.53	$18.37
20	16.15	17.62	18.67	19.68	20.63
25	18.21	19.90	21.15	22.33	23.45
30	20.81	22.82	24.33	25.75	27.12
35	24.14	26.56	28.41	30.19	31.88
40	28.45	31.38	33.70	35.93	38.07
45	34.01	37.59	40.50	43.32	46.04
50	41.31	45.69	49.40	52.99	56.48
55	50.99	56.41	61.11	65.71	70.22
60	64.03	70.74	76.73	82.67	88.54
65	81.82	90.08	97.69	105.34	112.97

The extra mortality under the extra-percentage method is relatively small at the early ages, unless the percentage of extra mortality is high, since the normal (or base rate) mortality at such ages is small. As the base death rate increases, however, the margin for extra mortality increases very greatly. This explains why the method is appropriate for substandard risks whose impairments are expected to produce an increasing rate of extra mortality. Like the increase-in-age method, extra percentage substandard tables should, in theory, be used only when the hazard is expected to increase at a greater rate. In practice, however, they are used for all types of impairments that are expected to worsen as the years go by.

The reserves under policies issued in accordance with **extra percentage tables** must be calculated on the basis of the mortality assumptions underlying the premiums, which requires separate classification records and tabulations. Depending on company practice and state law, surrender values may be based on the special mortality table or may be the same as surrender values under policies issued to standard risks. Many companies do not make the extended term insurance nonforfeiture option (which is discussed in chapter 8) available under extra-percentage-table policies, especially at the higher percentages, and

those that do compute the period on the basis of the higher mortality rate even when only the normal surrender value is allowed.

Extra percentage tables are sometimes used as a basis for determining the extra premiums needed under other methods of underwriting substandard risks. Thus, the risk may first be assigned to an extra percentage table, after which the rating is translated into the equivalent age markup. This is a convenient way to determine the necessary step-up in age when statistics on the additional mortality expected from a particular impairment are available.

Example

A substandard health condition that is expected to result in an increasing rate of extra mortality with aging is an appropriate situation for either the increase-in-age approach or the extra-percentage method.

Flat Extra Premium

A third method of underwriting substandard risks is by assessing a flat extra premium. Under this method, the standard premium for the policy in question is increased by a specified number of dollars per $1,000 of insurance. Assessed as a measure of the extra mortality involved, the flat extra premium does not vary with the age of the applicant. It may be paid throughout the premium-paying period of the policy, or it may be terminated after a period of years when the extra hazard has presumably disappeared.

flat extra premium

The flat extra premium method is normally used when the hazard is thought to be constant (deafness or partial blindness, for example) or decreasing (as with a family history of tuberculosis or the aftermath of a serious illness or surgical operation, in which case the flat extra is usually temporary in duration). The **flat extra premium** is widely used to cover the extra risk associated with certain occupations and avocations. When used for this purpose, the extra premium usually ranges from $2.50 to $10 per $1,000 of insurance. Unless a permanent impairment is involved, the extra premium is generally removed if the insured leaves the hazardous occupation or avocation.

At first glance, a flat extra premium for an extra hazard that adds an approximately constant amount to the rate of mortality at each age appears to be a fair arrangement. In practice, however, it works out equitably only if an allowance is made for the fact that the amount at risk is not a level sum under most policies. Except for term policies, the net amount at risk decreases with each year that elapses. Thus a flat extra premium becomes

an increasing percentage of the amount at risk and, in effect, provides for an increasing extra risk.

When the extra risk is constant, the extra premium for a cash value contract should diminish each year in the proportion that the amount at risk decreases. To avoid the labor and expense that would be involved in such an annual adjustment, and in recognition of the fact that the flat extra premium is an approximation, most companies compute the flat extra addition on the basis of the average amount at risk. Some companies vary the extra premium with the plan of insurance, charging less for high cash value policies than for policies with lower reserve elements.

The flat extra premium is not reflected in policy values and dividends. It is assumed that the entire amount of the extra premium is needed each year to pay additional claims and expenses. The dividends and guaranteed values are identical to those of a comparable policy without the flat extra premium. Thus, the policyowner must regard the flat extra premium as an irrecoverable outlay, a costly way to get even except through premature death.

Liens

lien

When the extra mortality to be expected from an impairment is of a distinctly decreasing and temporary nature, such as that associated with convalescence from a serious illness, neither an increase in age, a percentage addition to the rate of mortality, nor a flat extra premium is an appropriate method of dealing with the risk. A more suitable method—from a theoretical standpoint, at least—is to create a lien against the policy for a number of years, the amount and term of the **lien** depending on the extent of the impairment. If adequate statistics are available, it is possible to calculate the term and amount of the lien that are equivalent to the extra risk undertaken. If such a method is utilized, the policy is issued at standard rates and is standard in all respects except that, should death occur before the end of the period specified, the amount of the lien is deducted from the proceeds otherwise payable. The method is frequently refined to provide for a yearly reduction in the amount of the lien on the theory that the hazard is decreasing.

The lien method has a psychological appeal, in that few persons who are refused insurance at standard rates believe themselves to be substandard risks and tend to resent the company's action in classifying them as such. If the only penalty involved is a temporary reduction in the amount of protection, most applicants are willing to go along with the company's decision, confident that they will survive the period of the lien and thus "prove" the company to have been wrong. The plan appeals to the applicant's sporting instinct.

A practical and serious disadvantage of the method is that a comparatively large lien is necessary to offset a relatively small degree of extra mortality. Furthermore, the reduction occurs in the early years of the policy, when the need for protection is presumably the greatest. Frequently, the beneficiary has no knowledge of the lien, and the company's failure to pay the face amount of the policy may be the source of great disappointment and resentment, to the detriment of the company's reputation in the community. There is also a possibility that the lien is in conflict with laws in certain states that prohibit any provision that permits the company to settle a death claim with a payment smaller than the face amount. These laws are known as "no-lesser-amounts" statutes.

Other Methods

A method of dealing with substandard risks when the degree of extra mortality is small or when its nature is not well known is to make no extra charge but to place all of the members of the group in a special class for dividend purposes, adjusting the dividends in accordance with the actual experience. This method can accommodate only those impairments that produce an extra mortality that does not exceed the normal dividend payments. Moreover, a sufficiently large number of such risks must be underwritten to yield an average experience.

Some impairments can be dealt with by merely limiting the plan of insurance. The extra mortality associated with certain impairments is largely postponed to advanced middle age or old age. These impairments can be underwritten at no extra charge by issuing single premium or modified endowment contracts that have minimal amount at risk before the impact of the extra mortality. Being moderately overweight is a typical impairment that is adaptable to the endowment plan at standard rates.

REMOVAL OF SUBSTANDARD RATING

Frequently, a person who is classified as a substandard risk and insured on that basis by one company subsequently applies for insurance with another company—or even the same company—and is found to be a standard risk in all respects. Under these circumstances, the person's natural reaction is to request the removal of the substandard rating. The question is whether the company should remove the rating.

Theoretically, the rating should not be removed unless the impairment on which it was based was known to be temporary or was due to occupation or residence. At the time the policy was originally issued, the insured was placed in a special classification of risks whose members were presumably impaired to approximately the same degree. It was known

by the company that some of the members of the group would die within a short period, while others would survive far beyond their normal expectancy. It was likewise known that the health of some of the members would deteriorate with the passage of time, while some members would grow more robust. By the time the insured under consideration is in normal health, the health of many others in the original group has undoubtedly worsened. Many of them cannot now get insurance on any terms, while others are insurable only at a greater extra premium than that charged. If the company reduces the premiums for those whose health has improved, it should be permitted to increase the premiums of those whose health has deteriorated. Because the premiums of those in the latter category cannot be adjusted upward, the premiums of those in the former category should not be reduced.

As a practical matter, however, the company is virtually forced to remove the substandard rating of a person who can demonstrate current insurability at standard rates. If it does not do so, the policyowner will almost surely surrender the extra-rate insurance and replace it with insurance at standard rates in another company. Knowing this, most companies calculate their initial substandard premiums on the assumption that the extra premium will have to be removed for people who subsequently qualify for standard insurance. Thus, the common practice is to remove the extra premium upon proof that the insured is no longer substandard.

Where an extra premium has been imposed on account of occupation, residence, or a temporary risk, it is proper to discontinue the extra premium upon termination of the condition that created the extra hazard without prior adjustment in the substandard premium. It is necessary to exercise care in these cases, however, particularly when the source of the rating was occupation or residence. There is always a possibility that the insured may subsequently return to the hazardous occupation or residence, or that his or her health has already been affected adversely. Hence, it is customary in such cases to require that a specified period of time, such as one or 2 years, must elapse after cessation of the extra hazard before the rating will be removed. Occasionally, a medical examination is also required. At the end of the period, the adjustment is usually made retroactively to the change of occupation or residence.

Removal of a Substandard Rating Often Requires

- Waiting period of one or 2 years

- Medical examination(s)

VALUE OF SUBSTANDARD INSURANCE

substandard insurance

The majority of life insurance companies in North America offer insurance to substandard risks. Several important companies that formerly confined their operations to standard risks are now willing to accept substandard risks. Some companies, however, refer to insurance on people who are substandard risks as classified insurance, rather than extra-rate or substandard insurance. There is a natural reluctance to call such business substandard insurance because the term suggests that the insurance is lacking in some of the essential qualities of standard insurance. This, of course, is not the case.

Substandard insurance is of great social importance since it makes insurance protection available to millions of American families that would otherwise be without it. Approximately 6 percent to 7 percent of all new policies are issued on a substandard basis. Extensive investigations into the rates of mortality prevailing among various types of substandard groups are continually being undertaken, resulting in further extensions of this class of business and in revisions of the terms upon which the insurance is offered. It is perhaps fair to conclude that life insurance is now available to all except those subject to such excessive rates of mortality as to entail premiums beyond their ability or willingness to pay.

CHAPTER REVIEW

Key Terms and Concepts

substandard risks
extra percentage tables
flat extra premium

lien
substandard insurance

Chapter 15 Review Questions

1. When an individual who was placed in a substandard classification lives to old age, it is often argued that the company made an error in its treatment of that case. Explain why this is not necessarily an indication that an error in classification was made. [1]

2. List the three broad additional hazard groups that most companies assume sub-standard risks fall into, and give examples of additional hazards that would cause life insurance applicants to fall into each of these three categories. [2]

3. Using the increase-in-age method of dealing with substandard risks, explain the following:

    (a) how this method provides for the extra mortality of a substandard risk;

    (b) types of risks for which it is considered appropriate to use this method;

    (c) why this method is appealing for an insurance company; (d) why this method is attractive to the applicant. [3]

4. Using the extra-percentage tables method of dealing with substandard risks, explain the following:

    (a) how this method provides for the extra mortality of a substandard risk;

    (b) types of risks for which it is considered appropriate to use this method;

    (c) why the gross premiums derived under this method do not increase in propor-tion to the degree of extra mortality involved; (d) what implications this method has for the determination of policy reserves and cash surrender values, and the availability of and/or determination of the coverage period for the extended term nonforfeiture option. [3]

5. Using the flat-extra-premium method of dealing with substandard risks, explain the following:

6. Using the lien method of dealing with substandard risks, explain the following: (a) how this method provides for the extra mortality of a substandard risk; (b) types of risks for which it is considered appropriate to use this method; (c) why this method has a psychological appeal to applicants; (d) the disadvantages associated with this method. [3]

7. In addition to the increase in age, extra percentage tables, flat extra premium, and lien methods, what other methods are available for dealing with the extra mortality of substandard risks? [3]

8. Explain the reasons (both theoretical and practical) for and against removing a sub-standard rating when a person classified as a substandard risk subsequently applies for insurance with another company (or even with the same company) and is found to be a standard risk in all respects. [4]How do insurers attempt to cope with the lack of insurable interest in writing insurance on the lives of very young children? [5]

Chapter 15 Review Answers

1. *If 1,000 persons, each of whom is suffering from a particular physical impairment, are granted insurance, it is certain that the death rate among them will be greater than the death rate among a group of people the same age who are free from any discernible impairments. To allow for the higher death rates that will certainly occur within the substandard group, the company must collect an extra premium from—or impose special terms on—all who are subject to the extra risk because it is not known what members of the group will be responsible for the extra mortality. It is not expected that every member of the group will be responsible for the extra mortality. It is not expected that every member of the group will survive for a shorter period than the normal life expectancy. In fact, it is a certainty that this will not be the case; it is known merely that a larger proportion of people in a normal group will attain normal life expectancy. The fact that certain members of the impaired group reach old age is, therefore, no indication that an error was made in their cases. If they had paid no extra premium, a still higher premium would have been required from the others. Generally speaking, nothing could or should be refunded to members of a substandard group who live beyond the normal life expectancy, provided that the extra premiums charged (or other special terms imposed) were a true measure of the degree of extra hazard represented by the group.*

2. *The majority of companies proceed on the assumption that each substandard risk falls into one of three broad groups:*

    *   *In the first group, the additional hazard increases with age (for example, high blood pressure).*

    *   *In the second group, the additional hazard remains approximately constant at all ages (for example, occupational hazards).*

    *   *In the third group, the additional hazard decreases with age (for example, many impairments attributable to past illnesses and surgical operations).*

3. a. *Under the increase-in-age method, the applicant is assumed to be a number of years older than his or her real age, and the policy is written accordingly. The number of years older is usually determined by adding the amount estimated as necessary to provide for the extra mortality to the net premium for the applicant's actual age, and then finding the premium in the standard table that most closely matches that total, and deriving the rate-up from the standard age in the table. The policy would contain the same surrender and loan values and would be entitled to the same dividends, if any, as any contract of that type issued at the increased age.*

    b. *This method of dealing with substandard risks is suitable only when the extra risk is a decidedly increasing one and will continue to increase indefinitely at a greater rate. Although few impairments give rise to such a consistent and rapid increase in the rate of mortality as provided in the rated-up age method, the method is considered to be appropriate for all types of substandard risks where the extra mortality, in general, increases with age.*

    c. *The chief appeal of the method for the insurance company is its simplicity. Policies can be dealt with for all purposes as standard policies issued at the assumed age. No separate set of records is required; no special calculations of premium rates, cash and other surrender values, reserves, and dividends are involved.*

    d. *The higher cash values and higher dividends (if participating) are attractive to the applicant. The policy will have a more rapid build up of surrender values than one issued at the actual age of the insured.*

4. a. *The extra-percentage-tables method classifies risks into groups based on the expected percentage of standard mortality and charges premiums that reflect the appropriate increase in mortality. The number of substandard classifications may vary from three to 12, depending to some extent on the degree of extra mortality the company is willing to underwrite. In effect, a special mortality table reflecting the appropriate degree of extra mortality is prepared for each substandard classification, and a complete set of gross premium rates is computed for each classification.*

    b. *This is the most common method of dealing with risks that present an increasing hazard.*

    c. *Perhaps the most notable feature of the extra-percentage-table premiums is that they do not increase in proportion to the degree of extra mortality involved. There is a twofold explanation of this result. In the first place, the rates charged the policy-owner are gross premium rates, and the amount of loading does not increase from one rate classification to the other, except for commissions and premium taxes but remains constant (with minor exceptions). In the second place, the percentage of extra*

mortality is computed on the basis of actual—rather than tabular—mortality. The premiums for standard risks are calculated on the basis of the 1980 CSO Table, which contains a considerable overstatement of mortality at the young and middle ages, but additions to standard premiums to arrive at the substandard rates reflect only the excess mortality for the substandard classifications over the actual mortality. Hence, the rates for the substandard classifications are not proportionally greater than even the net premiums for the standard risks.

    d.   The reserves under policies issued in accordance with extra-percentages tables must be calculated on the basis of the mortality assumptions underlying the premiums, which requires separate classification records and tabulations. Depending on company practice and state law, surrender values may be based on the special mortality table or may be the same as surrender values under policies issued to standard risks. Many companies do not make the extended term insurance nonforfeiture option available under extra-percentage-table policies, especially at the higher percentages, and those that do compute the period on the basis of the higher mortality rate even when only the normal surrender value is allowed.

    (a) how this method provides for the extra mortality of a substandard risk;

    (b) types of risks for which it is considered appropriate to use this method;

    (c) how companies adjust for the use of a flat extra premium to handle constant extra risk for policies with increasing cash values in order to approximate equitable treatment of the policyowners; (d) the effect that this method has on policy values and dividends. [3]

  5. a.   Under the flat extra-premium method, the standard premium for the policy in question is increased by a specified number of dollars per $1,000 of insurance. Assessed as a measure of the extra mortality involved, the flat extra premium does not vary with the age of the applicant. It may be paid throughout the premium-paying period of the policy, or it may be terminated after a period of years when the extra hazard has presumably disappeared.

    b.   The flat extra-premium method is normally used when the hazard is thought to be constant (deafness or partial blindness, for example) or decreasing (as with a family history of tuberculosis or the aftermath of a serious illness or surgical operation, in which case the flat extra is usually temporary in duration). The flat extra premium is widely used to cover the extra risk associated with certain occupations and

avocations. Unless a permanent impairment is involved, the extra premium is generally removed if the insured leaves the hazardous occupation or avocation.

c. *When the extra risk is constant, the extra premium for a cash value contract should diminish each year in the proportion that the amount at risk decreases. To avoid the labor and expense that would be involved in such an annual adjustment, and in recognition of the fact that the flat extra premium is an approximation, most companies compute the flat extra addition on the basis of the average amount at risk. Some companies vary the extra premium with the plan of insurance, charging less for high cash value policies than for policies with lower reserve elements.*

d. *The flat extra premium is not reflected in policy values and dividends. It is assumed that the entire amount of the extra premium is needed each year to pay additional claims and expenses. The dividends and guaranteed values are identical to those of a comparable policy without the flat extra premium.*

6. a. *The lien method creates a lien against the policy for a number of years, the amount and term of the lien depending on the extent of the impairment. If adequate statistics are available, it is possible to calculate the term and amount of the lien that are equivalent to the extra risk undertaken. If such a method is utilized, the policy is issued at standard rates and is standard in all respects except that, should death occur before the end of the period specified, the amount of the lien is deducted from the proceeds otherwise payable. The method is frequently refined to provide for a yearly reduction in the amount of the lien on the theory that the hazard is decreasing.*

   b. *The lien method is appropriate to use when the extra mortality to be expected from an impairment is of a distinctly decreasing and temporary nature, such as that associated with convalescence from a serious illness.*

   c. *The lien method has a psychological appeal, in that few persons who are refused insurance at standard rates believe themselves to be substandard risks and tend to resent the company's action in classifying them as such. If the only penalty involved is a temporary reduction in the amount of protection, most applicants are willing to go along with the company's decision, confident that they will survive the period of the lien and thus "prove" the company to have been wrong. The plan appeals to the applicant's sporting instinct.*

   d. *A practical and serious disadvantage of the method is that a comparatively large lien is necessary to offset a relatively small degree of extra mortality. Furthermore, the reduction occurs in the early years of the policy, when the need for protection is presumably the greatest. Frequently, the beneficiary has no knowledge of the lien, and the company's failure to pay the face amount of the policy may be the source of great*

disappointment and resentment, to the detriment of the company's reputation in the community. There is also a possibility that the client is in conflict with laws in certain states that prohibit any provision that permits the company to settle a death claim with a payment smaller than the face amount. These laws are knows as no-lesser-amounts statutes.

7.   *Other methods available for dealing with the extra mortality of substandard risks are*

   •   *to make no extra charge but to place all of the members of the group in a special class for dividend purposes, adjusting the dividends in accordance with the actual experience. This method can be used for dealing with substandard risks when the degree of extra mortality is small or when its nature is not well known. This method can accommodate only those impairments that produce an extra mortality that does not exceed the normal dividend payments. Moreover, a sufficiently large number of such risks must be underwritten to yield an average experience.*

   •   *to merely limit the plan of insurance. The extra mortality associated with certain impairments is largely postponed to advanced middle age or old age. These impairments can be underwritten at no extra charge by issuing single premium or modified endowment contracts that have a minimal amount at risk before the impact of the extra mortality.*

8.   *Theoretically, the substandard rating should not be removed unless the impairment on which it was based was known to be temporary or was due to occupation or residence. At the time the policy was originally issued, the insured was placed in a special classification of risks whose members were presumably impaired to approximately the same degree. It was known by the company that some of the members of the group would die within a short period, while others would survive far beyond their normal expectancy. By the time the insured under consideration is in normal health, the health of many others in the original group has undoubtedly worsened. If the company reduces the premiums for those whose health has improved, it should be permitted to increase the premiums of those whose death has deteriorated. Because the premiums of those in the latter category cannot be adjusted upward, the premiums of those in the former category should not be reduced.*

As a practical matter, however, the company is virtually forced to remove the substandard rating of a person who can demonstrate current insurability at standard rates. If it does not do so, the policyowner will almost surely surrender the extra-rate insurance and replace it with insurance at standard rates in another company.

Where an extra premium has been imposed because of occupation, residence, or a temporary risk, it is proper from both a theoretical and a practical perspective to discontinue the extra premium upon termination of the condition that created the extra hazard. It is necessary to exercise care in these cases, however, particularly when the source of the rating was occupation or residence.

Reinsurance

By Dan M. McGill

Revised by Jeremy S. Holmes and James F. Winberg

Learning Objectives

An understanding of the material in this chapter should enable the student to

1. **Explain what reinsurance is and identify the parties to a reinsurance agreement.**

2. **List and explain the various reasons why life insurance companies use reinsurance.**

3. **Explain how the yearly renewable term, coinsurance, and modified coinsurance plans of proportional reinsurance work; describe the advantages and disadvantages of each, and compute the primary company's and the reinsurer's shares of the death benefit payment under the yearly renewable term and coinsurance plans.**

4. **Explain how stop-loss, catastrophe, and spread-loss plans of nonproportional reinsurance work.**

5. **Explain the differences between facultative and automatic reinsurance agreements.**

6. **Describe and explain the effects of the provisions commonly found in reinsurance agreements, including those related to the cession form, claims settlement, recapture of insurance, duration of the agreement, insolvency of the primary company, experience rating, and supplementary coverages.**

reinsurance

primary company

reinsurer

cession

retrocession

Reinsurance is a device by which one insurance company or insurer transfers all or a portion of its risk under an insurance policy or a group of policies to another company or insurer. The company that issued the policy initially is called the direct-writing or **primary**

company (also ceding company); the company or organization to which the risk is transferred is called the assuming company or **reinsurer**.

The act of transferring the insurance from the direct-writing company to the reinsurer is called a **cession**.[1] If the reinsurer should, in turn, transfer to one or more companies all or a portion of the risk assumed from the primary company, the transaction is referred to as a **retrocession**. Thus, the primary insurer cedes insurance to a reinsurer, which may then retrocede the coverage to still other companies.

PURPOSES OF REINSURANCE

assumption reinsurance

indemnity reinsurance

In life insurance, reinsurance may be undertaken for one of two general reasons: (1) to transfer all or a specific portion of a company's liabilities or (2) to accomplish certain broad managerial objectives, including favorable underwriting results and the reduction of surplus drain from writing new business. Reinsurance undertaken for the purpose of transferring all or a substantial portion of a company's liabilities is called portfolio or **assumption reinsurance**. Reinsurance arranged for general business purposes is referred to as **indemnity reinsurance**.

Assumption Reinsurance

There are a number of reasons for assumption reinsurance. A traditional use has been to bail out insurance companies that find themselves in financial difficulties. Rather than liquidate the company, with almost certain losses to policyowners, two companies frequently work out a procedure whereby a solvent insurer assumes the policy liabilities of the company in distress in exchange for the assets underlying the liabilities and the right to receive future premiums under the policies. If the assets are not sufficient to offset the liabilities—a likely circumstance—the reinsurer may place a lien against the cash values of the ceded policies until the deficiency can be liquidated through earnings on the policies. A merger is another situation in which all the business of one company may be ceded to another.

---

1. The term cession also refers to a document executed by the primary company in accordance with the reinsurance agreement that describes the risk being transferred and provides a schedule of reinsurance premiums and allowances, if any.

In many instances, assumption reinsurance involves only a segment of the ceding company's business. For example, a combination company[2] may decide to restrict its future operations to ordinary insurance and arrange to cede all of its outstanding industrial business to another company. Likewise, a company may decide to withdraw from one or more states and, in so doing, reinsure all policies outstanding in that geographical area. Assumption reinsurance is always tailored to the particular facts and requirements of the case under consideration and does not lend itself to generalization. Hence, it will not be further discussed in this book.

Indemnity Reinsurance

Indemnity reinsurance is characterized by a series of independent transactions whereby the primary insurer transfers its liability with respect to individual policies, in whole or in part, to the reinsurer. It is extremely widespread and may be used for any one of several reasons.

Limiting the Amount of Insurance on One Life

retention limits

The most fundamental and prevalent use of indemnity reinsurance is to avoid too large a concentration of risk on one life. All companies, including the giants of the industry, have deemed it prudent to limit the amount of insurance that they will retain on any one life. These maxima, called **retention limits**, reflect the judgment of company management as to many factors, but they are strongly influenced by the volume of insurance in force, the amount of surplus funds,[3] and the proficiency of the underwriting personnel. The limits range from $1,000 in small, recently established companies to well over $20 million to $30 million in the largest companies.[4] There may be various limits within one company, depending upon the plan, age at issue, sex, and the substandard classification. Retention tends to be smaller at the lower and upper age groups and for plans under which the risk element is relatively large. It is clearly in a company's interest to retain as much of the risk as is consistent with safety, so the retention limit or limits are usually raised as the insurance in force and amount of surplus funds grow. To remain competitive and to retain the services of a qualified agency force, a company must be in a position to accept applications

---

2. A combination company writes both ordinary and industrial insurance.
3. A rule of thumb, subject to many exceptions, is that the retention limit should be equal to one percent of capital and surplus.
4. Some newly established companies reinsure all their business for a number of years, although the companies may be motivated by reasons other than (or in addition to) the avoidance of mortality risk.

for any reasonable amount of insurance, regardless of its retention limit. Thus, a company must have facilities for transferring amounts of insurance in excess of the amount that it is willing to retain at its own risk.

Example

For a company with $5 million retention limits

Policy Size	Amount Retained	Amount Reinsured
$2 million	$2 million	—
$7 million	$5 million	$2 million

Stabilizing Mortality Experience

A closely related use of reinsurance, as yet limited in scope but receiving increasing attention, is to stabilize the primary company's overall mortality experience. This function is associated with so-called nonproportional reinsurance, one form of which transfers to the reinsurer all or a specified percentage of that portion of aggregate mortality claims for a given period in excess of a stipulated norm. Another form of nonproportional reinsurance provides protection against an undesirable concentration of risk on several lives, such as might be found among the passengers of a jet airliner or the employees of an industrial plant.

Reducing the Drain on Surplus

A third use of indemnity reinsurance is to reduce the drain on surplus caused by writing new business. As pointed out earlier, the expense of putting a new policy on the books greatly exceeds the first-year gross premium. This alone creates a strain on surplus, but when the insurer must also set aside funds to cover all or a portion of the first-year reserve, the strain is intensified. Under certain plans of reinsurance (to be discussed later), the burden of meeting first-year expenses and reserve requirements can be shifted to the reinsurer, thus permitting the primary company to write all the acceptable business produced by its agency forces.

Utilizing the Reinsurer's Expertise

A fourth use of indemnity reinsurance is to take advantage of the reinsurer's underwriting judgment. This is most likely to occur with applications from impaired lives. Some types of impairments are encountered so infrequently that even the largest companies do not

have much opportunity to develop any experience with them. Those responsible for the selection of risks, upon encountering such an impairment, cannot evaluate the risk with the same degree of confidence they feel in dealing with the more common varieties of impaired risks. For their own peace of mind, they are likely to seek the benefit of reinsurance, knowing that the selection of impaired risks is a special service of reinsurance companies. Even if the impairment is a common one and the underwriter has no hesitation about classifying the risk, the case may be submitted to one or more reinsurers to demonstrate to the soliciting agent that the most favorable terms were granted.

A company may also enter into a reinsurance agreement with another company to receive advice and counsel on underwriting matters, rates, and policy forms. This purpose is usually associated with small, newly organized companies that cannot afford a large enough staff to deal with all aspects of its operations. In the relationship between the primary company and the reinsurer, the latter becomes thoroughly conversant with the primary company's operations and is in a position to provide expert advice. While extremely valuable, this service of indemnity reinsurance is usually subsidiary to the fundamental function of spreading the risk.

Transferring Substandard Insurance

A fifth application of indemnity insurance, closely related to the fourth, is to transfer all policies of substandard insurance. This use is brought into play when the primary insurer does not write substandard insurance on any basis. Yet in order to offer a full range of services to its agency force, the company may work out an arrangement whereby it can channel all applications from substandard risks to a reinsurer equipped to classify and underwrite such risks. A variation of this arrangement is to reinsure all substandard insurance policies that fall within a class above a stipulated percentage of anticipated mortality, such as 200 percent.

Finally, with group insurance and pension plans, the company with which the master contract is placed may transfer portions of the coverage to several other insurers under instructions from the policyowner. Such an arrangement is specially fashioned and arises because the policyowner, for business reasons, wishes to divide the coverage among several insurers while looking to one for overall administration of the case.

PROPORTIONAL REINSURANCE

proportional reinsurance

A number of plans have been developed for transacting indemnity reinsurance. The basic or traditional plans, designed for individual risks, are called **proportional reinsurance**, because under these plans a claim under a reinsured policy is shared by the primary company and the reinsurer in a proportion determined in advance. The precise manner in which a claim payment is shared depends on the type of plan employed.

Types of Plans

Proportional reinsurance is provided under two distinct plans: yearly renewable term insurance and coinsurance. A variation of the latter plan, called modified coinsurance, has also been developed.

Yearly Renewable Term Insurance

yearly renewable term plan

The **yearly renewable term plan** derives its name from the fact that the primary company, in effect, purchases term insurance on a yearly renewable basis from the reinsurer. The amount of term insurance purchased in any particular reinsurance transaction is the net amount at risk year by year under the face amount of insurance transferred to the reinsurer. This can be illustrated by a $1 million ordinary life policy issued on a male aged 35 by a company with a retention limit of $200,000. Under such circumstances $800,000 of insurance would ostensibly be transferred to the reinsurer. However, in the event of the insured's death, the reinsurer would pay not $800,000 but only the net amount of risk under an $800,000 policy. If the insured should die during the first policy year, the reinsurer would be liable for $800,000 less $8,820.96, the first-year terminal reserve[5] under the policy in question. If death occurred during the 8th policy year, the reinsurer would remit $727,213.52 to the primary company—the face amount less the 8-year terminal reserve of $77,786.48. The reserves under the $800,000 of life insurance transferred to the reinsurer are held by the primary insurer and, in the event of the insured's death, would be added to the reinsurer's remittance to make up the full payment of $800,000 due under the

---

5.   The figure is the full net level premium reserve under the 1980 CSO aggregate table plus 4 percent interest. Small and medium-sized companies, which are an important segment of the reinsurance market, almost invariably use the Commissioners Reserve Valuation Method. On that reserve basis, there would be no reserve under an ordinary life policy at the end of the first year, so the amount at risk would be the face of the policy.

reinsured portion of the original policy. The primary insurer would, of course, also be solely responsible for payment of the $200,000 of coverage it retained—which, in turn, would be composed of the net amount at risk and the accumulated reserves under $200,000 of coverage.

Whenever a policy is to be reinsured on a yearly renewable term basis, either the primary company or the reinsurer prepares a schedule of the amount at risk for each policy year under the face amount being reinsured. The reinsurer quotes a schedule of yearly renewable term premium rates that will be applied to the net amount at risk year by year. These rates are extremely competitive and usually reflect the lower mortality associated with the selection process.

The premiums are generally graded upward with duration under a wide variety of schedules. Some schedules grade the premium upward over a period as long as 15 years. There may be no charge other than a policy fee of nominal amount—for example, $5 or $10 for the first year of reinsurance coverage. The premium schedule may also reflect, through a policy fee or in some other manner, the amount of insurance involved. The expense loading is lower than in direct premiums since the primary company pays all commissions, medical fees, and other acquisition expenses connected with the policy. (Under most reinsurance agreements, the premium tax is borne by the reinsurer in the form of a "refund" to the primary company.) As a further cost concession, some agreements of this type provide that the primary company share in any mortality savings on the reinsured business. Because it holds all the reserves, the primary company is responsible for surrender values, policy loans, and other prematurity benefits.

Yearly Renewable Term Insurance Reinsurance

- Primary insurer retains reserves for portion of policy reinsured.

- Reinsurer charges premium on at-risk portion of reinsured amount ($500,000 reinsured), if primary insurer maintains $30,000 reserve for portion reinsured, it results in $470,000 at risk amount.

- Reinsurer liability is limited to at-risk amount if insured dies.

- Primary insurer allowed to retain more of the premium.

- Primary insurer liability for a claim is the full amount retained, plus the reserve for the reinsured portion.

There are several advantages associated with the yearly renewable term basis of reinsurance. It permits the primary company to retain most of the premiums, giving rise to a more

rapid growth in assets—a matter of special concern to small and medium-sized companies. For the same reason, it may be favored when the reinsurer is not licensed to transact business in the domiciliary state of the primary company, which would mean that the primary company would not be permitted to deduct the reserves on the reinsured policies from its overall reserve liability. (The same situation may lead to the use of a modified coinsurance arrangement.) This plan of reinsurance is also easier to administer than the more complicated coinsurance arrangements. Finally, it is thought to be more suitable for nonparticipating insurance where costs are fixed in advance.

Coinsurance

coinsurance plan

Under the **coinsurance plan** the primary company transfers (or cedes) the proportion of the face amount of insurance called for in the cession form, but the reinsurer is responsible not only for the net amount at risk but also for its pro rata share of the death claim. In the example cited under yearly renewable term insurance, the reinsurer is liable for the payment of $800,000, irrespective of the policy year in which the insured died. The reinsurer is also responsible for its pro rata share of the cash surrender value and other surrender benefits. In effect, the reinsurer is simply substituted for the primary company with respect to the amount of insurance reinsured. The primary or ceding company, however, remains liable to the policyowner for the full amount of any benefits if the reinsurer becomes insolvent or otherwise cannot pay its share of claims.

ceding commission

The primary or ceding company pays the reinsurer a pro rata share of the gross premiums collected from the policyowner,[6] and the reinsurer accumulates and holds the policy reserves for the amount of insurance ceded. Inasmuch as the ceding company incurs heavy expenses in putting the original policy on the books, it is customary for the reinsurer to reimburse the primary insurer for the expenses attributable to the amount of insurance reinsured. This reimbursement takes the form of a **ceding commission**, which includes an allowance for commissions paid to the soliciting agent of the ceding company, premium taxes paid to the insured's state of domicile,[7] and a portion of the overhead expenses of the

---

6. There are exceptions to this practice. Sometimes when the ceding insurer offers both participating and nonparticipating policies, all reinsurance will be arranged on the basis of the ceding company's nonparticipating gross premium rates in order to avoid the complexity of dividend accounting.

7. In most—if not all—states, the ceding company is not permitted to deduct premium taxes on amounts of insurance transferred to reinsurers. By the same token, reinsurers are not required to pay premium taxes on insurance

ceding company. Paying a portion of the primary company's overhead recognizes the fact that not only does a reinsurer incur relatively lower expenses on that portion of the face amount assumed by it, but the average amount of insurance per reinsurance certificate is also larger than the average size of the primary insurer's policy. Hence, the administrative expense per $1,000 of insurance is lower on that portion of the insurance reinsured than on the ceding company's normal business, and the reinsurer is willing to share the savings with the company that originated the business. There is normally no sharing of medical and other selection expenses, based on the theory that such expenses are incurred on a per-policy basis and vary only slightly with the amount of insurance. The amount of the ceding commission is negotiated between the ceding insurer and the reinsurer.

If the original policy is participating, the reinsurer must pay dividends on the portion of insurance it assumes according to the primary company's dividend scale. This can prove burdensome if the net investment earnings of the reinsurer do not approximate those of the primary company or if the mortality under the ceded policies is not as favorable as that underlying the dividend scale. As a matter of fact, the mortality rates on reinsured policies as a whole tend to be higher than those on direct business, possibly because of the larger amounts of insurance involved and the less rigid underwriting standards of the many small and medium-sized companies that rely heavily on reinsurance. The anticipated higher mortality is taken into account in arriving at the ceding commission.

Coinsurance Sharing

- Proportional sharing of premiums
- Proportional sharing of reserve liability
- Proportional sharing of dividends (if policy is participating)
- Reinsurer issues ceding commission to the primary insurer for acquisition costs incurred on the portion reinsured
- Primary insurer responsible for policy loans

In the event that the original policy is terminated voluntarily, the reinsurer is liable for its pro rata share of the cash surrender value. If the policy is surrendered for reduced paid-up insurance, the reinsurer may remain liable for its proportionate share, or its share may be reduced by paying the appropriate cash surrender value to the primary insurer. Should the policy be exchanged for extended term insurance, the reinsurer usually retains its

assumed under reinsurance agreements.

proportionate share of liability, although its share may be reduced by any policy indebt-edness. The reinsurer does not ordinarily participate in policy loans, settlement options, or installment settlements under family income or maintenance policies. The reinsurer's obligation in the event of the insured's death is discharged by a single-sum payment to the ceding company.

Modified Coinsurance

modification of the coinsurance method

Many companies regard the reinsurer's accumulation of substantial sums of money as an unessential feature of a reinsurance arrangement and one that can be disadvantageous to the primary company. Apart from a company's natural desire to retain control of the funds arising out of its own policies, it may be apprehensive about entrusting another company to accumulate the funds necessary to discharge the primary company's obligations under a policy. This apprehension is heightened by the knowledge that the primary insurer's basic liability to the policyowner or beneficiary is not affected by the reinsurer's inability to make good on its obligation to the primary company. This problem is of more immediate concern when the reinsurer is not licensed to operate in the primary company's home state. In many states the primary company is not permitted to include sums due from the reinsurer as assets in its balance sheet. These considerations have led to a **modification of the coinsurance method**, under which the primary company retains the entire reserve under the reinsured policy.

Under this arrangement, the ceding company pays the reinsurer a proportionate part of the gross premium, as under the conventional coinsurance plan, less whatever allowances have been arranged for commissions, premium taxes, and overhead. At the end of each policy year, however, the reinsurer pays over to the ceding company a sum equal to the net increase in the reserve during the year, less one year's interest on the reserve at the beginning of the year. In more precise terms, the reinsurer pays over an amount equal to the excess of the terminal reserve for the policy year in question over the terminal reserve for the preceding policy year, less interest on the initial reserve for the current policy year. It is necessary to credit the reinsurer with interest on the initial reserve since a part of the increase in the reserve during the year is attributable to earnings on the funds underlying the reserve, which are held by the ceding company. The reserves are usually credited with interest at the rate used in the primary company's dividend formula or, in the case of non-participating insurance, a rate arrived at by negotiation.

Under this arrangement, the reinsurer never holds more than the gross premium, as adjusted for allowances, for one year. Under one variation of this method, the anticipated

increase is deducted in advance from the gross premium. In many reinsurance transactions using the modified coinsurance plan, the foregoing adjustments are based on the aggregate mean reserves, rather than on the individual terminal reserves. Apart from the reserve adjustment, the modified coinsurance basis is identical to the straight coinsurance basis, and the description of the coinsurance arrangement in the preceding section is equally applicable to the modified form.[8]

The modified coinsurance plan bears such a strong resemblance in net effect to the yearly renewable term basis of coinsurance that one might question why modified coinsurance would ever be used. One answer is that the premium paid by the primary company is geared to the premium received from the policyowner, rather than being arrived at through negotiation. The second answer is more complex but rests on the fact that under a modified coinsurance plan, reinsurance costs reflect the incidence of expense and surplus drain incurred by the primary company. Under the yearly renewable term plan, the ceding company is responsible for maintaining the reserves at the proper level. Under the modified coinsurance arrangement, however, the reinsurer, out of the premium received from the primary company, must each year turn back a sum equal to the increase in reserves (less one year's interest on the reserve at the beginning of the year), as well as the ceding commission. Over the lifetime of the reinsured policy, the total cost of modified coinsurance and yearly renewable term should be approximately the same, but the net cost of reinsurance in the early years is normally less under modified coinsurance.

NONPROPORTIONAL REINSURANCE

nonproportional reinsurance

The great bulk of life reinsurance is transacted on the basis of proportional reinsurance as described above. However, in recent years increasing interest has developed in an approach that relates the reinsurer's liability to the mortality experience on all or a specified portion of the primary company's business, rather than to individual or specific policies of insurance. Widely used in property-casualty insurance, this approach is referred to as nonproportional reinsurance, because the proportion in which the primary company and the reinsurer will share losses is not determinable in advance. This type of nonproportional reinsurance coverage is available from both American and European reinsurers in three forms: stop-loss reinsurance, catastrophe reinsurance, and spread-loss reinsurance.

---

8.   In the settlement of claims under the modified coinsurance plan, the reinsurer is charged with the face amount of insurance transferred to it but credited with the reserve on that sum.

Stop-Loss Reinsurance

stop-loss reinsurance

Stop-loss reinsurance is highly developed in casualty insurance but it is still in a growth stage in life insurance, serving primarily as a supplement to conventional reinsurance rather than as a substitute for it. Thus, plans follow no fixed pattern. In essence, however, stop-loss reinsurance arrangements undertake to indemnify the primary company if its mortality losses in the aggregate, or on specified segments of its business, exceed by a stipulated percentage what might be regarded as the normal or expected mortality. The agreements commonly invoke liability on the reinsurer's part if the primary company's aggregate mortality exceeds by more than 10 percent the "normal" mortality, which, of course, must be defined explicitly—or implicitly—in the agreement. Normal mortality is usually defined as a specified percentage of the tabular mortality for the categories of business covered by the agreement. Thus, if the mortality under the policies subject to a particular stop-loss reinsurance agreement is running around 50 percent of the 1980 CSO Table, the agreement might stipulate that the reinsurer will absorb all losses in excess of 110 percent of the normal level of mortality, defined as 50 percent of the 1980 CSO Table rates. Another way to express the reinsurer's obligation is to stipulate that the reinsurer will indemnify the primary company for all claims in excess of a specified percentage of tabular mortality, such as 60 percent of the 1980 CSO Table.

Under some agreements, the reinsurer indemnifies the primary company for only a specified percentage (for example, 90 percent) of the excess mortality, an arrangement intended to encourage careful underwriting by the primary company. Under most agreements, the reinsurer's liability during any contract period, generally a calendar year, is limited to a stipulated dollar amount. Under any of these arrangements, if the mortality for the contract period is below the level at which the reinsurer's obligation would attach, the reinsurer makes no payment to the primary company.

Stop-Loss Features

- Reinsurer assumes all losses over an agreed threshold (exceeds normal claims expectation)

- Threshold is tied to both a stated level of standard mortality table experience and more than 100 percent of primary insurer's past mortality experience

- Price and terms negotiated

This approach to reinsurance lends itself to great flexibility, since the agreements can be written to cover only selected portions of the primary company's business with varying levels of mortality and with varying duration periods. The premium for stop-loss reinsurance is arrived at by negotiation and involves the use of highly refined actuarial techniques, as well as a large portion of judgment. The basic appeal of this coverage is that it provides protection against adverse mortality experience arising out of an unexpectedly large number of small claims or an unexpected increase in the average size of claims. It is a form of reinsurance on the amounts at risk retained under conventional reinsurance agreements. Because the unit cost of protection under this approach is less than under proportional reinsurance, a company can reduce its total outlay for reinsurance by increasing its retention limits under conventional agreements and reinsuring the retained amounts under stop-loss arrangements. Another advantage of this approach is its relative ease of administration, attributable to the absence of individual policy records.

Adherents to conventional (proportional) reinsurance arrangements see many practical disadvantages to stop-loss reinsurance. They point out that it is short-term, rate-adjustable, cancelable coverage available under conventional arrangements. They call attention to the limit on the reinsurer's liability, as well as exclusion of the war risk. They emphasize the restrictions on the primary company's underwriting practices necessarily imposed by the reinsurer. Finally, they question for a number of reasons whether any cost savings will, in fact, be realized in the long run.

At its present stage of development in the United States, stop-loss reinsurance serves primarily as a supplement to conventional reinsurance arrangements rather than as a substitute for them.

Catastrophe Reinsurance

catastrophe reinsurance

Like stop-loss reinsurance, **catastrophe reinsurance** was first developed for property-casualty insurance lines. As its name implies, it usually provides for payment by the reinsurer of some fixed percentage, ranging from 90 to 100 percent, of the aggregate losses (net of conventional reinsurance) in excess of a stipulated limit in connection with a single accident or catastrophic event, such as an airplane crash, explosion, fire, or hurricane. Catastrophe reinsurance is clearly intended to serve only as a supplement to proportional reinsurance agreements. The level of losses at which the reinsurer's liability attaches may be expressed in terms of dollar amount or number of lives. The contract usually covers a period of one year and limits the reinsurer's liability for that period. The coverage is attractive to insurance companies that have a concentration of risks in one location, such as

the reinsurer; the other is retained by the primary company. The form is identical for both facultative and automatic insurance. In effect, it is the individual contract of insurance; the entire reinsurance agreement is incorporated into it by reference.

cession form

The **cession form** describes the basis on which the reinsurance is being effected—that is, whether it is yearly renewable term insurance, coinsurance, modified coinsurance, or some other type. If one of the coinsurance arrangements is being used, provision is made for paying a ceding commission to the primary or ceding company.

Provision is also made for the manner in which premiums are to be paid. All premiums are generally payable on an annual basis subject to prorated refunds in the event of terminations other than on policy anniversaries. The reinsurer bills the primary insurer monthly for reinsurance premiums falling due during that month. The bill also includes first-year premiums arising from cessions of reinsurance received since the date of the previous billing and refunds of premiums due to policy cancellations, as well as other small adjustments that arise from time to time.

Claims Settlement

The policyowner is not a party to the reinsurance agreement and looks to the issuing company to fulfill the obligation of the contract.[11] Consequently, the reinsurance agreement stipulates that any settlement made by the primary insurer with a claimant is binding on the reinsurer,[12] whether the reinsurance was originally automatic or was accepted facultatively by the reinsurer. Despite this contractual right to settle claims at its discretion, the primary insurer will invariably consult with the reinsurer in doubtful cases.

If the policy is to be settled on an installment basis, the reinsurer will nevertheless discharge its liability by paying a lump sum to the primary insurer. This is true not only of settlement option arrangements but also of contracts, such as the family income and retirement income policies, which provide for settlement on an installment basis. If a policy is settled for less than the face amount, such as might happen from a misstatement of age or the compromise of a claim of doubtful validity, the reinsurer shares in the savings.

---

11.   Under portfolio reinsurance, policyholders are usually given the right to proceed directly against the reinsurer in pressing a claim for settlement.

12.   An exception is made when the entire risk is carried by the reinsurer. Under such circumstances, the agreement provides for consultation with the reinsurer before an admission or acknowledgment of a claim by the primary company.

Under a facultative arrangement the primary company submits a copy of the application from the insured, together with all supporting documents, to the prospective insurer. The primary insurer also submits a form that specifies the basis on which reinsurance is desired and the proportion of the face amount that the originating company proposes to retain. This form, which constitutes the offer for reinsurance, supplies all information about the risk in the possession of the primary company, including the amount of insurance already in force on the risk. The agreement normally provides that the reinsurer will phone, telegram, or facsimile its acceptance or rejection to the primary company.

jumbo clause

Under an automatic arrangement the reinsurer is obligated to accept a specified amount of reinsurance, including amounts for supplemental coverage on the basis of the primary company's underwriting appraisal. The maximum amount that can be transferred automatically to the reinsurer depends on the quality of the ceding company's underwriting staff, as well as its limits of retention. It is fairly common for the reinsurer to obligate itself to accept automatically up to four or more times the primary company's retention. However, when the retention limits of the primary company are fairly high, the reinsurer may limit its obligation to an amount equal to the primary company's limit. The agreement specifies that the originating company will retain an amount of insurance equal to its retention limit and will not reinsure it elsewhere on a facultative basis.[10] In other words, if the primary company should decide to retain less than the full retention indicated for the particular classification in which the risk falls, the reinsurer is relieved of its obligation under the automatic agreement, and the entire transaction will have to be handled on a facultative basis. The agreement also usually includes a so-called **jumbo clause**, which stipulates that if the total amount of insurance in force on an applicant's life in all companies—including policies applied for—exceeds a specified amount, reinsurance is not automatically effected. The agreement normally makes provision for facultative reinsurance of those risks not eligible, for one reason or another, for automatic reinsurance.

Cession Form

The reinsurance agreement stipulates that the primary insurer, after delivering its policy to the insured and collecting the first premium, is to prepare a formal cession of reinsurance (in duplicate), which gives the details of the risk and schedule of reinsurance premiums, including the ceding commission, if any. One copy of the cession form goes to

---

10. Such a provision is obviously not included in an agreement under which the ceding company is to transfer all amounts of substandard insurance written by it.

of risk that will be subject to reinsurance, the extent of the reinsurer's liability, and the procedures by which the transactions are to be carried out. These agreements are broadly classified as either facultative or automatic.

Types of Agreement

facultative agreement

The **facultative agreement** establishes a procedure whereby the primary insurer may offer risks to the reinsurer on an individual case basis. The essence of the arrangement is that the primary company is under no obligation to offer—and the reinsurer is under no duty to accept—a particular risk. Each company reserves full freedom of action, and each risk is considered on its merits. The arrangement takes its name from the fact that each party retains the "faculty" to do as it pleases with respect to each specific risk.

A pending life insurance application on which the primary insurer is seeking reinsurance on a facultative agreement basis will probably be rejected if no reinsurer accepts the case. Seeking reinsurer approval sometimes delays the primary insurer's underwriting.

An agent who tries to hurry up the acceptance may actually be pushing the case to rejection. Allowing more time to find a reinsurer may increase the likelihood the coverage is issued.

automatic agreement

The **automatic agreement**, on the other hand, binds the primary insurer to offer—and the reinsurer to accept—all risks that fall within the purview of the agreement. The automatic agreement sets forth a schedule of the primary insurer's limits of retention and provides that whenever the primary company issues a policy for an amount in excess of the limit for each policy, the excess amount is to be reinsured automatically. The primary company does not submit the underwriting papers to the reinsurer, and the reinsurer does not have the option of accepting or rejecting the risk.[9]

---

9.   In recent years, a modified type of automatic agreement has been developed under which the reinsurer's obligation becomes fixed only after the reinsurer has had an opportunity to screen its files for any unfavorable information relating to the risk. The primary company sends the reinsurer a notice of intention to bind, and unless the reinsurer notifies the primary company of unfavorable information on the risk within a specified time, the reinsurance automatically goes into effect. This method, without slowing down the primary company's underwriting and issuing procedures, makes the reinsurer's confidential files, built up over many years of operation, available to the issuing company. Moreover, there are some automatic agreements, under which the primary company submits the underwriting papers to the reinsurer, which has the option of declining to reinsure the risk.

might arise under a group insurance policy. The risk involved is essentially accidental death attributable to a catastrophic occurrence.

While the reinsurer's liability under a catastrophe type of agreement is high, the probability of loss was perceived to be low prior to the attack on the World Trade Center on September 11, 2001. Hence, the premiums for this type of coverage have generally been low. Premium increases will be imposed and the viability of this coverage may be more limited in the future. The expense element of the premium is minimized through the use of aggregate reporting procedures.

Spread-Loss Reinsurance

spread-loss reinsurance

A final type of nonproportional reinsurance is **spread-loss reinsurance**. Under this type of agreement, the reinsurer collects an annual premium of a stipulated minimum amount, of which a certain portion (such as 20 percent) is allocated to expenses and profit, with the balance credited to a refund account until the account reaches a specified maximum figure, such as the sum of 3 years' premiums. During any calendar year when the primary company's aggregate death claims (net of conventional reinsurance payments) exceed a specified limit, the reinsurer pays the claims in excess of the limit but adjusts the premium to reflect the claims experience. The agreement provides that any amounts paid by the reinsurer for a given year, plus 20 percent, must be returned to the reinsurer by the primary company during the next 5 years.

The spread-loss agreement can be terminated by either party, with proper notice, at the end of any contract year, except that the primary company cannot terminate the arrangement under circumstances that would cause a loss to the reinsurer. In other words, the reinsurer must be permitted to recover all payments made to the primary company. It is apparent that the main purpose of this type of reinsurance is to spread the financial effects of an unfavorable mortality experience in any one year over a period of 5 years. About the only risk the reinsurer takes is the continued solvency of the primary company. Consequently, the mathematical basis of the premium charge is completely different from the other two forms of nonproportional reinsurance.

REINSURANCE AGREEMENT

Arrangements between ceding insurers and reinsurers are generally formalized by a reinsurance agreement (also called a reinsurance treaty). Such agreements describe the classes

If the primary insurer contests a claim, the reinsurer bears its proportionate share of the expenses incurred.

Reduction in the Sums Reinsured

Once a sum of insurance has been reinsured, the reinsurer is at risk for that amount as long as the amount retained by the primary company remains in force, subject to two important exceptions. One exception is in instances where the total amount of insurance on a particular risk is reduced after a portion of the insurance has been reinsured. This can result from the maturity or expiration of policies in accordance with their terms or through the voluntary termination of policies by nonpayment of premiums. Some agreements provide that the full amount of the reduction will come out of the sum reinsured (up to the amount reinsured), while other agreements call for proportionate reductions in the amounts held by the two insurers.

recapture of insurance

The other exception applies to increases in the primary insurer's limits of retention and is especially significant to young and growing insurance companies. The provision states that if the primary company increases its limits of retention, it may make corresponding reductions in all reinsurance previously transferred. In the case of a $5 million policy written by a company with a $1 million retention limit, $4 million would originally have been reinsured. If the primary company later increases its retention limit for that particular class of policy to $2 million, it would be permitted to recover $1 million of the $4 million that had been reinsured. This is referred to as the **recapture of insurance**.

Recapture Provision

Recapture is usually permitted only after the policies involved have been in force for a specified period of time. This restriction is clearly designed to enable the reinsurer to recover its acquisition expenses. It is customary to restrict recapture of insurance arranged under a renewable term plan to policies in force for 5 or more years, while amounts ceded on a coinsurance basis must typically remain in force for 10 or more years before being subject to recapture. The recapture provision provides an effective method of recovering amounts of insurance previously reinsured when the primary company holds the reserves, as under the yearly renewable term and modified coinsurance arrangements, but it may be ineffective under the coinsurance plan, since the reinsurer is obligated to release only the cash values—not the reserves—for the amounts recaptured. If there is a differential between the surrender value and the reserve under a policy, which is likely, the primary

company may conclude that it is not worthwhile to recapture the insurance, at least until the differential between the surrender value and the reserve is insignificant.

Duration of the Agreement

Subject to the provisions described in the preceding section, a reinsurance agreement remains effective for reinsured policies as long as the original insurance continues in force. For new insurance, however, most agreements make provision for cancellation by either party with 90 days' notice. During that period, the agreement remains in full force and effect, and the reinsurer must accept all new insurance exceeding the retention limit with an automatic treaty. It is anticipated that the primary company can make other reinsurance arrangements within a period of 90 days.

Insolvency of the Primary Insurer

In general, reinsurance agreements are regarded as contracts of indemnity, and the reinsurer's liability is measured by the actual loss sustained by the primary insurer. An important exception is in the case of the primary insurer's insolvency. Virtually all agreements provide that the reinsurer must remit in full to the insolvent carrier that issued the original policy, even though the claim against the insolvent company will have to be scaled down. Many states, including New York, will not permit a primary company to treat amounts due from reinsurers as admitted assets or to deduct reserves held by reinsurers from its policy liabilities unless the reinsurance agreement requires the reinsurer to discharge its own obligation in full in the event the primary company becomes insolvent.

It is important to note that a claimant under a reinsured policy issued by a company that is insolvent at the time of the claim is not permitted to bring action directly against the reinsurer but must look to the insolvent carrier's general assets for the settlement of the claim. On the other hand, when the issuing company is insolvent, the reinsurer is given the specific right to contest claims against the primary insurer in which it has an interest, with all defenses available to the reinsurer that are available to the primary insurer.

Experience Rating

It is becoming increasingly common for reinsurance agreements to contain a provision permitting a primary company to share in any mortality gains or losses arising under reinsured policies. This is a form of experience rating found in many lines of insurance, including the various group coverages written by life companies. In this case, the primary company is treated as the policyowner, and the mortality refund (or surcharge, as the case might

be) is calculated on the combined experience under all reinsured amounts with a particular reinsurer. The practice originated in the 1920s but was generally discontinued in the 1930s because of the disastrous claims experience on "jumbo" risks. In recent years, there has been renewed interest in the arrangement, and there are many variations in practice. A common arrangement is to have the primary insurer participate in any gains or losses on reinsurance amounts below a specified limit and not participate in the experience on amounts in excess of such limit. The purpose of this variation is to permit the primary company to share in the favorable mortality experience of the bulk of reinsured risks but to avoid the undesirable fluctuations in its overall experience that might result from unpredictably heavy mortality among very large risks. (Note that arrangements that permit the primary insurer to share the gains from favorable mortality experience on reinsured risks lessen the importance of recapture provisions.)

Mortality refunds are a matter of accounting between insurance companies and should not be confused with dividends to policyowners, although under participating policies, all or a portion of the savings may be passed on indirectly to policyowners. Agreements that provide for sharing mortality savings on reinsured risks with the primary company are usually referred to as experience-rated agreements.

Supplementary Coverages

The reinsurance agreement covering life risks may or may not apply to supplementary coverages, such as accidental death benefits and total disability benefits. If the basic agreement is facultative, it is likely to cover supplementary benefits as well as the life risk; if it is automatic, a separate agreement may be used for the supplementary coverages, particularly the accidental death benefits.

Many companies have lower limits of retention for accidental death benefits than for basic life risks. For example, a company may be willing to retain $400,000 of coverage under a basic life policy but only $100,000 of accidental death coverage. Therefore, a policy for $200,000 with accidental death provisions would require reinsurance for the supplementary coverage but not for the basic coverage. For this reason the reinsurance of accidental death benefits may be set up under a special agreement.

Reinsurance may be provided on either a coinsurance or yearly renewable term basis, depending on the plan used for basic life risks. If the coinsurance plan is used, the premium for the accidental death benefits is based on the premium charged the insured, less a first-year and renewal expense allowance. If the renewable term plan is used, the premium is usually a flat rate per $1,000, irrespective of age of issue or the type of contract issued to the policyowner. The benefits are reinsured on a level-amount basis, because only nominal

reserves are accumulated in connection with such coverage. Disability benefits may likewise be reinsured on either a coinsurance or a yearly renewable term basis. The premium is the same as that charged the insured, less a first-year and renewal-expense allowance. It is customary to limit the reinsurance of disability benefits to an amount not exceeding that attaching to the face amount of life coverage reinsured.

Substandard Reinsurance

The general principles governing reinsurance of standard risks are also applicable to substandard insurance. For substandard reinsurance on either the coinsurance or the modified coinsurance basis, the primary or ceding company pays the reinsurer appropriate portions of the additional premiums collected from the policyowner, subject to a ceding commission for reimbursement of the ceding company's acquisition expenses. If the reinsurance is accomplished on the yearly renewable term basis and the substandard risk is classified according to a multiple of standard mortality, the reinsurance premiums are usually calculated on the same multiple of the standard reinsurance rate. If the policyowner is charged a flat extra premium, the primary insurer pays the reinsurer the same premium as for a standard risk, plus an appropriate share of the flat extra premium. The flat extra premiums, however, are not reduced as the net amount at risk declines.

CHAPTER REVIEW

Key Terms and Concepts

reinsurance
primary company
reinsurer
cession
retrocession
assumption reinsurance
indemnity reinsurance
retention limits
proportional reinsurance
yearly renewable term plan
coinsurance plan
ceding commission

modification of the coinsurance
   method
nonproportional reinsurance
stop-loss reinsurance
catastrophe reinsurance
spread-loss reinsurance
facultative agreement
automatic agreement
jumbo clause
cession form
recapture of insurance

Chapter 16 Review Questions

1. What are the two general reasons reinsurance may be undertaken in life insurance? [2]

2. What are the reasons for using assumption reinsurance? [1]

3. List and explain the reasons for which a life insurance company may use indemnity reinsurance. [2]

4. What factors strongly influence company management in setting limits on the amount of insurance that the company will retain on any one life (that is, in setting retention limits)? [2]

5. Describe two ways nonproportional reinsurance can be used to stabilize a primary company's overall mortality experience. [2]

6. Explain the following for the yearly renewable term plan of reinsurance:

    (a) how the plan works, including how the primary company and reinsurer share death payments and reserves;

    (b) characteristics of the premium schedules;

    (c) the advantages associated with this type of plan. [3]

7. Explain how the coinsurance plan of reinsurance works, including how the primary company and reinsurer share death payments, reserves, surrender benefits, premiums, expenses, and (for participating policies) dividends. [3]

8. Suppose a $1 million ordinary life policy with a 10th-year policy reserve of $15,000 is issued by a company with a $300,000 retention limit. Under each of the following reinsurance plans, what are the primary company's and reinsurer's shares of the $1 million death benefit if the insured dies during the 10th policy year?

    (a) yearly renewable term plan;

    (b) coinsurance plan. [3]

9. Explain the reasons why many companies regard the reinsurer's accumulation of substantial sums as an unessential feature of a reinsurance arrangement and one that can actually be disadvantageous to the primary company. [3]

10. Explain the following for the modified coinsurance plan of reinsurance: (a) how the plan works, including how it is similar to and different from the coinsurance plan of reinsurance; (b) reasons it might be preferred to the yearly renewable term plan for meeting a company's reinsurance needs. [3]

11. Explain how each of the following types of nonproportional reinsurance works:

    (a) stop-loss reinsurance;

    (b) catastrophe reinsurance;

    (c) spread-loss reinsurance. [4]

12. Identify the following for stop-loss reinsurance:

    (a) advantages of this approach;

    (b) disadvantages seen by adherents to conventional (proportional) reinsurance. [4]

13. Compare facultative and automatic reinsurance agreements with regard to:

    (a) the primary company's obligation to offer, and the reinsurer's obligation to accept, a particular risk;

    (b) the procedures and considerations involved in determining the amount of risk that can be transferred to the reinsurer. [5]

14. Describe the following features of a reinsurance agreement, and indicate the responsibilities each places on the primary company and/or the reinsurer:

(a) cession of reinsurance (cession form);

(b) procedure for claims settlement;

(c) procedures for handling reductions in the sums reinsured, including the provision for recapture of insurance;

(d) the duration of the agreement;

(e) procedures in the event of the primary company's insolvency;

(f) provision for experience rating;

(g) treatment of supplementary coverages. [6]

Chapter 16 Review Answers

1. *In life insurance, reinsurance can be undertaken for one of two general reasons: (1) to transfer all or a specific portion of a company's liabilities (called portfolio or assumption reinsurance) or (2 to accomplish certain broad managerial objectives, including favorable underwriting results and the reduction of surplus drain from writing new business (referred to as indemnity reinsurance).*

2. *There are a number of reasons for assumption reinsurance. A traditional use has been to bail out, rather than liquidate, insurance companies that find themselves in financial difficulties. A merger is another situation in which all the business of one company can be ceded to another. In other cases, assumption reinsurance may be used if a combination company were to decide to restrict its future operations to ordinary insurance and discontinue its industrial business, or if a company were to decide to withdraw from one or more states.*

3. *Indemnity reinsurance is used for several reasons:*

   • *to limit the amount of insurance on one life. The most fundamental and prevalent use of indemnity reinsurance is to avoid too large of a concentration of risk on one life. All companies have deemed it prudent to limit the amount of insurance that they will retain on any one life.*

- *to stabilizing mortality experience. Nonproportional reinsurance can be used to stabilize the primary company's overall mortality experience.*

- *to reduce the drain on surplus caused by writing new business. The expense of putting a new policy on the books greatly exceeds the loading in the first-year gross premium. This alone creates a strain on surplus, but when the insurer must also set aside funds to cover all or a portion of the first-year reserve, the strain is intensified. Under certain plans of reinsurance, the burden of meeting first-year expenses and reserve requirements can be shifted to the reinsurer, thus permitting the primary company to write all of the acceptable business produced by its agency forces.*

- *to utilize the reinsurer's expertise. In this case of applications on lives with infrequently encountered impairments, the underwriter is likely to seek the benefit of reinsurance, knowing that the selection of impaired risks is a special service of reinsurance companies. Also, a small, newly organized company may enter into a reinsurance agreement with another company to receive advice and counsel on underwriting matters, rates, and policy forms.*

- *to transfer substandard insurance. When the primary insurer does not write substandard insurance on any basis and yet wishes to offer a full range of services to its agency force, the company may work out an arrangement whereby it can channel all applications from substandard risks to a reinsurer equipped to classify and underwrite such risks. A variation of this arrangement is to reinsure all substandard insurance policies that fall within a class above a stipulated percentage of anticipated mortality, such as 200 percent.*

- *to divide group insurance and pension business among several companies. The company with which the master contract is placed may transfer portions of the coverage to several other insurers under instructions from the policyowner. Such an arrangement is specially fashioned and arises because the policyowner, for business reasons, wishes to divide the coverage among several insurers while looking to one for overall administration of the case.*

4. *Retention limits reflect the judgment of company management as to many factors, but they are strongly influenced by the volume of insurance in force, the amount of surplus funds, and the proficiency of the underwriting personnel.*

5. One form of nonproportional reinsurance transfers to the reinsurer all or a specified percentage of that portion of aggregate mortality claims for a given period in excess of a stipulated norm. Another form of nonproportional reinsurance provides protection against an undesirable concentration of risk on several lives, such as might be found among the passengers of a jet airliner or the employees of an industrial plant.

6. a. The yearly renewable term plan derives its name from the fact that the primary company, in effect, purchases term insurance on a yearly renewable basis from the reinsurer. The amount of term insurance purchased in any particular reinsurance transaction is the net amount at risk year by year under the face amount of insurance transferred to the reinsurer. In the event of the insured's death, the reinsurer would pay an amount equal to the net amount at risk (face amount minus the terminal reserve) on the amount of insurance transferred to the reinsurer, and the primary insurer would pay an amount equal to the terminal reserve on the amount of insurance transferred to the reinsurer plus the amount of insurance (net amount at risk plus terminal reserve) for the coverage it retained. Because it holds all the reserves, the primary company is responsible for surrender values, policy loans, and other prematurity benefits.

    b. The reinsurer quotes a schedule of yearly renewable term premium rates that will be applied to the net amount at risk year by year. These rates are extremely competitive and usually reflect the lower mortality associated with the selection process. The premiums are generally graded upward with duration under a wide variety of schedules reflecting the following characteristics:

        • Some schedules grade the premium upward over a period as long as 15 years. There may be no charge other than a policy fee of nominal amount—for example, $5 or $10 for the first year of reinsurance coverage.

        • The premium schedule may also reflect, through a policy fee or in some other manner, the amount of insurance involved.

        • The expense loading is lower than in direct premiums because the primary company pays all commissions, medical fees, and other acquisition expenses connected with the policy.

        • As a further cost concession, some agreements of this type provide that the primary company share in any mortality savings on the reinsured business.

    c. There are several advantages associated with the yearly renewable term basis of reinsurance. It permits the primary company to retain most of the premiums, giving rise to a more rapid growth in assets—a matter of special concern to small- and medium-sized companies. For the same reasons, it may be favored when the reinsurer is not

licensed to transact business in the domiciliary state of the primary company, which would mean that the primary company would not be permitted to deduct the reserves on the reinsured policies from its overall reserve liability. This plan of reinsurance is also easier to administer than the more complicated coinsurance arrangements. Finally, it is thought to be more suitable for nonparticipating insurance where costs are fixed in advance.

7.   *Under the coinsurance plan, the primary company transfers (or cedes) the proportion of the face amount of insurance called for in the cession form, but the reinsurer is responsible not only for the net amount at risk but also for its pro rata share of the death claim. The reinsurer is also responsible for its pro rata share of the cash surrender value and other surrender benefits. In effect, the reinsurer is simply substituted for the primary company with respect to the amount of insurance reinsured. The primary or ceding company, however, remains liable to the policyowner for the full amount of any benefits if the reinsurer becomes insolvent or otherwise cannot pay its share of claims.*

The primary or ceding company pays the reinsurer a pro rata share of the gross premiums collected from the policyowner, and the reinsurer accumulates and holds policy reserves for the amount of insurance ceded. Inasmuch as the ceding company incurs heavy expenses in putting the original policy on the books, it is customary for the reinsurer to reimburse the primary insurer for the expenses attributable to the amount of insurance reinsured. This reimbursement takes the form of a ceding commission. The amount of the ceding commission is negotiated between the ceding insurer and the reinsurer.

If the original policy is participating, the reinsurer must pay dividends on the portion of insurance it assumes according to the primary company's dividend scale.

In the event that the original policy is terminated voluntarily, the reinsurer is liable for its pro rata share of the cash surrender value. If the policy is surrendered for reduced paid-up insurance, the reinsurer may remain liable for its proportionate share, or its share may be reduced by paying the appropriate cash surrender value to the primary insurer. Should the policy be exchanged for extended term insurance, the reinsurer usually retains its proportionate share of liability, although its share may be reduced by any policy indebtedness.

8.   a.   *With a yearly renewable term plan, the primary company's share of the death benefit is $310,500, and the reinsurer's share is $689,500. Because $300,000 of the $1 million of insurance is retained by the primary company, the reinsurer pays an amount equal*

to the net amount at risk on the $700,000 of insurance above the retention limit. Because the 10th-year reserve on the $1 million of coverage is $15,000, the reserve on the $700,000 of insurance above the retention $10,500 (that is, [$15,000'$1,000,000] x $700,000). Thus, the net amount at risk on the $700,000 of insurance is $689,500 (that is, $700,000 – $10,500). This $689,500 is the reinsurer's share of the death benefit. The primary company is responsible for an amount ($310,500 equal to the $10,500 reserve on the $700,000 of insurance above the retention, plus the $300,000 of coverage it retained.

b. With the coinsurance plan, the primary company's share of the $1 million death benefit is $300,000, the amount of coverage it retained, and the reinsurer's share is $700,000, the amount of insurance above the primary company's retention.

9. Many companies regard the reinsurer's accumulation of substantial sums of money as an unessential feature of a reinsurance arrangement and one that can be disadvantageous to the primary company. Apart from a company's natural desire to retain control of the funds arising out of its own policies, it may be apprehensive about entrusting another company to accumulate the funds necessary to discharge the primary company's obligations under a policy. This apprehension is heightened by the knowledge that the primary insurer's basic liability to the policyowner or beneficiary is not affected by the reinsurer's inability to make good on its obligation to the primary company. This problem is of more immediate concern when the reinsurer is not licensed to operate in the primary company's home state. In many states, the primary company is not permitted to include sums due from the reinsurer as assets in its balance sheet.

10. a. Under the modified coinsurance plan of reinsurance, the primary company retains the entire reserve under the reinsured policy. The ceding company pays the reinsurer a proportionate part of the gross premium, as under the conventional coinsurance plan, less whatever allowances have been arranged for commissions, premium taxes, and overhead. At the end of each policy year, however, the reinsurer pays over to the ceding company a sum equal to the net increase in the reserve during the year, less one year's interest on the reserve at the beginning of the year. In more precise terms, the reinsurer pays over an amount equal to the excess of the terminal reserve for the policy year in question over the terminal reserve for the preceding policy year, less interest on the initial reserve for the current policy year. It is necessary to credit the reinsurer with interest on the initial reserve because a part of the increase in the reserve during the year is attributable to earnings on the funds underlying the reserve, which are held by the ceding company. The reserves are usually credited with interest at the rate used in

the primary company's dividend formula or, in the case of nonparticipating insurance, a coinsurance basis is identical to the straight coinsurance basis.

b.   *The modified coinsurance plan might be preferred to the yearly renewable term basis of coinsurance for several reasons:*

  - *The first reason is that the premium paid by the primary company is geared to the premium received from the policyowner, rather than being arrived at through negotiation.*

  - *The second reason is more complex but rests on the fact that under a modified coinsurance plan, reinsurance costs reflect the incidence of expense and surplus drain incurred by the primary company. Under the yearly renewable term plan, the ceding company is responsible for maintaining the reserves at the proper level. Under the modified coinsurance arrangement, however, the reinsurer, out of the premium received from the primary company, must each year turn back a sum equal to the increase in reserves (less one year's interest on the reserve at the beginning of the year), as well as the ceding commission. Over the lifetime of the reinsured policy, the total cost of modified coinsurance and yearly renewable term should be approximately the same, but the net cost of reinsurance in the early years is normally less under modified coinsurance.*

11. a.   *While plans follow no fixed pattern, stop-loss reinsurance arrangements undertake to indemnify the primary company if its mortality losses in the aggregate, or on specified segments of its business, exceed by a stipulated percentage what might be regarded as the normal or expected mortality. The agreements commonly invoke liability on the reinsurer's part if the primary company's aggregate mortality exceeds by more than 10 percent the "normal" mortality, which, of course, must be defined explicitly—or implicitly—in the agreement. Normal mortality is usually defined as a specified percentage of the tabular mortality for the categories of business covered by the agreement.*

    Under some agreements, the reinsurer indemnifies the primary company for only a specified percentage (for example, 90 percent) of the excess mortality, an arrangement intended to encourage careful underwriting by the primary company, Under most agreements, the reinsurer's liability during any contract period, generally a calendar year, is limited to a stipulated dollar amount. Under any of these arrangements, if the mortality for the contract period is below the level at which the reinsurer's obligation would attach, the reinsurer makes no payment to the primary company.

b.   *Catastrophe reinsurance usually provides for payment by the reinsurer of some fixed percentage, ranging from 90 to 100 percent, of the aggregate losses (net of conventional reinsurance) in excess of a stipulated limit in connection with a single accident*

or catastrophic event, such as an airplane crash, explosion, fire, or hurricane. The level of losses at which the reinsurer's liability attaches may be expressed in terms of dollar amount or number of lives.

    c.   *Under a spread-loss reinsurance agreement, the reinsurer collects an annual premium of a stipulated minimum amount, of which a certain portion (such as 20 percent) is allocated to expenses and profit, with the balance credited to a refund account until the account reaches a specified maximum figure, such as the sum of 3 years' premiums. During any calendar year when the primary company's aggregate death claims (net of conventional reinsurance payments) exceed a specified limit, the reinsurer pays the claims in excess of the limit but adjusts the premium to reflect the claims experience. The agreement provides that any amounts paid by the reinsurer for a given year, plus 20 percent, must be returned to the reinsurer by the primary company during the next 5 years. The spread-loss agreement can be terminated by either party, with proper notice at the end of any contract year, except that the primary company cannot terminate the arrangement under circumstances that would cause a loss to the reinsurer.*

12. a.   *Stop-loss reinsurance has several advantages:*

      •   *This approach lends itself to great flexibility, because the agreements can be written to cover only selected portions of the primary company's business with varying levels of mortality and with varying duration periods.*

      •   *The basic appeal of this coverage is that it provides protection against adverse mortality experience arising out of an unexpectedly large number of small claims or an unexpected increase in the average size of claims. It is a form of reinsurance on the amounts at risk retained under conventional reinsurance agreements.*

      •   *Because the unit cost of protection under this approach is less than under proportional reinsurance, a company can reduce its total outlay for reinsurance by*

increasing its retention limits under conventional agreements and reinsuring the retained amounts under stop-loss arrangements.

- *Due to the absence of individual policy records, this approach is relatively easy to administer.*

b. *Adherents to conventional (proportional) reinsurance arrangements see many practical disadvantages to stop-loss reinsurance.*

- *They point out that it is short-term, rate-adjustable, cancelable coverage available under conventional arrangements.*

- *They call attention to the limit on the reinsurer's liability, as well as exclusion of the war risk.*

- *They emphasize the restrictions on the primary company's underwriting practices necessarily imposed by the reinsurer.*

- *Finally, they question for a number of reasons whether any cost savings will, in fact, be realized in the long run.*

13. a. *The facultative agreement established a procedure whereby the primary insurer may offer risks to the reinsurer on an individual case basis. The essence of the arrangement is that the primary company is under no obligation to offer—and the reinsurer is under no duty to accept—a particular risk. Each company reserves full freedom of action, and each risk is considered on its merits.*

The automatic agreement, on the other hand, binds the primary insurer to offer—and the reinsurer to accept—all risks that fall within the purview of the agreement. The agreement sets forth a schedule of the primary insurer's limits of retention and provides that whenever the primary company issues a policy for an amount in excess of the limit for each policy, the excess amount is to be reinsured automatically.

b. *Under a facultative arrangement, the primary company submits a copy of the application from the insured, together with all supporting documents, to the prospective insurer. The primary insurer also submits a form that specifies the basis on which reinsurance is desired and the proportion of the face amount that the originating company proposes to retain. This form, which constitutes the offer for reinsurance, supplies all information about the risk in the possession of the primary company, including the amount of insurance already in force on the risk. The agreement normally provides*

that the reinsurer will phone, telegram, or facsimile its acceptance or rejection to the primary company.

Under an automatic arrangement, the primary company does not submit the underwriting papers to the reinsurer, and the reinsurer does not have the option of accepting or rejecting the risk. The reinsurer is obligated to accept a specified amount of reinsurance, including amounts for supplemental coverage on the basis of the primary company's underwriting appraisal. The maximum amount that can be transferred automatically to the reinsurer depends on the quality of the ceding company's underwriting staff, as well as its limits of retention. It is fairly common for the reinsurer to obligate itself to accept automatically up to four or more times the primary company's retention. However, when the retention limits of the primary company are fairly high, the reinsurer may limit its obligation to an amount equal to the primary company's limit. The agreement specifies that the originating company will retain an amount of insurance equal to its retention limit and will not reinsure it elsewhere on a facultative basis. In other words, if the primary company should decide to retain less than the full retention indicated for the particular classification in which the risk falls, the reinsurer is relieved of its obligation under the automatic agreement, and the entire transaction will have to be handled on a facultative basis. The agreement also usually includes a so-called jumbo clause, which stipulates that if the total amount of insurance in force on an applicant's life in all companies—including policies applied for—exceeds a specified amount, reinsurance is not automatically effected. The agreement normally makes provision for facultative reinsurance of those risks not eligible, for whatever reason, for automatic reinsurance.

14. a. *The reinsurance agreement stipulates that the primary insurer, after delivering its policy to the insured and collecting the first premium, is to prepare a formal cession of reinsurance (in duplicate), which gives the details of the risk and schedule of reinsurance premiums, including the ceding commission, if any. One copy of the cession form goes to the reinsurer; the other is retained by the primary company. The cession form describes the basis on which the reinsurance is being effected, and if one of the coinsurance arrangements is being used, provision is made for paying a ceding commission to the primary or ceding company. Provision is also made for the manner in which premiums are to be paid.*

   b. *The reinsurance agreement stipulates that any settlement made by the primary insurer with a claimant is binding on the reinsurer, whether the reinsurance was originally automatic or was accepted facultatively by the reinsurer. Despite this contractual right to settle claims at its discretion, the primary insurer will invariably consult with the reinsurer in doubtful cases. If the policy is to be settled on an installment basis, the*

reinsurer will nevertheless discharge its liability by paying a lump sum to the primary insurer. If a policy is settled for less than the face amount, such as might happen from a misstatement of age or the compromise of a claim of doubtful validity, the reinsurer shares in the savings. If the primary insurer contests a claim, the reinsurer bears it proportionate share of the expenses incurred.

c.   *Once a sum of insurance has been reinsured, the reinsurer is at risk for that amount as long as the amount retained by the primary company remains in force, it is subject to two important exceptions. One exception is in instances where the total amount of insurance on a particular risk is reduced after a portion of the insurance has been reinsured. This can result from the maturity or expiration of policies in accordance with their terms or through the voluntary termination of policies by nonpayment of premiums. Some agreements provide that the full amount of the reduction will come out of the sum reinsured (up to the amount reinsured), while other agreements call for proportionate reductions in the amounts held by the two insurers.*

The other exception applies to increases in the primary insurer's limits of retention and is especially significant to young and growing insurance companies. The provision states that if the primary company increases its limits of retention, it may make corresponding reductions in all reinsurance previously transferred. This is referred to as the recapture of insurance. Recapture is usually permitted only after the policies involved have been in force for a specified period of time. This restriction is clearly designed to enable the reinsurer to recover its acquisition expenses.

d.   *Subject to the provisions described in the preceding answer, a reinsurance agreement remains effective for reinsured policies as long as the original insurance continues in force. For new insurance, however, most agreements make provision for cancellation by either party with 90 days' notice. During that period, the agreement remains in full force and effect, and the reinsurer must accept all new insurance exceeding the retention limit with an automatic treaty. It is anticipated that the primary company can make other reinsurance arrangements within a period of 90 days.*

e.   *Virtually all agreements provide that the reinsurer must remit in full to the insolvent carrier that issued the original policy, even though the claim against the insolvent company will have to be scaled down. It is important to note that a claimant under a reinsured policy issued by a company that is insolvent at the time of the claim is not permitted to bring action directly against the reinsurer but must look to the insolvent carrier's general assets for the settlement of the claim. On the other hand, when the issuing company is insolvent, the reinsurer is given the specific right to contest claims*

against the primary insurer in which it has an interest, with all defenses available to the reinsurer that are available to the primary insurer.

f.   *It is becoming increasingly common for reinsurance agreements to contain a provision permitting a primary company to share in any mortality gains or losses arising under reinsured policies. This is a form of experience rating. In this case, the primary company is treated as the policyowner, and the mortality refund (or surcharge, as the case might be) is calculated on the combined experience under all reinsured amounts with a particular reinsurer. In recent years, a common arrangement is to have the primary insurer participate in any gains or losses on reinsurance amounts below a specified limit and not participate in the experience on amounts in excess of such limit. The purpose of this variation is to permit the primary company to share in the favorable mortality experience of the bulk of reinsured risks but to avoid the undesirable fluctuations in its overall experience that might result from unpredictably heavy mortality among very large risks.*

g.   *The reinsurance agreement covering life risks may or may not apply to supplementary coverages, such as accidental death benefits and total disability benefits. If the basic agreement is facultative, it is likely to cover such as accidental death benefits and total disability benefits. If the basic agreement is facultative, it is likely to cover supplementary benefits, as well as the life risk; if it is automatic, a separate agreement may be used for the supplementary coverages, particularly the accidental death benefits. Many companies have lower limits of retention for accidental death benefits than for basic life risks. For this reason, the reinsurance of accidental death benefits may be set up under a special agreement. Reinsurance may be provided for supplementary coverages on either a coinsurance or yearly renewable term basis, depending on the plan used for basic life risks.*

Chapter 17
Policy
Illustrations

By Dan M. McGill

Revised by C.W. Copeland and Edward E. Graves

Learning Objectives

An understanding of the material in this chapter should enable the student to

1. **Describe the importance of interest adjustments to amounts from different years in policy illustrations.**

2. **Understand the Professional Practice Guideline and the Life Insurance Illustration Questionnaire, and explain the difference between them.**

3. **Identify the issues that may lead to direct regulation of policy illustration content and organization.**

POLICY ILLUSTRATIONS

Life insurance sales nearly always rely on multiple-year policy illustration sheets. There are some basic similarities among policy illustrations, such as a listing of the annual premium and the policy's cash value for each policy duration up to 20 years after policy issuance. However, despite the similarities, there were no uniform standards applicable to policy illustrations prior to 1997. The organization of illustrative information within a single report varies drastically from one insurance company to another even if the same information is contained in the report.

Policy illustrations or ledger sheets usually cover at least 10 years of data and often cover 15 or 20 years. The years are usually presented in a single column of such an illustration, with the figures in this column referring to the number of years after the date of policy issuance. Some illustrations present both the years column and an attained-age column in order to show the age of the insured at each displayed policy duration. There are, however, some illustrations that present only the attained-age information and do not present the years of duration since policy issuance. Presentation of only one of these columns is not a serious omission because the omitted column can be derived from the column that is included in the illustration.

The one convention that is very frequently followed is to represent separate years on separate rows of the policy illustration. Each column generally represents a separate category of data such as age, premium, cash value, loan, death benefit, and so forth.

Participating Policy Premiums

The following is an example of one of the simpler illustrations showing only policy year, gross annual premium, dividends, and net premium after dividends. Policy illustration 1 in Table 17-1 does not even present the cash values for the policy.

There are some shortcomings with even this simple type of illustration. The summation of premium payments from the different years is inappropriate unless the values are adjusted by an interest factor to make them comparable. In fact, it is inappropriate to combine any dollar amounts from different time periods unless they are adjusted for interest.

It is appropriate to add or subtract values from the same time period. In the example, the dividends are deducted from the gross premium due in the same period in order to correctly determine the net premium due. These net-premium-due values can all be adjusted for interest to determine what beginning balance would be needed in an interest-bearing account to pay all of the net-premium-due amounts as they become payable. This adjusted amount is the present value of all 20 net-premium payments. When a 5 percent interest rate is used, the present value of these net premiums due is $2,273. In other words, an account with a present balance of $2,273, which is earning 5 percent interest, would be sufficient to pay all 20 premiums because the interest earnings of $1,484 plus the starting fund balance would cover the aggregate payments of $3,757.

Another way of adjusting payments from different time periods is to calculate the accumulated values. This calculation merely adjusts all payments to the end of the selected time period. The same result is obtained by depositing each net premium due into an interest-bearing account and letting the interest accumulate in the account. The balance in the account at the end of the period is the accumulated value for the specified interest rate, time period, and payments. This accumulated value for the example in policy illustration 1, based on 5 percent interest for the full 20 years, is $6,032. This value may be thought of as an opportunity cost of the premium payments. The policyowner is giving up the equivalent of the accumulated value that could have been invested had it not been allocated to life insurance premiums.

Table 17-1
Policy Illustration 1

$50,000 Graded Premium Paid-Up at Age 95 Policy			
Insured: Female, Aged 32		Initial Annual Premium: $170	
Year	Gross Annual Premium	Dividend Used to Reduce Premiums	Premium Due
1	$170	$0	$170
2	170	50	120
3	175	52	123
4	180	53	127
5	185	53	132
	880	208	672
6	190	54	136
7	195	55	140
8	200	56	144
9	205	57	148
10	215	58	157
	1,885	488	1,397
11	230	59	171
12	245	60	185
13	260	61	199
14	275	65	210
15	295	70	225
	3,190	803	2,387
16	315	75	240
17	340	80	260
18	360	90	270
19	390	100	290
20	420	110	310
	$5,015	$1,258	$3,757
Dividends shown are not guarantees of future dividends. They are merely based on the current level of dividends, which may change in the future.			

Obviously, the particular interest rate used has a strong influence on the adjusted present values and accumulated values. There is an inverse relationship between the interest rate and the resultant present values. That is, higher interest rates result in lower present values,

and lower interest rates produce higher present-value amounts. To illustrate this point, reconsider the present value given above. The value was $2,273 when based on 5 percent interest. The calculated present value of the same premiums was $1,524 based on 10 percent interest. Similarly, the accumulated value of those 20 net premiums was $6,032 when based on 5 percent interest, but would have had an accumulated value of $10,252 if it had been based on 10 percent interest. This demonstrates the direct relationship between interest rates and accumulated values. Higher interest rates produce higher accumulated values and lower interest rates produce lower accumulated values.

The choice of the proper interest rate is both important and difficult. The difficulty arises from the fact that the rate chosen should represent actual after-tax investment rates of return for the particular policyowner over the selected future period. Any attempt to represent unknown future interest rates is necessarily an estimate or a guess. It is important to select an interest rate that is a relatively accurate representation of actual rates over the period because slight changes in the interest rate result in significant changes of the present values and accumulated values being calculated and compared.

interest-adjusted indexes

The **interest-adjusted indexes** required by law in nearly every state specify an interest rate of 5 percent. The concern of these state statutes or regulations is not the accuracy of the interest rate in representing the actual future interest but rather a need for comparability of indexes for different policies. Interest adjusted indexes based on different interest rates are not directly comparable. Thus, the prescribing of one interest rate results in comparison indexes that can be used without needing any further adjustments.

Ledger statements and policy illustrations that do not include interest adjustments are really based on an implicit assumption that the interest rate is zero and the inflation rate is zero. Dollar amounts from different time periods are comparable without adjustment if, and only if, funds can be borrowed without paying interest and if prices remain stable or unchanged over the time interval. The subtotals in the first illustration after every 5 years are examples of unadjusted values from different years that have been added together. Similar illustrations that include policy cash values often imply that the coverage is free because the cash value eventually exceeds the aggregate premiums paid unless the premiums are adjusted for interest. Many policy illustrations are intended to preserve the traditional net-cost policy comparisons that ignore interest. Illustrations that present interest-adjusted figures are preferable because of their enhanced accuracy over unadjusted values.

There are many types of policy illustrations. The simplest types, which are similar to the illustration already discussed, merely show how much will have to be paid out-of-pocket to keep the policy in force. Many illustrations omit the suggested dividends but contain cash value and death-benefit values. It is very common for policy illustrations to show increasing death benefits based on the application of policy dividends to purchase paid-up additional insurance. The use of dividends to purchase one-year term insurance is another method of increasing the policy death benefit without altering the policy.

The more complex policy illustrations can be separated into the following five categories: minimum-deposit policies, split-dollar policies, comparisons of two policies, policies with side investment funds or annuity contracts, and universal life policy illustrations. Many of these illustrations are dependent on the policyowner's marginal tax rate for federal income taxes.

Policy illustrations that have more than four columns of values often derive some of their data from information that is not provided in the illustration. The relationship between columns is sometimes defined in the footnotes to the policy illustration, but often the relationships between columns are only partially described, if at all.

Combination Coverage

Policy illustration 2 in Table 17-2 is an example showing where policy dividends are used to purchase additional coverage. The basic policy is for $18,000 of whole life insurance, supplemented with additional paid-up coverage purchased with dividends. There are no figures in the illustration to indicate the level of the policy dividends, but there is a footnote indicating that the dividend levels assumed for the calculation are not guaranteed. The first column merely lists the policy year or duration. The second column shows the gross annual premium that is constant for this policy. The illustration does not show that any funds were borrowed from the policy cash value.

The third column of illustration 2 is labeled "total paid-up value." This label is ambiguous because it does not indicate whether the paid-up value is for the dividend additions only or for both coverages as a result of applying the cash values of both coverages. Study of the illustration reveals that a paid-up value occurs in the second policy year before there is any cash value associated with the coverage purchased with dividends. Thus, it can be deduced that the total paid-up value is the amount of fully paid-up coverage the policyowner is eligible for if the total cash value is applied to the purchase. This illustration is based on the assumption that the policyowner will not exercise any policy loans during the 20 years displayed.

The column titled "guaranteed cash value end of year" is relatively easy to interpret. The word guaranteed indicates that this is the scheduled cash value for the base whole life policy. Values for the supplemental coverage cannot be guaranteed because the dividends used to purchase the additional coverage are not guaranteed.

The "enhancement reserve fund" column essentially shows the cash value for the paid-up supplemental policies purchased with policy dividends. The "total cash value end of year" column merely lists the sum of the guaranteed cash value and the enhancement reserve fund.

The last two columns in illustration 2 show the relationship between the premium paid and the annual increase in the policy cash value. During the first through eighth policy years the policy premium exceeds the incremental increase in the cash value. The cash value increases exceed the policy premium in the ninth and all subsequent policy years. Although this comparison may lead some consumers to think they are getting their coverage free after the ninth policy year, such an interpretation is incorrect because the cash value is not made available to the policyowner other than as policy loans that are subject to compound interest charges.

The three column totals in illustration 2 have the same flaw as those in the previous illustration: they are only appropriate if both interest rates and inflation rates are zero. The accumulated value of the $320 annual premium after 20 years is $11,110 based on 5 percent interest, or $20,161 if it is based on a 10 percent interest rate. The accumulated value of the last column in illustration 2 is only $557 if based on a 5 percent interest rate. This is less than the column sum of $1,039 because of the negative quantities in the first 8 years, which accrued larger negative balances until they were counterbalanced in subsequent years with positive values. The accumulated value is $1,076 for a 10 percent interest rate.

The only important concept to be discerned from this illustration is that the premium is sufficient to create an internal buildup of funds in the policy, which also earns investment income. These internal funds are essential for the level-policy mechanism to work.

deceptive sales practices

Policy illustrations can get very complex. It is important to use a marginal tax rate in the policy illustration that is the same as the marginal tax rate for the prospective policyowner. Minor variations in the tax rate can result in significant changes in the after-tax costs to the policyowner and other involved participants. Illustrations based on tax rates that are significantly different from those of the prospect are misleading and could be considered **deceptive sales practices**. The size limitations of standard office stationery tend to limit the amount of information that can be displayed on a single sheet. Consequently, many related items are not included in policy illustrations.

It is essential to show both the corporate information and the individual insured information for this type of illustration.

Table 17-2							
Policy Illustration 2							
Combination of Whole Life and Additional Coverage Purchased with Policy Dividends							
	Whole Life		**$18,000**				
	Additional Coverage		**7,000**		**Insured: Female, Aged 40**		
	Death Benefit		**$25,000**		**Annual Premium: $320**		
Year	**Gross Annual Premium**	**Total Paid-Up Value**	**Guaran- teed Cash Value End of Year**	**Enhance- ment Reserve Fund**	**Total Cash Value End of Year**	**Total Cash Value Increase End of Year**	**CV Increase Less Net Payment**
1	$320	$0	$0	$0	$0	$0	$–320
2	320	285	101	0	101	101	–219
3	320	1,098	402	0	402	301	–19
4	320	1,863	704	0	704	302	–18
5	320	2,577	1,005	0	1,005	301	–19
6	320	3,291	1,324	0	1,324	319	–1
7	320	3,958	1,642	0	1,642	318	–2
8	320	4,583	1,960	0	1,960	318	–2
9	320	5,926	2,296	7	2,303	343	23
10	320	5,926	2,647	44	2,691	388	68
11	320	6,570	2,983	90	3,073	382	62
12	320	7,228	3,334	146	3,480	407	87
13	320	7,907	3,703	215	3,918	438	118
14	320	8,569	4,072	296	4,368	450	130
15	320	9,214	4,440	391	4,831	463	143
16	320	9,846	4,809	498	5,307	476	156
17	320	10,494	5,194	619	5,813	506	186
18	320	11,131	5,580	755	6,335	522	202
19	320	11,755	5,965	905	6,870	535	215
20	320	12,398	6,367	1,072	7,439	569	249
	$6,400					$7,439	$1,039
The current dividend scale is expected to continue, and it is now adequate to provide the needed $7,000 of benefits as term insurance for the first 8 policy years, then as whole life additions. The dividends are not guaranteed.							

Universal Life

The final illustration presents an early version of a universal life policy. This particular policy provides a death benefit of $100,000 until the policy cash value exceeds $95,000. Thereafter a death benefit will be $5,000 higher than the policy cash value. Policy illustration 3 in the table below shows the annual premium of $1,300 is paid for 25 years. The illustrations for universal life policies may include (as this one does) a column for partial withdrawals. These are policyowner withdrawals of funds from the policy cash value that are not policy loans and do not accrue interest, nor are they expected to be returned to the policy. Because universal life policies can have both policy loans and partial withdrawals, it is likely that some illustrations will have columns for both. If the total of all partial withdrawals ever exceeds the total premiums paid for the policy, the excess will be subject to federal income tax.

The premium less withdrawals column in illustration 3 is a non-interest-adjusted column indicating the cumulative amount of past premiums paid after reductions for any partial withdrawals of funds. The present value of these premiums over 25 years and of withdrawals in the subsequent 5 years is $10,512 based on 5 percent interest. If the premiums had been deposited in a 5 percent interest-bearing account, that account would still have a balance of $45,432 after the five annual withdrawals of $6,500 each. Based on 10 percent interest, the same calculations indicate a present value of $10,478 and an accumulated value of $182,835. These adjusted figures negate the impression that the policyowner will have no investment in the policy at the end of the 30 years, as the unadjusted numbers might imply.

This illustration is quite different from a traditional policy illustration in that it has three separate cash value columns, each calculated for a different assumed rate of interest earnings for the cash value. The "guaranteed cash value" column is comparable to the traditional examples because it is based on the interest rate guaranteed in the policy. However, even the "guaranteed cash value" column has its own properties for universal life policies because the premium level is usually inadequate if the cash value interest earnings do not exceed the guaranteed rate. That is why the cash values peak at $11,449 in the 19th policy year and decline to zero by the 26th policy year.

The column showing the assumed cash value is calculated using the assumption that the cash value will earn 9 percent interest every year. At that level of investment earnings or higher, the $1,300 premium for 25 years is clearly adequate to keep the policy in force. This scenario would develop ever-increasing cash values for the policy. There are no guarantees or suggestions that the investment earnings will always equal or exceed 9 percent. This is merely an example of how the cash value would grow if the actual earnings turn out to be exactly 9 percent each policy year.

Table 17-3
Policy Illustration 3

Universal Life

Death Benefit: $100,000
Planned Annual Premium $1,300

Insured: Female, Aged 40, nonsmoker

				End of Year			
Policy Year	Annual Premium	Partial Withdrawal	Premiums Less With-drawals	Guar. Cash Value	Assumed Cash Value*	Current Cash Value**	Current Death Benefit
1	$1,300	$0	$1,300	$114	$153	166	$100,000
2	1,300	0	2,600	943	1,175	1,212	100,000
3	1,300	0	3,900	1,773	2,275	2,357	100,000
4	1,300	0	5,200	2,604	3,473	3,627	100,000
5	1,300	0	6,500	3,438	4,769	5,025	100,000
6	1,300	0	7,800	4,262	6,161	6,555	100,000
7	1,300	0	9,100	5,077	7,659	8,233	100,000
8	1,300	0	10,400	5,873	9,287	10,091	100,000
9	1,300	0	11,700	6,649	11,048	12,140	100,000
10	1,300	0	13,000	7,393	12,956	14,405	100,000
11	1,300	0	14,300	8,107	15,040	16,924	100,000
12	1,300	0	15,600	8,777	17,308	19,719	100,000
13	1,300	0	16,900	9,392	19,781	22,288	100,000
14	1,300	0	18,200	9,551	22,482	26,288	100,000
15	1,300	0	19,500	10,439	25,427	30,138	100,000
16	1,300	0	20,800	10,845	28,645	34,431	100,000
17	1,300	0	22,100	11,164	32,159	39,218	100,000
18	1,300	0	23,400	11,371	36,006	44,566	100,000
19	1,300	0	24,700	11,449	40,218	50,546	100,000
20	1,300	0	26,000	11,380	44,847	57,252	100,000
21	1,300	0	27,300	11,133	49,933	64,777	100,000
22	1,300	0	28,600	10,685	55,533	73,238	100,000
23	1,300	0	29,900	10,011	61,704	82,766	100,000
24	1,300	0	31,200	9,058	68,524	93,521	100,000
25	1,300	0	32,500	7,792	76,075	105,617	100,000
26	1,300	6,500	26,000	0	75,659	110,198	115,198
27	1,300	6,500	19,500	0	75,284	115,288	120,288
28	1,300	6,500	13,000	0	74,973	120,945	125,945
29	1,300	6,500	6,500	0	74,704	127,229	132,229
30	1,300	6,500	0	0	74,400	134,213	139,213

The guaranteed cash value is based on a 4% interest rate.

*Interest rate used for assumed cash value is 9%

**Interest rate used for current cash value is 11%

The "current cash value" column is another example of how the cash value will increase at an even higher interest rate if that rate is earned every policy year. The interest rate used in illustration 3 for the current cash value is 11 percent each year. These columns are just demonstrations of what compound interest can do at sustained high levels. During the 1981–82 high-interest-rate period, there were companies using rates as high as 14 percent in their illustrations. There were many arbitrary predictions during that time, one being that interest rates would never again drop below 12 percent. These predictions have already proven to be erroneous. It is unrealistic to expect interest rates to stay at historically high levels over any protracted period of time. There is a very low probability that the cash value of the policy in illustration 3 will reach $134,000 in the 30th policy year. It is questionable whether even a 9 percent rate of return is achievable over such an extended period. The assumed cash value of $74,000 after 30 years may turn out to be overly optimistic.

As previously stated, this policy is of the earlier design and would not be offered with such a narrow final amount of at-risk death protection. The policies issued after the tax law change in October 1986 would provide a larger spread between the cash value and the death benefit. The cash value in the illustrated policy is too high for the $100,000 death benefit in the 24th policy year if the amounts in the "current cash value" column are actually attained. If the cash value of the policy attains the amounts in the "assumed cash value" column, there will be no problem of satisfying the test for life insurance in Sec. 101(f) of the Internal Revenue Code.

There are many other possibilities that could be illustrated for universal life policies and traditional policies. Universal life policies can be used in any type of situation in which whole life policies can be used. Whether they would be the preferred policy can only be determined after analysis and realistic estimation of future interest earnings in the policy. (The required space for further illustrations puts them beyond the scope of this chapter.)

The most important thing to remember about illustrations is that the values in the columns should be adjusted for interest before adding column values. When the illustration does not include interest-adjusted values, it is advisable to provide present values and accumulated values—at representative values—for the after-tax cash outlay columns. Another element of extreme importance is the use of appropriate marginal tax rates in illustrations that match the applicable tax rate to the prospective policyowner.

The proliferation of illustrations since the early 1980's prompted calls for standards or guidelines. The Society of Financial Service Professionals took the initiative and adopted a *Professional Practice Guideline,* which is a checklist of guidelines for sales material and presentations. Although these guidelines were not intended to be minimum standards, they did give explicit guidance on many issues concerning illustrations. This document

was adopted by the membership of the Society of Financial Service Professionals at its 1988 annual meeting. It was one of the first steps on the slow journey to establishing some standards for policy illustrations.

The principal items addressed in the checklist were interest rates, mortality expenses, dividends, benefit changes, surrender charges, waiver-of-premium benefit base, policy comparisons, and issues of replacement. This document can be used to ensure that all relevant questions have been explained to a prospect. Obviously, not every item will always be applicable. For example, dividends might not be involved in a proposal because of the type of coverage under consideration.

Life Insurance Illustration Questionnaire

Life Insurance Illustration Questionnaire

The Society took further initiative regarding policy illustrations in 1992 by adopting the **Life Insurance Illustration Questionnaire**. It was intended to stimulate agents to question and more thoroughly understand the intricacies of illustrations so they could better explain them to purchasers and prospects. The questions were directed to the insurance company regarding the assumptions and methodology underlying the responding insurer's illustrations. Nearly all of the major life insurance companies responded to the questionnaire and provided their answers to their own agents.

Insurance companies are reluctant to provide their questionnaire responses to agents from competing companies or to the consuming public. This is understandable because of both competitive concerns and the detailed nature of the information itself. It would take even the best of agents a lot of time and effort to explain the intricate information provided in the questionnaire response of any one insurance company.

The American Society of CLU and ChFC had no power to impose a standard for illustrations, but its development of the Professional Practice Guidelines and the Life Insurance Illustration Questionnaire helped prod the National Association of Insurance Commissioners (NAIC) to adopt standards for life insurance policy illustrations in 1996.

Policy illustrations are projections of what could happen under a policy if actual experience serendipitously mirrored all the assumed factors used to calculate the illustration. However, it is almost a certainty that actual experience will deviate from the illustration on multiple factors. The actual future numbers for each—cash values, premiums, and death benefits—can vary drastically from those shown in an illustration.

A study of policy illustrations by a task force of the Society of Actuaries, released in 1992, showed the following major findings:

- Policy illustrations work well to educate clients in the mechanics of how policies work.

- Policy illustrations are not an adequate tool for comparing costs of policies from different insurance companies. Illustrations do not create accurate projections of future performance because of differences in assumptions and the problems of estimating future parameters.

Another opinion was provided in the October 26, 1992, edition of Probe by John C. Angle, FSA. He proposed that rather than trying to educate producers and consumers about interpreting illustrations, it is advisable to issue a prospectus for the policy that would disclose in minute detail how the insurance company determines each aspect of the policy and reveal any subsidization being provided. Such disclosure is already being provided for variable life insurance policies.

POLICY ILLUSTRATION REGULATIONS

model regulation

With the stated purpose of protecting consumers and fostering consumer education, in 1996 the National Association of Insurance Commissioners (NAIC) adopted a **model regulation** pertaining to life insurance illustrations. This was the NAIC's first attempt to set standards for policy illustrations. By January 1, 1997, two states (North Carolina and Utah) had already adopted the model regulation, and 13 additional states (California, Colorado, Delaware, Iowa, Louisiana, Nebraska, North Dakota, Ohio, Oklahoma, Oregon, Pennsylvania, South Carolina, South Dakota) adopted some form of the regulation that became effective in 1997. Alabama, Illinois, Kansas, Maryland, Nevada, New York, Washington, and Wisconsin had illustration regulations that became effective in 1998, and today all of the states have adopted the regulation in some form.

The new model regulation has had an impact on illustrations in all states because many life insurance companies have moved toward using the same illustration model in every state. Thus, they do not need different software systems for each state. They are making all their illustrations conform to the most stringent state's requirements.

The new regulation does not apply to variable life, credit life, or life insurance with a face amount of less than $10,000. It does not apply to either individual or group annuity

contracts. The new regulation applies to all nonvariable group and individual life insurance policies and certificates for more than $10,000 of death benefit.

The regulation requires the insurance company to declare to the state insurance department for each policy form whether or not it intends to use illustrations to market that form of coverage. A copy of each illustration the insurer intends to use must be forwarded to the state insurance department. Each illustration used in the sale of a life insurance policy covered by the new regulation must be clearly labeled "life insurance illustration" and must include the following:

1. name of the insurance company

2. name and business address of the insurer's agent

3. name, age, and sex of the proposed insured

4. the underwriting or rating classification upon which the illustration is based

5. the generic name of the policy (for example, whole life, universal life, and so on)

6. the initial death benefit amount

7. the dividend option election or application of nonguaranteed elements if applicable

The NAIC Model regulation prohibits insurers and their agents from the following:

1. representing the policy as anything other than a life insurance policy

2. using or describing nonguaranteed elements in a manner that is misleading or has the capacity or tendency to mislead

3. stating or implying that the payment or amount of nonguaranteed elements is guaranteed

4. using an illustration that does not comply with the illustration regulation

5. using an illustration that is more favorable to the policyowner than the illustration based on the illustrated scale of the insurer

6. providing an applicant with an incomplete illustration

7.   representing in any way that premium payments will not be required for each year of the policy in order to maintain the illustrated death benefits, unless that is the fact

8.   using the term "vanish," "vanishing premium," or a similar term that implies the policy becomes paid up, to describe a plan for using nonguaranteed elements to pay a portion of future premiums

9.   using an illustration that is not "self-supporting"

The NAIC model illustration regulation specifies that all illustrations must be dated as of the date prepared. All pages must be marked to indicate both the individual page number and the total number of pages in the illustration (for example, "page 3 of 7"). The illustration must clearly indicate which elements are guaranteed and which are nonguaranteed. Any amount available upon surrender shall be the amount after deduction of surrender charges. Items presented in illustrations can be in the form of charts, graphs, or tabular values.

Each illustration must be accompanied by a narrative summary that describes the policy, premiums, and features, and defines column headings used in the illustration. The summary should also state that actual results might be more or less favorable than those shown in the illustration.

Universal Life Policies

The regulation states that illustrations for universal life policies must comply with the regulation requirements and additionally that the insurance company must issue annual reports to policyowners after the policy is issued. These annual reports must specify the beginning and ending dates for the reporting period.

The content of the annual reports is specified in the NAIC model regulation:

- all transactions affecting the policy during the reporting period (debits and credits) and a description of each (for example, premiums paid, interest credited, loan interest debited, mortality charges, expenses debited, rider transactions, and so on)
- cash values at the beginning and end of the period
- death benefit at the end of the reporting period (for each life covered)
- the cash surrender value at the end of the period after deduction of surrender charge (if any)

- the amount of outstanding policy loans, if any, at the end of the report period
- a special Notice to Policyowners if the policy will not maintain insurance in force until the end of the next reporting period unless further premium payments are made

The regulation further stipulates that policyowners have the right to request an in-force illustration annually without charge. The insurer must provide information regarding where and how to direct such requests and must supply a current illustration within 30 days of the request. Such illustrations are to be based on the insurer's present illustrated scale.

Annual Certifications

Each insurer's board of directors must appoint at least one illustration actuary, who will certify that the illustrations are in compliance with the illustration regulation and are insurer-authorized. The regulation states the qualifications of an illustration actuary, including membership in good standing of the American Academy of Actuaries.

The illustration actuary must annually certify the method used to allocate overhead and expenses for all illustrations and file such certification with the insurance commissioner and with the insurer's board of directions. Further, the illustration actuary is required to report any mistakes found in previous certifications to both the commissioner and the board of directors. The insurance commissioner must also be notified of any change in the illustration actuary and the reasons for the change.

The model regulation sets forth limits on the methodology for calculating illustrations. These limits are intended to curb some of the overly optimistic projections that a few insurers were utilizing in recent years in the absence of any standards or constraints. Most of the new constraints are contained in the definitions of currently payable scale, disciplined current scale, and illustrated scale.

These definitions are as follows:[1]

- *currently payable scale:* a scale of nonguaranteed elements in effect for a policy form as of the preparation date of the illustration or declared to become effective within the next 95 days.
- *disciplined current scale:* a scale of nonguaranteed elements constituting a limit on illustrations currently being used by an insurer that is reasonably based on actual recent historical experience, as certified annually by an illustration actuary

---

1.   From section 4, Life Insurance Illustrations Model Regulation.

designated by the insurer. Further guidance in determining the disciplined current scale as contained in standards established by the Actuarial Standards Board may be relied upon if the standards

- are consistent with all provisions of this regulation,

- limit a disciplined current scale to reflect only actions that have already been taken or events that have already occurred,

- do not permit a disciplined current scale to include any projected trends of improvements in experience or any assumed improvements in experience beyond the illustration date, and

- do not permit assumed expenses to be less than minimum assumed expenses.

- Illustrated scale: a scale of nonguaranteed elements currently being illustrated that is not more favorable to the policyowner than the lesser of

- the disciplined current scale, or

- the currently payable scale.

METHODS OF COMPARING LIFE INSURANCE POLICY COSTS

Net Cost Method

net cost method

There are as many different methodologies of comparing life insurance policies as there are generic types of coverage. Historically the traditional **net cost method** was widely utilized. Its methodology is quite simple, easy to understand, and even easy to calculate. The starting point is a specification of the duration of coverage to be evaluated. Often this was for either 10 years or 20 years of coverage. The actual mechanics of the evaluation involve taking all of the net premiums paid under the policy and adding them together, then subtracting the cash surrender value for the interim being considered and all dividends paid over that interval. One of the reasons this method is so easy to understand is that it does not take into account the time value of money. In other words, it ignores interest.

The final cost derived under net cost method can be considered the amount the insurance company retains. The main criticism of this methodology is that after 20 years the net cost is usually negative. That is, the cash value amounts at the end of the interval plus dividends

paid over the interval exceed the aggregate of premiums paid. The implication is that the policyowner has received insurance free of charge. The serious shortcoming of using this methodology is that it gives equal weight to payment amounts that may be separated by 10 or 20 years. By doing so, it totally ignores the opportunity costs of earnings forgone because the funds were not invested in an investment account. (See Table 17-6.)

The net cost method is not appropriate for comparing policies, whether they are the same type or different types. It is totally unacceptable under the state statutes and regulations for purposes of making replacement evaluations. In fact, under some state statutes insurance agents are prohibited from using the net cost method.

Interest-adjusted Indexes

interest-adjusted indexes

The logic of using **interest-adjusted indexes** is similar to that of the traditional net cost approach with the exception that interest-adjusted indexes explicitly take into account the time value of money. The National Association of Insurance Commissioners developed the interest-adjusted cost indexes and also derived model laws requiring their use. These statutes were drafted and adopted during the 1970s prior to the high interest and inflation rates experienced in the late 1970s and early 1980s. Almost every one of the statutes mandates that the rate of interest to be used is 5 percent annually.

Essentially, the interest-adjusted method takes all payments for premiums and treats them as if they had been put into interest-bearing accounts to accumulate interest until the end of the interval for evaluation. In a like manner, all dividend payments are carried as if they are deposited in an interest-bearing account, and that account balance is calculated for the end of the interval of evaluation. After all premium payments and all dividend payments have been adjusted to the end of the comparison interval, the policy cash value and accumulation dividends are subtracted from the accumulated value of all the premiums paid.

The next step is to take that future net cost and divide it by the future value of an annuity due, based on the specified interest rate and the period of time being evaluated. At 5 percent interest the factor to use for a 10-year evaluation is 13.2068. Likewise the factor to divide into the future value amount over a 20-year interval, again assuming a 5 percent interest rate, is 34.7193. The result represents the level annual cost for the policy. This will still be an aggregate amount that must be converted to a per-thousand amount, which is accomplished by dividing the level annual cost amount by the number of thousands of dollars in the policy death benefit. (For example, the aggregate level annual cost for a $50,000 policy is 50 times greater than it would be for a $1,000 policy. We would therefore

divide the level annual policy cost by 50 to determine the level annual cost per thousand dollars of coverage.)

These future values appear on most sales presentation materials utilized by insurance agents. For that reason there is usually no need to calculate them independently. The numbers presented will be based on the 5 percent mandated interest rate and the methodology described in the statutes. The same methodology works for any other interest rate the evaluating party thinks is appropriate.

The future value factor for an annuity due can easily be derived on a financial calculator using the beginning-of-period mode. Merely specify the number of periods in the evaluation interval (such as 10 or 20) on the N key, and enter the interest rate on the I key and the payment amount of $1.00 on the PMT key. Press the FV key to solve for the future value. The resulting factor is then divided into the net future value of the accumulated premium amounts in excess of the accumulated dividends and end-of-period cash value. If there are terminal dividends available at the end of the interval, they are subtracted from the accumulated premiums before dividing by the annuity due factor to determine the surrender cost index. (See Table 17-7.)

Determining the payment cost index is similar to calculating the surrender cost index except that there is no recognition of the end-of-period cash value. Under this index calculation, dividends over the internal and terminable dividends at the end of the interval are the only items subtracted from the accumulated premium amounts. This gives a future value of net premiums that is then divided by the annuity due factor for the appropriate period and appropriate interest rate. Future values contained in agents' sales materials are usually based on either a 10- or 20-year interval and a 5 percent annual interest rate. (See Table 17-8.)

Sample Comparison

A simple example of a fictitious policy is presented in Table 17-9. In the example there is a premium of $15 per year over a 10-year interval and a dividend of $0.00 the first year and $1.00 the second year, increasing by $1.00 each year until it reaches $9.00 in the 10th policy year. The accumulation at 5 percent of all premiums paid is $198.10; the accumulation of all dividends is $54.14. Subtracting the accumulated value of dividends from the accumulated value of premiums yields a future value of net premiums equal to $143.96. Subtracting the cash value at the end of 10 years ($120) from that amount yields a future value of net cost equal to $23.96. This future net cost is then divided by the future value of an annuity due for 10 years, or 13.2068, which yields a surrender cost index of $1.814676. In the same table we can see that by ignoring the cash value, the payment cost index becomes $10.90.

Calculations under interest-adjusted indexes can be done by hand, but they are easier and quicker when done on a computer or financial calculator. Index values are sensitive to the interval being evaluated and the insured's age of issue for the policies being compared.

These cost indexes are an acceptable means of comparing similar policies. Usually the policy with the smaller numerical values for surrender cost and payment cost indexes is preferable to policies with higher index values. The method is not acceptable, however, for comparing dissimilar policies—for example, a term policy with a whole life policy. It is also not well suited for evaluating policy replacements.

Cash Accumulation Method of Comparison

cash accumulation comparison method

The **cash accumulation comparison method** is much more complex than either the net cost method or the interest adjusted methods and requires a computer to make the calculations. A significant amount of data must be entered into the computer program in order to calculate the results accurately. One of the strengths of this method is that it is acceptable to compare permanent insurance policies with term policies. It can also be used for evaluation of replacement proposals.

The technique is simply to accumulate the premium differences between the policies being compared, while holding the death benefits of both policies constant and equal. For example, to compare a cash value contract with a term contract, set the death benefits equal at the beginning of the period, and use the yearly premium differences between the whole life policy and the term policy as the amount to deposit into a side fund to accumulate at interest. The calculation is basically a buy-term-and-invest-the-difference approach to comparing the policies. At the end of the interval being evaluated, the side fund accumulation amount can be compared to the cash value in the whole life or other form of cash value insurance policy. The policy with the greater accumulation at the end of the comparison interval is considered the preferable of the two contracts. (See Tables 17-10 to 17-14.)

As noted before, this comparison method really requires a computer in order to be efficient. Not only does the difference in premium have to be allocated to a side fund and accumulated interest, but there is also a necessary adjustment of the amount at risk. The side fund accumulated with the term policy acts much like the cash value in the whole life policy, and the amount of term coverage being purchased has to be adjusted so that when it is added to the side fund it will exactly equal the death benefit under the permanent policy to which it is being compared. Using a computer, once a spreadsheet has been built

with all of the logic to make the necessary comparisons, it is just a matter of plugging in new values for premiums, cash values, and accumulation account amounts.

Equal Outlay Method

equal outlay method

The **equal outlay method** is somewhat similar to the cash accumulation method. The same amount of premium dollars is expended, on the one hand for a cash value contract and on the other for a term policy. The amount by which the cash value contract premiums exceed the term premiums is deposited into a side fund, and the difference in premium amounts is accumulated at specified interest rates. Then the death benefit of the term insurance plus the accumulated side fund amounts are compared with the death benefit under the cash value contract in which dividends, if any, have been used to purchase paid-up benefit amounts, and the value of those paid-up additions. Under this type of comparison, the policy producing the greater death benefit is considered the preferable contract. (See Tables 17-15 to 17-19.)

Both this method and the cash accumulation method are very sensitive to the interest rate chosen for purposes of the side fund accumulation. Manipulating the interest rate can skew the comparison results. The higher the interest rate used, the more the equal outlay method will tend to favor the lower premium policy with the side fund combination.

Comparisons That Isolate Interest Rates

There are three other comparison methods that all utilize an assumed cost of coverage to isolate an interest rate for comparison purposes. One of the problems of comparing any life insurance policies is that there are degrees of freedom in the parameters involved. We cannot make a single-factor comparison without choosing assumptions for the other factors and doing so in a way that those factors are also comparable. In other words, if we want to calculate a policy's internal cost of insurance, we have to make some assumptions about interest rates; if we want to calculate interest rates, we have to make some assumptions about the cost of insurance.

Comparative Interest Rate Method

comparative interest rate method

The **comparative interest rate method** is really a modification of the cash accumulation method, whereby we are calculating the interest rate that would make a term insurance

policy side fund exactly equal to the cash value policy's surrender value at the end of the evaluation period. The comparative interest rate method looks for the interest rate that would make the buy-term-and-invest-the-difference comparison exactly equivalent in the death benefits provided. To make that calculation both the outlays for premiums and side funds and the death benefit levels must be held equal. This method is often referred to as the Linton yield method, named for actuary Albert Linton, who first published the approach in the early 1900s. (See Table 17-20.) Its primary drawback is the complexity of the calculation, which requires not only a computer program to accurately calculate the interest rate desired but also a large amount of policy information that must be entered into the program before it can be run.

Another caution with using software for this type of comparison is that each comparison should use the same assumed term premium rates to derive the interest rate. Otherwise, there will have been manipulation (intentional or unintentional) of the interest rates derived by the calculations. The policy generating the highest comparative interest rate is assumed to be the preferable policy when making comparisons by this method.

Belth Yearly Rate-of-Return Method

Belth yearly rate-of-return method

Joseph Belth, a retired professor of insurance and publisher of the Insurance Forum newsletter, has developed more cost comparison approaches than any other scholar known to this author. This chapter presents two of his many different policy comparison approaches. (See Table 17-21.) He is quick to point out that there is no perfect comparison method because the wide range of objectives that insurance policies address requires that different levels of priority be placed on the death benefits and cash values in different situations. Each methodology puts its primary emphasis on the elements considered to be the highest priorities for that particular approach.

Under the **Belth yearly rate-of-return method** only one year of the policy is considered in making an individual calculation. Such a calculation can be made for each and every year of coverage over the given interval. The objective is to identify the benefits provided by the policy during that year (the end-of-year cash value plus the dividends paid during the year and the net death benefit for the policy year) and the investments in the policy necessary to derive those benefits (a combination of the beginning-of-the-year cash value and the premium paid for that year of the policy). The yearly rate-of-return formula divides the sum of the benefits by the sum of the investments and then subtracts the number one from that amount. This process is repeated for each year over the comparison interval. The policy with the highest rates of yearly return in the largest number of years over the observation

interval is considered the preferable policy. The calculation under the Belth yearly rate-of-return method depends on a realistic assumed term rate, not a manipulated rate that is intentionally much too high or low that it skews the results. This method does not necessarily make it easy to identify a predominant policy. The highest yearly rate of return may change back and forth among the policies being compared.

Belth Yearly Price-of-Protection Method

Belth yearly price method

Under the **Belth yearly price method** we must assume an investment or interest rate and thereby calculate the cost of protection. Again, the calculations are made one year at a time for each of the years in the comparison interval (usually 10 or 20 years as in most other comparison methods). Using this methodology, the beginning cash value plus the current premium are accumulated at the assumed rate of interest to derive a theoretical year-end surrender value. After computing the theoretical end-of-year value from the beginning cash value and the premium plus interest, we subtract the actual end-of-year cash value plus dividends paid during the year. This is the difference assumed to have been available to pay mortality charges.

$$\text{Cost per } \$1,000 = \frac{(P + CVP) \times (1 + i) - (CSV + D)}{(F - CSV) \times (0.001)}$$

P	=	Premium
CVP	=	Cash surrender value previous year
i	=	Net after-tax interest rate
CSV	=	Cash surrender value current year
D	=	Dividend current year
F	=	Face amount of coverage

The next step is to divide the difference between theoretical year-end values and actual year-end values plus dividends by the amount at risk per $1,000 of coverage. The actual formula looks quite formidable, but when its terms are defined, it is really quite simple and straightforward.

After making a yearly price-of-protection calculation for each policy being compared for each year in the comparison interval, it is then a matter of identifying the policy with the lowest cost of protection for the largest number of years over that interval. In most cases

that policy would be the preferable one of those under consideration.[2] The benchmark prices derived by Professor Belth (see table) are based on United States population data, rather than on insured lives data, and represent a relatively high cost of providing death benefits only; there is no allowance for company overhead or operations.

In most cases term rates for standard-issue policies to people in good health will be below these benchmark prices, which are only a crude yardstick and should not be used as the criterion for automatically rejecting a policy. These benchmark prices would have no validity at all for evaluating rates on policies issued or proposed to persons in poor health who are charged associated higher premiums. Such premiums might legitimately be multiples of the benchmark prices.

Table 17-4	
Joseph Belth's Benchmark Prices for $ 1,000 of Insurance	
Age	Benchmark Price/ $ 1,000
Under Age 30	$1.50
30–34	2.00
35–39	3.00
40–44	4.00
45–49	6.50
50–54	10.00
55–59	15.00
60–64	25.00
65–69	35.00
70–74	50.00
75–79	80.00
80–84	125.00

Both Belth methods of policy comparison are appropriately used for comparing similar and dissimilar policies. With some modification these methods are even appropriate for comparing replacement evaluations. Part of their attractiveness is their simplicity and their ability to be calculated without the need of a computer. Calculations are actually simple enough they can be done by hand; nevertheless, the process can be expedited with a good calculator or a computer.

---

2.   Insurance Forum, June 1982, p. 168.

TABLES

Table 17-5 Corridor Test for Cash Value Life Insurance		
Age	Death Benefit Must Exceed Cash Value by This Multiple	Cash Value May Not Exceed This % of Death Benefit
0 to 40	2.50	0.40
41	2.43	0.41
42	2.36	0.42
43	2.29	0.44
44	2.22	0.45
45	2.15	0.47
46	2.09	0.48
47	2.03	0.49
48	1.97	0.51
49	1.91	0.52
50	1.85	0.54
51	1.78	0.56
52	1.71	0.58
53	1.64	0.61
54	1.57	0.64
55	1.50	0.67
56	1.46	0.68
57	1.42	0.70
58	1.38	0.72
59	1.34	0.75
60	1.30	0.77
61	1.28	0.78
62	1.26	0.79
63	1.24	0.81
64	1.22	0.82
65	1.20	0.83
66	1.19	0.84
67	1.18	0.85
68	1.17	0.85

Table 17-5		
Corridor Test for Cash Value Life Insurance		
Age	Death Benefit Must Exceed Cash Value by This Multiple	Cash Value May Not Exceed This % of Death Benefit
69	1.16	0.86
70	1.15	0.87
71	1.13	0.88
72	1.11	0.90
73	1.09	0.92
74	1.07	0.93
75 to 90	1.05	0.95
91	1.04	0.96
92	1.03	0.97
93	1.02	0.98
94	1.01	0.99
95	1.00	1.00
Source: IRC Sec.7702(d)(2)		

Table 17-6
Traditional Net Cost

10-Year Traditional Net Cost		20-year Traditional Net Cost	
Dividends	$2,178	Dividends	10,487
Cash value	14,820	Cash value	35,900
Total	16,998	Total	46,387
Less		Less	
Premiums paid	21,870	Premiums paid	43,740
Cost	4,872	Cost	-2,647
Divide by $1,000's face	48.72	Per $1,000	-26.47
Divide by number of years	4.872	Per $1,000 per year	-1.3235

$100,000 Whole Life Policy Issue Age 48 Male Participating						
Policy Year	Age	Premium	Cash Value	Dividend	Accum. Dividend	Accum. Premium
1	48	$2,187	$0	$0	$0	$2,296
2	49	2,187	1,456	76	76	4,708
3	50	2,187	2,963	120	200	7,239
4	51	2,187	4,516	170	380	9,898
5	52	2,187	6,119	185	584	12,689
6	53	2,187	7,775	217	830	15,620
7	54	2,187	9,470	280	1,151	18,697
8	55	2,187	11,210	325	1,534	21,928
9	56	2,187	12,992	390	2,001	25,321
10	57	2,187	14,820	415	2,516	28,883
11	58	2,187	16,698	455	3,097	32,624
12	59	2,187	18,625	550	3,801	36,551
13	60	2,187	20,605	615	4,606	40,675
14	61	2,187	22,638	707	5,544	45,005
15	62	2,187	24,720	775	6,596	49,552
16	63	2,187	26,857	845	7,771	54,326
17	64	2,187	29,042	952	9,111	59,339
18	65	2,187	31,276	1,020	10,587	64,602
19	66	2,187	33,559	1,140	12,256	70,128
20	67	2,187	35,900	1,250	14,119	75,931

Table 17-7
Interest-adjusted Net Surrender Cost Index

10-Year Surrender Cost Index		20-Year Surrender Cost Index	
Dividends	$2,515.779	Dividends	$14,119.04
Cash value	14,820	Cash value	35,900
Total	17,335.78	Total	50,019.04
Less		Less	
Premiums paid	28,883.24	Premiums paid	75,931.00
Cost	11,547.46	Cost	25,911.97
Divide by $1,000's face	115.4746	Per $1,000	259.1197
Divide by number of years (13.2068)	8.743575	Per $1,000 per year (34.7193)	7.463274

$100,000 Whole Life Policy Issue Age 48 Male Participating						
Policy Year	Age	Premium	Cash Value	Dividend	Accum. Dividend	Accum. Premium
1	48	$2,187	$0	$0	$0	$2,296
2	49	2,187	1,456	76	76	4,708
3	50	2,187	2,963	120	200	7,239
4	51	2,187	4,516	170	380	9,898
5	52	2,187	6,119	185	584	12,689
6	53	2,187	7,775	217	830	15,620
7	54	2,187	9,470	280	1,151	18,697
8	55	2,187	11,210	325	1,534	21,928
9	56	2,187	12,992	390	2,001	25,321
10	57	2,187	14,820	415	2,516	28,883
11	58	2,187	16,698	455	3,097	32,624
12	59	2,187	18,625	550	3,801	36,551
13	60	2,187	20,605	615	4,606	40,675
14	61	2,187	22,638	707	5,544	45,005
15	62	2,187	24,720	775	6,596	49,552
16	63	2,187	26,857	845	7,771	54,326
17	64	2,187	29,042	952	9,111	59,339
18	65	2,187	31,276	1,020	10,587	64,602
19	66	2,187	33,559	1,140	12,256	70,128
20	67	2,187	35,900	1,250	14,119	75,931

Table 17-8 Interest-adjusted Net Payment Cost Payment Index			

10-Year Surrender Cost Index		20-Year Surrender Cost Index	
Accum. dividends	$2,515.779	Accum. dividends	$14,119.04
Accum. premiums	28,883.24	Accum. premiums	75,931.00
Future value of net premiums	26,367.46	Future value of net premiums	61,811.96
Convert to per $1,000	263.6746	Per $1,000	618.1196
Divide by factor	13.2068	Per $1,000 per year	
19.96507		(34.7193)	17.80334
Payment index	19.96507	Payment index	17.80334

$100,000 Whole Life Policy Issue Age 48 Male Participating						
Policy Year	Age	Premium	Cash Value	Dividend	Accum. Dividend	Accum. Premium
1	48	$2,187	$0	$0	$0	$2,296
2	49	2,187	1,456	76	76	4,708
3	50	2,187	2,963	120	200	7,239
4	51	2,187	4,516	170	380	9,898
5	52	2,187	6,119	185	584	12,689
6	53	2,187	7,775	217	830	15,620
7	54	2,187	9,470	280	1,151	18,697
8	55	2,187	11,210	325	1,534	21,928
9	56	2,187	12,992	390	2,001	25,321
10	57	2,187	14,820	415	2,516	28,883
11	58	2,187	16,698	455	3,097	32,624
12	59	2,187	18,625	550	3,801	36,551
13	60	2,187	20,605	615	4,606	40,675
14	61	2,187	22,638	707	5,544	45,005
15	62	2,187	24,720	775	6,596	49,552
16	63	2,187	26,857	845	7,771	54,326
17	64	2,187	29,042	952	9,111	59,339
18	65	2,187	31,276	1,020	10,587	64,602
19	66	2,187	33,559	1,140	12,256	70,128
20	67	2,187	35,900	1,250	14,119	75,931

Table 17-9					
Interest-adjusted Cost Method					
Premiums			**Dividends**		
Year	Per Year	Accum. @ 5%	Per Year	Accum. @ 5%	Cash Value
1	$15	$15.75	0	$0	$0
2	15	32.29	1	1.05	0
3	15	49.65	2	3.20	23
4	15	67.89	3	6.51	34
5	15	87.03	4	11.04	43
6	15	107.13	5	16.84	56
7	15 ·	128.24	6	23.99	75
8	15	150.40	7	32.54	100
9	15	173.67	8	42.56	115
10	15	198.10	9	54.14	120
TOTALS	150	198.10	45	54.14	120

Surrender Cost Index		Payment Cost Index	
Future value of premiums	$198.1018	Accum. premiums	$198.1018
		Less accum. dividends	-54.13574
Minus FV of dividends	54.13574	FV of net premiums	$143.9661
FV of net premiums	$143.9661		
Less net cash value	– 120		
FV of net cost	$23.96606		
Divide by annuity factor	13.2068	Divide by annuity factor	13.2068
Surrender Cost Index	1.814676	Payment Cost Indes	10.9009

Table 17-10
Cash Accumulation Comparison Method

Male Aged 48—$100,000 Whole Life
Dividends Buy Paid-up Additions
Annual Renewable Term (ART) Decreased to Equalize Death Benefits
Interest Rate 3% (on accumulations)

Policy Year	WL Premium	ART Premium	Prem Diff.	Accum. Diff. @ 3%	WL Cash Values	Term Plus Side Fund	WL + Paid-up Adds.	ART Face Amount
1	$2,187	$365	$1,822	$1,877	$0	$100,000	$100,000	$98,123
2	2,187	386	1,801	3,788	1,456	100,075	100,075	96,287
3	2,187	409	1,778	5,733	2,963	100,203	100,203	94,470
4	2,187	434	1,753	7,710	4,516	100,527	100,527	92,817
5	2,187	460	1,727	9,720	6,119	100,972	100,972	91,252
6	2,187	491	1,696	11,759	7,775	102,321	102,321	90,562
7	2,187	528	1,659	13,820	9,470	104,408	104,408	90,588
8	2,187	574	1,613	15,896	11,210	107,549	107,549	91,653
9	2,187	628	1,559	17,979	12,992	111,463	111,463	93,484
10	2,187	685	1,502	20,066	14,820	114,876	114,876	94,810
11	2,187	753	1,434	22,145	16,698	119,071	119,071	96,926
12	2,187	838	1,349	24,199	18,625	124,156	124,156	99,957
13	2,187	946	1,241	26,203	20,605	130,507	130,507	104,304
14	2,187	1,071	1,116	28,138	22,638	136,789	136,789	108,651
15	2,187	1,226	961	29,972	24,720	143,896	143,896	113,924
16	2,187	1,427	760	31,654	26,857	152,719	152,719	121,065
17	2,187	1,679	508	33,127	29,042	162,745	162,745	129,618
18	2,187	1,942	245	34,374	31,276	170,345	170,345	135,971
19	2,187	2,483	-296	35,100	33,559	183,682	183,682	148,582
20	2,187	3,127	-940	35,185	35,900	196,132	196,132	160,947

Table 17-11
Cash Accumulation Comparison Method

Male Aged 48—$100,000 Whole Life
Dividends Buy Paid-up Additions
Annual Renewable Term (ART) Decreased to Equalize Death Benefits
Interest Rate 5% (on accumulations)

Policy Year	WL Premium	ART Premium	Prem Diff.	Accum. Diff. @ 5%	WL Cash Values	Term Plus Side Fund	WL + Paid-up Adds.	ART Face Amount
1	$2,187	$365	$1,822	$1,913	$0	$100,000	$100,000	$98,087
2	2,187	386	1,801	3,900	1,456	100,075	100,075	96,175
3	2,187	408	1,778	5,963	2,963	100,203	100,203	94,240
4	2,187	433	1,754	8,104	4,516	100,527	100,527	92,423
5	2,187	457	1,730	10,325	6,119	100,972	100,972	90,647
6	2,187	486	1,701	12,628	7,775	102,321	102,321	89,693
7	2,187	521	1,666	15,008	9,470	104,408	104,408	89,400
8	2,187	564	1,623	17,463	11,210	107,549	107,549	90,086
9	2,187	615	1,572	19,987	12,992	111,463	111,463	91,476
10	2,187	666	1,521	22,583	14,820	114,876	114,876	92,293
11	2,187	729	1,458	25,243	16,698	119,071	119,071	93,828
12	2,187	806	1,381	27,955	18,625	124,156	124,156	96,201
13	2,187	905	1,282	30,698	20,605	130,507	130,507	99,809
14	2,187	1,019	1,168	33,460	22,638	136,789	136,789	103,329
15	2,187	1,159	1,028	36,212	24,720	143,896	143,896	107,684
16	2,187	1,342	845	38,910	26,857	152,719	152,719	113,809
17	2,187	1,570	617	41,504	29,042	162,745	162,745	121,241
18	2,187	1,804	383	43,981	31,276	170,345	170,345	126,364
19	2,187	2,300	-113	46,061	33,559	183,682	183,682	137,621
20	2,187	2,885	-698	47,631	35,900	196,132	196,132	148,501

Table 17-12							
Cash Accumulation Comparison Method							
Male Aged 48—$100,000 Whole Life							
Dividends Buy Paid-up Additions							
Annual Renewable Term (ART) Decreased to Equalize Death Benefits							
Interest Rate 7% (on accumulations)							
Policy Year	WL Premium	ART Premium	Prem Diff.	Accum. Diff. @ 7%	WL Cash Values	Term Plus Side Fund	WL + Paid-up Adds.	ART Face Amount
1	$2,187	$365	$1,822	$1,950	$0	$100,000	$100,000	$98,050
2	2,187	385	1,802	4,014	1,456	100,075	100,075	96,061
3	2,187	407	1,780	6,200	2,963	100,203	100,203	94,003
4	2,187	431	1,756	8,513	4,516	100,527	100,527	92,014
5	2,187	454	1,733	10,964	6,119	100,972	100,972	90,008
6	2,187	481	1,706	13,556	7,775	102,321	102,321	88,765
7	2,187	514	1,673	16,296	9,470	104,408	104,408	88,112
8	2,187	553	1,634	19,185	11,210	107,549	107,549	88,364
9	2,187	600	1,587	22,226	12,992	111,463	111,463	89,237
10	2,187	646	1,541	25,431	14,820	114,876	114,876	89,445
11	2,187	701	1,486	28,801	16,698	119,071	119,071	90,270
12	2,187	769	1,418	32,334	18,625	124,156	124,156	91,822
13	2,187	857	1,330	36,020	20,605	130,507	130,507	94,487
14	2,187	956	1,231	39,859	22,638	136,789	136,789	96,930
15	2,187	1,077	1,110	43,837	24,720	143,896	143,896	100,059
16	2,187	1,236	951	47,924	26,857	152,719	152,719	104,795
17	2,187	1,433	754	52,085	29,042	162,745	162,745	110,660
18	2,187	1,628	559	56,329	31,276	170,345	170,345	114,016
19	2,187	2,060	127	60,408	33,559	183,682	183,682	123,274
20	2,187	2,563	−376	64,235	35,900	196,132	196,132	131,897

Table 17-13
Cash Accumulation Comparison Method

Male Aged 48—$100,000 Whole Life
Dividends Buy Paid-up Additions
Annual Renewable Term (ART) Decreased to Equalize Death Benefits
Interest Rate 10% (on accumulations)

Policy Year	WL Premium	ART Premium	Prem Diff.	Accum. Diff. @ 10%	WL Cash Values	Term Plus Side Fund	WL + Paid-up Adds.	ART Face Amount
1	$2,187	$365	$1,822	$2,005	$0	$100,000	$100,000	$97,995
2	2,187	385	1,802	4,188	1,456	100,075	100,075	95,887
3	2,187	405	1,782	6,566	2,963	100,203	100,203	93,637
4	2,187	428	1,759	9,158	4,516	100,527	100,527	91,369
5	2,187	448	1,739	11,987	6,119	100,972	100,972	88,985
6	2,187	473	1,714	15,071	7,775	102,321	102,321	87,250
7	2,187	501	1,686	18,432	9,470	104,408	104,408	85,976
8	2,187	535	1,652	22,093	11,210	107,549	107,549	85,456
9	2,187	574	1,613	26,076	12,992	111,463	111,463	85,387
10	2,187	610	1,577	30,149	14,820	114,876	114,876	84,457
11	2,187	652	1,535	35,149	16,698	119,071	119,071	83,922
12	2,187	703	1,484	40,297	18,625	124,156	124,156	83,859
13	2,187	767	1,420	45,888	20,605	130,507	130,507	84,619
14	2,187	836	1,351	51,963	22,638	136,789	136,789	84,826
15	2,187	918	1,269	58,554	24,720	143,896	143,896	85,342
16	2,187	1,026	1,161	65,687	26,857	152,719	152,719	87,032
17	2,187	1,157	1,030	73,388	29,042	162,745	162,745	89,357
18	2,187	1,265	922	81,741	31,276	170,345	170,345	88,604
19	2,187	1,555	632	90,610	33,559	183,682	183,682	93,072
20	2,187	1,867	320	100,023	35,900	196,132	196,132	96,109

Table 17-14
Cash Accumulation Comparison Method

Male Aged 48—$100,000 Whole Life
Dividends Buy Paid-up Additions
Annual Renewable Term (ART) Decreased to Equalize Death Benefits
Interest Rate 12% (on accumulations)

Policy Year	WL Premium	ART Premium	Prem Diff.	Accum. Diff. @ 12%	WL Cash Values	Term Plus Side Fund	WL + Paid-up Adds.	ART Face Amount
1	$2,187	$364	$1,823	$2,041	$0	$100,000	$100,000	$97,959
2	2,187	384	1,803	4,306	1,456	100,075	100,075	95,769
3	2,187	404	1,783	6,819	2,963	100,203	100,203	93,384
4	2,187	425	1,762	9,610	4,516	100,527	100,527	90,917
5	2,187	445	1,742	12,714	6,119	100,972	100,972	88,258
6	2,187	467	1,720	16,167	7,775	102,321	102,321	86,154
7	2,187	492	1,695	20,005	9,470	104,408	104,408	84,403
8	2,187	521	1,666	24,271	11,210	107,549	107,549	83,278
9	2,187	554	1,633	29,012	12,992	111,463	111,463	82,451
10	2,187	582	1,605	34,292	14,820	114,876	114,876	80,584
11	2,187	613	1,574	40,170	16,698	119,071	119,071	78,901
12	2,187	649	1,538	46,712	18,625	124,156	124,156	77,444
13	2,187	694	1,493	53,990	20,605	130,507	130,50	76,517
14	2,187	736	1,451	62,094	22,638	136,789	136,789	74,695
15	2,187	783	1,404	71,117	24,720	143,896	143,896	72,779
16	2,187	844	1,343	81,156	26,857	152,719	152,719	71,563
17	2,187	912	1,275	92,322	29,042	162,745	162,745	70,423
18	2,187	936	1,251	104,802	31,276	170,345	170,345	65,543
19	2,187	1,087	1,100	118,610	33,559	183,682	183,682	65,072
20	2,187	1,208	979	133,939	35,900	196,132	196,132	62,193

Table 17-15
Equal Outlay Comparison Method

Male Aged 48—$100,000 Whole Life
Dividends Purchase Paid-up Additions
Interest Rate 3%

Policy Year	WL Premium	ART Premium	Prem Diff.	Accum. Diff. @ 3%	WL Cash Values	Term Plus Side Fund	WL + Paid-up Adds.
1	$2,187	$372	$1,815	$1,869	$0	$101,869	$100,000
2	2,187	401	1,786	3,765	1,456	103,765	100,075
3	2,187	433	1,754	5,685	2,963	105,685	100,203
4	2,187	468	1,719	7,626	4,516	107,626	100,527
5	2,187	504	1,683	9,588	6,119	109,588	100,972
6	2,187	542	1,645	11,570	7,775	111,570	102,321
7	2,187	583	1,604	13,569	9,470	113,569	104,408
8	2,187	626	1,561	15,584	11,210	115,584	107,549
9	2,187	672	1,515	17,612	12,992	117,612	111,463
10	2,187	722	1,465	19,649	14,820	119,649	114,876
11	2,187	777	1,410	21,691	16,698	121,691	119,071
12	2,187	838	1,349	23,731	18,625	123,731	124,156
13	2,187	907	1,280	25,762	20,605	125,762	130,507
14	2,187	986	1,201	27,772	22,638	127,772	136,789
15	2,187	1,076	1,111	29,749	24,720	129,749	143,896
16	2,187	1,179	1,008	31,680	26,857	131,680	152,719
17	2,187	1,295	892	33,549	29,042	133,549	162,745
18	2,187	1,428	759	35,337	31,276	135,337	170,345
19	2,187	1,671	516	36,929	33,559	136,929	183,682
20	2,187	1,943	244	38,288	35,900	138,288	196,132

Table 17-16 Equal Outlay Comparison Method							
Male Aged 48—$100,000 Whole Life Dividends Purchase Paid-up Additions Interest Rate 5%							
Policy Year	WL Premium	ART Premium	Prem Diff.	Accum. Diff. @ 5%	WL Cash Values	Term Plus Side Fund	WL + Paid-up Adds.
1	$2,187	$372	$1,815	$1,906	$0	$101,906	$100,000
2	2,187	401	1,786	3,876	1,456	103,876	100,075
3	2,187	433	1,754	5,912	2,963	105,912	100,203
4	2,187	468	1,719	8,012	4,516	108,012	100,527
5	2,187	504	1,683	10,180	6,119	110,180	100,972
6	2,187	542	1,645	12,416	7,775	112,416	102,321
7	2,187	583	1,604	14,721	9,470	114,721	104,408
8	2,187	626	1,561	17,097	11,210	117,097	107,549
9	2,187	672	1,515	19,542	12,992	119,542	111,463
10	2,187	722	1,465	22,058	14,820	122,058	114,876
11	2,187	777	1,410	24,641	16,698	124,641	119,071
12	2,187	838	1,349	27,289	18,625	127,289	124,156
13	2,187	907	1,280	29,998	20,605	129,998	130,507
14	2,187	986	1,201	32,759	22,638	132,759	136,789
15	2,187	1,076	1,111	35,563	24,720	135,563	143,896
16	2,187	1,179	1,008	38,400	26,857	138,400	152,719
17	2,187	1,295	892	41,256	29,042	141,256	162,745
18	2,187	1,428	759	44,116	31,276	144,116	170,345
19	2,187	1,671	516	46,864	33,559	146,864	183,682
20	2,187	1,943	244	49,463	35,900	149,463	196,132

| Table 17-17 |
| Equal Outlay Comparison Method |

| Male Aged 48—$100,000 Whole Life |
| Dividends Purchase Paid-up Additions |
| Interest Rate 7% |

Policy Year	WL Premium	ART Premium	Prem Diff.	Accum. Diff. @ 7%	WL Cash Values	Term Plus Side Fund	WL + Paid-up Adds.
1	$2,187	$372	$1,815	$1,942	$0	$101,942	$100,000
2	2,187	401	1,786	3,989	1,456	103,989	100,075
3	2,187	433	1,754	6,145	2,963	106,145	100,203
4	2,187	468	1,719	8,415	4,516	108,415	100,527
5	2,187	504	1,683	10,804	6,119	110,804	100,972
6	2,187	542	1,645	13,321	7,775	113,321	102,321
7	2,187	583	1,604	15,970	9,470	115,970	104,408
8	2,187	626	1,561	18,758	11,210	118,758	107,549
9	2,187	672	1,515	21,692	12,992	121,692	111,463
10	2,187	722	1,465	24,778	14,820	124,778	114,876
11	2,187	777	1,410	28,021	16,698	128,021	119,071
12	2,187	838	1,349	31,426	18,625	131,426	124,156
13	2,187	907	1,280	34,995	20,605	134,995	130,507
14	2,187	986	1,201	38,730	22,638	138,730	136,789
15	2,187	1,076	1,111	42,630	24,720	142,630	143,896
16	2,187	1,179	1,008	46,692	26,857	146,692	152,719
17	2,187	1,295	892	50,915	29,042	150,915	162,745
18	2,187	1,428	759	55,291	31,276	155,291	170,345
19	2,187	1,671	516	59,714	33,559	159,714	183,682
20	2,187	1,943	244	64,155	35,900	164,155	196,132

Table 17-18
Equal Outlay Comparison Method

Male Aged 48—$100,000 Whole Life
Dividends Purchase Paid-up Additions
Interest Rate 10%

Policy Year	WL Premium	ART Premium	Prem Diff.	Accum. Diff. @ 10%	WL Cash Values	Term Plus Side Fund	WL + Paid-up Adds.
1	$2,187	$372	$1,815	$1,997	$0	$101,997	$100,000
2	2,187	401	1,786	4,161	1,456	104,161	100,075
3	2,187	433	1,754	6,506	2,963	106,506	100,203
4	2,187	468	1,719	9,048	4,516	109,048	100,527
5	2,187	504	1,683	11,804	6,119	111,804	100,972
6	2,187	542	1,645	14,794	7,775	114,794	102,321
7	2,187	583	1,604	18,037	9,470	118,037	104,408
8	2,187	626	1,561	21,558	11,210	121,558	107,549
9	2,187	672	1,515	25,381	12,992	125,381	111,463
10	2,187	722	1,465	29,530	14,820	129,530	114,876
11	2,187	777	1,410	34,034	16,698	134,034	119,071
12	2,187	838	1,349	38,922	18,625	138,922	124,156
13	2,187	907	1,280	44,222	20,605	144,222	130,507
14	2,187	986	1,201	49,965	22,638	149,965	136,789
15	2,187	1,076	1,111	56,184	24,720	156,184	143,896
16	2,187	1,179	1,008	62,911	26,857	162,911	152,719
17	2,187	1,295	892	70,183	29,042	170,183	162,745
18	2,187	1,428	759	78,036	31,276	178,036	170,345
19	2,187	1,671	516	86,407	33,559	186,407	183,682
20	2,187	1,943	244	95,317	35,900	195,317	196,132

Table 17-19
Equal Outlay Comparison Method

Male Aged 48—$100,000 Whole Life
Dividends Purchase Paid-up Additions
Interest Rate 12%

Policy Year	WL Premium	ART Premium	Prem Diff.	Accum. Diff. @ 12%	WL Cash Values	Term Plus Side Fund	WL + Paid-up Adds.
1	$2,187	$372	$1,815	$2,033	$0	$102,033	$100,000
2	2,187	401	1,786	4,277	1,456	104,277	100,075
3	2,187	433	1,754	6,755	2,963	106,755	100,203
4	2,187	468	1,719	9,491	4,516	109,491	100,527
5	2,187	504	1,683	12,514	6,119	112,514	100,972
6	2,187	542	1,645	15,859	7,775	115,859	102,321
7	2,187	583	1,604	19,558	9,470	119,558	104,408
8	2,187	626	1,561	23,653	11,210	123,653	107,549
9	2,187	672	1,515	28,189	12,992	128,189	111,463
10	2,187	722	1,465	33,212	14,820	133,212	114,876
11	2,187	777	1,410	38,777	16,698	138,777	119,071
12	2,187	838	1,349	44,941	18,625	144,941	124,156
13	2,187	907	1,280	51,767	20,605	151,767	130,507
14	2,187	986	1,201	59,324	22,638	159,324	136,789
15	2,187	1,076	1,111	67,688	24,720	167,688	143,896
16	2,187	1,179	1,008	76,939	26,857	176,939	152,719
17	2,187	1,295	892	87,171	29,042	187,171	162,745
18	2,187	1,428	759	98,482	31,276	198,482	170,345
19	2,187	1,671	516	110,877	33,559	210,877	183,682
20	2,187	1,943	244	124,456	35,900	224,456	196,132

Table 17-20
Linton Yield Method—20 Year

Male Aged 48—$100,000 Whole Life
Dividends Purchase Paid-up Additions
Annual Renewable Term (ART) Decreased to Equalize Death Benefits
Interest Rate 3.132% (on accumulations)

Policy Year	WL Premium	ART Premium	Prem Diff.	Accum. Diff. @ 3.132%	WL Cash Values	Term Plus Side Fund	WL + Paid-up Adds.	ART Face Amount
1	$2,187	$365	$1,822	$1,879	$0	$100.000	$100.000	$98,121
2	2,187	386	1,801	3,795	1,456	100,075	100,075	96,280
3	2,187	409	1,778	5,748	2,963	100,203	100,203	94,455
4	2,187	434	1,753	7,735	4,516	100,527	100,527	92,792
5	2,187	460	1,727	9,759	6,119	100,972	100,972	91,213
6	2,187	491	1,696	11,814	7,775	102,321	102,321	90,507
7	2,187	528	1,659	13,896	9,470	104,408	104,408	90,512
8	2,187	573	1,614	15,995	11,210	107,549	107,549	91,554
9	2,187	627	1,560	18,105	12,992	111,463	111,463	93,358
10	2,187	683	1,504	20,222	14,820	114,876	114,876	94,654
11	2,187	752	1,435	22,336	16,698	119,071	119,071	96,735
12	2,187	836	1,351	24,429	18,625	124,156	124,156	99,727
13	2,187	944	1,243	26,477	20,605	130,507	130,507	104,030
14	2,187	1,068	1,119	28,460	22,638	136,789	136,789	108,329
15	2,187	1,222	965	30,347	24,720	143,896	143,896	113,549
16	2,187	1,422	765	32,086	26,857	152,719	152,719	120,633
17	2,187	1,672	515	33,622	29,042	162,745	162,745	129,123
18	2,187	1,934	253	34,936	31,276	170,345	170,345	135,409
19	2,187	2,472	−285	35,736	33,559	183,682	183,682	147,946
20	2,187	3,113	−926	35,900	35,900	196,132	196,132	160,232

Table 17-21
Belth Yearly Cost and Yearly Return Methods

Male Aged 48—$100,000 Whole Life
Dividends Buy Paid-up Additions
Annual Renewable Term (ART) Decreased to Equalize Death Benefits
Interest Rate 3.132% (on accumulations)

Policy Year	WL Premium	ART Rate	Divi-dends	WL Cash Values	WL Cash Values	Yearly Benefit	Yearly Invest-ment	Yearly Return %
1	$2,187	3.72	$0	$0	$372	$2,187	-82.99	$22.96
2	2,187	4.01	76	1,456	1,927	2,187	−11.88	7.76
3	2,187	4.33	120	2,963	3,503	3,643	−3.84	7.65
4	2,187	4.68	170	4,516	5,133	5,150	−0.33	7.56
5	2,187	5.04	185	6,119	6,777	6,703	1.11	7.82
6	2,187	5.42	217	7,775	8,492	8,306	2.24	7.91
7	2,187	5.83	280	9,470	10,278	9,962	3.17	7.84
8	2,187	6.26	325	11,210	12,091	11,657	3.72	7.94
9	2,187	6.72	390	12,992	13,967	13,397	4.25	7.87
10	2,187	7.22	415	14,820	15,850	15,179	4.42	8.25
11	2,187	7.77	455	16,698	17,800	17,007	4.66	8.46
12	2,187	8.38	550	18,625	19,857	18,885	5.15	8.04
13	2,187	9.07	615	20,605	21,940	20,812	5.42	7.97
14	2,187	9.86	707	22,638	24,108	22,792	5.77	7.58
15	2,187	10.76	775	24,720	26,305	24,825	5.96	7.59
16	2,187	11.79	845	26,857	28,564	26,907	6.16	7.52
17	2,187	12.95	952	29,042	30,913	29,044	6.43	7.08
18	2,187	14.28	1,020	31,276	33,277	31,229	6.56	7.19
19	2,187	16.71	1,140	33,559	35,809	33,463	7.01	6.58
20	2,187	19.43	1,250	35,900	38,395	35,746	7.41	5.98

OUTLOOK

It is important to note that even though all states have the model regulation, there will still be wide variation in acceptable underlying assumptions. Illustrations will never be an accurate prediction of future results or policy performance. Actual future situations will be heavily influenced by the economy and by the investment performance of the specific insurance company's actual portfolio.

Illustrations are useful for showing how a policy works and how sensitive a policy is to given changes in factors such as interest, mortality, or expenses. However, illustrations are of limited value for comparing different policies (whether from the same insurer or from different insurers).

The new regulation will no doubt eliminate some of the past abuses in illustrations where the assumptions were based on unfettered pie-in-the-sky optimism. The new restrictions do not constrain illustrations to such an extent that we can compare apples to apples. It is still important to study all the questions about the underlying assumptions.

CHAPTER REVIEW

Key Terms and Concepts

interest-adjusted indexes
deceptive sales practices
Universal Life
Life Insurance Illustration
   Questionnaire
model regulation
net cost method

interest-adjusted indexes
cash accumulation comparison
   method
equal outlay method
comparative interest rate method
Belth yearly rate-of-return method
Belth yearly price method

Chapter 17 Review Questions

1. Describe the relationship between interest rates and accumulated values in policy illustrations. [1]

2. What is the implicit assumption underlying policy illustrations that do not include interest adjustments? [2]

3. Describe the major elements of the NAIC Life Insurance Illustrations Model Regulation. [3]

4. Describe the duties of an illustration actuary under the NAIC model regulation pertaining to illustrations. [3]

5. What is the implicit assumption underlying policy illustrations that do not include interest adjustments? [2]

6. Describe the major elements of the NAIC Life Insurance Illustrations Model Regulation. [3]

7. Describe the duties of an illustration actuary under the NAIC model regulation pertaining to illustrations. [3]

Chapter 17 Review Answers

1. *There is an inverse relationship between the interest rate and the accumulated values in policy illustrations. That is, higher interest rates result in lower present values, and lower interest rates produce higher present-value amounts.*

2. *Ledger statements and policy illustrations that do not include interest adjustments are really based on an implicit assumption that the interest rate is zero and the inflation rate is zero.*

3. *The major elements of the NAIC Life Insurance Illustrations Model Regulation are as follows:*

    • *The new regulation applies to all nonvariable group and individual life insurance policies and certificates for more than $10,000 of death benefit.*

    • *The regulation requires the insurance company to declare to the state insurance department for each policy form whether or not it intends to use illustrations to market that form of coverage. A copy of each illustration the insurer intends to use must be forwarded to the state insurance department.*

    • *Each illustration used in the sale of a life insurance policy covered by the new regulation must be clearly labeled "life insurance illustration" and must include certain*

specified pieces of information about the company, the agent, the proposed insured, the policy and its benefit features.

- The NAIC Model Regulation prohibits insurers and their agents from misrepresenting various specified types of information to the client.

- The illustration must clearly indicate what elements are guaranteed and what elements are nonguaranteed.

- Any amount illustrated as being available upon surrender will be the amount after deduction of surrender charges.

- Each illustration must be accompanied by a narrative summary that describes the policy premiums and features and defines column headings used in the illustration.

- The summary should also state that actual results may be more or less favorable than those shown in the illustration.

- The regulation states that illustrations for universal life policies must comply with the regulation requirements, that the insurance company must issue annual reports to policyowners after the policy is issued, and specifies the content of those annual reports.

- The regulation further stipulates that policyowners have the right to request an in-force illustration annually without charge.

- Each insurer's board of directors must appoint at least one illustration actuary, who will certify that the illustrations are in compliance with the illustration regulation and are insurer-authorized. The regulation states the qualifications of an illustration actuary, including membership in good standing of the American Academy of Actuaries.

- The model regulation sets forth limits on the methodology for calculating illustrations.

4. The illustration actuary must certify that the illustrations are in compliance with the illustration regulation and are insurer-authorized. The illustration actuary must annually certify the method used to allocate overhead and expenses for all illustrations and file such certification with the insurance commissioner and with the insurer's board of directions. Further, the illustration actuary is required to report any mistakes found in previous certifications to both the commissioner and the board of directions.

5. Ledger statements and policy illustrations that do not include interest adjustments are really based on an implicit assumption that the interest rate is zero and the inflation rate is zero.

6. *The major elements of the NAIC Life Insurance Illustrations Model Regulation are as follows:*

    - *The new regulation applies to all nonvariable group and individual life insurance policies and certificates for more than $10,000 of death benefit.*

    - *The regulation requires the insurance company to declare to the state insurance department for each policy form whether or not it intends to use illustrations to market that form of coverage. A copy of each illustration the insurer intends to use must be forwarded to the state insurance department.*

    - *Each illustration used in the sale of a life insurance policy covered by the new regulation must be clearly labeled "life insurance illustration" and must include certain specified pieces of information about the company, the agent, the proposed insured, the policy and its benefit features*

    - *The NAIC Model Regulation prohibits insurers and their agents from misrepresenting various specified types of information to the client.*

    - *The illustration must clearly indicate what elements are guaranteed and what elements are nonguaranteed.*

    - *Any amount illustrated as being available upon surrender will be the amount after deduction of surrender charges.*

    - *Each illustration must be accompanied by a narrative summary that describes the policy premiums and features and defines column headings used in the illustration.*

    - *The summary should also state that actual results may be more or less favorable than those shown in the illustration.*

    - *The regulation states that illustrations for universal life policies must comply with the regulation requirements, that the insurance company must issue annual reports to policyowners after the policy is issued, and specifies the content of those annual reports.*

    - *The regulation further stipulates that policyowners have the right to request an in-force illustration annually without charge.*

    - *Each insurer's board of directors must appoint at least one illustration actuary, who will certify that the illustrations are in compliance with the illustration regulation and are insurer-authorized. The regulation states the qualifications of an illustration actuary, including membership in good standing of the American Academy of Actuaries.*

    - *The model regulation sets forth limits on the methodology for calculating illustrations.*

7. The illustration actuary must certify that the illustrations are in compliance with the illustration regulation and are insurer-authorized. The illustration actuary must annually certify the method used to allocate overhead and expenses for all illustrations and file such certification with the insurance commissioner and with the insurer's board of directions. Further, the illustration actuary is required to report any mistakes found in previous certifications to both the commissioner and the board of directions.

Chapter 18
Types of Life Insurance Carriers

Revised by: Jon S. Hanson & C.W. Copeland

Learning Objectives

An understanding of the material in this chapter should enable the student to

1. **Describe the differences between stock and mutual life insurers and how the conversion from one to the other is executed.**

2. **Identify the types of life insurance providers other than commercial life insurance companies.**

3. **Describe the internal organization of life insurance companies.**

4. **Describe various methods of creating affiliations among companies in the life insurance business, including the special role of holding companies**

In light of the different demands and circumstances in a vigorous and free society, it is only natural that various types of organizations have emerged as providers of life insurance. These organizations may be categorized into three broad groups:

- commercial life insurers

- other private providers of life insurance

- government agencies[1]

COMMERCIAL LIFE INSURANCE POLICIES

Most life insurance in force today is written by commercial life insurance companies. Although theoretically coverage could be issued by an individual or a partnership, to ensure the promise of security it is essential that the insurance provider be permanent in order to be around when its long-term obligations come due. Since the corporate form of organization tends to be more permanent than other alternatives (a corporation's existence continues beyond the death of any or all of its owners), it is the only form of business organization sanctioned by state law to underwrite life insurance.

---

1. The description of these major categories of insurance providers in this chapter does not and cannot encompass all possible variations that now exist or may arise in the future.

Generally speaking, there are two different types of life insurance corporations, stock and mutual insurers. Both types of insurer must meet the formation, licensing, capital and/or surplus, and other state law requirements to do business.

Stock Life Insurance Companies

Profit Orientation

To obtain the initial operating capital necessary to enable a new company to begin to operate, the founders of a stock insurer sell shares of stock in the company that is being created. (In the future, if more funds are needed, additional shares may be offered for sale.) The people who purchase transferable ownership interests in the shares of stock own the insurer. If the company operates successfully, the value of the stockholders' investments will grow. Hence, they may profit both by income from periodic payments (stockholder dividends) and gains arising from the sale of their stock. On the other hand, if the insurer is unsuccessful, the stockholders may lose some or all of their investment.

Whatever the ultimate result, a stock insurer is organized and operated primarily for the purpose of earning profits for its stockholders. In its quest for profits, a stock life insurer offers a wide range of products and services that benefit not only the insurance-consuming public (policyowners, insureds, and beneficiaries) but also the public at large (insurance protection, savings mechanisms, sources of investment funds for business and government, and employment opportunities).

Management Accountability

The stockholders elect the board of directors that in turn appoints and oversees the management and operation of the company.[2] Although it is not unknown for dissatisfied stockholders to vote to replace board members and thereby change control of the company, because of the number and dispersion of stockholders, direct replacement of the board is very difficult and, therefore, rare.[3]

---

2. Owners of common stock are entitled to one vote per share. In addition, there may be a class of stockholders known as preferred stockholders who normally possess no right to vote for the board of directors but who must be paid their dividends before the common stockholders receive dividends.

3. As is typical with noninsurance corporations, a moderate-to-large stock insurance company, with its numerous and widely scattered stockholders, is likely to be controlled by its management group through management's ability to obtain proxies.

Nevertheless, management is subject to other forms of accountability that restrict trading the insurer's stock in the open market. The investment community constantly monitors management performance. Changes in stock prices, among other things, reflect stockholder views on management performance. If stockholders believe that the performance is poor, they can sell their stock, which drives the share price down and leaves management vulnerable to a hostile takeover.[4] Thus, a stock company's management is under real and constant pressure to generate an acceptable level of earnings that translate into stockholder dividends and increase the value of the stock.

At the same time, policyowner interests are neither irrelevant nor ignored. Although policyowners in most stock insurance companies lack legal control over management,[5] successful business operations in a competitive marketplace require a certain degree of customer satisfaction and a good business reputation. Furthermore, life insurers are subject to comprehensive state insurance regulations aimed at fostering policyowner interests.[6]

Distribution of Surplus to Shareholders

surplus

The **surplus** of a stock life insurer is the amount by which the insurer's assets exceed the sum of its liabilities and capital (capital is the amount of money the stockholders have invested in the company). Stockholders share in the insurer's surplus either through liquidation of the company or the payment of stockholder dividends.

Liquidation. Although an insurer may be liquidated in a situation that benefits stockholders, liquidation typically occurs when an insurer becomes financially impaired with little prospect for recovery. After the insurer closes down and the assets are gathered pursuant to a court order for liquidation, any assets remaining after satisfying the insurer's liabilities are distributed to the stockholders. Usually, however, few if any assets remain for such distribution.

---

4.   A takeover attempt affords stockholders an opportunity to sell shares at a more favorable price than they would otherwise obtain and/or to wait out the takeover attempt and the possible institution of new management.

5.   In some companies, limited policyowner control is permitted by granting participating policyowners the right to elect some, albeit a minority, of the board of directors. Such an insurer blends both stock and mutual attributes and sometimes has been termed a "mixed" company.

6.   Unfortunately, on occasion, stock life insurance companies have been used in less laudable ways for personal aggrandizement with little concern for the insurance-consuming public the companies profess to serve. Deterring, screening out, and removing such insurers from the marketplace are ongoing functions of insurance regulation.

Stockholder Dividends. Cash dividends are the usual means by which stockholders receive part of the insurer's surplus. A gain in the company's surplus may arise from a specific provision for profit in the gross premiums charged for its policies or from favorable interest, mortality, and expense experience compared to the assumptions in the establishment of premium rates. Management may elect to pay a portion of its surplus to stockholders in the form of dividends as compensation for the use of their capital funds, it may retain surplus to enhance policyowner security against future adverse contingencies, or it may utilize surplus to finance insurer operations, such as new business, acquisitions, and so forth. If shareholders are dissatisfied with their stockholders dividends or the growth in the value of their stock, as noted above, they may either sell their shares or seek to replace the existing board of directors.

Nonparticipating Policies

nonparticipating policies

Traditionally, stock life insurers issue **nonparticipating policies** for which they charge fixed premiums. These policies are sometimes referred to as guaranteed cost policies because they involve neither future increases in premiums nor refunds. (Stock companies cannot issue assessable policies that would permit an insurer to demand an increase in the premium to recapture losses.) Under a nonparticipating policy, policyowners do not share in the profits the insurer experiences (hence the term nonparticipating). In stock companies issuing only nonparticipating policies, the entire net worth of the insurer, while available for the protection of policyowners against adverse developments, represents assets held for the ultimate benefit of the shareholders.

Participating Policies

Many stock life insurers currently issue (or have at one time issued) participating life insurance[7] either exclusively or in addition to nonparticipating policies. As explained earlier, under a participating policy the policyowner shares (participates) in the insurer's gains through policyowner dividends. Most states impose no special regulation on participating insurance sold by stock insurers. In the absence of any special charter provisions, statutory restrictions, or other legally binding agreements, the insurer's entire net worth, after payment of dividends to participating policyowners, is held for the ultimate benefit of the

---

7. It is sometimes difficult to ascertain what constitutes a participating policy. Some insurers pay dividends on nonparticipating policies. Others have reduced the participating policy gross premium to virtually the competitive level of nonparticipating gross premiums, resulting in very small projected policyowner dividends.

shareholders. However, the charters of some stock companies and a few states limit the extent to which stockholders of the company may benefit from profit on the participating business.

Surplus Allocation by Stock Insurers Issuing Participating Policies

- Stockholder dividends to owners of stock

- Policyowner dividends to owners of participating policies

- Increases or decreases in surplus holdings

Mutual Life Insurance Companies

Policyowner Orientation

Like a new stock company, a mutual insurer needs funds to operate. However, it issues no stock and has no stockholders. Instead, the initial funds come from the first premiums paid by the original policyowners or monies the insurer borrows. However, it is difficult to attract a sufficiently large number of individuals who are willing to apply for insurance and pay the first premium to a company that is not yet in existence and unable to issue policies until it has the specified number of applications, premiums, and the minimum initial surplus required by statute. Although mutual insurers play a major historical role in the life insurance business, because of these reasons and the lack of a profit incentive in their formation, few (if any) new mutual insurers are being formed. A new mutual insurer may emerge, however, from the conversion of an existing stock company to a mutual company (a process called mutualization).

In theory, the policyowners own and control a mutual company, but the actual ownership continues to be a subject of debate.[8] Nevertheless, it is clear that a mutual company's policyholders possess certain rights, including the rights to vote and to share in the insurer's surplus. The company is obligated to operate in their interests, and its primary purpose is to provide reliable and low-cost insurance to its policyowners.

---

8.   In purchasing a policy, the policyowner does not acquire an ownership interest that is freely transferable on the open market. Furthermore, whatever status a policyowner has, whether as an owner or member of the company, such status continues only so long as his or her policies are in force. It has been said that technically the assets and income of a mutual insurance company are owned by the company and that policyowners are contractual creditors, rather than owners.

Management Accountability

The management of a mutual insurer is virtually immune to pressure from policyowners. With no publicly traded ownership interests, the threat of outside takeover is not a factor. Although policyowners have the right to vote for the board of directors, each policyowner is entitled to only one vote, regardless of the number or size of policies he or she owns. Moreover, a collective effort by a diffuse body of policyowners is most difficult; the cost to an individual of organizing a challenge to management will most likely far exceed any possible financial return. Consequently, the mutual insurers' directors and management wield control that is virtually unhindered by the exercise of the policyowner's right to vote. Nevertheless, they must be cognizant of policyowner interests to be successful.

Mutual insurers are subject to the protections afforded by state insurance regulation. However, they are not subject to the conflicting pressures of also having to satisfy stockholder interests.

Participating Policies/Sharing in Surplus

Mutual life insurers issue participating policies. Although they are theoretically owners of a mutual insurer, participating policyowners do not have individual access to the insurer's surplus. Rather, the assets represented by the surplus are held by the company for the benefit of the policyowners as a group. Except through the insurer's possible liquidation or demutualization, an individual policyowner participates in the surplus via distribution of a policyowner dividend declared by the company's board of directors. Management has broad latitude in declaring dividends, albeit subject to regulatory constraints and mandates. Because the participating policyowner typically pays a premium higher than that for a comparable nonparticipating policy, the policyowner dividend usually reflects this excess amount plus a share in the insurer's gain in operations.

Generally, mutual companies issue only participating policies, but some mutuals also issue nonparticipating policies. It is not uncommon for a mutual company to issue some of its nonforfeiture options and dividend options on a nonparticipating basis. Nonparticipating term insurance riders are sometimes attached to basic participating policies. A few mutual companies have even offered a regular line of nonparticipating life insurance, although some states have restricted or prohibited them from doing so.

A question often raised by prospective buyers is whether they should purchase life insurance from a stock or a mutual company. The relative desirability tends to focus on the comparative financial strength and the price of protection afforded by the two types of insurers. Although there are some theoretical differences, the debate generally has more

academic than practical interest. The basic factors determining an individual insurer's financial solidity and price competitiveness are the quality of its management, management's philosophy toward allocating gains in a way that reduces policyowner costs, and the insurer's regulatory supervision, rather than inherent differences between the stock and mutual forms of organization.

At the end of 2007, there were an estimated 1,009 United States legal reserve life insurance companies. Approximately 77 percent were stock companies; the remaining 121 companies were mutuals. Mutual life insurers, which are usually older and larger, possessed over 20 percent of the assets and wrote nearly 19 percent of the life insurance in force.[9] However, some very large mutual life insurers have switched over to a stock company form of organization. Demutualization explains the shrinking share of the business attributable to mutual life insurers.

Conversion: Mutualization/Demutualization

Mutualization of Stock Companies

In times past, some stock insurance companies have converted to the mutual form of organization. The primary reasons for conversion have been management's desire to gain freedom from stockholder demands or to avoid being taken over by another company through a change in stock ownership. (Because a mutual has no stock, a potential purchaser has no stock to buy.) In essence, mutualization involves retiring the insurer's outstanding capital stock and transferring control of the insurer to the policyowners.

The laws in several states outline the procedure for mutualization. Generally, after the mutualization plan is developed by management and ratified by the board of directors, it must be approved by the insurance commissioner of the insurer's state of domicile, by the stockholders, and by the policyowners in accordance with the provisions of state law. The plan must include the price of the shares and the terms under which they will be purchased. (The price must be sufficiently high to induce the stockholders to sell but not so high that the insurer will lack adequate surplus to continue operations soundly.) The plan typically establishes a trust to receive the shares from the stockholders. Because the stockholders representing a majority of the stock must approve the plan initially, the bulk of the stock is usually turned over to the mutualization trustee promptly after the adoption of the plan. This places control of the insurer in the hands of the trustee until the last shares are received, at which time the stock may be canceled and the insurer is fully mutualized.

---

9.   *2008 Life Insurance Fact Book*, American Council of Life Insurance, pp. 2–3.

Although in theory the process of mutualization is quite simple, in practice some stock-holders may refuse to surrender their shares, perhaps because they feel that the price is too low. However, unless they are successful in court, the stockholders ultimately have little alternative but to turn in their stock since no other market for their shares usually exists after adoption of the mutualization plan. Nevertheless, the complete process may take a long time, and mutualization has not proven to be very popular in recent years.[10] However, some mutual companies have recently acquired stock companies and became mutual holding companies.

Demutualization of Mutual Companies

An estimated 105 mutual life insurance companies converted to the stock form of organization between 1930 and 1969.[11] Sixteen mutual life insurers did so over the 25-year period from mid-1966 to mid-1991.[12] Nevertheless, prior to the 1980s, demutualization generated relatively little regulatory concern, as evidenced by the lack of laws or regulations in many states governing the process. In recent years, however, an insurer's organizational form has been perceived as highly important in the increasingly competitive marketplace because of its impact on the insurer's ability to raise capital and adapt to changing marketplace conditions. Consequently, a growing number of mutual insurers have either undertaken or are considering demutualization. Some companies have sought new legislation to enable mutual life insurers to become holding companies for stock life insurers.

Reasons for Demutualization

The reasons underlying demutualization stem primarily from the perceived competitive disadvantages of the mutual form of organization.

Ability to Raise Capital. First, the mutual insurer's ability to raise capital is limited essentially to retained earnings from underwriting gains and investment income and to borrowing. In contrast, stock insurers not only can draw on retained earnings but they also can raise capital by offering common, preferred, and convertible stock for sale; by financing alternatives such as convertible debentures and warrants; and by utilizing the full range of debt instruments. The ability to raise investment capital more easily puts a

---

10   During the 25-year period from mid-1966 to mid-1991, only two stock life insurers converted to the mutual form of organization (there were none between 1991–1998). *Life Insurance Fact Book* , p. 108.

11.   J. Binning, "Conversion of Mutual Insurance Company," 6 Forum 127 (1971), as cited in John C. Gurley and James R. Dwyer, *An Analysis of the Insurance Regulatory Aspects of Demutualization,* (Chicago: Lord, Bissell and Brook, 1984), p. 1.

12.   *1992 Life Insurance Fact Book*, p. 108.

stock insurer in a better position to grow rapidly in insurance writings, to finance development of new insurance products, and to avoid statutory or practical limitations inherent in debt financing. Furthermore, access to outside capital may better enable an insurer to strengthen a weak financial statement.[13] The importance of full access to capital has increased with the integration of financial services.[14]

Expansion Flexibility. Second, because of its ability to buy, sell, or exchange its own stock, a stock insurer possesses greater flexibility to expand through acquisitions or diversification. Unlike mutual insurers, stock companies can create upstream holding companies that facilitate expansion into other businesses, perhaps even non-insurance-related businesses, beyond the confines of insurance regulations. Effective diversification in the financial services, in fact, depends on use of an upstream holding company. For example, in the absence of an upstream holding company, a life insurer's acquisition of a bank would be subject to the investment restrictions placed on life insurance companies. It could also render the insurer itself a bank holding company subject to federal banking as well as state insurance regulations. (See discussion of holding companies later in this chapter.)

Noncash Employee Incentives. Third, the stock form of organization offers additional noncash incentive compensation (for example, stock options and payroll-based stock ownership plans) to attract and retain key officers, directors, and employees.

Tax Advantage. Fourth, with the Deficit Reduction Act of 1984, the tax advantages insurers used to enjoy have eroded significantly. The Act limited the deductibility of dividends mutual insurers pay to policyowners. This (and other changes) shifted more of the industry's federal tax burden to the mutual companies. Many mutuals view the federal tax law as biased in favor of stock insurers. Conversion to a stock company might result in tax savings.

However, before a mutual company opts to demutualize, it should carefully consider alternative (and perhaps better) ways to achieve its objectives prior to embarking on the difficult process of conversion. The cost and the complexity of demutualization are monumental (valuation and allocation of surplus to policyowners, along with legal, regulatory, actuarial, accounting, and tax problems). The cost of demutualization and the required

---

13. A 1984 survey indicated that 80 percent of mutual life insurers with assets exceeding $2 billion, as well as 43% of other mutual life insurers participating in the survey, were considering demutualization. Approximately 22% of property and liability insurers surveyed were also considering it. Ernst and Whinney, Demutualization: A Survey of Mutual Insurers, 1984, pp. 2–3, as cited in Gurley and Dwyer, An Analysis of the Insurance Regulatory Aspects of Demutualization, p. 1.

14. As financial integration continues, the demand for capital to fund more sophisticated computer systems, increase sales and distribution capabilities, and improve access to potential customers accelerates. In the absence of funds for such investments, mutual life insurers may suffer a decline in their competitive position.

distributions to policyowners could significantly deplete the insurer's surplus, thus severely impairing its ability to function. In addition, following conversion, by virtue of its being a stock company, the insurer becomes accountable to stockholders and vulnerable to hostile takeovers.[15] Moreover, once a mutual insurer converts to a stock company, it is subject to the ongoing expense and problems of complying with federal and state securities laws from which mutuals are now largely exempt.

Abuses in and Regulation of Demutualization

The history of demutualization includes several cases of abuse in the distribution of a mutual company's surplus or the transfer of ownership or control flowing from the conversion. On several occasions, managers effected a conversion for the purpose of transferring control of the company to themselves with little infusion of capital on their part. The distribution of surplus redounded not to the benefit of the policyowners who traditionally are deemed to be the mutual insurer's owners but to the existing management.

The perceived inequitable results of such conversions generated legislative responses, including several state laws prohibiting demutualization. In 1923, the National Association of Insurance Commissioners (NAIC) reflected the then prevailing sentiment by proposing a model law prohibiting a mutual insurer from converting to a stock company. Other states enacted laws that, while permitting demutualization, were designed to prevent recurrence of past abuses.

More recently, some states have repealed the total prohibition of demutualization. These and other states have enacted new laws to strengthen protections and vest substantial authority in the insurance commissioner to monitor the conversion process and safeguard the interests of the mutual policyowners.[16] State willingness to shift from the earlier prohibitory approach stems from (1) the recognition that conversion to a stock company may be essential to some mutual insurers' viability and survival in today's competitive marketplace and (2) increased confidence in the state's ability to fashion a regulatory framework that balances legitimate business objectives and policyowner interests.

---

15.   Some maintain that market discipline and management accountability to stockholders foster greater efficiency in company operations and better treatment of policyowners.

16.   As of 1991, 41 states had statutes permitting mutual life or property/casualty insurers (usually both) to directly convert to the stock form of organization. Two states prohibited direct conversion, and seven states had no conversion law.

Alternative Modes of Demutualization

Currently, most states regulate insurer demutualization either directly or indirectly. Generally, the law of the insurer's domicile governs.[17]

Although there are basically three alternative approaches to demutualization—some form of direct or pure conversion, merger, or bulk reinsurance[18]—the basic steps in the process are similar. A specified number of the board of directors must prepare and adopt a plan and submit it to the insurance commissioner in the insurer's state of domicile. The insurer must demonstrate that the demutualization is fair and equitable to the policyowners, that there are sound reasons for the conversion, and that the reorganization is in the interest of the company and the policyowners and not detrimental to the public. The commissioner may order an examination of the insurer and obtain an independent appraisal value of the company. After review, public hearing, and approval by the commissioner, policyowners are given notice of the conversion and an explanation of what they will receive in exchange for giving up their membership rights in the insurer. If the requisite number of policyowners vote in favor of the plan, and the insurer obtains final approval from the commissioner, the company proceeds to implement the conversion. If the company will be issuing securities to the public, it may also be required to register them with the Securities and Exchange Commission and state securities commissioner(s) before their sale.

Usual Steps in the Conversion Process

- Submit plan to insurance commissioner

- Valuation of company

- Review

- Public hearings

- Approval of plan by commissioner

---

17. When large numbers of policyowners reside in other states, commissioners of those states may attempt to exercise some influence over the terms of the conversion plan.

18. As an alternative to demutualization, a mutual insurer might organize or acquire a stock subsidiary or a downstream holding company that in turn owns one or more stock life insurance companies. If the operations of such subsidiary are substantial enough, it may be possible for a mutual insurance company group to raise a significant amount of capital by offering stock in the subsidiary to public investors. If this approach is viable, it avoids some of the problems associated with demutualization, including vulnerability to a hostile takeover.

Pure Conversions. The pure conversion approach involves amending the mutual insurer's articles of incorporation to reorganize the company from a mutual to a stock form of organization. A majority of states now have statutes expressly authorizing a mutual insurer to directly convert to a stock company. Virtually all of these states condition the conversion on obtaining the approval of the commissioner, whose function is to ensure that the mutual insurance company's policyowners are treated equitably. Generally, such laws preclude plans vesting control in or distribution of surplus to management and mandate that surplus be distributed to the policyowners.

Determining the portion of surplus to which an individual policyowner is entitled, however, is difficult because (1) a mutual company does not record the amount that an individual policyowner has forgone when the company retained earnings in lieu of paying policyowner dividends and (2) portions of surplus are attributable to former, rather than current, policyowners. In varying degrees of specificity, the pure conversion laws govern the procedures to accomplish the conversion. Although the requirements differ among states, some of the laws prescribe (1) the method of valuing the distributable surplus, (2) the proportionate amount of total surplus that must be distributed to policyowners, (3) which policyowners are entitled to receive the distributed surplus,[19] (4) the determination of each policyowner's share of the surplus, (5) the form of surplus distribution (cash and/or stock),[20] and (6) the percentage of policyowners necessary to approve the conversion.

If a state neither expressly prohibits nor expressly authorizes conversion, a second possible (albeit risky) pure conversion approach is a common law conversion—that is, a mutual insurer converts to a stock company simply by amending its articles of incorporation. However, many general laws and some insurance case laws pertaining to corporate mergers and consolidations hold that a corporation cannot effect such corporate structural changes in the absence of express statutory authority. Thus, the validity of common law conversions is highly suspect whether challenged by the insurance commissioner or disgruntled policyowners.

---

19. Some authorities believe that because all of the policyowners, living and dead, contributed to the surplus, all policyowners or their heirs should share in the distribution. Others believe that only current policyowners should participate. Still others conclude that only policyowners who have had policies in force for a minimum specified period (3 or 5 years, for example) should participate in the distribution.

20. If the insurer distributes the surplus in cash, it may severely weaken its financial condition and its ability to raise additional capital. On the other hand, distributing shares of stock in the converted company might shrink the number of stockholders to an unmanageable or very costly proportion.

In states where a mutual company is established under a special charter or enactment, it may be possible to achieve a pure conversion through a statutory amendment of the company's charter.

Conversion by Merger or Bulk Reinsurance. States that expressly prohibit a mutual insurer's pure conversion to a stock company and states that have no pure conversion authorization statute may afford mutual companies the option of a merger or bulk reinsurance. To effect demutualization through a statutory merger, the mutual insurer organizes or purchases a stock company, the two companies merge, and the stock company is the survivor. The mutual company, therefore, ceases to exist. Under the bulk reinsurance approach, the mutual insurer cedes all of its insurance business and transfers all of its assets and liabilities to a stock insurer that the mutual company has organized or acquired. After the transaction, the mutual insurer is dissolved.

Both statutory merger and bulk reinsurance conversions must be approved by the insurance commissioner and in some states by the mutual policyowners. Again, management has to demonstrate that the terms of the proposed transaction are fair to the policyowners. Pursuant to either statutory prescription or commissioner discretion, the commissioner is likely to evaluate many of the same factors codified in the pure conversion statutes in determining whether the mutual policyowners are treated fairly.

Licensing/Readmission Problems

If the conversion is by a merger or bulk reinsurance arrangement, some very difficult practical readmission problems could arise if the surviving stock company is not licensed to do insurance business in the states where the mutual insurer had been licensed. Many insurance departments have taken the position that the mutual company's certificate of authority is not transferred to the surviving stock corporation. Thus, many states require the surviving stock company to file for admission to do business in that state, submit all of its policy forms, pay all fees, and make all statutory deposits required of new foreign insurers. This takes time, and unless it is done in advance of the actual demutualization, the new insurer might be unable to do business in many states for some time.

Furthermore, many states impose a "seasoning" requirement on insurers. An insurer applying for admission to do business in the state must have been actively engaged in the business of insurance for a specified period (typically 3 years). If the surviving stock company is newly created and lacks previous operating experience, it may be unable to obtain a license to do business until after the seasoning period. (Some states waive the seasoning requirement in the demutualization situation.) In some states, if the surviving corporation

has been in existence for less than a year, in the absence of an annual statement, the insurance department will not even review the company's application for admission.

Post-demutualization Problems

- Mutual company licenses may not be transferred to successor stock company

- May have to seek all new licenses as if a new company with no experience

- May have to wait out a 3-year seasoning period before new licenses are issued

When the conversion from a mutual to a stock company is achieved by the pure conversion procedure, these readmission problems are more likely to be avoided because the new stock company is not a separate new entity. One court has held that the mere amendment of articles of incorporation does not create a new company.[21] However, this conclusion may not be accepted by a particular state.

Other Nongovernmental Providers

Although most life insurance in the United States is written by commercial companies, there are other nongovernmental providers of life insurance, including fraternal benefit societies, assessment societies, and savings banks. Because these other providers write only a small portion of the total amount of life insurance in the United States, their treatment here will be very brief.

Fraternal Benefit Societies

Fraternal life insurance is issued by fraternal benefit societies that were formed to provide social and insurance benefits to their members. They provide life insurance on a basis similar to that offered by commercial insurers. The modern fraternal life insurance certificate or contract is akin to a commercial company policy and contains most of the provisions found therein.

Assessment Associations

Although most assessment associations today utilize the level premium and do not operate solely on an assessment basis, these providers do not establish actuarially based premiums as do commercial and fraternal life insurers and can still levy assessments when

---

21. *Bergeson v. Life Insurance Corporation of America*, 265 F.2d 227, 234 (10th Cir. 1959).

needed. On occasion problems have arisen when policyowners have been unaware of the association's right to charge such assessment.

Savings Banks

In 1907 Massachusetts enacted a law authorizing savings banks in that state to establish life insurance departments to sell over-the-counter life insurance and annuity contracts to persons residing or working in the state. The Massachusetts law sought to provide a system of low-cost insurance by eliminating the sales costs of agents' commissions and home collection of industrial insurance premiums. In 1938 and 1941 respectively, New York and Connecticut enacted similar legislation. Efforts to establish savings bank life insurance in other states have proven unsuccessful. Savings banks have the authority to sell the normal types of ordinary policies, annuities, and group insurance. The terms of the contracts are similar to those of commercial life insurers. However, the maximum amount of insurance any one applicant can obtain is limited by law in each state.[22]

GOVERNMENT-PROVIDED LIFE INSURANCE

Governmental agencies offer various forms of life insurance protection. These agencies include the Department of Veterans Affairs, the Social Security Administration, and the State of Wisconsin. Because these governmental agencies are not the main thrust of this book, the treatment of these agencies and the forms of life insurance protection they offer will be necessarily brief.

Department of Veterans Affairs

Since World War I, the United States government has made life insurance available to current and former members of the armed services. More recently, Congress created Servicemen's Group Life Insurance (SEGLI) to provide members of the uniformed services on active duty with life insurance written on a group basis through private life insurance companies. SEGLI in the maximum amount of $100,000 (periodically increased from the original $10,000 maximum) is provided automatically to essentially all members of the armed forces unless such persons affirmatively elect no insurance or insurance in reduced amounts. No evidence of insurability is required. The coverage continues during active

---

22. The current maximum limit for individual life insurance coverage is $100,000 in Connecticut, $250,000 in Massachusetts, and $50,000 in New York. In all three states, the maximum limit is an aggregate limit on any one life whether there are one or more policies issued by one or more savings banks.

duty through 120 days after separation from the service. The individual is free to name any beneficiary he or she chooses.

Under the Veterans Insurance Act of 1974, Congress also created a program of postseparation insurance that will automatically convert SEGLI to a 5-year nonrenewable term policy known as Veterans Group Life Insurance (VGLI). At the end of the term period, the insured may convert VGLI to an individual commercial life insurance policy at standard rates with any of the participating insurers.

Social Security Administration

Governments, both state and federal, play an important role in providing economic security to individuals and families. Although this book focuses primarily on private life insurance, because Social Security is so pervasive that it affects the design and sale of life insurance products, a short discussion of the program is appropriate.

The Social Security Administration, an agency of the Department of Health and Human Services, administers the Social Security OASDI (Old Age, Survivors, and Disability Insurance) program. The availability of coverage under the OASDI program is tied to gainful employment. For the worker and members of his or her family to be entitled to benefits, the worker must have achieved insured status. There are three categories of insured status: (1) fully insured, (2) currently insured, and (3) disability insured. The benefits that are available depend on the individual worker's insured status. OASDI provides retirement, disability, and spouse's and child's benefits to retired and disabled workers and their families, and widow(er)'s, mother's/father's, parent's, child's, and lump-sum death benefits to survivors of a deceased worker if he or she dies while insured under the program. After a worker's death, a modest separate $255 lump-sum burial allowance is paid to the surviving spouse or other designated person.[23]

---

23. For more detailed treatment see CLU course HS 326 Planning for Retirement Needs, The American College, (revised annually).

INTERNAL ORGANIZATION OF LIFE INSURANCE COMPANIES

Effective organization is fundamental to an insurer's ability to develop and manage a life insurance operation that serves the needs of its insurance-consuming public on a sound and profitable basis.[24] Successful organization includes these four elements:

- clear allocation of responsibility
- clear delegation of the authority to carry out the responsibilities allocated
- accountability for the good or poor performance of responsibilities
- coordination of activities to achieve company goals

However, there is no one best organizational structure suitable for all life insurers all the time. Companies differ substantially in size, objectives, range of products, geographical areas of operation, and so forth. Furthermore, the exact form of any organizational pattern depends on the circumstances of the company's formation and evolution and on the personalities involved. Since most life insurance in force today is written by commercial life insurance companies, the following material on the internal organization of life companies is focused primarily on commercial insurers.

Organizational Structure

Levels of Authority

Subject to constitutional, statutory, and regulatory constraints, and to the company charter or bylaw authorizations and limitations, the stockholders in a stock company and the policyowners in a mutual company are a commercial life insurance company's ultimate source of authority. However, they usually do not direct the actual operations of their company but elect a board of directors to whom they give the authority for the company's conduct.

authority

Authority can be defined as the right to control, command, and decide or otherwise settle issues. Most organizations have various levels of authority. At each level those possessing authority delegate specific responsibilities to their subordinates to make decisions and

---

24.   Another important element in the organizational structure of a life insurance company is the nature of its sales operations.

take certain actions. There are typically four levels of authority: the board of directors, executive officers, managers, and supervisors.

Board of Directors. The stockholders, or the policyowners if the insurer is a mutual company, elect and when necessary may replace the insurer's board of directors. The minimum number of directors is usually specified in the company's charter and sometimes by state law. The board and its various committees are the highest level of authority in the company.

Board members represent the interests of those who elected them. The board establishes corporate policy, appoints the chief executive officer and other executives of the company, delegates to them whatever authority and responsibilities it deems appropriate, holds them accountable for the performance of their responsibilities, evaluates company results and finances, fosters long-range planning, authorizes major transactions such as acquisitions or mergers, and declares dividends. The board meets periodically, approves or disapproves recommendations of its committees and company officials, and considers important matters concerning the conduct of the business.

Example

Mutual Insurance Company management suggests demutualization.

The board of directors must authorize demutualization before formal steps can be taken to demutualize and will delegate authority for the necessary actions.

The board of directors will also establish a committee responsible for monitoring the demutualization process. In addition, it may get directly involved in the process of seeking approval from the insurance commissioner.

To facilitate the exercise of its responsibilities and maintain closer and more frequent contact with key company operations, the board is usually divided into a number of standing committees. Committees handle whatever actions need to be taken between board meetings. The committees report to the board.

To enable the committees to perform their functions efficiently, one or more executive officers are often assigned to each committee. These officers are responsible for bringing background information, proposed recommendations, and the matters requiring committee action to each committee's attention. Not uncommonly, an executive officer is empowered to act for a committee between meetings on any matters within the committee's authority and to report his or her action at the next committee meeting.

The number of board committees and the scope of their duties vary from company to company. However, they commonly include the executive committee (sometimes called the insurance committee), the investment committee (sometimes referred to as the finance committee), the audit committee, the tax committee, and sometimes a claims committee.

The executive committee focuses on matters bearing on the insurer's general business. It deals with overall company policy, lines of business sold, territories in which the company operates, policies affecting company employees, other matters not assigned to a different committee of the board, and long-range planning.

The investment committee establishes the insured's investment policy, including the types of investments in which company funds are to be placed and the allocation of assets among the different types of investments (bonds, stocks, mortgages, and real estate). Although day-to-day investment activities are conducted by the insurer's investment department, the committee oversees all investment practices; the investment department proposes major investment transactions, which are then subject to committee approval or disapproval. The committee may also select the banks into which company funds are to be deposited and determine the amount of funds to be maintained in each account.

The audit committee oversees the insurer's accounting operations, supervises internal and external audits, and reviews the company's periodic financial statements. One of its primary functions is to ensure the integrity of the financial information used by the board in its decision-making activities and made available to outsiders, including federal and state regulators. The committee is also responsible for retaining a professional, independent outside auditing firm to perform periodic audits. (Internal audits may be conducted by the company's own accounting personnel.) Because this committee serves as the guardian of the integrity of the insurer's financial reports, company officers do not normally serve as members. Some states bar them from doing so.

The tax committee analyzes and evaluates the tax implications of various company policies, programs, and practices. It also keeps abreast of any relevant tax legislation.

The claims committee exercises general control over the payment of claims. This includes determining policy as to questionable or contestable claims.

Although it usually places considerable reliance on management recommendations, the ultimate responsibility for the insurer's legal and ethical conduct rests with the board. Simply rubber stamping management recommendations and actions may, therefore, result in personal liability for board members. With several insolvencies and the questionable management conduct of several property, casualty, and life insurance companies over the

past decade, the responsible exercise of the board's authority has become a sensitive and important issue that board members cannot afford to ignore.

Executive Officers. The second level of authority within a life insurance company is its executive officers. Although the board has the highest level of authority, it vests broad administrative authority over the company in a chief executive officer (CEO), typically the president or chairman of the board. The CEO is primarily responsible for the selection, termination, and supervision of his or her subordinate officers and department heads.

The executive officers, usually vice presidents or senior vice presidents, report to the CEO and are responsible for carrying out company policies and general company management. In addition to serving on board committees and being part of the executive management team, executive officers usually have authority over a major division of company operations.

Managers. The third level of authority in a typical life insurance company is the managerial level. Company managers at this level focus on a particular phase of the company's activities, rather than on the operations of the insurer as a whole or a broad division of the company. These officers are responsible for translating company policy into plans for day-to-day operations and making decisions on matters within the scope of authority delegated to them.

Supervisors. Supervisors occupy the fourth level of authority. They manage the daily activities of subdivisions in various departments, directly supervise nonmanagement employees, and implement their manager's plans.

Span of Control

span of control

The people a manager directly supervises represent the manager's **span of control**.[25] The number of subordinates one manager can effectively supervise depends on a variety of factors. The simpler and more repetitive the tasks, the more people a manager can supervise easily. The greater the skills and competence of the manager and his or her subordinates, the broader the span of control the manager can handle. The higher the rate of turnover among subordinates (and, therefore, the need for more training) and the more widely dispersed subordinates are, the narrower the span of the manager's control.

---

25. Drawn from Kenneth Huggins and Robert Land, *Operations of Life and Health Insurance Companies,* 2d ed. (LOMA Life Management Institute, Inc., 1992), pp. 71–74.

Whether a manager's span of control is broad or narrow, however, every employee should know for whom he or she works and to whom he or she is accountable.

A company utilizing broad spans of control requires fewer levels of management. Communication tends to be better. Decisions can be made more quickly because several levels of management are not involved. However, a flat (fewer levels of management) structure may result in managers or supervisors being responsible for more activities or people than they can effectively manage. By contrast, if a company adopts a narrow span-of-control philosophy, each supervisor or manager oversees only a few subordinates. Although this can enhance supervision, it may also boost company expenses because of additional management layers and increase communication problems from the top of the company down to the lower levels and from the lower levels up to the top. Historically, insurance companies have leaned toward several, rather than few, levels of management and narrow, rather than broad, spans-of-control. Recently, however, many insurers have begun to organize (or reorganize) to reduce the number of levels between the company president and entry-level positions.

Example

To promote a wider span of control, some companies have eliminated regional home offices and moved all functions back to a single home office.

Bases of Organization

A life insurance company's successful operation depends on the performance of several basic functions. Products must be developed and made ready for sale. A system to sell products must be created and implemented. Customers must be serviced. Claims must be paid. Funds received must be invested in a way that ensures the availability of sufficient funds to meet the insurer's obligations when they become due. An insurer may be organized in a variety of ways to perform these functions.

Traditionally, life insurers have been organized on a functional, product, or geographical basis, or a combination of these organizational formats.

Function

function

The term **function** refers to a distinct type of work, an element or step in a process, or some aspect of operations or management requiring special technical knowledge.

Organization by function involves allocating closely coordinated activities to a single unit or department. The major functional areas of a life insurance company are marketing, actuarial, underwriting, customer service, claim administration, accounting, investments, legal, human resources, and information systems. A company organized by function establishes a separate department to perform each of these functions.

Product

Organization by product involves allocating work according to the products sold. Each line is administered by a major division of the company (for example, ordinary, group, or industrial insurance). Consequently, each division assumes responsibility for various functional activities with respect to that product, although some functions, such as investments, might continue to be handled centrally.

Geography

Under organization by territory, responsibilities are allocated to divisions in the company based on geographical areas. A company may divide its operations by states or regions. If the insurer does business in Canada, there may be a United States division and a Canadian division. Within each territorial division, the insurer may further divide its operations by functions and/or by products.

Profit Center

profit centers

In recent years, other forms of organization have emerged. Some insurers now organize their activities around **profit centers**—segments of the company that control their own revenues and expenses and make their own decisions about operations. (Segments that are not profit centers are service centers, which provide support to the profit centers.) The profit center approach focuses on improving efficiency by controlling costs and thereby becoming more competitive and profitable. Profit centers tend to be organized by product because the insurer's product lines are the prime generators of the company's revenues. Because each profit center is responsible for its own readily measurable performance, one benefit of this approach is that decisions can be made lower in the organizational chain. Possible disadvantages of the approach are a lack of coordination between different elements of the company, duplication of efforts, and lost economies of scale.[26]

26. Ibid., pp. 82–83. Sometimes support functions are incorporated into a profit center so that each center has its own

Functional Areas of a Life Insurance Company

Because life insurers have traditionally been organized on a functional basis and since certain functions need to be performed regardless of the form of organization, this section will briefly describe a functionally organized insurer. Keep in mind, however, that the following discussion is not intended to depict an actual company. It is presented to illustrate the functional form of organization. In addition, numerous interdepartmental committees can be employed to better coordinate activities as between departments.

Functional Departments

The marketing/agency department is responsible for the sale of new business, the conservation of existing business, and providing field services to policyowners. The department supervises the activities of the insurer's field force; recruits, selects, and trains agents; and conducts market analysis, advertising, and sales promotions. It also works with the actuarial and legal departments to develop new products, policy forms, and agent-company contracts.

The primary responsibility of the actuarial department is to see that the company's insurance operations are conducted on a sound financial basis. This includes determining appropriate premium rates and establishing adequate policy reserves. The department generally handles the insurer's mathematical operations, develops new policies and forms (including nonforfeiture values), analyzes earnings, provides statistical data from which the annual dividend scale is established, and conducts mortality, lapse, and other studies. The chief actuary and other company officers are jointly responsible for the accuracy of the annual financial statements required by the various insurance departments, especially the portions relating to policy liabilities and other items determined by actuarial calculation. Actuaries also typically participate in corporate strategic planning.

The underwriting department establishes standards for the acceptance or rejection of applicants for insurance and for applying these standards to ensure that the actual mortality the company experiences does not exceed that assumed in calculating the premium rates. Underwriting relies on medical underwriting judgment as to good health and lay underwriting judgment as to other factors relevant to an applicant's insurability. The home office underwriting department collaborates with medical and actuarial personnel in establishing general underwriting standards, is responsible for communicating matters

---

actuarial, underwriting, and information systems. Such centers have been termed strategic business units (SBUs). An SBU operates as a separate profit center, deals with its own customers, has its own management and support functions, and plans its own activities.

concerning the selection of risks to the field force, and may be responsible for negotiating and managing reinsurance agreements (agreements through which the company transfers some or all of an insurance risk or risks to another insurer).

The customer or policyowner services department furnishes home office services to the insurer's field force and to customers, including policyowners, beneficiaries, and employees. Customer service personnel fulfill requests for information, assist in interpreting policy language, answer questions about policy coverage, and make changes requested by policyowners (new addresses, beneficiary designations, or mode of premium payments, for example). The department also computes and processes policy loans, non-forfeiture options, and dividends. In some companies, the department processes commission payments to the insurer's agents, sends premium notices, and collects premium payments.

Actuarial Responsibilities

- Financial soundness

- Appropriate premium rates

- Adequate reserves

- New product development

- Statistical evaluations

- Setting dividend scale

- Mortality and lapse studies

- Participate in strategic planning

The claim administration department processes the claims against the company. Claim examiners review the claims filed by policyowners or beneficiaries, verify their validity, and authorize payments to the proper persons. Claims denied may result in litigation.

The accounting department establishes, supervises, and maintains the insurer's accounting and control procedures. It maintains the company's general accounting records, controls receipts and disbursements, oversees the company's budgeting process, and administers the payroll. It performs audits both in the field and in the home office. In conjunction with the actuarial department, the department prepares the financial statements used both internally and submitted to the regulatory agencies. The comptroller is one of the officers who certify the accuracy of the annual financial statements required by state insurance

departments. The accounting department is also responsible for matters concerning federal, state, and local taxes. It may, in addition, perform various expense analyses and other statistical operations not undertaken by the actuarial department.

The investment department implements the insurer's investment program under policies established by the board of directors and under the supervision of the investment committee. The department constantly evaluates existing and new investments, recommends whether to hold or sell, and may negotiate with brokers, investment bankers, or directly with borrowers. Authorized members of the department buy and sell stocks, bonds, mortgages, real estate, and other assets. The investment department also advises the president and the board about possible acquisitions and mergers.

The legal department is responsible for the insurer's legal matters, including compliance with federal and state laws and regulations. This encompasses not only traditional general corporate and insurance law but also antitrust, securities, labor, pension, and tax law. The legal department evaluates current and proposed legislation and regulations affecting the company. It advises on questionable claims, oversees litigation, performs a variety of legal activities relating to the insurer's investment transactions, works with the accounting and auditing department to determine the company's tax obligations, and participates in the development of policy forms, agents' contracts, investment transactions, and other contractual forms used by the company.

The human resources department handles matters concerning the insurer's employees. The department develops company policy on hiring, training, and dismissal of employees. It ascertains appropriate levels of compensation, assures compliance with federal and state employment laws, and administers employee benefit plans.

Over the last 30 years or so, the computer has become an indispensable tool in life insurance company operations. The information systems department develops and maintains the company's computer systems. It assists other departments in developing or buying the computer systems and software they need to furnish information, maintain records, and administer products. The department also maintains company records in computerized files, provides data for the preparation of financial statements, and conducts analyses of various systems and procedures used throughout the company.

Committees Various Insurers Might Establish

- Marketing committee to evaluate the need for product revisions or new products

- Budget committee to prepare the annual budget (the ultimate budget is subject to approval by the board of directors)

- Corporate communications (often called public relations) committee to coordinate company activities on advertising, publicity, and public relations

- Research committee, and a human resources committee to provide interdepartmental coordination with the human resources department in such areas as personnel policies and training

Interdepartmental Committees

A company may appoint a number of interdepartmental committees to coordinate the activities of various departments or to conduct an activity that falls outside a particular department's domain or requires input from two or more departments.

AFFILIATIONS

For a variety of reasons, life insurers buy or are purchased by other companies, merge with other insurers, or enter into strategic alliances with other companies. The basic purpose of these affiliations is to strengthen company operations and activities to increase efficiency and profitability. The rapidly changing world of financial services has spurred insurers to undergo various corporate restructurings and to undertake transactions that enhance their competitive position by expanding into new product or geographical areas and that help them survive the challenges of new competitors entering into traditional insurance areas.

Acquisitions: Friendly and Hostile Takeovers

An acquisition occurs when a company, an individual, a group of individuals, or some other group buys a controlling interest in a company. Mutual insurers can acquire but cannot be acquired since there is no stock to be purchased. Stock insurers can both acquire and be acquired.

The reasons for an acquisition vary greatly. Sometimes the stock acquired is solely for investment purposes, and the acquired company's management continues to direct the company operations. In other situations, the benefits of merging with another company

may be the motivation for the acquisition. In these cases, the new controlling stockholder(s) may either retain the existing management or install new management.

The acquisition of a company can be friendly or hostile. In a friendly takeover the acquiring company offers to purchase a company. The company to be purchased agrees to the acquisition and the price for the stock. The board of directors of the company to be acquired approves the offer and publicly recommends to its stockholders that the offer be accepted. The acquisition requires the approval of both the stockholders and the insurance commissioner in each state in which any insurers involved in the acquisition are domiciled. The Securities and Exchange Commission (SEC) and the antitrust authorities may also be involved.

A hostile takeover occurs when the acquirer proceeds with a takeover even though the board of directors of the company to be acquired (the target company) refuses the acquisition offer. To obtain a controlling interest the acquiring company makes a tender offer—a public offer to purchase the target company's securities directly from the shareholders at a specified price—thereby circumventing the board of directors. As further discussed below, under the federal securities laws, the company making the tender offer files information with the SEC about the reasons for the acquisition, any plans to liquidate the target company or sell a major portion of its assets, and the source of funds for the acquisition. The acquirer then publicly announces the offer to purchase the target's stock at a specified price, usually significantly in excess of the market value of the stock. Not uncommonly, the purchase is conditioned on the acquirer's ability to obtain a certain percentage of the target company's shares within a specified period of time (to assure the acquirer of at least practical controlling interest if and when the tender offer is successful). If the takeover succeeds, the acquiring company obtains control, can elect a new board of directors, and can decide on management policy.[27]

A leveraged buyout (LBO) is one strategic process of acquiring a company. In an LBO, the acquiring company finances the acquisition primarily through borrowing. After a successful takeover, the acquirer repays the debt from money generated by the acquired company's operations or through the sale of some of the acquired company's assets.

---

27.   Hostile takeovers often involve long and expensive legal and financial battles. The target company may make a counteroffer to buy enough of the stock to prevent the acquirer from obtaining controlling interest. The target company's board may attempt to convince its stockholders that the takeover would not enhance the long-term value of the stock. If the target believes that it cannot prevent a hostile takeover, it may seek a takeover by a purchaser more to its liking (often called a white knight).

Mergers

merger

A **merger** occurs when two or more companies are legally joined together to become one. One company may be absorbed by another—the surviving—company, or two or more existing companies may be merged into an entirely new company.

The advantages of a merger depend on the circumstances. An insurer in weakened financial condition, for example, may seek a stronger partner to help the insurer overcome its financial difficulties or gain access to additional surplus to fund expansion and growth. An insurer that has decided to offer new products or services may determine that it would be more feasible to merge with an existing company that already offers those products and/or services than to expend the time and money to develop them itself. An insurer that wants to expand into new geographical areas may find that joining an insurer already licensed and marketing in those areas is a more rapid and economical mode of expansion. Because unit costs decrease as the size of operations increases, a merger is also attractive to a company that wants to reduce the price of its products and increase profits through economies of scale. Moreover, large and growing companies often attract both security-minded customers and high-quality management and other personnel.

Mergers may also have significant drawbacks. A merger often incurs enormous legal and accounting costs. It can cause great anxiety among managers and employees, resulting in either the loss of key people or the cost in time and money to retain them. When merging companies are in different locations, there can be substantial costs to move personnel, as well as the inevitable costs of employee turnover. Many business relationships will need to be reviewed and perhaps reestablished, including contracts with agents. Difficulties will undoubtedly arise in efforts to blend different managements, corporate philosophies, and company systems. Finally, there is the danger that the perceived benefits of the merger may not be realized, at least to the extent the companies had contemplated, and that this will create new difficulties.

A merger between two or more insurance companies involves several steps. First, potential merger partners must be found and evaluated; usually, an independent actuarial or investment banking firm examines each company's financial condition. Then the boards of directors must approve the plan of merger, typically by a two-thirds majority vote of the stockholders or, if a mutual company, by two-thirds of the policyowners. Stockholders who disapprove must be paid a fair market value for the forced surrender of their stock if the merger actually occurs. The state insurance regulatory authorities in the insurer(s)' domiciliary state(s) must also approve the merger. The final merger document must be filed in the

new or surviving company's state of domicile and a new or amended certificate of incorporation must be obtained. The merging companies' assets and liabilities must be transferred to the new or surviving company. And, finally, the new or surviving company must obtain licenses in all states where it does business.

Holding Companies

When a company acquires one or more companies (purchases a sufficient amount of stock to possess controlling interest), the acquired companies become subsidiaries of the acquirer, the parent company. The group of companies has formed a holding company system, and the parent company is the holding company.

holding company

A **holding company** is any person or organization (firm) that directly or indirectly controls an authorized insurer. (Control commonly means the power to vote 10 percent or more of the insurer's voting securities.) An insurance holding company system consists of two or more affiliated persons or organizations (firms), one of which is an insurer (that is, a holding company system is an insurer, its parent, subsidiaries and/or other affiliated organizations).

Trend Toward Holding Companies

Traditionally, insurers operated as independent, free-standing entities or as a part of insurance company groups. Originally, the holding company concept was utilized to acquire a group of companies in related lines. By the late 1960s, however, this changed in the insurance industry as a result of two trends.

First, to improve earnings and long-term growth, many insurers sought to diversify by venturing into new lines of insurance (for example, a life company acquiring a property and liability insurer) or into noninsurance enterprises, commonly in the financial services area (acquiring securities/broker-dealer organizations, mutual fund management companies, consumer finance companies and other related institutions). Several life insurers found that forming a holding company system gave them greater ability to diversify their services and products, imposed fewer restrictions on their investments, and enhanced their capital-raising flexibility.

Second, several life insurers were taken over by other insurers or noninsurance company acquirers and thus became part of a conglomerate (a group of unrelated businesses under the control of a holding company). Sometimes being part of the conglomerate contributed to the insurer's strength. On occasion, however, the acquirer was less interested in the

insurer's well-being than in gaining access to the insurer's accumulation of liquid assets and substantial cash flows.

Nature of Holding Companies

A holding company may be an insurer or a general business corporation. As noted before, a mutual insurer, by its very nature, is not subject to acquisition by another company purchasing shares of the insurer's stock since there are no shares. However, a mutual insurer (or a stock insurer if it so chooses) can become involved in a downstream holding company system by creating or acquiring subsidiaries, perhaps including a downstream holding company, which, in turn, can acquire other enterprises as subsidiaries. The mutual insurer sits atop the holding company structure. A downstream holding company has fewer insurance regulatory concerns since the parent insurer, which continues to control its own destiny as well as that of any subsidiaries acquired downstream, remains directly subject to insurance regulatory control.

By contrast, there are upstream holding company systems in which the holding company acquires the insurer's stock. Stock insurers tend to become involved in upstream holding company systems in one of two ways. First, a stock insurer can organize an upstream noninsurance holding company that sits atop the intercorporate structure. The insurer's board of directors and management, or appropriate portion thereof, becomes the board and management of the holding company; the insurer becomes its subsidiary. As a noninsurance company, generally speaking, the new parent is outside the scope of insurance regulation. It can engage in a host of activities through its different subsidiaries, including insurance business, other financially related businesses, and totally unrelated enterprises. Second, as noted earlier, a stock insurer can become involved, either voluntarily or involuntarily, in an upstream holding company system by being acquired by an outside company that becomes the insurer's upstream holding company.

Alliances

Although acquisitions, mergers, and holding companies are common, insurers have also formed strategic alliances—which involve less drastic structural changes—to accomplish some of the same objectives. A strategic alliance is an ongoing relationship in which two or more independent organizations share the risks and rewards. Through this alliance, a life insurer gains access to the resources of other firms but still retains its independence.

Insurers have a long tradition of entering into some form of strategic alliance with other business firms—foreign and domestic insurers, securities firms, third-party administrators,

commercial banks, and so forth. Through cooperation with other firms, an insurer can improve its ability to handle the increased competition from traditional competitors, the integration of financial services, and the globalization of the financial service marketplace.

Regulation

As mentioned earlier, firms can diversify or grow through internal development, by acquisition, or by merger. Often, acquisitions or mergers prove to be the more attractive routes. Although they have corporate advantages, because acquisitions and mergers may involve changing management, company structure, and perhaps even the competitive nature of the marketplace, they can give rise to public policy issues that come to the attention of the state insurance regulators, federal antitrust enforcement authorities, and the SEC.

State Insurance Regulation

Regulatory Concerns. Although acquisitions and mergers have long been subject to state insurance department regulatory approval, the rash of insurance company takeovers—many of them hostile—in the late 1960s heightened regulatory concerns. These takeovers usually involved tender offers, which enabled the acquiring company to avoid dealing directly with the target company's resistant management. Unlike affiliations involving willing partners, such as two companies agreeing to merge, tender offers were essentially unregulated.

Regulators became concerned when affiliations of insurers with noninsurance companies pursuing different interests began to occur, which gave control of the insurers to noninsurance parents outside of insurance regulatory control. Their concern increased when noninsurance holding companies that lacked insurance experience, focus, and orientation toward safeguarding policyowner interests started to acquire and control stock insurers. During the ensuing years, regulators' concern proved to be justified. Actual and potential abuses in these affiliations included rapacious acquirers looting insurers' assets, raiding insurer surplus to finance either the holding company itself or the operations of other holding company subsidiaries, subtle threats to insurer solvency, and circumvention of various state requirements enacted to protect the insurance-buying public.

At the same time, however, regulators acknowledged that the interests of the public, policyowners, and shareholders might not be compromised by—perhaps even be benefited by—permitting insurers (1) to engage in activities that would enable them to better use their management skills and facilities, (2) to diversify into new lines of business, (3) to have free access to capital markets to fund diversification programs, (4) to implement sound tax

planning, and (5) to serve the public's changing needs by being able to compete with a comprehensive range of financial services. Nevertheless, regulators recognized that public, policyowner, and shareholder interests could be adversely affected if (1) persons seeking control of an insurer utilized that control contrary to policyowner and public interests, (2) the acquisition of an insurer substantially lessened competition, (3) an insurer in a holding company system entered into transactions or relationships with affiliated companies on unreasonable or unfair terms to the insurer, or (4) an insurer paid dividends to the noninsurance parent or other shareholders that jeopardized the insurer's financial condition.[28]

Holding Company Act. As regulatory concerns mounted, both the regulators and the insurance industry moved to develop a legislative response. In 1969, following legislative enactments in New York and Connecticut, the NAIC adopted a model Insurance Holding Company Systems Regulatory Act (hereafter referred to as the Holding Company Act) and a model regulation setting forth rules and procedural requirements to assist in carrying out the provisions of the act.[29] All states regulate the acquisition of insurance companies in some way, whether as a part of the act or separately from it. Furthermore, all states have enacted some type of holding company law, most of which are patterned after the NAIC model act (although not necessarily adopting all of the amendments made to it).

To exercise control over holding company situations, the model act (1) facilitates insurer diversification, (2) requires disclosure of relevant information relating to changes in the insurer's control and commissioner approval of such changes, (3) requires insurer disclosure of material transactions and relationships between the insurer and its affiliates, including certain dividends distributed by the insurer, and (4) establishes standards governing material transactions between the insurer and its affiliates. To avoid unnecessary multiple and conflicting regulation of insurers, the model act applies only to domestic insurers, except where otherwise specifically stated.

---

28. Appendix to the NAIC Model Holding Company Act containing an alternate (optional) section setting forth findings.

29. This activity was triggered by the declaration of an extraordinarily large cash dividend by a fire and casualty insurance company shortly after it had been acquired. Regulators envisioned that this means of extracting funds from insurers, if left unchecked, would not only limit the capacity of insurers to write business, but would also jeopardize the adequacy of an insurer's surplus. At the same time, many insurer managements became increasingly interested in holding company structures for a variety of reasons. For example, the property and liability business had been unprofitable, giving rise to management's desire to be able to employ the industry's capital more profitably elsewhere. From a defensive perspective, life insurance stocks were thought to be relatively cheap, thereby rendering such insurers vulnerable to takeovers. Some viewed holding company legislation as a defensive mechanism against hostile takeovers.

Insurer Diversification. From the insurance industry's perspective, the traditional investment law limitations precluded or severely constrained insurer's ability to diversify and grow. This contributed to the pressure for insurers to organize holding company systems with the insurer as a subsidiary of a noninsurer parent that had the flexibility to acquire or establish subsidiaries in diversified fields. In response, the Holding Company Act relaxed some of the investment restraints but did so within a somewhat controlled environment.

Approval of Acquisitions and Mergers. Under the Holding Company Act, any person or organization (firm) acquiring securities that would result in obtaining direct or indirect control of a domestic insurer or entering into an agreement to merge with a domestic insurer must file specific information with the commissioner and obtain his or her approval before the acquisition or merger can be effected.[30] The information, as required by supplementary regulation, must include the method of acquisition; the identity and background of the applicant and individuals associated with the applicant; the nature, source, and amount of funding used for the acquisition or merger; future plans for the insurer; and financial statements. The information that must be provided to the commissioner not only alerts the target insurer to the potential takeover but also gives the insurer's management a better opportunity to make its case to the shareholders about whether or not to accept the offer.

Registration of Insurers. Every insurer that is a member of an insurance holding company system and licensed to do business in the state (except a foreign insurer already subject to substantially the same disclosure requirements and standards in its domiciliary state) must register with the commissioner. Each registered insurer must keep the required information current.

Standards Governing Transactions between the Insurer and Its Affiliates. Transactions within a holding company system are subject to several standards, including the fairness and reasonableness of terms, charges, and fees for service. Expenses must be allocated to the insurer according to customary insurance accounting practice, and accurate and clear records must be maintained as to the nature, details, and reasonableness of transactions between affiliates. The insurer's surplus for policyowners, following dividends or distributions to affiliates, must be reasonable in relation to the insurer's liabilities and financial needs.

Insurer Management. As early as 1972, some commissioners urged the adoption of management standards giving the insurer's officers control over all facets of the insurance

---

30.   However, the model act avoids imposing commissioner approval requirements in situations involving the acquisition of a holding company that, even though controlling a domestic insurer, is not primarily engaged in the business of insurance either directly or through its subsidiaries.

operation, rather than permitting a general corporation's board of directors to usurp this function. The 1985 amendments to the act include provisions to this effect, stating that the insurer's officers and directors continue to be responsible for the insurer's management and must manage the insurer in a manner that ensures the insurer's separate operating identity.

Enforcement. In addition to various ways to monitor compliance with provisions of the holding company law—reviewing the various information filings, examining insurers and sometimes insurers' affiliates, and compelling the submission of books, records and other information[31]—the commissioner has a host of sanctions with which to enforce the act, including monetary penalties and recoveries, cease-and-desist orders, and license revocation. Furthermore, if it appears that any insurer or any director, officer, employee, or agent willfully violated the act, the commissioner may cause criminal proceedings to be instituted. The insurer is subject to dollar penalties; individuals are subject to fines, and if fraud is involved, imprisonment.

If violations of the act threaten a domestic insurer's solvency or make further transaction of business hazardous to policyowners, the commissioner may proceed under the state's rehabilitation and liquidation law.[32] If the commissioner believes a violation makes the continued operation of an out-of-state insurer contrary to policyowner interest, after a hearing, he or she may suspend or revoke the insurer's license to do business.

In the 1980s, numerous insurers became insolvent or nearly so. Although a majority of insolvencies involved property and liability insurers, the life insurance industry was not immune. The record of insolvent insurance companies is replete with self-dealing abuses in relationships between insurers, their parent holding companies, and their affiliates, involving intercompany loans, dividends, management contracts, and investments. Regulators and liquidators were concerned that they did not have adequate access to the interrelated corporate networks' books and records affecting insurer operations and were thereby deterred from effective regulatory action. A series of amendments to the Holding Company Act in the 1980s reflect regulatory responses to such abuses.

---

31. In 1988 the NAIC annual statement was amended to require detailed information on the inflow and outflow of funds between affiliated companies in an insurance holding company system. The disclosure of this information is designed to enhance the regulators' ability to monitor self-dealing transactions.

32. If an order for rehabilitation or liquidation is entered, the receiver may recover from a parent, affiliated company or person who otherwise controlled the insurer the amount of distribution paid by the insurer or any payment of bonuses, extraordinary salary adjustments, and the like that the insurer made to a director, officer, or employee if the distribution or payment was made within a year of the petition for rehabilitation or liquidation (unless the recipient did not know that it might adversely affect the insurer's ability to meet its obligations).

Federal Antitrust Treatment of Acquisitions and Mergers

In the United States the first wave of corporate mergers occurred around the turn of the century. The only federal antitrust statute at the time was the Sherman Act. However, the need to prove either a conspiracy in restraint of trade or some type of monopolization activity rendered the act a somewhat less-than-effective deterrent to anticompetitive mergers. Consequently, Congress enacted Section 7 of the Clayton Act, which was ultimately amended to prohibit a corporation from directly or indirectly acquiring the stock or assets of another corporation if, in any line of commerce in any section of the country, it substantially lessened competition or tended to create a monopoly.[33] Unlike the Sherman Act, which requires finding actual anticompetitive effects, the test under Section 7 is probable effect in order to combat incipient monopolistic tendencies.

Prior to the 1960s, the Department of Justice and the Federal Trade Commission (FTC) showed little interest in challenging insurance company acquisitions and mergers, perhaps because there were few of them or that it was difficult to overcome a McCarran Act defense. In the early 1960s, however, a few lower court decisions sanctioned the application of federal antitrust law to insurance acquisitions. Although the Supreme Court has not definitively determined whether the McCarran Act bars federal antitrust jurisdiction in many situations and even though good legal arguments support such a bar, as a practical matter, the potential for applying the federal antitrust law to insurance company acquisitions and mergers has become a fact of life.

To the extent that federal antitrust jurisdiction is not barred by the McCarran Act, the issue becomes whether a state insurance regulator applying holding company law is preempted by federal antitrust law. Since the Sherman and Clayton Acts were enacted long before the antitrust laws were deemed applicable to insurance, it appears unlikely that the Supreme Court would find Congressional intent to preempt. As to the conflict test under the preemption doctrine, antitrust law seeks to prohibit anticompetitive acquisitions and mergers. If the insurance commissioner disapproves the transaction, there will be no conflict with antitrust law. However, if the commissioner approves what antitrust law prohibits and if the McCarran Act defense to antitrust actions is inapplicable, preemption of the holding company law is probable. In short, unless Congress acts in some way to change the existing balance, dual assertion of federal antitrust law and state insurance acquisition and merger regulatory authority promises to continue in the years ahead.

---

33.   15 U.S.C.A. Sec. 18.

McCarran-Ferguson Act of 1945

In 1944, the U.S. Supreme Court held that Congress had authority to regulate the insurance industry, overruling past precedent in this area. The McCarran-Ferguson Act of 1945 stated that regulation of insurance would remain with the states provided the states actually regulated it. The National Association of Insurance Commissioners (NAIC) worked with the states to establish regulatory bodies to maintain the primacy of state law in the insurance industry. The federal government can and does influence state laws through the prospect of federal regulation in the absence of adequate state controls. The act has seen extensive legislative scrutiny in recent years with bills promoting both an outright repeal of the act and a national charter for insurance companies.

Federal Securities Law: The Williams Act

The emergence of the tender offer technique and the frequency of its use revealed a deficiency in the disclosure of information to investors. Therefore, in 1968 Congress enacted the Williams Act as an amendment to the Securities Exchange Act of 1934. (In 1970, this act was made applicable to insurance securities.) The central philosophy of the Williams Act is disclosure. Among other things, the act requires that upon the commencement of a tender offer, the offeror must file pertinent information with the SEC and provide such information to the target company's shareholders and management. All shares tendered must be purchased at the same price. The offer commences at the time of the first public announcement, and it must remain open for at least 20 days.

Congress believes that the Williams Act strikes a fair balance between the party making the takeover bid and the management of the target company by enabling both to present their cases to the shareholders. More important, compelling timely, full, and fair disclosure puts the shareholders in a position to make informed decisions.

In the absence of McCarran Act protection, insurance commissioner authority to approve or disapprove an acquisition pursuant to a tender offer is questionable under the preemption doctrine. Even though the commissioner reviews a tender offer from the perspective of protecting the policyowners, a disapproval of a tender offer precludes the offer itself. This directly affects those shareholders who want to accept the offer. Thus, insurance commissioner disapproval would appear to constitutionally prohibit what Congress authorizes and fosters—the shareholders' freedom to make informed decisions about accepting or rejecting a tender offer for their shares.[34]

---

34.   See Edgar v. Mite , 457 U.S. 624 (1982).

Consequently, the states' ability to protect policyowners from adverse acquisitions by tender offers most likely depends on the scope of the McCarran Act in such situations. In SEC v. National Securities, Inc.,[35] the Supreme Court found that an insurance commissioner's approval of an acquisition under an insurance holding company law's standard of the transaction's fairness to the shareholders was the regulation of securities, not the regulation of the "business of insurance." Hence, the application of the Securities Exchange Act proxy rules were not barred by the McCarran Act. This decision has been cited in the proposition that acquisitions and mergers are not part of the business of insurance as that term is used in the McCarran Act.

However, in most acquisition and merger situations, the application of the holding company law focuses on standards to ensure the protection of policyowners and the competitiveness of the insurance marketplace.

Although the National Securities decision suggests that this application constitutes regulating the business of insurance, the more recent judicial narrowing of this language leaves the issue in some doubt. In the meantime, states continue to regulate acquisitions and mergers under their holding company laws.

CHAPTER REVIEW

Key Terms and Concepts

surplus

nonparticipating policies

authority

span of control

function

profit centers

merger

holding company

Chapter 18 Review Questions

1. Why is the corporate form of organization appropriate for life insurance companies? [1]

2. How does management accountability in a stock insurer differ from that in a mutual insurer? [1]

---

35. 393 U.S. 453 (1969).

3. How do stockholders share in an insurance company's surplus? [1]

4. How do policyowners of participating policies share in the insurance company's surplus? [1]

5. How does a stock insurance company become a mutual insurance company?[1]

6. Why would a mutual company desire to demutualize and become a stock insurance company? [1]

7. How do the three alternative approaches to demutualization differ? [1]

8. What licensing or readmission problems might arise when conversion from mutual to stock insurer involves merger or bulk reinsurance arrangements? [1]

9. In addition to commercial companies, what are the other types of nongovernmental providers of life insurance? [2]

10. What governmental agencies offer various forms of life insurance? [2]

11. What four elements should be included in the organizational structure if a firm wishes to attain effective operations? [3]

12. (a) What are the principal responsibilities of a company's board of directors?

    (b) What standing committees are typically established to assist the board in carrying out its responsibilities?

    (c) How do these committees assist the board? [3]

13. What responsibilities do the following levels of authority in an organization typically perform? (a) executive officers; (b) managers; (c) supervisors. [3]

14. What factors affect the number of subordinates one manager can effectively supervise? [3]

15. What are the ways that insurance company organizations have traditionally been structured? [3]

16. a. What are the functional departments typically found in insurance companies organized on the functional basis?

    b. What are the activities undertaken in these functional departments? [3]

17. What are the differences between friendly and hostile takeovers? [3]

18. a. What are the steps in completing a merger between two or more insurance companies?

    b. What are the possible advantages resulting from a merger? [3]

19. a. How do downstream holding company systems differ from upstream holding company systems?

    b. What two trends led to an increased use of holding companies in the insurance industry? [3]

20. a. For what reasons did state regulators seek greater regulatory authority over insurance holding companies?

    b. What regulatory control over holding company situations does the model Holding Company Act grant? [3]

21. How does the Holding Company Act affect actions that would result in any person or organization obtaining direct or indirect control of an insurer? [4]

22. What sanctions are available to insurance commissioners to enforce the provisions of a holding company law? [4]

23. What is the role of the federal government in acquisitions and mergers involving holding companies and insurers? [4]

24. What is the Williams Act, and how does it affect insurance regulation involving acquisitions of insurance companies? [4]

25. How do stock and mutual companies often differ regarding the period over which they amortize acquisition expenses? [11]

Chapter 18 Review Answers

1. *The corporate form of organization is the only form of business organization sanctioned by state law to underwrite life insurance because it tends to be more permanent than other alternatives (a corporation's existence continues beyond the death of any or all of its owners).*

2. *The stockholders elect the board of directors that in turn appoints and oversees the management and operation of the company. Although it is not unknown for dissatisfied stockholders to vote to replace board members and thereby change control of the company, because of the number and dispersion of stockholders, direct replacement of the board is very difficult and, therefore, rare. Nevertheless, the investment community constantly monitors management performance. Changes in stock prices, among other things, reflect stockholder views on management performance. If stockholders believe that the performance is poor, they can sell their stock, which drives the share price down and leaves management vulnerable to a hostile takeover. Thus, a stock company's management is under real and constant pressure to generate an acceptable level of earnings that translate into stockholder dividends and increase the value of the stock.*

    The management of a mutual insurer is virtually immune to pressure from policyowners. With no publicly traded ownership interests, the threat of outside takeover is not a factor. Although policyowners have the right to vote for the board of directors, each policyowner is entitled to only one vote, regardless of the number or size of policies he or she owns. Moreover, a collective effort by a diffuse body of policyowners is most difficult; the cost to an individual of organizing a challenge to management will most likely far exceed any possible financial return. Consequently, the mutual insurers' directors and management wield control that is virtually unhindered by the exercise of the policyowner's right to vote. Nevertheless, they must be cognizant of policyowner interests to be successful.

3. *Stockholders share in the insurer's surplus either through liquidation of the company or the payment of stockholder dividends.*

4. *Except through the insurer's possible liquidation or demutualization, an individual policy-owner participates in the surplus via distribution of a policyowner dividend declared by the company's board of directors.*

5. *A stock insurance company becomes a mutual by going through a conversion process called mutualization. In essence, mutualization involves retiring the insurer's outstanding capital stock and transferring control of the insurer to the policyowners. Generally, after the mutualization plan is developed by management and ratified by the board of directors, it must be approved by the insurance commissioner of the insurer's state of domicile, by the stockholders, and by the policyowners in accordance with the provisions of state law. The plan typically establishes a trust to receive the shares from the stockholders. The bulk of the stock is usually turned over to the mutualization trustee promptly after the adoption of the plan. This places control of the insurer in the hands of the trustee until the last shares are received, at which time the stock may be canceled and the insurer is fully mutualized.*

6. *There are several reasons for demutualization:*
    -   *for the ability to raise investment capital more easily*
    -   *for greater flexibility to expand through acquisitions or diversification*
    -   *for availability of additional noncash incentive compensation (for example, stock options and payroll-based stock ownership plans) to attract and retain key officers, directors, and employees*
    -   *for conversion to a stock company might result in tax savings due to the shifting of more of the industry's federal tax burden to the mutual company by the Deficit Reduction Act of 1984*

7. *Although the steps in the process are similar, the three alternative approaches to demutu-alization differ as follows:*
    -   *The pure conversion approach involves amending the mutual insurer's articles of incorporation to reorganize the company from a mutual to a stock form of organization.*
    -   *To effect demutualization through a statutory merger, the mutual insurer organizes or purchases a stock company, the two companies merge, and the stock company is the survivor. The mutual company, therefore, ceases to exist.*
    -   *Under the bulk reinsurance approach, the mutual insurer cedes all of its insurance business and transfers all of its assets and liabilities to a stock insurer the mutual*

company has organized or acquired. After the transaction, the mutual insurer is dissolved.

8. *If the conversion is by a merger or bulk reinsurance arrangement, the following very diffi-cult practical licensing and readmission problems could arise if the surviving stock com-pany is not licensed to do insurance business in the states where the mutual insurer has been licensed.*

   - *Many states require the surviving stock company to file for admission to do business in that state, submit all of its policy forms, pay all fees, and make all statutory deposits required of new foreign insurers, which takes time and may delay the stock company's ability to do business in many states.*

   - *Many states impose a "seasoning" requirement on insurers. An insurer applying for admission to do business in the state must have been actively engaged in the business of insurance for a specified period (typically 3 years). If the surviving stock company is newly created and lacks previous operating experience, it may be unable to obtain a license to do business until after the seasoning period.*

9. *Although most life insurance in the United States is written by commercial companies, there are other nongovernmental providers of life insurance, including fraternal benefit societies, assessment societies, and savings banks.*

10. *Governmental agencies that offer various forms of life insurance protection include the Department of Veterans Affairs, the Social Security Administration, and the State of Wisconsin.*

11. *Effective operations require the organizational structure of the firm to include these four elements:*

    - *clear allocation of responsibility*

    - *clear delegation of the authority to carry out the responsibilities allocated*

    - *accountability for the good or poor performance of responsibilities*

    - *coordination of activities to achieve company goals*

12. *a.* *The board establishes corporate policy, appoints the chief executive officer and other executives of the company, delegates to them whatever authority and responsi-bilities it deems appropriate, holds them accountable for the performance of their*

responsibilities, evaluates company results and finances, fosters long-range planning, authorizes major transactions such as acquisitions or mergers, and declares dividends.

b. Board committees commonly include the executive committee (sometimes called the insurance committee), the investment committee (sometimes referred to as the finance committee), the audit committee, the tax committee, and sometimes a claims committee.

c. To facilitate the exercise of its responsibilities and maintain closer and more frequent contact with key company operations, the board is usually divided into a number of standing committees. Committees handle whatever actions need to be taken between board meetings. The committees report to the board.

13. a. Although the board has the highest level of authority, it vests broad administrative authority over the company in a chief executive officer (CEO), typically the president or chairman of the board. The CEO is primarily responsible for the selection, termination, and supervision of his or her subordinate officers and department heads. The executive officers, usually vice presidents or senior vice presidents, report to the CEO and are responsible for carrying out company policies and general company management. In addition to serving on board committees and being part of the executive management team, executive officers usually have authority over a major division of company operations.

b. Company managers focus on a particular phase of the company's activities, rather than on the operations of the insurer as a whole or a board division of the company. These officers are responsible for translating company policy into plans for day-to-day operations and making decisions on matters within the scope of authority delegated to them.

c. Supervisors manage the daily activities of subdivisions in various departments, directly supervise nonmanagement employees, and implement their manager's plans.

14. The people a manager directly supervises represent the manager's span of control. The number of subordinates one manager can effectively supervise depends on a variety of factors. The simpler and more repetitive the tasks, the more people a manager can supervise easily. The greater the skills and competence of the manager and his or her subordinates, the broader the span of control the manager can handle. The higher the rate of turnover among subordinates (and, therefore, the need for more training) and the more widely dispersed subordinates are, the narrower the span of the manager's control.

15. *Traditionally, life insurers have been organized on a functional, product, or geographical basis, or a combination of these organizational formats. In recent years, other forms of organization have emerged. Some insurers now organize their activities around profit centers-segments of the company that control their own revenues and expenses and make their own decisions about operations.*

16. *a. and b. The typical functional departments and their activities are*

   • *The marketing agency department is responsible for the sale of new business; the conservation of existing business; the provision of field services to policyowners; the supervision of the activities of the insurer's field force; the recruitment, selection, and of training agents; and the conducting of market analysis, advertising, and sales promotions. It also works with the actuarial and legal departments to develop new products, policy forms, and agent company contracts.*

   • *The primary responsibility of the actuarial department is to see that the company's insurance operations are conducted on a sound financial basis. This includes the appropriate premium rates and establishing adequate policy reserves; determination of the development of new policies and forms; the analysis of earnings; the provision of statistical data from which the annual dividend scale is established; and the conducting of mortality, lapse, and other studies. Actuaries also typically participate in corporate strategic planning.*

   • *The underwriting department establishes standards for the acceptance or rejection of applicants for insurance and for applying these standards to ensure that the actual mortality the company experiences does not exceed that assumed in calculating the premium rates. The home office underwriting department collaborates with medical and actuarial personnel is establishing general underwriting standards, is responsible for communicating matters concerning the selection of risks to the field force, and may be responsible for negotiating and managing reinsurance agreements.*

   • *The customer or policyowner services department furnishes home services to the insurer's field force and to customers, including policyowners, beneficiaries, and employees.*

   • *The claim administration department processes the claims against the company. Claim examiners review the claims filed by policyowners or beneficiaries, verify their validity, and authorize payments to the proper persons. Claims denied may result in litigation.*

   • *The accounting department establishes, supervises, and maintains the insurer's accounting and control procedures. It maintains the company's general accounting*

records; controls receipts and disbursements; oversees the company's budgeting process; administers the payroll; and performs audits both in the field and in the home office. In conjunction with the actuarial department, the department prepares the financial statements used both internally and submitted to the regulatory agencies. The accounting department is also responsible for matters concerning federal, state, and local taxes. It may, in addition, perform various expense analyses and other statistical operations not undertaken by the actuarial department.

- *The investment department implements the insurer's investment program under policies established by the board of directors and under the supervision of the investment committee.*

- *The legal department is responsible for the insurer's legal matters, including compliance with federal and state laws and regulations, evaluation of current and proposed legislation and regulations affecting the company, providing advice on questionable claims, oversight of litigation, performance of a variety of legal activities relating to the insurer's investment transactions, work with the accounting and auditing department(s) to determine the company's tax obligations, and participation in the development of policy forms, agents' contracts, investment transactions, and other contractual forms used by the company.*

- *The human resources department handles matters concerning the insurer's employees, including the development of company policy on hiring, training, and dismissal of employees; ascertaining appropriate levels of compensation; assuring compliance with federal and state employment laws; and administering employee benefit plans.*

- *The information systems department develops and maintains the company's computer systems; assists other departments in developing or buying the computer systems and software they need to furnish information, maintain records, and administer products; maintains company records in computerized files; provides data for the preparation of financial statements; and conducts analyses of various systems and procedures used throughout the company.*

17. *The acquisition of a company can be friendly or hostile. In a friendly takeover, the acquiring company offers to purchase a company. The company to be purchased agrees to the acquisition and the price for the stock. The board of directors of the company to be acquired approves the offer and publicly recommends to its stockholders that the offer be accepted. The acquisition requires the approval of both the stockholders and the insurance commissioner in each state in which any insurers involved in the acquisition are domiciled.*

The Securities and Exchange Commission (SEC) and the antitrust authorities may also be involved.

A hostile takeover occurs when the acquirer proceeds with a takeover even though the board of directors of the company to be acquired (the target company) refuses the acquisition offer. To obtain a controlling interest, the acquiring company makes a tender offer—a public offer to purchase the target company's securities directly from the shareholders at a specified price—thereby circumventing the board of directors. Under the federal securities laws, the company making the tender offer files information with the SEC about the reasons for the acquisition, any plans to liquidate the target company or sell a major portion of its assets, and the source of funds for the acquisition. The acquirer then publicly announces the offer to purchase the target's stock at a specified price, usually significantly in excess of the market value of the stock. If the takeover succeeds, the acquiring company obtains control, can elect a new board of directors, and can decide on management policy.

18. a.   *A merger between two or more insurance companies involves several steps:*

- *First, potential merger partners must be found and evaluated.*

- *Then the boards of directors must approve the plan of merger, typically by a two-thirds majority vote of the stockholders or, if a mutual company, by two-thirds of the policyowners.*

- *Stockholders who disapprove must be paid a fair market value for the forced surrender of their stock if the merger actually occurs.*

- *The state insurance regulatory authorities in the insurer(s)' domiciliary state(s) must also approve the merger.*

- *The final merger document must be filed in the new or surviving company's state of domicile and a new or amended certificate of incorporation must be obtained.*

- *The merging companies' assets and liabilities must be transferred to the new or surviving company.*

- *Finally, the new or surviving company must obtain licenses in all states where it does business.*

b.   *The advantages of a merger depend on the circumstances.*

- *An insurer in weakened financial condition may seek a stronger partner to help the insurer overcome its financial difficulties or gain access to additional surplus to fund expansion and growth.*

- *An insurer that has decided to offer new products or services may determine that it would be more feasible to merge with an existing company that already offers those products and/or services than to expend the time and money to develop them itself.*

- *An insurer that wants to expand into new geographical areas may find that joining an insurer already licensed and marketing in those areas is a more rapid and economical mode of expansion.*

- *Because unit costs decrease as the size of operations increases, a merger is also attractive to a company that wants to reduce the price of its products and increase profits through economies of scale.*

c.   *Large and growing companies often attract both security-minded customers and high-quality management and other personnel.*

19. a.   *A mutual insurer (or a stock insurer if it so chooses) can become involved in a downstream holding company system by creating or acquiring subsidiaries, perhaps*

including a downstream holding company, which, in turn, can acquire other enterprises as subsidiaries. The mutual insurer sits atop the holding company structure. A downstream holding company has fewer insurance regulatory concerns because the parent insurer, which continues to control its own destiny, as well as that of any subsidiaries acquired downstream, remains directly subject to insurance regulatory control.

By contrast, there are upstream holding company systems in which the holding company acquires the insurer's stock. Stock insurers tend to become involved in upstream holding company systems in one of two ways. First, a stock insurer can organize an upstream noninsurance holding company that sits atop the intercorporate structure. Second, a stock insurer can become involved, either voluntarily or involuntarily, in an upstream holding company system by being acquired by an outside company that becomes the insurer's upstream holding company.

b.   *Two trends that led to an increased use of holding companies in the insurance industry are:*

- *To improve earnings and long-term growth, many insurers sought to diversify by venturing into new lines of insurance or into noninsurance enterprises. Several life insurers found that forming a holding company system gave them greater ability to diversify their services and products, imposed fewer restrictions on their investments, and enhanced their capital-raising flexibility.*

- *Several life insurers were taken over by other insurers or noninsurance company acquirers and, thus, became part of a conglomerate (a group of unrelated businesses under the control of a holding company).*

20. *State regulators sought greater regulatory authority over insurance holding companies for the following reasons:*

- *The rash of insurance company takeovers—many of them hostile—in the late 1960s usually involved tender offers, which enabled the acquiring company to avoid dealing directly with the target company's resistant management. These tender offers were essentially unregulated.*

- *When affiliations of insurers with noninsurance companies pursuing different interests began to occur, they often gave control of the insurers to noninsurance parents outside of insurance regulatory control.*

- *Noninsurance holding companies that lacked insurance experience, focus, and orientation toward safeguarding policyowner interests started to acquire and control stock insurers. Actual and potential abuses in these affiliations included rapacious acquirers*

looting insurers' assets, raiding insurer surplus to finance either the holding company itself or the operations of other holding company subsidiaries, subtle threats to insurer solvency, and circumvention of various state requirements enacted to protect the insurance-buying public.

21. *To exercise control over holding company situations, the model act (1) facilitates insurer diversification, (2) requires disclosure of relevant information relating to changes in the insurer's control and commissioner approval of such changes, (3) requires insurer disclosure of material transactions and relationships between the insurer and its affiliates, including certain dividends distributed by the insurer, and (4) establishes standards governing material transactions between the insurer and its affiliates.*

22. *The commissioner has a host of sanctions with which to enforce the act, including monetary penalties and recoveries, cease-and-desist orders, and license revocation. Furthermore, if it appears that any insurer or any director, officer, employee, or agent willfully violated the act, the commissioner may cause criminal proceedings to be instituted. The insurer is subject to dollar penalties; individuals are subject to fines, and if fraud is involved, imprisonment. If violations of the act threaten a domestic insurer's solvency or make further transaction of business hazardous to policyowners, the commissioner may proceed under the state's rehabilitation and liquidation law. If the commissioner believes a violation makes the continued operation of an out-of-state insurer contrary to policyowner interest, after a hearing, he or she may suspend or revoke the insurer's license to do business.*

23. *Federal antitrust law seeks to prohibit anticompetitive acquisitions and mergers. The potential for applying the federal antitrust law (the Sherman Act and Section 7 of the Clayton Act) to insurance company acquisitions and mergers has become a fact of life. Unless Congress acts in some way to change the existing balance, dual assertion of federal antitrust law and state insurance acquisition and merger regulatory authority promises to continue in the years ahead.*

24. *In 1968, Congress enacted the Williams Act as an amendment to the Securities Exchange Act of 1934. The act, whose central philosophy is disclosure, was designed to handle an existing deficiency in the disclosure of information to investors encountered with the emergence of the tender-offer technique. Among other things, the act requires that upon the commencement of a tender offer, the offeror must file pertinent information with the SEC and provide such information to the target company's shareholders and management. All*

shares tendered must be purchased at the same price. The offer commences at the time of the first public announcement, and it must remain open for at least 20 days.

In 1970, the Williams Act was made applicable to insurance securities. Congress believes that the act strikes a fair balance between the party making the takeover bid and the management of the target company by enabling both to present their cases to the shareholders. More important, compelling timely, full, and fair disclosure puts the shareholders in a position to make informed decisions.

25. Stock companies usually amortize their first-year expenses over a shorter period than do mutual insurers.

Financial Statements

Revised by: C.W. Copeland & Harry D. Garber

Learning Objectives

An understanding of the material in this chapter should enable the student to

1. **Identify the key audiences that use life insurance company financial statements and explain each user group's interest and objectives.**

2. **Describe the purpose of, and the information presented in, the statement of financial position (balance sheet), the income statement, and the statement of cash flows.**

3. **Explain the differences in statutory accounting's SAP and general GAAP accountings emphasis and focus.**

4. **Explain the principal differences between statutory accounting practices and GAAP.**

5. **Describe the differences in the form of presentation in statutory and GAAP financial statements.**

Securities and Exchange Commission (SEC)

Life insurance company financial statements have evolved to meet the needs of its various audiences. To understand the structure and content of these statements, a good place to start is with the needs and goals of these audiences. They include investors, the **Securities and Exchange Commission (SEC),** state insurance regulators, creditors, security analysts, rating agencies, policyowners, company management, and agents and employees of the company. Each of these audiences has different interests, and the financial statements for each audience have different objectives. Not unexpectedly, the objectives overlap in many respects.

CONSIDERATIONS IN LIFE INSURANCE COMPANY ACCOUNTING

Let's consider the interests and objectives of each of these distinct audiences.

Users of Life Insurance Company Financial Statements

Investors are interested in the current level of and the prospective growth in the earnings of public companies in order to value these companies for investment purposes. Because

investments can be made in debt instruments (for example, bonds) and in equity securities (for example, common or preferred stock), investors are also interested in an enterprise's current and prospective financial strength.

The Securities and Exchange Commission (SEC) seeks to ensure that the financial statements and accounting rules used by publicly held companies, including stock life insurance companies, provide investors and other users with the required level of information. Fair and consistent presentation across industries is the norm; however, certain industries, such as insurance, have requirements tailored to their unique characteristics.

State insurance regulators are principally interested in the ability of the life insurance companies that operate in their jurisdictions to meet current and future obligations to policyowners and owners of other contracts with the insurer. This means that the regulators' focus is on the near-term and long-term financial safety and solvency of the company. To this end, they seek to assure that the financial statements filed by life insurance companies are based on conservative accounting principles and practices.

Creditors are interested in the likelihood that the amounts owed to them will be paid. Creditors include bondholders and suppliers of equipment and services to the life insurance company. Creditors whose obligations are due currently need information on the company's current liquidity position and/or its expected near-term cash flow from operations. This information, however, is rarely available in a timely fashion from the company's financial statements. Long-term bondholders are interested in assessing the ability of the life insurance company (or its parent company) to pay bond interest and principal due in the future. Although published financial statements can provide some of this information, these creditors usually require additional information not unlike that provided to the rating agencies described below.

Security analysts are an audience with similar but more expansive information requirements than investors. Although large corporate and mutual fund investment managers do their own research using financial statements and other public and private information available about a company, individual investors often rely heavily on the analyses and recommendations of the leading brokerage and investment banking firms' industry security analysts.

Rating agencies are another audience for life insurance company financial statements. Their focus is the company's present financial position and how it may evolve in the future. It is important to these rating agencies that financial statements of companies in an industry be comparable and provide consistent results over the years. Because the principal agencies (A. M. Best, Standard and Poors, Duff and Phelps, and Moody's) depend

mostly on their own in-depth data-gathering visits and interviews with the company's senior management, their needs for information do not impose additional requirements on the structure or content of the life insurance company's published financial statements. Other rating services, which depend almost entirely on published financial statements and other publicly available information, may find their analytical capability and the quality of their ratings limited by the information contained in these sources.

Policyowners and prospective policyowners are primarily concerned with two aspects of a company's position and performance. One is the company's ability to meet its benefit guarantees to policyowners; the second is the company's performance in those areas that will affect future charges to policyowners for insurance coverage. Key performance areas include investment income, mortality costs, expenses, and persistency. Policyowner interest is most acute at the time of purchasing an insurance contract (which often involves comparisons among several companies), but this interest may continue throughout the lifetime of a contract. A life insurance company's policyowners therefore are interested in financial statements that permit them to assess the company's safety and solvency and to compare the current levels and trends of the company's performance in the areas that affect policyowner costs (investment income, mortality, expenses, and persistency) with those of other companies. Businesses, particularly those acting in a fiduciary or quasi-fiduciary capacity as policyowners or sponsors of 401(k) or other benefit plans, have an obligation to deal only with insurance companies with unquestionable positions of safety and solvency.

Members of the insurance company management, as well as the company's board of directors, are interested in having financial statements that fairly portray the company's financial position and progress, particularly as they relate to its principal life insurance competitors. The financial statement should not only fairly measure the results of an individual company's operations but should also ensure comparability among companies. In particular, measurements of current year earnings should neither favor nor disfavor companies that are making investments in capacity or growth for future profits versus companies that are profiting largely from past investments. If financial statements do not recognize the appropriate value of investments in capacity or growth, companies may focus too much on short-term actions to the detriment of long-term performance.

Agents and employees share the interests of company management, policyowners, and in the case of stock companies, shareholders. As representatives of the company, their most immediate concern is that financial statements accurately inform policyowners about operational results and financial strength. Agents, in particular, must advise clients and respond to clients' questions on issues of company safety and solvency and on policy funding

adequacy. Very often, the agent's advice and counsel must be given in competition with other agents and brokers, placing greater intensity and focus on these issues.

In addition to the different perspectives of the several audiences described above, the structure of life insurance company financial statements is shaped by the nature of the business the company conducts. Most contracts issued by life insurance companies involve long-term commitments. Policy accumulations are invested for long periods of time, and many contracts remain in force for decades. Because the company's actual financial results for each block of contracts can be determined only after it has run its full course, measuring financial results on in-force contracts often depends as much on the assumptions and accounting conventions used as it does on cash receipts and payments (premiums received, investment income received, death claims and surrender values paid, and expenses paid). This factor shapes life insurance company financial statements as much or more than the goals and objectives of the various audiences for these statements.

The remainder of this chapter describes the structure and content of life insurance companies' published financial statements. It will become clear that these statements largely, but not fully, satisfy the objectives of certain of these audiences and leave others largely unfulfilled. Despite the significant expansion in the amount of information provided in financial statements in recent years, no statement (or set of statements) can economically meet all needs. As indicated above, the shortfalls in the ability of financial statements to meet the objectives of a particular audience can sometimes be bridged by additional information or in-depth visits, but this is not always practical.

Various User Groups of Life Insurance Financial Statements

- Investors

- SEC

- Insurance regulators

- Creditors

- Security analysts

- Rating agencies

- Policy owners

- Agents and employees

Form and Composition of Life Insurance Company

Financial Accounting Standards Board (FASB)

Financial statements are a primary means for a life insurance company, or for that matter any enterprise, to communicate information to the audiences described earlier. In one of its financial accounting concepts statements, the **Financial Accounting Standards Board (FASB)** identified three objectives of financial reporting. These are paraphrased below:

- to provide information that is both useful and comprehensible to audiences in making rational investment, credit, and similar decisions

- to provide information that is helpful in assessing the amounts, timing, and uncertainty of prospective cash receipts from sales of products or services and from investments (dividends, interest, and sales or redemption of securities)

- to provide information about a company's economic resources (assets), claims on those resources (liabilities), and the effects of transactions, events, and circumstances that change those resources and claims

Financial statements have evolved over time strongly inluenced by the Financial Accounting Standards Board (FASB) and now encompass many reports, schedules, exhibits, and explanations. The three most common and significant reports are as follows:

- statement of financial position

- income statement

- statement of cash flows

Statement of Financial Position

balance sheet

The statement of financial position, more commonly called the **balance sheet**, lists the company's assets, liabilities, and its equity position at the end of the fiscal period. Comparable balance sheet numbers are also shown for one or 2 prior years. (For life insurance companies, the calendar year is the fiscal year; the statement date is December 31 of that year.)

Assets are economic resources that the company owns or controls. Assets include cash, investments (stocks, bonds, mortgages, and real estate), real property used in the business (buildings, parking lots, and so on), and premiums and other amounts receivable from customers. There are events or transactions that can cause a change in the value of an asset

that a life insurance company holds. For example, the market price of a common stock can go up (or down) and can increase (or decrease) the value of the company's investment in that stock relative to its original cost. Similarly, in the case of the investment-income-receivable asset, experience has shown that the amount due and accrued will not always be collected, particularly if the business is behind in its payments. Therefore, total investment income due and accrued will be reduced by an estimate of the amount that will not be received to determine the appropriate asset value.

Certain assets, such as buildings, furniture, computers, and equipment, are usually worth less as they age. For financial reporting purposes, a useful life is determined for each such asset or asset class and the cost of the asset is written off or depreciated over its productive years. Depreciation is an expense in the income statement and a reduction in the asset's carrying value. Over time, the cumulative amount of depreciation for an asset grows until, at the end of its useful life, the statement or book value of the asset is reduced to zero (or some residual or salvage value if resale is possible). When applied to intangible assets such as goodwill, the term amortization is used to describe a similar process.

Liabilities, on the other hand, are obligations to transfer assets or to provide services to others: policyowners and contract owners, creditors, employees, suppliers, or taxing authorities. Liabilities include such items as policyowners' account balances and future benefits payable, short- and long-term debt, dividends not yet paid to policyowners and/or shareholders, and taxes payable.

In the insurance industry, the terms liability and reserve are often used interchangeably. However, these terms have distinctly different meanings in other accounting contexts and for other industries. For example, policy reserves (discussed in detail in chapter 12) are liabilities. The allowances for uncollectible investment income mentioned above are often called reserves, but they are classified with and used to reduce assets.

Equity is, very simply, the difference between assets and liabilities. A company's equity is the book measurement of the ownership interest. The insurer's own common and nonredeemable preferred stock, the related paid-in capital, and its retained earnings/surplus are typical components of equity.

Equity is increased when the owners of a business make additional investments in the company or when a company's net earnings are retained in the business instead of being returned to the owners as dividends. Equity is decreased when a company has a net loss from operations, pays dividends to shareholders, or otherwise returns assets to its owners.

asset valuation reserve (AVR)

The distinction between liabilities and equity is not always clear. For example, redeemable preferred stock has characteristics of both debt and equity. The **asset valuation reserve (AVR)** is reported as a liability in the annual statements filed with state regulators, but it is often treated as equity. (The asset valuation reserve (AVR) is discussed more fully later in this chapter.)

Income Statement

income statement

Unlike the statement of financial position, which presents the company's position on the date of the statement, the **income statement** (which is also referred to as the statement of operations, or statement of earnings) presents the company's revenues, expenses, and earnings (losses) for the accounting period specified (a fiscal year or a fraction thereof). Earnings serve to build the company's equity and, in the case of stock companies, to provide the funds for distribution as dividends to shareholders. Year-to-year trends in a company's earnings, which are usually expressed as earnings per share of stock outstanding, are a principal factor affecting the stock market's evaluation of the value (price) of the company's stock.

Revenues are inflows of cash or other assets that result from an enterprise's business operations and are reported on the income statement. In the case of a life insurance company, major sources of revenue include premiums and other contract charges and income from its investments. Expenses, on the other hand, are outflows or other uses of assets (or incurred liabilities) required to provide products and services to a company's clients. Benefits paid to policyowners or contract owners, salaries, commissions, employee benefits, and taxes are a few of the more significant expenses life insurers report in the income statement.

In financial reports, a distinction is drawn between revenues and expenses from the insurance company's normal ongoing business activities and its gains and losses. One distinguishing characteristic of gains and losses is that they are usually the direct result of specific management actions. For example, when an investment is sold, the difference between the amount the company receives and the current carrying value of the investment represents a gain or loss. Similarly, the discontinuance or sale of a business may produce a gain or loss. Security analysts tend to treat gains and losses differently from (and place less importance on) income from regular business operations in evaluating a company's economic performance.

Statement of Cash Flows

In addition to the balance sheet and income statement, a life insurance company's financial statement contains a cash flow statement and supplementary material that provides additional details regarding the balance sheet and income statements. The cash flow statement and the supplementary material will be discussed in greater detail in a later section of this chapter.

GAAP and Statutory Financial Statements: Approaches

Although the goals and objectives of the several audiences for life insurance company financial statements are now well understood, this was not always the case. Life insurance company statements have evolved in form and content as these audiences have grown in influence and their requirements have become more clearly defined and articulated.

Statutory Accounting and Reporting

Until the 1960s, state regulators were the only group with a substantial interest in life insurance companies' published financial statements. There were few major stock life insurance companies and limited investor interest in such companies. The Accounting Principles Board, the predecessor of today's Financial Accounting Standards Board, had just come into being in September 1959 and would not issue its first opinion until 1962. There had been no major life insurance company insolvencies since the Great Depression, and most individual life insurance was sold in situations in which there was little policyowner concern about insurer safety and solvency and, given the relatively low level of price competition, whether the company's illustrations of future policy performance would be realized.

statutory accounting practices (SAP)

In this environment, the state insurance departments defined the contents of the only published financial statements for life insurance companies. The statutory financial statements they prescribed, commonly called the NAIC blank or the "blue blank" (because of the color of its cover), must still be filed by life insurance companies in each state in which they are licensed to do business. The statutory statement places primary emphasis on solvency and stability. As a result, this statement focuses principally on the balance sheet. The **statutory accounting practices (SAP)** are a form of liquidation-basis accounting—that is, accounting as if the insurer is expected to cease operations in an orderly fashion in the near future. SAP tends to value both assets and liabilities conservatively. Some of the traditional statutory accounting practices include immediately charging furniture and equipment purchases directly against surplus, immediately expensing all costs (including policy

and contract acquisition costs), and computing policy reserves on the basis of conservative (low) interest rates. The effect of this emphasis on the balance sheet is a lessening of the value of the income statement as a source of information and dependable trends.

Statutory accounting and reporting requirements are established by each state's legislature, which enacts the insurance laws and authorizes the regulations that govern insurance companies in that state. The state insurance department, headed by an insurance commissioner, interprets and enforces the prescribed statutory requirements. A life insurance company must comply with the requirements in each state in which it does business. Even though each state independently enacts its individual body of law, much similarity exists because of the influence of the National Association of Insurance Commissioners (NAIC), an organization made up of state insurance department regulators.

Those Influencing Statutory Accounting

- NAIC
- State legislators
- Insurance commissioners
- FASB

NAIC blanks

The NAIC helps to promote uniformity among the states. Model laws and regulations are developed by the NAIC that each state is then encouraged to pass. The NAIC has also codified statutory accounting practices into policy manuals and produces an annual statement guide that covers the information to be included in every report, schedule, and exhibit that make up the **NAIC blanks.** The NAIC blank is mandated for both stock and mutual life insurance companies.

generally accepted accounting practices (GAAP)

Until the advent of **generally accepted accounting practices (GAAP),** many life insurance companies also published a condensed version of the statutory financial statement to include in the company's annual report. Mutual life companies produce such statutory statements to this day. This condensed statement, while still compiled in accordance with statutory accounting practices, more closely resembled the traditional financial statement found in the annual reports of noninsurance enterprises which report using generally accepted accounting practices. However, while the balance sheets and income statements of life insurance companies looked similar to those of noninsurance enterprises, the

numbers were based on two separate and distinct accounting methodologies. Uniformity in the underlying accounting policies and procedures used by insurers was needed to achieve comparable financial statements.

GAAP Accounting and Reporting

During the 1960s, investors showed an increased interest in life insurance companies as potential investments. At the same time, analysts' frustration with the statutory financial statements was growing. The accounting practice that required acquisition costs to be written off immediately tended to tint the income statements of fast-growing companies negatively. As a result, security analysts developed several different rule-of-thumb adjustments to the statutory operating statements and used the "adjusted" income to advise investors in purchases and sales of life insurance company stock.

It soon became clear to the SEC and the American Institute of Certified Public Accountants (AICPA) that an environment in which state insurance regulators established accounting rules for life insurance companies and analysts developed different techniques for adjusting the resulting income statements for investment recommendations was not healthy. Investors needed a more controlled, standardized information flow. The AICPA was asked to develop an accounting structure for life insurance companies that would be in accord with the set of GAAP developed for other types of enterprises. This effort was completed in the early 1970s.

The GAAP statement seeks the best possible measure of a company's past performance to provide users (investors, creditors, company managements, rating agencies, and so forth) with information to evaluate potential future performance. The focus of GAAP reporting is on the income statement and the statement of cash flows and on making the results of operations between periods easy to compare.

The underlying accounting principle influencing GAAP is to match income and expense so that profits emerge over the lifetime of a life insurance policy in a pattern that is more reasonably related to the policy margins than the profits would have been if all costs had been charged off in the year of sale, as they are under SAP. (Some FASB and SEC actions in the early 1990s diluted the focus on the income statement to some degree but did not disturb the essential nature of GAAP for life insurance companies.)

GAAP accounting standards usually apply to all United States business enterprises and to foreign operations that have United States filing requirements. In some instances, special guidance is developed on an industry-wide basis; the insurance industry is a case in point.

The authoritative accounting pronouncements that, taken as a whole, make up GAAP have been developed and enforced by three bodies. Like its predecessors, FASB has been the principal GAAP-standard-setting body since 1973. The AICPA, through its statements of position, accounting and auditing guides, and similar technical services, interprets existing GAAP. Finally, the SEC continues to affect GAAP through its direct and indirect influence on FASB, its own codified accounting and reporting policies, and case-by-case actions on the accounting practices used by companies seeking approval of registration statements.

During the development of the GAAP accounting structure for life insurers, there was a split between the mutual and stock segments of the industry. The mutual segment argued that GAAP accounting was not required for mutual companies, which were not investor-owned, and that the proposed GAAP treatment of policy dividends as a policy benefit was not in accord with mutual company dividend practices.

The mutual companies were successful in convincing the SEC and the other standard-setting organizations that the new GAAP structure should not be applied to them. As a result, stock companies have prepared both statutory and GAAP financial statements since 1973, while mutual companies at that time issued only statutory financial statements.

Over the years, mutual companies have been required to file more financial statements with the SEC, frequently because of an increasing amount of separate account activity and various kinds of asset-based financings and public debt offerings. The noncomparability of the mutual company's statutory financial statements and the stock company's GAAP financial statements was, in the view of the SEC, a concern.

Therefore, the exemption for mutual insurers was examined and FASB was asked to develop and implement a GAAP structure for mutual life insurance companies, which has not been implemented since 2012.

Those Influencing GAAP Accounting
• AICPA
• SEC
• FASB

LIFE INSURANCE COMPANY FINANCIAL STATEMENTS

Substantive GAAP/Statutory Differences

Some of the principal differences between statutory accounting practices and GAAP are described below.

Deferred Acquisition Costs

Under GAAP, acquisition costs are capitalized and amortized over the life of the book of policies or contracts. These costs can be amortized in proportion to anticipated premiums (in the case of traditional life insurance) or in proportion to estimated gross profits (in the case of deposit-type contracts, such as universal life and deferred annuities). As discussed previously, under statutory accounting practices, these costs are expensed in the year incurred.

Furniture and Equipment and Similar Assets

With GAAP, purchases of furniture, equipment, and similar assets are treated as assets and are depreciated over their useful lives. Under statutory accounting practices, except for computer hardware and related operating systems, these purchases are charged directly against surplus in the year of purchase. The statutory accounting treatment of computer systems purchases is similar to the GAAP treatment.

Federal Taxes

Using statutory accounting practices, federal income taxes are charged as incurred (based on the net taxable income reported in the company's federal income tax returns). Under GAAP, in addition to the charge for federal income taxes incurred, a net deferred tax liability (or asset) is established to recognize the estimated future tax effects of temporary differences between the measurements of revenue and expenses and of assets and liabilities required under the applicable tax laws and the measurements of these items required under GAAP. A deferred tax liability (or the increase in such a liability during a year) increases the federal tax charge against income; the reverse is true for a deferred tax asset.

The effect of the deferred tax approach is to adjust the federal tax charge in the GAAP financial statement so that it is consistent with the pretax revenue and expense and the asset and liability measurements reflected in the GAAP statement, rather than the

comparable measures in the federal income tax return. As an example, if a company uses accelerated real estate depreciation for tax purposes but straight-line depreciation for GAAP statement purposes, a deferred tax liability would be recorded for the excess of accelerated tax depreciation over financial reporting depreciation.

Asset Valuation

Valuation allowances are established under GAAP accounting to adjust asset values for improvements in value deemed to be other than temporary. These valuation allowances reflect the losses that company management expects to realize on the sale or other disposition of the asset, on foreclosure (in the case of mortgage loans), on the borrower's failure to meet scheduled payments, or from shortfalls of cash flows (on investment real estate). The establishment of a valuation allowance or the increase in such an allowance is recorded as a charge to income.

interest maintenance reserve (IMR)

Traditionally, valuation allowances that are part of specific categories of assets have not been established under statutory accounting practices. Instead, an asset valuation reserve is established as a liability. The purposes of the AVR are to absorb both realized and unrealized gains and losses on substantially all invested assets other than policy loans and to serve as a general reserve for possible asset losses. (Gains and losses that are due to changes in the level of interest rates since the date of the investment's acquisition are captured in the **interest maintenance reserve (IMR)**, a companion reserve to the AVR.) Each year the AVR is increased by formula-based contributions and by the realized and unrealized net capital gains on securities, mortgages, and real estate, and it is decreased by the capital losses on these investments. The formula contributions vary depending on the relationship of the AVR balance to the defined maximum level. If the reserve balance is small compared to the defined maximum, a larger annual contribution is required than if the balance is greater than the defined maximum.

Although statutory accounting does not call for the establishment of valuation allowances for individual investments or investment categories, there is a growing trend among companies to establish such allowances and to reduce the carrying values for those assets in their statutory financial statements. Any such reduction in asset value, which would be treated as an unrealized capital loss in statutory accounting, would reduce the company's AVR and would have no current-year effect on the company's earnings or surplus.

One final note on asset valuation: Responding to the savings and loan and bank failures of the late 1980s, in 1993 the SEC and FASB adopted a requirement (FASB 115) that, except in

rare circumstances, securities be carried at market value. This requirement applies only to GAAP financial statements. Insurers and other financial institutions are unhappy about the standard because it forces an insurer's surplus accounts, as the residual balancing account on the balance sheet, to become more volatile.

Policy Reserves

Policy reserves are computed differently under SAP and GAAP. Historically, statutory policy reserves were computed using interest rates, mortality tables, and valuation standards prescribed by state statutes and regulations, while GAAP policy reserves for insurance contracts were computed using interest, mortality, and persistency assumptions established by the company's actuary at policy issue (usually based on the company's own experience). More recent trends in statutory practices have expanded the range of acceptable interest and mortality assumptions, which in turn permit the application of somewhat more actuarial judgment. In addition, the statutory and GAAP approaches to accumulation-type products (for example, universal life and deferred annuities) tend to be similar.

Subsidiaries

Investment in a subsidiary is treated for statutory purposes as a common stock, but the value of the investment is usually based on cost adjustments for the life insurance company's share of income or losses after the date of acquisition. (If the subsidiary is also an insurance company, a statutory measure of income or loss is used.) GAAP requires consolidation (inclusion of the subsidiary on a line-by-line basis) of all majority-owned subsidiaries unless control is likely to be temporary or does not rest with the majority owner. This GAAP accounting practice has the effect of increasing each applicable asset, liability, revenue, and expense measure in the life insurance company's financial statements by the corresponding amounts from the operations of majority-owned subsidiaries.

Nonadmitted Assets

nonadmitted assets

The concept of **nonadmitted assets** applies only to the statutory balance sheet. Under the insurance laws or some state regulations, certain assets or portions thereof are considered to have no value for statutory reporting purposes and are reflected as a direct reduction of surplus.

Example

<u>Nonadmitted Assets</u>

Furniture and equipment, such as computers, are assets, which tend to have very little value when sold at an auction for quick liquidation. It is this focus on liquidation valuation that prompted the creation of the category "nonadmitted assets" required by the insurance regulators.

Special Reserves; Loss Recognition

Statutory accounting practices do not impose significant restraints on the establishment of reserves for specific concerns or contingencies, although sometimes such a reserve must be treated as a designated element of surplus, rather than as a liability. (This is consistent with the focus on achieving a conservative measurement of a company's financial position.) In general, any losses that arise from establishing a special reserve or provision are charged directly against surplus under statutory accounting practices.

Under GAAP, accounting for such a loss contingency can occur only if it is probable that both an asset has been impaired (or a liability has been incurred) and the amount of the loss can be estimated with reasonable accuracy. In contrast to statutory accounting practices, these losses are charged against income in the current year, rather than being charged directly to shareholder equity, and they are reported as a reduction of an asset or as a liability.

Differences in GAAP/Statutory Form

The previous section covered the principal differences between statutory accounting practices and GAAP accounting practices. These are the *substantive* differences between the two different approaches to life insurance financial reporting. In addition to these, there are also differences in the form of presentation of statutory and GAAP financial statements.

The basic statutory financial statement (the so-called "blue blank") has the three basic statement forms (a balance sheet, an income statement, and a cash flow statement) plus a large set of supplementary exhibits, schedules, and notes. The form of this package, which is prescribed in precise detail by the NAIC, tends to be specific to life insurance companies, quite detailed, and resistant to change. (This resistance to change is evident in the new lines, new pages, and new exhibits or schedules that are added instead of reformatting or eliminating existing material.) The GAAP financial statement is also composed of the three basic statement forms, plus a set of explanatory notes. Compared with the blue blank, however, the form of this package is much less oriented to the life insurance industry,

has much less detail, and permits more tailoring of the notes to a company's specific circumstances.

Each stock company prepares a statutory financial statement and a GAAP financial statement. A mutual company must prepare a statutory financial statement, and some also prepare a hybrid type of statement using the GAAP format and statutory numbers. This hybrid statement permits clearer public communication, and it is used, for example, in annual corporate reports, and sales prospectuses.

To highlight the differences between SAP and GAAP, the illustrative balance sheets in Table 19-1 and the income statements in Table 19-2 (in the illustrative income statements section later in this chapter) compare the GAAP numbers for a hypothetical company with the statutory numbers in a hybrid format.

Illustrative Balance Sheets

The following table presents illustrative GAAP and statutory (hybrid format) balance sheets for a hypothetical life insurance company. The text that follows describes each of the main entries on that balance sheet, along with the reasons for differences between the GAAP and statutory amounts.

The illustration in the table is for a large stock life insurance company without a downstream, majority-owned, noninsurance subsidiary. As explained earlier, under GAAP reporting, such a subsidiary would have to have been consolidated on a line-by-line basis, with a resulting distortion of the GAAP-statutory comparisons for the life insurance company being illustrated.

Table 19-1
Balance Sheet (Statement of Financial Position-Amounts in $ Millions)

	GAAP	Statutory (Hybrid Format)
Assets		
Investments		
Fixed maturities	17,470	18,000
Equity securities	400	400
Mortgage loans	12,390	12,690
Real estate	1,330	1,200
Policy loans	3,400	3,400
Short-term investments	150	150
Other invested assets	2,465	2,300
Total investments	37,605	38,140
Cash and cash equivalents	765	385
Deferred policy acquisition costs	3,100	
Accrued investment income	550	575
Premiums and other receivables	90	330
Property and equipment	140	20
Other assets	350	415
Separate account assets	17,600	17,300
Total assets	60,200	57,165
Liabilities		
Policyowners' account balances	24,400	34,660
Future policy benefits	11,875	1,800
Other policyowners' funds	800	350
Policyowners' dividends payable	200	5
Short-term debt	5	260
Long-term debt	1,060	
Federal income taxes payable	210	210
Current	350	
Deferred	900	500
Other liabilities	17,500	17,200
Separate account liabilities		
Total liabilities	57,300	54,985

Table 19-1 Balance Sheet (Statement of Financial Position-Amounts in $ Millions)		
Commitments and Contingencies Asset valuation reserve (AVR)		580
Shareholders' Equity (Surplus)		
Common stock	5	5
Capital in excess of par	445	445
Retained earnings	2,375	
Surplus		
Special surplus fund		80
Unassigned surplus		1,070
Net unrealized investment gains	75	
Total shareholders' equity	2,900	1,600
Total Liabilities and Shareholders' Equity	60,200	57,165

Balance Sheet Entries

Fixed-maturity investments consist of publicly traded debt securities, privately placed debt securities, and redeemable preferred stock. Fixed maturities that are intended to be held to maturity are generally carried at amortized cost under GAAP. The difference, if any, between the original cost and the face amount and maturity value of the investment is reduced ratably over the life of the security. When a fixed-maturity investment is purchased at an amount above its face value, that premium is amortized to reduce the value to its final redemption value. The annual amortization of premium is recorded as a reduction of interest income. If a fixed-maturity investment is purchased at an amount below its face value, the discount is accrued each year by increasing the value of the security and the interest income.

Fixed maturities are carried in the annual statutory statements at values determined primarily by the NAIC Valuation of Securities manual; in GAAP statements fixed maturities are generally carried at amortized cost or, if in or near default, at market value. The GAAP carrying values of publicly traded securities are adjusted for sustained impairments in value by actual writedowns; privately traded debt securities generally reflect such adjustments by means of a valuation allowance, although the use of writedowns is also acceptable. The GAAP and statutory amounts may differ because of differences between the NAIC values and the company's estimates of value, and either amount might be larger.

equity securities

Equity securities consist primarily of common stocks and nonredeemable preferred stocks. Under statutory accounting, equity securities are reported at the values published in the NAIC Valuation of Securities manual, which is the NAIC market-value determination for each stock. For GAAP, common and nonredeemable preferred stocks are reported at market; temporary changes in those securities' market value are recognized as unrealized gains or losses in shareholder equity. Equity securities include investments in subsidiaries that, for statutory purposes, are usually reported on the equity basis (that is, cost adjusted for the company's share of income or losses after the date of acquisition). GAAP requires consolidation (including the subsidiary on a line-by-line basis) of majority-owned subsidiaries. This has the effect for GAAP of increasing the corresponding assets, liabilities, revenues, and expense line items and reducing the equity securities amount. In general, except for companies with consolidated subsidiaries, the GAAP and statutory amounts for this line should be very close.

Mortgage loans on real estate are generally reported under SAP at the unpaid principal balances, net of unamortized premiums or discounts. Premium amortization or discount accrual on mortgage loans is spread over the life of the loan in a manner similar to that for fixed maturities. Under GAAP, mortgage loans are similarly reported, less an allowance for amounts estimated to be uncollectible. The change in this valuation allowance is reported as a realized investment gain or loss. In general, therefore, the GAAP measure of this asset will be less than the statutory measure.

Real estate reported in the statutory financial statements includes three categories: real estate occupied by the company, investment real estate, and real estate acquired to satisfy debt. Under SAP, real estate occupied by the insurer and investment real estate are carried at cost, less accumulated depreciation and encumbrances (mortgage or other debt related to the property). Real estate acquired when a mortgage loan is foreclosed (not repaid) is valued at the estimated fair value of the property at the time of the acquisition, but it is not valued at more than the unpaid balance of the foreclosed loan.

On a GAAP basis, real estate is classified as either an investment or as real estate used in the insurer's operations (which is treated as property and equipment), depending on its primary use. Real estate investments are reported at cost, less accumulated depreciation and an allowance for impairment of value. Rent earned from real estate is recorded as investment income when earned and reported with related expenses on an accrual basis. Depreciation on real estate is recorded as part of the operating cost of the property. Real estate encumbrances are treated as liabilities.

If there are no encumbrances on owned real estate, the GAAP numbers will tend to be lower (because of the different treatment of real estate used in the company's operations), but this difference may be more than offset by the amount of encumbrances.

Policy loans are loans collateralized by the cash values of the underlying policies and are stated at unpaid principal balances. Policy loans receive the same treatment in statutory and GAAP accounting.

Short-term investments are investments maturing within one year such as commercial paper and money market instruments. They are carried at amortized cost. Short-term investments receive the same treatment in statutory and GAAP accounting.

Other invested assets are invested assets not included in the aforementioned investment categories. The principal investments are real estate joint ventures and partnerships. These assets are valued on an equity basis (cost adjusted for the company's share of income or losses after the date of acquisition). In the absence of real estate encumbrances, the GAAP and statutory amounts should be similar.

Cash and cash equivalents in statutory accounting are limited to monetary items, such as cash, demand deposits, and savings deposits. In GAAP, cash and cash equivalents include monetary items and Treasury bills, commercial paper, money market funds, and federal funds sold. (Federal funds are commercial bank deposits at Federal Reserve Banks. Any excess reserve that one bank maintains on deposit can be lent on an overnight basis to another member bank.) Cash and cash equivalents are valued similarly under statutory and GAAP accounting. The GAAP amount will be larger than the statutory amount if the company holds any of the types of investments treated as cash and cash equivalents by GAAP but not by SAP.

Deferred policy acquisition costs are capitalized and amortized for GAAP reporting. Under statutory accounting, these expenses are charged against income in the year in which they are incurred.

Accrued investment income is income earned but not yet received on investments. It includes interest income on bonds, mortgage loans, policy loans, short-term investments, and dividends declared on common and preferred stock investments. Accrued investment income is treated similarly under statutory and GAAP accounting, and therefore there should be no material differences in this asset amount under the two accounting methods.

Premiums and other receivables are principally premiums due from policyowners but not yet paid by the balance sheet date. In the case of statutory accounting, this entry also includes the net premiums (the premiums determined without provision for expenses) on

traditional life insurance policies and annuity contracts that are due between the statement date and the next policy anniversary. This modification of due premium is necessary because the statutory reserves on these policies are determined on the assumption that the full net annual premium is paid on the policy anniversary. In addition, this line includes fees and policy charges due under universal life and annuity contracts. Because statutory accounting includes an expanded definition of due premiums (to balance the traditional statutory reserve calculation methodology), the statutory amount will be considerably greater than the GAAP amount. (For other types of businesses, statutory and GAAP financial treatment is similar.)

Property and equipment is property owned and occupied by the company, leasehold improvements, furniture and fixtures, and computer equipment. Under GAAP accounting, purchases of property and equipment are treated as assets and are depreciated over their useful lives. Under statutory accounting, except for computer systems, these expenditures are charged directly against surplus in the year of purchase. The statutory accounting treatment for computer systems is similar to the GAAP treatment. Typically, the GAAP amount for property and equipment is much larger than the statutory amount.

Other assets are miscellaneous assets that do not fall into the categories discussed above. These assets have generally comparable accounting treatments. Therefore, the amounts shown in the statutory and GAAP financial reports should be similar if the same assets are used in both reports. There may be some differences, however, because of different definitions for some of the balance sheet entries discussed above. For example, assets under corporate-owned life insurance would be included in this item in statutory reporting but might be classified as investment assets in GAAP.

separate account assets

Separate account assets are segregated from those of the general account for the purpose of funding variable life insurance, variable annuities, pensions, and other benefits. The assets of separate accounts are similar to those of the insurer and may consist of fixed maturities, stocks, short-term investments, mortgages, and real estate. The investments of separate accounts are usually valued based on fair market value.

The assets associated with variable life insurance, variable annuities, and qualified plans are reported separately from the insurance company's general portfolio. Separate account assets are not subject to the restrictions that limit investments in stock and encourage investments in bonds and mortgages. Separate account assets tend to be heavily invested in equities.

Except for real estate encumbrances, which are netted against the related real estate for statutory reporting and treated as a liability for GAAP reporting, separate account assets receive similar treatment in statutory and GAAP reporting. Therefore, these amounts should be the same unless the company has a separate account with leveraged real estate. In that case the GAAP amount will be greater by the amount of the outstanding debt.

Policyowners' account balances and future policy benefits are an insurance company's principal liabilities and represent the reserves established to provide future benefits that will become payable under the provisions of the insurance policies and annuity contracts in force. The GAAP reserves and account balances will ordinarily exceed comparable statutory amounts.

Other policyowners' funds, for statutory reporting, include amounts deposited and accumulated for guaranteed interest contracts, dividends left on deposit (dividend accumulations), and other items of a similar nature. Certain policyowner obligations that are treated as other policyowner funds for statutory reporting are included in policyowner account balances for GAAP, and therefore the GAAP amount for this item will usually be less than the statutory amount. For example, the liability for supplementary contracts without life contingencies is included on this line for statutory reporting and in policyowners' account balances for GAAP reporting.

Policyowners' dividends payable are the company's liability for dividends due but not paid prior to the end of the accounting period, plus a provision for the accrued portion of dividends that will become payable in the following year. For statutory reporting on individual policies, the accrued portion is the full amount of dividends that will be payable in the following calendar year on policies in force at the end of the year. For GAAP reporting on individual policies, the accrued amount is the portion of the dividend that would have accrued since the last policy anniversary if the dividend had accrued evenly over the policy year. (The remainder of the liability is, in effect, a part of the GAAP reserve for future policy benefits.) In these circumstances, the GAAP amount for this item will be less than the statutory amount. For group insurance contracts, the accrued portion of the dividend under both GAAP and statutory reporting is determined for the elapsed portion of the year and is based on the experience of the period.

Short-term and long-term debt represent contractual obligations to pay money on demand or on a fixed or determinable date. For statutory reporting, long-term debt, such as mortgages and other debts on real property, is netted against the related asset. GAAP reports such debt as a liability. Accordingly, the GAAP amount will usually be larger than the statutory amount.

Federal income taxes payable have a current component and, for GAAP only, a deferred component. Current federal income taxes payable are accrued taxes as of the statement date. Deferred taxes, which apply only to GAAP reporting, were discussed in detail earlier in this chapter. Statutory and GAAP reporting methods for current taxes are similar; the only difference should be in reporting the deferred tax item under GAAP.

Other liabilities represent liabilities that are not related to the policyowners, such as general expenses due and accrued, commissions due and accrued, and employee and agent postretirement benefit liabilities. GAAP and SAP treat amounts due and accrued and qualified pension plan liabilities the same way. With respect to other postretirement benefits (for example, pension benefits in excess of the federal qualified plan limits and postretirement life and health insurance benefits), there is a difference between GAAP and statutory reporting. Moreover, in some cases, the statutory reporting is not well defined. The tendency in statutory reporting is to move toward the GAAP model of earlier recognition of these costs. Until this happens, however, the GAAP amount for this liability will usually exceed the statutory amount.

Separate account liabilities consist of the reserves established for the variable life insurance, variable annuities, pensions, and other benefits funded through separate accounts. The reserve amounts vary directly with the investment performance of the separate account assets. The separate account liabilities will generally be smaller than the separate account assets, usually an indication that a portion of the company's surplus is invested in these accounts. The measure of the separate account liabilities under GAAP reporting is larger than the measure under statutory reporting.

The asset valuation reserve is a general purpose investment reserve that is unique to statutory financial reporting. The purpose and basis of this reserve was described earlier.

Commitments and contingencies are items that are not recorded in the financial statements but that do have a risk of loss. A loss contingency may be recognized through a charge to income. Disclosure of the accrual of and sometimes the amount of the loss contingency is necessary. In cases where no amount has been charged to income or the exposure to loss exceeds the amount accrued, additional disclosure of the contingency may be necessary. Commitments and contingencies, including such items as future commitments to lend funds and financial guarantees, are disclosed in the footnotes of both GAAP and statutory financial statements.

Shareholders' equity is common stock, capital in excess of par, and retained earnings/surplus. Common stock represents the par value of the common stock issued; capital in excess of par is the amount in excess of the par value paid for the stock when the stock was first

issued to owners or investors; retained earnings/surplus is the company's accumulated net income or loss, less any shareholder dividends paid. The net unrealized investment gains entry under GAAP represent the unrealized gains (or losses) on certain equity securities that have not been reflected in the financial statements. The difference between GAAP and statutory total shareholder equity amounts is the net effect of all of the differences between these two sets of accounting practices.

Illustrative Income Statements

Table 19-2 shows statutory and GAAP income statements for the same hypothetical company. The following are descriptions of the several lines of the illustrative income statements and the reasons for any differences between the GAAP and statutory amounts.

Table 19-2
Income Statement (Statement of Operations) (Amounts in $ Millions)

	GAAP	Statutory (Hybrid Format)
Revenues		
Premiums	1,725	5,075
Universal life and investment-type product policy fee income	600	
Investment income, net	3,080	2,980
Investment gains (losses), net	(150)	(125)
Commissions, fees, and other income	25	25
Total revenues	5,280	7,955
Benefits and Other Deductions		
Policyowners' benefits paid or provided for	2,055	6,430
Interest credited to policyowners' account balances	1,440	
Allocation to (from) AVR		70
Policyowners' dividends	340	330
Other operating costs and expenses	875	825
Total benefits and other deductions	4,710	7,655
Income from continuing operations before federal income taxes	570	300
Federal income tax expense	(195)	(100)
Net income	375	200

Income Statement Line Entries

Premiums are defined very differently in statutory and GAAP reporting. Under statutory reporting, both premiums received under traditional life and health insurance policies and deposits under universal life and annuity accumulation contracts are classified as premiums. Under GAAP reporting, only the premiums associated with traditional life and health policies are classified as premiums; the other premiums are treated like bank deposits—that is, there is no income amount recorded when the deposits are received or any charge for deposits withdrawn. Under both statutory and GAAP reporting, premium amounts include payments on both new and renewed business, and these amounts are reduced by premiums paid on reinsurance purchased (ceded). The statutory amount will be larger than the GAAP amount primarily because of this definitional difference and secondarily because the total premiums for traditional life insurance are somewhat greater. (See discussion above for balance sheet item "premiums and other receivables.")

Universal life and investment-type product policy fee income, a GAAP-only concept, represents the amount of fee income for the period related to these types of products. This fee income includes premium-based charges, mortality charges, and withdrawal charges on surrender of policies or contracts. This item arises from the basic deposit-type treatment of these contracts under GAAP.

Investment income, net, is the largest component of revenues under GAAP and the next-to-the-largest component under statutory accounting. The sources of investment income are interest income, dividends, and other income earned on investments. Investment income is presented net—that is, expenses related to the investment are subtracted from the related income. On a statutory basis, real estate is reported net of encumbrances; therefore, the interest expense on such debt reduces statutory investment income. Similarly, the effect of consolidating certain investments on a line-by-line basis for GAAP reporting versus the equity presentation for SAP will create additional differences between GAAP and statutory investment income.

Investment gains (losses), net, are measured differently under statutory and GAAP reporting. With respect to the gain (loss) on investments sold or otherwise disposed of during the year, the accounting treatment is similar under statutory and GAAP reporting, although the numbers may differ if the assets sold or disposed of have specific valuation allowances under GAAP. Realized and unrealized gains (losses) on investments held by the company are included in this item for statutory reporting. Under GAAP reporting, unrealized gains (losses) are not included in this item but instead are credited (charged) directly to capital. In addition, in GAAP reporting, provisions for, or increases in, valuation allowances and writedowns on invested assets are included in realized gains and losses.

Commissions, fees, and other income are miscellaneous sources of income not included in the above items. They can be created the same way under GAAP and SAP. When there are differences, GAAP tries to match them with the associated coverage period whereas SAP tries to match them with the associated premium-paying period.

Policyowner benefits paid or provided for represent the amounts paid or set aside for death benefits, annuity benefits, surrender benefits, and matured endowments. These benefits are reported on an incurred basis under both SAP and GAAP. They include benefit payments due but unpaid at the balance sheet date, reported claims for which payment has been delayed pending completion of processing, claims resisted, and an estimate of the claims incurred during the year that had not been reported to the company by the balance sheet date. This item also includes the increases in reserves for policyowner benefits (for statutory reporting) and the increases in reserves for traditional life insurance policies (for GAAP reporting). Under GAAP, surrenders of accumulation-type products are treated as a return of a deposit and not included in this item. Accordingly, the GAAP amount should be less than the statutory amount.

Interest credited to policyowners' account balances is the amount of interest credited to policyowner account balances for accumulation-type products. It is recognized separately only for GAAP reporting.

Allocation to (from) AVR is the current period's charge (credit) for the net increase (decrease) during the accounting period in the asset valuation reserve for fixed maturities, common and preferred stock, mortgage loans, real estate, and joint ventures. (See earlier discussion of the AVR.) This applies only to statutory reporting.

Policyowner dividends are the charges for dividends to policyowners for the accounting period. This entry includes dividends paid in cash, as well as dividends applied to pay premiums or to increase policy values. Under statutory accounting, the charge is determined as the apportionment for dividends to be paid during the following year, adjusted for the difference between the dividends paid during the year and the apportionment at the end of the preceding year. Under GAAP accounting, the charge is the amount of dividends becoming due and payable during the current accounting period plus (less) the increase (decrease) in year-end dividend accruals. The statutory and GAAP amounts should not differ materially.

Other operating costs and expenses include operating and other pretax costs that do not fall into the earlier categories. Under statutory reporting, this item is composed principally of operating expenses. Under GAAP it also includes the interest on encumbrances. Operating expenses can be influenced to some extent by either shortening or lengthening

the period over which acquisition costs are recovered. By increasing the length of the acquisition cost deferral period, an insurer can lower the operating expenses and consequently increase the reported gain from operations. Similarly, shortening the deferral period for acquisition costs will usually increase the operating costs and reduce gains from operations.

Federal income tax expense is the charge against earnings for federal income taxes. In statutory reporting, this is basically the charge for taxes payable on the operations during the accounting period. In GAAP reporting, the amount of this item is essentially the federal tax charge that would have been incurred on the amount of GAAP pretax income.

Cash Flow Statements

cash flow statement

Like the income statement, the **cash flow statement** presents the several elements of the company's cash flow for the fiscal year ending on the statement date. The GAAP (and hybrid statutory) cash flow statement divides the life insurance company's cash flow into three parts:

- cash flow from insurance operations including investment income earned on existing investments
- cash flow from investing operations including the proceeds from maturity or sale of investments, along with the reinvestment of these proceeds
- cash flow from financing, including the sale by the company of bonds or stocks for corporate finance purposes, the repurchase of outstanding bonds or stocks, and the payments of dividends to shareholders

The cash flow statement is very important for nonfinancial businesses because cash usually represents a scarce resource in business operations and investment. (Business growth usually entails growth of inventories and receivables with commensurate cash requirements.) For life insurance companies, the cash flow statement has traditionally not been of great importance because the normal operations of these companies typically produce strong, positive cash flows. In the early 1990s, interest in life insurance companies' liquidity and in cash flow statements was heightened by the failures of two major life companies that were attributed largely to policyowner "cash runs" that could not be satisfied by these companies' (relatively inflexible) portfolios of invested assets.

The cash flow statement in the blue blank statutory accounting form does not follow the three-part breakdown of the GAAP (and hybrid statutory) report. Rather, it resembles an income statement form but with each line item measured on a cash basis.

Schedules and Notes

In addition to the three standard statement forms, each audited GAAP statement (and each hybrid statement), contains a set of notes that enhance or explain the statements in general or that provide additional data or explanations for specific line items. The statutory blue blank has a more abbreviated set of notes but contains several exhibits and many supporting schedules. These notes, exhibits, and schedules support or expand on specific entries in the three basic blue blank financial report forms and provide additional operational information.

The supplementary information in both the GAAP (and hybrid) financial statements and the statutory blue blank includes the following:

- a description of the company's accounting policies and practices
- an analysis of invested assets
- an analysis of investment income and of capital gains and losses on investments
- an analysis of expenses
- analyses of revenue and earnings by line of business (statutory) and by business segment (GAAP)
- an analysis of the company's pension plan charge
- additional information on leases, litigation, and contingent liabilities

Similarly, the exhibits and schedules that are part of the statutory blue blank include information about the following items that are not covered specifically in the GAAP financial statement:

- the amounts of life insurance sold and in force
- the income on annuity contracts sold and in force
- details on policyowner benefits, reserves, and liabilities
- a 5-year display of certain sales, coverage in force, and financial information

CHAPTER REVIEW

Key Terms and Concepts

Securities and Exchange Commission
  (SEC)
Financial Accounting Standards Board
  (FASB)
balance sheet
asset valuation reserve (AVR)
income statement
statutory accounting practices (SAP)

NAIC blanks
generally accepted accounting practices (GAAP)
interest maintenance reserve (IMR)
nonadmitted assets
equity securities
separate account assets
cash flow statement

Chapter 19 Review Questions

1. List the various audiences that have a need for information in life insurance
    company financial statements, and describe the interests and objectives of
    each of these distinct audiences. [1]

2. What are the three objectives of financial reporting identified by the Financial
    Accounting Standards Board (FASB)? [1]

3. List the three most common and significant financial statements that have
    evolved over time, and describe the purpose and general content of each. [2]

4. Describe the events or transactions that can cause a change in the value of
    an asset that a life insurance company holds. [2]

5. What are the possible uses of the earnings that result when a company's
    revenues exceed its expenses for the fiscal year? [2]

6. Explain the roles the state legislatures, the state insurance departments,
    and the National Association of Insurance Commissioners (NAIC) play in
    the establishment and implementation of statutory accounting and reporting
    requirements. [2]

7. Describe the differences in the form of presentation of statutory and GAAP financial statements. [3]

8. Explain how GAAP and statutory cash flow statements differ in the format used to organize and report a life insurer's cash flows. [4]

9. Explain why cash flow statements for life insurance companies:

    a.   have traditionally not been seen as being of great importance;

    b.   have recently attracted considerable interest. [5]

Chapter 19 Review Questions

1. •   *investors—current and future earnings and financial strength*

    •   *SEC—required level of disclosure, fair, and consistent*

    •   *insurance regulators—short-term and long-term safety and solvency*

    •   *creditors—current liquidity, expected near-term cash flow, ability to pay bond interest and principal in future*

    •   *security analysts—current and future earnings and financial strength*

    •   *rating agencies—present financial condition and likely future changes consistency and comparability to other insurers*

    •   *policyowners and buyers—ability to pay benefits and efficiency of investment income, mortality costs, expenses*

    •   *company management—financial position and progress relative to competitors, current year's earnings investment in capacity or growth for future, long-term performance*

    •   *agents and employees—operational results and financial strength, accuracy of reports, safety, solvency, policy funding adequacy*

2. *Three objectives of financial reporting identified by the FASB:*

    a. to provide information that is both useful and comprehensible to audiences in making rational investment, credit, and similar decisions

    b. to provide information that is helpful in assessing the amounts, timing, and uncertainty of prospective cash receipts from sales of products or services and from investments (dividends, interest, and sales or redemption of securities)

    c. to provide information about a company's economic resources (assets), claims on those resources (liabilities), and the effects of transactions, events, and circumstances that change those resources and claims

3. *The three most common and significant financial statements that have evolved over time are*

    a. statement of financial position (balance sheet). This statement lists the assets, liabilities, and equity position at the end of the year (what they control, what they owe, and the difference).

    b. income statement (statement of operations). Presents the company's revenues, expenses, and earnings (losses) for the accounting period specified.

    c. statement of cash flows. Presents the receipts and disbursement of funds during the accounting period specified. It helps to indicate company liquidity.

4. *Depreciation is one accounting transaction that reduces the value of assets over the time they are held. Intangible assets can be either increased in value or decreased in value as discounts or premiums are amortized (such as bonds).*

5. *Additional investment in the company or retention of net earnings are both sources of increased equity. On the other side, equity will be decreased by losses from operations, pays dividends, or increases debt more than increases in assets.*

6. *State legislatures enact laws specifying how reserves and assets are reported. These are often variations of model laws recommended by the NAIC. The insurance departments are responsible for the development of regulations to clarify the statutes and for the enforcement of the laws and regulations. The NAIC also creates and recommends model regulations that state insurance departments can adopt "as is" or modify at their own discretion.*

7. *SAP statements depict a more conservative valuation of the company. Revenue is only recognized in full when they are created even if they cover future operating periods.*

   GAAP accounting attempts to match revenues and expenses with the operating periods they represent by accrual adjustments, such as prepaid expenses and prepaid premiums.

8. *The GAAP cash flow statement is broken down into three parts:*
   - *cash flow from insurance operations*
   - *cash flow from investments*
   - *cash flow from financing*

   The statutory cash flow statement is organized like the income statement.

9. a. *Traditionally, life insurers had very predictable positive cash flows with very little liquidity concerns.*

   b. *Some life insurer failures and negative cash flows from policyowner demands in recent years have created more concern about liquidity. Flexible premiums and recurrent disintermediation have reduced predictability of cash flows.*

Ratings

Revised by: Harry D. Garber & C.W. Copeland

Learning Objectives

An understanding of the material in this chapter should enable the student to

1. **Describe the claims-paying ability ratings assigned to life insurers by the four principal rating services, including the rating definitions used, the rating processes followed, and the rating criteria employed to measure current financial strength and future performance.**

2. **Explain how the IRIS is used to identify companies for whom regulatory review and perhaps regulatory oversight is appropriate.**

3. **Explain how the risk-based capital approach operates, including how the amount of risk-based capital is computed for a life insurer, how the need for regulatory intervention is determined, what degrees of regulatory intervention may be indicated, and what issues this regulatory tool leaves untested.**

4. **Describe the limitations and problems encountered when using information in published financial statements and published comparative performance analyses to compare life insurance companies' financial strength, earnings growth, and pricing performance.**

From 1906 until the mid-1980s, A.M. Best, a rating service that specialized in the insurance industry, was the recognized rating service for life and property-liability insurance companies. Most large insurance companies had a top rating (then A+) from A.M. Best, and those that did not were at a disadvantage in marketing their products.

During the 1980s, the three multi-industry rating services (Standard and Poor's, Duff and Phelps, and Moody's) began for the first time to rate large numbers of life insurance companies. Duff and Phelps insurance rating services were taken over by Fitch Ratings. These ratings are known as claims-paying ability or financial strength ratings. They are an outgrowth of the ratings that had been assigned traditionally by these agencies to the long-term debt, commercial paper, and preferred stock issues of companies, including insurance companies. The major difference is that a claims-paying ability rating represents

an assessment of a company's ability to meet its obligations to all of its policyowners, while the traditional rating related to a particular bond or stock issue. Coming at a time of concern about the solvency of the life insurance industry resulting from the failures of Executive Life and Mutual Benefit, the many bank failures, and the collapse of the commercial real estate market, the substantial growth in the number of life insurance companies rated by these widely respected, traditional rating agencies had a strong impact on the industry and its customers.

RATINGS

The three multi-industry rating services have substantially similar claims-paying ability rating definitions, although they often differ on the rating assigned to a particular life insurance company. The broad rating classes used and their definitions are as follows:

- Triple A (AAA)—the highest claims-paying ability rating; capacity to honor insurance contracts extremely strong and highly likely to remain so over a long period of time

- Double A (AA+, AA, AA–)—very strong capacity to honor insurance contracts; differs only in small degree from the highest rating category

- Single A (A+, A, A–)—strong capacity to honor insurance contracts, although such capacity may be susceptible to the adverse effects of changes in circumstances over a long time period

- Triple B (BBB+, BBB, BBB–)—ability to meet insurance contract obligations considered to be adequate under most circumstances but likely to exhibit less stability in changing economic conditions over long time periods than the higher rating categories

- Double B (BB+, BB, BB–), Single B (B+, B, B–)—ability to honor insurance obligations under stressful circumstances regarded as speculative

- C ratings—ability to honor insurance obligations extremely speculative, and policyowners, in many cases, may not receive timely payment of their claims; company vulnerable to liquidation and may be under regulatory supervision

- D ratings—company has been placed under an order of liquidation

The above rating definitions are paraphrases of the definitions published by Standard and Poor's. Fitch uses virtually the same rating categories and definitions.

Moody's and A.M. Best use categories and definitions that are similar to those used by Standard and Poor's and Fitch. The principal differences are in category designations, as follows:

- Moody's uses l, 2, and 3 to modify the ratings (for example, Moody's A l is equivalent to S&P's A+, Moody's A2 is equivalent to S&P's A, and so on).

- Instead of BBB, BB, and B, Moody's uses Baa, Ba, and B, respectively.

The rough equivalences of the A.M. Best and S&P categories are shown in Table 20-1.

Table 20-1 Rating Equivalences			
A.M. Best	**S&P**	**Fitch**	**Moody's**
Superior (A++, A+)	AAA	AAA	Aaa
Excellent (A, A–)	AA	AA	Aa1 – Aa3
Very good (B++, B+)	A	A	A1 – A2
Good (B, B–)	BBB	BBB	A3 – Baa1
Fair (C++, C+)	BB	BB	Baa2 – Baa3
Marginal (C, C–)	B	B	Ba1 – Ba2

The distribution of A.M. Best's ratings and those of the three multi-industry rating services as of late 2010 are shown in Table 20-2[1].

Table 20-2 Distribution of Ratings of Life Insurance Companies				
	Fitch	**Moody's**	**Standard and Poor's**	**A.M. Best**
AAA	2.4%	3.5%	2.7%	14.9%
AA	32.0	26.9	28.9	53.14
A	54.6	52.6	52.6	23.0
BBB	6.6	9.3	8.1	5.4
Below BBB	4.4	7.7	7.7	3.6
	100%	100%	100%	100%
Number of companies rated	288	171	331	938

---

1.   Insurance Forum, September 2010, p.112

Because there are differences in the distribution of the four services' ratings, be careful in drawing conclusions from this comparison because the population of the companies rated by any two rating services differs, sometimes significantly. Given that the risk of failure to meet policyowner obligations differs very little between the top three broad rating classes (AAA, AA, and A), the industry as a whole is highly rated in its capacity to meet policyowner obligations.

watch list

When there has been a material change in the company's circumstances that the rating agency has not had the opportunity to evaluate fully or if there are expected future events that could have a significant effect on the company's position, the rating agency will often place the company on a **watch list**. The published notice of this watch list action will usually indicate whether there are positive, negative, or developing expectations. An expected capital contribution from a parent company is a positive future event; reported losses from a natural disaster that are materially higher than would have been expected for that company is an example of a negative event that will require additional evaluation.

RATING PROCESS

The rating process, as conducted by Standard and Poor's, Moody's, and Fitch, usually involves the following distinct steps:

- an advance review by rating agency analysts of statutory and GAAP financial statements for the last few years and related material. (The statutory blue blank is the principal financial statement source used for rating purposes; the GAAP statements are used as supplementary information. See chapter 24 for a discussion of SAP and GAAP accounting.)

- a meeting of rating agency analysts with the company's senior officials and managers. The meeting will include a meeting with the company's chief executive officer and the company officials responsible for the business areas that are most likely to affect the final rating.

- a review by a committee of experienced insurance analysts of the material and observations gathered in the on-site visit to determine a tentative rating. The result will be communicated to the company, which can request an additional review if it believes that material information was not fully considered.

- publication of the final rating once it has been established by the rating agency, along with suitable explanations, particularly if the rating has been changed

There are slight variations in this general process among the three multi-industry rating services, and there can be other variations depending on the rated company's circumstances. For example, one rating agency invites company officials, at the beginning of the third step above, to meet with members of the committee that will make the rating decision.

Companies seeking ratings for the first time usually have the option of withdrawing the rating request if they do not agree with the agency's rating decision. For a company with an existing claims-paying ability rating, this is almost never an option because the public perception of a decision not to be rated would probably be worse than the rating itself.

The A.M. Best process includes the same elements as those of the other rating services, but the order of the steps differs because A.M. Best releases its annual ratings in the spring of the year. In addition, A.M. Best does not require visits with company officials each year.

Rating Criteria

The criteria used by the four principal rating services in reaching their rating decisions, not surprisingly, have a large degree of commonality. They involve elements that are quantitative and elements that are largely qualitative. The quantitative elements frequently involve comparisons to industry norms developed independently by each of the services. Because a claims-paying ability rating is an evaluation of the company's ability to meet obligations maturing in the future, even the quantitative elements (which are necessarily based on the company's past performance) must be tempered by qualitative judgments.

Because statutory blue blank reports are available for all life insurance companies, the quantitative analyses of the rating services are presently based on data drawn from these reports. GAAP financial statements are used to provide certain supplementary information and have taken on more importance in the rating process.

Measurements of Present and Future Financial Strength

A claims-paying ability rating must measure the company's present financial strength (relative to its obligations for future policyowner claims) and whether the company's financial performance is likely to increase or decrease this financial strength in the future. In describing the elements that are taken into account by the rating services, it is useful to categorize them into elements that are used principally to measure the company's current

financial strength and elements that are used principally to form an opinion about the company's future financial performance. (Of course, most of these elements will, at least to some extent, affect both a company's present position and its future performance.)

Elements to Measure Current Financial Strength

The elements that principally measure a company's current position are

- capital
- liquidity
- asset/liability values
- other insurance/investment risks

Capital is required to provide the safety margin (over and above the amount of reserves and other liabilities) to assure that the company will be able to invest (in its businesses), to grow, and to meet its commitments. The amount of capital depends on the size of the company and on the riskiness of the company's investment portfolio and insurance lines. For example, an investment strategy that emphasizes high-yield bonds requires more capital than a strategy that emphasizes government bonds. Similarly, Guaranteed Investment Contracts (GICs), which guarantee a return to contract owners, require more capital than variable contracts in which the investment earnings of a separate account are passed through to policyowners.

liquidity

Liquidity is the company's ability to make large and unpredictable payouts to policyowners or to meet other obligations. To determine if a company is in a good liquidity position, the rating service looks at the amount of the company's cash and short-term investments (usually those maturing in less than one year) and the likelihood of sudden cash calls. For example, a company with a large block of annuity contracts on which the cash surrender values are available without penalty presents a greater risk than a company whose book of business consists largely of life insurance policies sold to meet estate planning needs.

Asset/liability values are a key element. Because the company's asset and liability values are taken into account in measuring the amount of the company's capital, the degree of conservatism in their measurement is a very important factor to the rating services in reaching a decision. The key question on assets is the degree to which the asset values reflect appropriate reserves for likely or potential losses; in the case of liabilities, the question is whether the reserves have an adequate margin for future interest requirements and/

or insurance losses. For example, if the company's investment earnings are currently insufficient to cover the interest requirements of its guaranteed interest contracts (GIC) and are not expected to be sufficient in the future, a reserve equal to the contract funds would not, by itself, be adequate. (A judgment about reserve and liability adequacy should be made with respect to the aggregate of all reserves and liabilities because a shortage in one area may be covered by excesses in others.)

Other insurance/investment risks include the degree of asset or insurance concentration risk, the use of reinsurance to reduce risk, and the company's vulnerability to reinsurer default. A concentration of investments in a particular geographical area or business/industry or a concentration of life insurance in force on a relatively small number of insureds increases risk and is the subject of rating agency review. Reinsurance ceded can reduce large life and health insurance risks to the company but only to the extent that the reinsurer is financially strong.

Elements to Measure Future Financial Strength

The following are the key elements that the rating services focus on to form opinions about the company's future financial performance:

- management/strategy
- company's capabilities
- ability to finance

The management/strategy element involves a review of the experience and accomplishments of the company's senior management and a review of the company's future strategy in relation to the competitive dynamics of the industry, the company's ability to execute the strategy, and the availability of the financial and other resources needed to implement the strategy successfully. Many aspects of this evaluation are obviously qualitative in nature but supplemented by the available quantitative data. The key issue for the rating agency is whether the company has the leadership, the market positioning, the competitive advantages, and the resources to execute its strategy successfully, and if it does not appear to have the ingredients to be fully successful, what the consequences are of partial success or failure.

The company's capabilities element for a life insurance company is an analysis of the various elements of competitive advantage and sources of profit. This element is a critical factor in assessing the company's ability to increase revenue and profits and to maintain or improve its financial position. The key considerations include the company's (1) marketing and sales capability and positioning, (2) investing skills and the ability to achieve

market-level spreads between investment income earned and interest credited on policyowner funds, (3) underwriting system and skills and the ability to achieve market-level
spreads between mortality/morbidity charges to policyowners and the claims incurred,
(4) efficiency in marketing company products and servicing the business in force, and
whether these efficiency levels will enable the company to achieve and to maintain the
unit expense levels incorporated in its pricing structure, and (5) ability to achieve competitive policy persistency levels with the accompanying beneficial effects on revenue growth
and unit costs.

The ability to finance element is the company's ability to raise the capital it may need to
finance its strategic plan and general growth or to strengthen a capital position that is
presently sub-par or that may be eroded by future adverse events. In addition to the capital
that could be generated within the company, the rating agency also considers the state of
the capital markets, the ability and intent of a parent company (of the insurance company)
to provide capital and the (limited) options a mutual life insurance company has to raise
capital.

The four rating services examine each of these elements, although their approaches vary
and their examinations may not entail all of the detail suggested by these descriptions.
Nevertheless, it should be clear that a full analysis and understanding of a life insurance
company's current and future financial position requires gathering and analyzing much
more information than is available in the company's published financial statements.

REGULATORY MEASURES

A primary function of state regulators is to ensure that to the extent possible companies
will be able to meet their current and future obligations to policyowners. Life insurance
companies will have the financial capability to meet these obligations as long as they are
solvent and operate with sufficient safety margins to ensure future solvency. In recent years
the NAIC has concentrated on developing tools to identify companies that are currently
solvent but have adverse operating trends or potentially insufficient capital to withstand
a period of sustained losses. The purpose of these tools is to identify companies whose
position and operations should be reviewed by state regulators. In many (or most) cases
of the companies so identified, no regulatory action will be required because the regulatory review will have shown that the adverse operating trends that triggered the review
are not material or that the company has already taken appropriate actions to remedy the
problems. In other cases the regulators will find that the triggering conditions are material
and that the company has not adequately addressed them. In these circumstances the

regulators will oversee the development and implementation of a plan to remedy these conditions or trends.

The two types of tools state regulators currently use are the insurance regulatory information system (IRIS) ratios and, starting with 1993, risk-based capital (RBC). Unlike the ratings of the rating services that are intended to be measures of company risk, these regulatory tools are not, and are not intended to be, such measures of risk. Additional investigation by regulators is required to determine if a company that "failed" the tests must take any actions and what these actions should be. Failure of these tests does not by itself indicate that a company has a significant risk of insolvency or impairment. This is true regardless of whether or not regulators make the company take remedial actions.

IRIS Ratios

IRIS ratios

The **IRIS ratios** are successors to the early warning system developed by the state insurance regulators about 20 years ago. They identify companies for whom regulatory review and perhaps regulatory oversight is appropriate.

IRIS involves 12 ratios for life and health insurance companies. Each ratio is computed as a percentage, and depending on the ratio, it may be positive or negative. The specific IRIS ratios are presented in Table 20-3, along with the usual range for each ratio. To establish the usual ranges for the IRIS ratios, state regulators reviewed the ratios for companies that had become insolvent or had experienced financial difficulties in recent years. The NAIC expects that in any year 15 percent of the companies will fall outside the usual ranges on four or more ratios.

There are no specific rules that determine the degree of regulatory response for a company whose results fall outside the usual ranges in a number of the IRIS tests. The response depends on such factors as the number of outside-the-usual-range results, their severity, the trends in the number and severity of previous outside-the-usual-range results, and the effects of previous reviews and actions.

Risk-based Capital

The capital standards imbedded in state law for life insurance companies have traditionally been quite low, ranging from a few hundred thousand dollars in some states to $2 million in New York. Moreover, such standards have never adequately recognized company size or risk.

In the early 1990s the NAIC developed, in consultation with industry experts, a risk-based capital (RBC) measure. As indicated earlier, this measure is used to determine whether and to what degree regulatory intervention is required. The RBC measure first became a requirement with the 1993 financial statements.

Table 20-3		
IRIS Ratios for Life and Health Insurance Companies		
Ratio	**Title**	**Usual Range**
1	Net Change in Capital and Surplus Ratio (percentage of growth in capital and surplus, excluding new paid-in capital and surplus)	–10% to 50%
1A	Gross Change in Capital in Surplus Ratio (percentage growth in capital and surplus)	–10% to 50%
2	Net Gain to Total Income Ratio (including capital gains and losses)	Greater than 0%
3	Not used	—
4	Adequacy of Investment Income Ratio (ratio of investment income to interest required on reserves and credits on deposit funds)	125% to 900%
5	Nonadmitted to Admitted Assets Ratio	Less than 10%
6	Real Estate to Capital and Surplus Ratio	Less than 200% (a) Less than 100% (b)
7	Investment in Affiliates to Capital and Surplus Ratio	Less than 100%
8	Surplus Relief Ratio (ratio of net reinsurance allowances to capital and surplus)	–99% to 30% (a) –10% to 10% (b)
9	Change in Premium Ratio (growth in premiums)	–10% to 50%
10	Change in Product Mix (change in percentage of total premiums each product represents)	Less than 5%
11	Change in Asset Mix (similar to ratio #10 but for asset classes)	Less than 5%
12	Change in Reserving Ratio (reserving ratio in rates of increase in reserves to single and renewal premiums; computed for individual life only)	–20% to 20%
(a) companies with more than $5 million of capital and surplus		
(b) companies with $5 million or less of capital and surplus		

Under the RBC approach, a company determines the RBC standard amount of capital and surplus (based on the RBC formulas) each year. It then compares its actual capital and surplus, including the asset valuation reserve (AVR), to the computed RBC measure.

The regulatory response, if any, depends on the results of this comparison. A company whose actual capital and surplus exceeds the computed RBC standard requires no regulatory action. If the company's actual capital and surplus falls between 75 percent and 100 percent of the computed RBC standard, the company is required to file a plan of the actions it intends to take to eliminate this gap with its state regulators. If the company's actual capital and surplus falls between 50 percent and 75 percent of the computed RBC standard, the home state regulator has an obligation to undertake a detailed review of the company's operations and to mandate corrective actions. If the company's actual capital and surplus is below 50 percent of the computed RBC standard, the company is considered to be a candidate for seizure by the state regulator.

Categories of Risk

During the 20 years leading up to the NAIC's formal adoption of the RBC standards, there was a steady evolution in the identification and evaluation of the risks facing life insurers. The actuarial profession classified risks into these four categories:

- C-I risks (the risks of asset default)
- C-2 risks (insurance risks, principally mortality and morbidity)
- C-3 risks (interest rate deficiency risks)
- C-4 risks (other business risks)

In recent years Lincoln National Life Insurance Company and Moody's rating service developed and published capital and surplus standards by assigning weights to the amounts of assets and liabilities in specific categories and, in some cases, to the amounts of specific income and disbursement elements. There was considerable overlap in their approaches to evaluating capital requirements, and these approaches, along with formulas developed by the Minnesota and New York insurance departments, provided a useful starting point for the NAIC in developing the RBC methodology.

Assets. The RBC risk-assessment basis recognizes all of the four types of risk described earlier. The risk factor that is the most important in terms of the proportion of the company's RBC it represents is the asset default risk (C-I). Computations of the RBC objective for asset default risk take the following items into account:

- types of assets
- quality mix of assets, including the NAIC rating classes for bonds
- degree of diversification in an asset class
- mix of asset maturities

For example, the bond factors (before adjustment) range from 0.3 percent for AAA bonds to 30 percent for bonds in default. These basic rates are then multiplied by the applicable degree of diversification factor (based on the number of issuers whose bonds are held in the portfolio). For less than 50 issuers, this factor is 2.5; for 200 issuers the factor is l.45; for 500 issuers, the factor is 1.16. For other key asset classes, the basic factors applied to the amounts of assets to determine the asset default risk are as follows: for mortgages, 0.l percent to 20 percent, depending on quality level and company experience; for common stock, 30 percent; for owned real estate, 10 percent to 15 percent, but 20 percent if held in a partnership; and for cash and short-term investments, .3 percent. For large companies the asset default risk (C-l) constitutes almost 75 percent of the total calculated RBC standard. For smaller companies the percentage of the RBC standard attributable to C-l risk factors is somewhat smaller.

Insurance. The insurance risk (C-2) element is intended to provide additional protection (over and above the required reserves) for adverse trends and experience in life insurance mortality and/or health insurance morbidity or for premium inadequacies. The life insurance factors, which are applied to the net life insurance risk, decrease as the company's insurance risk amount increases; this element, therefore, is a relatively more important component of the RBC standard for smaller companies than it is for larger companies. The health insurance factors are applied to premiums and vary by both type of health insurance coverage (hospital and medical insurance, disability income, and so on) and premium volume, with lower ratios applying to premium amounts in excess of $25 or $50 million per year for coverage. For both life and health insurance, smaller factors apply to group insurance than to individual coverages. The C-2 factors represent about 10 percent to 15 percent of the RBC standard for larger companies and, as noted above, a relatively greater percentage for smaller companies.

Interest. The interest risk (C-3) is determined by applying factors to the amounts of insurance reserves. These factors depend on the level of risk (low, medium, or high) and on whether the company has received an unqualified actuarial opinion. Low-risk reserves include individual life insurance reserves and individual annuity reserves that cannot be withdrawn or that have a low withdrawal risk because of a market value adjustment feature. Individual annuity reserves permitting surrenders at book value but with large surrender charges (5 percent or more) are considered to be medium risk. The interest-risk factors range from about 10 percent of the total RBC standard for larger companies down to less than 5 percent for smaller companies for whom the insurance risk is relatively more important.

Business. The business risk (C-4) factors are 2 percent of life insurance premiums and annuity considerations and 0.5 percent of health insurance premiums. This element generally constitutes 5 percent or less of the total RBC standard for companies of all sizes.

RBC Adjustment Formula

In recognition of the fact that there are interrelationships among the different types of risks and that the separate risk calculations may overstate the total risk requirement, the total of the four risk elements is adjusted using the following formula:

$$RBC = [(\text{asset risk} + \text{interrest risk})^2 + (\text{insurance risk})^2]^{1/2} + \text{business risk}$$

The result is to reduce the RBC capital standard to about 80 percent to 90 percent of what it would have been without this adjustment. As an example, let's assume that a company has determined the following preadjustment RBC standards:

Asset risk	$750 million
Insurance risk	200 million
Interest risk	125 million
Business risk	50 million

After the adjustment, the RBC standard is $948 million, compared to $1.125 billion when the standard components are independently calculated.

Testing RBC Effectiveness

Because the RBC standard is relatively new, there has been little opportunity yet to test RBC effectiveness in helping companies and regulators prevent life insurance company failures and policyowner losses. Clearly, it is an improvement on the previous minimal capital standards. But whether a standard with such heavy emphasis on responding to the asset-risk lessons of the late 1980s and early 1990s will serve the industry and regulators well in the unknown (and certainly different) world of the twenty-first century without substantial modification is still to be determined. (For example, could the more conservative investment philosophy prompted by the emphasis on the asset-risk component of the RBC significantly increase the interest rate deficiency risk or substitute the asset-liability mismatching risk for the asset-default risk?) The other critical dimension will be state regulators' effectiveness in monitoring the progress or, in some cases, guiding the improvement efforts of companies whose capital and surplus fall below the computed RBC standard.

The purpose of the RBC calculations and comparisons is to identify companies where regulatory oversight and action may be beneficial in preventing future failures and policyowner losses. There is no compelling evidence, however, that a company whose capital and surplus approximates the computed RBC standard has significantly greater risk than a company with substantially more capital and surplus (say, 150 percent of the computed RBC minimum standard). Except for companies with very weak current capital positions, the risk of future failure usually depends more on future business actions and results than on current capital strength.

Since 1993, a company's statutory financial statement must disclose its total adjusted capital (the amount of the company's capital and surplus for purposes of the RBC comparison) and its authorized control level of capital (the amount of capital below which the regulators are authorized to seize the company), which is 50 percent of the computed RBC standard. RBC results are intended to be kept confidential, and there are explicit prohibitions on the use of RBC results in a company's sales promotions and advertising. Nevertheless, it will not be difficult for outside parties to prepare lists showing the ratio of each company's actual capital and surplus to the computed RBC standard and for these lists to become available to policyowners and prospective policyowners.

COMPARATIVE PERFORMANCE MEASURES

Most life insurance products are long term, and policy benefits and policyowner costs are not fixed at issue but depend on postissue company actions. Such actions include changes in the dividend scale (for participating business) and changes in interest crediting rates, mortality charges, or expense charges on accumulation and variable-type products.

As the insurance market has become more and more competitive, many policyowners, agents, and advisers have evidenced an increased interest in measures of insurance companies' financial position and performance. Companies' interest in comparing their performance to their peer companies' performance in several key areas has also increased. In addition to the analyses made by individual companies, several organizations have begun to measure and promulgate such comparative information. For the most part, these comparisons are based on information drawn from the statutory blue blank financial statements, which are available for all companies—mutual and stock—and contain more information related to pricing decisions than do the GAAP or hybrid financial reports. However, these published analyses can rarely, if ever, be used to demonstrate or measure real differences between companies or to highlight a company's standings among its peers. At best, they can be used as general directional pointers.

Financial Position and Performance Measures

The published comparisons tend to focus on a company's financial strength, earnings growth, and sales and growth of the insurance lines.

With respect to financial strength, many measures have been developed and published over the years to compare the relative financial strength of the leading life insurance companies. These have, typically, been ratios of capital (usually defined as surplus plus the asset valuation reserve) to one or more measure of risk (assets, reserves, and so forth). As companies diversified their investment portfolios by type and quality and their liabilities became equally diverse, these broad general ratios have become virtually meaningless. This diversity must be brought into any competitive calculations, but even then the results must be used with great caution because the relative risk measures assigned to different types of assets and liabilities are themselves often arbitrary. The RBC standard, which is probably the most sophisticated approach to such a standard, is used by the regulators only to highlight companies for further investigation and, if necessary, action. The rating agencies never base ratings solely on current measures of financial strength (unless the company is bordering on insolvency) but look at the combination of current financial strength and current and future earnings power.

With respect to earnings growth, the standards used most frequently are the various earnings-per-share measures included in the GAAP financial statements. Statutory measures of income are less valuable because of SAP's emphasis on conservative measurement of assets and liabilities and the prevalence of certain types of reinsurance transactions.

Regarding sales and growth in business, the statutory statement contains information that can provide bases for reasonably good comparisons among companies. A better service is the Life Insurance Management and Research Agency (LIMRA), which surveys a large group of companies to obtain consistent measures of new business for different types of coverage.

Pricing Performance Comparisons

Information on companies' performance in the key areas (investment return, mortality and morbidity, expenses, and persistency) that affect prices and nonguaranteed benefits is of great interest to competitors, customers, agents, and advisers. Many firms develop and publish various types of comparative measures to provide insights to these interested parties. Most are of limited value.

The reason these comparisons are limited in value is that modern pricing techniques recognize the particular characteristics of the markets the companies serve and the unique costs of providing coverage in those markets. Often there are trade-offs among different cost factors. For example, much business insurance is written on a guaranteed-issue basis, with the additional mortality cost covered by reduced commissions and underwriting cost savings. Most analyses of a company's experience and intercompany comparisons drawn from data in financial reports, on the other hand, must necessarily aggregate results for all markets the company addresses and, in some cases, for all lines of business. If a company that has a sizable amount of the business insurance described above is compared on an aggregate basis with a company that sells all of its insurance with full underwriting and full commissions, the former will show higher average mortality and lower average expenses. Although this statement is true, it has no significance because the customer purchases a product designed for a particular market, and the information required to compare the past and anticipated experience of the two companies in that market is almost never available from the companies' financial statements.

Theoretically, therefore, much information can be determined from a company's financial reports, but as described above, the information is usually too aggregated to be relevant to the company's pricing decisions in the market(s) of interest to the agent or policyowner. For example, in the case of investment income, companies usually have several portfolios of investments, each backing one or more classes of business. In addition, if the company prices on a "new money" basis, the overall portfolio rate does not reflect the rates for different classes of business. It is impossible to determine from the financial statements what investment return a company is earning on the assets associated with a particular class of business or how this performance compares with the comparable business of other companies.

The problem is even more complex in the case of mortality experience. Mortality expectations vary by age, sex, type of underwriting (for example, medical, paramedical, non-medical, or guaranteed issue), and number of years since issue. Although the blue blank statements do show the net mortality costs (death claims incurred less reserves held) for the financial period, the information is of little value without an understanding of the company's expected mortality costs (based on the distribution of business by risk class) and its pricing objectives, which are simply not available from the published financial statements. There is a similar problem with respect to morbidity under health insurance policies, although the smaller level of policy accumulations and the absence of cash values mean that there is a closer connection between the premiums charged and the expected morbidity.

With respect to expenses, the statutory blue blank discloses the amounts of a company's commissions, general insurance expenses, and taxes for each principal line of business. There are also exhibits that present additional details on the components of these three expense categories but without a full breakdown by line of business. It is possible therefore to determine many ratios of expenses to various measures for a life insurance company's book of business. While these expense ratios can give a general indication of a company's expense situation, they cannot mark the company's exact standing with any degree of precision. The problem is the same as that described for mortality. Expenses vary significantly by policy year (acquisition costs are vastly higher than renewal administration costs), size of policy, type of coverage (variable universal contracts involve more service and administrative costs than term insurance, for example), type of customer (individual versus business), and market served. The pricing used by the company ordinarily reflects these differences. Unless two life insurance companies have remarkably similar portfolios of business, it is impossible to determine from any general expense ratios gathered from information in their financial statements whether a company is meeting its pricing expense objectives or whether there is a significant difference in the expense levels of two companies that would affect future pricing actions.

Because there is no way of knowing how any two companies match up in terms of their business profiles and expense objectives, the published expense ratios developed from financial statements must be used with extreme caution. Even intercompany expense studies within the industry are often difficult to understand and interpret because of different organizational approaches and accounting classifications.

CHAPTER REVIEW

Key Terms and Concepts

watch list
liquidity
IRIS ratios

Chapter 20 Review Questions

1. What is the major difference between a claims-paying ability rating assigned by a multi-industry rating service to a life insurance company and the ratings traditionally

assigned by such a rating service to the long-term debt and preferred stock issues of companies, including insurance companies? [1]

2. Describe (a) the broad rating classes used by the three key multi-industry rating services and A.M. Best, (b) including any major differences. [1]

3. a. Describe the steps usually included in the rating process that the three key multi-industry rating services follow, and

    b. explain how and why the process A.M. Best uses differs. [1]

4. Describe the respective roles statutory and GAAP financial statements play in the quantitative analyses the four principal rating services conduct, and explain how and why those roles may change in the future. [1]

5. List and describe the elements the rating services take into account to:

    a. measure a company's current financial strength;

    b. enable the rating service to form an opinion about a company's future financial strength. [1]

6. What is the purpose of regulatory tools such as IRIS (insurance regulatory information system) ratios and risk-based capital standards, and what are the implications and consequences for a company these tools identify? [2]

7. How is IRIS used to identify companies for whom regulatory review is appropriate, and what factors determine the degree of regulatory response to such companies? [2]

8. Describe how the RBC (risk-based capital) approach determines whether and to what degree regulatory intervention is required. [3]

9. List the four types of risk considered in determining the amount of risk-based capital and surplus required for a particular life insurance company, and for each type of risk describe (1) the factors taken into account in measuring that risk and (2) the relative importance of that type of risk for typical life insurance companies. [3]

10. Describe the limitations and problems in using information in published financial statements and comparative performance analyses to compare the financial strength, earnings growth, and pricing performance of life insurance companies. [4]s

Chapter 20 Review Answers

1. *The major difference is that a claims-paying ability rating represents an assessment of a company's ability to meet its obligations to all of its policyowners, while the traditional rating related to a particular bond or stock issue.*

2. *The broad rating classes used and their definitions are as follows:*

    *   *Triple A (AAA)—the highest claims-paying rating; capacity to honor insurance contracts extremely strong and highly likely to remain so over a long period of time*

    *   *Double A (AA+, AA, AA–)—very strong capacity to honor insurance contracts; differs only in a small degree from the highest rating category*

    *   *Single A (A+, A, A–)—strong capacity to honor insurance contracts, although such capacity may be susceptible to the adverse effects of changes in circumstances over a long time period*

    *   *Triple B (BBB+, BBB, BBB–)—ability to meet insurance contract obligations considered to be adequate under most circumstances but likely to exhibit less stability in changing economic conditions over long time periods than the higher rating categories*

    *   *Double B (BB+, BB, BB–), Single B (B+, B, B–)—ability to honor insurance obligations under stressful circumstances regarded as speculative*

    *   *C ratings—ability to honor insurance obligations extremely speculative, and policyowners, in many cases, may not receive timely payment of their claims; company vulnerable to liquidation and may be under regulatory supervision*

    *   *D ratings—company has been placed under an order of liquidation*

    The principal differences are in category designations, as follows:

    *   *Moody's uses 1, 2, and 3 to modify the ratings (for example, Moody's A1 is equivalent to S&P's A+, Moody's A2 is equivalent to S&P's A, and so on).*

    *   *Instead of BBB, BB, and B, Moody's uses Baa, Ba, and B, respectively*

3.   a.   The rating process, as conducted by Standard and Poor's, Moody's, and Fitch, usually involves the following distinct steps:

  - A review of statutory and GAAP financial statements for the last few years and related material is conducted in advance by rating agency analysts.

  - Rating agency analysts meet with the company's senior officials and managers. The meeting includes a meeting with the company's chief executive officer and the company officials responsible for the business areas that are most likely to affect the final rating.

  - A committee of experienced insurance analysts reviews the material and observations gathered in the on-site visit to determine a tentative rating. The result is communicated to the company, which can request an additional review if it believes that material information was not fully considered.

  - Once the final rating has been established by the rating agency, the rating, along with suitable explanations, is published, particularly if the rating has been changed.

     b.   The A.M. Best process includes the same elements as those of the other rating services, but the order of the steps differs because A.M. Best releases its annual ratings in the spring of the year. In addition, A.M. Best does not require visits with company officials each year.

4.   Because statutory financial reports are available for all life insurance companies, the quantitative analyses of the rating services are presently based on data drawn from these reports. GAAP financial statements are used to provide certain supplementary information for stock life insurance companies. When GAAP reporting becomes required for mutual companies, it is likely that GAAP financial information will take on more importance in the rating process.

5.   a.   The elements rating services take into account that principally measure a company's current position are

  - Capital, which is required to provide the safety margin (over and above the amount of reserves and other liabilities) to assure that the company will be able to invest (in its businesses), to grow, and to meet its commitments. The amount of capital required depends on the size of the company and on the riskiness of the company's investment portfolio and insurance lines.

  - Liquidity is the company's ability to make large and unpredictable payouts to policyowners or to meet other obligations. To determine if a company is in a good

liquidity position, the rating service looks at the amount of the company's cash and short-term investments (usually those maturing in less than one year) and the likelihood of sudden cash calls.

- *Asset/liability values are taken into account in measuring the amount of the company's capital. The degree of conservatism in their measurement is a very important factor to the rating services in reaching a decision. The key question on assets is the degree to which the asset values reflect appropriate reserves for likely or potential losses. In the case of liabilities, the question is whether the reserves have an adequate margin for future interest requirements and/or insurance losses.*

- *Other insurance/investment risks include the degree of asset or insurance concentration risk, the use of reinsurance to reduce risk, and the company's vulnerability to reinsurer default.*

b. *The following are the key elements on which the rating services focus to form opinions about the company's future financial performance:*

- *Management/strategy. This element involves a review of the experience and accomplishments of the company's senior management and a review of the company's future strategy in relation to the competitive dynamics of the industry, the company's ability to execute the strategy, and the availability of the financial and other resources needed to implement the strategy successfully. The key issue for the rating agency is whether the company has the leadership, the market positioning, the competitive advantages, and the resources to execute its strategy successfully, and if it does not appear to have the ingredients to be fully successful, what the consequences are of partial success or failure.*

- *Company's capabilities. For a life insurance, this involves an analysis of the various elements of competitive advantage and sources of profit. This element is a critical factor in assessing the company's ability to increase revenue and profits and to maintain or improve its financial position. The key considerations include the company's (1) marketing and sales capability and positioning, (2) investing skills and the ability to achieve market-level spreads between investment income earned and interest credited on policyowner funds, (3) underwriting system and skills and the ability to achieve market-level spreads between mortality/morbidity charges to policyowners and the claims incurred, (4) efficiency in marketing company products and servicing the business in force, and whether these efficiency levels will enable the company to achieve and to maintain the unit expense levels incorporated in its pricing structure, and (5) ability to achieve competitive policy*

persistency levels with the accompanying beneficial effects on revenue growth and unit costs.

- *Ability to finance. This element is the company's ability to raise the capital it may need to finance its strategic plan and general growth or to strengthen a capital position that is presently subpar or that may be eroded by future adverse events. In addition to the capital that could be generated within the company, the rating agency also considers the state of the capital markets, the ability and intent of a parent company (of the insurance company) to provide capital and the (limited) options a mutual life insurance company has to raise capital.*

6. *Unlike the ratings of the rating services that are intended to be measures of company risk, IRIS and RBC regulatory tools are not intended to be measures of risk. Additional investigation by regulators is required to determine if a company that "failed" the tests must take any actions and what these actions should be. Failure of these tests does not by itself indicate that a company has a significant risk of insolvency or impairment.*

7. *IRIS involves 12 ratios for life and health insurance companies. Each ratio is computed as a percentage and, depending on the ratio, it may be positive or negative. State regulators establish the usual ranges for the IRIS ratios by reviewing the ratios for companies that had become insolvent or had experienced financial difficulties in recent years. A company whose results fall outside the usual ranges in a number of the IRIS tests may be identified as requiring regulatory review and perhaps regulatory oversight.*

   There are no specific rules that determine the degree of regulatory response for a company whose results fall outside the usual ranges in a number of the IRIS tests. The response depends on such factors as the number of outside-the-usual-range results, their severity, the trends in the number and severity of previous outside-the-usual-range results, and the effects of previous reviews and actions. However, additional investigation by regulators is required to determine if a company that "failed" the tests must take any actions and what these actions should be.

8. *Under the RBC approach, a company determines the RBC standard amount of capital and surplus (based on the RBC formulas) each year. It then compares its actual capital and surplus, including the asset valuation reserve (AVR), to the computed RBC measure. The regulatory response, if any, depends on the results of this comparison. A company whose actual capital and surplus exceeds the computed RBC standard requires no regulatory action. If the company's actual capital and surplus falls between 75 percent and*

100 percent of the computed RBC standard, the company is required to file a plan of the actions it intends to take to eliminate this gap with its state regulators. If the company's actual capital and surplus falls between 50 percent and 75 percent of the computed RBC standard, the home state regulator has an obligation to undertake a detailed review of the company's operations and to mandate corrective actions. If the company's actual capital and surplus is below 50 percent of the computed RBC standard, the company is considered to be a candidate for seizure by the state regulator.

9. The following four types of risks are considered in determining the amount of risk-based capital and surplus required for a particular life insurance company:

    •   risks of asset default. This is the most important risk factor in terms of the proportion of the company's RBC it represents. Computations of the RBC objective for asset default risk take the following items into account:

        −   quality mix of assets, including the NAIC rating classes for bonds

        −   degree of diversification in an asset class

        −   mix of asset maturities

For large companies, the asset default risk constitutes almost 75 percent of the total calculated RBC standard. For smaller companies, the percentage of the RBC standard attributable to asset default risk factors is somewhat smaller.

    •   insurance risks, principally mortality and morbidity. This element is intended to provide additional protection (over and above the required reserves) for adverse trends and experience in life insurance mortality and/or health insurance morbidity or for premium inadequacies. Because the life insurance factors, which are applied to the net life insurance risk, decrease as the company's insurance risk amount increases, this element is a relatively more important component of the RBC standard for smaller companies than it is for larger companies. The health insurance factors are applied to premiums and vary by both type of health insurance coverage (hospital and medical insurance, disability income, and so on) and premium volume. For both life and health insurance, smaller factors apply to group insurance than to individual coverages. The insurance risk factors represent about 10 percent to 15 percent of the RBC standard for larger companies and a relatively greater percentage for smaller companies.

    •   interest rate deficiency risks. The interest risk is determined by applying factors to the amounts of insurance reserves. These factors depend on the level of risk (low, medium, or high) and on whether the company has received an unqualified actuarial opinion. Low-risk reserves include individual life insurance reserves and individual annuity

at book value but with large surrender charges (5 percent or more) are considered to be medium risk. The interest-risk factors range from about 10 percent of the total RBC standard for larger companies down to less than 5 percent for smaller companies for whom the insurance risk is relatively more important.

- *other business risks. The business risk factors are 2 percent of life insurance premiums and annuity considerations and 0.5 percent of health insurance premiums. This element generally constitutes 5 percent or less of the total RBC standard for companies of all sizes.*

10. *The limitations and problems in using information in published financial statements and comparative performance analyses in comparing each of the following types of performance for life insurance companies are:*

- *Financial strength. Measures of financial strength have typically been ratios of capital (usually defined as surplus plus the asset valuation reserve) to one or more measures of risk (assets, reserves, and so forth). As companies diversified their investment portfolios by type and quality and their liabilities became equally diverse, these broad general ratios have become virtually meaningless. This diversity must be brought into any competitive calculations, but even then the results must be used with great caution because the relative risk measures assigned to different types of assets and liabilities are themselves often arbitrary. Earnings growth. The standards used most frequently are the various earnings-per-share measures included in the GAAP financial statements.*

- *Statutory measures of income are less valuable because of SAP's emphasis on conservative measurement of assets and liabilities and the prevalence of certain types of reinsurance transactions.*

- *Pricing performance. The reason these comparisons are limited in value is that modern pricing techniques recognize the particular characteristics of the markets the companies serve and the unique costs of providing coverage in those markets. Most analyses of a company's experience and intercompany comparisons drawn from data in financial reports, on the other hand, must necessarily aggregate results for all markets and company addresses and, in some cases, for all lines of business. Aggregated data has no significance because the customer purchases a product designed for a particular market, and the information required to compare the past and anticipated experience of the two companies in that market is almost never available from the companies' financial statements. Therefore, while much information can be determined from a company's financial reports, the information is usually too aggregated to be*

relevant to the company's pricing decisions in the market(s) of interest to the agent or policyowner.

Chapter 21
Life Insurance Company Investments

Revised by: Francis H. Schott & C.W. Copeland

Learning Objectives

An understanding of the material in this chapter should enable the student to

1. **Identify the forces that have stimulated changes in life insurer investments and products.**

2. **Understand the dynamic nature of the investment process.**

3. **Describe some of the more prominent changes in life insurer investments since 1975.**

4. **Describe how the regulation of life insurer investments has been modified in recent decades.**

5. **Identify the commercial insurance rating companies, and explain why they have been so successful.**

6. **Explain how life insurance investing has become more conservative.**

7. **Understand the concept of asset liability matching.**

8. **Understand what a yield curve represents.**

9. **Describe recent trends regarding life insurer investments.**

Over the past 30 years the role of investment performance and policy has evolved from being a mere adjunct of product and sales management to becoming the lifeblood of a life insurance company. Instead of insurance driving investment, we encountered since the 1990s a dynamic interaction of the two sides of the business. The recession that started in the fourth quarter of 2008 has resulted in lower investment returns than those of the previous 5 decades. Since 2008, the Federal Reserve has limited interest rates on bonds to less than the interest rate guarantees in many life insurance contracts which is problematic for the insurers. Overall success depends on the profitable integration of the accumulation and disposition of funds.

HISTORICAL PERSPECTIVE

Effects of Inflation and Technology

The historic development of higher priority on investment management and coordination with product features was caused by the sharp acceleration of inflation in the late 1970s and early 1980s and the attendant near tripling of interest rates between 1975 and 1982. Long-term investments in bonds and mortgages had dominated insurance portfolios as the counterpart to whole life policies, the main accumulation product. These investments, with an average maturity of roughly 20 years, turned out to leave the industry behind in terms of yield on the savings element of life insurance as market rates of interest adjusted to inflation. Large parts of the industry became noncompetitive in attracting funds and subject to heavy outflows through surrenders and policy loans as policyowners took their savings elsewhere.

Initially in self-defense but later as an aggressive sales tool, the industry developed universal life and other products to compete with the then higher current yields by passing investment yields directly through to policyowners, encouraging in turn a scramble for high-yield investments and competition for funds based on interest rates. The nature of insurance contracts makes it nearly impossible for an insurer to make major and significant changes instantaneously. Two significant tactics were utilized to speed up such adjustments: (1) the start-up of brand new subsidiary insurance companies with the entire portfolio invested at current yields and (2) the exchange of old, in-force policies with new contracts containing lower premiums and variable interest rates for policy loans.

Interest-rate-based competition survived the relatively short period of historically high yields, which ended by the late 1990s. The investment field is now dealing with the consequences of low interest rates that are expected to increase slowly as the economy recovers from the recession. One of these consequences is the broadening of buyers' choices for insurance products and investment vehicles for the life insurance savings dollar. Another is an increase in the number of life companies that failed as sharpening competition cut into product margins and encouraged heightened investment risk-taking. Still another result is that annuities, with their highly visible yield link, have become more important than insurance in generating investable funds. The average maturity of the typical insurer's portfolio has also been cut in half, to roughly 10 years, both to minimize the yield lag if accelerating inflation returns and to accommodate the escape clauses in their contracts that corporate and individual policyowners now demand in anticipation of resurgent high interest rates and high inflation rates.

segmentation of the general account

equity kickers

On the more technical side of portfolio management, investment executives have had to learn and implement new technical and analytical skills. First and foremost, they have had to evaluate the liability characteristics of different insurance products with respect to a more detailed and complex set of risk classification categories to arrive at correct maturity and risk characteristics of the corresponding assets. One aspect of this process has been termed **segmentation of the general account** (grouping assets according to their risk characteristics and establishing criteria to maintain prescribed ratios of holdings in each of these segmentation categories). Second, the rising risk of policyowners' massive and instantaneous withdrawal of funds has required not only shorter asset maturities but also protective techniques (such as staggered maturities) and the increased use of liquid instruments (such as U.S. Treasury and agency securities). In addition, options, futures, and other partial offsets to a riskier environment have become routine among many companies. Finally, the search for inflation protection has led some companies into enlarged equity positions in the general account, mainly through the use of **equity kickers**,[1] warrants, or similar devices attached to debt instruments.

financialization

The **financialization**[2] of life insurance portfolios has created new problems for regulators, policyowners, and investors. Excess debt generated during the 1980s among corporations and commercial real estate interests was spurred to dangerous levels by the supercharged speculation by individual investors based on expectations of continued high levels of inflation. This was extensive among depository institutions such as savings and loan companies, but to a moderate degree also among competition-driven insurance companies. Consequently, insurance regulators backed off in the late 1980s and early 1990s from the liberalization in the early 1980s of the quantitative investment rules that had long been a characteristic of insurance laws. The trend in the 1990s was in the opposite direction—toward detailed limitations on the insurer's portfolio composition. Lowering the allowable proportion of low grade (junk) bonds is but one example. Substantial discretion—a prudent-man rule—continues to prevail for much of portfolio management. Since

---

1.   An equity kicker involves lender participation in part of the change in value of an asset when sold, as an added inducement to loan the funds needed to purchase the asset.

2.   Financialization is the creation of securities backed by an insurer's asset holdings, such as collateralized mortgage obligations, where the yield on the assets is paid to the security owner. They are often called pass-through securities.

2008, a major concern has been the extremely low yields on all types of debt instruments (bonds, mortgages, treasuries, and so on). The collapse of real estate values in late 2008 has brought into question the value of such items as equity kickers.

Interaction Between Regulators and Rating Agencies

rating agencies

As financial pressures increased through narrowing spreads on traditional insurance products, fierce competition in new product yields, and the rising cost of outside capital, commercial **rating agencies** entered the life insurance field for the first time in a serious and sustained manner. After the failures at Baldwin United and Charter Securities in the mid-1980s, ratings became important in the markets and to the companies. The negative publicity generated by a few major insurance company failures in the early 1990s (Executive Life, Mutual Benefit Life, Confederation Life) prompted both insurance agents and insurance consumers to increase their insistence on dealing only with insurers having the highest-quality ratings.

An interaction of regulators and rating agencies developed as each sought to generate early warnings for the public, policyowners, and investors. Much of the attention of both regulators and rating agencies was focused on the investment portfolio.

The overexuberance and debt overhang that resulted in the recession beginning in 2008 was especially apparent in rising mortgage delinquencies, falling real estate prices and a moderate rise in nonperforming bond holdings. The entire experience of failures and widespread writedowns led the insurance regulators toward broadened asset reserves effective in late 2009. The NAIC has tightened up its self-examination procedures to make sure that agreed-upon laws and regulations are actually enforced in each state.

Meanwhile, the search for new capital—simply to grow modestly or just to stay in business, quite apart from regulation—began to dominate industry thinking in late 2009 and continues in this decade. Traditional conservatism reasserted itself in all phases of insurance management. Nevertheless, two decades of rapid evolution have strengthened and broadened the investment function in many important ways. Investment officers have acquired a far greater knowledge of market instruments, are more flexible and adaptable in their use of instruments and techniques, participate more in insurance product development and marketing, and are wiser to the perils of the marketplace. Should the country's economic performance improve in the second decade of the 21st century, investment management is poised to take advantage of developing opportunities and, one hopes, will not forget the lessons of the prior two decades. The reliance on rating agencies has been somewhat

shaken by the subprime mortgage fiasco that led to a worldwide economic collapse in 2008. The rating agencies had been giving AAA ratings to very low quality mortgage backed securities. The high default rate on these securities continues to slow the economic recovery.

LIFE INSURANCE PORTFOLIO MANAGEMENT

Role of the Industry in Investment Markets

Some of the changes generated by life insurance's increased investment orientation are revealed by changes in the industry's aggregate assets. (See table below.)

Table 21-1 Distribution of Assets of U.S. Life Insurance Companies	1975		2012	
	$ billions	% of total	$ billions	% of total
Government securities	15.2	5.2	458.9	7.9
Corporate securities	105.8	36.6	1,893.5	32.8
Mortgages	89.2	30.8	937.3	16.2
Stocks	28.1	9.7	1,725.2	29.9
Real estate	9.6	3.3	30.6	0.5
Policy loans	24.5	8.5	130.7	2.3
Miscellaneous	17.0	5.9	601.1	10.4
Total	289.4	100.0	5,777.3	100.0
Source: American Council of Life Insurance (ACLI) Fact Book, 1976 and 2013. Reprinted with permission.				

The first—and a crucial—observation is that despite economic instability and rapid change, the growth rate of industry assets over the 32-year period from 1975 to 2007, at over 9.4 percent annually, has been ahead of the inflation rate and comfortably in line with the average of other financial institutions. Since 2008, industry growth has decreased significantly but most of the companies have been able to maintain a strong financial position. Only three life insurers received bailout funds from the government to survive and they are repaying or have repaid the funds.

The life insurance industry has also done better than commercial banks because the industry has successfully adapted its products to the public's greater financial orientation.

On the other hand, insurance has not grown as rapidly as mutual funds and money market funds because liquidity and flexibility in response to changing consumer demand have only gradually become life insurance industry attributes.

Changes in Investment Characteristics

guaranteed interest contracts (GICs)

Investments generally considered long term (corporate bonds and mortgages combined) accounted for over two-thirds of total investments in 1975 but were down to about 49 percent in 2012. The industry continues to be a leading supplier of corporate debt and commercial mortgage funds. Yet the shift toward annuities and **guaranteed interest contracts (GICs)**[3] as sources of funds, together with the need for liquidity in a volatile external environment, has led to major changes in the characteristics of these GIC investments.

First, the average maturity of the nonmarketable part of long-term investments has been cut sharply. Crudely and imprecisely, as average maturity was halved, the annual turnover rate of the portfolio was doubled in the 37-year period covered in Table 21-1 to roughly 10 percent. This permits a more frequent "fresh look at your money," including its use to pay off liabilities instead of reinvesting.

securitized mortgages

Second, both bonds and mortgage investments have been heavily redirected toward public securities rather than toward directly negotiated deals with debtors. Thus, marketable bonds (including privately issued mortgage-backed bonds) have gained heavily at the expense of direct placements, and **securitized mortgages** (especially including pass-through securities and collateralized mortgage obligations [CMOs] of federal housing agencies) have virtually become the exclusive life insurance method of investing in residential mortgages (10.1 percent of assets in 2012). (Efforts to securitize commercial mortgages are hampered by the individualized characteristics of commercial structures and by high underwriting costs associated with parcel-by-parcel securitization.)

Unfortunately, life insurer holdings of securitized mortgages has in some cases become a threat to solvency. Securitized mortgages and all other financial derivatives were exempted from oversight or regulation in the Graham-Leach-Bliley Act passed in 1999. That federal law also repealed the Glass-Steagall Act and thus permitted financial institutions

---

3. GICs are frequently negotiated with employers as one of the employee options available in qualified plans. The contract specifies the investment earnings it will pay a year at a time (in advance). Usually these one-year guarantees are covered by existing asset holdings.

to compete with any other type of financial institution. This breakdown of separation between banks, insurers, investment banks, stock brokerages and other financial institutions was not accompanied by a change in the regulatory boundaries which had been built around the restrictions of the Glass-Steagall Act. These factors contributed to the subprime mortgage debacle that eventually resulted in the credit freeze and market declines that emerged in September 2008 and beyond.

Many securitized mortgage packages were composed of mortgages that were not of high quality but the originators of the packages passed them off in the marketplace as high quality. The rating agencies relied on these false representations and gave the packages AAA ratings. Sales of the securitized mortgages in the secondary markets spread these instruments all over the globe with holders unaware they held inferior investments because they trusted the AAA ratings. As mortgage defaults started mounting, the value of the packages declined. The true value of the packages was hard to determine. The declines in value have threatened the solvency of some institutional holders because they have reported their holdings under the mark-to-market rules of accounting. Life insurer holdings of securitized mortgages are subject to the same problems of valuation.

A special report from the A.M. Best Company reflecting the assets of 101 life insurance companies at the end of 2009 indicated that the subset of companies held 11.4 percent of assets as collateralized mortgage obligations and 13.6 percent of assets as mortgage loans. This is significantly higher than the life insurance fact book figures for 2008 representing all life insurers operating in the U.S. The difference is a combination of a one year time interval and the investment characteristics of the total population and the 101 company subset.

Third, the doubling of United States government securities in their share of life insurance investments over the period studied is confirmation of the liquidity drive of the industry. (Over one-third of the $634.3 billion of Government Securities held in 2008 consisted of federally backed mortgage securities, where good yield or "portfolio fit" with liabilities may have counted as heavily as liquidity per se.) The holdings of government securities has declined since 2008 from 13.6 percent of assets to 7.8 percent of assets in 2010 because of the very low yields created on those since 2008.

Separate Accounts, Pooled Separate Accounts

separate accounts

Common stocks in insurance companies' general accounts are limited to 10 percent of assets under New York insurance law, which tends to dominate investment regulations throughout the country. The desirable liquidity characteristic of equities is deemed to be

largely offset by the problem of substantial price and total-return fluctuations of common stocks. The industry's general account holdings have remained well below the ten percent legal limit at 2.0 percent, but total holdings have risen to above 10 percent to 29.7 in 2012 because **separate accounts** (linked to pensions, variable life, variable universal life, and variable annuities) have gained relative to the general account. In such accounts, the nonguaranteed return of best-effort stock market investing flows through directly to the client. Separate accounts originated with the competition for corporate pension funds. Common stocks account for as much as 50 percent of aggregate pension fund assets because it is hoped that long-term equity gains may reduce the cost of pensions to companies. Hence, insurance companies had to be granted separate-account powers (in the 1960s) to compete effectively for pension fund management.

Since the mid-1980s, the growth of investment choices and client discretion in growing individual products, such as variable life, variable universal life, and variable annuities, has provided vehicles for life insurance investment in common stocks—pooled separate accounts of individual clients. Bond funds for such clients are also growing. In the mid-1980s separate accounts passed the 10 percent mark as a share of life insurance assets, and they gained further in the 1990s—a clear manifestation of the rising importance of investment management in attracting funds to insurance companies. Separate accounts are advantageous to the industry because the risk-based capital standards implemented in 1994 treat such accounts lightly; the client, not the company, bears the risk. By 2012, separate accounts had grown to over 36 percent of total industry assets and within the separate accounts over 79 percent was allocated to stocks.

Enhanced Liquidity

disintermediation

The growth of policy loans during **disintermediation**[4] periods was the original reason for turning toward enhanced liquidity in life insurance portfolios. When market interest rates were above those that insurance companies were able to charge contractually, as occurred during tight-money episodes, it paid the insured to take out a policy loan. (The proceeds could be invested at a rate above that paid to the insurance company, or borrowing at rates in excess of the cost of a policy loan could be avoided.) Legal and regulatory changes, combined with redesigned contracts, have enabled companies to whittle down the policy loan share of assets. Loan rates are now indexed to a bond market rate, or if they are fixed, tend

---

4.   Disintermediation is the withdrawal of funds from financial institutions by the depositor/owners so they can invest directly in securities at high current yields. It usually occurs when interest rates go up very rapidly.

to be at 8 percent. Yet concerns about liquidity, disintermediation and policy loan earnings remain. A special report by the A.M. Best Company in 2010 indicated that the life insurance industry had suffered decreased liquidity in 2008 but liquidity had increased some by the end of 2009.

Investment Organization and Principles

Life insurance investment has always been a spread business in the sense that management seeks a yield on investments in excess of the implicit rate credited to policies as their cash value grows over the years. Until universal life became a factor in the mid-1990s, however, this spread was known to very few and understood by even fewer. Business judgments and accounting factors relating to mortality, commissions, and operating expenses often helped to mask the investment yield spread and related issues. Once interest rates and/or equity performance became explicit, competition forced an all-around sharpening of pencils, and margins in general became smaller. Meanwhile, the product portfolio was constantly expanding during the last two decades, and differential characteristics among products forced product-by-product asset management.

One obvious way to manage assets on a product-by-product basis is the individualization of product accounts. Thus, whole life, universal life, single-premium life, variable life, variable universal life, single-premium annuities, equity indexed annuities, and GICs for corporate savings plans can each be considered a specialized asset/liability problem subject to individual solutions. This may involve establishing product-differentiated subsidiaries of a parent company, formal separate accounts, or internal segmentation of the general account. Creating product-differentiated subsidiaries or separate product accounts typically requires much legal work and regulatory approval. Segmentation, however, is almost entirely at management's discretion, provided that the company makes no attempt to avoid its de facto responsibility for all liabilities, regardless of its internal accounting.

Investment management's first task in segmentation is to develop criteria by which to distinguish investment policy by product. The scheme in Table 21-2 helps to illustrate the criteria and possible outcomes of such deliberations.

back-end withdrawal penalties

This scheme is far from noncontroversial. Moreover, it is only a sample of products and criteria. Thus the intuitive results—such as life insurance requires less liquidity than annuities and GICs, and total yield requirements are highest in the most investment-oriented and interest-sensitive products—are subject to further evaluation. For example, the specific withdrawal provisions of the company's single-premium deferred annuities (SPDAs) and

the term distribution of the portfolio make a difference. Stiff **back-end withdrawal penalties**, a long stretch-out phase for the expiration of such penalties, and a large percentage of annuities to which the penalties still apply all work toward making the portfolio less susceptible to withdrawal and, therefore, to liquidity requirements, and vice versa. Because product and asset characteristics interact, they must be determined by simultaneous equations.

The recency of product differentiation and asset segmentation suggests that much in the type of scheme outlined here remains subject to review on the basis of future experience, especially for investment-sensitive products. The average duration of the huge amount of SPDAs put on the books in the last two decades is unknown, as is the percentage of outstanding SPDAs still subject to surrender charges. Nor have all of the new products yet undergone a full interest rate and economic cycle. Nevertheless, asset/liability management by product is a vital step forward in making (eventually profitable) business decisions, and enough time has passed to permit verification of the direct relevance of surrender terms to the likelihood of actual withdrawal.

Table 21-2
Sample Characteristics of "Appropriate" Investment Portfolios by Product

	Liquidity Need	Duration	Total Yield Needs
Whole life	–	+	–
Universal life	=	+	=
Single-premium deferred annuities (SPDAs)	+	–	+
Guaranteed interest contracts (GICs)	=	–	+
= (portfolio average)			
+ (above portfolio average)			
– (below portfolio average)			
Source: Author's consultations with life insurance investment officers.			

Practical Investment Decisions and Problems

yield curve

A study of yield curves offers a crude, yet instructive, approximation of the practicalities of modern investment management. At any given moment, an almost infinite variety of interest rates of the market confronts the financial intermediary who seeks funds for

investment. To protect against interest rate risk means matching assets and liabilities, at least approximately, along the **yield curve** (defined as an array of interest rates by maturity of the underlying debt).

The normal yield curve is sloped upward because price and credit risk—as well as uncertainty itself—tend to increase with maturity. The steepness of this upward slope, however, varies sharply with the business cycle phase. Generally the slope is steepest at or near the bottom of the cycle and flattens as full employment and inflation dangers approach. About one-fifth of the time from 1970 to 2004 the yield curve was inverted—that is, short rates exceeded long rates, typically under the influence of the extremely restrictive monetary policy during inflation and interest rate peaks. Normal yield curves prevailed for most of the 1990s and the current decade. However, the interest rates have plunged since the onset of the recession in 2008 and have been maintained at historically low levels by the Federal Reserve Bank. The yields on treasury issues actually became negative in parts of 2009 and 2010.

Figure 1
Yield Curve (November 6, 2012)

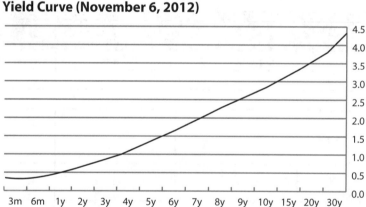

U.S. Treasuries are Treasury bills (up to and including one year), Treasury notes (2-year to 10-year securities), and bonds (up to 30 years). Sources: Federal Reserve.

The preceding figure offers a yield curve for United States government bonds as of November 6, 2012. The yields are significantly lower than in more normal times prior to 2008. The Federal Reserve Bank has deliberately held interest rates low since 2008. A difference of one quarter point in average yield on the portfolio can be highly significant to an insurance company's bottom line.

In August 2008, the rates for treasury bills ranged from 1.68 percent at 3-month maturities to 4.63 percent for 30-year maturities. The AAA-rated corporate seasoned bonds rate was 5.73 percent and the Baa-rated corporate seasoned bonds rate was 7.22 percent. By November of 2008 the rate on all duration treasuries had fallen lower than the August 2008 rates. However, the rates on seasoned Corporate bonds had increased to 6.34 percent for AAA and 9.22 percent for Baa as a result of the credit freeze and market downturn that started in September 2008.

In November 2012, rates on Treasury issues had dropped to 0.11 percent for 3-month maturities and to 2.9 percent for 30-year maturities. The yields on AAA-rated corporate seasoned bonds had dropped to 4.23 percent and as of the end of 2014, no significant change had occurred.

Investment Diversity

The first and most important point is that life insurance companies now operate throughout the maturity spectrum as they seek outlets for withdrawable funds generated by investment-sensitive insurance products. As late as the early 1970s, the industry operated almost exclusively at the long end of the yield curve (with only a marginal involvement at the shortest end).

joint ventures

A second key point is that the industry has also diversified by type of investment. As mentioned earlier, there has been a rise in public corporate bonds (compared to private placements) securitized mortgages, and directly negotiated deals. One may add junk bonds for general account or separate account investment, a greater variety of common stock and bond portfolios for pension or new-product investments (growth, income, or balanced accounts, for example), and the increased involvement of a few companies in equity real estate through such devices as **joint ventures** with developers (the insurance company receives a share of the equity in return for supplying a long-term mortgage). This investment diversity has added to the complexity of investment operations in a new-product environment for insurance. It has also created new wrinkles in investments that enhance the ability to ferret out additional niches of funds (with or without a major insurance component).

Attendant Risks

It stands to reason that increased complexity brings difficult problems. Among these, the actual process of matching maturities of assets and liabilities stands out. The first difficulty

is that retail insurance sales cannot be matched with regularity and precision in an investment operation that has to be wholesale to be efficient. The very nature of an insurance company therefore creates a degree of mismatch. The second difficulty is that the actual maturity of liabilities may be misjudged or be in fact unpredictable. The disintermediation episodes of the 1970s and 1980s showed that even whole-life-based liabilities could suddenly "mature" by having contracts surrendered or cash reserves borrowed against if market rates exceeded inside rates by a large margin. The first decade of this century proved that the prepayment risk on high-interest securities is a very real one when the general interest rate level turns down as it did after 2001. A third (and fundamental) difficulty is that the cost of acquiring the liabilities may preclude precise maturity matching at orthodox credit risk levels.

Failure to resolve this last difficulty was at the bottom of most insurance company crash landings of the late 1980s and early 1990s. The "best" solution—foregoing the business—may be unacceptable to top management. Other noninvestment answers include reducing the expense margins necessary to acquire and administer the liabilities (possible but painful) and stiffening the backload penalties for withdrawals and thus reducing their probability (also possible but subject to the same competitive pressures that caused the problem in the first place).

The temptation, therefore, is to do one of the following: (1) risk a mismatch by taking in assets with longer maturities than the most probable maturity of liabilities, which improves the calculated financials in a normal yield-curve environment or (2) take additional credit risk, thus obtaining higher returns at any given maturity of the yield curve. A third risk is diversifying investments insufficiently, which may or may not be directly related to the yield curve. Thus in the failure of Executive Life (California and New York, 1991), First Capital Life of California (1991), and Fidelity Bankers Life (Virginia, 1991) extra yield was obtained through excessive credit risk and concentration in junk bonds. (At Executive Life, maturity matching appeared to be very good until suspicions led to mass withdrawals, especially of SPDA funds, regardless of back-end penalties.) In the case of Mutual Benefit Life (New Jersey, 1991) an unusual concentration in one asset class and location—Florida mortgages—constituted a maturity mismatch, as well as an excessive credit risk, during a major commercial real estate recession. The extremely low interest rates since 2008 have induced many life insurers to hold higher levels of cash and cash equivalents than has historically been the case.

Some Technical Aspects of Investment Management

The keen competition among asset managers has forced life insurance portfolio management to adopt highly technical and sophisticated evaluation and simulation models. The rapid evolution of academic finance and computer calculating capacity has also been a major factor in making the rigorous analysis feasible. Monte Carlo computer simulations allow analysts to quickly look at thousands of possible scenarios for evaluating alternatives.

Duration Balancing

duration

In practice, asset/liability matching is approximated through duration balancing of blocks of business (general account segments or their subsets). **Duration**, a traditional concept of bond finance, measures the weighted average maturity to term of a series of cash flows arising from an obligation. (For example, the less frequent interest and principal repayments are, the longer the duration of a bond. Thus, duration can differ among two bonds of identical average and final maturity.) The duration of the corresponding liabilities tends to be even more difficult to estimate than that of assets, but even assets can deviate from initially calculated duration if restructuring or defaults occur, or if they have prepayment or call options. Thus the reinvestment risk for the large blocks of mortgage-backed securities acquired in recent years is considerable. The underlying mortgages can typically be prepaid when interest rates decline and new securities can be substituted only at lower interest rate earnings while rates payable on the corresponding liabilities may not be equally adjustable.

In addition, duration itself changes with interest rate changes so the value of any portfolio will tend to diverge from initial calculations. A concept known as convexity measures the variability of portfolio asset durations in response to interest rate changes. Convexity helps to define acceptable limits on the asset side to the almost inevitable mismatches of duration of liabilities.

Barbell Strategy

barbell strategy

Barbell strategy is a concept applied in both liquidity and risk management. A portfolio may be forced into sufficient liquidity by having one concentration of assets at the shortest end of the yield curve while another concentration at the long end provides excess return over the yield requirements of the corresponding liabilities and thus offers

a profit potential. Precisely the same strategy may be applied in concentrating on low-risk and high-risk assets rather than accepting middle-range risk throughout the portfolio. The measured weighted risk can, therefore, remain acceptable even while investment managers hope to exploit the potential extra return of, say, junk bonds or equity warrants. (Barbell strategy bears a family resemblance to traditional life insurance investment at only the shortest and longest maturity ends. Naturally, a barbell-weighted portfolio will not perform as hoped when the yield curve steepens. The long securities may decline in value, while the short securities gain little, if any, in price.)

Hedging

hedging

Derivative securities transactions have multiplied immensely in financial markets and have gradually been practiced in life insurance investment management. New York insurance law restricts such transactions by characteristics and amounts; only **hedging** (and not speculating) is permitted, and amounts outstanding may not exceed 15 percent of admitted assets. Financial futures, options, and interest rate swaps have come into use, with hedging through Treasury bond futures contracts developing into a very broad and liquid market—possibly constituting the most frequent operation.

Suppose an insurance company has negotiated for a block of GIC money to be acquired 3 months hence at a rate guaranteed to the client for the next 5 years. Because the company does not yet have the cash to invest, it hedges by purchasing a 5-year U.S. Treasury bond futures contract at a yield known today to approximate (not necessarily match exactly) the guaranteed interest rate, with a forward delivery date roughly matching that of the expected funds delivery. The price change of the futures contract will then tend to inversely match the difference between the rate the company guaranteed at contract time and the rate actually available for investment when the cash is received. The insurance company has thus hedged the open position it assumed at the time of acquiring future funds and guaranteeing the rate it will pay.

The example above oversimplifies the process and the calculation and overstates the certainty of the result, but it accurately describes a practical method of reducing interest rate risk. One of the major possible refinements is the use of a combination of hedges—synthetic hedges—to closely approximate the terms of an interest rate guarantee that may have been extended but for which a direct public-market equivalent may not be available.

Covered Call Options

covered call

The sale of **covered call options** against a portfolio of options marketable bonds illustrates permitted use of options. In broad markets, as exist for United States Treasuries, there will almost invariably be buyers of the right to purchase bonds at a predetermined "strike" price. This price may slightly or substantially exceed the actual cash price. Selling the option enhances current income on the bonds beyond their stated yield, but it gives up potential future price gains to the purchaser of the option. The operation is virtually riskless if the company holds the exact optioned bonds in its portfolio, and it is appropriate provided the client—whether the insurance operators or an outside investment client—understands the trade-off to obtain the extra yield from the covered call option.

Efficient Frontier Calculations

efficient frontier

Modern portfolio theory can also be applied to common stock strategy. Offering investment management to pension clients through commingled or individual separate accounts requires insurance companies to handle **efficient frontier** calculations and to manage accordingly. It is assumed that risk and total return on equities will rise or fall jointly, and risk is typically measured by the price variability (the beta) of the stock relative to an average or index of stocks. (A beta larger than one means that the stock fluctuates more widely than the market; a beta smaller than one indicates that the stock fluctuates less widely.) Exposing the trade-off between risk and return determines the point on a constructed convex efficient frontier line that corresponds to the client's preference and thus attracts his or her business. If the preference turns out to be a simple averaging of stocks in the market, the company can develop and offer an index fund with expected results similar to the market as a whole.

While analyses clarify risks and technical operations ameliorate these risks, neither analysis nor execution is cost free. Typically, the potential gain is reduced along with the risk, and although uncertainty is reduced, it is not eliminated. Thus, investment management can avoid extremes, but the fact remains that obtaining satisfactory investment earnings involves risks. The risks increase sharply if a significant contribution to a company's bottom line is expected from the investment function. Such expectations may lead to untoward investment risk. Once bottom-line pressures are caused by insurance product terms and/or expenses that cannot be satisfied with conservative investments, investment management may be tempted to go out on a limb. When good investment judgment is overridden,

technical expertise becomes largely irrelevant. Regulators and rating agencies have become increasingly alert to this problem since the past investment-related failures.

REGULATION OF LIFE INSURANCE INVESTMENTS

Overview and Brief History

Life insurance investments are regulated in all 50 states, as are most aspects of insurance law and supervision. Until a few years ago, New York state law dominated investment regulation because of New York City's central role in financial markets and because for many years companies doing business in New York state accounted for about three-quarters of all United States insurance sales. In 1996, however, a model insurance investment law (defined limits version) was prepared under the aegis of the National Association of Insurance Commissioners (NAIC) with the goal of having it adopted by all 50 states. It was followed in 1998 by another NAIC model insurance investment law (defined standards version).

Actual regulation has gone through three phases: reliance on traditional measures and methods prior to the 1980s (albeit with gradual refinements), substantial liberalization during most of the 1980s, and a search for modern and possibly tightened standards in recent years. These phases reflect the place of insurance in finance and its standing as a long-regulated industry. The market disruption by inflation and interest rate volatility beginning in the 1970s played a key role in confronting the industry and its regulators with serious new problems. Other important factors unhinging traditional regulatory measures were the cross-invasion of each other's territory by previously distinct types of financial institutions and the closely interrelated technological advances in back-office productivity through computerized data collection, record keeping, and client service.

A further and truly decisive factor contributing to the liberalization phase of the 1980s, however, was the nation's general turn toward deregulation. The movement was fostered initially in the 1970s by the hope that less regulation would mean more competition and, therefore, help to keep prices down in industries that had been closely regulated (trucking, air travel, commissions in securities transactions, and so on). By the early 1980s, the movement had gained impetus, and liberalization crept closer to the insurance industry via federal laws giving depository institutions interest-rate freedom and easing asset restrictions. This liberalization greatly influenced insurance regulators, although state-by-state regulation necessarily meant a much slower transition than in federally regulated industries.

By the late 1980s, the pendulum was beginning to swing back, and this trend accelerated in the early 1990s. Investment factors were a key to the latest change. Insolvencies, which had been few prior to 1987, accelerated. An ACLI study in 1990 found that 31 of 68 insolvency cases from 1985 to 1990 were related in part to investment problems, although other factors—fraud, underpricing—were even more frequent causes. (These various factors are of course not mutually exclusive.) By the early 1990s, however, investment problems had quite possibly become the leading cause of insolvencies. In addition, as will be noted later, insurance rating agencies' closer attention to insurance portfolios and their frequent downgradings based on investment problems implied that regulators might drop "behind the curve" and not be near the optimal mix of yield and risk unless they redoubled their investment analysis. Thus, a push toward conservatism through regulation and supervision gained momentum in the 1990s. Risk-based capital standards, another regulatory item adopted in 1994, were closely related to investment supervision since portfolio problems had given rise to capital deficiencies in the major insolvency cases of 1991. The risk-based capital model ties the minimum capital requirements to the risk characteristics of the investment portfolio. Many insurers have reacted by shifting more of their investments into higher-quality, lower-volatility assets. The low yields available during the first decade of the 21st century have presented new challenges and promoted more use of the derivative investments encouraged by the 1999 Graham-Leach-Bliley Act. That act also allowed other financial institutions (banks, investment bankers, stock brokers, broker-dealers, and others) to compete directly with life insurers This was the ultimate in deregulation which played a significant part in the recession of 2008 and beyond.

Traditional Regulation

Pre-1970s regulation emphasized that policy reserves, conservatively valued, should fully cover insurance liabilities. (Since changes in law and regulation have been gradual—even marginal—many of the traditional requirements still apply.)

In the key New York State law, therefore, quality and diversification were enforced through investment prescriptions and proscriptions. Major latitude was granted for long-term, private-sector earning assets, such as corporate bonds and commercial and residential mortgages (total mortgages had a very generous quantitative limit of 50 percent of assets), as well as for United States government securities. Other investments, judged more risky and/or less reliable as to earnings, were—and remain—rather strictly limited. Thus, common stock can constitute only 10 percent of general account assets, as noted, even after several liberalizations over the decades; investment real estate is at 20 percent; foreign investment is at 3 percent (although a separate 10 percent limit applies to Canadian holdings); and, very significantly, a leeway clause permits a liberalized 10 percent of assets to be held

outside the otherwise applicable limits, thereby granting significant discretion to go into novel or generally more risky investments such as derivatives introduced after 1999.

Qualitative Constraints

qualitative constraints

Qualitative constraints. Within the quantitative freedom for corporate bonds and mortgages, qualitative standards still apply. Bonds must meet the issuer's earnings test, and lower-grade holdings are curbed. Commercial mortgages are subject to a 75 percent loan-to-value limit. Both bonds and mortgages are limited as to the percentage of assets for which any one debtor can account. (The leeway clause permits an out in specific cases, provided it is not yet fully used—for example, a mortgage loan can be 90 percent of appraised value if 15 percentage points are charged to the leeway, also known as the "basket clause.") Obviously the subprime mortgage problems were created by securitized mortgages that did not satisfy these criteria. The life insurers were not the originators of these securitized mortgages of questionable quality. However, they may have acquired some of the tainted securitized mortgages that were rated AAA but composed of many lower grade mortgages in the secondary markets.

It is clear that an earnings test for bonds or a loan-to-value ratio for mortgages tends to emphasize the past or the present rather than to be an impossible-to-obtain reliable future forecast. The calculus of routine regulation does not encompass adverse general market developments. Thus, judgment strongly influences management's investment decisions. While company capital and its adequacy are the bottom-line test for investment risk, regulators have sought to build intermediate barriers to cushion the effect of adverse portfolio developments. The market fiasco of late 2008 has severely tested these safety margins.

Reserve Accounts

mandatory security valuation reserve (MSVR)

interest maintenance reserve (IMR)

asset valuation reserve (AVR)

The first line of these defenses used to be the **mandatory security valuation reserve (MSVR)**, which was a buffer (shock absorber) between the decline in value of market-traded securities and insurer surplus and capital. The MSVR has been supplanted by two reserve accounts (discussed more fully later in this chapter): (1) **interest maintenance reserve (IMR)** and (2) **asset valuation reserve (AVR)**. Their combined function

is essentially the same as the previous MSVR. The IMR and AVR recognize that there are multiple sources of asset value fluctuation risk, and theynseparate out the interest rate risk of fixed-interest securities. The NAIC, through a Securities Valuation Office, evaluates the quality rating of the bonds in insurance company portfolios.

Common stocks command MSVR holdings in a manner similar to the new AVR require-ments. In fact, the stiff provisions of the rules applicable to equities have been a significant factor in curbing common stocks in the general account. The rules, reflecting the perceived wide fluctuations of equity prices, make it difficult to credit the gains from capital values to the policyowner, which make up a large proportion of the total return from equities over the long term. Curiously, however, equity real estate or mortgages have not been subject to the MSVR in traditional insurance regulation, perhaps on the theory that equity real estate was a minor holding and mortgages were not risky if they were restricted by loan-to-value rules.

Writedowns

writedowns

A second line of regulatory defense has required **writedowns** of company assets as a consequence of adverse developments. Basically, bonds and mortgages are permitted to be held at cost and not at market value, thus stabilizing investment values. But an NAIC decision to recognize major writedown problems and/or outright default of troubled investments points to any inadequacies in the remaining IMR and AVR or company capital.

Liberalization and the Beginning of Retraction

By the early 1980s, although not abandoned, a great many quantitative rules had been liberalized. As discussed earlier, larger portions of total assets in equities in real estate, in foreign holdings, and in leeway investments had gradually been permitted. Liberalization reached a high point in 1983 when New York insurance law substituted a prudent-man rule for many of the inside prescriptions within each category of permitted assets (although the general quantitative limits by asset categories remained in effect). Actual and potential abuses soon forced reconsideration of liberalized regulation.

below-investment-grade bonds

Below-investment-grade bonds (by the standards of bond rating agencies) had long con-stituted a substantial part of life insurance portfolios without creating any hazards. These bonds were companies' direct-placement issues that had not yet reached the financial

ratios required for investment grade but could pass the earnings test(s) of insurance regulation. The lead insurance companies' close scrutiny of the borrower in such financings, combined with the earnings test(s), virtually assured very few credit problems in such a bond portfolio.

The merger and acquisition and leveraged buyout craze of the 1980s changed this situation materially. Coming at a time when new product needs drove insurance companies into the public market, high-yield, high-risk junk bonds infiltrated insurance portfolios. By 1987, perceiving impending danger, the New York Insurance Department issued an edict limiting such bonds to 20 percent of assets. This regulation was later broadened so that by 1992 the 20 percent limit had additional internal components further restricting holdings (including direct placements) by officially defining riskiness in progressive steps. These rules went beyond preliberalization regulations and, in effect, declared that similarly graded past MSVR requirements were not sufficient.

Another important step in modifying liberalization also occurred during the mid-1980s. New York State adopted Regulation 126, a rule requiring justification for the interest rate and cash-flow assumptions underlying the asset/liability match of interest-sensitive products. Aggressive companies had bid up the interest rates they offered on GICs, SPDAs and universal life during the high-rate environment of the early 1980s. Such guarantees on liabilities created surplus strain (weakening of capital ratios) because the earnings assumptions for the corresponding assets were held down by state regulation. High portfolio earnings of the blocks of funds involved were required in order to meet the guarantees and to eliminate the initial capital strain. In addition, the withdrawal privileges often extended for new products, qualified as they might be, generated potential cash-flow problems over questions of asset/liability matching with respect to maturities and values. The New York regulation asked company valuation actuaries to perform adequacy tests under a variety of interest rate scenarios over the life of defined blocks of business. The formulation and enforcement of this rule were key factors in helping regulatory and company actuaries reach an understanding with the investment side of the house about the dynamics of investment-sensitive products.

Model Investment Law, Expanded Asset/Interest Reserves, Risk-based Capital Standards

In addition to several substantial company failures directly related to investment problems, as noted before, the 1990s witnessed a continuing severe commercial real estate recession. Nonperforming real estate loans rose to a post-Great Depression peak of about 7 percent in 1992.

Furthermore, the moderate economic growth in the 1990s prolonged the unusually large credit problems in the corporate sector, despite a solid recovery of general bond values associated with a major decline of interest rates. Thus, investment regulation of insurance companies remains a challenge to state insurance departments—a challenge accentuated by the increasing role of rating agencies in evaluating company acceptability in the general insurance market. In particular, the regulators and the regulated alike have become aware that perceptions of a company's soundness, including its ratings, might be as important in avoiding runs (and ruin) as any objective standards applied by the regulators. The erroneous ratings of mortgage securities since 2001 have eroded confidence in the integrity of the rating agencies.

Reversion to Strict Rules

The repercussions from the crises among depository institutions were yet another factor in the insurance regulation of the 1990s, especially the emphasis on risk relative to capital in evaluating the need for and tightness of an institution's supervision. With the NAIC's Model Investment Law, anticipating potential company problems by appropriate regulation became the dominant theme.

model investment law

The **model investment law** carefully defines allowed asset classes and establishes concentration limits within these classes, somewhat similar to previous regulations. Even prior to a final draft of the model investment law, the MSVR was transformed into an Asset Valuation Reserve, in which all classes of assets, including real estate, are exposed to reserving rules. In addition, the accumulation rules are stiffer.

Simultaneously, companies were subjected to a new reserve requirement, the Interest Maintenance Reserve. The IMR makes it mandatory to amortize security valuation gains from interest rate changes over the remaining life of a security, rather than having the gains contribute to the profits (or surplus) in the year in which they occur. This new provision will slow up the realization of profits originating in the interest rate declines of the early 1990s, but it will presumably also provide a cushion for interest-rate-caused losses in each sustained upturn of rates.

It appears likely that the eventual investment rules will vary with a company's capitalization, with strongly capitalized companies enjoying greater freedoms than weakly capitalized ones. As one example, weaker companies might be confined to publicly traded corporate bonds and negotiable private-placement bonds, whereas stronger companies could invest in private placements. Furthermore, for purposes of investment latitude, a

company's capitalization might be measured not only by capital and surplus versus total assets but also by the ratio of capital to risk-weighted assets. The risk weighing might in turn be influenced by asset concentration ratios, such as an unusually large proportion of mortgages in one location or a large ratio of below-investment-grade bonds.

Difficult Issues

Some very sticky issues delayed until 1996 the final draft and adoption of the Investments of Insurers Model Act. One such issue was the required integration of risk-based capital standards with the model law. (The risk-based capital standards, for which state-by-state adoption was being sought by the NAIC in the 1993–94 time frame, cover risks beyond those relating to investments alone. Other risks requiring capital include withdrawal potential on the insurance liability side and possible state guaranty fund calls.)

Another issue is the permissible extent of the use of derivative instruments and the disclosure requirements associated with their use. These issues prompted the 1998 NAIC model investments law. It seems clear that protection, rather than speculation, will remain the key to permissibility, but the distinction is more easily stated in theory than applied in practice. Advancing financial technology, from which insurance companies cannot be isolated, is in itself a problem since regulation is almost necessarily a step behind bright operators. (Gaps may also develop in understanding the latest techniques between these bright operators on the one hand, and top management and the directors on the other—a difficult internal company problem that occurs frequently.) Still another difficulty is the required length of any phase-in period for regulations more restrictive than the existing ones. The Graham Leach Bliley Act passed in 1999 provided that there would be no oversight or regulation of derivative instruments which conflicts with the insurance regulations. Those derivative instruments played a major role in the recession of 2008, especially the erroneously rated securitized mortgages, the credit default swaps, and the interest default swaps.

Reversion to strict rules appears desirable for many reasons. Reassuring the public of life insurance's soundness is the most important one; discovering and pursuing early warning supervision systems is a close corollary. Still, innovation in product design and investment policy should be encouraged, not suppressed. It is impossible to draw a rigid line around the insurance industry when financial service institutions are characterized by increasing and highly competitive overlaps. The risk of failure—indeed, occasional actual failure—increases with the attraction of talented and spirited young people to the investment function and to the insurance industry in general. The problem is to confine greed, susceptibility to imprudence, and ambition itself to limits compatible with the productive function of investments within the conservative societal role of insurance. It is helpful that

the competitors, especially the banking industry, are likewise experiencing more stringent tightening of capital adequacy and lending rules in the wake of the abuses within their industry.

LIFE INSURANCE INVESTMENTS AND COMMERCIAL RATING AGENCIES

Reasons for Rating Agencies' Important Role

Rating agencies' appraisals of life insurance investments have played an important role in the markets since the 1990s for three main reasons. First, the raters themselves have emerged from an industry-only interest to key players in the course of a single decade. The only traditional rating service, A.M. Best, even though it had a monopoly, languished in the shadows till the mid-1980s. The other three current leaders—Standard & Poor's, Moody's, and Fitch—all began their insurance-industry-specific services during the 1980s. (Weiss Research is a fourth and even more recent—and controversial—arrival.) Fitch Ratings later purchased the insurance rating operations of Duff and Phelps.

Second, the very fact of insurers' and raters' broadening interest in the ratings is directly related to the growing integration of insurers with the financial markets as both borrowers and lenders. The need for insurance companies to have the ability to issue commercial paper and to obtain bank credit lines was caused by periodic disintermediation problems, by the shortening of liability maturities, and perhaps most important for the future, by the need for access to capital through public equity and bond markets. Insurance companies suddenly needed ratings, a fact the raters correctly perceived as a profit opportunity.

Third, the vagaries of the business cycle—with special emphasis on the downside of commercial real estate and junk bonds in a recession—played a key role in the rise of life insurance defaults. Therefore, investment portfolios immediately became a challenge to rating agencies. Once educated in facts and regulations, rating agencies soon began to produce elaborate tests, models and analyses on all the factors relevant to portfolio management—liquidity, asset/liability matching (including cash-flow testing), bond and real estate quality, and actual and possible delinquencies and defaults, as already discussed. The rating agencies had the ability and incentive to go beyond insurance supervisors' rules and regulations. In particular, the leading raters coming from the securities industry (Standard & Poor's and Moody's) brought criteria from outside institutional and market finance to bear upon the insurance industry, thereby educating their new clients in turn.

Impact of Ratings

Controversy began almost as soon as the number of raters and their published ratings began to rise in the mid-1980s. The element of judgment, common to most raters, opened the door to disagreements among equally qualified appraisers in much the same way in which investment portfolios differ even among managers with identical objectives. When the rating agencies used strictly quantitative tests to evaluate investments (and other factors) in their analysis, the very lack of supplementary qualitative judgment became a source of criticism. Ratings, thus, became publicity items at the exact time (1986–1991) when life insurance failures became significant.

The ratings services scrambled as junk bond and real estate problems multiplied. Downgradings typically followed a company's disclosure of extra reserving for investment problems, of outright writedowns, or of poor quarterly or annual results often associated with investment problems. Competition among insurance company field sales forces quickly spread the bad (or good) news, raising sharply the importance of high ratings in attracting new funds. The cause and effect of downgradings were sometimes indistinguishable since downgradings themselves, even if justified in the eyes of the rating agencies by mounting portfolio problems, could trigger runs on a company and force asset sales at distress prices.

By the early 1990s it was clear that the importance of ratings reinforced the return to conservatism in investment policy and supervision. But several questions have yet to be answered. The low investment returns during the first decade of the 21st century prompted more aggressive use of derivative investments and led to the subprime mortgage problems and the credit freeze of 2008. The rating agencies have subsequently come under strong criticism for their laxity prior to 2008. Rating agencies reacted by lowering many company ratings to reflect the collapse of equity prices and the questionable values of securitized mortgage holdings. The revelations of the subprime mortgage fiasco and the questionable ratings have undermined confidence in the ratings agencies.

Liquidity Safety Net

The most important of these questions is whether the insurance industry needs a source of liquidity to tide a company over a temporary market and/or ratings-induced rough spot. Might Executive Life have survived had it been able to participate in the recovery of the junk-bond market after new supplies abruptly ceased in 1991? Would Mutual Benefit Life's real estate have come into its own in the mid-1990s? Might a conditional liquidity arrangement be preferable to impairment and liquidation proceedings or to forced mergers and/or the activation of guarantee funds? As an analogy, Federal Reserve credit is one of the options available to banking entities judged to be capable of recovering, and its quantity

and terms have occasionally been stretched to help banks through crises before 2008. In the fourth quarter of 2008, The Federal Reserve Bank was authorized to purchase assets and equities from troubled financial institutions under the Troubled Asset Relief Program (TARP).

The longer-term nature of nearly all life insurance portfolios leaves them vulnerable to a threatened run on an insurance company. Insurers have no safety net, no outside source of funds to help them through a crisis. The guarantee funds in each state kick in only after the regulators have taken control of a troubled insurer. Therefore, the influence of published ratings and their changes will remain a major force in an insurer's survival. It has been proved that capital-strong companies can survive a downgrading, especially at or near the top of the rating grades. Weaker companies, however, may have to adopt new and possibly severe restraints on their investment portfolios in order to avoid potentially ruinous asset squeezes. Marketing considerations reinforced by regulatory developments and rating pressures will continue to move the industry in the direction of investment conservatism.

The 2008 federal TARP bailout program for financial institutions was expanded to include life insurers that have a federal regulatory connection, that is, control of a bank or thrift. This prompted some life insurers to acquire a bank or a thrift to be eligible for the federal bailout funds. Prior to the creation of the 2008 bailout, there were 47 life insurers that owned either a bank or a thrift. But only 3 life insurers received bailout funds and those companies had repaid all of the funds by the end of 2010.

Glimpse into the Future

Few people would have dared predict the low interest rates of the current decade, especially the elevation of the investment function to its current importance, as a consequence of the product revolution. The credit freeze and market downturn of late 2008 came as a complete surprise to most participants in the financial services arenas. Clearly, caution is in order with respect to predictions for the future. Nevertheless, some trends may continue into the next decade.

Continued Conservatism

The most important of these trends is the swing toward investment conservatism in reaction to the swinging 1990s and the real estate bubble of the past decade. Capital standards and the Model Investment Law will require such conservatism; continuous attention to ratings and their influence on marketing will reinforce it. There is a distinct possibility, however, that the reactionary securities regulation prompted by the credit freeze, market

downturn and loss of confidence in combination with these factors will carry too far a trend that in itself is logical and desirable. As a result, the important role that life insurance investments has played in the long-term capital markets and in support of emerging companies may be diminished, to the detriment of national economic growth—especially if life insurers shift all of their assets to top-quality issues and abandon the intermediate-quality assets they have typically financed in past decades.

In fact, the industry might have to raise so much outside capital to satisfy the new standards being imposed by insurance regulators that its historical net contribution to national investment might fall sharply in the coming decade, along with the change toward high-grade investments. The acceleration of the previously snail-like process of demutualization because of the need for outside capital was a sign of the times in 1992 when the Equitable, one of the largest companies, joined the demutualization parade, primarily to help cure a serious capital deficiency. Other mutuals have also demutualized in order to augment internal retained capital by going public. One mutual insurer (Prudential) was able to raise $300 million by issuing a new form of notes to institutional investors in mid-1993. This indicates that at least some of the strongest mutual insurers may raise capital on Wall Street without having to demutualize. By 2002, even Prudential had demutualized. There is the argument that the 2008 events pushed some of the holdout mutuals to convert to stock companies. As of today, the hold out mutual companies seem to be more than surviving as consumers turn to more of the guarantees of traditional life insurance contracts.

One consequence of the new conservatism was that the recovery of commercial real estate was delayed by insurer investment officers' reluctance or inability to renew their commitment to a sector subject to high capital requirements and asset reserves. The 20 percent average vacancy rate for office space in the early 1990s took the rest of the decade to settle to a more normal 8 percent to 10 percent. Other substantial real estate surpluses existed in hotel and shopping center space. Overbuilding of the 1980s, partly because of weakened underwriting standards, had come home to roost. Thus, life insurers had to emphasize defensive management of the existing mortgage and equity real estate portfolio. While in the last decade real estate financing became frenzied and fed an overheated real estate market that ended abruptly when the defaults started lowering yields on securitized mortgages, most life insurers kept their investments in this sector at a very low level. Those insurers with a high level of securitized mortgages have experienced an unwanted but understandable level of defaults.

Similar considerations, although less extreme, could arise in the relation of corporate financing to life insurance investments. As leading life insurers curbed their appetite for risky loans in response to regulatory and marketing forces, the interest rate margins available on well-secured loans to stable businesses shrank sharply, regardless of whether these

margins were measured against the cost of funds or against the alternative of government (or government-backed) securities. Conservatism itself thus increased the squeeze on life insurance earnings, and this conservatism will have to run its course to purge the excesses of the past decade.

Money Management Diversification

A second important trend is further life insurance diversification into money management *per se*. The enormous progress of investment skills among insurance officers and of the investment selection aspects of life insurance products can be readily extended into the noninsurance field. A key incentive is the relatively low capital requirements in fee-for-service operations. A great number of leading insurers have created or acquired mutual fund affiliates and/or independent pension management firms to utilize the sophisticated investment skills of their employees more fully. The field forces of numerous insurers have also developed more refined financial planning knowledge and skills. In effect, many life insurance agents have become financial planners with full portfolio capability, including securities licenses.

The integration of this diversification and expansion into traditional life insurance marketing operations presents major problems in both home-office and field force organization and management. The differences in marketing tactics and commission structure—indeed in corporate culture—cannot be bridged easily. One clearly emerging development in home-office organization is to establish semi-independent investment subsidiaries; in effect, money market and securities portfolio management is declared another segment of investment operations, often more distinct organizationally than general account segments or separate accounts among themselves.

Investment Operation Overlap

A third trend for the turn of the century is the increasing overlap of investment operations among different types of institutions. This trend is part of the larger issue of broadening franchises and direct competition among previously unassociated groups of institutions. But while the 1990s produced much consolidation in banking, the legal separation between banking and insurance was eliminated by Congress with the passage of the Graham-Leach-Bliley Act in 1999. This removal of legal and regulatory barriers is significant, but important public policy concerns and private turf considerations are likely to keep some barriers intact. On the other hand, the marriage of investment banking and brokerage with life insurance proceeded forward in the current decade—a logical development, given the trend toward broad-service financial management within the insurance

industry. Management skills to make the disciplines compatible are proving difficult to acquire. The Citigroup combination is the first example of a large insurer, a large bank, and a large securities firm joining forces. Citigroup has divested some of the insurance units since the original combination.

In 2008, there were 47 life insurers that owned banks or thrifts when the Federal Government proposed the $700 billion rescue program. The subsequent requirement that only those life insurers with some federal regulatory oversight would be eligible for bailout funds, prompted some life insurers to acquire banks or thrifts in order to avail themselves of the bailout funds. Some life insurers indicated they were not interested in taking that step to avail themselves of bailout funds. In the end, only 3 life insurers obtained rescue funds and they repaid all of the funds by the end of 2010.

Internationalization

internationalization

A fourth important trend is the further **internationalization** of the investment business. Leeway provisions of existing laws or the new Model Investment Law are likely to be used increasingly to take advantage of investment opportunities in the European common market, the developing North American common market, and in dynamic Asian economies. Newly acquired portfolio management skills are also being marketed by several leading United States insurers to generate United States real estate and securities portfolios for foreign institutional investors. Last but not least, the imposition of more stringent United States capital standards for life insurers is certain to be followed by a search for new sources of capital. Leading foreign capital markets are a likely source, and foreign insurers might perceive new opportunities for combinations with United States firms. (Again, the demutualization experience of the Equitable in 1992 may point the way as most of the total additional capital raised in 1991–2001 came from a foreign source, the French AXA insurance group.)

Some United States life insurers have partnered with Chinese insurance companies since 1999. The laws of China limit non-Chinese companies to no more than a 49 percent ownership of companies operating in China. This restriction could be liberalized in the future to comply with World Trade Organization standards.

The market in India is now open to life insurance competition (both internal and foreign). This is the result of legislation that phased out the government monopoly previously enjoyed by the Life Insurance Corporation of India.

In sum, new challenges and opportunities in life insurance investment management are readily apparent in the coming decade, notwithstanding the conservative reaction to the 1980s. Consolidation and expansion alternate with the business cycle, more so on the investment side than on the product side of life insurance. Thus, it appears that the retrenchment of the 1990s will continue to be followed by further enhancement of the relative importance of the investment function of life insurance.

CHAPTER REVIEW

Key Terms and Concepts

segmentation of the general account	hedging
equity kickers	covered call
financialization	efficient frontier
rating agencies	qualitative constraints
guaranteed interest contracts (GICs)	mandatory security valuation reserve (MSVR)
securitized mortgages	
separate accounts	interest maintenance reserve (IMR)
disintermediation	asset valuation reserve (AVR)
back-end withdrawal penalties	writedowns
yield curve	below-investment-grade bonds
joint ventures	model investment law
duration	internationalization
barbell strategy	

Chapter 21 Review Questions

1. Explain how the high inflation rates of the previous decades affected life insurance companies. [1]

2. What tactics have life insurers used to speed up the transition to new policy types to accommodate strong and changing forces in the investments arena? [2]

3. Describe some of the changes many life insurers have made in their investment portfolios to protect against possible future surges of inflation. [3]

4. Why are insurer investment managers more concerned about insurance products' liability characteristics now than they were in past decades? [3]

5. What events stimulated increased reliance on commercial rating agencies by purchasers of life insurance products? [4]

6. Describe the steps insurance regulators have taken in the last decades to improve life insurer financial strength. [4]

7. Describe the most prominent changes in life insurer investment holdings from 1975 to 2009. [3]

8. What have the trends been in life insurer portfolios' average asset maturity and annual turnover rates? [6]

9. What types of investment assets have life insurers moved away from in recent years? [3]

10. What category of assets do many life insurers use to increase the liquidity of their portfolios? [2]

11. Explain why life insurance companies usually have less than 10 percent of the assets in their general accounts allocated to common stocks. [4]

12. Describe the changes that have enabled life insurers to decrease the proportion of their assets tied up with policy loans. [2]

13. Explain what the term inverted yield curve means. [8]

14. Describe the types of investments life insurers have added to their traditional portfolios to increase diversity. [6]

15. Explain why it is difficult for life insurers to match the maturities of assets and liabilities. [7]

16. Explain how borrowers' prepayment of mortgages (in full) has a negative impact on the insurer that originally loaned the funds and still holds the mortgage. [1]

17. Describe the current structure of life insurance investment regulations, and indicate why it has been changing. [4]

18. Describe the general types of constraints that traditional regulation imposed on life insurers' investments. [4]

19. Cite some examples of liberalized life insurer investment regulation during the 1980s. [4]

20. Explain how investment regulation has become more stringent for life insurers. [4]

21. Identify the more widely known life insurer rating agencies. [5]

22. What were the major factors prompting the rating agencies to downgrade many life insurers in recent years? [9]

23. Explain why life insurers may choose to reduce or curtail investing in some categories of assets that they have supported strongly in recent decades. [9]

24. Describe four trends in life insurance investments discernible in the past two decades. [9]

Chapter 21 Review Answers

1. *The sharp acceleration of inflation in the late 1970s and early 1980s and the attendant near tripling of interest rates between 1975 and 1982 caused the role of investment performance and policy to evolve from being a mere adjunct of product and sales management to becoming the lifeblood of a life insurance company. Instead of insurance driving investment, there is now a dynamic interaction of the two sides of the business. Overall success depends on the profitable integration of the accumulation and disposition of funds.*

2. *Two significant tactics have been utilized by life insurers to speed up the transition to new policies: (1) the start-up of brand new subsidiary insurance companies with the entire portfolio invested at current yields and (2) the exchange of old, in-force policies with new contracts containing lower premiums and variable interest rates for policy loans.*

3. *Changes many life insurers have made in their investment portfolios to protect against possible future surges of inflation include*

   - *cutting significantly the average maturity of their investment portfolios*

   - *evaluating the liability characteristics of different insurance products with respect to a more detailed and complex set of risk classification categories to arrive at correct maturity and risk characteristics of the corresponding assets*

   - *moving to shorter asset maturities and protective techniques (such as staggered maturities) and the increased use of liquid instruments (such as U.S. Treasury and agency securities)*

   - *ncreasing use of options, futures, and other partial offsets to a riskier environment*

   - *enlarging equity positions in the general account, mainly through the use of equity kickers, warrants, or similar devices attached to debt instruments*

4. *In anticipation of resurgent high interest rates and high inflation rates, corporate and individual policyowners now demand escape clauses in their contracts. As a result, insurer investment managers must evaluate the liability characteristics of their company's different insurance products to arrive at a portfolio of assets with matching maturity and risk characteristics.*

5. *Increased reliance on commercial rating agencies was stimulated by the failure of a few major insurance companies in the early 1990s.*

6. *Steps taken by insurance regulators to improve life insurer financial strength include placing more detailed limitations on the insurer's portfolio composition broadening asset reserves requiring careful calculation of investment factors within the risk-based capital standards developing a National Association of Insurance Commissioners (NAIC) Model Investment Law tightening up of the NAIC's self-examination procedures to make sure that agreed-upon laws and regulations are actually enforced in each state*

7. *The most prominent changes in life insurer investment holdings from 1975 to 1996 include*

    -   *Investments generally considered long term (corporate bonds and mortgages combined) accounted for over two-thirds of total investments in 1975 but were down to about 62 percent in 1996.*

    -   *Moreover, there have been major changes in the characteristics of these long-term investments.*

        -   *The average maturity of the "nonmarketable" part of long-term investments has been cut sharply*

        -   *Both bonds and mortgage investments have been heavily redirected toward public securities rather than toward directly negotiated deals with debts*

    -   *The share of life insurance investments represented by United States government securities has tripled over the period.*

    -   *Total holdings of common stocks have risen because separate accounts have gained relative to the insurers' general account.*

    -   *Legal and regulatory changes, combined with redesigned contracts, have enabled companies to whittle down the policy loan share of assets.*

8. *From 1975 to 1999, life insurer portfolios' average maturity was halved and the annual turnover rate was doubled to roughly 10 percent.*

9. *In recent years, life insurers have moved away from the "nonmarketable" part of long-term investments, direct placements, mortgages, and policy loans.*

10. *Many life insurers use U.S. government securities to increase the liquidity of their portfolios.*

11. *Commonstocksinlifeinsurancecompanies'generalaccountsarelimitedto10percentof assets under New York insurance law, which tends to dominate investment regulations throughout the country.*

12. *Legal and regulatory changes, combined with redesigned contracts, have enabled companies to whittle down the policy loan share of assets. Loan rates are now indexed to a bond market rate, or if they are fixed, tend to be at 8 percent.*

13. *A yield curve is defined as an array of interest rates by maturity of the underlying debt. The normal yield curve is sloped upward because price and credit risk-as well as uncertainty*

itself—tend to increase with maturity. With an inverted yield curve, short rates exceeded long rates.

14. *The life insurance industry has diversified by type of investment. There has been a rise in public corporate bonds (compared to private placements), securitized mortgages, and directly negotiated deals. Also, insurers have invested in junk bonds for general account or separate account purposes, and a greater variety of common stock and bond portfolios for pension or new-product investments (growth, income, or balanced accounts, for example). There has been increased involvement of a few companies in equity real estate through such devices as joint ventures with developers (the insurance company receives a share of the equity in return for supplying a long-term mortgage).*

15. *There are several reasons why it is difficult for life insurers to match the maturities of assets and liabilities:*

    - *The first difficulty is that retail insurance sales cannot be matched with regularity and precision in an investment operation that has to be wholesale to be efficient. The very nature of an insurance company, therefore, creates a degree of mismatch.*

    - *The second difficulty is that the actual maturity of liabilities may be misjudged or be, in fact, unpredictable.*

    - *A third (and fundamental) difficulty is that the cost of acquiring the liabilities may preclude precise maturity matching at orthodox credit risk levels.*

16. *If the mortgages held by an insurer are prepaid in full when interest rates decline, new securities can be substituted only at lower interest rate earnings, but the rates payable on the insurer's corresponding liabilities may not be equally adjustable.*

17. *Following the liberalization phase of the 1980s, the pendulum began to swing back toward conservatism in investment regulation in the late 1980s, and this trend accelerated in the early 1990s. The key changes in the structure of life insurance investment regulation have been more conservative regulation and supervision of investments, as well as the introduction of risk-based capital standards. These changes were brought about by the leading role investment problems played in life insurance company insolvencies, as well as the implication that regulators might drop "behind the curve," which arose as insurance rating agencies increased their downgradings based on investment problems.*

18. *Traditional investment regulation emphasized a number of constraints designed to enforce quality and diversification:*

- *Quantitative constraints. While major latitude was granted for long-term, private-sector earning assets, such as corporate bonds and commercial and residential mortgages (total mortgages had a very generous quantitative limit of 50 percent of assets), as well as for United States government securities, other investments, judged more risky and/or less reliable as to earnings, were—and remain—rather strictly limited. For example, under New York law common stock can constitute only 10 percent of general account assets.*

- *Qualitative constraints. Within the quantitative freedom for corporate bonds and mortgages, qualitative standards still apply. For example, bonds must meet the issuer's earnings test, and lower-grade holdings are curbed. Both bonds and mortgages are limited as to the percentage of assets for which any one debtor can account.*

- *Reserve accounts. The mandatory security valuation reserve (MSVR), which has been supplanted by two reserve accounts: (1) interest maintenance reserve (IMR) and (2) asset valuation reserve (AVR), was a buffer (shock absorber) between the decline in value of market-traded securities and insurer surplus and capital. The stiff provisions of the MSVR (and now the AVR) rules applicable to equities have been a significant factor in curbing common stocks in the general account. The rules, reflecting the perceived wide fluctuations of equity prices, make it difficult to credit the gains from capital values (which make up a large proportion of the total return from equities over the long term) to the policyowner.*

- *Writedowns of company assets as a consequence of adverse developments*

19. *By the early 1980s, although not abandoned, a great many quantitative rules had been liberalized. For example, larger portions of total assets in equities, in real estate, in foreign holdings, and in leeway investments had gradually been permitted. Liberalization reached a high point in 1983 when New York insurance law substituted a "prudent-man" rule for many of the inside prescriptions within each category of permitted assets (although the general quantitative limits by asset categories remained in effect).*

20. *Since the early 1980s, investment regulation has become more stringent in several ways:*

- *By 1987, perceiving impending danger from high-risk junk bonds, the New York Insurance Department issued an edict limiting such bonds to 20 percent of assets. This regulation was later broadened so that by 1992 the 20 percent limit had additional internal components further restricting holdings (including direct placements) by*

officially defining riskiness in progressive steps. These rules went beyond preliberaliza-tion regulations and, in effect, declared that similarly graded MSVR requirements were not sufficient.

- *Another important step in modifying liberalization also occurred during the mid-1980s. New York state adopted Regulation 126, a rule requiring justification for the interest rate and cash-flow assumptions underlying the asset/liability match of inter-est-sensitive products. The New York regulation asked company valuation actuaries to perform adequacy tests under a variety of interest rate scenarios over the life of defined blocks of business. The formulation and enforcement of this rule were key factors in helping regulatory and company actuaries reach an understanding with the investment side of the house about the dynamics of investment-sensitive products.*

- *With the NAIC's Model Investment Law, anticipating potential company problems by appropriate regulation has become the dominant theme. The model law carefully defines allowed asset classes and establishes concentration limits within these classes, somewhat similar to previous regulations.*

- *Even prior to a final draft of the model law, the MSVR was transformed into an Asset Valuation Reserve, in which all classes of assets, including real estate, are exposed to reserving rules. In addition, the accumulation rules are stiffer.*

- *Simultaneously, companies were subjected to a new reserve requirement, the Interest Maintenance Reserve. The IMR makes it mandatory to amortize security valuation gains from interest rate changes over the remaining life of a security, rather than having the gains contribute to the profits (or surplus) in the year in which they occur. This new provision will slow up the realization of profits originating during interest rate declines, but it will presumably also provide a cushion for interest-rate-caused losses in each sustained upturn of rates.*

- *It appears likely that the eventual investment rules will vary with a company's capital-ization, with strongly capitalized companies enjoying greater freedoms than weakly capitalized ones.*

21. *The more widely known life insurer rating agencies include A.M. Best, Standard & Poor's, Moody's, and Fitch.*

22. *Downgradings typically followed a company's disclosure of extra reserving for investment problems, of outright writedowns, or of poor quarterly or annual results often associated with investment problems.*

23. *Life insurers may choose to reduce or curtail investing in some categories of assets that they have supported strongly in recent decades for a number of reasons including:*

- *the avoidance of having their ratings downgraded*

- *the requirement some categories of assets have for considerably more capital under the risk-based capital rules than others*

- *the growing strictness of investment regulation*

- *the need for greater liquidity*

24. *The following are four trends in life insurance investments:*

- *Continued conservatism. The most important of these trends is the swing toward investment conservatism in reaction to the swinging 1980s. Capital standards and the Model Investment Law require such conservatism; continuous attention to ratings and their influence on marketing reinforces it.*

- *Money management diversification. A second important trend for the 1990s was further life insurance diversification into money management per se. The enormous progress of investment skills among insurance officers and of the investment selection aspects of life insurance products was readily extended into the noninsurance field. A key incentive were the relatively low capital requirements in fee-for-service operations. A great number of leading insurers acquired mutual fund affiliates and/or independent pension management firms to utilize the sophisticated investment skills of their employees more fully. The field forces of numerous insurers also developed more refined financial planning knowledge and skills. In effect, many life insurance agents became financial planners with full portfolio capability, including securities licenses.*

- *Investment operation overlap. A third trend for the 1990s was the increasing overlap of investment operations among different types of institutions. This trend was part of the larger issue of broadening franchises and direct competition among previously unassociated groups of institutions.*

- *Internationalization. A fourth important trend was the further internationalization of the investment business. Leeway provisions of existing laws or the new Model Investment Law were used increasingly to take advantage of investment opportunities in the European common market, the developing North American common market, and in dynamic Asian economies. Newly acquired portfolio management skills were also being marketed by several leading United States insurers to generate United States real estate and securities portfolios for foreign institutional investors. Last, but not least, the imposition of more stringent United States capital standards for life insurers was certain to be followed by a search for new sources of capital. Leading foreign*

capital markets were a likely source, and foreign insurers were likely to perceive new opportunities for combinations with United States firms.

Chapter 22
Life Insurance Marketing

Revised by: C.W. Copeland, Ram S. Gopalan, Robert M. Baranoff, and Denise C. Marvel

Learning Objectives

An understanding of the material in this chapter should enable the student to

1. **Explain the structure of life insurer marketing departments.**

2. **Describe the structure of the field organization, including the variety of producers, the relationship between agent and company, and the selection and development of producers.**

3. **Explain why it is important to control marketing expenses.**

4. **Describe some of the forces that can affect life insurance marketing in the future.**

The highly respected management consultant and writer Peter Drucker writes in his book *People and Performance,* "Because its purpose is to create a customer, the business enterprise has two—and only these two—basic functions: marketing and innovation. Marketing and innovation produce results; all the rest are 'costs.'"[1]

So it is with life insurance companies. Until the end of the last century, all of the marketing function and much of the innovation function were the responsibilities of the marketing department. It was here that all activities designed to attract new customers and retain existing customers were performed, including creating innovative new products and innovative ways to distribute those products.

STRUCTURE OF MARKETING DEPARTMENTS

In previous times, marketing departments were simple structures. Distribution was a line function and the marketing support functions such as research, product development, advertising and sales promotion, policyowner service, distribution personnel training and development, and marketing administration were staff functions, designed to help agents—for all practical purposes, the sole distribution channel in use—find and keep customers.

Many companies retain the traditional structure described above. Others have separated manufacturing from distribution and have set up individual distribution organizations as

---

1. Peter Drucker, People and Performance (Tyler, TX: The Leadership Network, 1989).

profit centers independent of any other function. Some companies have a different marketing function for every distribution channel they employ. Still other companies structure their marketing function according to product line, the markets they serve, the geographic region they operate in, or the size—in volume or in personnel—of the distribution outlets involved.

The bottom line is that companies will organize their marketing function in the way that they feel is best for them based on their target markets, products, distribution system, strategic goals, capabilities, and culture.

Regardless of structure, there are various functions that marketing departments try to perform. First and foremost, they try to create demand for the company's products. But they also try to know their customers and distributors well enough to design products that meet the needs of both parties, while still returning a profit to the company. They try to do whatever they can to ease the process along. Thus, the nondistribution marketing functions (sometimes called "marketing services" or "marketing support") include such things as research, planning, product development, advertising and sales promotion, market development (that is, lead generation), etc. Also, home office training and development for field producers may also be housed in marketing or may be contained within the distribution area. And in many cases, the actual building of the products takes place in a separate actuarial area, but not without significant input from the marketing department. Finally, policyowner service may or may not be part of marketing; with the move toward more comprehensive call centers that handle both sales and service, this may indeed be more commonly located within the marketing department in the future.

THE DISTRIBUTION FUNCTION

A life insurance company must have a continuing, incoming flow of new profitable revenue, and this is accomplished through the distribution of its products, or to use Drucker's terminology, by creating and keeping customers. There are many ways of doing this since a life insurance company's products can be—are in fact—sold the same ways in which any product can be sold, from vending machines in airports to direct solicitations in the mail to offers on the Internet.

Today, the majority of life insurance companies use a number of different distribution channels (counting different variations on the personal producer theme as distinct channels). The geographic area in which a life insurance company can sell varies from a single state to the entire world, but regardless of how big the area is, a company must be able to exert some control over its distribution system while at the same time providing support services to the system. In the smallest company, one operating in a limited geographic

area, the chief marketing officer and a small staff in the home office marketing department can provide this control and support. However, it is much more common for a company to be active over a very large area and to have a large marketing department that operates in a hierarchical organizational structure.

Under the chief marketing or distribution officer, there are typically a number of layers of subordinates—depending on the size and complexity of the company's operation—with decreasing amounts of authority. The lowest tier, usually located in a specific geographic region of the country, controls and supports a specified number of field outlets. If that sounds obscure, that is because it is; the different combinations of contractual and reporting relationships between the field and the home office can be counted in the hundreds.

Need for a Field Organization

The first companies to sell life insurance in the United States had no agents. They sold only a small number of life insurance policies each year, and it seemed as if the business would never achieve any notable success. But in 1842 the directors of the Mutual Life Insurance Company of New York made a decision to appoint soliciting agents to sell their product, and the business has never been the same. J. Owen Stalson, in his classic, *Marketing Life Insurance*, writes as follows:

> Just advertising, just sales promotion, would, I believe, have won but little for the companies; it was the agent, supported in his efforts by advertising and sales promotion, which put life insurance in the ascendancy after 1842.

Those words, written more than 60 years ago about an event that happened more than 160 years ago, are as true today as they were then. Ninety-eight percent of all new individual life insurance premium comes from policies sold by an individual producer, and only 2 percent comes from policies sold without an individual producer's involvement. This is true despite all the money and effort that have been spent in recent years on the development and implementation of mass marketing approaches, such as marketing through credit cards, associations, lending firms, direct mail, and the Internet.

It should be noted, however, that the proportion of individual policies being sold without the use of a producer is higher than the two percent of premium that those sales account for; the number often quoted is about 10 percent. Furthermore, sales made by quoting services are included as broker-mediated sales, since those services are indeed run by brokers (or brokerage general agents) with licensed salespeople staffing the phones. It should also

be pointed out that a few individual companies have been quite successful with a direct response distribution strategy.

Functions of the Field Organization

Until new distribution channels achieve the success that producers have achieved, the great majority of companies maintain a producer distribution system in order to survive. The use of individual producers is often criticized because the commissions and other remuneration paid to producers are perceived as unnecessarily increasing the cost of life insurance to policyowners. Such criticisms generally claim that the cost is a direct expense to policyowners for which they receive no corresponding benefit. Defenders of the system counter that producers render many types of services that would not be available if there were no producers, not the least of which is advice and recommendations about which product is best. In any event, distribution channels that do not employ commissioned producers are attractive to companies because they offer the promise of lower costs; thus, there is a constant search for successful alternatives to the individual producer.

The greatest obstacle to finding an effective substitute for agents is that consumers, in general, rarely apply for life insurance (irrespective of the need for it) until they are solicited. Producers perform an important service merely by calling attention to the need for protection and by persuading prospects to apply for it. Good producers also analyze applicants' needs and advise them about the most suitable types of policies, the amounts of protection required, the cost and method of premium payment, the more important provisions of the contract, the optional ways benefits can be paid after death, and the appropriate choice of and rights regarding a beneficiary. If prospects own a number of policies, the good producer will make suggestions for coordinating these policies along with government and employer-sponsored benefits to create a total plan for financial protection against all risks.

Good agents, in their advisory role, will also explain how life insurance can be used in many creative ways to achieve desired aims in such diverse areas as funding education, relieving tax burdens, continuing businesses, supplementing Social Security, paying off obligations, dissolving partnerships equitably, enhancing credit, financing business buy-sell agreements, canceling mortgages, and funding pensions.

Nor does the work of good producers end with the sale and delivery of the policy. Life insurance needs are not static but require frequent review and adjustment to meet changing conditions. This is particularly true of beneficiary provisions. Therefore, the relationship established by a producer with a client is a long and mutually beneficial one.

Variations on a Theme

Not all companies' personal producer or agent distribution systems look the same. Indeed, this channel has many variations.

multiple-line exclusive agents (MLEA)

independent marketing organizations (IMOs)

super producers

- Ordinary agents (sometimes referred to as agents within an "agency-building" system) are producers who devote at least 75 percent of their time selling primarily individual life products for one company that generally provides financing, training, supervision, sales support, and office facilities (also called housing). There are approximately 108,100 ordinary agents, and their share of new life premiums is 39 percent.

- Home service agents are producers who spend at least 75 percent of their time selling ordinary and industrial individual life for one company that provides financing, training, supervision, sales support and office facilities. Unlike the ordinary agents described above, home service agents sell in an assigned territory called a debit and sometimes collect premiums at the insured's house or office. There are approximately 14,500 home service agents, and their share of new life premiums is 2 percent.

- **Multiple-line exclusive agents (MLEA)** are producers who sell individual life, but usually their primary products are property and casualty products. MLEA agents sell for one company that provides financing, training, supervision, sales support, and office facilities. There are approximately 67,750 multiple-line exclusive agents and their share of new life premiums is 6 percent.

- Personal-producing general agents (PPGAs) are producers who receive both a producer's commission and the overriding commission that would usually go to a manager or general agent on personally produced business. Many are single-individual operations but some personal producing general agents hire and support a number of subproducers. PPGAs often specialize in one or a few market niches and typically have contracts with several companies offering products appropriate for those niches. They often have a primary company relationship, usually reflecting the niche they serve most frequently. Sometimes companies require a minimum production level to keep these PPGA contracts. Over time, large national organizations called **independent marketing organizations (IMOs)** have

evolved that likewise specialize in certain market niches, providing training and marketing materials to their agents and finding products from carriers that are appropriate to those niches. These independent marketing organizations usually recruit highly successful experienced agents. The share of new life premiums from PPGAs and IMOs is 22 percent.

- Brokers are full-time insurance producers who work independently and have no primary relationship or minimum production requirements with any company. There are two important distinctions between brokers and PPGAs: brokers do not receive overriding (general agent) commissions, and there is neither a tendency nor an intent for the company to achieve a primary-carrier status with brokers.

- Independent agents are primarily property and casualty producers who have no primary relationship with a company. Brokers and independent agents' share of new life premiums is 25 percent, the bulk of that going to brokers.

- Stockbrokers should be included among producers because an increasing number of them sell annuities, single premium life, and variable products. Stockbrokers account for about 3 percent of new life premiums.

- Financial planners are producers who can usually be placed in one of the categories above, although an increasing number of planners work on a fee-only basis (sometimes fulfilling the insurance portion of the plan with commission-free, or "no-load," products). Although there is no agreed-upon definition of financial planners, it is usually understood that they provide clients with a total financial plan that includes everything from investments to insurance, and they usually have a planning-oriented designation (that is, ChFC or CFP).

- **Super producers** are a special kind of producer—one with sophisticated product knowledge and technical support. A major segment of this group comprises the "super agents" of life insurance—those with whom we associate producer groups and producer-owned reinsurance companies. Although all super producers would fall into one of the categories above, they really represent a distribution system within a distribution system because they are different, with their special compensation arrangements, joint case work, country-wide partnerships, equity ownerships, influence on product development, technical expertise, shared knowledge, and even proprietary software.

Still other distribution channels use producers in a different way or do not use them at all.

worksite marketing

direct response marketing

- Banks are a growing presence in the life insurance business as more and more financial institutions create, buy, or form a joint alliance with an insurance company or agency to create an insurance and investment presence in the bank. Usually, the structure of the bank agency falls into one of the categories above, although it is possible in some places to buy insurance from a salaried, licensed bank employee. Banks account for approximately 15 percent of new annuity considerations, but only about one percent of new life premium.

- **Worksite marketing** is another growing distribution channel. It consists of individuals who will go to a work place and, with the endorsement of management, conduct sales interviews with employees on site, with premiums being paid through payroll deduction. Usually, individual producers from the categories above will make the sale to management in worksite marketing, while a specially-formed unit of salaried or commissioned enrollers will sign up the rank-and-file employees.

- Retail establishments are another source of life insurance sales. Typically, producers sell either in their own office or in the prospect's home, office, or an insurance facility in a department or grocery store. An individual salesperson is usually involved, although he or she may be salaried rather than paid a commission. This approach is more popular in Europe than in the United States and is sometimes referred to as "brand assurance" because part of the appeal to prospects is the brand recognition of the retail establishment.

- **Direct response marketing** accounts for only two percent of new life premium income, but LIMRA estimates that 10 percent of new life policies sold in the United States are sold on a direct basis. Thus, direct sales still meet the needs of a sizable market. Direct response marketing consists of making sales to consumers through the mail, media advertising, telemarketing, or the Internet. The process typically includes standardized sales messages made to consumers, orders taken, products delivered, and payments remitted without a face-to-face meeting between prospect and salesperson. Some insurance companies rely completely on direct response systems to distribute their products while other companies use direct response as just one of several distribution methods. As time progresses, direct response marketing is becoming more and more advanced technologically. Direct response firms engage heavily in market research and testing, and they maintain extensive computer-driven information retrieval and telemarketing operations. The emphasis in such operations is instant access to customers' records to make

sales or provide service. Most products distributed through direct response methods are designed to serve large market segments, are very affordable, and are uncomplicated in design and administration.

- Internet selling is the latest channel to be added to the distribution mix. Just about all insurers have an Internet presence and a significant proportion of them make it possible to buy over the Internet. However, the main use of insurance company Internet sites is for education, service, and information. In addition, there are a number of Web-based operations ("quoting services" or "aggregators") that will give online insurance quotes for a number of competing life insurance companies. In many cases, insurance can be purchased through these sites, effectively making them online brokers.

STRUCTURE OF FIELD ORGANIZATIONS

agencies

As we have noted, although direct methods of marketing products do exist, their success has been limited, and in reality, the overwhelmingly dominant distribution method is the individual producer who makes face-to-face sales. Because these producers operate in field offices (typically called **agencies**) in locales wherever a market for life insurance exists, this method of distribution is called the agency system.

The agency system has two main branches. In the first, a company builds its own agency distribution system by recruiting, financing, training, motivating, housing, and supervising new agents to represent it "exclusively." This branch of the agency system is identified with the descriptive adjective "agency-building," or "career agency." In the second, a company taps into the existing pool of agents created by the building branch referred to above to create an "instant sales force." This branch is referred to as being "independent."

The driving force in either of these branches is an individual who represents the company on the local level, either as an employee or an independent contractor, and who is the company's local sales force manager.

In the agency-building system, the individual in charge is typically called a manager or general agent, and it is he or she who does the recruiting of new, inexperienced recruits and develops them into a sales force. In the second branch of the agency system—the nonbuilding agencies—companies win an established producer's attention through the use of an intermediary who acts as a sort of "manufacturer's representative"—either as an

employee or independent contractor—and convinces established producers to sell their company's products through one type of arrangement or another.

Producers in the field are arrayed in an almost countless variety of organizational structures based on company policy in the building companies and on the arrangement between the manager, general agent, and/or manufacturer's representative in the independent companies. For the most part, however, existing field structures fall into one of the following general broad categories:

- Agency building—managerial. In this type of field organization, the manager (along with a staff of second-line managers) is a direct extension of the company, and his or her role is strictly to hire, train, and manage a sales staff. In some companies production by the manager is either discouraged or not allowed, while in other companies it is allowed but not usually expected. Expenses tend to be borne entirely by the company. This form of organization is usually for home-service agents, multiple-line exclusive agents and, to a lesser degree, ordinary agents. Managers in a managerial agency building system are compensated by salary, overrides, and/or commissions on personal production, depending on what the company wants the manager to do.

- Agency building—general agent. The goal in this type of field organization is also to build a sales staff, but the person in charge, usually called a general agent, is an independent contractor and is compensated primarily for building the agency's staff, although personal production is common. Instead of the company paying expenses directly, quite often the general agent is given an expense allowance and is then expected to manage his or her own agency expenses. The ordinary agent is the dominant producer in this structure.

- Regional director approach (RDA)—personal-producing general agent. This type of structure is favored by companies that prefer to have primary-carrier relationships with their PPGAs. Inherent in the evolution of this strategy was the concept of exclusive representation. However, because of the pressure of competition for qualified PPGAs, exclusive representation or exclusive territorial rights rarely exist today. Companies that employ this approach hire only experienced producers and are not committed to new agent development in any way. They provide little, if any, continuing generic education or training, some product orientation, and no office facilities or supervision. As the name of this type of structure implies, PPGAs are hired and supervised by regional directors.

- Managing general agent approach—personal-producing general agent. This type of structure originated with independent agents in the casualty insurance business. There, an independent general agent representing a company in a particular

region was authorized to appoint other independents to represent the company. While wielding more "clout" with the carrier, the managing general agent (MGA) operated essentially as a regional agency for the company and usually had territorial rights as well as certain powers. The MGA also often specialized in a particular product. The MGA concept differs from the RDA approach because the MGA is an independent contractor authorized by the company to appoint PPGAs, and there is much less primary company orientation. Typically the MGA is a franchisee who represents one company for a particular product in a particular territory. Because their producers are already paid the override, MGAs are compensated on a percentage of commissions and assume such administrative expenses as recruiting and mailing costs.

- Brokerage supervisor approach. The brokerage supervisor is a company employee who solicits business from producers with whom that company has no primary relationships. Brokerage supervisors are most often associated with agency-building companies—providing them with an additional distribution option—and with life affiliates of property-casualty companies where they primarily target independent property-casualty agencies. Companies that use this approach tend to offer a full line of products and rely on their ability to provide technical help to producers whose main business is not life insurance, such as property-casualty agents and stockbrokers. Because brokerage supervisors are usually housed in the field, they are able to solve local producers' problems when and where they occur.

- Independent brokerage general agent approach. This approach provides companies access to a producer through an independent brokerage general agent (BGA) who is authorized to solicit business for the company and to appoint producers on its behalf. BGA companies tend to be ones that offer specialty products or that provide process-oriented service, including liberal underwriting and speedy policy issue and commission payment, to producers who often are agents of other companies or full-time life brokers. BGAs offer some administrative services, usually represent several carriers for the same product, and are paid by overrides on business generated through their efforts while their producers are compensated by basic commissions.

Before we leave the subject of the structure of field organizations, it should be noted that some companies have provided their field forces with a larger number of products to sell or have expanded their distribution capacities without having an impact on their existing field force. Companies have done so by entering into manufacturer-distributor agreements with nonaffiliated companies. Under these agreements one company distributes products manufactured by the other company. Such agreements offer companies product

diversification and the ability to capture outside business. The manufacturing company gets additional distribution capacity and easier access to producers; the distributing company adds income sources for its producers, enhances its agents' service capabilities, and has a chance to test market products without the cost and effort required to develop the product itself.

RELATIONSHIP BETWEEN AGENT AND COMPANY

At one time it was common for the agent to contract with the general agent or manager. Today, however, the common practice is for the agent to contract with the company. The contract describes the authority, scope, and limits of the agent's job, and it determines the agent's legal relationship with the company, the restrictions concerning representation of other companies, and the compensation arrangements.

The contract's compensation provision is frequently handled by attaching a commission schedule or agreement. This attachment facilitates modifications of the commission provisions for new types of policies, changes in rates and cash value structures, and other changes in marketing strategies, such as raising or lowering commissions on certain products to encourage or discourage their sale.

Newly licensed agents, of course, have no immediate commission income. They are paid a specified amount until they can earn enough to survive on commissions, reach a designated time limit, or are terminated. Usually the amount paid is on the condition that the recruit fulfill specific minimum requirements in regard to such things as hours worked, interviews held, and training sessions completed. A validation schedule outlines the sales requirements that an agent must meet in order to continue being subsidized.

Agents, in certain situations or for particular reasons, may also be paid noncommission compensation. For most agents, this noncommission compensation is in the form of such programs as group life and health insurance, pension funding, and similar fringe benefits, as well as production, persistency, or activity bonuses or nonmonetary contest rewards such as gifts or trips. When home-service agents collect premiums at the policyowner's home or office, they are paid for performing this function.

MARKETING COSTS AND PROFITABILITY

If a company is in a market with a unique (and properly priced) product, service level, or distribution advantage that cannot be easily duplicated by the competition or if it has a captive market, the company should be profitable, regardless of the circumstances. However, those kinds of situations are very rare. For most companies profitability can be achieved only through the use of superior financial fundamentals. This is simple to illustrate: In a broad sense, profit equals revenues less expenses. In other words, profit comes from high revenues and low expenses. Revenues are properly managed by controlling the fundamental factors associated with getting new business: field productivity, agent retention, and the persistency of policies sold.

productivity

Productivity refers to how much business agents write. Agents may sell many different types of products—life insurance, annuities, disability income, mutual funds, small group insurance, and so on. Agents' product mix varies, depending on the needs of the market they serve and the products they have available to them.

Companies can use a number of different methods of measuring agent productivity such as number of contracts sold, premiums or other deposits, and commissions earned. Measuring productivity using the number of contracts sold may be misleading because not all products require the same level of effort to sell and not all provide the same level of profitability to the company. For example, a $50,000 life insurance single premium and a $50,000 mutual fund deposit are not necessarily equivalent in value to the company.

One measure of agent productivity that cuts across product lines is first-year commissions. First-year commission rates generally vary based on the effort involved in selling the contract and the value of that sale to the company. According to LIMRA surveys, the typical experienced agent (five or more years of service with the company) in a high-productivity company earns around $60,000 in first-year commissions. The typical experienced agent in a low-productivity company earns in the neighborhood of $15,000-25,000 in first-year commissions.

retention

Retention refers to how long an agent stays with a company. Typically, 4 years after contracting 100 new agents, an agency-building company with average retention still has 16 of them under contract. However, in companies with good retention, the 4-year retention rate is about 30 percent. (These numbers tend to be higher for MLEA companies and lower for home service companies.) High retention rates have a direct bearing on company

profitability in three ways: (1) The company avoids the expenses associated with recruiting and training additional new agents, (2) established agents have higher productivity than less experienced agents, and (3) the policies written by agents who stay with the company tend to have better persistency than those written by failing agents.

persistency

Persistency refers to how long policies remain in force and the policyowners pay premiums on them. The industry average for "13-month persistency" is around 85 percent—that is, about 85 percent of the industry's policies will still be in force 13 months after they are written. In other words, 85 percent of the time the insured pays the first premium of the second year of the policy; thus, the policy remains in force at least beginning the second year.

Control of Marketing Expenses

marginal pricing

The other factor in the profitability equation is expenses. It is impossible to market without expenses; therefore, the key to profitability on this side of the ledger is to control marketing expenses. The principal trap companies fall into that keeps them from managing expenses as well as they could is **marginal pricing**—allocating less than full fixed costs or less than full overhead costs to a product. Marginal pricing can be used sometimes, but never over a long time period and never with core products. Too often companies use marginal pricing to gain entry into a market, planning to remedy the situation later. This rarely works, however, because the marginal pricing is aimed at capturing a target market share that seldom materializes, because cost improvement measures that will make a product profitable are only rarely realized, or because competitive conditions force the price to remain low.

While the building branch of the agency system would tend to have higher costs because of its expenses for recruiting and developing agents, these expenses are often offset by the higher commissions and support service costs incurred by companies utilizing independent agents. LIMRA studies show that when all types of companies are analyzed, there are high-cost companies and low-cost companies in each distribution system, and there is a band of relatively profitable companies that cuts across all distribution systems. This tends to indicate that with good quality management, any distribution system can be profitable.

It is obvious just how important producers are to the achievement of profitability, especially in regard to retention and productivity. For the most part, and whether or not they

now sell in a building or independent organization, how producers were recruited into the business and developed in the performance of their skills is a key to how well they succeed. Almost without exception, all producers share the same early recruitment and developmental experiences.

RECRUITING, SELECTING, AND DEVELOPING PRODUCERS

Field office heads and their second-line managers are responsible for bringing new people into the life insurance business. It begins by the recruiter's establishing a clear picture of the type of person he or she wants to recruit. It is usually based on the market the producer will be working in and the type of individual who has achieved success in similar circumstances.

It is not the recruiter's purpose initially to be very selective; that comes later. The object at this point is to accumulate as many names as possible. To do this, recruiters use all of the sources at their disposal—personal contacts; referrals from other producers, clients, and friends of the agency; college and personnel placement offices; and newspaper ads.

Selection-Rejection Process

After the recruiter gets an individual's name and that individual exhibits some interest in a life insurance career, the process becomes very selective. It usually contains three stages: obtaining all the facts relating to the candidate's background, experience, and personal qualifications; using an organized system for verifying and evaluating the facts; and devoting an adequate amount of time and effort to judge the facts and make an intelligent decision. These stages are accomplished through the implementation of a detailed selection-rejection process that has the following specific steps:

- a quick preliminary interview to determine if there are any obvious reasons why the candidate should be rejected and to convince the candidate to take an aptitude test
- the administration of an objective aptitude test that accurately predicts the chances of an individual's likelihood of success in the job of producer (and conforms to all equal opportunity rules and regulations)
- completion of a legal application form
- an evaluation interview in which the company can gain further information about the candidate and the candidate can learn about the job

- interviews with other people, if appropriate, such as spouses, other producers, and references
- a follow-up interview to clear up any questions on the part of either the recruiter or candidate

In addition to these selection steps, there are two additional ones that a recruiter should take to make sure the candidate is right for the job. One is precontract training—having the candidate actually do certain parts of the job before making a commitment. The other is giving the candidate a complete, honest, and realistic description of the job, including both the good and the bad aspects of the position.

Training Recruits

Newly contracted agents enter the financing period referred to earlier in this chapter and follow a validation schedule that details what they must produce to remain under contract. They are also required to follow a training program that usually includes attending a school (often held in the home office) and completing specific learning assignments determined by the agency office. Of course, before actually going out and selling, recruits must also obtain the licenses required by the agency or company.

Generally speaking, a new agent's training will cover these five areas:

- life insurance basics
- sales techniques and use of computer software in the sales process
- company and agency procedures
- product knowledge
- company history, goals, plans, and policies

Often a new agent will make sales calls with the head of the agency, a second-line manager, or an experienced agent. There are industry-supported educational and skill-building courses available to new producers (commercial programs are also available). As agents progress in their careers, there are additional programs that lead to professional designations. Since modern agents sell technically and financially complex products, training and development is an ongoing process. In addition, companies and agencies provide a wide range of programs to motivate their salespeople. These include regular meetings, production awards, print recognition, and the opportunity to qualify for sales conventions that are typically held in resorts or exotic locales.

The amount of supervision that producers require varies greatly. New agents generally require more supervision than do veteran agents. Common to all agents, however, is the formulation of a sales quota, construction of plans to achieve that quota, and periodic reviews to measure the producer's progress toward reaching the quota. Such quotas, plans, and reviews are usually not limited to a single measure but can include all or some of the following: premiums written, commissions earned, face amount sold, average premium per sale, number of policies, persistency rate, and activity (which includes prospects contacted, interviews conducted, sales literature mailed, telephone calls placed, sales interviews held, service calls made, and closings attempted). A producer's continuing development is also part of periodic reviews.

Administrative, Technical, and Sales Support

Several levels of support are provided to help producers make sales. Often, the amount of administrative support—secretarial help, proposal generation, and mailings—given to a producer depends on his or her production level, with a high-producing agent earning his or her own private secretary or administrative assistant. Technical support is given to producers in the form of computer-generated policy illustrations, computer analysis of client finances, computer-controlled sales and performance measuring, and word-processed mailings. In more computer-literate operations, computers are also used for maintaining client information databases, prospecting among existing policyowners, and policy creation. Advanced sales support is provided to help producers sell a product or sell to a market with which they are not familiar or that requires special knowledge. This is common in group insurance, pension, sophisticated upscale, and business situations.

Educational Support

Agency managers and directors usually support professional educational programs such as LUTC, CLU, and ChFC.[2] Some insurance companies have established incentive programs to encourage agents to pursue these designations and increase their knowledge. Studies have repeatedly confirmed that professional designation holders are generally more

---

2. CLU stands for Chartered Life Underwriter, which is a designation granted by The American College (270 Bryn Mawr Avenue, Bryn Mawr, PA 19010). The program requires students to pass 8 examinations covering courses dealing with taxes, finance, insurance, pensions, and related material, and to have 3 years of experience. ChFC stands for Chartered Financial Consultant, which is a designation also granted by The American College. This 8-part program focuses more on the planning process. LUTC stands for Life Underwriter Training Council, an organization now part of The American College, which produces sales training courses and grants the designations LUTC and LUTCF.

successful than nonholders in terms of sales and compensation. The NAIFA/LIMRA Survey of Producer Opinion confirms that there is a direct correlation between the compensation agents receive and whether they hold a professional designation. (Compensation is also correlated with whether they have received a college education and how long they have served in the insurance industry.)

Some agencies require their agents to complete one or more professional designations within a short time after joining the sales force. If the company and agency deal with variable life and equity products such as mutual funds, the new agents will be given educational support to prepare for the examinations they must pass in order to sell those products. The Securities and Exchange Commission (SEC) mandates the examinations that are nowdeveloped and managed by the Financial Industry Regulatory Authority (FINRA) which supplanted the National Association of Securities Dealers (NASD). The examinations were developed and manged by the NASD when the original mandate was issued by the SEC.[3] There are also educational programs provided by the Million Dollar Round Table (MDRT) and the Association of Advanced Life Underwriting (AALU).[4] And as more and more producers become involved in financial planning, companies are increasingly encouraging agents to get planning designations, such as ChFC (Chartered Financial Consultant) or CFP (Certified Financial Planner).

FUTURE OF LIFE INSURANCE MARKETING

There have been major revolutions in life insurance marketing, most notably the introduction of soliciting agents in the 1840s, the rise of the debit agent in the 1880s, the advent of group insurance in the 1930s, and the growth of nonexclusive producer companies since the end of World War II. Radical change, therefore, is not unknown in life insurance marketing, and it might happen again. However, evolution seems to be more likely than revolution, and that evolution will be triggered by forces already in place that are sure to have some impact on how life insurance will be marketed in the future.

---

3.   The SEC regulates all securities publicly traded in the United States. It requires that these products be sold only by licensed persons and that a prospectus be supplied to potential purchasers before the sale transaction. The FINRA (formerly NASD) has a series of tests, each geared to a specific product group or subgroup. These tests must be passed in order to obtain the FINRA license (formerly NASD license) needed to sell equity products.

4.   Million Dollar Round Table (325 Touhy Avenue, Park Ridge, Il 60068) is an organization open only to the top 20 percent of agents, based on sales volume. The Association of Advanced Life Underwriting (AALU) is a membership organization affiliated with the National Association of Independent Financial Advisors (NAIFA). (Both organizations are at 1922 F Street NW, Washington, DC 20006.)

Increased Competition

One of these forces is an increase in competition. Since passage of the Gramm-Leach-Bliley Financial Services Modernization Act (GLB), insurance products need no longer be manufactured by traditional insurance companies. Now bank holding companies and stock brokerage firms, for example, can own insurers and, instead of just distributing someone else's product, can sell their own insurance product. (It should be noted that, conversely, many insurance companies are starting or purchasing their own bank and trust companies.) To compete in this new environment, mergers and acquisitions are creating huge financial services conglomerates that consist of a bank, investment company, and insurance company, with the ultimate aim of cross-selling each other's products. Some industry observers suggest that companies in the future will fall into one of two types: huge multinational financial services giants or niche players, both large and small.

Globalization

Not only are other types of financial institutions entering the life insurance arena, but the life insurance business is becoming a global business, with foreign insurers invading the United States and vice versa. Many foreign insurers bring with them a different marketing orientation, and their approach, especially their historic relationship with banks in other countries, could force United States insurers to modify their distribution methods, especially in light of GLB.

Demographic Shifts

There is also a major demographic shift going on in the United States and other parts of the world. The consequences are that the work force will grow more slowly than at any time since 1930 and the average age of the work force will rise, meaning that the pool of younger workers entering the labor market will shrink. Also, more women will continue to enter the work force and minorities will be a larger share of new entrants into the work force. Finally, immigrants will represent the largest percentage increase in the work force since World War I. Such changes are bound to affect how life insurance is sold in the future.

A Move Toward Living Benefits

Due to these shifting demographics, the focus of life insurance companies is turning more toward living benefits than death benefits. For example, the ratio of workers paying into the Social Security system to retired payment recipients will continue to decline, putting a strain on the public system and requiring more reliance on private sector products for

retirement. The key result of this trend is that the business will be selling more annuities and other retirement and savings-oriented products than life insurance. Since these products have lower margins and pay lower commissions, there is some concern that, as core products, they will not be able to support the cost of existing distribution systems.

Another result of the aging of the population is the increased interest in long-term care (LTC) products. The public does not know much about these products yet, but they have enjoyed double-digit growth as individually sold products. The Federal government will soon be offering long-term care to its employees and their families for optional purchase. This may signal a growth in consumer knowledge of the product. As a result of this stance by the Federal government, LTC may soon become a benefit commonly offered at the worksite on an employee-pay-all basis.

Changes in Distribution Systems

Finally, the life insurance industry finds itself in a financial squeeze. As a result of competition from outside the business, the loss of comfortable product margins, and the rise of giant financial services companies, insurers need to increase surplus, compete on the basis of price, and operate under tighter financial controls, suppressing investment returns. They are making concerted efforts to find the least expensive ways to distribute products. They are experimenting with any distribution system that shows promise while recognizing that they must meet or better the competition's performance. Otherwise, market share will decrease and acquisition costs will rise.

In the past companies could live with inefficiencies because of the product margins in place at the time. Those margins are gone and, most likely, will never return. Therefore, companies must refine and exploit the market-segment product-distribution system linkage. Historically, the distribution systems now in use gravitated to the markets they service without prior planning or direction. It is time now, say proponents of the approach, to attack these markets with planning and direction. This has led to distribution system pluralism—that is, the many different distribution systems described earlier (and others yet to be developed) have been implemented across individual companies rather than just across the entire industry. A recent regional experiment has a major life insurer selling life insurance through the giant retailer Walmart. Purchasers buy a prepaid card at the retailer and send it with a completed questionnaire to the insurer for underwriting evaluation and possible policy issue.

CHAPTER REVIEW

Key Terms and Concepts

multiple-line exclusive agents (MLEA)   agencies
independent marketing organizations   productivity
   (IMOs)   retention
super producers   persistency
worksite marketing   marginal pricing
direct response marketing

Chapter 22 Review Questions

1. a. What activities are included in an insurer's marketing department?

    b. What are these activities designed to do? [1]

2. a. Why does a life insurance company need a field organization of individual producers?

    b. What services do producers perform for consumers? [1]

3. What are the basic differences among the producers active in life insurance companies' field sales operations? [2]

4. What are the various agency distribution systems in life insurance? [2]

5. What are the general broad categories into which existing field structures fall? [2]

6. What provisions are generally found in the contract between the agent and the insurer? [2]

7. What effect do high retention rates have on company profitability? [3]

8. a. What are the three stages in the selection-rejection process of producer recruitment?

    b. What steps can be taken to facilitate these stages? [3]

9. What areas does a new agent's training generally cover? [3]

10. What professional educational programs should companies and managers encourage agents to pursue? [4]

11. What impact will increased competition have on the way life insurance will be marketed in the future? [4]

Chapter 22 Review Answers

1. a. *The activities in the marketing department include the eight specific functions listed below:*

    - *research*
    - *product development and pricing*
    - *distribution*
    - *communications, including advertising and sales promotion*
    - *policyowner service*
    - *distribution personnel training and development*
    - *marketing management and administration*
    - *distribution support services*

    b. *These activities are designed to attract new customers and retain existing customers.*

2.   a.   *The need for a field organization of individual producers arises from the following:*

- *the company's desire to secure the largest amount of new business possible*

- *the company's social duty to provide adequate life insurance protection for all who need it, and therefore, to perform in the greatest possible degree the function for which it is organized*

    b.   *Producers perform the following services for consumers:*

- *calling attention to the need for protection and persuading prospects to apply for it analyzing applicants' needs and advising them about the most suitable types of policies, the amounts of protection required, the cost and method of premium payment, the more important provisions of the contract, the optional ways benefits can be paid, and the appropriate choice of and rights regarding a beneficiary*

- *making suggestions for coordinating various policies owned by the prospect with governmental and employer-supplied benefits to create a total plan for financial protection against all risks*

- *explaining how life insurance can be used in many, many creative ways to achieve desired aims in such diverse areas as funding education, relieving tax burdens, continuing businesses, supplementing Social Security, paying off obligations, dissolving partnerships equitably, enhancing credit, financing business buy-sell agreements, canceling mortgages, and funding pensions*

- *reviewing and adjusting insurance coverage to meet changing conditions*

3.   *The basic differences among the producers active in life insurance companies' field sales operations are as follows:*

- *Ordinary agents are producers who devote at least 75 percent of their time selling primarily individual life products for one company that generally provides financing, training, supervision, sales support, and office facilities.*

- *Home service agents are producers who spend at least 75 percent of their time selling ordinary and industrial individual life for one company that provides financing, training, supervision, sales support, and office facilities. These agents sell in an*

assigned territory called a debit and sometimes collect premiums at the insured's house or office.

- *Multiple-line exclusive agents are producers who sell individual life, as well as property and casualty products, for one company that provides financing, training, supervision, sales support, and office facilities.*

- *Personal-producing general agents (PPGAs) are producers who receive both a producer's commission and the overriding commission that would usually go to a manager or general agent on personally produced business. Many are single-individual operations but some PPGAs hire and support subproducers. PPGAs typically have contracts with several companies but often have a primary company relationship. They sometimes have to maintain a minimum production level to keep these contracts.*

- *Brokers are full-time insurance producers who work independently and have no primary relationship or minimum production requirements with any company. There are two important distinctions between brokers and PPGAs: brokers do not receive overriding (general agent) commissions, and there is neither a tendency nor an intent for the company to achieve a primary-carrier status with brokers.*

- *Independent agents are primarily property and casualty producers who have no primary relationship with a company.*

- *Financial planners are producers who can usually be placed in one of the categories above. Although there is no agreed-upon definition of financial planners, it is usually understood that they provide clients with a total financial plan that includes everything from investments to insurance.*

- *Stockbrokers sell some annuities, single premium life, and variable products.*

- *Super producers are a special kind of producer-those with sophisticated product knowledge and technical support. Although all super producers would fall into one of the categories above, they really represent a distribution system within a distribution system simply because they are different, with their special compensation arrangements, joint case work, country-wide partnerships, equity ownership's, influence on product development, technical expertise, shared knowledge, and even proprietary software.*

4. *The agency system has two main branches:*

- *building agencies. A company builds its own agency distribution system by recruiting, financing, training, motivating, housing, and supervising new agents to represent it "exclusively." The individual in charge is typically called a manager or general agent,*

and it is he or she who does the recruiting of new, inexperienced recruits and develops them into a sales force.

- *nonbuilding agencies. A company taps into the existing pool of agents created by the building branch referred to above to create an "instant sales force." Companies win an established producer's attention through the use of an intermediary who acts as a sort of "manufacturer's representative"—either as an employee or independent contractor—and convinces established producers to sell their company's products through one type of arrangement or another.*

5. *Almost all of the existing field structures fall into one of the following general broad categories:*

- *Agency building—managerial. In this type of field organization, the manager (compensated by salary, overrides, and/or commissions on personal production) is a direct extension of the company, and his or her role is strictly to hire, train, and manage a sales staff. In some companies, production by the manager is either discouraged or not allowed, while in some companies it is allowed but not usually expected. Expenses tend to be borne entirely by the company. This form of organization is usually for home-service agents, multiple-line exclusive agents, and to a lesser degree, ordinary agents.*

- *Agency building—general agent. The goal in this type of field organization is also to build a sales staff, but the person in charge, usually called a general agent, is an independent contractor and is compensated primarily for building the agency's staff, although personal production is common. Quite often, the general agent is given an expense allowance and is then expected to manage his or her own agency expenses. The ordinary agent is the dominant producer in this structure.*

- *Regional director approach (RDS)—personal-producing general agent. This type of structure is favored by companies that prefer to have primary-carrier relationships with their PPGAs. Companies that employ this approach hire only experienced producers and are not committed to new agent development in any way. They provide little, if any, continuing generic education or training, some product orientation, and no office facilities or supervision. As the name of this type of structure implies, PPGAs are hired and supervised by regional directors.*

- *Managing general agent approach—personal producing general agent. The managing general agent (MGA) concept differs from the RDA approach because the MGA is an independent contractor authorized by the company to appoint PPGAs, and there is much less primary company orientation. Typically, the MGA is a franchisee who represents one company for a particular product in a particular territory. Because their*

producers are already paid the override, MGAs are compensated on a percentage of commissions and assume such administrative expenses as recruiting and mailing costs.

- *Brokerage supervisor approach. The brokerage supervisor is a company employee who solicits business from producers with whom that company has no primary relationships. Brokerage supervisors are most often associated with agency-building companies—providing them with an additional distribution option—and with life affiliates of property-casualty companies where they primarily target independent property-casualty agencies. Companies that use this approach tend to offer a full line of products and rely on their ability to provide technical help to producers whose main business is not life insurance, such as property-casualty agents and stockbrokers. Because brokerage supervisors are usually housed in the field, they are able to solve local producers' problems when and where they occur.*

- *Independent brokerage general agent approach. This approach provides companies access to a producer through an independent brokerage general agent (IBGA) who is authorized to solicit business for the company and to appoint producers on its behalf. IBGA companies tend to be ones that offer specialty products or that provide process-oriented service, including liberal underwriting and speedy policy issue and commission payment, to producers who typically are agents of other companies. IBGAs offer some administrative services, usually represent several carriers for the same product, and are paid by overrides on business generated through their efforts while their producers are compensated by basic commissions.*

6. *The agent's contract with the company describes the authority, scope, and limits of the agent's job, and it determines the agent's legal relationship with the company, the restrictions concerning representation of other companies, and the compensation arrangements.*

7. *High retention rates have a direct bearing on company profitability in two ways: (1) the company avoids the expenses associated with recruiting and training additional new agents and (2) established agents have higher productivity than less experienced agents.*

8. a. The selection-rejection process of producer recruitment usually contains three stages:

    - obtaining all the facts relating to the candidate's background, experience, and personal qualifications

    - using an organized system for verifying and evaluating the facts

    - devoting an adequate amount of time and effort to judge the facts and make an intelligent decision

    b. The following steps can be taken to facilitate these three stages:

    - a quick preliminary interview to determine if there are any obvious reasons why the candidate should be rejected and to convince the candidate to take an aptitude test

    - the administration of an objective aptitude test that accurately predicts the chances of an individual's likelihood of success in the job of producer (and conforms to all equal opportunity rules and regulations)

    - the completion of a legal application form

    - an evaluation interview in which the company can gain further information about the candidate and the candidate can learn about the job

    - interviews with other people, if appropriate, such as spouses, other producers, and references

    - a follow-up interview to clear up any questions on the part of either the recruiter or candidate

    - precontract training—having the candidate actually do certain parts of the job before making a commitment

    - giving the candidate a complete, honest, and realistic description of the job, including both the good and the bad aspects of the position

9. Generally, a new agent's training will cover these five areas:

    - life insurance basics

    - sales techniques

    - company and agency procedures

    - product knowledge

    - company history, goals, plans, and policies

10. *Agency managers and directors usually support professional educational programs, such as LUTC, CLU, and ChFC.*

   If the company and agency deal with variable life and equity products, such as mutual funds, the new agents will be given educational support to prepare for the examinations they must pass in order to sell those products. The Securities and Exchange Commission (SEC) mandates the examinations that are developed and managed by the National Association of Securities Dealers (NASD). There are also educational programs provided by the Million Dollar Round Table (MDRT) and the Association of Advanced Life Underwriting (AALU).

11. *Any increase in insurance sales activities by noninsurance organizations, which have a totally different marketing orientation, could alter the ways insurance marketers operate. Furthermore, the life insurance business is becoming a global business with foreign insurers invading the United States and vice versa. Many foreign insurers also have a different marketing orientation, and their approach, especially their relationship with banks, could force United States insurers to modify their distribution methods.*

Chapter 23

Time Value of Money

By Dan M. McGill

Revised by Norma Nielson and Donald Jones

Learning Objectives

An understanding of the material in this chapter should enable the student to

1. **Explain the concepts of compound interest and simple interest.**

2. **Understand, explain, and calculate present values (discounting).**

3. **Understand, explain, and calculate future values (accumulating)**

4. **Explain how changes in interest rates and time periods affect present values and future values**

5. **Calculate the present values and the future values of various annuities (series of annual payments).**

Money held today is worth more than money promised in the future. The premiums, products, and financial operations of life insurance companies not only reflect life contingencies but also depend heavily on this time value of money—particularly when a company collects level premiums over the life of a policy, accumulating sums of money that it manages for many years before that money is disbursed. Companies invest these funds in income-producing assets with the earnings credited on a compound interest basis to benefit policyowners. Three different examples of interest rate crediting are as follows:

- internal policy accumulations

- policy dividend accumulations

- policy proceeds left at interest

Each of these may differ from the other and all will fluctuate with economic conditions. To illustrate the concept, this chapter deals only with level interest assumptions, but insurance companies must accommodate nonlevel interest patterns. Premiums, surrender values, reserves, and dividends all reflect the differing value of money over extended periods.

Because interest earnings play such a vital role in the pricing practices and operations of a life insurance company, it is essential to consider the concept further. In order to explain their products to customers and assure that policy illustrations are appropriate, agents need a clear understanding of the relationship between interest rates and the financial features of life insurance. Today's financial calculators and computer spreadsheets make these computations readily accessible to everyone in the financial community.

DEFINITION OF TERMS

interest

principal

> **Interest** represents the difference between the **principal**—the value of the original capital invested—and the amount that must be repaid by the borrower after a specified term. To an investor interest is the income from invested capital. To a borrower it is the price paid for the use of money.

future value

> Interest income is usually expressed as a percentage rate of the principal per year. Thus, if an invested principal of $100 earns $5.50 during a 12-month period, the rate of return is 5.5 percent. The rate of interest may be expressed in various forms, but in this chapter we will express it as either a percentage—for example, 5.5 percent—or as its equivalent decimal fraction—0.055. To obtain the interest earnings on any given principal sum for a specified period, multiply the appropriate decimal fraction by the principal sum. For example, the interest earnings on $1 invested for one year at 5.5 percent is $1 \times 0.055 = \$0.055$, or 5½ cents. The equation $S = P(1 + i)$ represents the amount to which any given principal sum will accumulate in one year when invested at a specified rate of interest. In the equation, S represents the **future value** or sum at the end of the year; P represents the principal at the beginning of the year or present value; i is the rate of interest. If the principal is $1, the equation can be simplified to $S = 1 + i$. Once the amount to which $1 will accumulate in one year is known, the future value of any principal sum can be determined by multiplying it by that factor. Figure 23-1 shows the accumulation of interest on a principal amount of $100.

> The same reasoning applies to the death benefit payable under a life insurance policy. A payment deferred for one year by the beneficiary would earn interest under the policy's interest-only option. With 5.5 percent interest the payment received on a $100,000 policy would be that original face amount plus interest at 5.5 percent for the one-year delay period. The eventual payment amount would be computed as $100,000 \times 1.055 = \$105,500$.

Figure 23-1
Simple Interest

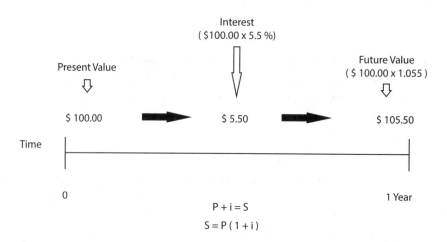

The term **simple interest** is used if interest is paid on only the original principal invested. If interest earnings are not distributed but are added to the original principal and reinvested at the same interest rate or a different rate of interest, the result is compound interest. **Compound interest** is simply interest on interest. While interest may be compounded annually, semiannually, monthly, daily, or at other agreed-upon intervals, only annual compounding is illustrated in this chapter.

COMPOUND INTEREST FUNCTIONS

Life insurance calculations use compound interest. Premium and reserve computations assume that companies keep funds continuously invested until those funds are paid out in settlement of claims. The company's computations further assume that interest earnings are added to the original principal and reinvested. To understand the relationships, it will be helpful to examine four basic compound interest series.

Future Values

The first series shows the amount to which a principal sum of $10,000 invested for a number of years (or other units of time) will increase over time. This applies compound interest to accumulate interest earnings. Figure 23-2 illustrates this concept. If you invest $10,000 at 5.5 percent for one year, the combined amount of principal and interest at the end of the year, according to the simple formula previously stated, will be $10,000 × 1.055, or $10,550. If the $10,550 is then invested for another year at 5.5 percent, the combined amount of principal and interest at the end of the second year will be $10,550 × 1.055, or $11,130. This is equivalent to multiplying $10,000 by 1.055^2 where the exponent—indicated in this example by the superscript "2"—denotes the number of times the base—in this case 1.055—is multiplied by itself. If the sum of $11,130 is again invested for another year at 5.5 percent, the principal and interest at the end of the third year will be $11,130 × 1.055, or $11,742, which is the equivalent of multiplying $10,000 by 1.055^3. If this process continues, the accumulated principal and interest will always equal the sum obtained by multiplying $10,000 by 1.055 raised to an exponent equal to the number of years of compound interest earned.

The future value of any principal sum invested for any period of time at any rate of interest can be computed by the same process. If S represents the future value, or sum, at the end of the period, i the rate of interest, P the principal invested, and n the number of years, the general formula becomes $S = P (1 + i)^n$. If the principal is $1, as is shown in most compound interest tables, the formula is $S = (1 + i)^n$. Table 23-1 shows the accumulated amount of 1 at the end of each of 30 years at various rates of compound interest. A student who wants to compute the future value of $500, for example, at the end of 23 years with interest at 5.5 percent compounded annually looks up the factor (the number in the table opposite 23 years in the column headed 5.5 percent), 3.4262, and multiplies that factor by 500. This produces the answer of $1,713.10.

Instead of reading 3.4262 from a compound interest table, the y^x function of a calculator could be used. To solve the same problem, a calculator that uses algebraic notation, such as the TI BA-II Plus, would require the following set of key strokes:

Pressing the '=' key then produces the answer, the factor 3.4262. For calculators like the HP 12-C, using "reverse Polish" notation, the future value factor is found with the following series of key strokes:

Those with ready access to a computer spreadsheet, such as Lotus 1-2-3 or excel, would enter the formula (1.055)^23 into a spreadsheet cell and press ENTER to obtain the needed solution.

Likewise, future value problems can be solved using a financial calculator. For most calculators with financial function keys, the future value of an initial $500 principal at the end of 23 years with interest at 5.5 percent compounded annually requires the following key strokes to produce the $1,713.10 answer:

Figure 23-2
Compound Interest

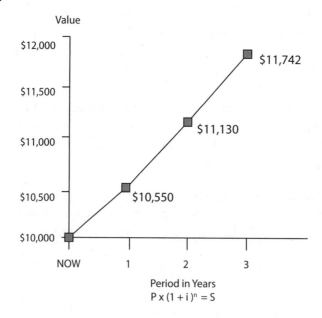

Table 23-1
Future Value of 1 at Various Rates of Compound Interest

$$(1+i)^n$$

Year	3.5%	4.0%	4.5%	5.0%	5.5%
1	1.0350	1.0400	1.0450	1.0500	1.0550
2	1.0712	1.0816	1.0920	1.1025	1.1130
3	1.1087	1.1249	1.1412	1.1576	1.1742
4	1.1475	1.1699	1.1925	1.2155	1.2388
5	1.1877	1.2167	1.2462	1.2763	1.3070
6	1.2293	1.2653	1.3023	1.3401	1.3788
7	1.2723	1.3159	1.3609	1.4071	1.4547
8	1.3168	1.3686	1.4221	1.4775	1.5347
9	1.3629	1.4233	1.4861	1.5513	1.6191
10	1.4106	1.4802	1.5530	1.6289	1.7081
11	1.4600	1.5395	1.6229	1.7103	1.8021
12	1.5111	1.6010	1.6959	1.7959	1.9012
13	1.5640	1.6651	1.7722	1.8856	2.0058
14	1.6187	1.7317	1.8519	1.9799	2.1161
15	1.6753	1.8009	1.9353	2.0789	2.2325
16	1.7340	1.8730	2.0224	2.1829	2.3553
17	1.7947	1.9479	2.1134	2.2920	2.4848
18	1.8575	2.0258	2.2085	2.4066	2.6215
19	1.9225	2.1068	2.3079	2.5270	2.7656
20	1.9898	2.1911	2.4117	2.6533	2.9178
21	2.0594	2.2788	2.5202	2.7860	3.0782
22	2.1315	2.3699	2.6337	2.9253	3.2475
23	2.2061	2.4647	2.7522	3.0715	3.4262
24	2.2833	2.5633	2.8760	3.2251	3.6146
25	2.3632	2.6658	3.0054	3.3864	3.8134
26	2.4460	2.7725	3.1407	3.5557	4.0231
27	2.5316	2.8834	3.2820	3.7335	4.2444
28	2.6202	2.9987	3.4297	3.9201	4.4778
29	2.7119	3.1187	3.5840	4.1161	4.7241
30	2.8068	3.2434	3.7453	4.3219	4.9840

Despite the fact that different strokes are needed to solve mathematical formulas, the key strokes for financial functions are similar for algebraic notation and reverse Polish calculators (although the former may require that a CPT [computer] key be pressed before the FV key). If you do not obtain the correct answer, check your calculator to be certain it is set for beginning-of-year computations.

The spreadsheet solution with an initial $500 principal amount is a simple extension of the formula (1.055)^23. Enter the formula (1.055)^23*500 to verify the $1,713.10 answer.

Relationship between Interest Rate and Accumulation Period to Future Values

If a higher rate of interest is used in the compounding process, or if a longer period of accumulation is used, a higher future value results. (While this is a somewhat obvious statement in the context of future value, it is important to make this explicit statement here because similar relationships that the student will encounter later in this chapter are less obvious.)

Present Values or Discounted Values

present values

discounting

The second series, called **present values**, calculates the value today that is equivalent to a given sum due at a designated time in the future. This process is called **discounting**. The process of discounting is particularly vital to life insurance company operations since the companies deal heavily in future promises. Their contracts provide for benefits to be paid in the future. Companies finance these benefits through premium income and future interest earnings. Their very solvency depends on establishing an equivalence between future benefit payments and receipts from premiums and investments. This equivalence is established through the discounting process whereby all values are reduced to a common basis. That common basis is present value.

The discounting process implicitly recognizes that a dollar due one year from now is worth less than a dollar due now. And a dollar due 5 years from now is worth less than a dollar due in one year. Money in hand can be invested to produce more money or capital. The difference in value between money in hand and money due in the future depends on the rate of return that can be obtained from invested capital. Also, the longer the period before the future money will be received, the greater the expected interest earnings and the greater the difference between the value of the present and future capital.

The present value of an amount due at a specified date in the future is that principal sum that, if invested now at an assumed rate of interest, would accumulate to the required amount by the due date.

Derivation of Present Values

As explained earlier, the amount to which a given sum will accumulate is found by multiplying the principal by 1 plus the rate of interest raised to an exponent equal to the number of interest-compounding time units in the period (years in our example). If, instead, the amount at the end of the period is given, the beginning principal may be found by dividing the future amount by 1 plus the rate of interest raised to the proper exponent. For example, $1 invested for one year at 5.5 percent interest will accumulate to $1.055 by the end of the year. If the process is to be reversed, the principal is found by dividing $1 by 1.055. If the amount due 2 years from now is $11,130, the present value of the amount at 5.5 percent compounded annually is $11,130 ÷ (1.055)^2 = $11,130 ÷ 1.1130 = $10,000. Similarly, if $10,000 is due one year from now, it is worth only $10,000 ÷ 1.055, or $9,479, today, based on an interest rate of 5.5 percent.

Example

$1 accumulating interest at 5.5 percent annually has a future value of $1.71 (original $1 plus $0.71 interest).

$1.71 payable 10 years from now has a present value of $1 if the annual interest rate is 5.5 percent.

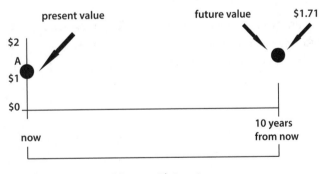

5.5 percent interest

If $10,000 is to be paid 2 years from now, its value now is only $10,000 $\div$ $(1.055)^2$ = $10,000 $\div$ 1.1130 = $8,985. Figure 23-3 illustrates this derivation. Conversely, $8,985 invested at 5.5 percent compound interest will, at the end of 2 years, amount to $10,000.

The present value of 1 at 5.5 percent compound interest can be derived for any number of years and arranged in tabular form for convenience by use of this general formula,

$$P = \frac{S}{(1+i)^n}$$

In standard actuarial notation the present value of 1 due n years from now is represented by the symbol v^n where $v = 1/(1+i)$ and n = number of years:

$$v^n = \left[\frac{1}{(1+i)}\right]^n$$

These values are shown for 30 years in Table 23-2 or can be computed easily using a financial calculator or computer spreadsheet.

Once you have a table of values for v^n, the present value of any amount due at the end of any number of years is determined by multiplying the future amount by the appropriate value of v^n. Thus, the present value of $1,000 due 15 years from now is, at 5.5 percent compound interest, $1,000 $\times$ 0.4479, or $447.90.

Once again, the financial calculator can produce the same answer. For the present value of $1,000 to be received at the end of 15 years with interest at 5.5 percent compounded annually requires the following key strokes:

1000   FV   15   N   5.5   i   0   PMT

Figure 23-3
Present Value

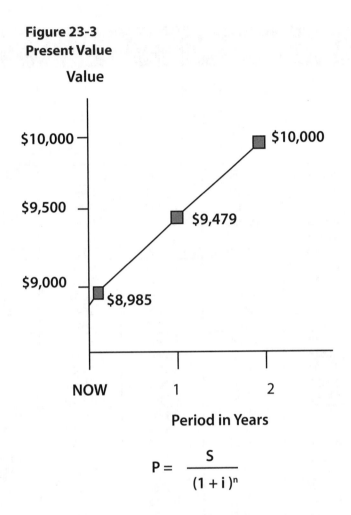

$$P = \frac{S}{(1 + i)^n}$$

Pressing the PV key, or the CPT and PV keys, yields an answer of $447.93 (the 3 cents difference between table value and the calculation value is due to the rounding in the table values). The spreadsheet user would enter the formula (1/1.055)^15*1000 to obtain this solution.

Table 23-2
Present Value of 1 at Various Rates of Compound Interest

$$v^n = \left[\frac{1}{(1+i)} \right]^n$$

Year	3.5%	4.0%	4.5%	5.0%	5.5%
1	0.9662	0.9615	0.9569	0.9524	0.9479
2	0.9335	0.9246	0.9157	0.9070	0.8985
3	0.9019	0.8890	0.8763	0.8638	0.8516
4	0.8714	0.8548	0.8386	0.8227	0.8072
5	0.8420	0.8219	0.8025	0.7835	0.7651
6	0.8135	0.7903	0.7679	0.7462	0.7252
7	0.7860	0.7599	0.7348	0.7107	0.6874
8	0.7594	0.7307	0.7032	0.6768	0.6516
9	0.7337	0.7026	0.6729	0.6446	0.6176
10	0.7089	0.6756	0.6439	0.6139	0.5854
11	0.6849	0.6496	0.6162	0.5847	0.5549
12	0.6618	0.6246	0.5897	0.5568	0.5260
13	0.6394	0.6006	0.5643	0.5303	0.4986
14	0.6178	0.5775	0.5400	0.5051	0.4726
15	0.5969	0.5553	0.5167	0.4810	0.4479
16	0.5767	0.5339	0.4945	0.4581	0.4246
17	0.5572	0.5134	0.4732	0.4363	0.4024
18	0.5384	0.4936	0.4528	0.4155	0.3815
19	0.5202	0.4746	0.4333	0.3957	0.3616
20	0.5026	0.4564	0.4146	0.3769	0.3427
21	0.4856	0.4388	0.3968	0.3589	0.3249
22	0.4692	0.4220	0.3797	0.3418	0.3079
23	0.4533	0.4057	0.3634	0.3256	0.2919
24	0.4380	0.3901	0.3477	0.3101	0.2767
25	0.4231	0.3751	0.3327	0.2953	0.2622
26	0.4088	0.3607	0.3184	0.2812	0.2486
27	0.3950	0.3468	0.3047	0.2678	0.2356
28	0.3817	0.3335	0.2916	0.2551	0.2233
29	0.3687	0.3207	0.2790	0.2429	0.2117
30	0.3563	0.3083	0.2670	0.2314	0.2006

One final note about present values is important for anyone working or investing in the financial marketplace. Sometimes banks and other commercial organizations use approximation methods that produce results slightly different from those obtained by the precise determination of present values described here. For example, interest may be deducted

in advance. For small amounts and short terms the differences produced by the alternate methods of discounting are inconsequential.

Relationship between Interest Rate and Discounting Period to Present Values

The relationship between interest rates and discounting period to present value is an inverse one. The magnitude of the difference between present and future values depends on the interest rate that is used for discounting. Assuming a higher rate of interest means that more interest is made or lost over time. That means the present values of future amounts are smaller for higher interest rates.

Example

$100 to be paid 20 years from now (Future Value) has a present value of $100 × (the present value factor for 20 years and the given interest rate)

5.5 percent interest for 20 years factor is 0.3427

3 percent interest for 20 years factor is 0.5537

PV at 5.5 percent = $100 × 0.3427 = $34.27

PV at 3 percent = $100 × 0.5537 = $55.37

Higher interest rates produce lower present values.

Future Value of Annual Payments

annuity

The third compound interest series deals with the future value of periodic equal annual payments. This stream of annual payments is called an **annuity**.

Beginning-of-Year Future Values

annuity due

An annuity with payments at the beginning of the period is called an **annuity due**. Premium payments on most life insurance policies, although they include a mortality factor as well as interest, are one common example of beginning-of-period payments. Figure 23-4 shows the future values based on a 5.5 percent interest rate of four $1 payments made at

the beginning of the year. Adding together the future values of the four payments—$1.055 + $1.113 + $1.1742 + $1.2388 gives us the $4.5810 future value of all four payments.

This process can be continued for any number of years to produce a table of annuity values. The elements of Table 23-3 are created by simply adding the elements of Table 23-1. To illustrate, the first five figures in the 5.5 percent column of Table 23-1 are reproduced in Table 23-1 extract.

Figure 23-4
Future Value of an Annuity with Beginning-of-Year Payments

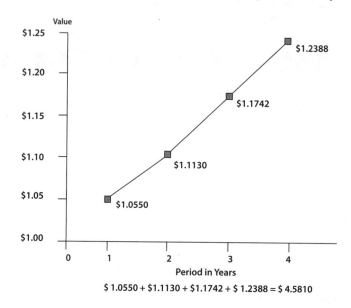

$ 1.0550 + $1.1130 + $1.1742 + $ 1.2388 = $ 4.5810

Year	5.5%	$(1.055)^n$
1	1.0550	$(1.055)^1$
2	1.1130	$(1.055)^2$
3	1.1742	$(1.055)^3$
4	1.2388	$(1.055)^4$
5	1.3070	$(1.055)^5$

Table 23-3:
Future Value of 1 per Year at Various Rates of Compound Interest Annuity Due—Payments Made at the Beginning of Year

$$S_n = (1 + i) + (1 + i)^2 + ... + (1 + i)^n$$

Year	3.5%	4.0%	4.5%	5.0%	5.5%
1	1.0350	1.0400	1.0450	1.0500	1.0550
2	2.1062	2.1216	2.1370	2.1525	2.1680
3	3.2149	3.2465	3.2782	3.3101	3.3423
4	4.3625	4.4163	4.4707	4.5256	4.5811
5	5.5502	5.6330	5.7169	5.8019	5.8881
6	6.7794	6.8983	7.0192	7.1420	7.2669
7	8.0517	8.2142	8.3800	8.5491	8.7216
8	9.3685	9.5828	9.8021	10.0266	10.2563
9	10.7314	11.0061	11.2882	11.5779	11.8754
10	12.1420	12.4864	12.8412	13.2068	13.5835
11	13.6020	14.0258	14.4640	14.9171	15.3856
12	15.1130	15.6268	16.1599	16.7130	17.2868
13	16.6770	17.2919	17.9321	18.5986	19.2926
14	18.2957	19.0236	19.7841	20.5786	21.4087
15	19.9710	20.8245	21.7193	22.6575	23.6411
16	21.7050	22.6975	23.7417	24.8404	25.9964
17	23.4997	24.6454	25.8551	27.1324	28.4812
18	25.3572	26.6712	28.0636	29.5390	31.1027
19	27.2797	28.7781	30.3714	32.0660	33.8683
20	29.2695	30.9692	32.7831	34.7193	36.7861
21	31.3289	33.2480	35.3034	37.5052	39.8643
22	33.4604	35.6179	37.9370	40.4305	43.1118
23	35.6665	38.0826	40.6892	43.5020	46.5380
24	37.9499	40.6459	43.5652	46.7271	50.1526
25	40.3131	43.3117	46.5706	50.1135	53.9660
26	42.7591	46.0842	49.7113	53.6691	57.9891
27	45.2906	48.9676	52.9933	57.4026	62.2335
28	47.9108	51.9663	56.4230	61.3227	66.7114
29	50.6227	55.0849	60.0071	65.4388	71.4355
30	53.4295	58.3283	63.7524	69.7608	76.4194

The first number in the Table 23-1 extract is the same as the first figure in the 5.5 percent column of Table 23-3 To obtain the second number in Table 23-3—2.1680—add the first two numbers in Table 23-1 extract. The third number in the Table 23-1 extract, 1.1742, is added to 2.1680 to produce 3.3423, the third number in Table 23-3 in the 5.5 percent column except for a difference due to rounding. Add 1.2388 to this to yield 4.5811, the fourth number in the 5.5 percent column in Table 23-3 and so on. To repeat, the values in Table 23-3 assume payments of $1 occur at the beginning of each year.

End-of-Year Future Values

ordinary annuity

An annuity with payments at the end of each period is called an **ordinary annuity**. A homeowner's mortgage with its payment due at the end of the first month is a common example of an ordinary annuity. Figure 23-5 illustrates a 4-year ordinary annuity. Figure 23-5 can be compared with Figure 23-4 to better understand the difference between this and a 4-year annuity due. Three of the four payments align perfectly, with a payment of $1 at the end of year 0 in Figure 23-5 corresponding exactly to a payment of $1 at the beginning of year 1 in Table 23-4 and so on.

The correspondence between most of the payments, illustrated in Figure 23-6 eliminates the need for a separate table. Table 23-3 with its beginning-of-year values can also be used to find the future value of a series of annual payments made at the end of each year. An adjustment is made to reflect the difference in timing of the first and last payments. An example follows to clarify the method.

To derive ordinary-annuity future values from annuity due values, use the factor from the annuity due table for one period less than the actual number of payments and add 1.0000 to that factor. The result will be the present value factor for an ordinary annuity. For example, to find the factor for a 5-year ordinary annuity, add 1.0000 to the future value factor for a 4-year annuity due of $1 per year.

Figure 23-5
Future Value of an Annuity with End-of-Year Payments

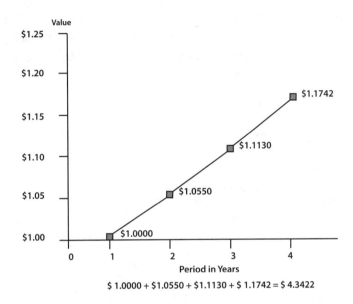

$ 1.0000 + $1.0550 + $1.1130 + $ 1.1742 = $ 4.3422

Suppose you need to find the amount to which $1,000 per year, payable for 5 years at the end of each year, will accumulate by the end of the last period at 5.5 percent interest. Since the first payment is not due until one year from now, interest will be earned for only 4 years. From Table 23-3, the amount of $1 per annum in advance at 5.5 percent interest for 4 years is $4.5811. The last of the five payments, however, will be made at the end of the period and will not earn any interest. This last payment of $1 added to $4.5811 yields $5.5811, the amount of $1 per annum payable at the end of each year over a 5-year period at 5.5 percent interest. Since $1 payments made in this manner will amount to $5.5811, then $1,000 payments made in the same manner will, obviously, amount to $1,000 × 5.5811, or $5,581.10.

Calculator and Spreadsheet Functions

Most financial calculators can be set directly to do either beginning-of-year or end-of-year calculations of the future value of an annuity. The end-of-year calculator solution to finding the future value of $1 per year for 5 years and annual compounding of interest entails the following keystrokes:

When the user presses the FV (or CPT and FV) button, the calculator produces the answer of 5.5811, which is 1 plus the 4th-year value from Table 23-3.

Computer spreadsheet functions usually assume end-of-year payments. The typical spreadsheet function to obtain the same answer is formatted @FV(payment, interest rate, term of years). This problem is solved with the formula @FV(1,0.055,5). Spreadsheet users enter the interest rate as a decimal rather than as a percent.

Figure 23-6

Comparing Future Values

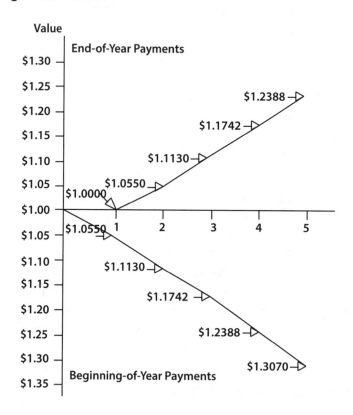

Test your spreadsheet or calculator's financial functions to be certain that you understand whether it is performing computations that assume payment at the beginning of a year or the end of a year. Enter the three factors specified above for 5 years of payments at 5.5 percent interest. If the answer is 5.5811, then the computation assumes end-of-year payments. If the answer is 5.8881, then the computation assumes beginning-of-year payments. The HP-12C calculator is easily set for beginning- or end-of-period payments through the

function and the BEG or END key. The BA-II Plus calculator is set by using the 2nd, BGN, and SET keys.

Another way to check your calculator or spreadsheet assumption about timing of payments is to solve for the future value of a single payment of $1 at an interest rate greater than zero. If the payments are assumed to be at the end of the period, the calculated FV will be $1. If the payment is assumed to be made at the beginning of the period, the calculated FV will be greater than $1 because of the interest earned during the period.

Also be certain you understand how interest is being compounded. Many manual calculations assume annual compounding. Some calculators, including the HP-12C and the BA-II Plus, can be set for monthly, weekly, or other compounding intervals. The interest rate must be appropriately adjusted to coincide with the length of the compounding period.

Present Value of Annual Payments

The fourth and final compound interest series determines the present value of a number of equal annual payments at various rates of interest. This series is used by life insurance companies to find amounts payable under the settlement options[1] that liquidate insurance proceeds over several years. An understanding of this series is particularly important here so that we can extend it in the next chapter to include computations that combine these values with life contingencies.

Derivation of Present Values

Table 23-4 showing the present value of annuity payments is derived from the values presented in Table 23-2 in the same manner that Table 23-3 was derived from the values in Table 23-1 As in Table 23-2, the values in this series are for annual payments of $1 due at the end of each year (ordinary annuity). (Adjustments similar to those described in the previous section can be made to derive the present value of payments due at the beginning of each year.) Remember that in Table 23-2 at 5.5 percent interest, the present value of $1 payable one year from now is $0.9479. The present value of the second payment of $1 due 2 years from now is $0.8985; the payment due in 3 years is worth $0.8516 now. The present value of all three payments is, of course, the sum of the present values of each taken separately, or $2.6980, as depicted in Figure 23-7.

---

1.   Settlement options are discussed in chapter 8.

Figure 23-7
Present Value of a 3-Year Annuity with End-of-Year $1 Payments

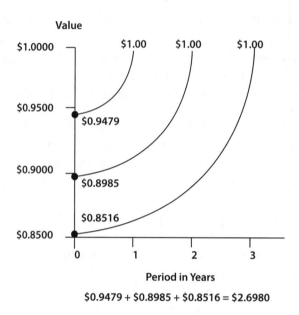

$0.9479 + $0.8985 + $0.8516 = $2.6980

The present value factors in Table 23-4 are based on the assumption that each $1 payment is made at the end of the period. Many life insurance calculations involve payment streams that are made at the beginning of the period, such as premium payments. When the number of payments, the interest rate, and amount of each payment are all the same, the present value of an annuity due is higher than the present value of a corresponding immediate annuity. This is purely a result of the earlier timing of the payments.

In order to convert ordinary-annuity present value factors into annuity due present value factors, first, find the ordinary-annuity factor for the appropriate interest rate and for one payment period less than the total number of payments to be made. Then, add 1.000 to that factor to represent the $1 payment at the beginning of the stream. The result is a present value factor representing the specific annuity due payments of $1 per period.

Table 23-4
Present Value of 1 per Year at Various Rates of Compound Interest Immediate Annuity—Payment at End of Year

$$a_n = v + v^2 + \ldots + v^n$$

Year	3.5%	4.0%	4.5%	5.0%	5.5%
1	0.9662	0.9615	0.9569	0.9524	0.9479
2	1.8997	1.8861	1.8727	1.8594	1.8463
3	2.8016	2.7751	2.7490	2.7232	2.6979
4	3.6731	3.6299	3.5875	3.5460	3.5052
5	4.5151	4.4518	4.3900	4.3295	4.2703
6	5.3286	5.2421	5.1579	5.0757	4.9955
7	6.1145	6.0021	5.8927	5.7864	5.6830
8	6.8740	6.7327	6.5959	6.4632	6.3346
9	7.6077	7.4353	7.2688	7.1078	6.9522
10	8.3166	8.1109	7.9127	7.7217	7.5376
11	9.0016	8.7605	8.5289	8.3064	8.0925
12	9.6633	9.3851	9.1186	8.8633	8.6185
13	10.3027	9.9856	9.6829	9.3936	9.1171
14	10.9205	10.5631	10.2228	9.8986	9.5896
15	11.5174	11.1184	10.7395	10.3797	10.0376
16	12.0941	11.6523	11.2340	10.8378	10.4622
17	12.6513	12.1657	11.7072	11.2741	10.8646
18	13.1897	12.6593	12.1600	11.6896	11.2461
19	13.7098	13.1339	12.5933	12.0853	11.6077
20	14.2124	13.5903	13.0079	12.4622	11.9504
21	14.6980	14.0292	13.4047	12.8212	12.2752
22	15.1671	14.4511	13.7844	13.1630	12.5832
23	15.6204	14.8568	14.1478	13.4886	12.8750
24	16.0584	15.2470	14.4955	13.7986	13.1517
25	16.4815	15.6221	14.8282	14.0939	13.4139
26	16.8904	15.9828	15.1466	14.3752	13.6625
27	17.2854	16.3296	15.4513	14.6430	13.8981
28	17.6670	16.6631	15.7429	14.8981	14.1214
29	18.0358	16.9837	16.0219	15.1411	14.3331
30	18.3920	17.2920	16.2889	15.3725	14.5337

Figure 23-8 depicts a 3-year annuity due of $1 per year. The first payment is not discounted because it is made now and worth the full $1 amount. The second payment is one year away and is worth $0.9479 now when discounted at 5.5 percent interest. The third payment is worth $0.8985 now. All three $1 payments have a present value equal to the sum of their individual present values ($2.8464 in this example). The difference between the present value of the 3-year annuity due and the corresponding ordinary annuity does not seem important. However, consider the amount involved if each annual payment is for $10 million instead of $1. The difference in timing amounts to $1,484 million, which is one year of additional interest earned when each payment is made one year earlier.

By the process of cumulative addition, the present value of a series of annual payments of $1 for any number of years can be found. Table 23-4 shows these values at various rates of interest for durations up to 30 years. The value for 2 years in Table 23-4 is the sum of the first two values in Table 23-2. The value for 3 years is the sum of the first three values in Table 23-2 (2.6979, which is the same present value depicted in Figure 23-7), and so on.

Application of the Values

Annuity values, typically based on a present value of $1, are used in several different ways by life insurance companies. For example, determining what payment amount each $1 of death benefit can buy if paid to the beneficiary in 20 annual end-of-year installments under the fixed-period settlement option earning 5.5 percent interest requires the present value of $1 per annum for 20 years, which is $11.9504. This number is then divided into $1 to yield $0.08368. Stated differently, at 5.5 percent compound interest, $1 will provide 8.4 cents at the end of each year for 20 years. Therefore, each $1,000 of death benefit would provide $1,000 × 0.08368, or $83.68 per year for 20 years.

From a different perspective, $11.95 of savings invested at 5.5 percent will provide $1 per year for 20 years. The first payment will occur one year from now; payments will continue for 19 years. At the end of 20 years none of the money will remain. Similarly $14.53 will provide $1 annual payments for 30 years.

Annuity values also can be used to determine the amount available from larger investments. If $11.95 will provide $1 per year for 20 years, then $1,000 will provide an annual payment of $1,000 ÷ 11.95 = $83.68. The rule is as follows: To find the amount of annual payments due at the end of each year that a given principal sum will provide, divide the sum by the present value of $1 per year at the applicable rate of interest for the period.

Figure 23-8

Present Value of a 3-Year Annuity with Beginning-of-Year $1 Payments

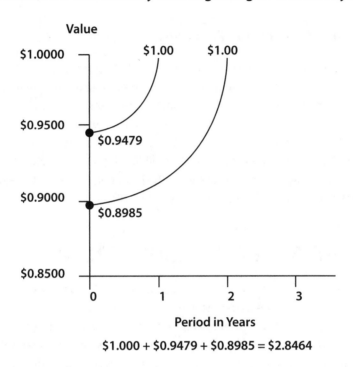

$1.000 + $0.9479 + $0.8985 = $2.8464

Amounts payable under life insurance settlement options are payable at the beginning of the year.[2] Likewise, annual premiums are due at the beginning of the year. Therefore, life insurance companies must modify the values shown in Table 23-4 to reflect the present value of a series of periodic payments due at the beginning of the year. The adjustment involved is simple and very similar to the adjustment made for future values.

Consider, for example, a series of annual payments of $1 due at the beginning of each year for 25 years. The first payment is due immediately and is worth $1. Twenty-four additional payments remain, the first of which is due one year from now. The present value of the entire series is obtained by adding $1 to the present value of $1 per annum (end of year from Table 23-4) for one year less, in this case, 24 years. The result at an interest rate of 5.5 percent is $13.1517 + $1, or $14.1517.

---

2.   As a matter of fact, life insurance settlement options usually provide for monthly payments, which necessitates a further modification.

Calculator and Spreadsheet Functions

Financial calculators and spreadsheets are also used to perform present value computations. The financial calculator solution to valuing a temporary annuity that pays $1 per year at the end of each of 20 years at 5.5 percent interest requires input similar to that used for future value computations: When the PV (or CPT and PV) button is pressed, the present value of $1 per annum for 20 years is $11.9504, as before. If this is divided into 1, the annual payment for 20 years purchased by $1 is $0.08368. The typical computer spreadsheet function to obtain the same answer is formatted @PV (payment, interest rate, term of years). This problem is solved with the formula @PV(1,0.055,20).

CURRENT INTEREST ASSUMPTIONS

In the broad financial market the interest rate paid reflects the degree of risk associated with the future payment. The riskier the venture, the higher the interest rate paid. The more secure the principal, the lower the interest rate paid. Many of the illustrations in this chapter assume 5.5 percent interest. This rate is only representative of rates that could be used by companies in computing premiums and reserves on their various products.

The actuaries designing a permanent cash value life insurance product must select the interest rate carefully, as it will be guaranteed for the lifetime of the contract and subject to a statutory maximum. While companies tend to select a conservative rate, perhaps one percentage point less than they expect to earn on their investments over a long period, they also must offer rates that are competitive with other insurers and with other financial intermediaries. Permanent life insurance contracts in force today have been issued over a period of many decades. Interest rate guarantees in those policies range from 2.0 percent to nearly 6 percent.

Flexible premium contracts like universal life also quote interest rate guarantees with this same range, but they derive most of their marketing appeal from the possibility that they will pay rates higher than those guaranteed. As demonstrated in chapter 12 reserves under such contracts are recalculated on a similar interest basis.

CHAPTER REVIEW

Key Terms and Concepts

interest	present values
principal	discounting
future value	annuity
simple interest	annuity due
compound interest	ordinary annuity

Chapter 23 Review Questions

1. Explain the difference between simple interest and compound interest. [1]

2. Using the values in Table 23-1 of the text, calculate the amount to which $2,000 would grow by the end of 15 years if it earned 5 percent compound interest. [3]

3. Describe what effect either increasing the interest rate or lengthening the period of accumulation has on the future value of a specific present sum. [3]

4. Explain why $600 of commission received one year from now is worth less than $600 of commission received now. [4]

5. Using the values in Table 23-2 of the text, calculate the present value of $2,000 to be received at the end of 15 years, assuming 5 percent interest. [2]

6. Describe what effect either increasing the interest rate or lengthening the discounting period has on the present value of a specific future value. [4]

7. Using the values in Table 23-3 of the text, calculate the future value of an annuity due of $2,000 per year for 15 years at 5 percent interest. [5]

8. Using the values in Table 23-3 of the text, calculate the future value of an ordinary annuity of $2,000 per year for 15 years at 5 percent interest. [5]

9. Using the values in Table 23-4 of the text, calculate the present value of an annuity due of $2,000 per year for 15 years at 5 percent interest. [5]

10. Using the values in Table 23-4 of the text, calculate the present value of an ordinary annuity of $2,000 per year for 15 years at 5 percent interest. [5]

11. Using the values in Table 23-2 of the text, calculate the total present value of a series of three payments where $100 is to be received at the end of one year, $200 is to be received at the end of 2 years, and $300 is to be received at the end of 3 years, assuming 4.5 percent interest. [5]

12. Using the values in Table 23-4 of the text, calculate how much per year a $100,000 lump sum will provide in level annual payments over 15 years if it is invested at 5.5 percent interest and the payments are to be made at the end of each year. [5]

Chapter 23 Review Answers

1. *Simple interest only applies to the original principal invested. Any interest earned is not added to the principal so that the interest payment will remain constant in each future period unless the simple interest rate changes or the amount of principal changes.*

   Compound interest results from adding interest payments to the beginning principal and paying interest on both the original principal and the prior interest earnings. Interest is paid on interest under compound interest.

   In the first period, there is no difference between simple interest and compound interest. After the first period, the compound interest will apply to a larger amount (interest from last period plus principal at beginning of last period). Both principal amount and interest payments will increase in each new period.

	Period 1		Period 2		Period 3	
	Principal	Interest	Principal	Interest	Principal	Interest
10% simple interest	$100	$10.00	$100	$10.00	$100	$10.00

	Period 1		Period 2		Period 3	
	Principal	*Interest*	*Principal*	*Interest*	*Principal*	*Interest*
10% compound interest	100	10.00	110	11.00	121	12.10

2. At the end of 15 years, the beginning sum of $2,000 would grow to $4,157.80 (that is, 2.0789 x $2,000 = $4,157.80).

3. Either increasing the interest rate or lengthening the period of accumulation will increase the future value of a specific present sum.

    Examples—$1,000 present sum invest

    a. at 10 percent for 10 years will accumulate to $2,593.74

    b. at 12 percent for 10 years will accumulate to $3,105.85

    c. at 10 percent for 11 years (longer period) will accumulate to $2,853.12

    d. at 12 percent for 11 years (both higher interest rate and longer period) will accumulate to $3,478.55

4. Because of the time value of money, any future receipt is worth less today than the amount that will be received in the future. The present value is the discounted value of the future amount. The discount rate reflects the potential investment return that could be earned if the funds were available right now. The discount rate may also reflect anticipated inflation, which reduces the purchasing power of the funds over the delay period before receipt of the funds.

    The $600 commission discounted for 5 percent for one year becomes $571.44 (that is, 0.9524 x $600 = $571.44).

    If the $600 had been received now, it could have been invested at 5 percent and grown to $630 by the next year (1.05 x $600 = $630).

5. The present value of $2,000 to be received at the end of 15 years, if discounted at 5 percent, is $962.00 (that is, 0.4810 x $2,000 = $962.00).

6. Either increasing the interest rate or lengthening the discounting period will decrease the present value of any specific future value.

    For example, for someone who desires to accumulate $1,000 in the future by making a deposit into an interest-bearing account, the corresponding present values are

    a. $385.54 invested today at 10 percent for 10 years will accumulate to $1,000

    b. $321.97 invested today at 12 percent (higher interest rate) for 10 years will accumulate to $1,000

    c. $350.49 invested today at 10 percent (longer period) for 11 years will accumulate to $1,000

    d. $287.48 invested today at 12 percent (longer period and higher interest rates) for 11 years will accumulate to $1,000

7. The future value of an annuity due of $2,000 per year for 15 years at 5 percent interest is $45,315.00 (that is, 22.6575 x $2,000 = $45,315).

8. The future value of an ordinary annuity of $2,000 per year for 15 years at 5 percent interest is $43,157.20 (that is, [20.5786 + 1] x $2,000 = $43,157.20). Note: To convert the annuity factor from due to immediate, use the factor for one less year (14 here) and add 1.0000.

9. The present value of an annuity due of $2,000 per year for 15 years at 5 percent interest is $21,797.20 (that is, [9.8986 + 1] x $2,000 = $21,797.20). Note: To convert the annuity factor from immediate to due, use the factor for one less year (14 here) and add 1.0000.

10. The present value of an ordinary annuity of $2,000 per year for 15 years at 5 percent interest is $20,759.40 (that is, 10.3797 x $2,000 = $20,759.40).

11. The present value of the three payments assuming 4.5 percent interest is $541.71, calculated as follows:

    0.9569 x $100 = $ 95.69
    0.9157 x $200 = 183.14
    0.8763 x $300 = 262.89
                    = $541.72

12. *A $100,000 lump sum will provide level annual payments at the end of the next 15 years at 5.5 percent interest of $9,962.54 (that is, $100,000 / 10.0376 = $9,962.54).*

Chapter 24
Annuities

By Dan M. McGill

Revised by Edward E. Graves and Joseph W. Huver

Learning Objectives

An understanding of the material in this chapter should enable the student to

1. **Describe and understand the various types of annuity contracts, including single and joint lives, immediate and deferred designs, and fixed or indexed or variable benefits.**

2. **Explain how increased longevity has affected the safety margins in mortality tables**

3. **Describe and understand equity-indexed annuities.**

The term annuity is derived from the Latin word annus, meaning year, and hence connotes an annual payment. A broader and more contemporary definition, however, is that an annuity is a periodic payment to commence at a specified or contingent date and to continue throughout a fixed period or for the duration of a designated life or lives. The person whose life governs the duration of the payments is called the annuitant. The annuitant may or may not be the person who receives the periodic payments, although he or she usually is. The income under the annuity contract may be paid annually, semiannually, quarterly, or monthly, depending on the conditions of the agreement. Normally the income is paid monthly.

annuity certain

life annuity

whole life annuity

temporary life annuity

If the payments are to be made for a definite period of time without being linked to the duration of a specified human life, the agreement is known as an **annuity certain** (exemplified by mortgages and bank loans). If the payments are to be made for the duration of a designated life, the agreement is called a **life annuity** or, more accurately, a single-life annuity. It is also referred to as a **whole life annuity** to distinguish it from a **temporary life annuity**, under which payments terminate with the death of the designated individual or at the expiration of the specified period of time, whichever occurs earlier. The word life in the title of an annuity indicates that the payments are based on life contingencies or

continue only as long as a designated person is alive. This chapter is concerned primarily with life annuities created by insurance companies.

NATURE OF ANNUITIES

Comparison with Life Insurance

The primary function of life insurance is to create an estate or principal sum; the primary function of an annuity is to liquidate a principal sum, regardless of how it was created. Despite this basic dissimilarity in function, life insurance and annuities are based on the same fundamental pooling, mortality, and investment principles.

In the first place, both life insurance and annuities protect against loss of income. Life insurance furnishes protection against loss of income arising out of premature death; an annuity provides protection against loss of income arising out of excessive longevity. It might be said that life insurance provides a financial hedge against dying too soon, while an annuity provides a hedge against living too long. From an economic standpoint, both contingencies are undesirable. A second common feature is the utilization of the pooling technique. Insurance is a pooling arrangement whereby all make contributions so that the dependents of those who die prematurely are partially compensated for loss of income; an annuity is a pooling arrangement whereby those who die prematurely make a contribution on behalf of those who live beyond their life expectancy and would otherwise outlive their income. A third common feature is that the contributions in each case are based on probabilities of death and survival as reflected in a mortality table. For reasons that will be apparent later, the same mortality table is not used for both sets of calculations. Finally, under both arrangements, contributions are discounted for the compound interest that the insurance company will earn on them.

The Annuity Principle

The annuity concept is founded on the unpredictability of human life. A person may have accumulated a principal sum for his or her old-age support that, assuming that the sum is to be liquidated over his or her remaining years, should be adequate for the purpose. Such a result, however, requires estimating the length of the individual's lifetime. He or she might have average health and vitality for his or her age and could expect to live exactly the calculated life expectancy (derived from a mortality table). But because the individual could not be sure of not surviving beyond this predicted life expectancy, to be on the safe side, he or she would have to plan to spread the accumulated principal over a much

longer period than he or she is likely to live. Even then there would be some danger of surviving the period and finding the assets and income totally consumed prior to death. On the other hand, the individual might die after only a few years, leaving funds to his or her estate that could have and should have been used to provide the person with more comforts during his or her lifetime. If the individual were willing to pool savings with those of other people in the same predicament, the administering agency, relying on the laws of probability and large numbers, could provide each of the participants with an income of a specified amount as long as he or she lives—regardless of longevity. No one could outlive his or her income. Such an arrangement, however, implies a willingness on each participant's part to have all or a portion of his or her unliquidated principal at the time of death used to supplement the exhausted principal of those who live beyond their life expectancy.

Each payment under an annuity is composed partly of principal and partly of the income on the unliquidated principal. For each year that goes by, a larger proportion of the payment is composed of principal. If a person exactly lives out his or her life expectancy, as computed at the time the individual enters on the annuity, the principal will be completely exhausted with the last payment prior to death. If the person lives beyond his or her life expectancy, each payment will be derived from funds forfeited by those who die before attaining their life expectancy. It is an equitable arrangement since at the outset no one can know into what category he or she will fall. There is no other arrangement under which a principal sum can—with certainty—be completely liquidated in equal installments over the duration of a human life.

Classifications of Annuities

Annuities may be classified in many different ways, depending on the point of emphasis. For most purposes, they can be classified by the following:

- number of lives covered
- time when payments commence
- method of premium payment
- nature of the insurer's obligation

Number of Lives Covered

joint annuity

joint-and-survivor annuity

This is a simple dichotomy and refers only to whether the annuity covers a single life or more than one life. The conventional form is a single-life annuity. If the contract covers two or more lives, it may be a joint annuity or a joint-and-survivor annuity. A **joint annuity** provides that the income will cease upon the first death among the lives involved; it is seldom issued. A **joint-and-survivor annuity**, on the other hand, provides that the income will cease only upon the last death among the lives covered. In other words, payments under a joint-and-survivor annuity continue for as long as either of two or more specified persons lives. This is a very useful contract, and it enjoys a wide market. Annuity contracts involving more than two lives are rarely sold.

Time When Payments Commence

immediate annuity

Annuities may also be classified as immediate or deferred. An **immediate annuity** is one in which the first payment is due one payment interval after the date of purchase. If the contract provides for monthly payments, the first payment is due one month after the date of purchase; if annual payments are called for, the first payment is due one year after the date of purchase. However, in all these cases the annuity is "entered on" immediately. The first payment begins to accrue immediately after purchase. An immediate annuity is always purchased with a single premium; the annuitant exchanges a principal sum for the promise of an income for life or for a term of years, as the case might be.

The immediate annuity has been supplanted in importance by the deferred annuity, under which a period longer than one payment interval must elapse after purchase before the first benefit payment is due. As a matter of fact, there is normally a spread of several years between the date of purchase and the time when payments commence. This contract is usually, but not always, purchased with periodic premiums payable over a number of years, up to the date income benefits commence. It is suitable for many people, including a person of ordinary means who wants to accumulate a sum for his or her old age.

Method of Premium Payment

deferred annuity

Deferred annuities may be purchased with either single premiums or periodic premiums. Originally an annuity was envisioned as a type of contract one would buy with a lump sum, accumulated perhaps from a successful business venture or possibly inherited, in exchange for an immediate income of a stipulated amount. Immediate annuities are still purchased with a lump sum, but most annuities today are purchased on an installment basis. High income taxes and estate taxes as well as inflation have made it difficult for most people to accumulate the purchase price (consideration) for a single-premium annuity. The **deferred annuity** provides an attractive and convenient method of accumulating the necessary funds for an adequate old-age income.

Nature of the Insurer's Obligation

pure annuity

straight life annuity

The dichotomy here is pure versus refund annuities. A **pure annuity**, frequently referred to as a **straight life annuity**, provides periodic—usually monthly—income payments that continue as long as the annuitant lives but terminate at that person's death. The annuity is considered fully liquidated upon the death of the annuitant, no matter how soon that may occur after purchase, and no refund is payable to the deceased annuitant's estate. Moreover, no guarantee is given that any particular number of monthly payments will be paid. This nonrefund feature may be applied to either an immediate or a deferred annuity. In other words, it is possible to obtain a contract under which no part of the purchase price will be refunded even if the annuitant dies before the income commences. On the other hand, the contract could call for a refund of all premiums paid, with or without interest, in the event of the insured's death before commencement of the annuity income, with no refund feature after the annuitant enters on the annuity. In the description of a deferred annuity, therefore, it is necessary to distinguish between the accumulation and liquidation periods in labeling the contract as pure or refund.

refund annuity

A **refund annuity** is any type that promises to return (in one manner or another) a portion or all of the purchase price of the annuity. These contracts take several forms, the most important of which are discussed in the next section.

SINGLE-LIFE ANNUITIES

Immediate Annuities

The discussion in this section is not limited to immediate annuities in the technical sense but also includes the liquidation phase of deferred annuities. In other words, it is a description of the various arrangements under which a principal sum can be liquidated on the basis of life contingencies. The principles involved are equally applicable to the life-income options of life insurance contracts where the death benefit funds the lifelong payments.

Pure Annuities

As stated above, a pure annuity is one that provides periodic benefit payments of a stipulated amount as long as the annuitant lives, with the payments ceasing upon the death of the annuitant. The consideration paid for the annuity is regarded as fully earned by the insurance company by the time the benefit payments begin. The payments may be made monthly, quarterly, semiannually, or annually. The more frequent the periodic payments, the more costly the annuity is in terms of annual income. That is, 12 monthly payments of $100 each, the first due one month hence, are more costly than one annual payment of $1,200 due one year hence. This is due to the greater expense of drawing 12 checks, loss of interest by the insurance company, and the greater probability that the annuitant will live to receive the payments. If the annuitant should die 6 months and one day after purchasing the annuity, he or she would receive six monthly payments of $100 each in one case and nothing in the other. The principle would hold true regardless of the year in which the annuitant dies. Occasionally, annuities are made apportionable—that is, they provide for a pro rata fractional payment covering the period from the date of the last regular payment to the date of death. This feature necessitates an increase in the purchase price since premiums for the usual type of annuity are calculated on the assumption that there will be no such pro rata payment.

Pure Annuities

- Lifetime benefits only

- No refunds

- No benefits after annuitant dies

The pure annuity provides the maximum income per dollar of outlay and for that reason is perhaps most suitable for people with only a limited amount of capital. According to

typical actuarial assumptions, $1,000 of capital will provide monthly income between $7 and $10 for males and between $6 and $9 for females under a straight life annuity to those aged 65. If payments are guaranteed for 10 years, whether the annuitant lives or dies, the monthly income will be reduced approximately $.50 for each $1,000 increment.[1] On an investment of $100,000, the difference in monthly income will be $50, which might be the difference between dependency and self-sufficiency for an elderly person. For a person aged 70 the difference in monthly income from $100,000 will be $100, and at 75 the difference will be $175—too large to ignore.

At younger ages, however, because of the high probability of survival, the difference in income between an annuity without a refund feature and one with a refund feature is extremely small. A person aged 35 can obtain an annuity with a 5-year guarantee for the same cost as a pure annuity and an annuity with a 10-year guarantee at the sacrifice of only a few cents of monthly income per $1,000 of outlay. Even someone aged 55 can obtain a 10-year guarantee at a reduction in monthly income of less than 50 cents. In general, therefore, males under 60 and females under 65 should not purchase a pure annuity unless a limited amount of capital makes it imperative. Below those ages, annuitants' chances of surviving the typical periods of guaranteed payments are so good that they gain little in monthly income by giving up the refund feature.

Refund Annuities

Most people have strong objections to placing a substantial sum of money into a contract that promises little or no return if they should die at an early age. Therefore, to make annuities salable insurance companies have found it necessary to add a refund feature. The refund feature may take two general forms: a promise to provide a certain number of annuity payments whether the annuitant lives or dies, or a promise to refund all or a portion of the purchase price in the event of the annuitant's early death.

life annuity certain

Life Annuity Certain. This type of contract goes under various names, including **life annuity certain**, life annuity certain and continuous, life annuity with installments certain, life annuity with a period certain guarantee, and life annuity with minimum guaranteed return. The essence of the agreement is that a stipulated number of monthly payments will be made whether the annuitant lives or dies, and payments will continue for the whole

---

1.   The income figures in this chapter reflect the amounts of monthly life income payable per $1,000 of capital accumulated with an insurance company through periodic premiums. Because of expense allowances, the same income cannot be obtained from a lump-sum payment of $1,000 to an insurance company at the ages mentioned.

of the annuitant's life if he or she lives beyond the guaranteed period. Contracts may be written with payments guaranteed for 5, 10, 15, or 20 years, although not all insurers offer such a wide range of choices. A few companies will even guarantee payments for 25 years.

This type of refund annuity is composed of two elements: an annuity certain and a pure deferred life annuity. The annuity certain covers the period of guaranteed payments and, true to its characteristics, provides the payments whether the annuitant is alive or not. The deferred life annuity becomes effective at the end of the period of guaranteed payments and provides benefits only if the annuitant survives the term of the annuity certain. The benefits are deferred and are contingent upon the annuitant's being alive to receive them. Therefore, the second portion of the company's promise can properly be described as a pure deferred life annuity. If the annuitant does not survive the period of guaranteed payments, no payments are made under the deferred life annuity, and no refund is forthcoming. If the annuitant does survive the term of the annuity certain, the deferred life annuity provides benefits for the remainder of the annuitant's life.

Example

Jack purchased a life annuity with a 10-year-certain guarantee. At his death, he had collected monthly benefits for 8 years. An additional 2 years of monthly benefits continued to the contingent beneficiary.

An annuity with a period certain is always more expensive per dollar of income than a straight life annuity since it is not based solely on life contingencies. Some of the payments are a certainty; the only cost-reducing factor is the compound interest earned on the unliquidated portion of the purchase price. Therefore, the longer the term of the period certain—or to put it more specifically, the longer the period of guaranteed payments—the more costly this type of refund annuity will be, or the lower the yield on the purchase price. Since it is not based solely on life contingencies, the cost of an annuity certain does not depend on the age of the annuitant; it varies directly with the length of the term. At any particular age, however, the longer the period of guaranteed payments, the less expensive the deferred life annuity will be since the higher the age at which the deferred life annuity commences, the smaller the probability that the annuitant will survive to that age. This means that the larger the number of guaranteed payments, the smaller the portion of the purchase price going into the deferred life annuity.

installment refund annuity

Installment Refund Annuity. There are two important types of contracts that promise to return all or a portion of the purchase price. The first is called the **installment refund**

annuity. This contract promises that if the annuitant dies before receiving monthly payments equal to the purchase price of the annuity, the payments will be continued to a contingent beneficiary or beneficiaries until the full cost has been recovered. According to the rates of a sample of insurers, $100,000 will provide a monthly life income between $650 and $950 on the installment refund basis to a male annuitant aged 65 at the time of purchase. If the annuitant dies after receiving 100 payments ($65,000 to $95,000), the payments will be continued to a contingent beneficiary until an additional $35,000 to $5,000 is paid out, making an aggregate of $100,000. If he dies after 13 years, there will be no further payments since the entire purchase price will already have been recovered. It is understood, of course, that payments to the annuitant continue as long as he lives even though the purchase price may long since have been recovered in full.

cash refund annuity

Cash Refund Annuity. The contract may promise, upon the death of the annuitant, to pay to the annuitant's estate or a contingent beneficiary a lump sum that is the difference, if any, between the purchase price of the annuity and the sum of the monthly payments, in which case the contract is called a **cash refund annuity**. The only difference between the cash refund and installment refund annuities is that in the former, the unrecovered portion of the purchase price is refunded in a lump sum at the time of the annuitant's death; in the latter, the monthly installments are continued until the purchase price has been completely recovered. The cash refund annuity is naturally somewhat more expensive because the insurance company loses the interest it would have earned while liquidating the remaining portion of the purchase price on an installment basis.

A frequently asked question is how a life insurance company can afford to promise to return the annuitant's investment in full whether he or she lives or dies and yet continue monthly payments to annuitants who have already recovered their investment. It would seem that every dollar paid to an annuitant in excess of his or her investment would have to be offset by the forfeiture of a dollar by an annuitant who died before recovering the purchase price. The answer lies in compound interest. Note that the insurance company does not promise to pay out benefits equal to the purchase price plus interest. Under this type of refund annuity the interest earnings on the unliquidated portion of the premiums of all annuitants receiving benefits provide the funds for payments in excess of any particular annuitant's purchase price (investment).

50 percent refund annuity

Fifty Percent Refund Annuity. Used in limited scope, an annuity contract that guarantees a minimum return of one-half of the purchase price is a compromise between the straight life

annuity and the 100 percent refund annuity. Logically enough, such a contract is called a **50 percent refund annuity**. Under its terms, if the annuitant dies before receiving benefits equal to half of the cost of the annuity, monthly installments are continued until the combined payments to both the annuitant and a contingent beneficiary equal half of the cost of the annuity. If the beneficiary so elects, it is customary to provide that he or she can receive the present value of the remaining payments in a lump sum. Since the guarantee under this contract is smaller than that under the 100 percent refund annuity, the cost is lower. Conversely, the income per dollar of purchase price is larger.

Example

Larry paid $200,000 for a 50 percent refund annuity. He had received an aggregate of $80,000 in benefit payments at the time of his death. The remaining $20,000 of the refund guarantee will be paid to the contingent beneficiary.

A form of annuity sometimes written provides that, regardless of the number of payments received prior to the annuitant's death, 50 percent of the cost of the contract will be returned in the form of a death benefit. This contract is not a refund annuity in the strict sense. Instead, one-half of the premium is used by the company to provide a straight life annuity, and the other half is held on deposit. Earnings from the half held on deposit are used to supplement the annuity benefits provided by the other half of the premium. At the annuitant's death the premium deposit is returned to the annuitant's estate or to a designated beneficiary in the form of a death benefit.

modified cash refund annuity

Modified Cash Refund Annuity. Finally, another variation of the refund annuity is found among contributory pension plans. Called a **modified cash refund annuity**, it promises that if the employee dies before receiving retirement benefits equal to the accumulated value of his or her contributions with or without interest, the difference between the employee's benefits and contributions will be refunded in a lump sum to the employee's estate or a designated beneficiary. In other words, the refund feature is based on the employee's contributions and not on the portion of the total cost of the annuity paid by the employer.

Comparisons of Annuity Types. The range of monthly income amounts provided under various forms of annuities per $1,000 of premium accumulations are shown in the following table. The principal sum of $1,000 does not refer to a single premium of that amount paid at the various ages but to a sum accumulated through periodic premiums that contain an allowance for expenses or through the maturity by death of an insurance

contract purchased with gross premiums. In other words, these benefits, which may be augmented by dividends, are based on premiums without policy fees and could not be purchased with a lump-sum payment on quite so favorable a cost basis, but they do illustrate the variations in yield among the various annuity forms.

The following table illustrates the inconsequential cost of a refund feature at younger ages and its high cost at advanced ages. It is interesting to note that at the higher ages, both the installment refund and the cash refund forms are less expensive—or, conversely, yield more—than a life annuity with a 10-year guarantee. At the advanced ages they cost less than even a 15-year guarantee. Remember, however, that the benefits under each of the forms are the actuarial equivalent of those under all the other forms, and the annuitant must choose the form that is most appropriate to his or her financial and family circumstances.

Table 24-1
Range of Monthly Annuity Benefits Available per $1,000 of Purchase Price (Immediate Annuities)

		Male Age				
Type	**Range**	**60**	**65**	**70**	**75**	**80**
Life	Low	$6.42	$7.00	$8.33	$9.60	$12.18
Life	High	9.32	10.00	11.26	12.82	15.12
10-Year Certain + Life	Low	5.60	6.50	7.32	8.26	9.00
10-Year Certain + Life	High	9.03	9.50	10.26	10.94	11.60
Refund	Low	5.89	6.50	7.46	8.27	9.61
Refund	High	9.06	9.50	10.50	11.55	12.87
		Female Age				
Type	**Range**	**60**	**65**	**70**	**75**	**80**
Life	Low	$5.20	$5.20	$7.12	$8.38	$9.90
Life	High	8.66	8.66	10.11	12.60	10.00
10-Year Certain + Life	Low	5.07	5.07	6.52	7.51	8.37
10-Year Certain + Life	High	8.52	8.52	9.67	10.46	11.08
Refund	Low	5.44	5.44	6.18	7.58	8.27
Refund	High	8.52	8.52	9.85	11.00	11.74
Source: Best's Flitcraft Compend 1993 (Note: No current updates available)						

With the computing power available today it is possible for insurance companies to design annuity contracts with any length of period certain or with a refund guarantee for any

specified portion from none to all of the purchase price. In practice, however, each insurer is likely to offer only a few options regarding period certain choices and refund portions. The costs of getting regulatory approval are probably the single most important impediment to offering a full spectrum of choices.

Deferred Annuities

It is helpful in considering deferred annuities to distinguish between the accumulation period and the liquidation period. The preceding discussion of immediate annuities related entirely to the liquidation phase of annuities. It was assumed that the funds needed to provide the various income payments were on hand, and no consideration was given to the manner in which the funds had been accumulated.

Accumulation Period

accumulation period

With deferred annuities, however, there is always an **accumulation period** during which funds are accumulated with the insurance company to reach the amount necessary to provide the benefits promised at a specified future date. The sum may be accumulated through a lump-sum premium to which compound interest is added during the intervening years, or it may be accumulated through a series of periodic premiums. If the premiums are made periodically, they can range almost anywhere between a rigid schedule of level payments and (at the other extreme) flexible payments where the timing and amount of each payment is at the discretion of the purchaser.

Figure 24-1
Deferred Annuity

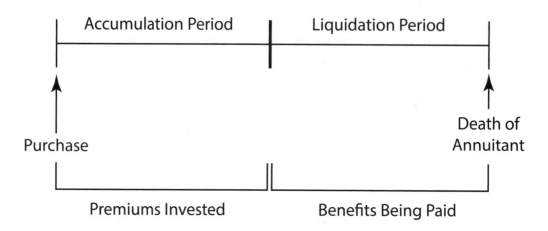

Because it is impossible to predict the amount available to fund benefits, annuity contracts that allow flexibility in premium payments during the accumulation phase cannot specify in advance the level of benefit payments that will be paid during the liquidation phase. Instead, they specify the amount of benefit per each $1,000 of fund balance when the annuity switches over to the liquidation phase. The fund itself is merely an accumulation device similar to a defined-contribution pension plan prior to retirement.

Almost without exception deferred annuities sold to individuals promise to return all premiums with or without interest in the event of the annuitant's death before "entering on" the annuity. The usual contract provides for a return of either gross premiums without interest or the cash value (whichever is larger). Such a contract, therefore, is a type of refund annuity with respect to the period of accumulation.

Liquidation Period

liquidation period

Everything about immediate annuities discussed earlier applies with equal force to the **liquidation period** of deferred annuities. Once the necessary funds have been accumulated and the annuitant is ready to enter on the annuity, he or she usually has the option of taking the income under any of the benefit plans described. Thus, annuitants might

choose a straight life annuity, a life annuity with guaranteed installments, an installment refund annuity, or a cash refund annuity. As a matter of fact, they may be given the choice of taking cash in lieu of a life income. It is not inconsistent for annuitants to choose a pure or straight life annuity for the liquidation phase of an annuity that was a refund type of annuity during the accumulation phase. Conceivably, some individuals might purchase an annuity that provides for no refund during the period of accumulation and elect to liquidate it on a refund basis. Most annuitants, however, prefer the refund basis during both the accumulation and the liquidation phases.

A deferred annuity that had fixed level premiums, known as a retirement annuity, was an annuity form that was widely available in the past. It was popular back when nearly all annuity contracts had heavy front-end expense loadings. A wide range of options permitted the annuitant to adjust the contract during the deferral period to changes of circumstances not anticipated when the contract was purchased. The retirement annuity was an early step in the development of increased annuity contract flexibility. The more flexible and lower-cost annuities available today have nearly eliminated the fixed-premium retirement annuity from the market.

Structuring the Contract

The premiums for an annuity contract may be quoted in units of $100 annual premium or in terms of the annual premium needed to provide a monthly life income of $10 at a designated age. In the first case, the premium will be an even amount, and the income will vary with the age of issue and the age at which the income will commence. In the second case, the income will be a fixed even amount, and the premium will vary.

The structure of the deferred-annuity contract can best be understood by the following example. In accordance with the rate basis of several leading companies, for each $10 unit of monthly life income to be paid to a male annuitant at age 65 with payments guaranteed for 10 years, between $1,052 and $1,538 must be accumulated by age 65, regardless of the age at which the annuitant purchases the annuity.[2] Obviously, the younger the age at which the annuitant begins to contribute toward the accumulation objective, the smaller each annual contribution or deposit can be. To accumulate $15,380—the amount needed to provide $100 per month at age 65 with payments guaranteed for 120 months—a man aged 25 will have to contribute only $112 per year to age 65, while a man aged 45 will have to deposit $441 per year.[3] A man aged 55 will have to deposit $1,195 per year for 10 years.

---

2. Rate basis: 1983 Individual Annuity Mortality Table.
3. These deposits, or level premiums, include a charge for insurance company expenses and vary among companies

The level premiums or deposits, as they are usually called, are accumulated at a rate of compound interest equal to or greater than the specified long-term rate guaranteed in the contract—usually between 3 percent and 5 percent. Some deferred-annuity contracts also include a short-term (such as one, 2, 3, or 5 years) interest rate guarantee that is competitive with current investment yields and higher than the guaranteed long-term rate. These short-term interest rate guarantees are often combined with a bail-out provision allowing the contract to be terminated without a surrender charge if the interest rate actually being credited falls below a stipulated rate (often 2 percentage points [200 basis points] below the short-term guaranteed rate). The bail-out provision may seem much more attractive than it really is for two reasons: (1) It is highly unlikely that competitors will be able to pay higher rates if and when the release is triggered, and (2) a cash-out will be subject to income taxes and possibly a 10 percent penalty tax.

In the event of the annuitant's death before age 65 (or whatever the maturity date) the company will return either the accumulated gross premiums without interest or the cash value, whichever is larger. The cash value is equal to the gross premiums improved at a guaranteed rate of interest after deducting a charge for expenses. After about 10 years, the cash value exceeds the accumulated value of premiums paid (without interest) and thus becomes the effective death benefit. (It is of interest to note that, while this is an annuity contract, there is an insurance element during the accumulation period in that the death benefit exceeds the cash value.)

The annuitant may withdraw the full cash value at any time during the deferral period, whereupon the contract terminates and the company has no further obligation. Under some contracts the annuitant may borrow against the cash value, which would not bring about a termination of the contract.

Liquidation Option

liquidation options

Liquidation Options. At the maturity date the annuitant may elect to have the accumulated sum—$15,380 in the example—applied under any of the annuity forms offered by the company, even though the premium deposits were predicated on the assumption that the income would be provided under a life annuity with 120 guaranteed installments. Depending on the option elected, the actual monthly income might be more or less than the amount originally anticipated. Moreover, the annuitant is usually given the privilege

whose policies have the same maturity value. The deposits illustrated are for a contract on which dividends are paid prior to maturity.

of taking cash in lieu of an annuity. This is known as the cash option, and it exposes the company to serious adverse selection. Persons in poor health tend to withdraw their accumulations in cash, while those in excellent health usually choose an annuity. To offset this selection if the annuitant selects the cash option, some companies provide a retroactive reduction in the investment earnings rate applied to accumulations under a deferred annuity. The resultant penalty can be a substantial dollar amount, and it usually also applies to exchanges of annuity contracts.

Under most contracts the annuitant may choose to have the benefit payments commence at an earlier or a later date than the one originally specified in the contract with a subsequent adjustment in the amount of monthly benefits. It should be recognized that the privilege of having the income begin at an earlier age than the age specified in the contract is an option to convert the cash value to an immediate annuity. There is usually no age limit below which the benefit payments cannot begin, although the option is subject to the general requirement that the periodic income payments equal or exceed a stipulated minimum amount.

On the other hand, there is usually an upper age limit, sometimes as high as age 80 or as low as age 70, beyond which commencement of the income benefits cannot be postponed. The option to postpone the commencement of benefit payments may be particularly attractive if the annuitant is still in good health at the original maturity date and plans to work for a few more years. The life income payable at any particular age, whether the maturity date is moved ahead or set back, is the same amount that would have been provided had the substituted maturity date been the one originally selected and funded with the actual amount accumulated.

JOINT ANNUITIES

There are basically two types of joint annuities. One provides income benefits only until the death of the first of two or more annuitants. The other continues benefit payments until the last of the named annuitant dies.

Joint Life Annuity

A joint life annuity is a contract that provides an income of a specified amount as long as the two or more persons named in the contract live. In other words, the income ceases at the first death among the covered lives. As a result, the coverage is relatively inexpensive.

This contract has a very limited market. It might be appropriate for two persons, elderly sisters, for example, who have an income from a stable source large enough to support one but not both of the sisters. If they can purchase a joint life annuity in an amount adequate to support one sister without disturbing the other income, the combined income will be adequate for their needs while both sisters are alive. Upon the death of one of the sisters, the income from the original source will meet the survivor's needs. Such a contract is always sold as a single-premium immediate annuity.

Another use of joint life annuities is to provide income while a spouse or other caregiver must give custodial care to one of the annuitants. In a few cases parents may dislike their children's spouses so strongly that they establish a trust payable to the natural child only if he or she survives the resented in-law. A joint life annuity could provide support until the trust funds become available to the beneficiary.

Joint-and-Last-Survivor Annuity

A joint-and-last-survivor annuity is a far more appealing contract than the joint life annuity because the income under this form of annuity continues as long as any of the two or more persons named live. It is ideal for a husband and wife.

For most combinations of ages, the joint-and-last-survivor annuity is the most expensive of all annuity forms. To provide an income of $100 per month on the joint-and-survivor basis to a man and woman both aged 65, for example, requires an accumulation of $18,350. If the man is 65 and the woman 60, a sum of $19,827 is needed to provide $100 per month on the joint-and-survivor basis. Compare those figures to the $14,285 required to provide a life income of $100 per month with no refund feature to only a man aged 65.

The joint-and-survivor annuity can be purchased as a single-premium immediate annuity, in which event the cost will be somewhat higher than the accumulation figures quoted above, or it may be one of the optional forms made available under an annual-premium deferred annuity. A joint-and-survivor annuity may also be made available for the settlement of life insurance and endowment proceeds.

Although a typical contract does not contain a refund feature, most insurance companies offer a contract under which 120 monthly installments are guaranteed, and a few offer 240 guaranteed installments. When so written, if the last survivor dies before the minimum number of payments has been made, the remaining installments will be continued to a contingent beneficiary. As under single-life annuities, the contingent beneficiary may be permitted to take the present value of the remaining installments. When both husband and wife are 65, a life income of $100 per month with 120 guaranteed installments requires

an accumulation of $18,560—only $210 more than such an annuity without a refund feature.

In its conventional form the joint-and-survivor annuity continues the same income to the survivor as is payable while both annuitants are alive. A common modification, which reduces the cost, provides that the income to the survivor will be decreased to two-thirds of the original amount on the theory that the survivor does not require as much income as the two annuitants. This contract or option, as the case may be, is called a joint-and-two-thirds annuity. Such a contract written in an original amount of $100 on the lives of a husband and wife, both aged 65, requires an accumulation of slightly more than $15,960. The benefits can be duplicated by placing a single-life immediate annuity in the appropriate amount on each annuitant and a conventional joint-and-survivor annuity on both lives. Thus an immediate annuity on each life for $100 per month and a joint-and-survivor annuity in the amount of $100 per month will provide $300 per month as long as both annuitants live and $200 per month to the survivor.

Example

Harry and Jenny have just purchased a joint-and-two-thirds annuity. The benefit currently being paid while they both live is $6,000 monthly. After either of them dies, the survivor will receive $4,000 monthly until he or she dies.

In a joint-and-one-half annuity the income to the survivor is reduced to one-half the original amount. This form has not had the popular appeal of the joint-and-two-thirds annuity. The computing capacity at insurance companies makes it possible to design the survivor benefit to be any specified proportion of the predeath benefit. Consequently many insurers have introduced more than the one-half and two-thirds options.

The joint-and-last-survivor form is widely used by private pension plans to pay the retirement benefits to married plan participants. It is common to provide that where the joint-and-two-thirds annuity has been elected by the employee, the income is to be reduced only if the employee dies first. If the wife or other dependent dies first, the employee continues to receive the full income. Federal law now requires written consent of the non-employee spouse in order to drop the survivorship benefit.

VARIABLE ANNUITIES

variable annuity

The conventional concept is that an annuity provides payments of a fixed amount over a specified period or throughout the lifetime of one or more persons. The persistent inflation over recent decades, however, has focused attention on the need for protecting the purchasing power of annuity benefits. This has given rise to a type of contract that attempts to achieve that objective by providing benefits that vary with changes in the insurer's investment performance, which in turn often coincide approximately to changes in the purchasing power of the dollar. Such a contract has appropriately been named a **variable annuity.**

If a contract is to provide benefits with stable purchasing power, it must provide more dollars when prices rise and fewer dollars when prices decline. Theoretically this could be achieved by adjusting the benefits to changes in an appropriate price index, such as the Consumer Price Index published by the Bureau of Labor Statistics. This is not practical from the standpoint of the insurance companies, however, since there is no mechanism by which the value of the assets backing the annuity can be adjusted automatically, or otherwise, to changes in the dollar value of the annuity promises. As a practical solution, contracts have been developed that provide benefits adjusted to changes in the market value of the assets—typically, common stocks—in which the annuity reserves are invested. The theory is that over a long period of time, the market value of a representative group of common stocks tends to conform rather faithfully to changes in the consumer price level. Moreover, inasmuch as the insurance company's liabilities to its annuitants are expressed in terms of the market value of the assets offsetting the liabilities, funds for the payment of annuity benefits will be available in the proper proportions at all times.

Supporters of the variable annuity feel that annuitants need some kind of protection against inflation, and they believe that a common stock investment program administered by a life insurance company is the best approach yet developed. Critics of the variable annuity approach question whether continuing inflation is inevitable, and even if it is, whether common stock investments provide an effective hedge against rising prices.

Guarantees

Some insurance companies have introduced minimum income guarantees and minimum withdrawal guarantees for their variable annuity contracts. However, this has driven up the price and such guarantees often make it difficult or impossible for the insurance company to obtain reinsurance for these contracts. Consequently, since 2008 with the downturn in

investment returns, most insurers that have previously provided minimum guarantees for income and withdrawal amounts on variable annuity contracts are now eliminating such provisions in their new contracts or significantly increasing the charge for the guarantee. Another response has been to drastically reduce the level of these minimum guarantees in the new contracts. Existing variable annuities that contain such guarantees cannot be unilaterally altered by the insurance company. However, some companies have refused to accept any additional contributions to the existing contracts. There have been some companies offering to purchase back deferred annuity contracts with income or withdrawal guarantees that are too expensive to maintain with the current market returns on investments under the Federal Reserve restrictions since 2008.

Accumulation Units

accumulation unit

At present, variable annuities are most often issued on a deferred basis. During the accumulation period, premium payments—or deposits, as they are frequently called—are applied to the purchase of accumulation units. The **accumulation unit** is assigned an arbitrary value, such as $10, at the inception of the plan, and the initial premiums purchase accumulation units at that price. Thereafter, the units are revalued each month to reflect changes in the market value of the common stock that makes up the company's variable annuity portfolio. On any valuation date, the value of each accumulation unit is determined by dividing the market value of the common stock underlying the accumulation units by the aggregate number of units. Dividends are usually allocated periodically to the participants and applied to the purchase of additional accumulation units, although they may simply be reinvested without allocation and permitted to increase the value of each existing accumulation unit. Capital appreciation or depreciation is always reflected in the value of the accumulation units, rather than in the number of units. (In other words, both realized and unrealized gains and losses are reflected for individual participants through an increase or decrease in the value of their accumulation units.) A portion of each premium payment is deducted for expenses, and the remainder is invested in accumulation units at their current market value.

Table 24-2
Variable Annuity Accumulation Units Deferred Annuity Purchased at Age 35 at $200 per Month (Rounded to two decimal places)

Year	Age	Unit Value	New Units	Total Units	Total Value
1	35	$1.00	2,400.00	2,400.00	$2,400.00
2	36	1.08	2,232.56	4,632.56	4,980.00
3	37	1.16	2,076.80	6,709.36	7,753.50
4	38	1.24	1,931.91	8,641.26	10,735.01
5	39	1.34	1,797.12	10,438.38	13,940.14
6	40	1.07	2,242.99	12,681.37	13,569.07
7	41	1.15	2,086.50	14,767.88	16,986.75
8	42	1.24	1,940.93	16,708.81	20,660.76
9	43	1.88	1,276.60	17,985.41	33,812.56
10	44	2.12	1,132.08	19,117.48	40,529.06
11	45	2.28	1,053.09	20,170.57	45,968.74
12	46	2.45	979.62	21,150.20	51,816.39
13	47	2.63	911.28	22,061.47	58,102.62
14	48	2.83	847.70	22,909.17	64,860.32
15	49	3.04	788.56	23,697.73	72,124.84
16	50	3.27	733.54	24,431.27	79,934.21
17	51	3.52	682.36	25,113.63	88,329.27
18	52	3.78	634.76	25,748.39	97,353.97
19	53	3.50	685.71	26,434.10	92,519.37
20	54	3.25	738.46	27,172.57	88,310.84
21	55	3.00	800.00	27,972.57	83,917.70
22	56	3.60	666.67	28,639.23	103,101.24
23	57	4.01	598.50	29,237.74	117,243.32
24	58	4.97	482.90	29,720.63	147,711.55
25	59	5.76	416.67	30,137.30	173,590.85
26	60	6.25	384.00	30,521.30	190,758.13
27	61	7.16	335.20	30,856.50	220,932.51
28	62	7.90	303.80	31,160.29	246,166.32
29	63	8.09	296.66	31,456.96	254,486.78
30	64	8.14	294.84	31,751.80	258,459.62

A hypothetical accumulation is shown in Table 24-2. In this example the initial purchase is made at age 35 with a gross consideration (premium) high enough to cover a $200

acquisition each month after paying insurer expenses. The assumptions behind the Table 24-2 numbers are that the accumulation units change value once each year and that a full $200 is available each month to acquire more units. The units in this example grow at approximately 7.5 percent most years but fluctuate more or less than that in some years, as stock prices are prone to do over short intervals. In this case, there is an accumulation of $258,459.62 at the end of the 30th year (end of age 64 or beginning of age 65) consisting of 31,751.8 accumulation units.

Annuity Units

annuity units

At the beginning of the liquidation period, the accumulation units are exchanged for **annuity units**. The number of annuity units that will be acquired by the annuitant depends on the company's assumptions as to mortality, dividend rates, and expenses, and upon the market value of the assets underlying the annuity units. In essence, the number of annuity units is determined by dividing the dollar value of the accumulation units ($258,459.62 in our example) by the present value of a life annuity at the participant's attained age in an amount equal to the current value of one annuity unit (assumed to be $35 in this case). Although the number of accumulation units of a particular person increases with each premium payment and each allocation of dividends, the number of annuity units (7,384.6 in this case) decreases; however, the number of units drawn down each period remains constant throughout the liquidation period. The units are revalued each year, however, reflecting the current market price of the common stock, and the mortality, investment, and expense experience for the preceding year.[4] The dollar income payable to the annuitant each month is determined by multiplying the number of annuity units by the current value of each unit. During the annuity—or liquidation—period, the higher the market price of the stock and the greater the dividends, the greater the dollar income of the annuitant will be. During the accumulation stage, however, it is to the annuitant's advantage for stock prices to be relatively low since he or she will thus be able to acquire a larger number of accumulation units for each premium payment.

Some of the more recent variable annuity contracts differ from the above by using only one unit rather than two, by discounting for mortality before as well as after retirement, and by limiting variations in the unit value to investment experience only.

---

4.   More precisely, the value of an annuity unit at the end of each fiscal year is obtained by dividing the current market value of the funds supporting the annuity units by the present value of the total number of annuity units expected to be paid over the future lifetimes of all participants then receiving annuity payments, in accordance with the assumptions as to mortality, investment earnings, and expense rates for the future.

Surrender Provisions

A participant in a variable annuity plan should not normally be permitted to surrender his or her accumulation units for cash or to take other action that might involve temptations to play the stock market. When the variable annuity is used as part of a pension plan, surrender values are not generally made available. When the variable annuity is sold as an individual contract, surrender privileges are made available but on a much more restricted basis than in connection with ordinary annuities. Under all plans the current value of the accumulation units is payable to a designated beneficiary (if any) or the estate, usually as a continuing income, but a lump-sum settlement is possible upon the death of the participant during the accumulation period.

In a landmark decision,[5] the United States Supreme Court held that an individual variable-annuity contract is a security within the meaning of the Securities Act of 1933 and that any organization that offers such a contract is an investment company and subject to the Investment Company Act of 1940. Hence, any company that offers individual variable-annuity contracts is subject to dual supervision by the Securities and Exchange Commission and the various state insurance departments. Persons selling variable annuities must pass the series 6 licensing exam of the Financial Industry Regulatory Authority (FINRA).

INDEXED ANNUITIES (EQUITY & FIXED)

equity-indexed annuities

> **Equity-indexed annuities** are fixed, deferred-annuity products introduced in the mid-1990s to enhance the appeal of fixed annuities. Fixed annuities were very attractive during the high interest rate era of the 1980s and early 1990s. However, their appeal waned as interest rates dropped and stock market yields significantly surpassed the yields in traditional fixed annuities.

Product Evolution

Some insurance companies have introduced fixed-indexed annuities as a product that still offers guaranteed minimum interest rates and equity-indexed annuities that will pay a higher return if the specified stock index increases enough to provide a higher yield.

---

5. Securities and Exchange Commission v. Valic, 359 U.S. 65 (1959).

These products are promoted as the best of both worlds—fixed-interest debt investments (bonds) and equities (stocks). They are designed to appeal to persons who want to participate in higher investment yields without bearing the full investment risk that must be assumed in the purchase of a variable annuity.

Variable annuities are still the only annuity products that provide most of the full yield of the equity investments to the owner/annuitant. The equity-indexed annuity provides only a portion of the capital gain of the stocks making up the applicable index (commonly the Standard & Poor's 500 Index). Since the formulas look at the value of the index only at specified dates (usually anniversary dates), there is no way to capture the dividend income (if any) of those stocks in the formula approach used in the equity-indexed annuities. It is difficult for prospective purchasers of these annuities to find accurate information about past performance of the capital-gain portion of the index because most sources report the combined total return—both capital gain and income from dividends. Over the past 20 years a relevant portion of the total return of the S&P 500 has been from the income portion.

Participation Rate Formula

Prospective purchasers of equity-indexed annuities need to understand that their potential return based on increases in the value of the index is determined by the actual formula approach set forth in the contract. Generally this formula includes participation rate as well as an increase in the index from the beginning of the term to the acceptable anniversary-date value of the index. Some contracts use the increase in the index to the anniversary date during the specified term period (ranging from one year to 8 years, depending on the specific contract) when the index reached its highest value. The participation rate is a percentage (usually less than 100 percent) of the defined increase that will be used to calculate the crediting amount. This participation rate is set by the insurer and is subject to change. Some companies do not even specify the current participation rate in their promotional materials. Often the participation rate is guaranteed for a specified first term, such as 5 or 7 years. The insurance company reserves the right to change the participation rate at the expiration of each term but usually guarantees the then-current rate for the subsequent term.

Most contracts anticipate a series of terms of uniform length, much like renewals of 5-year term life insurance. However, some contracts reserve the insurer's right to modify the term period available for continuation at the expiration of any existing term. In most designs, the higher increase from the index calculation is available only at the end of the applicable term unless the owner dies or the contract is converted to benefit-payout status

(annuitized) before the end of the term. The higher value based on the index will not apply if the contract is terminated before the end of the term.

The participation rate is very important in that it restricts the amount of the index gain that can be applied (if any) to get more than the guaranteed yield. There is also a link between the participation rate and the guaranteed interest rate. Higher participation rates may be available from some insurers if the purchaser will accept a lower guaranteed interest rate. One company guarantees that the participation rate will never be lower than 25 percent. Example illustrations are often based on 80 percent or 90 percent participation rates. It is reasonable to assume that participation rates range from 25 percent to 90 percent. The participation rate cannot be changed more than once per year under most contracts.

Another aspect of the indexed benefit is that some contracts include a cap on the crediting rate that can be applied to the accumulated value of the contract. This may be a single stated percentage applicable to the whole participation period (contract term). It can be stated as an annual equivalent that in turn determines the aggregate limit for the full participation period. The existence of such a cap prevents even the full formula participation in times of very rapid index increases.

As a protection on the downside, most contracts specify a floor of zero percent as the minimum interest crediting rate applicable to the accumulated value. This prevents the application of a negative percentage in the formula to reflect plunges in the index value.

The intent is that the fixed-interest-rate guarantee is the worst possible outcome and if the equity index does better, the accumulation may be even better than the guaranteed accumulation. The marketing material touts this feature as presenting the best of both worlds. Equity-indexed annuities are clearly designed to appeal to purchasers who want higher yields than bonds have provided.

No Securities and Exchange Commission Regulation

Equity-indexed annuities satisfy another objective of the insurance companies. They are classified as fixed annuities and can be sold by agents who are not licensed to sell variable products. Thus, the agent has a product that is partly influenced by equity performance and that offers a minimum-accumulation guarantee. The agent can sell the product without having to acquire a new license and, thus, avoids the training requirement and commitment necessary to enter the variable-annuity market.

It is worthy of note that the Securities and Exchange Commission (SEC), approved rule 151A on December 17, 2008, which would have subjected indexed annuities to SEC

regulation as securities effective January 12, 2011. This proposed rule was challenged by a suit filed with the D.C. Circuit Court of Appeals on January 16, 2009. The court issued an order to vacate rule 151A on July 21, 2010, as a result of passage of the Dodd-Frank Wall Street Reform and Consumer Protection Act signed by President Obama on that date. The law exempts indexed annuities from treatment as securities by the SEC and they remain under the regulation and control of the respective State Insurance Commissioners. However, there may still be some involvement with securities regulation, because FINRA claims responsibility to enforce the suitability standards applicable to variable annuities to the sale of equity indexed annuities.

The 18 months of dispute over SEC control of indexed annuities created several changes in the market. Some companies dropped the indexed annuity product from their offerings while other companies started preparing their field force for securities licenses. The companies supporting the indexed annuities spent much time and effort to fight the rule 151A in the courts and to lobby for the new law, which exempted the contracts from SEC regulation as securities. It is anticipated that the companies that withdrew this product from the market will now reintroduce it with the kinowledge that it will not be treated as a security by the SEC even though FINRA may impose variable annuity suitability standards to equity indexed annuity sales.

The Guarantees

The minimum guarantees under equity-indexed annuities are lower than those for traditional fixed annuities. In fact, the rates actually guaranteed apply to less than the full amount paid as a premium. It is common to apply the guaranteed rate to 90 percent of the amount paid to purchase the annuity. That percentage (often 10 percent) not included in the guarantees can be used to cover insurer expenses. With this approach it usually takes 3 or 4 years before the guaranteed amount equals or exceeds the initial purchase amount. The guaranteed rate may result in only a 10 percent gain over a 7-year term when calculated on the full original purchase price. The specified interest rate applied each year to the contract value is set forth in the contract and remains fixed unless a negotiated change is later agreed to by both the contract owner and the insurance company.

Value of the Contract at End of Term

At the end of each term, or participation period, the value of the annuity will be the greater of the following three amounts:

- the contract value based on the minimum interest rate guarantees

- the accumulated value derived by applying the participation rate to the increase in the index on the applicable anniversary. This amount will be subject to any cap on maximum crediting rate and to any floor on minimum crediting rate.

- the purchase premiums paid up though the end of the term. (Partial withdrawals will be deducted from the premium amount.)

In many contracts the same procedure will be used to calculate the death benefit payable if the owner dies during the deferral phase of the contract.

Terminating an equity-indexed annuity before the end of a specified term will usually result in loss of the index-crediting option. The termination benefit will usually be the greater of the following two amounts:

- the guaranteed-interest contract value

- the aggregate purchase amount less adjustments for any partial withdrawals previously taken

Annuitization

The equity-indexed annuity can be converted to benefit-paying status at any time prior to the maximum age specified for mandatory benefit payout. For qualified annuity contracts the benefit payout must start after the annuitant reaches age 70 ½. For nonqualified annuities the benefit payout does not have to begin before age 85 with some insurers and may be pushed beyond that by an insurer in the future.

Tax law forces payout of qualified annuity contracts starting at whichever time is later:

- April of the year following the year in which the annuitant reaches age 70 ½

- April of the year following the year the annuitant retires

Many equity-indexed annuities in force were issued before the 1996 tax law change that permits delay of annuitization until retirement if that is later than age 70 ½. Consequently many equity-indexed annuity contracts used for IRA purposes or other qualified plan use will force the start of benefits before retirement for people working beyond that age.

The tax law does not mandate a maximum age for distributions to start for nonqualified annuities (those purchased with after-tax dollars). It is the insurer that imposes the maximum age constraints on nonqualified annuities.

The benefits-payout options are the same as those for any other type of fixed annuity contract.

The taxation of equity-indexed annuities is the same as that for any other type of fixed annuity contract.

Indexes

Although the most commonly used index is The Standard & Poor's 500 Composite Stock Price Index, some insurers use another index specified in the contract. These are generally established indexes that are regularly published in financial publications such as the Wall Street Journal. However, some insurers have chosen to use international indexes or a composite of two or more established indexes. This puts the definition of the index under the insurance company's control, and theoretically the company could change the definition of the index after the contract is created. This leaves open the possibility of intentional manipulation of the index in the future. The contracts often set forth an alternative index to be used in case the primary index ceases to exist in the future.

Asset Match

All financial products involve risks, and the equity-indexed annuity is no exception. The issuer needs to invest in assets that will provide an adequate return to honor the contractual promises.

Since the index participation promises some results that are above those of bond returns when the stock index outperforms the bond market, how will a company invest assets to produce the higher increment? The closest match will come by investing some funds in the same stocks that make up the index. However, some insurers have chosen to invest in derivatives and other financial assets that they feel will track well with the index even though these choices are not a composite of the items that make up the index. Over the long run there could be a significant difference between investment results and contractual obligations. If the investment results exceed the contractual obligations, there will be no problem honoring the annuity contract terms. On the other side, though, underperformance of asset returns relative to obligations could threaten the insurer's financial viability. Purchasers should feel more comfortable with issuing companies whose investments more closely resemble the index the benefits are related to.

The equity-indexed annuity concept is an acceptable composite approach to fixed annuities. It needs much more explanation than the traditional fixed annuity contract. If purchasers do not fully understand the features and the very limited extent to which these annuities participate in the index, they may later be very disappointed and revert to class action suits to seek redress. A small number of insurance companies are taking

a very aggressive stance on both indexes and investments that could potentially tarnish this product. That would be unfortunate because the concept is a sound one, and many insurers seem to be taking a responsible approach to both choice of the index to apply and the offsetting asset portfolio mix.

Equity-indexed annuities became highly visible in the market after 1998. In fact, there are now equity-indexed life insurance policies available in the marketplace. Time will tell how successfully equity-indexed products satisfy the needs and desires of the purchasing public. There have been many instances of litigation against these policies by owners who were not satisfied with the performance during a time of increasing index values or felt that there was inadequate disclosure of participation and crediting by the insurance agent who sold them the policy.

The Securities and Exchange Commission (SEC) held public hearings and open comment sessions during 2008 in an attempt to bring indexed annuities within the realm of SEC oversight and regulation as securities. This issue was no doubt a part of the regulatory backlash coming from the credit crunch and financial fiasco of 2008. The state insurance regulators are opposed to SEC regulation of indexed annuities and contend that the state regulators are doing an adequate job. This kind of dispute over regulatory boundaries is a natural outcome of the 1999 repeal of the Glass-Steagall Act by the Graham-Leach-Bliley Act. As of the writing of this text, states still have oversight of Equity-Indexed Annuities.

LONGEVITY INSURANCE

This is a relatively new product that is really an annuity contract. It is a deferred annuity contract that has no cash value or death benefit during the deferral period. It pays an income benefit for the remainder of the annuitant's lifetime if the annuitant survives the deferral period. If the annuitant dies before the end of the deferral period, there will be a total forfeiture of the purchase price.

The fact that there is no death benefit or cash value in this contract makes it a lower cost annuity than the standard deferred annuity contract. It appeals to individuals who are concerned about exhausting their assets before the end of their lifetime. A person retiring at age 65 who is confident that existing assets will support him or her until age 85 might purchase a longevity policy at age 65 with benefits scheduled to begin at age 85.

The purchase price will accumulate investment earnings over the deferral period and be supplemented by forfeitures of other annuitants that die during the deferral. There will be no income tax applicable during the deferral. Each income payment will be partially

subject to income tax as determined by the exclusion ratio. The non-taxed portion is considered to be a return of the purchase price, while the remainder is considered to be a gain and is subject to federal income tax.

The important factors in setting the price for this product are: the age of the annuitant at the time of the purchase, the length of the deferral period, the gender of the annuitant, and the desired income payment level. The purchase price can be surprisingly low if there is a long deferral period and income payments are scheduled to begin at a relatively high age. The full purchase price of longevity insurance is committed at the time of purchase, and there are no refund benefits for contract cancellation beyond any free look period.

ACTUARIAL CONSIDERATIONS

The insurance company's cost of providing annuity benefits is based on the probability of survival rather than the probability of death. In itself this fact would seem to have no greater significance than that the insurance company actuaries, in computing premiums for annuities, have to refer to the actuarial probabilities of survival rather than probabilities of death. As a matter of fact, however, writing annuities poses a unique set of actuarial problems.

In the first place, insurance companies have found that the mortality among persons who purchase annuities tends to be lower, age for age, than that of people who purchase life insurance. There may be several reasons for this, including the peace of mind that comes with an assured income for life, but certainly one of the most important is the selection practiced against the company. Individuals who know that they have serious health impairments rarely, if ever, purchase annuities. In fact, many persons contemplating purchasing immediate annuities subject themselves to a thorough medical examination to make sure that they have no serious impairments before committing their capital to annuities. On the other hand, people who know or suspect that they have an impairment usually seek life insurance. Whatever its origin, the mortality difference between life insurance insureds and annuitants is so substantial that special annuity mortality tables must be used for the calculation of annuity premiums.

Second, the trend toward lower mortality that has been such a favorable development with respect to life insurance has been very unfavorable with respect to annuities. Many annuity contracts run for 60 to 75 years, counting the accumulation period, and rates that were adequate at the time the contract was issued may, with the continued increase in longevity, prove inadequate over the years. All mortality tables, of course, contain a safety margin—which, for life insurance mortality tables, means higher death rates than those

likely to be experienced, and for annuity mortality tables, lower rates of mortality than anticipated. While a long-run decline in mortality rates increases the safety margin in life insurance mortality tables, it shrinks the margin in annuity mortality tables, sometimes to the point of extinction. Therefore an annuity mortality table that accurately reflects the mortality among annuitants at the time it was compiled gradually becomes obsolete and eventually overstates the expected mortality.

Finally, a high percentage of annuitants are women, who as a group enjoy greater longevity than men, which has intensified the first two factors mentioned above. It also forced companies to introduce a rate differential between male and female annuitants long before a rate differential based on sex was applied to the sale of life insurance policies. However, court decisions have required insurers to base some group annuity contracts on unisex mortality rates.

Revised Mortality Tables

Life insurance companies cope with these problems or complications in various ways. In the first place, they compute annuity considerations on the basis of mortality tables that reflect the annuitants' lower mortality. A number of annuity tables have been constructed and used since the 1937 Standard Annuity Table that was in common use until the 1950s. First, the Annuity Table for 1949, or some modification thereof, was widely used for writing individual annuities, but it has been supplanted by three newer tables: the 1955 American Annuity Table, then the 1971 Individual Annuity Table, the 1983 Individual Annuity Table, the Annuity 2000 Mortality Table, and currently the 2012 Individual Annuity Table on which all annuity calculations in this book are based.

For many years companies dealt with the specific problem associated with the continuing decline in mortality rates among annuitants by using age setbacks. In other words, a person was assumed to be one, 2, or 3 years younger than his or her actual age. Thus, a person who was actually 65 and had a normal life expectancy under a 3-year setback would be charged a premium based on age 62, thereby increasing the premium for a given amount of annuity income. Ages for females were usually set back 4 or 5 years in addition to the setback for males in recognition of the sex differential in mortality. Thus, if male ages were set back one year, female ages were set back as much as 6 years. If the reduction in mortality had been reflected equally at all ages, the setback technique could have been utilized indefinitely without serious distortion of the equities among annuitants at different ages. However, the reduction is not at a uniform rate at various ages, which has definitely limited the efficacy of the setback technique.

Ironically, the 1983 Individual Annuity Table was derived from separate male and female experience and has gender-distinct probabilities even though legal and social events have prompted many insurers to base their annuity products on unisex mortality. Comparison of the male and female mortality rates indicates that the practice of deriving female tables using an age setback of male tables as the only adjustment was a very crude approach to a very complex relationship. The practice should have entailed varying setbacks at each age to accurately adjust male mortality rates to represent longer-lived females.

An updated approach to the "problem" of declining mortality is an annuity table (2000 Annuity Mortality Table) that, by means of projection factors, attempts to forecast, and make suitable adjustments for, future reductions in mortality rates. For example, the Annuity Tables for 1949, 1955, 1971, 1983, and 2000 all contain a set of projection factors that can be used to adjust the mortality assumptions for all ages from year to year or, in lieu of that, to project the basic rates of mortality to some future date. The projections make allowances for anticipated future reductions in mortality. The most recent approach to addressing mortality changes is the 2012 Individual Annuity Reserve Table. The a2000 Table is a static mortality table. It is based on mortality experience from the 1980's and 1990's with projected mortality improvement to the year 2000 but not beyond. 2012 IAR, on the other hand, is a generational table that incorporates projections for future mortality improvements. This is accomplished by applying projection factors (Projection Scale G2) to the 2012 Individual Annuity Mortality Period Life (2012 IAM Period) Table. The latter is akin to the a 2000 Table. The new table applies to deferred annuities as well as those life annuities in payout status (immediate annuities as well as settlement options).

Higher Interest Assumptions

Historically insurance companies attempted to hedge future improvement in annuitant mortality by using an unrealistically low interest assumption in the premium formula. The rates were substantially lower than those used in the calculation of life insurance premiums. The effectiveness of this technique can be judged by the fact that an interest margin of .25 percentage point (25 basis points) is capable of absorbing a general reduction in mortality of 6 or 7 percent. Intensified competition among insurance companies and between insurance companies and investment media, however, has caused companies to adopt interest assumptions much closer to the level of their actual investment earnings. Considerations for individual deferred annuities are generally being computed today on the basis of interest assumptions running from 2.5 to 5.5 percent, while immediate annuities may be priced on the basis of slightly higher interest assumptions. The extremely low yields on portfolio assets since 2008 have forced interest assumptions even lower which has increased the price of immediate and deferred annuities sold since 2008.

Computing Premiums on a Participating Basis

A final approach to adjusting annuity mortality for anticipated future increases in life expectancy is to compute the premiums (or considerations) on a participating basis, which permits conservative assumptions (safety margins) with respect to all factors entering into the computations. Annual-premium annuities issued by mutual companies are almost invariably participating during the accumulation period and may be participating on some basis during the liquidation period. Some stock companies also issue annuities that are participating during the accumulation period. Single-premium immediate annuities, whether written by mutual or stock companies, are usually not participating.

USES OF THE ANNUITY

Because it is the single-premium life annuity that most frequently comes to mind when annuities are mentioned and since this form requires the deposit of a substantial sum of money, most people have the impression that annuities appeal only to the wealthy. This is not at all the case. The range of the annuity's usefulness is nearly as wide as that of the life insurance contract, and forms have been devised to fit virtually every conceivable need or circumstance.

The market for annuities is composed of two broad categories of individuals: those who have already accumulated an estate either through inheritance or by their own personal efforts, and those who are seeking to accumulate an estate. The first category may be sub-divided into the wealthy and those with only moderate resources.

In general, wealthy individuals purchase annuities as a hedge against adverse financial developments. Large estates can be wrecked through business reverses, unwise invest-ments, and reckless spending. Insurance company records abound with cases of individ-uals who at one time were wealthy but whose fortunes melted away, leaving payments from annuities purchased in their more affluent days as their sole source of income. There are also numerous cases of individuals who are dependent on relatives for whom they had purchased annuities during a more solvent period. Wealthy people, then, purchase annu-ities in a search for security. To them yield is a secondary consideration.

Yield, on the other hand, is a primary consideration for those persons, mostly middle-aged and elderly, who have accumulated a modest estate and hope that it will be the source of financial security during the remaining years of their lives. The life annuity, perhaps in the joint-and-survivor form, is the answer to the problem of this group, since it maximizes income by including a portion of the principal in each monthly payment and promises a

continuation of the benefit payments and some deferral of income taxes as long as the annuitant or annuitants live. Although some people in these circumstances are reluctant to invest their capital in an annuity because they want to leave an estate to their children or other close relatives, many parents feel that, having reared and educated their children, their greatest responsibility is providing for their own old-age maintenance, thus relieving the children of that burden. The annuity is an ideal instrument for accomplishing this objective.

Furthermore, there are situations in which the entire capital accumulation may not be needed to provide for the parents' old-age support. In such cases, a portion of the estate can be used to purchase an annuity of suitable form and size, making it possible for the remainder of the estate to be distributed to the children during the parents' lifetime, when it may be of the greatest use to the children. Most young people would probably prefer to receive a smaller share of their parents' estate when their need for capital is the greatest than to wait for a larger share when the need may be less urgent. Moreover, many parents, if they could safely do so, would prefer to distribute a portion of their estate to their children during the parents' lifetime so that they can witness the enjoyment it brings. Annuities can be used in a similar manner to provide living bequests to charitable, educational, and religious organizations.

The annuity is also an attractive savings medium for the person who has not yet accumulated an estate but wants to achieve financial independence in old age. Professional people find annuities especially attractive for that purpose. The same is true of athletes, entertainers, and others who enjoy a very large income but for a limited period of time. Annuities are an appropriate investment because they can be purchased through flexible periodic premiums or through single-premium deposits as the annuitant comes into possession of large sums.

STRUCTURED SETTLEMENTS

Over the past decade the courts have handed down guilty verdicts in at least 5,000 cases involving personal injury or wrongful death in which the negligent party was found liable for at least $1 million in damages. More than 95 percent of these cases were settled before they ever went to trial, although the settlement is still enforceable by the court. Most such cases were settled on a lump-sum basis.

Quite frequently the courts are seeking lifetime financial support for the injured party or throughout the minority of dependent heirs. Consequently it is usually acceptable to the court to have the liability paid in the form of periodic payments instead of as a single

lump-sum payment. Insurance companies can and do issue immediate annuity contracts that will guarantee the payments over the required lifetime or over the mandated support period. These contracts are specifically tailored to the needs of the injured or wronged parties (claimants).

While the concept of paying periodic payments over time for claimant damages can be traced to the 1950s, independent full-time structured settlement specialists were not common until the 1970s. Since then the number of cases using structured settlement contracts to satisfy the plaintiffs' claims has grown substantially. The most frequent cases in which a structured settlement may be appropriate usually involve general liability, medical malpractice, defective products, automobile accidents, or worker's compensation injuries.

Personal injury claim adjusters and/or defense attorney's work together with a structured settlement specialist to form a defense team. Their goal is to arrange settlements that will be appropriate and help to offset any damages suffered by the claimant, consistent with the issues of liability and the claimant's future needs (both known and unanticipated).

Suitable structured settlements will provide an adequate amount of immediate cash for liquidity needs, reimbursement for past expenses, legal fees, and other cash needs. If the recipient is unable to work, an income stream can be designed to fund normal living expenses, custodial and medical services, rehabilitation costs, and where appropriate, tuition for educational programs.

Annuities Utilized in Structured Settlements

The usual structured settlement provides for annuities to pay out periodic payments that meet the recipient's financial needs as much as possible. One of the primary advantages of structured settlements is that the periodic payments of income are received tax free by the claimant during his or her life and by the claimant's beneficiaries thereafter for the balance of any guarantee period. Two of the requirements for the claimant's income-tax-free treatment are the absence of any evidence of ownership by the annuitant of the annuities funding the structured settlement and the absence of constructive receipt or economic benefit in the annuity itself. Therefore, all timing decisions, as well as the exact amount of money, are predetermined by the defendant or its insurer, who are the legal owners of the annuity.

If the claimant has no reduction in life expectancy from the injuries that caused the claim, standard rates are applied on life annuities. Likewise, if there is no life contingency, standard rates are used for fixed-period annuities. (An example of a fixed-period annuity is payments of $1,000 a month for 5 years and $2,000 a month during years 6 through 10.

This is also referred to as a step-rate annuity.) Annuity benefit payments can generally be increased on a compound annual rate, ranging from 3 percent to 6 percent. In addition to life income guarantees, period-certain and joint life guarantees can be used, depending on the circumstances involved.

One of the most significant innovations that benefits both the claimant and the defendant is the rated age, or substandard life annuity (see figure). In a catastrophic injury case, the structured settlement broker submits the medical data to different insurance companies for evaluation. Each company makes its own judgment as to the claimant's life expectancy and bases its annuity quotes on that opinion. Because this is largely subjective, life expectancy estimates vary from one company to another, just as rated-up life insurance varies from one life insurance company to another. Then the broker presents the bids to the defendant and his or her legal counsel to make an informed selection. The life insurance company underwrites the proposed annuitant's current condition, including any preexisting health impairments.

The cost of a substandard annuity bears an inverse relationship to the cost of substandard life insurance. The lower the life expectancy, the lower the annuity cost and the higher the life insurance cost. A difference of 20 years in life expectancy could result in a 50 percent cost differential. Generally, this kind of annuity may be purchased only by defendants or their insurers in personal injury and wrongful death cases, and the number of insurers issuing such contracts is rather small. The claimant or plaintiff needs to cooperate in good-faith bargaining to achieve a fair settlement.

Figure 24-2
Premiums Required for Standard and Substandard Annuities to Provide $2,500/Month for Life, Increasing at 4%/Year for 30 Years

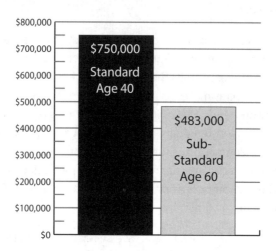

The substandard annuity provides the defense team with an extremely valuable financial vehicle. Less than one percent of the life insurance companies offer this discounted underwriting specialty.

Advantages of Structured Settlements

The advantages of a structured settlement for each of the individual entities involved are explained below.

For the Injured Party

Financial Security. The major advantage of a structured settlement for the injured party is financial security. A lifetime income is especially practical and desirable when a minor or someone acknowledged to be incompetent is involved. The approach is attractive, particularly to the court, whenever there is reason to be concerned about protecting the injured party's future finances. In cases of wrongful death, a structured settlement may be used to provide replacement earnings to the claimant's spouse and children.

Benefits that Match Needs. An injured party needs regular income to meet living expenses and medical care costs. On occasion, when future medical costs are estimated to be substantial but the timing of these costs is unknown, a medical trust, similar to an emergency fund recommended by financial planners, can be used. Typically, the medical

trust is created with the defendant as grantor under a trust agreement that is part of the settlement agreement.

Management of Benefits. Claimants and their families or guardians are usually not trained to manage large sums of money. Dissipation of funds through mismanagement, imprudent investment, unwise expenditures, misuse, or even neglect is a high risk. This risk is significantly reduced through the use of periodic payments in a structured settlement. Guaranteed Payment. Because the income payments are guaranteed for life or for a fixed period, the settlement can never be prematurely exhausted. There could be some reduction and delay in getting benefits if the insurer issuing the settlement agreement fails. Executive Life Insurance Co. is an example where the state guarantee funds are paying reduced benefits after a delay.

Income-Tax-Free Payments. Whether payments are in a lump sum or periodic, they represent personal injury damages, which are excluded from income tax under IRC Sec. 104(a)(2). (Further clarification of the tax-free nature of structured settlements is given in Rev. Ruls. 79–220, 79–313, and 77–230.)

Figure 24-3
Capital Needed to Produce $2,500 Net Monthly, Increasing at 4% per Year for 30 Years

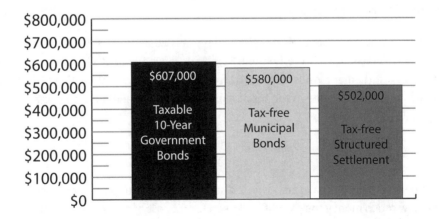

According to data from the Economic Report of the President, 1992, the 25-year average yield (1967–1990) of 10-year government bonds is 8.27 percent. This rate is assumed to apply to the settlement annuity tax free and to the government bond fund. The income tax rate used on the government bond fund is 28 percent. The long-term Standard & Poor's municipal bonds averaged a yield of 7.02 percent over the period 1967–1990; this rate

was used to calculate the municipal bond fund above. If the actual investment returns in future years are lower than these past yields, the amount of capital needed will increase. (In October of 2014, the 10 year government bond rate in the U.S. was 2.37 percent.)

The Periodic Payments Settlement Act of 1982 codified the above revenue rulings and clarified that the interest as well as the principal portion of periodic payments is income tax free. This same act not only amended IRC Sec. 104(a)(2) but also created IRC Sec. 130, which allowed for continuation of the tax-free treatment of qualified assignments. A qualified assignment allows the defendant or his or her insurer to assign the obligation to make the future payments to a third-party assignee. Usually, the assignee is an affiliate of the life insurance company providing the annuity payments and as assignee assumes the ultimate obligation from the defendant as assignor to make future payments guaranteed under the settlement agreement. The assignee typically is the parent of the life insurance company providing the annuity, an affiliate life insurance company, or an affiliate shell company incorporated to hold the assignments. With the assignment, the defendant or the insurer receives an absolute release and closes the file. The annuity is purchased by the assignee, and the claimant or plaintiff is perceived to receive an enhancement of security (even though it is the status of a general creditor) because life insurance companies and their affiliates are regarded as being more stable than property and casualty companies in terms of solvency.

For the Plaintiff Attorney

Attorneys are assured that their client's settlement is guaranteed and will not be subject to dissipation as is a lump-sum settlement. Some attorneys even believe that recommending a structured settlement insulates them from exposure to legal malpractice since they are not taking a sizable portion of the total value of the entire benefit payable as a lump sum right in the beginning.

For the Judge

Lump-sum settlements have an obvious disadvantage. The judge or jury must determine how much money the plaintiff will need for the rest of his or her life. If the plaintiff lives longer than expected, the lump sum is exhausted; if the plaintiff dies sooner than expected, his or her heirs could receive a windfall unintended in the settlement. Guaranteed periodic payments for life, however, assure the plaintiff of financial security regardless of when he or she dies and are therefore easier for a judge or jury to award.

For the Public

The public benefits from the structured settlement because the injured party will not become a ward of the state and will be assured of a guaranteed income and proper care. In addition, the delay of prolonged litigation is avoided, thereby reducing court costs and placing more burden on the already overloaded judicial system.

Disadvantages of Structured Settlements

If a life insurance company becomes insolvent, the insured may have to absorb all of the losses in excess of any Guarantor Association limitations. However, with the proviso that the insured is still insurable, he or she may replace life insurance coverage with another viable carrier. In the case of structured settlements, however, the income reduction from choosing a minimum benefit guarantee is not easily replaced. There may be insufficient funds from the insured's other assets to offset the benefit reduction.

Besides the structured settlement specialist's due diligence, the availability of a qualified assignment and compliance with the Uniform Periodic Payment of Judgments Act will mitigate any financial risks arising from a life insurer's insolvency. For obvious reasons, therefore, structured settlement specialists should select only the most secure and well-managed insurance companies.

Because there is no right to accelerate or decelerate future payments, problems can occur if more immediate cash is needed than the stream of payments will provide. This may be due to an unprecedented financial reversal, a medical necessity, an educational need, or inflation over and above expectations. The unfortunate fact is that the periodic payment schedule may not be changed. The original design of the structured settlement should therefore anticipate increasing payments annually, or at least periodically, building in periodic deferred lump sums, or including a medical trust for future medical and custodial needs. In addition to providing an adequate amount of immediate cash for the benefit of the injured party, a well-designed structured settlement will carefully consider the needs of the claimant's dependents.

Sample Structured Settlement Case

The following illustration involves a claimant, John Doe, aged 40, who is totally and permanently disabled due to an accident and will require substantial future medical and custodial care. In addition, his 3-year-old child, Annemarie, will require college funds since John Doe is no longer able to provide any income to save for this goal. As 50 percent of the total settlement, up-front cash of $1.125 million should be sufficient to pay the plaintiff

attorney's legal fees and to establish an emergency fund for John Doe. In addition, the income from a medical trust and a $1,000-a-month annuity should be adequate, according to the interpretation of the life care plan that was used as a guide to ascertain John Doe's capital needs for the future. Independent living income of $30,000 a year, increasing at 3 percent compounded interest annually, should provide enough funds to maintain the Doe family's routine cost of living and to help offset future inflation.

The average costs for room, board, and tuition at public and private universities were used to ascertain college fund requirements for Annemarie. These costs were then projected at the average inflation rate. Because many students take 5 years to complete their undergraduate college education, payments are forecast for a 5-year period. The proposed structured settlement is presented in Figure 24-4.

Structured Settlement Services

Prior to designing a structured settlement proposal tailored specifically to the claimant, the structured settlement specialist receives the pertinent data from the claims adjuster and/ or the defense attorney. The more data available for this purpose, the more appropriate the design is to the injured party's needs. The structured settlement specialist then provides proposals and present-value estimates of streams of income to the defense team, adopting the design to incorporate any variables they suggest. After a verbal settlement is reached, the structured settlement specialist usually provides the defense attorney with sample closing documents for reviews, such as a settlement agreement and release, a qualified assignment, and a medical trust agreement.

Very often the party purchasing a structured settlement is a property/casualty insurer providing liability coverage to the defendant. Structured settlement specialists devote a fair amount of effort and resources to informing possible purchasers of the potential savings available.

Profile of a Structured Settlement Specialist

Many structured settlement specialists have been claims representatives or claims adjusters. This is good experience for becoming a structured settlement specialist because so many aspects of structured settlements involve the resolution of the familiar claims process with personal injury law. The structured settlement company generally has a limited general agency relationship with approximately 12 life insurance companies who provide over 80 percent of the structured settlement annuities. Those 12 life insurers typically require a minimum production of structured settlement contracts each year from a

specialist in order to continue representing the insurer and selling their contracts. They are highly selective about the companies to which they extend the general agency, probably because of the highly technical nature of the business. None of the companies that have major life insurance sales forces allow their regular life and annuity field sales force to participate in structured settlements. Generally, these same life companies do not allow structured settlement companies to sell their regular life and annuity products.

Figure 24-4

Proposed Structured Settlement

Claimant: John Doe	Age: 40	Life Expectancy: 35 Years	
	Guaranteed Total Payments	Estimated Total Payments	Cost
Immediate Cash, including Legal Fees	$1,125,000	$1,125,000	$1,125,000
Medical Trust Fund			
Cash Seed	200,000	200,000	200,000
Annuity Seed (Payments of $1,000 monthly, compounding at 4% each year, starting in one month and continuing for the claimant's life, with the first 20 years guaranteed)	357,337	883,827	263,677
Independent Living Income (Payments of $2,500 monthly, compounding at 3% each year, starting in one month and continuing for the claimant's life with the first 20 years guaranteed)	806,111	1,813,862	583,707
College Funds for Daughter, Aged 3			
Payment at age 18	25,000	25,000	15,094
Payment at age 19	38,000	38,000	15,467
Payment at age 20	41,000	41,000	15,623
Payment at age 21	44,000	44,000	15,818
Payment at age 22	47,000	47,000	15,940
Totals	**$2,683,448**	**$4,217,689**	**$2,250,326**

National Structured Settlement Trade Association

The National Structured Settlement Trade Association was created in 1986, primarily by independent structured settlement broker companies. Its goals are to advance the expansion of structured settlement concepts, promote favorable legislation and regulations,

provide continuing education, develop guidelines for operational procedures, and establish a code of ethics for its members.

The year 1994 marked the first conferment of the association's certified structured settlement specialists. They completed studies in the following categories:

- structured settlements and periodic payment judgments
- casualty claim practices
- medical trusts
- evaluation of claims
- negotiation methods
- alternative investments
- macroeconomics
- business ethics

Uniform Periodic Payment of Judgments Act/Sec. 18

To promote the widespread use of structured settlements, the Uniform Periodic Payment of Judgments Act was approved in 1990 by the National Conference of Commissioners of Uniform State Laws. Sec. 18 of that act limits the number of life insurance companies that may qualify as structured settlement annuity providers as follows:

- The (Commissioner) shall publish a list of insurers designated by the (Commissioner) as qualified to participate in the funding of periodic payment judgments under Sec. 11. The list must be updated as often as necessary to keep current.

- In order for an insurer to be designated by the (Commissioner) as a qualified insurer, it must

  - request the designation
  - be an admitted insurer
  - have a minimum of $100 million of capital and surplus, exclusive of any mandatory security valuation reserve
  - have one of the following ratings from two or more of the following rating organizations:

    ◊ A.M. Best Company (A+, A+g, A+p, A+r, or A+s)

◊   Moody's Investors Service Claims Paying Rating (Aa3, Aa2, Aa1, or Aaa)

◊   Standard & Poor's Corporation Insurer Claims-Paying Ability Rating (AA-, AA, AA+ or AAA)

◊   Fitch Credit Rating Company Insurance Company Claims Payable Ability Rating (AA-, AA, AA+ or AAA)

Even though many of the states have not adopted the Periodic Payment of Judgments statute, structured settlement specialists tend to use the most financially secure, highly rated life insurance companies (those most likely to be approved under the act should it later be adopted). Any changes in the rating systems themselves, such as A++ of A.M. Best, will be phased in by the states who adopt the Uniform Act.

Postsettlement Opportunities for Other Advisers

Life insurance and financial advisers can certainly provide additional services for recipients of lump-sum settlements as well as structured settlements. The injured party is usually represented by an attorney who specializes only in personal injury cases. Frequently, the attorney refers his or her client to the local bank but in most cases does not get involved in any planning after the settlement. Life insurance and financial advisers can provide valuable postsettlement services.

While planning is even more critical if the injured party receives all of the proceeds in a lump sum, financial planning services are still necessary for those who receive a structured settlement of some up-front cash and the balance in periodic income. Keep in mind that most large settlements involve an injured party who is no longer able to work. Therefore financial planning is crucial not only to preserve capital but also to ensure an adequate income currently and in the future. Can you imagine an injured person who has no education or training in finance or investments trying to do it alone? Can you imagine an employer giving a check for $500,000 to an employee with the following words, "This represents the present value of all your future benefits toward your long-term disability plan. Even though you are only 45 we hope that you will make the right decisions on current and future investments because this is the last check you'll ever see from us."

Obviously, financial and estate planning are essential. In addition, the establishment of wills and trusts (and their periodic reevaluation) is also a vital service needed by accident victims whose income productivity has been impaired. Furthermore, with the creation of new insurance products (such as survivor life), a qualified life insurance adviser can help

create the necessary liquidity for estate taxes and clearance costs for individuals who may be disabled but still insurable.

CHAPTER REVIEW

Key Terms and Concepts

annuity certain
life annuity
whole life annuity
temporary life annuity
joint annuity
joint-and-survivor annuity
immediate annuity
deferred annuity
pure annuity
straight life annuity
refund annuity
life annuity certain

installment refund annuity
cash refund annuity
50 percent refund annuity
modified cash refund annuity
accumulation period
liquidation period
liquidation options
variable annuity
accumulation unit
annuity units
equity-indexed annuities

Chapter 24 Review Questions

1. Explain how annuities differ from life insurance, and indicate what fundamental principles apply to both annuities and life insurance. [1]

2. Describe four common classifications of annuity contracts. [1]

3. Describe the various types of benefit structures in single-life immediate annuities that are commonly available from life insurers. [1]

4. Indicate how deferred annuities differ from immediate annuities, and describe the various options available during the accumulation period. [1]

5. What types of requirements are commonly applicable to the liquidation options available under deferred-annuity contracts? [1]

6. Describe some of the benefit variations available under joint-and-last survivor annuity contracts. [1]

7. Describe the variable annuity concept, and explain how accumulation units differ from annuity units in these variable contracts. [1]

8. How do the surrender provisions under variable annuities differ from those of ordinary (fixed-dollar) annuities? [1]

9. What is the basic function of annuity contracts? [1]

10. Explain how increased longevity has affected the safety margins in mortality tables for: (a) annuities; (b) life insurance. [2]

11. Indicate some uses for which annuity contracts are well suited. [1]

12. Describe the equity portion of the equity-indexed annuity. [3]

13. What are the indexes commonly used in equity-indexed annuities, and which ones pose the potential for manipulation? [3]

14. How will the asset allocation associated with equity-indexed annuities affect the risk of performance? [3]

Chapter 24 Review Questions

1. *Annuities liquidate accumulated funds over a person's lifetime. Deferred annuities also promote accumulation of funds. Life insurance provides a cash benefit at the death of the insured. Both contracts relay on pooling, the time value of money, and mortality. Both protect against the loss of income.*

2. *Four common classifications of annuity contracts include*

    •   *number of lives covered*

    •   *time when payments start*

    •   *method of premium payment*

    •   *nature of insurer's obligation*

3. *Various types of benefit structures in single-life immediate annuities commonly available from life insurers include*

    •   *pure life annuity with benefits for remaining life*

    •   *refund annuity with benefits for remaining life, plus a guarantee that benefits will be paid after death if death occurs before the refund guarantee has been paid*

    •   *life annuity certain with benefit for remaining life, plus a benefit after death until the end of the period certain in those cases where the annuitant dies before the end of the period certain*

4. *Deferred annuities have an accumulation period that precedes the payout of benefits in the liquidation period. Immediate annuities only have a liquidation period. Deferred annuities can be purchased with*

    •   *single premium*

    •   *rigid periodic premiums*

    •   *flexible periodic premiums*

5. *The liquidation must start before some specified age (such as age 80), and there may be an adjustment in the accumulated amount if the benefit is taken as cash rather than some form of lifetime payments.*

6. *Joint-and-last survivor annuities can provide either the same level or some reduced level of benefits (for example, full, half, two-thirds) to the survivor after the other annuitant dies. The contract can also include a refund or period-certain guarantee if desired.*

7. *The assets backing variable annuities are invested in common stocks and other equities. The value of the accumulation fund depends on the investment performance of the variable funds. Premium contributions are used to purchase accumulation units at their value*

when each premium is received. The value of these units fluctuates with market prices of the portfolio.

When the variable annuity goes into the liquidation period, accumulation units are exchanged for annuity units. The number of annuity units remains constant for the remainder of the contract, but the value of the annuity units fluctuates with the market value of invested assets.

Benefit payments vary in relation to the changes in annuity unit values. The number of annuity units must remain constant for the pooling mechanism to work and to properly provide the benefits of survival.

8. *There are restrictions on surrenders to discourage participants of variable annuities from taking the funds and investing directly in the market. These may be in the form of market adjustment costs or limits on amounts available. No withdrawals are permitted if the variable annuity is part of a pension plan.*

   Fixed-dollar annuities usually have no restrictions on surrenders beyond surrender charges.

9. *The basic function of annuity contracts is to liquidate a principal sum in a scientific manner, regardless of how that sum was created.*

10. *Answers:*
    a. *Increased longevity erodes the safety margin in a mortality table for annuities.*
    b. *Increased longevity increases the safety margin in a mortality table for life insurance.*

11. *Annuity contracts are well suited for accumulating funds to provide a lifetime income, turning accumulated funds into a lifetime income, to provide a guaranteed income stream for a specific period, and as a vehicle for lump sum pension distribution (especially IRA annuities).*

12. *The equity portion of the equity-indexed annuity is the amount payable in excess of the guaranteed minimum interest rate. It is determine by the contract provisions regarding the reference index, the participation rate formula, and market conditions influencing the index.*

13. *The most commonly used index is the Standard and Poor's 500 Composite Stock Price Index. Other stock price indexes regularly published in the Wall Street Journal are sometimes used, and a few insurance companies have created their own index, such as a composite of 2 or more published indexes. The composite indexes have the potential of manipulation.*

14. *The assets chosen to represent the equity performance can be conservative, quite risky, or anywhere along the risk spectrum. As the difference between fixed interest investment yields and equity yields widens, insurers will be forced to pursue more risky investments in order to increase yields. If the portfolio returns do not equal the contractual guarantees, the insurer will be losing money on the equity index annuities.*

INDEX

Symbols

A